Smart Innovation, Systems and Technologies

353

Series Editors

Robert J. Howlett, *KES International Research, Shoreham-by-Sea, UK*
Lakhmi C. Jain, *KES International, Shoreham-by-Sea, UK*

The Smart Innovation, Systems and Technologies book series encompasses the topics of knowledge, intelligence, innovation and sustainability. The aim of the series is to make available a platform for the publication of books on all aspects of single and multi-disciplinary research on these themes in order to make the latest results available in a readily-accessible form. Volumes on interdisciplinary research combining two or more of these areas is particularly sought.

The series covers systems and paradigms that employ knowledge and intelligence in a broad sense. Its scope is systems having embedded knowledge and intelligence, which may be applied to the solution of world problems in industry, the environment and the community. It also focusses on the knowledge-transfer methodologies and innovation strategies employed to make this happen effectively. The combination of intelligent systems tools and a broad range of applications introduces a need for a synergy of disciplines from science, technology, business and the humanities. The series will include conference proceedings, edited collections, monographs, handbooks, reference books, and other relevant types of book in areas of science and technology where smart systems and technologies can offer innovative solutions.

High quality content is an essential feature for all book proposals accepted for the series. It is expected that editors of all accepted volumes will ensure that contributions are subjected to an appropriate level of reviewing process and adhere to KES quality principles.

Indexed by SCOPUS, EI Compendex, INSPEC, WTI Frankfurt eG, zbMATH, Japanese Science and Technology Agency (JST), SCImago, DBLP.

All books published in the series are submitted for consideration in Web of Science.

Yuzo Iano · Osamu Saotome ·
Guillermo Leopoldo Kemper Vásquez ·
Maria Thereza de Moraes Gomes Rosa ·
Rangel Arthur · Gabriel Gomes de Oliveira
Editors

Proceedings of the 8th Brazilian Technology Symposium (BTSym'22)

Emerging Trends and Challenges in Technology

 Springer

Editors
Yuzo Iano
Faculty of Electrical and Computer
Engineering
Unicamp
Campinas, São Paulo, Brazil

Guillermo Leopoldo Kemper Vásquez
Peruvian University of Applied Sciences
(UPC)
Lima, Peru

Rangel Arthur
Faculty of Electrical and Computer
Engineering
Unicamp
Campinas, São Paulo, Brazil

Osamu Saotome
Technological Institute of Aeronautics
Federal Fluminense University
Sao Jose dos Campos, São Paulo, Brazil

Maria Thereza de Moraes Gomes Rosa
Universidade Presbiteriana Mackenzie
São Paulo, Brazil

Gabriel Gomes de Oliveira ⓘD
Cidade Universitaria
Campinas, São Paulo, Brazil

ISSN 2190-3018   ISSN 2190-3026 (electronic)
Smart Innovation, Systems and Technologies
ISBN 978-3-031-31009-6   ISBN 978-3-031-31007-2 (eBook)
https://doi.org/10.1007/978-3-031-31007-2

This Springer imprint is published by the registered company Springer Nature Switzerland AG
The registered company address is: Gewerbestrasse 11, 6330 Cham, Switzerland

Foreword

With great satisfaction, I write this foreword for the Proceedings of the 8th Brazilian Technology Symposium—Emerging Trends and Challenges in Technology (BTSym'22), held virtually, for the second time, at the Mackenzie Campinas University, Brazil, in October 2022 and the UNAPUNO University, Peru, in November 2022. This event is in its eighth edition and has consolidated to become an excellent opportunity for researchers, professors, and students to present and discuss the results of their research works.

The event has been characterized since its first edition by the broad scope of the areas exposed and, within a virtual environment, it was possible to expand our network of researchers and encourage them to expose their papers, which deal with current and priority topics for Brazilian and world technological development, including subjects related to the various branches of innovation in industrial processes, robotics, telecommunications, buildings, urban infrastructure, product development, and biomedicines.

Events such as BTSym are an essential part of the research and innovation process. Firstly, these events contribute to the promotion of research activities, which are key to a country's technological development. The dissemination of research results, as promoted by BTSym, contributes to the transformation of research findings into technological innovation. In addition, these events facilitate the sharing of findings, leading eventually to the formulation of research networks, which accelerate the achievement of new results. Therefore, I would like to congratulate the BTSym General Chair, Prof. Dr. Yuzo Iano, and his group of collaborators for the important initiative of organizing the BTSym'22 and for providing the opportunity for authors to present their work to a wide audience through this publication. Finally, I congratulate the authors for the high-quality work presented in these proceedings.

Gabriel Gomes de Oliveira
Technical Program and Finance Chair of
Brazilian Technology Symposium

Preface

This book contains the Proceedings of the 8th Brazilian Technology Symposium—Emerging Trends and Challenges in Technology, held in Brazil in November 2022 and Peru in November 2022.

The Brazilian Technology Symposium is an excellent forum for presentations and discussions of the latest results of projects and development research in several areas of knowledge, in scientific and technological scope, including smart designs, sustainability, inclusion, future technologies, architecture and urbanism, computer science, information science, industrial design, aerospace engineering, agricultural engineering, biomedical engineering, civil engineering, control and automation engineering, production engineering, electrical engineering, chemical engineering, and probability and statistics.

This event seeks to bring together researchers, students, and professionals from the industrial and academic sectors, seeking to create and/or strengthen the linkages between issues of joint interest. Participants were invited to submit research papers with methodologies and results achieved in scientific level research projects, completion of course work for graduation, dissertations, and theses.

The 52 full chapters accepted for this book were selected from 145 submissions, and, in each case, the authors were guided by an experienced researcher with a rigorous peer-review process. Among the main topics covered in this book, we can highlight manufacturing processes, lean manufacturing, industrial costing models, sustainability and productivity, circular economy, workplace safety, control systems, Internet of Things, cyber-physical systems, Transportation Management System (TMS), logistic services analysis, digital supply chain, socio-economic impacts of technologies 4.0, robotics applications, artificial neural networks, Big Data, deep learning, computational vision, cybersecurity, soft-computing methodologies, technologies applied to cities development, smart cities, energy sustainability, Building Information Modeling (BIM), environment analysis, technologies applied to health, biomedical innovations, socio-economic impacts of COVID-19, technologies applied to education, academic development, civil aviation studies, and much more.

We hope you enjoy and take advantage of this book and feel motivated to submit your papers, in the future, to Brazilian Technology Symposium.

Best wishes,

Alex Midwar Rodriguez Ruelas
Proceedings Chair of Brazilian Technology
Symposium

Contributors

Organizing Committee

Alex Rodriguez Ruelas (Proceedings Chair)	LCV/DECOM/FEEC/UNICAMP
Alysson Gomes de Oliveira (Marketing Chair)	LCV/DECOM/FEEC/UNICAMP
Maria Thereza de Moraes Gomes Rosa (Vice-Associate-General Chair, BTSym)	Universidade Presbiteriana Mackenzie Campinas
Jorge Luiz da Paixão Filho (Vice-Associate-General Chair, BTSym)- Universidade Presbiteriana Mackenzie	Campinas
David Minango (Institutional Relationship Chair)	LCV/DECOM/FEEC/UNICAMP
Gabriel Gomes de Oliveira (Technical Program and Finance Chair)	LCV/DECOM/FEEC/UNICAMP
Lisber Arana (Institutional Relationship Chair)	LCV/DECOM/FEEC/UNICAMP
Osamu Saotome (Associate-General Chair, BTSym)	ITA
Rangel Arthur (Vice-General Chair, BTSym)	FT/UNICAMP
Yuzo Iano (General Chair, BTSym & WSGE)	LCV/DECOM/FEEC/UNICAMP

Executive Committee

Abel Dueñas Rodríguez (Midia Chair)	LCV/DECOM/FEEC/UNICAMP
Airton Vegette (Institutional Relationship Chair)	LCV/DECOM/FEEC/UNICAMP
Angélica F. G. (Institutional Relationship Chair)	LCV/DECOM/FEEC/UNICAMP

Daniel B. Katze (Institutional Relationship Chair)	LCV/DECOM/FEEC/UNICAMP
Daniellle Thiago Ferreira (Editorial Committee Chair)	LCV/DECOM/FEEC/UNICAMP
Elizangela Santos Souza (Editorial Committee Chair)	LCV/DECOM/FEEC/UNICAMP
Gabriel Caumo Vaz (Institutional Relationship Chair)	LCV/DECOM/FEEC/UNICAMP
Jennifer Chuin Lee (Designer Chair)	LCV/DECOM/FEEC/UNICAMP
João Carlos Gabriel (Vice-Associate-General Chair, BTSym)	Universidade Presbiteriana Mackenzie Campinas
Leticia Cursi (Institutional Relationship Chair)	LCV/DECOM/FEEC/UNICAMP
Lucas Alves (Institutional Relationship Chair)	LCV/DECOM/FEEC/UNICAMP
Luiz Vicente F. de Mello Filho (Vice-Associate-General Chair, BTSym)	Universidade Presbiteriana Mackenzie Campinas
Mariana Melo (Institutional Relationship Chair)	LCV/DECOM/FEEC/UNICAMP
Paulo Roberto dos Santos (Vice-Associate-General Chair, BTSym)	UniMetrocamp
Raquel J. Lobosco (Vice-Associate-General Chair, BTSym)	UFRJ
Thais Paiao (Institutional Relationship Chair)	LCV/DECOM/FEEC/UNICAMP
Telmo Cardoso Lustosa (Local Arrangements Chair)	LCV/DECOM/FEEC/UNICAMP
Ubiratan Matos (Institutional Relationship Chair)	LCV/DECOM/FEEC/UNICAMP

Scientific and Academic Committee

Alessandra Cristina Santos Akkari	Instituto Federal Sul-rio-grandense
Ana Cláudia Seixas	UNIFAL
Angela del Pilar Flores Granados	FEA/UNICAMP
Antonio Carlos Demanboro	PUC CAMPINAS
Celso Iwata Frison	PUC/Minas-Poços de Caldas

Cláudia Cotrim Pezzuto	PUC CAMPINAS
David Bianchini	LCV/DECOM/FEEC/UNICAMP
Edgard Luciano Oliveira da Silva	Universidade Estadual do Amazonas (UEA)
Edwin Valencia Castillo	Universidad Nacional de Cajamarca
Ernesto Karlo Celi Arevalo	UNPRG, Lambayeque, Perú
Erwin Junger Dianderas Caut	Instituto de Investigaciones de la Amazonía Peruana (IIAP)
Fábio Menegatti de Melo	PUC CAMPINAS
Gabriela Fleury Seixas	UEL
Grimaldo Wilfredo Quispe Santivañez	UERJ
Hugo Enrique Hernandez Figueroa	DECOM/FEEC/UNICAMP
Janito Vaqueiro Ferreira	DMC/FEM/UNICAMP
Jessie Leila Bravo Jaico	UNPRG, Lambayeque, Perú
João Carlos Gabriel	Universidade Presbiteriana Mackenzie
José Hiroki Saito	UFSCAR
Lia Toledo Moreira Mota	PUC CAMPINAS
Lucielen Santos	PURG
Luiz Vicente F. de Mello Filho	Universidade Presbiteriana Mackenzie
Marcos Fernando Espindola	IFSP São Paulo
Maria Thereza de Moraes Gomes Rosa	Universidade Presbiteriana Mackenzie
Marina Lavorato de Oliveira	PUC CAMPINAS
Néstor Adolfo Mamani Macedo	Universidad Nacional Mayor de San Marcos
Paulo Roberto dos Santos	UniMetrocamp
Osamu Saotome	ITA
Rangel Arthur	FT/UNICAMP
Raquel J. Lobosco	UFRJ
Silva Neto	UERJ
Suelene Silva Mammana	Universidade Presbiteriana Mackenzie
Talía Simões dos Santos	FT/UNICAMP
Telmo Cardoso Lustosa	LCV/DECOM/FEEC/UNICAMP
Victor A. M. Montalli	Faculdade São Leopoldo Mandic
Victor Murray	Universidad de Ingenieria y Tecnologia (UTEC)

Technical Reviewers Committee

Abel Alejandro Dueñas Rodriguez	LCV/DECOM/FEEC/UNICAMP
Adao Boava	Universidade Federal de Santa Catarina (UFSC)
Agord de Matos Pinto Júnior	DESIF/FEEC/UNICAMP

Airton José Vegette	LCV/DECOM/FEEC/UNICAMP
Alessandra Cristina Santos Akkari	Instituto Federal Sul-Rio-Grandense
Alex R. Ruelas	LCV/DECOM/FEEC/UNICAMP
Alex Restani Siegle	LCV/DECOM/FEEC/UNICAMP
Alysson Gomes De Oliveira	LCV/DECOM/FEEC/UNICAMP
Amilton da Costa Lamas	PUC CAMPINAS
Ana Cláudia Seixas	UNIFAL
Angela del Pilar Flores Granados	FEA/UNICAMP
Antônio José da Silva Neto	IPRJ/UERJ
Celso Fabrício Correia de Souza	LCV/DECOM/FEEC/UNICAMP
Cesar Henrique Cordova Quiroz	PUC CAMPINAS
Cláudia Cotrim Pezzuto	PUC CAMPINAS
Daniel Katz Bonello	LCV/DECOM/FEEC/UNICAMP
Daniel Rodrigues Ferraz Izario	LCV/DECOM/FEEC/UNICAMP
Daniela Helena Pelegrine Guimarães	EEL/USP
David Allan Ibarra	Universidad de las Fuerzas Armadas-ESPE
David Bianchini	LCV/DECOM/FEEC/UNICAMP
David Minango	LCV/DECOM/FEEC/UNICAMP
Diego Arturo Pajuelo	LCV/DECOM/FEEC/UNICAMP
Douglas do Nascimento	Marie Skłodowska-Curie Actions (MSCA)
Edgard Luciano Oliveira da Silva	EST/UEA
Edson Camilo	Eldorado Institute
Euclides Lourenço Chuma	LCV/DECOM/FEEC/UNICAMP
Everton Dias de Oliveira	UNIMEP
Fabiana da Silva Podeleski	UNISAL
Fábio Menegatti de Melo	PUC CAMPINAS
Francisco Fambrini	UFSCAR
Gabriel Caumo Vaz	LCV/DECOM/FEEC/UNICAMP
Gabriel Gomes de Oliveira	LCV/DECOM/FEEC/UNICAMP
Gabriela Fleury Seixas	UEL
Guilherme Barbosa Lopes Júnio	UFPE
João Carlos Gabriel	Universidade Presbiteriana Mackenzie
Josué Marcos de Moura Cardoso	LCV/DECOM/FEEC/UNICAMP
Juan Minango Negrete	LCV/DECOM/FEEC/UNICAMP
Jullyane Figueiredo	UFSC
Leonardo Bruscagini de Lima	LCV/DECOM/FEEC/UNICAMP
Leticia Dias Gomes	UDESC
Lisber Arana Hinostrosa	LCV/DECOM/FEEC/UNICAMP
Lucas Heitzmann Gabrielli	FEEC/UNICAMP
Luigi Ciambarella Filho	Universidade Veiga de Almeida/Develop Biotechnology

Luis Fernando Gonzalez	KonkerLabs
Luiz Antonio Sarti Junior	UFSCAR
Luiz Vicente Figueira de Mello Filho	Universidade Presbiteriana Mackenzie
Marcelo Jara	Eldorado Institute
Marcos Fernando Espindola	IFSP São Paulo
Maria Cecilia Luna	LCV/DECOM/FEEC/UNICAMP
Maria Thereza de Moraes Gomes Rosa	Universidade Presbiteriana Mackenzie
Marcius Fabius Henriques de Carvalho	PUC CAMPINAS
Miriam Tvrzska de Gouvea	Universidade Presbiteriana Mackenzie
Murilo Cesar Perin Briganti	LCV/DECOM/FEEC/UNICAMP
Osamu Saotome	ITA
Polyane Alves Santos	Instituto Federal Da Bahia
Rangel Arthur	INOVA/FT/UNICAMP
Raquel Jahara Lobosco	Federal University of Rio de Janeiro
Ricardo Barroso Leite	LCV/DECOM/FEEC/UNICAMP
Roger Prior Gregio	LCV/DECOM/FEEC/UNICAMP
Rosivaldo Ferrarezi	UNIP
Suelene Silva Piva	Universidade Presbiteriana Mackenzie
Telmo Cardoso Lustosa	LCV/DECOM/FEEC/UNICAMP
Victor Angelo Martins Montalli	Faculdade São Leopoldo Mandic-SLMANDIC

Acknowledgements

Our appreciation goes to a lot of colleagues and friends who assisted in the development of this book, Proceedings of the 8th Brazilian Technology Symposium—Emerging Trends and Challenges in Technology (BTSym'22).

First of all, I would like to thank all the members of the Organizing and Executive Committee for the commitment throughout the year. Several meetings were held, and many challenges were overcome for the accomplishment of the BTSym 2022. Also, and with great merit, I would like to thank all the Scientific and Academic Committee and Technical Reviewers Committee members for their excellent work, which was essential to ensure the quality of our peer-review process, collaborating with the visibility and technical quality of the BTSym 2022.

The Brazilian Technology Symposium is an event created by the Laboratory of Visual Communications of the Faculty of Electrical and Computer Engineering of the University of Campinas (UNICAMP). In this way, I would like to thank the MACKENZIE and UNAPUNO Universities, especially for supporting and hosting the BTSym'22 and BTSym'22 Satellite, respectively, which was fundamental for the successful accomplishment of the events.

We cannot thank Prof. MSc. Telmo Cardoso Lustosa, who passed away on September 9, 2022. Prof. Telmo has always helped us a lot since the first edition of BTSym with his great knowledge.

Finally, on behalf of Prof. Yuzo Iano, the General Chair of the Brazilian Technology Symposium, I thank all the authors for their participation in the BTSym'22; we sincerely hope to have provided a very useful and enriching experience in the personal and professional lives of everyone.

Best wishes,

Gabriel Caumo Vaz
Institutional Relationship Chair of
Brazilian Technology Symposium

Contents

Emerging Trends in Human Smart and Sustainable Future of Cities

Emerging Trends in Systems Engineering Mathematics and Physical Sciences

Artificial Neural Networks for Prediction of Hot Metal Production in a Blast Furnace

Wandercleiton Cardoso[1]([✉]) [iD], Renzo di Felice[1] [iD], Marcelo Margon[2] [iD],
Thiago Augusto Pires Machado[3] [iD], Danyelle Santos Ribeiro[4] [iD],
André Luiz Caulit Silva[5] [iD], and Ernandes Scopel[3] [iD]

[1] Università degli Studi di Genova, Genoa, Italy
wandercleiton.cardoso@dicca.unige.it
[2] Pontifícia Universidade Católica, Belo Horizonte, Brazil
[3] Instituto Federal do Espirito Santo, Vitoria, Brazil
[4] Università degli Studi Niccolò Cusano, Rome, Italy
[5] Fucape Business School, Vitoria, Brazil

Abstract. A blast furnace is a chemical reactor used in the steel industry to produce molten iron or hot metal. The size of this reactor is variable and can be more than 30 m high. It is coated with metal on the outside and refractory material on the inside. The reactor operates at high temperature and pressure. It is fed with coke, iron ore and fluxes in the upper part and air and auxiliary fuels are injected in the lower part. The rising gases react with the descending solids and melt the material. The production of pig iron also produces slag, which is normally used to make cement. This scientific article reports on the successful application of artificial neural networks in pig iron production. The neural network was modelled in MATLAB using 23 operational variables with 100 neurons. The validation of the mathematical model was carried out through statistical tests in the MINITAB software, which ensure the necessary statistical certainty for the validation of its application on an industrial scale.

Keywords: Forecast production · machine learning · neural network

1 Introduction

The process step for obtaining hot metal, the blast furnace, is the one with the highest energy consumption and operating costs and is therefore an element of great importance for the competitiveness of steel in the global scenario [1–3]. There are various industrial processes for producing pig iron, with the blast furnace being the most commonly used process in the world. The production process is very complex and has numerous control variables, namely: raw material, flame temperature, amount of heat, residence time of the solid material in the reactor, as well as thermal, chemical and dynamic parameters, which make machine learning difficult despite the advances in the application of artificial intelligence in the industrial sector [4–6]. Controlling a blast furnace using artificial intelligence is very complex despite the wide application of neural networks, which are versatile and reliable compared to various other machine learning techniques available on the market [7–9].

In the field of technology and modelling, in order to improve production conditions, in addition to predicting the effects of changes in production parameters, several models have been proposed for simulating blast furnaces, which require some simplifications in the conditions to be considered, which vary depending on the model proposed due to the complexity of the process. This highlights the importance of the continuous search for increasingly accurate and effective tools to monitor and predict operating and production conditions [10–12]. It is worth noting that the number of variables to be monitored, which can exceed 150, combined with the operating conditions of a blast furnace, makes it difficult, if not impossible, to obtain specific data during operation [12–14]. Depending on this situation, research into new methods for predicting such data has become the focus of studies in various institutions and research centres, especially mathematical modelling of the process [15–17].

Neural networks are versatile and reliable in simulating complex processes, such as blast furnaces, because it is possible to retrain the neural network and obtain new data so that the neural networks can acquire new predictive knowledge [18, 19]. In this sense, it is possible to develop neural networks that can be used in different blast furnaces, where the neural network only needs to be adapted to the new characteristics of the new blast furnace [20–22]. Considering that the operation of a blast furnace is complex and that neural networks can optimise the production process, it is important to work on the development of a source code that can monitor and control the production process of the reactor.

2 Materials and Methods

The data used are from a blast furnace that has an average daily production of 7,200 tonnes. According to Table 1, the operating data correspond to 150 operating days, 16 input variables and 7 output variables [23, 24].

The neural network was trained with the Matlab library "nnstart" and the Levenberg-Marquardt learning algorithm, single layer, 100 neurons and supervised learning. According to the literature, the number of neurons in the intermediate layer depends on the complexity of the problem, so it is difficult to determine exactly how many neurons should be used. Many similar works have found that a random number of neurons were used to find out what the optimal number would be. Therefore, there is no exact solution and no clear rule to determine the ideal number of neurons in each hidden layer [17–22].

Table 1. List of model input variables

Input data	Unit	Mean + std dev	Input data	Unit	Mean + std dev
Pellet	kg/t	754.4 ± 62.4	Coke ash content	%	8.9 ± 0.9
Sínter	kg/t	754.4 ± 50.2	Coke moisture	%	3.9 ± 0.7
Iron ore	kg/t	37.1 ± 27.4	Nitrogen	Nm^3/t	17.3 ± 11.1
Dolomite	kg/t	7.1 ± 4.6	Oxygen flow	Nm^3/t	14371 ± 419
Coke	kg/t	300.2 ± 26.4	Oxygen enrichment	%	4.1 ± 0.9
Pulverized coal	kg/t	198.1 ± 17.2	Flame temperature	°C	1,203 ± 21
Slag basicity	%	1.19 ± 0.03	Airspeed tuyère	m/s	221 ± 21
Blowing flow	Nm^3/min	4828.1 ± 587.2	Permeability	-	4.21 ± 0.21

3   Results

Figures 1, 2, 3, 4, 5, 6 and 7 show the results of the mathematical modeling:

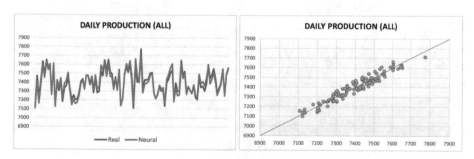

Fig. 1. Daily production

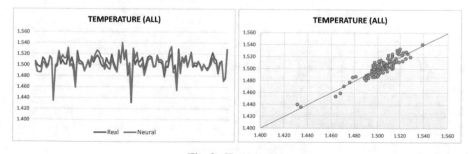

Fig. 2. Temperature

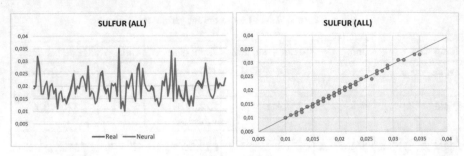

Fig. 3. Sulfur

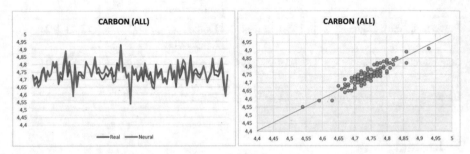

Fig. 4. Carbon

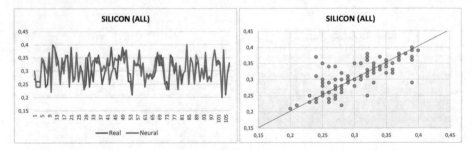

Fig. 5. Silicon

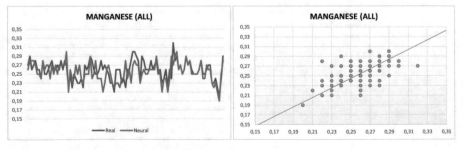

Fig. 6. Manganese

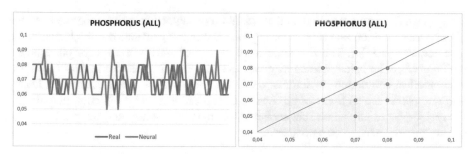

Fig. 7. Phosphorus

4 Discussion

The mathematical model showed a general correlation of 79.1% and only the output variable phosphorus content (Fig. 7) showed a low individual correlation of 27. However, to verify the functionality of the model for this variable, the hypothesis test, the 2-sample t-test, and the test of the two variances were performed with 99% confidence in the "Minitab® software", which confirms that the real and neural samples are identical, with the real mean equal to 0.07 ± 0.00 and the neural mean equal to 0.07 ± 0.01, with no atypical data points (outliers). The response of the neural network to the other variables (Figs. 1, 2, 3, 4, 5 and 6) was found to be excellent and the summary of the statistical analysis produced in the "Minitab® software" of the output variables is shown in Table 2.

Table 2. List of model input variables

Product	Output	Unit	Real value	Neural value	Correlation
Hot Metal	Daily production	tonnes/day	7397.5 ± 139.7	7397.0 ± 140.3	96.4%
	Temperature	°C	1520.9 ± 15.7	$1520.4 + 17.1$	90.9%
	Sulfur (S)	%	0.02 ± 0.01	0.02 ± 0.01	99.6%
	Carbon (C)	%	4.71 ± 0.05	4.74 ± 0.06	89.1%
	Silicon (Si)	%	0.31 ± 0.05	0.31 ± 0.05	77.3%
	Manganese (Mn)	%	0.26 ± 0.02	0.25 ± 0.02	71.5%
	Phosphorus (P)	%	0.07 ± 0.00	0.07 ± 0.01	27.9%

Sulphur and phosphorus are newcomers to pig iron and must therefore be removed from pig iron. Neural networks are able to monitor the production process and ensure the production of high quality hot metal. Sulphur and phosphorus mainly come from the metallurgical coke and operating parameters [25, 26]. The production of blast furnace slag affects the total solid carbon consumption. Therefore, it is important to control the quality of the raw material on a daily basis. In this simulation, the quality of the raw material remained constant throughout the simulation period [27–30]. The quality of the slag needs to be controlled so that it is fluid enough to flow and separate from the pig iron under appropriate conditions to promote efficient production of high quality pig iron and slag [30–34]. The neural network gave good results, except for phosphorus, which needs to be better studied as it was the only chemical element that showed low mathematical correlation. In summary, this work enabled the construction of a highly accurate neural model that can be used in the operational and production planning of the reactor, especially when fuel economy, operational stability and the production of quality pig iron need to be considered.

5   Conclusions

Considering the results, it is concluded that the developed artificial neural network is able to predict the quality of the pig iron produced, using 100 neurons and the logistic activation function. The mathematical correlation is good and the average values and standard deviations are similar when we compare the results of the database variables with the results provided by the neural networks. In future work, it is necessary to develop specific neural networks to monitor the values of sulphur and phosphorus, as this work has shown small shortcomings in monitoring these harmful elements for pig iron. The production of hot metal is a very difficult task. Therefore, it is only natural that the simulations are complicated to model, especially because the blast furnace combines several sub-processes that make model convergence difficult. The raw material is a variable that needs to be monitored and controlled, as the success of the model is highly dependent on this variable. In summary, the neural network is a tool that can be used in the production process of a blast furnace.

References

1. Chen, J.: A predictive system for blast furnaces by integrating a neural network with qualitative analysis. Eng. Appl. Artif. Intell. **14**, 77–85 (2001)
2. Demanboro, A.C., Bianchini, D., Iano, Y., de Oliveira, G.G., Vaz, G.C.: Regulatory aspects of 5G and perspectives in the scope of scientific and technological policy. In: Brazilian Technology Symposium, pp. 163–171. Springer (2023). https://doi.org/10.1007/978-3-031-04435-9_16
3. Iannino, V., Denker, J., Colla, V.: An application-oriented cyber-physical production optimisation system architecture for the steel industry. IFAC-PapersOnLine. **55**, 60–65 (2022)
4. Guo, D., Ling, S., Rong, Y., Huang, G.Q.: Towards synchronization-oriented manufacturing planning and control for Industry 4.0 and beyond. IFAC-PapersOnLine. **55**, 163–168 (2022)
5. Song, X.: Parameterized fragility analysis of steel frame structure subjected to blast loads using Bayesian logistic regression method. Struct. Saf. **87**, 102000 (2020)
6. Cardoso, W., Di Felice, R.: A novel committee machine to predict the quantity of impurities in hot metal produced in blast furnace. Comput. Chem. Eng. **163**, 107814 (2022)
7. Klingenberg, C.O., Borges, M.A.V., do Vale Antunes Jr, J.A.: Industry 4.0: what makes it a revolution? a historical framework to understand the phenomenon. Technol. Soc. **70**, 102009 (2022)
8. Cardoso, W., Barros, D., Baptista, R., Di Felice, R.: Mathematical modelling to control the chemical composition of blast furnace slag using artificial neural networks and empirical correlation. In: IOP Conference Series: Materials Science and Engineering, p. 32096. IOP Publishing (2021)

9. Beham, A., Raggl, S., Hauder, V.A., Karder, J., Wagner, S., Affenzeller, M.: Performance, quality, and control in steel logistics 4.0. Procedia Manuf. **42**, 429–433 (2020)
10. Cardoso, W., di Felice, R., Baptista, R.C.: A critical overview of development and innovations in biogas upgrading. In: Brazilian Technology Symposium, pp. 42–50. Springer (2022). https://doi.org/10.1007/978-3-031-08545-1_4
11. Hermann, M., Pentek, T., Otto, B.: Design principles for industrie 4.0 scenarios. In: 2016 49th Hawaii International Conference on System Sciences (HICSS), pp. 3928–3937. IEEE (2016)
12. Cardoso, W., Di Felice, R., Baptista, R.C.: Artificial neural network-based committee machine for predicting the slag quality of a blast furnace fed with metallurgical coke. In: Brazilian Technology Symposium, pp. 66–73. Springer (2022)
13. Itman Filho, A., Cardoso, W. da S., Gontijo, L.C., Silva, R.V. da, Casteletti, L.C.: Austenitic-ferritic stainless steel containing niobium. Rem. Rev. Esc. Minas. **66**, 467–471 (2013)
14. Garvey, A., Norman, J.B., Barrett, J.: Technology and material efficiency scenarios for net zero emissions in the UK steel sector. J. Clean. Prod. **333**, 130216 (2022)
15. Minango, P., Iano, Y., Chuma, E.L., Vaz, G.C., de Oliveira, G.G., Minango, J.: Revision of the 5G concept rollout and its application in smart cities: a study case in South America. In: Brazilian Technology Symposium, pp. 229–238. Springer (2023). https://doi.org/10.1007/978-3-031-04435-9_21
16. Rad, F.F., et al.: Industry 4.0 and supply chain performance: a systematic literature review of the benefits, challenges, and critical success factors of 11 core technologies. Ind. Mark. Manag. **105**, 268–293 (2022)
17. Cardoso, W., Di Felice, R., Baptista, R.C.: Artificial neural network for predicting silicon content in the hot metal produced in a blast furnace fueled by metallurgical coke. Mater. Res. **25**, (2022)
18. Lustosa, T.C., Iano, Y., de Oliveira, G.G., Vaz, G.C., Reis, V.S.: Safety management applied to smart cities design. In: Brazilian Technology Symposium, pp. 498–510. Springer (2020). https://doi.org/10.1007/978-3-030-75680-2_55
19. Cardoso, W., Di Felice, R., Baptista, R.C., Machado, T.A.P., Galdino, A.G. de S.: Evaluation of the use of blast furnace slag as an additive in mortars. REM-International Eng. J. **75**, 215–224 (2022)
20. Kim, D.-Y., Kumar, V., Kumar, U.: Relationship between quality management practices and innovation. J. Oper. Manag. **30**, 295–315 (2012)
21. Cardoso, W., Di Felice, R., Baptista, R.C.: Artificial neural networks for modelling and controlling the variables of a blast furnace. In: 2021 IEEE 6th International Forum on Research and Technology for Society and Industry (RTSI), pp. 148–152. IEEE (2021)
22. Pourmehdi, M., Paydar, M.M., Ghadimi, P., Azadnia, A.H.: Analysis and evaluation of challenges in the integration of Industry 4.0 and sustainable steel reverse logistics network. Comput. Ind. Eng. **163**, 107808 (2022)
23. Cardoso, W., Di Felice, R., Baptista, R.C.: Mathematical modeling of a solid oxide fuel cell operating on biogas. Bull. Electr. Eng. Informatics. **10**, 2929–2942 (2021)
24. Mazzoleni, M., et al.: A fuzzy logic-based approach for fault diagnosis and condition monitoring of industry 4.0 manufacturing processes. Eng. Appl. Artif. Intell. **115**, 105317 (2022)
25. Cardoso, W., Di Felice, R., Baptista, R.: Mathematical modelling to predict Fuel consumption in a blast furnace using artificial neural networks. In: Integrated Emerging Methods of Artificial Intelligence & Cloud Computing, pp. 1–10. Springer (2022). https://doi.org/10.1007/978-3-030-92905-3_1
26. Itman Filho, A., Silva, R.V., Cardoso, W.S., Casteletti, L.C.: Effect of niobium in the phase transformation and corrosion resistance of one austenitic-ferritic stainless steel. Mater. Res. **17**, 801–806 (2014)

27. Cardoso, W., et al.: Modeling of artificial neural networks for silicon prediction in the cast iron production process. Int. J. Artif. Intell. ISSN. 2252, 8938
28. Satyro, W.C., et al.: Industry 4.0 implementation: the relevance of sustainability and the potential social impact in a developing country. J. Clean. Prod. **337**, 130456 (2022)
29. Cardoso, W., Baptista, R.C.: Laves phase precipitation and sigma phase transformation in a duplex stainless steel microalloyed with niobium. Rev. Materia, **27** (2022)
30. Cardoso, W., Di Felice, R.: Prediction of silicon content in the hot metal using Bayesian networks and probabilistic reasoning. Int. J. Adv. Intell. Informatics. **7**, 268–281 (2021)
31. Rajab, S., Afy-Shararah, M., Salonitis, K.: Using industry 4.0 capabilities for identifying and eliminating lean wastes. Procedia CIRP. **107**, 21–27 (2022)
32. Cardoso, W., Machado, T.A.P., Baptista, R.C., de S Galdino, A.G., Pinto, F.A.M., de Souza Luz, T.: Industrial technological process for welding AISI 301 stainless steel: focus on microstructural control. In: Brazilian Technology Symposium, pp. 34–41. Springer (2022). https://doi.org/10.1007/978-3-031-08545-1_3
33. Cardoso, W., Di Felice, R.: Forecast of carbon consumption of a blast furnace using extreme learning machine and probabilistic reasoning. Chem. Eng. Trans. **96**, 493–498 (2022)
34. Cardoso, W., Di Felice, R., Baptista, R.C.: Perspectives on the sustainable steel production process: a critical review of the carbon dioxide (CO_2) to methane (CH_4) conversion process. International Series in Operations Research and Management Science (2023)

The Method of Ontological Designing of Complex Structural Events in the Study of Strikes of Aircraft with Wildlife

Nikolai I. Plotnikov[✉] [iD]

Scientific Research Project Civil Aviation Institute «AviaManager», 630078 Novosibirsk, Russian Federation
am@aviam.org

Abstract. This paper analyzes modern studies of strikes of aircraft with objects of wildlife or air-terrestrial animals: birds, bats, terrestrial mammals, and reptiles (Bird/Other Wildlife Strike). The paper presents a set of problems of the complexity of observing strikes. A method of ontological design is proposed, which contains an approach to reduce the uncertainty of describing complex structural events. A basic four-component strike observation model has been developed using the North American continental scale reports as an example. The study was carried out on the choice of a group of birds with the most significant in terms of the number of species and strike damage. The task of risk calculations establishes the possibility of reducing uncertainty and fuzzy event structure and creating metrics and calculations for risk management. The performed calculations of risks for groups of wildlife substantiate the development of a methodology to prevent risks. The development of a metric for observing the fuzziness of strike events is aimed at resolving the problem of interpreting incomplete, inaccurate information in strike reports. In this metric, the probabilities of actual damages and risks are calculated. The solution to the problem of calculating strike risks is carried out in the development of a relational matrix that contains data by parameters and indicators in selected scales. The results of the work are presented as algorithms for optimizing the mutual protection of aircraft and wildlife.

Keywords: Air transportation · Aircraft · Wildlife · Strike · Birds · Flight safety · Avian safety · Risk management

1 Introduction

The first accident in the history of aviation in a strike with a flock of birds was recorded by the Wright brothers on September 7, 1905, during tests by Orville Wright of the Flyer III aircraft [1]. In 1912, in California, in Long Beach, when a seagull hit the steering in a test flight of a Wright Model B-Pusher aircraft, the first plane crash occurred with the death of pilot Cal Rogers [2]. Research and development of modern methods of flight safety (FS) management are aimed at the establishment of aviation events (AE), investigation of aviation accidents (AA), and the study of statistics. Strike events have

© The Author(s), under exclusive license to Springer Nature Switzerland AG 2023
Y. Iano et al. (Eds.): BTSym 2022, SIST 353, pp. 11–35, 2023.
https://doi.org/10.1007/978-3-031-31007-2_2

a complex structure, high frequency, and relatively rare impact on flights with severe consequences.

This paper analyzes modern studies of strikes of aircraft with objects of wild nature (Wildlife) or air-terrestrial animals: birds, bats, terrestrial mammals, and reptiles (Bird/Other Wildlife Strike). The paper presents a set of problems of the complexity of observing strikes. A method of ontological design is proposed, which contains an approach to reduce the uncertainty of describing complex structural events. A basic four-component strike observation model has been developed using the North American continental scale reports as an example. The study was carried out on the choice of a group of birds with the most significant in terms of the number of species and strike damage. The task of strike risk calculations establishes the possibility of reducing uncertainty and fuzzy event structure and creating metrics and calculations for risk management. The performed risk calculations for the groups of wildlife substantiate the development of a methodology for observing strikes to prevent risks. The development of a metric for observing the fuzziness of strike events is aimed at resolving the problem of interpreting incomplete, inaccurate information in strike reports. In this metric, the probabilities of actual damages and strike risks are calculated. The solution to the problem of calculating strike risks is carried out in the development of a relational matrix that contains strike data by parameters and indicators in selected scales. The results of the work are presented as algorithms for optimizing the mutual protection of aircraft and wildlife.

2 Analysis of Aircraft Strike with Wildlife

2.1 Interaction of Aviation with Wildlife

In the subject under study, all aircraft are considered: airplanes, helicopters, and drones. The flight time starts from the taxiing and takeoff run to the end of the landing run. Therefore, strikes occur with air-terrestrial animals. The use of low-noise aircraft in commercial aviation is expected to reduce the ability of wildlife to recognize a strike hazard. Aircraft at greatest risk are light, low-altitude, high-speed, single-engine aircraft. The damage from strikes differs greatly from the speed of the aircraft and the mass of the body of the wildlife [3, 4]. Airport operators use many methods to reduce the likelihood and severity of strike risks, such as fencing off take-off and landing areas, local observations for compiling eBird databases, movement monitoring, and species identification. However, these measures are not very effective in relation to the observation of migratory movements of wildlife. Information about the location of the RBP based on expert observations and meteorological observation radars provides information on the resident and transit types of the wildlife. Radar observations provide information on the types of schooling and body weights of the wildlife. eBird data are based on the registration and reporting of previous strikes [5, 6].

2.2 Strike Risk Prevention Strategies

At present, the aviation world community has established the following strategies and measures to prevent the risks of aircraft strikes with wildlife.

Increasing the Strength of the Aircraft. Design and construction of aircraft elements with protection against damage and destruction. Designing different characteristics of windshields and engine inlet nozzles using high-strength materials and coatings that eliminate the worst-case scenarios of accidents. Certification of the airworthiness of the aircraft and structural elements with respect to strikes with wildlife is carried out by national and international aviation administrations [7–10]. The European Aviation Safety Agency (EASA) establishes strength certification for fuselage structures, windshields, and engines [9] of wide-body commercial aircraft [10] against impact kinetic energy requirements, which is defined by Eq. 1.

$$E_{kin} = 1/2 \cdot m \cdot (v)^2 \tag{1}$$

where (m) is mass, (v) is speed.

The kinetic energy certification criteria are set by EASA for large aircraft in the following values (Table 1).

Table 1. Certification criteria

Components	Kinetic energy criteria
Windshield	$E_{kin} = 1/2 \cdot 1, 8\, kg \cdot (v_{ref})^2$, v_{ref} - cruising speed at the corresponding route altitude
Hull	$E_{kin} = 1/2 \cdot 1, 8\, kg \cdot (0, 85 v_{ref}\, 2438\, \text{m})^2$, at the altitude of 2438 m
Engine	$E_{kin} = 1/2 \cdot m_{bird} \cdot (102.9\, \text{m/s})^2$, m_{bird} – bird body mass

Aircraft Space Freedom. Otherwise, remove the wildlife from the aircraft space. Design and organization of the aircraft movement space, minimizing strikes with wildlife. This strategy is being implemented in the following areas. (1) Organization of space. Airport fencing within five miles or greater distances of habitats and land use, wetlands, dredger containment sites, municipal solid waste landfills, and nature reserves that attract wildlife. (2) Regulatory actions. Development of regulatory documentation for ornithological flight safety. Formation of a database of strikes, statistical analysis, and participation in investigations. Evaluation of the bird hazard of airfields, development, and evaluation of the effectiveness of specialized means of protection against wildlife. (3) Ornithology. Organization of airport ornithological services, technical and biological means of scaring away birds in their habitats, formed by instincts over millions of years of evolution. The most productive is the content of the states of the "bird police" of hunting birds - saker falcons, golden eagles, pygmy eagles to "patrol" the sky over the airport. Creation of uncomfortable living conditions for wildlife. Extermination of insects and worms, cleaning of natural bird feeding areas near takeoff and landing areas, acoustic and bioacoustics installations, light signals, pyrotechnics, radio-controlled models of predators for scaring away, scarecrows, traps for trapping birds of prey, chemical means.

Wildlife Space Freedom. Otherwise, remove the aircraft from the wildlife space. Preservation of the wildlife habitat outside the aircraft movement space. Visual and radar observations, notification of airports about dangerous ornithological conditions. Designing airfields and take-off and landing areas, taking into account the historical areas of bird settlement and accounting for their migration. Development of a strike risk avoidance model based on a Geographic Information System (GIS), integrating data on geographical regions of habitat, migration, and feeding of various bird species, the U.S. Bird Avoidance Model (BAM) [5]. The analysis of numerous studies reliably establishes that the absolute number of aircraft strikes with wildlife occurs near the earth's surface during departure and arrival up to a height of 1000 m [11–14]. The implementation of strike avoidance is based on a comparison of the trajectory of the aircraft and the wildlife, similar to the Airborne Collision Avoidance System (ACAS | TCAS) [14], in which the space is structured into danger segments: caution, warning, and strike. Unlike ACAS | TCAS, which displays the exchange of distance information between aircraft, the strike avoidance system displays information from radars of the distance between the aircraft and the wildlife to make decisions about maneuver, departure, or approach delay and landing. Departure and arrival delays are related to runway and airport capacity calculations [15, 16]. Radars do not provide altitude information to calculate the Closest Point of Approach (CPA) for comparison with Predicted Bird Position (PBP) and Actual Bird Position (ABP). The distance between PBPs when the aircraft reaches the CPA is called the CPA distance (dCPA).

2.3 Content of the Problem

The International Civil Aviation Organization (ICAO) establishes aircraft flight safety requirements for the prevention of strike risks in the territories and near airports by fencing territories, displacement measures, scaring away, and liquidations, that is, to the detriment of the safety of the airborne flight [17]. Statistics based on the registration, recording, and analysis of strikes are considered incomplete since a significant part of the events is not recorded. The real number of strikes is several times more registered. According to the US Federal Aviation Administration (FAA) estimates from 1991–1997 to the present, about 20% of strikes that actually occur are recorded. Full statistics of strike observations is not maintained for various reasons: a) most of the strike are not critical, in the absence of damage to the aircraft, they may not be detected; b) lower priority of expenditures invested in security for this factor; c) a representative statistical sample of observations is preferred to complete statistics; d) insufficient formation and requirements for voluntary registration and accounting of the legal framework.

The requirements implemented by the Wildlife Control Units (WCU) have led to a reduction in the number of strikes at the airports themselves, but the upward trend continues outside them [6, 18]. To prevent strikes, observation radars of the ODP, weather radars, and the transmission of information from ATC to the crews of the aircraft Notice to Airmen (NOTAMs) are used [19, 20]. Radar data make it possible to establish statistical observations from a height above 200 m, they provide two-dimensional information about large flocks of birds [21, 22]. Aircraft crews and ATC services do not have volumetric information at low altitudes. The set of problems consists of the extreme complexity of observing, fixing, and registering the facts of strikes, and identifying groups and types of wildlife, which is required to develop strategies for the ecological balance of aviation and wildlife.

2.4 Method of Ontological Designing of Complex Structural Events

Method. The method of ontological designing (MOD) in this paper is considered a scientific approach to reducing the uncertainty in the description of complex structural objects and events [23, 24]. The basis of the method postulates the thesis that in order to control any object, it is necessary to identify its purpose through terms and definitions. Definitions set the features necessary for modeling and calculating the properties of an object, which is a condition of control. The method establishes a sequence of statistical analysis of events and information modeling for identifying the characteristics of objects and events necessary for calculating the risks of life safety management. Due to the lack of acceptable mathematical methods, symbolic formalization is used to formulate and solve the problem of this work. The purpose of the method is to establish measures to protect flights from strike events and reduce the risks of negative outcomes to acceptable levels. The method allows setting parameters, scales, and indicators for assessing the risks of adverse flight outcomes in possibilistic and probabilistic measures. The implementation of the method creates the possibility of reducing the risks of strikes in structured flight planning.

Task Statement. The purpose of this study is to design the strike event, which changes the complexity and fuzziness and allows the prevention of risks of hazard and the magnitude of event damage. The study contains the following tasks: a) analysis of the existing methods of observation, registration, accounting, and analysis of strikes between aircraft and aircraft; b) development of models of calculations of strike risks as the basis for the algorithms for software.

3   Designing and Modeling of the Strike Complex

This paper describes the model as a set of four components: space-time medium (M), aircraft (A), wildlife (W), and strike event (E) = (MAWE) (Fig. 1).

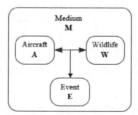

Fig. 1. Strike model

3.1 Initial Data

Information Sources. Formalized strike reports are produced by aircraft crews, air traffic controllers, ground handlers, airports, commercial aviation, and general aviation (GA) employees. Analyses for a certain period are compiled by government departments and international aviation organizations. Reports are generated only in cases of damage when strike events need to be recorded as incidents. The total number of strikes, especially minor and small bird strikes, remains virtually unknown. Databases (DB) contain incomplete, mutually inconsistent data. The largest databases were first created by the FAA in 1965. Systematized data collection, accounting, and analyses are formed in reports much later, starting in 1993. Until 1990, ICAO reported about 5,000 strikes annually. A comprehensive database of strikes was compiled in 1974–1988 by the US Air Force.

Strike Event Observation Space. The significance of the database lies in the completeness and accuracy of the data and depends on the space of the geographical scale of observations. This space in this paper is proposed to be structured into five levels: global, continental, national, regional, and local. Global observations are organized by international associations (ICAO). The continental level corresponds to the database created in the space of the continent. The national level corresponds to databases created in the space of a state. The regional level displays data at the scale of a distinct geographic region. The local level corresponds to the flight zone of the airport, aerodrome, or airfield. An example of the continental level of the DB [25] corresponds to the scale space of the North American continent and is used in the development of this work (Fig. 2).

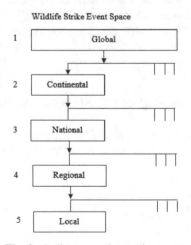

Fig. 2. Strike event observation space

The Number of Strikes. From 1985 to 2002, there were 52000 military aircraft strikes with birds, more than seven strikes a day, according to the US Air Force's Bird/Wildlife Aircraft Strike Hazard (BASH) Research Group. At the same time, 35 pilots died and 32 aircraft were destroyed. Losses were estimated at more than $30 million annually. The increase in strikes over the past three decades has been at an average of five percent due to an increase in air traffic (AT) of two to three percent annually. This paper analyzes data from the largest known reports compiled in the National Wildlife Strike Database (NWSD) FAA in collaboration with the US Department of Agriculture. For the period 1990–2020 238,652 strikes were recorded in the United States and a total of 243,064 strikes, including those assigned to the US military abroad [25].

3.2 Wildlife Objects (W)

In strike with aircraft, four groups of air-terrestrial (ATLs) animals (Wildlife Group) of 725 species were identified: 608 birds, 52 terrestrial mammals, 38 bats, and 27 reptiles [24]. Each group and species has characteristics: body weight, physical density, social behavior, flocking (herding) behavior, habitat use, feeding habits, movement patterns, and reactions to an approaching aircraft (Fig. 3).

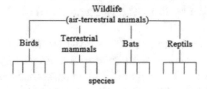

Fig. 3. Wildlife classification

About 90% of birds are legally protected under the Migratory Bird Treaty Act (MBTA) and the Mammals and Reptiles Acts at the state and local levels (Table 2).

Table 2. Number of registered aircraft strike with wildlife in the USA, 1990–2020 [25]

Wildlife groups	Quantity of species	Number of strikes	including strikes with aircraft damage
Birds	608	229551	16212
Terrestrial mammals	52	3561	1194
Bats	38	5006	26
Reptiles	27	534	3
Total	725	238652	17435

Further research, analysis, modeling, and calculations were carried out on the choice of a group of birds, as the most significant in terms of the number of species and strike damage. The calculation section below presents the rationale for this choice in the comparative calculation of strike magnitude risks across groups. Birds wildlife consists of the following parameters.

Species (Ws). Of the 608 identified birds, five species cause the most damage: pigeons (13%), raptors (12%), gulls (10%), waders (9%), waterfowl (6%), other species

(50%). 33 species of birds with an average weight of more than 2 kg with the highest probability of aircraft damage were identified. Of the terrestrial mammals, artiodactyls (deer) (90%) and carnivores (coyotes) (8%) cause the greatest damage.

Weight, kg (Ww). The number of strikes with birds weighing up to 0.5 kg is 25%, 0.5–2 kg is 60%, and more than 2 kg is 15%.

Age, years (Wa). Up to 1, 1–3, more than 3. The largest proportion of bird strikes are individuals less than one-year-old; the average is 1–3 years; the smallest is more than three years.

Behavior (Wb). Social behavior (flocking, herding) most affects the frequency of strikes and is determined by the combination of many characteristics of the wildlife. Flocking, number of individuals in a flock: 1, 2–10, 10–100, more than 100. There are no data on the behavior in known studies and reports.

3.3 Space-Time Media (M)

Space-time media consists of the following parameters.

Day (Md). Bird strikes by time of day occur: dawn (4%), day (62%), dusk (4%), and night (29%).

Seasons (Ms). January-March (11%), April-June (25%), July-September (40%), October-December (24%). Strikes with terrestrial mammals by the time of day occur: dawn (4%), day (26%), dusk (7%), night (52%); in seasons: January-March (7%), April-June (19%), July-September (50%), October-December (14%).

Altitude, m (Ma). Most (88%) bird strikes occur below 500 m, (9%) at 501–1000, (3%) at 1001–2000, and less than (1%) by 2000. Strikes at higher altitudes are more likely to damage aircraft than strikes at lower altitudes: 29% of strikes occur above 200 m and account for 45% of the damage. The record altitude for bird strikes is 31300 feet [25]. According to other sources, a world record was set when the aircraft collided at an altitude of 37000 feet with Ruppell's Vulture over Côte d'Ivoire [15]. Strikes with mammals occur near the earth's surface.

Landscape (Ml). Most strikes occur on: coast (50%), plains (20%), mountains (10%), and other (20%).

Weather (Mw). Clear, cloudy (fog), precipitation, rain (snow), wind (calm). Weather impact data are not available from known studies and reports. Bird strikes are known to occur more often in clear weather. Strikes with mammals occur more often at night in any weather.

3.4 Aircraft (A)

Aircraft as an object consists of the following parameters.

Flight (Af). 62% of bird strikes occur during aircraft arrival and 34% on departure: takeoff (17%), climb (16%), route (3%), landing (46%), run (17%), and taxiing (1%). Terrestrial mammal impacts: takeoff (17%), climb (2%), route (< 1%), landing (8%), run (55%), taxi, and park (2%).

Speed, km/h (As). At speeds less than 100 km/h, commercial aviation (3%), 100–200 km/h (50%), at speeds over 200 km/h (47%). In GA: at speeds less than 100 km/h

(16%), 100–200 km/h (62%), at speeds over 200 km/h (22%). Strikes with terrestrial mammals occur at taxi speed (2%), takeoff (33%), and landing and roll (63%).

Weight, kg (Aw). The number of strikes of aircraft weighing less than 2250 kg is (64%), 2250–5700 kg (23%), 5700–27000 kg (10%), and more than 27000 kg (3%).

3.5 Strike Event (E)

A strike event consists of the following parameters.

Element Damage (Eed). Aircraft elements occupy the following distribution of damage in bird strikes: nose cone (26%), windshield (15%), landing gear (15%), wings (propeller) (14%), engines (11%), and fuselage (11%). Other aircraft components (30%): headlights, tail, critical sensors such as pitot tubes, radars, communication antennas, navigation, and temperature sensors. With terrestrial mammals, damage prevails over propeller (46%), landing gear (14%), wings (main rotor) (10%), and other elements (30%).

Aircraft Damage (Ead). According to the classification of ICAO, damage to aircraft damage is assessed: no (93%), minor (3%), uncertain (2%), significant (2%), and destructive (<1%). In strikes with terrestrial mammals: minor (11%), uncertain (3%), significant (9%), and destructive (31%).

Effect on Flight (Eef). In bird strikes (95%), there are no consequences for flight, emergency landing (3%), aborted takeoff (1%), engine shutdown (<1%), or other (1%). In bird strikes, a frequent negative effect on a flight is running out or dumping fuel for a landing at the permitted landing weight and emergency landing. In strikes with terrestrial mammals, there are no effects on flight (93%), emergency landing (2%), aborted takeoff (5%), engine shutdown (1%), or other (8%).

Human Damage. Between 1988 and 2020, 327 people were injured in 251 strike encounters in the United States. 36 people died in 16 strikes. Around the world, as a result of strikes with wildlife in 1988–2020, more than 293 people died, and more than 271 civil and military aircraft were destroyed, with economic damage amounting to billions of dollars [25]. In the structure of the strike event, human damages are: injuries (human injuries), % (Ehi): < 5; victims (human fatalities), % (Ehf): < < 1. In the following content of the work, the calculations of damages from strikes of aircraft with wildlife are performed.

4 Strike Risk Calculation for Management Purposes

4.1 Calculation Task Statement

The task of calculating strike risks for management purposes establishes the possibility of reducing uncertainty and fuzzy event structure and creating metrics and calculations for risk management. For regulatory activities, modern theory and standards of risk management in aviation are used [14, 20, 26]. The standard [26] gives the following definition: "Safety risk. The predicted probability and severity of the consequences or outcomes of a hazard." The author of this paper outlined fundamental objections to the accepted terminology and proposed a different concept, definitions, and metrics for calculating life risks [27]. In accordance with the proposed concept, instead of measures of probability and severity of risks [26], the following metric is established.

The risk measure $(\overleftrightarrow{R})$ is determined by a set of fuzzy measures of hazard and the magnitude of the outcome of activity (Eq. 2):

$$\overleftrightarrow{R} : \{\tilde{\mu}_1 ExH\}, \{\tilde{\mu}_2 Ex^{\pm}M\} \tag{2}$$

where the measure $H\tilde{\mu}_1 Ex$ is denoted as a fuzzy measure of event hazard (H), the measure $\tilde{\mu}_2 Ex^{\pm}M$ is denoted as a fuzzy measure of event magnitude (M).

Definition 1. Qualification of the measure of hazard of the outcome $H\tilde{\mu}_1 Ex$. The hazard of an event is determined by measures of frequency in the areas of definition [uncertainty, certainty], [fuzziness, clarity], [discreteness, continuity] [24].

Definition 2. Qualification of the measure of the magnitude of the outcome $\tilde{\mu}_2 Ex^{\pm}M$. The magnitude of an event is determined by the measures of positive concepts (result, gain, luck), and/or negative concepts (harm, damage, loss), both, with the appropriate degrees: value, weight, importance, severity, and seriousness.

Definition 3. Risk quantification: a set of qualification measures of hazard and magnitude of the outcome are numerical estimates of values, the achieved formalization, suitable for subsequent calculation, risk quantification [27].

The event strike (E_S) cannot be observed directly, since it is a consequence of the interaction A-W in environment M, in which the strike occurs/does not occur/fuzzy occurs. A strike is an undesirable event, the general condition of which is written (Eq. 3).

$$E_S : \left| \left\{ \begin{array}{l} (M(A, W) \rightarrow f(E) | \textit{if the event occurs} \\ M(A, W) \rightarrow f'(E^{\sim}) | \textit{if the event fuzzy occurs} \\ M(A, W) \rightarrow f''(\overline{E}) | \textit{if the event is excluded} \end{array} \right\} \right. \tag{3}$$

where f, f', and f'' are the functions of solving the strike risk prevention problem.

For each environment $M_i \in M$, there are conditions $\in A$ and $W_i \in W$, when any event $E_i > 0$ in the phase space $\{E; \overline{E}\}$ is impossible if the solver function of limit protection and blocking danger $M_i \rightarrow \max f'$ is implemented. Detailing the solution to the problem consists in examining the parameters of the components of the MAWE model, related to the measures of hazard and measures of magnitude. This expertise is important and necessary for the calculation and risk management of events. The measure of the risk of random observation of the wildlife parameter W_H is written (Eq. 4).

$$\overleftrightarrow{R} : \{\tilde{\mu}_1 ExH\} \equiv (W_H, M) \tag{4}$$

where W_H is the statistical value of hazard (in the particular case, the probability) calculated by the i-th parameter of the wildlife; M is the statistical value of the environment parameters according to the eBird database.

The measure of the risk magnitude is written (Eq. 5).

$$\overleftrightarrow{R} : \{\tilde{\mu}_2 Ex^{\pm}M\} \equiv (W_M, A) \tag{5}$$

where W_M calculated magnitudes of the i th parameter of the wildlife; Λ are calculated values of aircraft parameters.

Similarly, calculations are carried out with respect to all parameters of the presented MAWE model. The calculation of the intensity of strike events is formalized by the following expression (Eq. 6).

$$Q^{Yi} = FN^{Yi}/EN^{Yi} \tag{6}$$

where Q^{Yi} is the intensity (coefficient) of strikes for the observed period (Yi-th year), EN^{Yi} is the number of flights of aircraft for the period, EN^{Yi} is the number of strike events for the period.

Further detailing of the solution to the problem is considered in the following content of the work.

4.2 Strike Risk Calculations by Wildlife Groups

The previously presented table [25] is used to perform the analysis and calculations. This table has been modified in the following way (Table 3).

Table 3. Strike risk calculations by wildlife groups

Wildlife groups	Quantity of species		Number of strikes		Strikes with damage		Analysis		
	A	A/T$_A$	B	B/T$_B$	C	C/T$_C$	B/A	C/A	C/B
Birds	608	0,84	229551	0,96	16212	0,93	378	27	0,07
Terrestrial mammals	52	0,07	3561	0,015	1194	0,068	68	23	0,34
Bats	38	0,05	5006	0,021	26	0,0015	132	0,7	0,005
Reptiles	27	0,04	534	0,002	3	0,00017	20	0,1	0,006
Total (T):	725	1,0	238652	1,0	17435	1,0	-	-	-

The columns are labeled: A - the number of species in the group, B - the number of strikes by groups, C - the number of strikes with aircraft damage, the total number (T) of numerical values by columns, T_A, T_B, T_C – calculated values by columns, B/A, C/A, C/B – ratios of values by columns. The following calculations are performed.

(A/T_A) - Calculation of the number of species of each group to the total number of species of all groups: birds −84%, land mammals 7%, bats −5%, reptiles −4%.

(A/T_B) - Calculation of the number of aircraft strikes of each group to the total number of strikes of all groups: birds −96%, land mammals 1.5%, bats −2.1%, reptiles −0.2%.

(C/T_C) - Calculation of the number of strikes with damage to aircraft of each group to the total number of strikes with damage to all groups: birds −93%, terrestrial mammals 6.8%, bats −0.15%, reptiles −0.017%.

Calculations $\{(A/T_A), (A/T_B), (C/T_C)\}$ and analysis [B/A, C/A, C/B] lead to the following conclusions:

Birds. In the observation of aircraft strikes (A/T_A) the group of birds absolutely prevails in terms of the number of species (84%), the number of strikes (96%), and the number of strikes with damage to the aircraft (93%) compared with other groups.

Terrestrial Mammals. Strikes of aircraft with terrestrial mammals due to body weight lead to significant damage $C/T_C = 6.8\%$. Their damaging effect C/B = 0.34 is five times greater than the damage from bird strikes C/B = 0.07. The number of terrestrial mammal species is 12 times less than the number of bird species, but the number of strikes with C/A = 23 damage is almost equivalent to C/A = 27 of bird damage. Therefore, damage rates do not depend on the number of species in groups.

Bats (Chiroptera). 625 species are known, but only 38 species have been recorded in reports of aircraft strikes [25]. Bat strikes B/A = 132 are significantly more frequent than B/A = 68 for terrestrial mammals and B/A = 20 for reptile strikes. Damage from strikes with bats C/B = 0.005 is two orders of magnitude less than with terrestrial mammals C/B = 0.34 and an order of magnitude less than with birds C/B = 0.07. Perhaps this is due to the behavior of large flocks and size anatomy: body length 2.9–40 cm, forearm length 2.2–23 cm, wingspan from 15 cm to 1.5 m, weight from 1.7 g to 1, 5 kg. [28].

Reptiles. Aircraft strikes with reptiles were recorded 48 times less than strikes with birds and an order of magnitude less than with terrestrial mammals and bats. This is probably due to the fact that strikes occur during a short period of aircraft flight time (taxiing, takeoff run, landing run), on the earth's surface, and the fencing of the territories of modern airports, which prevents the penetration of large species.

These calculations and analysis substantiate the importance of developing a monitoring methodology: (1) identifying aircraft strikes with wildlife, (2) identifying groups and types of wildlife, (3) fixing strikes, compiling reports, reporting, and analyses to prevent risks.

4.3 Development of Observation Metric of Fuzzy Strikes Events

Accounting for the events of aircraft strikes with wildlife is an extremely difficult task due to the fuzzy detection of strikes, accounting and identification of types of wildlife, establishing the degree of damage to the aircraft, and assessing the degree of impact on the flight, injuries, and deaths. The problems that arise in the interpretation of incomplete, inaccurate information or inconsistent reporting by national organizations illustrate the importance of reporting incidents. It is reported that the database contains only a part of the incidents that actually happened. It is estimated that only about 20% of strikes are reported to the FAA [25]. A significant proportion of the listed circumstances and factors remains unknown for detection and accounting; therefore, they can be calculated according to statistical data, heuristically and expertly. Below, it is proposed a method to overcome this problem by modeling the fuzzy observation metric of strike events. To develop the model, strike report data for the period 1990–2020 are used [25].

The proposed metric model has several levels of data accounting and relative percentages and elements of each factor. In the present work, an expert assessment of some factors was performed, the calculation of the absolute shares of damages, which is absent in the report [25] and many well-known studies. The purpose of the development is to calculate actual damage probabilities and strike risks.

1. Suppose that during the reporting period in a certain space for a certain period of time, the expected fuzzy number (N) = 100% of strikes between the aircraft and the wildlife is statistically observed.
2. Of the given integer, Nnrep80% were not reported and were reported Nrep20%. From this number, taken as a whole Nrep20% = 100%, the identified aircraft damage is Nrep_ad 7%, or from the initial amount (N) = 0.0286%.
3. The amount of damage in accordance with the ICAO classification is distributed as follows: minor (3%), uncertain (2%), substantial (2%), and destructive (<1%). Let us assume that only significant and destructive damages have an effect on flight, which is Nrep_damage 2%. This is from the original number (N) = 0.008116%.
4. From this number, taken as an integer Nrep_ad 2% = 100%, the effects on flight Nrep_ad_ef 5% are identified, which is (N) = 0.00032%.
5. Effects on flights are identified as follows: none and unknown (95%), emergency landing (3%), aborted takeoff (1%), other (1%), and engine shutdown (<1%). Ignoring the largest proportion of missing and unknown impacts (95%), the remaining impacts are about (5%), which is from the number (N) = 0.0000168% (Fig. 4).

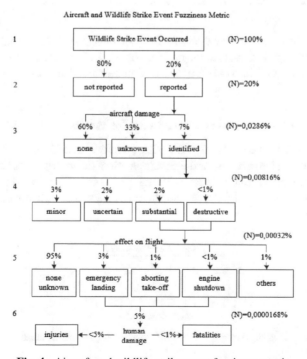

Fig. 4. Aircraft and wildlife strike event fuzziness metric

6. Human damage. Aviation accident statistics show that 95% of the people involved in a plane crash remain alive [30]. Therefore, injuries and fatalities are distributed in a ratio of 20:1, which is: injuries (N) = 0.0000159%, fatalities (N) = 0.0000009%.

To calculate the probability of damage from strikes of aircraft and wildlife data on air travel safety in the world for the last 70 years 1946–2020 are used [29]. From these data, a fragment was selected for the period 1988–2020, corresponding to the research task of this work. The average number of victims of air crashes from all causes or one accident per million flights (1:1000000) corresponds to the probability P = 10–6. The total number of victims for 1988–2020 is about 24000 people. The average annual number of victims is calculated to be about 750 people. The number of human fatalities due to the causes of aircraft strikes with wildlife for this period is 293 people [25], which is 0.0123 of the total number of casualties due to all causes and corresponds to a probability of about P = 10–8 (Table 4).

Table 4. Probabilities of human damages from strikes of aircraft with wildlife

Aviation accidents	Victims	Cases per flights	Probability
All reasons	24000	1:1 000 000	$P = 10^{-6}$
Aircraft strike with wildlife	293	1:100 000 000	$P = 10^{-8}$

The solution complex of strike observations in the form of a relational matrix, which contains the structural elements to the problem of calculating strike risks is carried out in the development of A of the MAWE model and quantitative data of strikes by parameters and indicators in selected scales.

4.4   Development of the Observation and Strike Matrix

To solve the problem of calculating strike risks, a matrix of MAWE model components is developed. General principles for the development of the matrix: (1) choice of space of observations: global, continental, national, regional, local; (2) a scaled known database of strike observations (eBird DB); (3) the choice of the wildlife group: birds, mammals, bats, reptiles (Fig. 5).

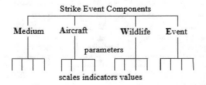

Fig. 5. Aircraft and wildlife strike component structure

This choice is important because of the significant difference in the data of aircraft strikes with different types of wildlife. All model MAWE components are structured into parameters in selected scales. Parameters are set as variables that allow setting calculation measures to prevent and mitigate the risks of an event.

For example, it is known that most strikes occur at low altitudes, therefore, by tracking the aircraft flight altitude parameter, it is possible to establish a metric of hazard, outcome, and magnitude of events. Scales display indicators and values of parameters. In the development of the matrix of this work, the above initial data [25] are used: the scale is continental (eBird DB), the wildlife group is birds, number of strikes with damage as a percentage (%). Symbols and abbreviations have been used to designate parameters. The dimension (number 1, 2, 3, and 4 table columns) of the scales is selected according to the criterion of the magnitude of the outcome of the event. For example, from the conditions for observing the speed of an aircraft, a flight is considered: from the start of the run to the end of the run. Taxiing bird strikes are rare (Table 5).

Table 5. Matrix of observation and calculation of the events of aircraft strikes and wildlife (birds). Continental scale [25]

MAWE	Parameters	Scales, values of indicators, %			
		1	2	3	4
Media (M)	Day (Md)	dawn	day	dusk	night
		4	**62**	4	30
	Seasons (Ms)	1–3	4–6	**7–9**	10–12
		11	25	**40**	24
	Landscape (Ml)	coast	plain	mountains	other
		50	20	10	20
	Weather (Mw)	clear	cloudy (fog)	rain snow)	wind (calm)
		often	regularly	periodically	sometimes
	Altitude, м (Ma)	**< 500**	501–1000	1001–2000	> 2000
		88	9	3	< 1
Aircraft (A)	Flight (Af)	takeoff	climb	cruise	approach (landing)
		17	16	3	**43 (17)**
	Speed, km/h (As)	< 100	100–200	> 200	
		3	**50**	47	
	Weight, kg (Aw)	< 2250	2250–5700	5700–27000	> 27000
		64	23	10	3
Wildlife (W)	Species (Ws)	**pigeons**	predators	gulls (waders)	waterfowl (other)
		13	12	10 (9)	6 (50)

(*continued*)

Table 5. (*continued*)

MAWE	Parameters	Scales, values of indicators, %			
		1	**2**	3	4
	Weight, kg (Ww)	< 0,5	**0,5–2**	> 2	
		25	**60**	15	
	Age, years (Wa)	< 1	1–3	> 3	
		sometimes	**regularly**	often	
	Behavior (Wb)	1	2–10	10–100	> 100
		sometimes	periodically	**regularly**	often
Event (E)	Elements (Eed)	nose (windshield)	chassis (wings, propeller)	engines	fuselage (other)
		26 (15)	15 (14)	**11**	11 (8)
	Aircraft damage (Ead)	none (unknown)	minor	significant	destructive
		93 (2)	3	2	**< 1**
	Effect on flight (Eef)	none	emergency landing	engines shutdown	aborted takeoff (other)
		95	3	**< 1**	1 (1)
	Human damage, %	Injuries (Ehi) < 5, fatalities (Ehf) < 1			
	Wildlife casualties	Annually 425,800 dead birds			

However, strikes with mammals and reptiles occur close to the earth's surface, so taxiing and even parking should be included in the matrix for these groups. The choice of indicators of aircraft damage elements can also be much wider. Flocking behavior means uniting in herd-packing forms of the social organization of populations. Weight determines the avian danger of damage. In observations, the lack of adaptation of young birds and a significant percentage of death are noted. The parameter of bird age is ecologically important but difficult to observe. From an ecological point of view, damage to an aircraft is identical to the death of a bird, calculated as damage to nature. It is not possible to enter an indicator of bird injury.

Let us note the important features of the developed model. The matrix contains parameters, scales, indicators, and values of quantities that are established empirically based on the results of statistical observations, analyses, and reports for the wildlife group birds [25]. Indicators and values are given in nominal scales, for example, "day (Md): dawn, day, dusk, night", and also in order scales, for example, "speed, km/h (As): < 100, 100–200, > 200". The scales are specific for each parameter, so the vertical columns of indicators cannot be mutually consistent. The values of all indicators are indicated as a percentage of the number of recorded strikes, except for the parameters "weather", "age" and "behavior", where the values are presented in natural language (NL) event frequency qualifiers [27]. Quantitative data for the "weather" parameter is missing in the reports. Similar matrices are compiled separately for each group of wildlife with a detailed adjustment of the parameters, scales, indicators, and values of the quantities that are given in the report [25].

In the development of a metric for observing the fuzziness of strike events, extreme difficulties were noted in compiling reliable statistical data. For example, the recording and reporting of strikes of wildlife with aircraft elements depend on the geographical scale of observations and have different data. The paper [30] gives the following strike frequency data: nose (8%), windshield (13%), engines (44%), wings (31%), and fuselage (4%). These data seriously differ from the data of [25]. A serious problem is the fact that the analyses and reports of observations provide only the "number of strikes" data. The quantitative data of these parameters do not match the actual risks established by experience. For example, the parameter "elements (Eed): nose 26%, windshield 15%, engine 11%". In practice, it has been established that the "windshield" and "engines", which are of lesser importance than the "nose", are the most critical elements of the vulnerability of the aircraft in strikes. Only seven percent of strikes are known to result in damage, so the "number of strikes with damage" data is needed for risk calculations. The subsequent content of this work is devoted to overcoming this problem.

4.5 Estimation of Accident Hazard and Magnitude of Strike Damage

This part of the work is intended to resolve the above problem of the mismatch between the scales of the developed observation matrix aircraft strike and wildlife and the lack of the "number of strikes with damage". Expertise is carried out: (1) evaluation of parameters related to measures of hazard and/or measures of magnitude; (2) evaluation of parameters, indicators, and their combinations that are critical for observations and strike risk calculations.

Risk Assessment. Hazard vs magnitude. In accordance with the above definitions of hazard and magnitude of risks, the procedure of expert evaluation of each of the parameters for compliance with measures of hazard and/or measures of the magnitude of the outcome of an event is performed. Differences in the signs of hazard and the magnitude of risks are fuzzy but necessary for subsequent calculations and the derivation of algorithms for their influence on the outcome of strike events. In the developed matrix, the report data are set as statistically verifiable, having the calculated values of the "number of strikes" in percent. That is, they have signs of magnitude. Example: parameter (Eed) "elements of damage": it is not possible to determine which element of the aircraft will be collided with wildlife. This parameter is random on the outcome of the event. Parameter (Eef) "effect on flight": according to the indicator "none" (95%), the parameter is random, according to other indicators "emergency landing, engine shutdown, aborted takeoff" 5% - indicators of magnitude. In general, indicators and signs of magnitude are those that can be quickly controlled by a person and correspond to facts, physical measurable properties of an event or object. Otherwise, the parameter is evaluated in measures of hazard (Table 6).

Table 6. Estimation of parameters: hazard (H), magnitude (M)

MAWE	Parameters	Estimation, %	
		(H)	(M)
	Day (Md)	70	30
Media (M)	Seasons (Ms)	50	50
	Landscape (Ml)	50	50
	Weather (Mw)	80	20
	Altitude, м (Ma)		100
	Flight (Af)		100
Aircraft (A)	Speed, km/h (As)		100
	Weight, kg (Aw)		100
	Species (Ws)	80	20
	Weight, kg (Ww)	90	10
Wildlife (W)	Age, years (Wa)	90	10
	Behavior (Wb)	100	
	Elements (Eed)	100	
	Aircraft damage (Ead)	95	5
Event (E)	Effect on flight (Eef)	95	5
	Human damage, % (Ehd)	100	
	Wildlife casualties, % (Ewc)	100	

In the assessment presented, four parameters of risk magnitude are specifically controlled by the crew and ATC: flight altitude, flight stage, aircraft speed, and weight. Other parameters can be assessed in terms of risks either hazard or magnitude. It is assumed that these assessments can be used to develop measures to prevent strike risks.

Assessment of Critical Parameters. Based on the derivation of critical parameters, the development of strike risk prevention algorithms is carried out.

Definition 4. Critical parameters are determined with the highest values of the "number of strikes" indicators, as well as the data "number of strikes with damage", established by expert and experimental means.

In studies, it was statistically established that the highest frequency of strikes occurs with birds of 0.5–2 kg. It has been experimentally determined that the most striking mass of a bird is determined to be 2.7 kg. In the identified 33 bird species, a correlation ($R2 = 0.82$) was established between the average body weight and the probability of aircraft injuries: for every 100 g of weight, the probability of injury increases by 1.22% [9]. It was revealed that the main danger is in the event of a strike of wildlife in the windshield and the aircraft engines. A large bird breaks the windshield at speeds of over 500 km/h and this can have fatal consequences for the life of the pilot and catastrophic destruction of the aircraft. The impact force of a bird weighing 100 g at an aircraft speed of 700 km/h reaches 20 tons. The risk of a pilot's death increases sharply at a speed of 400 km/h. Getting into the engine can lead to failure and disaster. The peculiarity of the consequences of strikes is that they can be either immediate or delayed. If destruction does not occur immediately, then destruction is possible during climb under the action of intra-cabin pressure and continued destruction of mechanical damage from high-speed air pressure in flight. An assessment has been made: the critical values of the indicators in the above matrix are highlighted in bold.

4.6 Aviation Safety vs Avian Safety

The solution to the problem of flight safety of aviation safety vs avian safety is similar to the solution to the problem of avoiding aircraft strikes in air traffic control. However, there is an important difference: in the strike avoidance problem, the motion of the aircraft is considered to be deterministic, which is possible for a formalized description, while in the problem of strikes between the aircraft and the wildlife, the motion of the wildlife is stochastic, the description of which is formally impossible. Observation parameters of aircraft and wildlife are general and specific for each object.

Damages Assessment. The following data are used to estimate and calculate the environmental damage caused by wildlife in strikes with aircraft, the conditions and assumptions are accepted. Wildlife damages mean the death of objects since there is no statistical record of injuries. Wildlife data with aircraft damage is used as evidence of the damage and death of wildlife. The calculations use statistical data on the ratios (coefficients) of strikes on the number of aircraft flights [25]. For certified commercial aviation airports for the years 2000–2020, the number of recorded strikes (hence, dead wildlife) per 100,000 flights is 21.29, including strikes with aircraft damage 1.25. According to the data of [31], the number of strikes that have occurred is five times more than the number taken into account, that is, 106.45 dead objects per 100,000 flights. In the behavior of the flocking parameter of birds, an indicator of 10–100 individuals is taken as statistically the most verifiable. For the sake of calculation, let us assume that 10 individuals from the flock die in each strike. For further calculations, the data of [25] are extrapolated to the global scale.

Currently, about 40 million commercial aviation flights take place in the world every year [32]. Calculations:

Damage to the wildlife: (40000000 flights) / (100000 flights) x (21.29 counted (106,45) strikes) x (10 birds) = 85160 (425800) counted (occurred) dead birds annually.

Aircraft damage vs wildlife damage: (1.25 / 100000 flights) = 0.0000125 vs (21.29 (106.45) / 100,000 flights) = 0.0002129 (0.0010645). Ratio: 0.0000125 / 0.0002129 (0.0010645) = 17032 (85.16).

Otherwise, the damages of wildlife exceed the damages of aircraft by 17 (85) times.

Human victims vs death of birds. Between 1988 and 2020, more than 293 people died in strikes around the world [25], on average, 9 people per year. Calculation: 85160 (425800) counted (occurred) dead birds / dead people (9) = 9 462 (47 311).

Otherwise, the number of victims of wildlife exceeds 9462 (47311) times the number of human victims. Almost 50000 birds die yearly in strikes between aircraft and wildlife per one human fatality. Let us summarize the calculations by comparing the annual number of casualties and damage to aircraft per 100000 flights with the estimated number of human fatalities (Table 7).

Table 7. Strike damage

	Damages	Number	1 / 2	1 / 3	Probability
1	Wildlife	85 160 (425 800)		9 462 (47 311)	$P = 10^{-5}$ (10^{-4})
2	Aircraft	21,29 (106,45)	17 (85)		$P = 10$–8
3	Human fatalities	9			$P = 10$–8

The performed calculations can be performed in more detail. First, separately perform calculations for groups and types of wildlife, for geographical scales. Calculations should take into account the GA data. For 100 000 GA flights, the number of strikes is 1.52, including 0.28 strikes with aircraft damage [25]. Strikes with damage account for about 6–7% in commercial aviation, and 18% in GA of the total number of recorded strikes. The total number of birds in the world is estimated at about 100 billion individuals [1]. From here, it is possible to structure and calculate the size of environmental damage.

4.7 Strike Event Algorithms

The MAWE model is described in the following scope and content of parameters (states). Medium (M) is observed in the totality of spatial-temporal parameters (Eq. 7).

$$M = \begin{cases} Time : (M_D, M_S); \; m_i, i = m_d, m_s \\ Space : (S_L, S_W, S_A); \; s_i, i = s_l, s_w, s_a \end{cases} \quad (7)$$

The aircraft (A) is observed in the set of parameters (Eq. 8).

$$A = (A_F, A_S, A_W); \; a_i, i = a_f, a_s, a_w \quad (8)$$

Wildlife object (W) is observed in the set of parameters (Eq. 9).

$$W = (W_S, W_W, W_B); \; w_i, i = w_s, w_w, w_b \quad (9)$$

The event strike (E_S) consists of sequentially connected states: (1) damage to critical elements of the aircraft (E_{ed}), (2) significant and destructive damage to the aircraft (E_{ad}), (3) unacceptable impacts on flight (E_{ad}), (4) negative outcome of the flight (Eq. 10).

$$\exists (E_i | E_{ed}) \rightarrow (E_{ad} | E_{af}) \rightarrow E_S \quad (10)$$

Definition 5. A strike event with a negative flight outcome is defined as a set of moral (human casualties) (E_H) and/or material damage (E_M) (Eq. 11).

$$E_S(E_i) = (E_H, E_M); \; e_i, i = e_h, e_m \tag{11}$$

Compilation of Strike Hazard Profiles. Based on the performed calculations, a profile (portrait) of the aircraft hazard for the wildlife is compiled as a strategic statement and solution of the problem for the geographic space, in the specific case of the airport (aerodrome) N. For this, a database is used with the characteristics of the parameters and features of a particular space. The profile is formulated in natural language (NL) with the addition of quantitative data. For the initial formulation, the structure of the description of the subject area and the quantitative data compiled in this paper are used. Hazard profile of aircraft with wildlife airport N:

"The risk of aircraft strikes with the wildlife of airport N has the highest probability and danger in the coastal zone during the day in August in clear weather from a flock of juveniles and adult gulls weighing one kilogram getting into the engine at an altitude of less than 500 meters at a speed of descent on approach and a pre-landing line."

The hazard profile is written by the algorithm in symbolic expression (Eq. 12).

$$M(A, W) = \left\{ M_i\big(M_{d_2}, M_{s_3}, M_{l_1}, M_{w_1}, M_{a_1}\big) \left[\begin{array}{c} A_i(A_{f_4}, A_{s_2}, A_{w_1}) \\ W_i(W_{s_1}, W_{w_2}, W_{A_2}, W_{b_3}) \end{array} \right] \right\} \rightarrow f(E_S) \tag{12}$$

where the components M_i, A_i, W_i contain parameters with critical indicators of the highest probability (danger) of strikes in accordance with the data of the developed observation matrix; digital designations of indexes of indicators correspond to the scale (column number) of the calculation matrix: M_{l_1} – coast, 50%; A_{s_2} – speed 100–200 km/h, 50%; W_{A_2} – age years.

This algorithm is the basis for the development of automated strike risk prevention systems. Profiles are compiled according to MAWE components, according to parameters and scales of indicator values.

4.8 Experimental Studies of Strikes

Expert assessments were carried out by the author of this work through questionnaires, surveys, and final discussions of the results.

Expert Assessments of Strikes. The main criterion for selecting experts is professional experience. The examination was attended by professional pilots with extensive flight experience. Among the experts were both active pilots and retired pilots. In different periods, interviews were conducted with several military pilots (1994–2012). Respondents were asked to answer the question: "How many strikes with wildlife have you had in your flight practice?" According to the respondents, almost without exception, they had cases of strikes with birds in flight. An average frequency has been established: strikes per flight hours (1/500), and strikes with damage per flight hours (1/4000).

Formalization of the Solution. When conducting expert assessments, formal conditions were fulfilled, called "mechanism of active expertise" [34, pp 183–184]. Suppose there are n experts evaluating pilot resource indicators using scalar values. Each expert reports an assessment (Eq. 13).

$$d \geq S_i \geq D, i = 1, n \tag{13}$$

where d is the minimum, and D is the maximum value of the indicator included in the field of ideas, definitions, knowledge, and experience of the expert.

Let us denote by r_i - the subjective statement of the indicator value. The final value of the indicator is displayed as $X = \pi(s)$ is a set of expert assessments $S = (S_1, S_2, \ldots, S_n)$. The procedure for the formation of $\pi(s)$ of the final grade is considered a monotonic function that satisfies the condition of the agreement of assessments (Eq. 14).

$$\forall_a \in [d, D]\pi(a, a, \ldots, a) = a \tag{14}$$

Let us assume that the subjectivity of the assessments corresponds to the true opinions $\{r_i\}_i \in N$ in accordance with the experience of each expert. The average score objectively and reliably corresponds to the estimated indicator (Eq. 15).

$$1/n \sum_{i=1}^{n} r_i \tag{15}$$

In this case, the options for manipulating $\pi(\cdot)$ are not considered, when the i-th expert insists on the eigenvalues of the indicators and will deliberately distort the values so that the average values $S_i \neq r_i$ are as close as possible to his statement r_i. Subjectivism of assessments was observed in the statements of the values of the minimum and maximum values. These problems were closed in group discussions.

Personal Experience.Personal Experience. Certainly, in the experience of most professional pilots, there have been close encounters and strikes in flight with birds and with animals. The author of this work is aware of the reliable fact of strikes with the cow of the AN-2 aircraft on the alignment during landing in the 1960s. The landing was completed successfully, but the cow was seriously injured by the footboard of the front door. In the author's professional flight practice, there were many strikes with birds, of which two strikes with serious consequences. The first strike with a large kite took place in 1968 at the aerial application of pesticides on an AN-2 aircraft at the exit turn from the rut at an altitude of about 50 m. A dent about 20 cm in diameter and about 5 cm deep remained on the duralumin edge of the attack on the left lower plane. The second meeting took place ten years later on an IL-18 with a flock of pigeons on the landing straight at Omsk airport. One of the pigeons hit the co-pilot's windshield and cut off his vision. After landing, the remains of the main part of the flock were found on the fuselage and the landing gear. The strike cost the lives of about two dozen pigeons at once. The facts of strikes were reported to dispatching and technical services.

5 Conclusion

The events of aircraft strikes with wildlife have a high frequency, extremely complex structure, and fuzzy content. These circumstances determine the complexity and costs of their observation and development of risk prevention measures. As the intensity of flights around the world increases, the total number of strikes will increase. The descriptions and structure of the subject area in this paper can be used as an approach for the development of manuals and manuals on ornithological flight safety management. The content of the work is based on the choice of a group of birds, which is recommended to be used when choosing other groups.

A new concept of risk calculations and an estimate of the randomness and magnitude of the observation parameters of the medium, wildlife, aircraft, and strike events are presented. Calculations show that in terms of the number of species, the number of strikes, and the number of strikes with damage, the group of birds prevails compared to other groups. Damage indicators do not depend on the number of species in groups. Due to their weight, damage from strikes with terrestrial mammals is five times greater than from strikes with birds. The development of a metric for observing the fuzziness of events makes it possible to calculate the probabilities of actual damages and strike risks. In the statistics of all accident causes, the events of strikes with the wildlife in this work are calculated by the probability of casualties for every 10–8 flights. Yearly almost 50000 birds die in strikes between aircraft and wildlife per one human fatality. A matrix and algorithms for observing and calculating strikes have been developed. Experimental studies have been carried out, which confirm the main results of statistical studies. The results of the work are algorithms as a base of computer programs for evaluating measures of flight protection from strike events and accident risks and adjusting forecasts taking into account the management decisions taken. It satisfies the need of airlines and airports to actively manage measures to protect flights from strike events and reduce the risks of accidents. Consumers are flight departments of airlines, ornithological services of airports, and emergency rescue services.

References

1. Sharing the skies. An Aviation Industry Guide to the Management of Wildlife Hazard Transport Canada, p. 366 (2004)
2. Thorpe, J.: Fatalities and destroyed civil aircraft due to bird strikes 1912–2002. International Bird Strike Committee, Warsaw (2003)
3. Van Gasteren, H., et al.: Aeroecology meets aviation safety: early warning systems in europe and the middle east prevent strikes between birds and aircraft. Ecography 42, 899–911 (2019)
4. Dolbeer, R.A., Begier, M.J.: Wildlife strikes to Civil Aircraft in the United States 1990–2017. Federal Aviation Administration National Wildlife Strike Database Serial Report Number 24, (2019)
5. Nilsson, C., et al.: Bird strikes at commercial airports explained by citizen science and weather radar data. J. Appl. Ecol. 58, 2029–2039 (2021). https://doi.org/10.1111/1365-2664.13971
6. Dolbeer, R.A.: Increasing trend of damaging bird strikes with aircraft outside the airport boundary: Implications for mitigation measures. Human-Wildlife Interactions 5, 235–248 (2011)

7. CFR 91.7 - Civil Aircraft Airworthiness; Federal Aviation Administration: Washington, DC, USA (2020)
8. EASA. Certification Specifications for Normal Aeroplanes; Amendment 5; European Aviation Safety Agency: Cologne, Germany, p. 750 (2017)
9. Oliveira, G.G., Iano, Y., Vaz, G.C., Chuma, E.L., Arthur, R.: Intelligent transportation: application of deep learning techniques in the search for a sustainable environment. In: Proceedings of the 2022 5th International Conference on Big Data and Internet of Things, pp. 7–12 (2022)
10. EASA. Certification Specifications and Acceptable Means of Compliance for Large Aeroplanes CS-25; Amendment 23; European Aviation Safety Agency: Cologne, Germany, p. 1135 (2019)
11. de Oliveira, G.G., Iano, Y., Vaz, G.C., Chuma, E.L., Gregio, R.P., Akkari, A.C.S.: Analysis of the ergonomic concept of public transportation in the city of campinas (Brazil). In: Stanton, N. (ed.) AHFE 2021. LNNS, vol. 270, pp. 453–459. Springer, Cham (2021). https://doi.org/10.1007/978-3-030-80012-3_52
12. Dolbeer, R.A., Begier, M.J., Miller, P.R., Weller, J.R., Anderson, A.L.: Wildlife strikes to civil aircraft in the United States 1990–2018; FAA National Wildlife Strike Database. Serial Report Number 25; FAA, U.S. Department of Agriculture: Washington, DC, USA, (2019)
13. McKee, J., Shaw, P., Dekker, A., Patrick, K.: Approaches to wildlife management in aviation. In: Angelici, F.M. (ed.) Problematic Wildlife, pp. 465–488. Springer, Cham (2016). https://doi.org/10.1007/978-3-319-22246-2_22
14. ICAO 2008–2015 Wildlife Strike Analyses (IBIS); Electronic Bulletin: Montreal, QC, Canada, 2017, p. 30 (2017)
15. European Organization for the Safety of Air Navigation. Bird Strike: Guidance for Controllers Sky Library (2018) https://skybrary.aero/articles/bird-strike-guidance-controllers
16. http://www.birdstrike.org. 3 August 2009
17. de Oliveira, G.G., Iano, Y., Vaz, G.C., Chuma, E.L., Negrete, P.D.M., Negrete, J.C.M.: Structural analysis of bridges and viaducts using the iot concept. an approach on dom pedro highway (Campinas-Brazil). In: Brazilian Technology Symposium, pp. 108–119. Springer (2022). https://doi.org/10.1007/978-3-031-08545-1_10
18. DeFusco, R.P., Unangst, E.T.J., Cooley, T.R., Landry, J.M.: ACRP report 145 applying an SMS approach to wildlife hazard management; airport cooperative research program; Transportation Research Board: Washington, DC, USA, p. 242 (2015)
19. MacKinnon, B.: Sharing the Skies. An Aviation Industry Guide to the Management of Wildlife Hazards; Transport Canada: Ottawa, ON, Canada, 2004, p. 366 (2004)
20. European Organization for the Safety of Air Navigation. ATFCM User Manual Network Manager. EUROCONTROL, Brussels, Belgium, p. 129 (2018)
21. Shamoun-Baranes, J., et al.: Innovative Visualizations Shed Light on Avian Nocturnal Migration. University of Amsterdam, p. 16 (2016)
22. Dokter, A.M., Liechti, F., Stark, H., Delobbe, L., Tabary, P., Holleman, I.: Bird migration flight altitudes studied by a network of operational weather radars. J. R. Soc. Interface, 8, 2330–1243 (2010)
23. Plotnikov, N.I.: Methods of resource modeling of organizational objects. In: Kwasiborska, A., Skorupski, J., Yatskiv, I. (eds.) ATE 2020. LNITI, pp. 116–130. Springer, Cham (2021). https://doi.org/10.1007/978-3-030-70924-2_10
24. Plotnikov, N.I.: The development of the subject domain observation complex for management purposes. In: 2018 XIV International Scientific-Technical Conference on Actual Problems of Electronics Instrument Engineering (APEIE). vol. 1, part 1, pp. 268–272 (2018). https://doi.org/10.1109/apeie.2018.8545868
25. Dolbeer, R.A., Begier, M.J., Miller, P.R., Weller, J.R., Anderson, A.L.: Wildlife strikes to civil aircraft in the US, 1990–2020. FAA Report 27, 141 (2021)

26. Annex 19 to the Convention on International Civil Aviation. Safety Management, 2nd ed. ICAO, p. 46 (2016)
27. Plotnikov, N.I.: Soft computing method in events risks matrices. In: Iano, Y., Saotome, O., Kemper, G., Mendes de Seixas, A.C., Gomes de Oliveira, G. (eds.) BTSym 2020. SIST, vol. 233, pp. 578–588. Springer, Cham (2021). https://doi.org/10.1007/978-3-030-75680-2_64
28. https://zmmu.msu.ru/bats/rusbats/order.html
29. https://tass.ru/infographics/9251?utm_source
30. Nicholson, R., Reed, W.S.: Strategies for Prevention of birdstrike events. AERO, Q3, pp.17–24 (2011) www.boeing.com/commercial/aeromagazin
31. Allan, J.R., Bell, J.C., Jackson, V.S.: An assessment of the world-wide risk to aircraft from large flocking birds. Bird Strike Committee-USA/Canada, First Joint Annual Meeting, Vancouver, BC (1999) https://digitalcommons.unl.edu/birdstrike1999/4
32. https://www.un.org/en/observances/civil-aviation-day
33. Novikov, D.A.: The Theory of Management of Organizational Systems. 2nd ed. Fizmatlit, Moscow, p. 584 (2007) (in Russian)

Effect Analysis of Service Entrance Box on the Wireless Communication Performance of Home Electric Power Meters

Rafael J. Minhoto[1]([✉])(iD), Carlos E. Capovilla[2](iD), Ivan R. S. Casella[2](iD), Alfeu J. Sguarezi Filho[2](iD), and Claudionor F. do Nascimento[3](iD)

[1] Centro de Tecnologia da Informação Renato Archer, Campinas, Brazil
`rafael.minhoto@cti.gov.br`
[2] Universidade Federal do ABC, Santo André, Brazil
`{carlos.capovilla,ivan.casella,alfeu.sguarezi}@ufabc.edu.br`
[3] Universidade Federal de São Carlos, São Carlos, State of São Paulo, Brazil
`claudionor@ufscar.br`

Abstract. Nowadays, the wireless communication system based on the IEEE 802.15.4 standard is one of the standards that can be used in the advanced metering devices of modern residential electric energy meters. In this paper, the authors present an analysis of the wireless communication system performance of these meters with open-area site measurements carried out in some streets of Sao Carlos, Brazil. This analysis was developed by employing a pair of communication boards, where, the first one, installed inside the service entrance metal box, was used to emulate a modern electric energy meter, and the second one was used to emulate an access point at a fixed height of 4.8 m within a pre-defined coverage area. The results have shown that the deployment and use of wireless communication in a modern residential electric power meter should be customized for each environment scenario to ensure, after installation, an adequate operation of the entire system.

Keywords: IEEE 802.15.4 · Wireless communication · Home electric power meter

1 Introduction

Smart metering is part of an energy policy with a focus on implementing new concepts that can provide consumers with friendly access to various services [1,2]. In this way, modern residential smart meters are among the enablers of this smart grid concept, providing consumers with greater control over their energy consumption [3,4].

Such modern smart meters are usually integrated with the system via a wireless communication interface. However, there is still a discussion about which

Y. Iano et al. (Eds.): BTSym 2022, SIST 353, pp. 36–44, 2023.
https://doi.org/10.1007/978-3-031-31007-2_3

communication technology would be the most attractive to be employed for the last-mile connection [5]. In view of this, Yongyong and Chenghao [6] suggest the wireless communication technology ZigBee as a potential candidate.

In this context, this paper presents an experimental analysis of the performance and range of wireless communication applied to a modern smart meter. The object of this study is to observe some parameters of wireless communication within a case study, in which a meter and its wireless communication system are installed inside the service entrance metal box, in an urban area of Sao Carlos, Brazil. For it, two communication devices, based on the standard IEEE Std. 802.15.4 at 915 MHz, are used.

The motivation for this work occurred due to the lack of homogeneity in the installation of the service entrance metal box in Group B customers, and, in this specific case, in the oldest buildings in the city.

This lack of homogeneity in the positioning of the installation of the service entrance metal box in the residence, combined with the variation of the external environment (relief, buildings, trees, etc.) and the impracticality of installing the antenna on the external side of the service entrance metal box for security reasons, compromise the deployment of a wireless network for the smart meter, eventually reducing the performance and range of communication, if a dedicated analysis for each environment is not adopted.

This paper has been divided into three sessions in addition to this introductory one. Section 2 presents the contextualization of the environment and the system, while Sect. 3 presents the measurement and analysis of the results. Finally, Sect. 4 concludes the paper.

2   Environment and System Context

The open-area site analysis aims to verify the range and quality of communication from pre-established distances, in a case study in the city of Sao Carlos (Brazil), and the aerial view of the test region is presented in Fig. 1.

Two standard IEEE Std. 802.15.4 boards were used for this analysis [7], with the first installed within the service entrance metal box and the second simulating the access point. The reference works for the open-area site measurements are by Clarke [8], Okumura [9], Hata [10], and Bultitude [11], in addition to works for IoT such as those by Khan [12], Silva [13] and Medeiros [14].

Two boards from Texas Instruments [15] were used for such tests. The model CC1352P-2 board was used as the receiver (RX), installed inside or outside the service entrance metal box, and coupled to a 3 dBi omnidirectional antenna. The antenna was aligned in the center of the window the service entrance metal box, this being the position chosen as the best possible for the setup. The entrance metal box was mounted perpendicular to the street, with the reading window facing west and the back, mounted on a brick wall, facing east, while the left side of the service entrance metal box faced north and the right side faced south.

At the other end of the link, a second model CC1352-R LPSTK board was used as a transmitter (TX) and coupled to an 8.15 dBi antenna. The antenna was fixed on a 4.8 m mobile mast to emulate the position and height of a utility-installed access point.

Fig. 1. Aerial View of the Test Region in Sao Carlos, Brazil.

3   Analysis of Results

The experimental analysis was divided into two approaches. The first approach presented here was performed using the CC1352P-2 board configured to transmit at 915 MHz, in continuous wave (CW), power of 10 dBm, in order to verify and compare the RF signal attenuation with the board outside and inside the service entrance metal box for the distances and positions defined in Fig. 1.

The first measurement was performed with the board without the service entrance metal box, and the results are shown in Fig. 2, while the second measurement, represented in Fig. 3, was performed with the board installed inside the service entrance metal box.

As a receiver, a spectrum analyzer model RF Explorer 3G was used, coupled to a half-wave dipole antenna, set at 915 MHz and installed on a mast 4.8 m long (the same mast on which one of the boards for the subsequent tests will be installed).

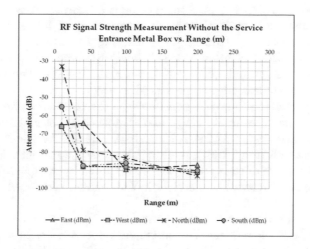

Fig. 2. RF signal strength measurement without the service entrance metal box.

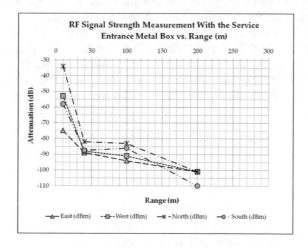

Fig. 3. RF signal strength measurement with the service entrance metal box.

Values higher than −103 dBm were discarded, since this is the maximum sensitivity of the receiver block of the CC1352P-2 board, according to the manufacturer's datasheet, for the following technical characteristics: frequency of 915 MHz, the data rate in the reception of 200 kbps, BER of 10^{-2} for 311 kHz RX bandwidth and 2-GFSK modulation. The maximum range with the board outside the service entrance metal box was 200 m, and the signal measured for the 300 m distance was greater than –103 dBm. For the measurements with the board inside the service entrance metal box, the maximum range was 100 m, and for the distance of 200 m, the signal level ranged from –100 to –110 dBm, being close to the limit of –103 dBm.

The second approach was performed using two boards, where the CC1352P-2 board was installed within the service entrance metal box as a receiver and the CC1352R board as a transmitter simulating an access point, as detailed in the system contextualization. For this analysis, some metrics were adopted to estimate the range and quality of the communication. The distances and positions defined are the same as presented in Fig. 1.

In this experimental analysis performed in the open-area site, two metrics were adopted, one to estimate range and the other to estimate the quality of the communication system IEEE Std. 802.15.4. The first metric is the Received Signal Strength Indicator (RSSI), used to determine the strength of the received RF signal. The range of the system can be estimated by comparing the value of RSSI with the sensitivity of the receiver in the configuration used which is –103 dBm [15].

The second metric is the Packet Error Rate (PER), used to determine the packet error rate at the receiver. The maximum value of PER, for a receiver of the TI - CC1352 family is ≤ 1%. The reading of the RSSI and PER were performed using the software from TI - CC1352 family boards. The measurements at the receiver were performed for two different data rates of 50 kbps and 200 kbps, in order to analyze the effect of data rate on system performance.

Tables 1 and 2 show the settings used on each card. The first test was performed with a 50 kbps data rate. The second test was performed with a data rate of 200 kbps, in the same positions used in the first test. In both cases, the relationship between the distance by the data rate [16]. The points indicated in Fig. 1 correspond to the source locations of the transmission.

Table 1. LPSTK Board Configuration.

Test	TX	TX
Mode	2-GFSK	GFSK 200 k
Freq.	915 MHz	915 Mhz
Pkts	10000	10000
Interval	No	No
Length	30	30

Table 2. CC1352P-2 Board Configuration.

Data Rate	RX 50 kbps	RX 200 kbps
Modulation	2-GFSK	2-GFSK
Freq.	915 MHz	915 Mhz
Deviation	25 kHz	50 kHz
RX Bandwidth	100 kHz	311 kHz

Figure 4 and Fig. 5 show the results of the measurements performed. The figures show the ratio of the RSSI measured at the reception of the CC1352P-2 board, by distance, for the data rate of 50 kbps and 200 kbps. Figure 4 presents the measurements in the four directions, for a 50 kbps data rate.

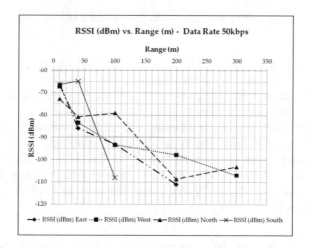

Fig. 4. RSSI vs. Range –50 kbps.

The longest range of communication occurred in the west and north directions. In the west direction, the service entrance metal box was installed perpendicular to the road, with the reading window facing that direction. The street is sloping, with buildings on only one side of the road, and possibly the scanning window has additionally contributed to a longer range in this direction. In the northern direction there were few buildings, undergrowth up to 100 m, and trees between 100 m and 300 m.

For the other directions, the range was smaller, especially for the southern direction, in which the maximum range was 100 m, being the direction with the highest density of buildings. For the eastern direction, the maximum reach was 200 m. In this direction, there were fewer buildings compared to the southern direction, with the street on a slope and the service entrance box with the back supported by brick.

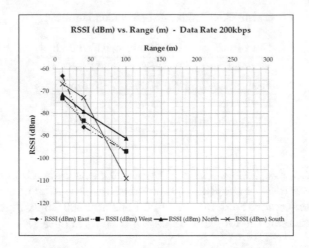

Fig. 5. RSSI vs. Range –200 kbps.

The measurements were repeated for a data rate of 200 kbps in the same directions and positions, as shown in Fig. 5. For all directions, there was a reduction in communication range, as expected, so the maximum communication range for a data rate of 200 kbps was limited to 100 m.

Besides the rise in data rate reducing the communication range, the rise in PER above 1% was the other factor reducing the communication range, caused by the rise in packet loss in the reception of the CC1352P-2 board. The estimation of the communication range was also limited by the value of PER. Table 3 presents the values of PER by distance, detailing such an observation in relation to the results obtained.

Table 3. Open-Area Site Measurements from PER (%) vs. Range (m).

Range (50 kbps)	10	40	100	200	300
PER East	0	**2.6**	0	**99.7**	**100**
PER West	0	0	1.7	**4.6**	**95**
PER North	0	0.4	0	**99.9**	**73.8**
PER South	0	0	**99**	**100**	–
Range (200 kbps)	**10**	**40**	**100**	**200**	**300**
PER East	0	0.2	**91.5**	**99.8**	–
PER West	0	0	**73**	**99**	**99**
PER North	0	0	**71**	0	**98**
PER South	0	0.1	**99**	–	–

4 Conclusion

This paper had the purpose of observing the effect of the service entrance metal box on the wireless communication of residential electric energy meters. A case study was carried out in the city of Sao Carlos (Brazil), in which different parameters of the wireless communication system were verified in several different directions along the environment.

The results show that the allocation of smart meters with an integrated communication system requires that the effects of the environment and the directions in which the access points on the poles will be installed are properly pre-analyzed, in order to ensure after implementation the perfect functioning of the wireless communication system within acceptable parameters in the desired directions.

Acknowledgment. This research was partially supported by CNPq, FAPEMIG, INERGE, and CAPES (Finance Code 001).

References

1. Ustun, T.S., Hussain, S.M.S.: Extending IEC 61850 communication standard to achieve Internet-of-Things in smartgrids. In: 2019 International Conference on Power Electronics, Control and Automation (ICPECA), pp. 1–6. IEEE (2019)
2. Bacega, P.R.d.O., Iano, Y., Carvalho, B.C.S.d., Vaz, G.C., Oliveira, G.G.d., Chuma, E.L.: Study about the applicability of low latency in HAS transmission systems. In: Brazilian Technology Symposium pp. 73–87. Springer (2023). https://doi.org/10.1007/978-3-031-04435-9_7
3. Neto, A.B., et al.: The BFS method in a cloud environment for analyzing distributed energy resource management systems. In: Brazilian Technology Symposium, pp. 349–362. Springer (2023). https://doi.org/10.1007/978-3-031-04435-9_35
4. Giaconi, G., Gunduz, D., Poor, H.V.: Privacy-aware smart metering: Progress and challenges. IEEE Signal Process. Mag. **35**, 59–78 (2018)
5. Srivilas, K., Pirak, C.: feasibility study and performance analysis of nb-iot communications for pea smart grid network. In: 2021 18th International Conference on Electrical Engineering/Electronics, Computer, Telecommunications and Information Technology (ECTI-CON), pp. 240–244. IEEE (2021)
6. Yongyong, Y., Chenghao, H.: Design of data acquisition system of electric meter based on ZigBee wireless technology. In: 2020 IEEE International Conference on Advances in Electrical Engineering and Computer Applications (AEECA), pp. 109–112. IEEE (2020)
7. IEEE SA, T.: IEEE Standard for Low-Rate Wireless Networks, Revision of IEEE Std 802.15.4-2015 (2020)
8. Clarke, R.H.: A statistical theory of mobile-radio reception. Bell Syst. Tech. J. **47**, 957–1000 (1968)
9. Okumura, Y.: The mobile radio propagation model "OKUMURA-Curve" and the world's first full-scale cellular telephone system. In: 2017 IEEE History Of Electrotechnology Conference (HISTELCON), pp. 107–112. IEEE (2017)
10. Hata, M.: Empirical formula for propagation loss in land mobile radio services. IEEE Trans. Veh. Technol. **29**, 317–325 (1980)

11. Bultitude, R.J.C., Bedal, G.K.: Propagation characteristics on microcellular urban mobile radio channels at 910 MHz. IEEE J. Sel. Areas Commun. **7**, 31–39 (1989)
12. Khan, M.F., Wang, G., Bhuiyan, M.Z.A., Li, X.: Wi-Fi signal coverage distance estimation in collapsed structures. In: 2017 IEEE International Symposium on Parallel and Distributed Processing with Applications and 2017 IEEE International Conference on Ubiquitous Computing and Communications (ISPA/IUCC), pp. 1066–1073. IEEE (2017)
13. Silva, B.J., Hancke, G.P.: Characterization of non-line of sight paths using 802.15. 4a. In: 2017 IEEE International Conference on Industrial Technology (ICIT), pp. 1436–1440. IEEE (2017)
14. Campos, M.M.M., Mattos, M.O., Macedo, R.S., Medeiros, A.A.M., Oliveira, W.V., Sousa, V.A., Jr.: People effects on IoT wireless channel characterization. Revista Principia - Divulgação Científica e Tecnológica do IFPB **53**, 141–149 (2021)
15. LAUNCHXL-CC1352P Evaluation board — TI.com. https://www.ti.com/tool/ LAUNCHXL-CC1352P (Accessed 25 Nov 2022)
16. McNamara, J.E.: Technical Aspects of Data Communication (1988). 3rd edn. Digital Press (1988)

A Digitally Controlled Delay Generator Implemented with Cyclone V FPGA Using Timing Analysis

Vlademir J. S. Oliveira[1]([⊠]) [iD], Elton F. Santos[1] [iD], Weverton R. Cajado[1] [iD],
Franklin H. Schmatz[1] [iD], and Wellington R. Melo[2] [iD]

[1] Universidade do Estado de Mato Grosso, Sinop, Brazil
vlademir.oliveira@unemat.br
[2] CTI - Renato Archer, Campinas, Brazil

Abstract. A digital delay generator can have a wide range and high resolution if divided into coarse and fine parts. In this paper, the implementation of a delay generator using counters and delay chains is presented using Field Programmable Gate Array (FPGA). The main contribution of the proposal is the implementation of delay chains with behavioral descriptions, applying a method to linearize them with no manual editing of the layout or routing, based on timing analysis. The building blocks consist of the digitally-controlled delay line (DCDL), employed for fine-tuning, a state machine for coarse-tuning, and the time-to-digital converter (TDC) to correct the error due to the unknown time interval between input and clock. The system is implemented on a Cyclone V SoC 5CSXFC6C6U23C8 device, with a 10-bit delay generator, achieving around 625 ps resolution in the LSB, and a range of 170 ns. The values measured of INL are $[-0.22, 1.91]$ in LSB.

Keywords: Digitally-Controlled Delay Lines (DCDL) · Time-to-Digital Converter (TDC) · Behavioral description · Field Programmable Gate Array (FPGA)

1 Introduction

Digitally controlled delay generators are widely used in timing experiments, test equipment, and clock deskew applications [1, 2]. These architectures are increasingly being found in all-digital versions, and the main approach to achieving high resolution is to use digitally-controlled delay lines (DCDL), that use delay chains. In this work, it is presented a counter-based architecture, referenced in [3] and [1], for widened range, and an adapted version of the DCDL proposed in [4] for getting high resolution. We propose the implementation of delay chains with behavioral description, using static time analysis to predict gate delays allowing delay chains to obtain better linearity. Time constraints provide a way to keep the path time between elements at specific values that guide the routing of those elements [5]. In this approach, the Intel® Quartus® Prime tool validates if the design has met the time constraints as designed. The design is set to slow 1100 mV 85 C model operating conditions corner for all analysis.

An issue with this approach is that the VHDL's optimization process eliminates logic redundancies in the circuit, and the delay chains are minimized [5]. These setups are very useful for improving performance, and many of them are set by default in the EDA tools. Delay chains are chains of elements with propagation delay and have multiple nets between the elements. As a solution, the "attribute keep" assignment is used to keep a wire name in the final netlist of the circuit [6]. It inserts a hard logic cell buffer to prevent a wire or a node from being taken away due to synthesis minimization.

This paper is organized as follows: the architecture and its main building blocks are described in Sect. 2. The details of architecture implementation using measurement results are in Sect. 3, and the conclusions are in Sect. 4.

2   Architecture Description

There is an error due to the unknown time interval between an input signal and the clock. Figure 1 illustrates the timing diagram of the proposed architecture. The total delay (t_{delay}) is digitally programmed by a binary value, whose more significant bit (MSB) controls the coarse delay (t_{coarse}) and the less significant bit (LSB) the fine delay (t_{fine}), thus

$$t_{delay} = n_{coarse} \times T + t_{fine} \tag{1}$$

where T is the clock period and n_{coarse} is the number of cycles.

Unfortunately, the error is added to the total delay and its value can range from 0 to T. The error value can be measured using a time-to-digital converter (TDC) [3] and the correction circuit can be implemented in VHDL. Thus, the proposed architecture is composed of a coarse delay generator (CDG), a fine delay generator (FDG), TDC, and a control logic.

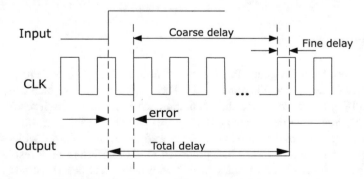

Fig. 1. Timing diagram of the proposed delay generator

Figure 2 shows the architecture proposed for the delay generator. The control logic performs the subtraction of the delay error by reducing the fine delay size in the total delay. The control logic input is divided into two parts: coarse control (C_{MSB}) and fine control (C_{LSB}), as well as its output is divided into two parts, R and S. If the error is smaller than the LSB of the control input (C_{LSB}), then $S = C_{LSB}$ - E, where S is the LSB of control logic and E is the error. However, if $E > C_{LSB}$, then $R = C_{MSB}$ -1 and $S =$ (TB - E) + C_{LSB}, where TB is a constant that represents the binary value of the clock period.

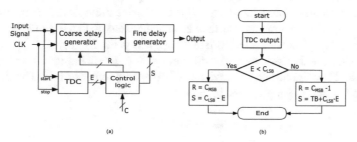

Fig. 2. Delay generator concept (a) architecture diagram (b) Control Logic flowchart.

2.1 Coarse Delay Generator

As shown in Fig. 3, to control the generated delay, a four-state state machine and a counter-based time measurement are used. The state machine starts and stops the counter while the delay is spent at discrete intervals equal to T, where T is the clock period.

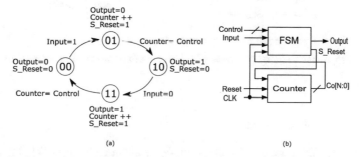

Fig. 3. Coarse delay generation (a) Finite State Machine (FSM) (b) block diagram

Figure 3 (a) shows the signals values in each state. In the states "01" and "11", the machine counts the clock cycles and compares them with the control vector value (from signal R), so the input signal change occurs n_{coarse} clock cycles later at the output, and

$$t_{coarse} = n_{coarse} \times T \qquad (2)$$

where t_{coarse} is the generated delay, and n_{coarse} is the decimal value of R.

Figure 3 (b) shows the block diagram of the circuit. The counter has N bits, just as the control should have as well.

The machine compares Co[N:0] with control[N:0] and, if they are equal, goes to state "10". When $n_{coarse} = 0$ the delay is zero, and the maximum delay is $(2^N - 1) \times T$.

2.2 Fine Delay Generator

In this work, the delay generator is created from a code with conditional "if-else" statements (see Fig. 4), based on the DCDL architecture proposed in [4]. Synthesis tools often implement sequential statements, such as "if-else" using multiplexers. A vector (IN) has been declared with n elements and then assigned buffers with the generate command. The attribute "keep" creates a buffer tree if assigned in the IN vector.

Thus, each combination selects a different path proportional to sel. This generates MUX up to $2^N = n$ multiplexers, where N is the sel number of bits. The delay is the same as in [4] and it is appropriate to define:

$$t_{fine} = t_0 + nT_{FDG} \tag{3}$$

where T_{FDG} is the resolution of FDG, and t_0 is the delay of buffers.

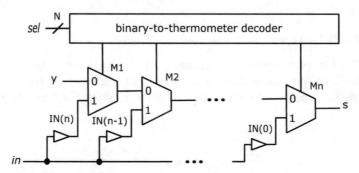

Fig. 4. Proposed fine delay generator with the chain of multiplexers generated by code.

2.3 Time-to-Digital Converter

High-resolution TDCs are usually based on delay chain techniques [7]. Tapped delay line with a single line has been employed, as illustrated in Fig. 5 [8]. The TDC line was designed using the VHDL generate statement to repeat 2N TDC units, where N is the number of bits in the encoder output, and behavioral description is used to generate each buffer and register pair (TDC unit). Then, the encoder has a vector of length 2^N at the input and N at the output. In order to detect a "001", and reduces bubbles, the code checks the following argument: *(sel(i-2) and sel(i-1)) and not sel(i))* = *'1'*, for each *i* position from 2 to 2^N and convert the corresponding position to the output.

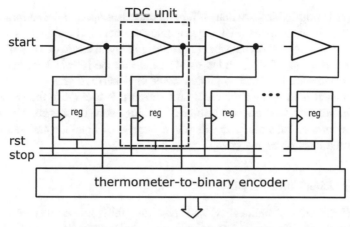

Fig. 5. Proposed tapped delay lines TDC.

3 Architecture Implementation

The digitally controlled delay circuits have been implemented on a Cyclone V SoC 5CSXFC6C6U23C8 device mounted in an Helio Board Rev1.2 from MPRESSION, with a 6-bits fine delay generator, a 4-bits coarse delay generator, and a 100 MHz crystal oscillator.

The fine delay generator must have a range greater than the clock period T so that the error correction can work. The clock with error is 50 MHz, so the period is T = 20 ns. The fine delay generator and TDC are designed with 6-bits, resulting in $2^6 = 64$ delay elements, and a range of $63 \times T_{FDG}$.

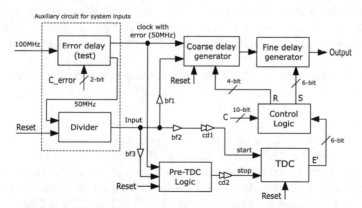

Fig. 6. Digitally controlled delay generator test setup.

The test setup of the delay generator is illustrated in Fig. 6. An FSM has been used to provide the clock with error (error delay), and a 5-bit counter (divider) to divide the frequency from 50 MHz to 1.5625 MHz providing the input signal. The pre-TDC, in this design, is simplified to only one buffer and one flip-flop, and the calibration delays (cd) are buffer chains generated via the generate command. The signals were obtained from an ADS1102CAL + digital storage oscilloscope with a rate of 1GS. The ambient temperature was around 25 °C, and the temperature on the IC was kept, with a cooler, around 34 °C measured with a Digital thermometer Hikari HT-455.

Our approach is to apply time-constraint commands to modify the placement and routing of the connections between the blocks. Timing analysis tools allow us to manage the design reports of constraints specified in Synopsis Design Constraints (SDC). The main constraint used is *set_net_delay*.

3.1 Design Using Timing Analysis

The DNL (Differential Nonlinearity) and INL (Integral Nonlinearity) were calculated using an Octave/Matlab script. The definition of nonlinearity based on [8], as well as $INL = cumsum(dnl)$ command, has been used. The input is the data vector with N length. The data is obtained from the critical path, also called the worst path through the report_path command. TCL scripts aid to get the data vector in the case of FDG and TDC (N = 64), through the time analysis tool.

The application of constraints in the FDG occurs mainly in the nets connected to the buffer tree. Scenario S0 is defined without constraint and scenario S1 with five or six constraints. The disadvantage of scenario S1 is that it increases the generated delays by up to 38%, affecting the resolution. However, the maximum values of DNL decrease by more than 50%. This approach was applied before the final adjustments in architecture in order to address only the blocks design. The delay range from 0.970 to 40.738 for S0, and from 0.499 to 56.186 for S1 in ns unit (simulated). The values obtained for min and max in LSB of DNL are [−1.29, 1.43] for S0, and are [−0.56, 0.54] for S1, and of INL are [−3.17, 1.70] for S0, and are [−1.23, 0.18] for S1. In the TDC, constraints are applied in the delay elements between the TDC inner units because the propagation of the START signal is an important feature in TDC. The DNL are [−0.65, 1.26] for S0, and are [−0.08, 0.12] for S1, and of INL are [−3.06, 0.40] for S0, and are [−0.22, 0.04] for S1.

The FDG circuits for S0 and S1 were tested using an oscilloscope to establish the resolution of architecture. The values measured for DNL are [−3.92, 3.55] for S0, and are [−1.47, 1.35] for S1, and of INL are [−2.23, 3.84] for S0, and are [−0.22, 1.91] for S1. The delay range from 0.2 to 19.6 ns for S0, and from 2.3 to 29.1 ns for S1. The average of the delay measured decreased because of the typical pessimism of time analysis. Therefore, the LSB for S1 is $T_{FDG} = (29.1-2.3)/63 = 425,4$ ps.

The final adjustments to the architecture design can be achieved using time analysis. First, we assumed that the ratio between the resolutions remains constant to estimate the delay values we used, for example $(56.186-0.499)/(29.1-2.3) = \mathbf{2.08}$, considering equivalent ambient temperatures, in order to relate the delay values obtained in the time analysis and the measured values. The main issues are the offset of TDC, and the resolution adjustment of FDG and TDC, both issues are designed using simulation. The offset usually occurs due to the non-symmetry between the critical paths beginning in START and STOP, which causes an offset in the output result of the TDC [9].

The control logic (see Fig. 6) calculates S comparing binary values, and the delay measured by the TDC (E') is used in the expression of E. Thus, if $E < C_{LSB}$, then $S = C_{LSB} - E$, and

$$E = (T'_{FDG}/T'_{TDC})E\prime + E_{off} \qquad (4)$$

where E_{off} is the binary value of the TDC offset error, T'_{FDG} and T'_{TDC} are the resolution values measured by a static timing analysis.

The method used to design the E (error correction between clock and input) requires linearity of the TDC and FDG delay chain circuits, so constraints are used to improve linearity. We use TCL scripts because each parameter adjustment causes a circuit layout change, so it is necessary to adjust linearity at the same time as the E_{off} value.

3.2 Tests and Discussions

Two designs with different E_{off} values were evaluated to illustrate the proposed method: design-1, with negative error, and design-2, with positive error. Design-1, which had 362 CLBs, used 7 buffers on cd1 and 5 buffers on cd2. Design-2, which had 363 CLBs, used 3 buffers on cd1 and 15 buffers on cd2. The error delay block (auxiliary circuit) generates delay values of 5, 10, 15, and 20 ns (values of error E) to test each design. The offset value of the TDC was calculated as

$$E_{off} = (t_{cd2} - t_{cd1})/T'_{TDC} \qquad (5)$$

where t_{cd1} e t_{cd2} are the delays of cd1 and cd2 obtained in timing analysis using the *report_path*.

The bf2 and bf3 are designed with the same *net* delay, while bf1 was made higher than bf2 and bf3 for the CDG to be after the TDC. The min and max *set_net_delay* constraints applied in the final adjustments for design-1 were: 0.380 and 1.000 between cd1 *nets*, 0.300 and 1.000 between cd2 *nets*, and for design-2 were: 0.450 and 1.100 between cd1 *nets*, 0.300 and 1.000 between cd2 *nets*. To correct the error using Eq. 4 it is convenient to make T'_{FDG}/T'_{TDC} approximately an integer. In this case, the FDG range was enlarged using the constraint *set_net_delay*, letting it be unitary. In design-1 we obtained $E_{off} \cong -1$ and $T'_{FDG} = T'_{TDC} \cong 1.30$, and design-2 obtained $E_{off} \cong 3$ and $T'_{FDG} = T'_{TDC} \cong 1.31$. The TDC was tested in order to verify the INL and the E_{off} value. INL below 0.125LSB or near zero was measured, and the value of E_{off} was confirmed.

The architectures were tested for two binary values of control, $C_{MSB} = 0010$ and $C_{MSB} = 1010$ with the fixed C_{LSB} at 011000. The theoretical total delay can be estimated as:

$$t_{delay} = n_{coarse} \times T + t_{fine} = n_{coarse} \times T + t_0 + nT_{FDG} \qquad (6)$$

We used the resolution's ratio of 2.08 (see Sect. 3.1). Thus, $T_{FDG} \cong 1.30/2.08$ for design-1 and $T_{FDG} \cong 1.31/2.08$ for design-2. The value of t_0 is picked by applying report_path between the CDG output and the FDG buffer tree. The average value for design-1 and design-2 is respectively 3.265/2.08 and 3.108/2.08 (ns).

The output and input signals of the proposed generator are measured using the X10 oscilloscope probe and the data are saved to determine the delays. Table 1 illustrates the results of the tests for two designs to show the error correction.

Table 1. Measured delay for $C_{LSB} = 011000$.

Test	t_{delay} (estimated)	E (ns)	t_{delay} (ns)
Design-1 with $C_{MSB} = 0010$	$2 \times 20 + 3.265/2.08 + 24 \times 1.30/2.08 = 56.57$ns	5	57.37
		10	56.84
		15	56.43
		20	56.58
Design-1 with $C_{MSB} = 1010$	$10 \times 20 + 3.265/2.08 + 24 \times 1.30/2.08 = 216.57$ns	5	216.53
		10	215.98
		15	216.57
		20	216.75
Design-2 with $C_{MSB} = 0010$	$2 \times 20 + 3.108/2.08 + 24 \times 1.31/2.08 = 56.61$ns	5	57,97
		10	57,33
		15	57,1
		20	57,11
Design-2 with $C_{MSB} = 1010$	$10 \times 20 + 3.108/2.08 + 24 \times 1.31/2.08 = 216.61$ns	5	217,66
		10	216,35
		15	217,52
		20	217,63

Note that, when E is 15 and 20 ns, E > C_{LSB}, TB = 32 in decimal (see the algorithm in Fig. 2). In both cases, the theoretically estimated values are close to the measured ones. The deviation due to nonlinearity is always less than $1.5 \times$ LSB, approximately $1.5 \times 1.3/2.08 = 0.94$ ns. The maximum variation with temperature was approximately 100 ps/°C. Quantization error is given by $T_{LSB}/\sqrt{12} = 180$ ps [8]. Thus, the deviation due to the nonlinearity of the FDG is the most critical

4 Conclusion

The implementation of a delay generator using counters and delay chains, in an approach that uses static timing analysis in the fine-tuning part is presented. The architecture can correct the error due to the unknown time interval between the input signal and the clock. The time analysis was used for adjustments in delays, such as skew problems and nonlinearities in the delay chains, making the whole project simulation-based. All analysis has used only one corner setup because we do not verify process, voltage, and temperature (PVT) variation. In future works, we will improve the trade-off between linearity and resolution in the method, and use constraints to improve variation with PVT, which will correct the main sources of inaccuracy.

Acknowledgment. This work is supported by Foundation for Research Support of Mato Grosso (FAPEMAT) and National Council for Scientific and Technological Development (CNPq).

References

1. Song, Y., Liang, H., Zhou, L., Du, J., Ma, J., Yue, Z.: Large dynamic range high resolution digital delay generator based on FPGA. In: 2011 International Conference on Electronics, Communications and Control (ICECC), pp. 2116–2118. IEEE (2011)
2. Cui, K., Li, X., Zhu, R.: A high-resolution programmable Vernier delay generator based on carry chains in FPGA. Rev. Sci. Instrum. **88**(6), 064703 (2017)
3. Li, J., Zheng, Z., Liu, M., Wu, S.: Large dynamic range accurate digitally programmable delay line with 250-ps resolution. In: 2006 8th International Conference on Signal Processing. IEEE (2006)
4. Giordano, R., Ameli, F., Bifulco, P.: High-resolution synthesizable digitally-controlled delay lines. IEEE Trans Nucl. Sci. **62**(6), 3163–3171 (2015)
5. Cheng, X., Song, R., Xie, G., Zhang, Y., Zhang, Z.: A new FPGA-based segmented delay-line DPWM with compensation for critical path delays. IEEE Trans. Power Electron. **33**, 10794–10802 (2017)
6. Intel® Quartus® Prime Pro and Standard Software User Guides. https://www.intel.com/content/www/us/en/support/programmable/support-resources/design-software/user-guides.html. Accessed 04 Aug 2022
7. Narasimman, R., Prabhakar, A., Chandrachoodan, N.: Implementation of a 30 ps resolution time to digital converter in FPGA. In: 2015 International Conference on Electronic Design, Computer Networks & Automated Verification (EDCAV), pp. 12–17. IEEE (2015)
8. Won, J.Y., Lee, J.S.: Time-to-digital converter using a tuned-delay line evaluated in 28- 40- and 45-nm FPGAs. IEEE Trans on Instrum. Meas. **65**(7), 1678–1689 (2016)
9. Yu, J., Dai, F.F., Jaeger, R.C.: A 12-bit vernier ring time-to-digital converter in 0.13 μm CMOS technology. IEEE J. Solid-State Circuits. **45**, 830–842 (2010)

Case Study of the Electric Power Supply System Between Punta Arenas Residential Complex and Talara's Refinery Through an Automatic Load Transfer System, Piura - Peru

Carlos Omar Quiñones Quispe[1]([⊠]) [iD], Marcos Pacheco Caparo[2] [iD], and Iván Delgado Huayta[1] [iD]

[1] National University of the Altiplano, Puno 21001, Peru
{cquinones,idelgado}@unap.edu.pe
[2] National University of Callao, Lima 07001, Peru
mjpachecoc@unac.edu.pe

Abstract. This work focuses on the electric power supply decoupling to the Punta Arenas residential complex in the Petroperú's Talara Refinery, where we can appreciate the stages that allowed the commissioning of a medium voltage utilization system (13.2 kV - 3ø) in order to supply electrical energy to the Punta Arenas residential complex from the primary electrical grid of the concessionaire ELECTRONOROESTE S.A. (ENOSA), which was originally fed from the main transformation substation of the Talara's Refinery. The Punta Arenas residential complex, where the administrative workers of the Petroperú's Talara Refinery reside, needed to know its electricity consumption independently, since it was being billed together with industrial consumption. This requirement was carried out through a SCADA system (Supervisory Control and Data Acquisition) to monitor the electrical energy consumption of the Punta Arenas residential complex from the concessionaire (ENOSA). And in the same way, an automatic load transfer switch was implemented, for an uninterrupted power supply, conserving as a backup the power supply of the main substation of the Talara's Refinery, according to the requirement of Petroperú.

Keywords: Automatic Transfer System · Medium voltage · SCADA · Utilization system

1 Introduction

At the Talara's refinery, it has been found that the energy power supply to the Punta Arenas residential complex (where the refinery's internal workers live) is initially fed from the Main Transformation Substation of the Talara's Refinery and it is required a power supply for home consumption and without interruptions (in this city there are repetitive blackouts); for that reason, there will be two energy supplies, one from the concessionaire ENOSA (ELECTRONOROESTE S.A.) and another from the main Substation of the Petroperú's Talara Refinery (as backup).

© The Author(s), under exclusive license to Springer Nature Switzerland AG 2023
Y. Iano et al. (Eds.): BTSym 2022, SIST 353, pp. 54–63, 2023.
https://doi.org/10.1007/978-3-031-31007-2_5

As background information, it is stated that for the design and implementation of sustainable, efficient, and more outage-resilient electricity supply chains, an optimization problem solution should be considered [1]; this takes into account the demand uncertainties with an adjustable and robust multi-objective. The objective of this kind of model was to be economic and environmental and show grid resilience. Other researchers propose the need to find market designs and electricity pricing schemes that facilitate the efficient functioning of the markets in different scenarios of penetration of non-conventional renewable sources [2–4] and contribute to the sustainability of the system and social welfare in the Colombian electricity market as a case study. Alternatively, other authors reflect on how the uncertainty of distributed renewable generation at a particular location affects the average purchase cost of public utilities and the cost reduction of a place [5], also it was shown that such uncertainty can lead to an increase in the average purchase cost per unit of electrical power from the public utility company that serves the operating district, (local impact), and a decrease on the average purchase cost per unit of electrical power from other public utilities in the same regional market (global impact).

Likewise, there is a novel modeling approach to assess the resilience of future power grids to climate hazards [6], two scenarios with centralized generation are shown, in which the impacts of a windstorm can disrupt connections; further development is also considered for future studies of the climate resilience of electricity systems; for instance, the impacts of climate hazards on a coupled electricity and transmission network. In the same way, recent academic research [7] recommends the smart grid service computing technique, along with a Personalized Recommender System (PRS) for retail electricity plans for residential users, where some strategies can be incorporated to alleviate the cold start problem. Another study describes the experience of several microgrid projects in Chile [8] at the same time that identifies risks, impacts, and control actions and discusses their replicability in the Latin American and Caribbean regions. Considering the co-construction process, we can say that it is a robust tool to exploit the potential for adaptation of microgrid projects to complex conditions and contexts. The co-construction methodology is not only focused on energy supply, but also on creating an environment of active participants in the energy solution. Finally, other reports suggest the supply of electrical power to vital consumers with an automatic transfer switch (ATS) [9], a system that, in the event of a faulty disruption, shifts the connection of the vital consumers to another one. In addition, it presents a reliable and accessible control solution proposed to supervise the electrical installations of vital consumers [10], since they require a permanent power supply. For that reason, the availability of a system with an automatic transfer switch is essential.

The contribution in this work consists of applying electrical systems technology to allow the separation of the power supply of industrial and residential electrical energy in the Talara's Refinery.

The implementation of the supply of materials, assembly, and commissioning of a utilization system at a voltage level of 13.2 kV – 3ø (medium voltage) was carried out, in such a way as to supply electricity to the Punta Arenas residential complex of ENOSA's primary networks.

In the same way, the implementation of a substation was carried out that allows the automatic switching of the electrical supply of both parties according to the requirement.

Finally, the implementation of a SCADA system was carried out to monitor the electricity consumption of Punta Arenas in front of the concessionaire (ENOSA).

2 Project Description

In this section, we will describe the implementation of the electrical energy supply to the Punta Arenas residential complex located within the facilities of the Talara – Petroperu refinery. It is located in the district of Pariñas, province of Talara, department of Piura – Peru.

- The first block of Fig. 1 explains the expansion of the ENOSA network and is carried out by means of centrifuged reinforced concrete poles of variable length along 967.56 m. Then the underground section for the intersection of streets along 260.7 m. linear until reaching the substation with the arrival cell to a 400 kVA ABB transformer of 13.2 kV ± 2.5%/2.4 kV. The 2.4 kV outputs are coupled to the primary networks of the Punta Arenas residential complex.
- In the second block of Fig. 1, there is the substation which was equipped with state-of-the-art monitoring, control, maneuvering, and protection devices. This substation has two 220 Vac low-voltage panels and another 24 Vdc panel for direct current and

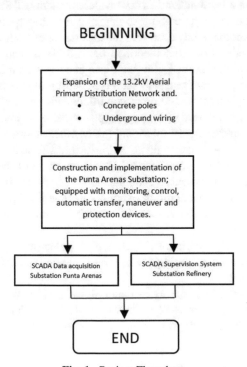

Fig. 1. Project Flowchart.

a UPS (Uninterruptable Power Supply) system. The supply of materials, assembly, and commissioning of an automatic load transfer panel at the medium voltage level has been carried out to supply (without interruptions) electrical energy to the Punta Arenas Condominium of ENOSA's Primary networks, having as backup the supply of the main substation of the Talara Refinery.

- In the third block of Fig. 1, a SCADA system has been implemented that first acquires the data in the Punta Arenas substation and transmits the information wirelessly to the main substation of the Talara refinery to have position monitoring of disconnectors and switches and of electrical parameters that will allow the continuous supervision of the operating parameters of the substation.

- In Fig. 2 we can see that the Talara refinery receives energy supply from the National Interconnected Electric System of Peru. On the other hand, you can also see the Malacas power plant, which supplies electricity to the city of Talara

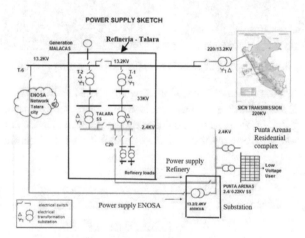

Fig. 2. Power supply sketch.

3 Substation

The substation is a conventional booth made of reinforced concrete, where the prefabricated 13.2 kV arrival cubicles, transformation cubicles, automatic transfer cubicles, 2.4 kV output cubicles, low voltage panels in AC (220 Vac), and DC were installed (24 Vdc) and the control and communications boards. This can be seen in Figs. 3 and 4.

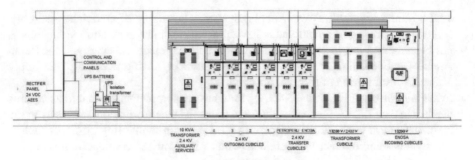

Fig. 3. Substation.

Fig. 4. Distribution of electric cubicles and substation photograph.

Figure 5 shows the automatic transfer between CB M (Circuit Breaker Main) and CB B (Circuit Breaker Backup), upon the loss of ENOSA's electrical power supply. The automatic switch is detected by the voltage sensors of the ENOSA network and the Petroperú network, which carry the signal to the ABB REF 545 module that controls

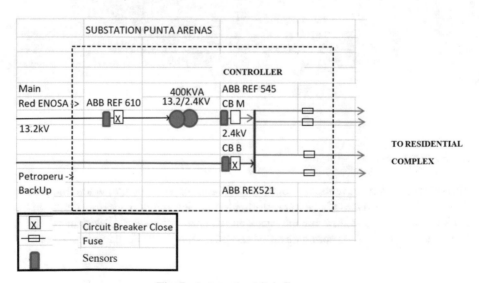

Fig. 5. Automatic switch diagram.

the automatic transfer. This controller determines the CB (Circuit Breaker) to open or close, having CB M as the main.

Figure 6 shows the automatic transfer system that is carried out to prevent Punta Arenas users from running out of electricity. If electrical energy is lost in CB M, the controller counts 10 s and proceeds to carry out the transfer: it opens CB M and then closes CB B, if the electrical energy returns to the Enosa network, then it opens CB B and then close CB M. Figure 7 is a photograph of the Transfer System powered by ENOSA and Petroperú.

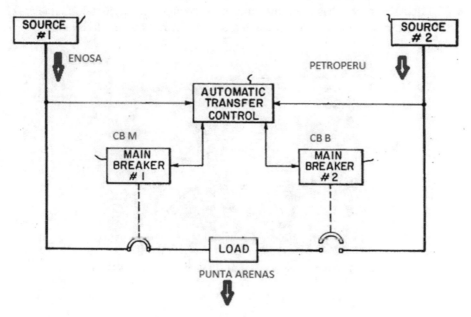

Fig. 6. Switching flow diagram.

Fig. 7. Photo of Automatic Transfer System powered by ENOSA and Petroperú.

4   Results

The general result is the Supply of electrical energy to the Punta Arenas residential complex independently between the electrical energy coming from ENOSA and Talara's Refinery. As seen in Fig. 8:

- The 13.2 kV primary grid connected to ENOSA has been implemented;
- The Punta Arenas Substation has been built and equipped with an automatic electrical load transfer system between ENOSA and PETROPERU;
- The SCADA system has been implemented to monitor the electrical parameters of the Punta Arenas Substation, located in the main Talara's refinery Substation.

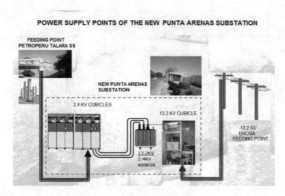

Fig. 8. Power supply points of the Punta Arenas substation

4.1   Communication and SCADA System

Figure 9 shows the architecture of communication and data acquisition through the equipment that performs the measurement of the different electrical parameters with an RS-485 communication protocol [11, 12]. This information is centralized in the AC800M PLC. These same data are transmitted to the main substation by a radio modem, with a 2.4 GHz radio link at a distance of approximately 1.1 km, where it is monitored on a computer with SCADA software.

A SCADA Supervision Software supplied by the company ABB (Asea Brown Boveri) has been used, which allows us to visualize the voltage and current readings of all cubicles, as well as the readings per phase and the THD harmonic distortion percentage for both voltages as for current. In Fig. 10, we can see the Human-Machine Interface and the voltage and current values for each input and output of the diagram that represents the Punta Arenas substation. In Fig. 11, we can observe the trend curves of active power, reactive power, phase currents, and voltages. The measurements obtained of the electrical parameters: voltages, currents, and powers were necessary to know the

Data acquisition at the Punta Arenas substation

Supervision at the main substation

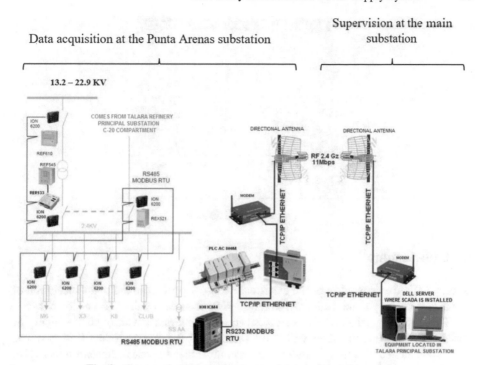

Fig. 9. Communication architecture and parameter measurement

consumption of electrical energy in the Punta Arenas residential complex, coming from the ENOSA concessionaire, as well as coming from the main substation of the Talara's refinery.

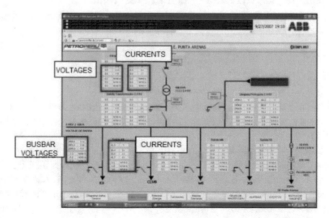

Fig. 10. SCADA Display

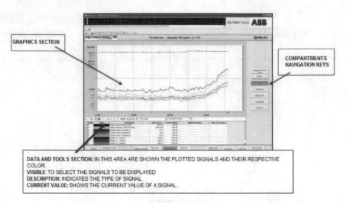

Fig. 11. Trend display.

5 Conclusions

In this work, the separation of the electrical energy supply from the main substation of Talara's Refinery and the supply from the ENOSA concessionaire was carried out.

The expansion of ENOSA's electrical grid was carried out through the laying of aerial and underground cables within the facilities of Petroperú's Talara Refinery. The implementation and commissioning of the Punta Arenas electrical substation were also carried out, with an automatic load transfer panel at the medium voltage level, to supply without interruptions, electrical energy to the Punta Arenas residential complex of the ENOSA primary networks. Communication equipment was implemented to have the monitoring of electrical parameters of volts, amps, powers, and consumption trend curves were obtained and visualized in a SCADA software, which will allow continuous monitoring and control of the parameters of operation of the substation, for an efficient and reliable operation, with a record of faults in real-time.

For future work, the project can be used for the subsequent treatment of Electricity Consumption Pricing.

References

1. Jabbarzadeh, A., Fahimnia, B., Rastegar, S.: Green and resilient design of electricity supply chain networks: a multiobjective robust optimization approach. IEEE Trans. Eng. Manag. **66**, 52–72 (2017)
2. Vargas, J., Franco, C.J., Jiménez, M.: Electricity pricing for renewable markets-a simulation approach for the colombian case. IEEE Lat. Am. Trans. **19**, 1995–2002 (2021)
3. Thiagarajan, Y., Pasupulati, B., de Oliveira, G.G., Iano, Y., Vaz, G.C.: A simple approach for short-term hydrothermal self scheduling for generation companies in restructured power system. In: Brazilian Technology Symposium, pp. 396–414. Springer (2022). https://doi.org/10.1007/978-3-031-08545-1_38
4. Gregio, R.P., et al.: Energy use in urban areas using neodymium magnets. In: Brazilian Technology Symposium, pp. 988–1005. Springer (2020). https://doi.org/10.1007/978-3-030-75680-2_107

5. Yi, H., Hajiesmaili, M.H., Zhang, Y., Chen, M., Liu, X.: Impact of the uncertainty of distributed renewable generation on deregulated electricity supply chain. IEEE Trans. Smart Grid. **9**, 6183–6193 (2017)
6. Fu, G., et al.: Integrated approach to assess the resilience of future electricity infrastructure networks to climate hazards. IEEE Syst. J. **12**, 3169–3180 (2017)
7. Luo, F., Ranzi, G., Wang, X., Dong, Z.Y.: Social information filtering-based electricity retail plan recommender system for smart grid end users. IEEE Trans. Smart Grid. **10**, 95–104 (2017)
8. Palma-Behnke, R., et al.: Lowering electricity access barriers by means of participative processes applied to microgrid solutions: the chilean case. Proc. IEEE. **107**, 1857–1871 (2019)
9. Sărăcin, C.G., Sărăcin, M., Zdrenţu, D.: Integration of residential alarm systems into electric power supplies of vital consumers. In: 2015 9th International Symposium on Advanced Topics in Electrical Engineering (ATEE), pp. 716–719. IEEE (2015)
10. Nishimura, E.H., Iano, Y., de Oliveira, G.G., Vaz, G.C.: Application and requirements of aiot-enabled industrial control units. In: Brazilian Technology Symposium, pp. 724–733. Springer (2022). https://doi.org/10.1007/978-3-031-08545-1_72
11. Neto, A.B., et al.: The BFS method in a cloud environment for analyzing distributed energy resource management systems. In: Brazilian Technology Symposium, pp. 349–362. Springer (2023). https://doi.org/10.1007/978-3-031-04435-9_35
12. Bacega, P.R.O., Iano, Y., Carvalho, B.C.S., Vaz, G.C., Oliveira, G.G., Chuma, E.L.: Study about the applicability of low latency in has transmission systems. In: Brazilian Technology Symposium, pp. 73–87. Springer (2023). https://doi.org/10.1007/978-3-031-04435-9_7

Application of Cluster Analysis to Electricity Generation Data from the Santo Antônio Hydroelectric Plant in the State of Rondônia, Brazil

João Gabriel Ribeiro[1]([✉]) [iD], Carlos Tadeu dos Santos Dias[2] [iD],
Sônia Maria de Stefano Piedade[2] [iD], Giovane Maia do Vale[1] [iD],
and Vlademir de Jesus Silva Oliveira[1] [iD]

[1] State University of Mato Grosso (UNEMAT-FACET-Electrical Engineering),
Sinop, Brazil
{joao.gabriel.ribeiro,vale.giovane,vlademir.oliveira}@unemat.br
[2] Statistics and Agronomic Experimentation, University of São Paulo
(USP-ESALQ), Piracicaba, Brazil
{ctsdias,soniamsp}@usp.br

Abstract. This work aims to build generation hourly electric power groups from the data of 50 existing turbines at the Santo Antônio hydroelectric plant located in the state of Rondônia, as well as to rank and analyze their potential through the application of multivariate techniques of Manhattan distance in the turbines combined with the method of hierarchical clustering of average linkage. Thus, the formation of 7 productive groups of electric energy generation at the plant was verified, in which the highest and lowest average, standard deviation, and total generation of groups are groups 1 and 7. And there is also an increasing ordination of these measures from groups 1 to 7, a result that can serve as another tool for monitoring potentials and bottlenecks of the power generation of the plant broken down into groups, and this methodology can be replicated year after year and in other hydroelectric plants in Brazil and around the world.

Keywords: Generation electric power · Turbine groups · Monitoring

1 Introduction

The generation, as well as the consumption of electric energy, has a primordial role in economic growth and the quality of life of any population. Several industrial, commercial, and service sectors have their development highly linked to the good progress of the generation and consumption of electric energy maintaining the existing demand and supplying the growing one.

© The Author(s), under exclusive license to Springer Nature Switzerland AG 2023
Y. Iano et al. (Eds.): BTSym 2022, SIST 353, pp. 64–74, 2023.
https://doi.org/10.1007/978-3-031-31007-2_6

However, more than the increase in energy consumption, it is the services generated by the energy that really lead to an improvement in well-being. It is also the purpose for which energy services are allocated which ultimately determines the level of economic development achieved by a country [1,2].

The assessment of energy potential in a country depends on the level of knowledge of its resources and reserves. The dimensioning of Brazilian reserves, or any other country, is intrinsic to the economic and technological conditions in which the assessment is made [2,3].

The Santo Antônio hydroelectric plant, located in the city of Porto Velho, capital of Rondônia, on the bed of the Madeira River, has been active since 2008 at its partial capacity, and its construction works were completed in 2016. The plant is a run-of-the-river type, that is, it stops accumulating large water reservoirs, using types of turbines to take advantage of the flow of the river, therefore, it has been operating with 50 bulb-type turbines, having today 3,568 megawatts of installed power and the capacity to generate energy from consumption estimated at 45 million Brazilians.

The plant in question is of great importance for the national interconnected system, as it is a base plant, contributes significantly to meeting the regional energy demand in Brazil, and also dedicates the energy generation of 6 of its turbines exclusively to the states of Rondônia and Acre.

Given the importance of this plant for Brazil, an analysis of the same was started, through the use of multivariate analysis methodologies, in which the 50 turbines/time series of hourly electrical energy generation in Megawatts were evaluated hour (MWh) of this plant in the year 2016, then, in the same year, the formation of clusters of hourly energy production of the hydroelectric plant from the generation of electric energy from its turbines was investigated, with the main objective of investigating the productive potential of generation electric energy of each of the groups built, which could be another tool for using the hydroelectric plant to map potential and bottlenecks them in their electricity generation.

2 Material and Methods

Data collection took place at the Santo Antônio hydroelectric plant. In a second step, the composition of an input data set was organized, in which the variable $X_{i,j}$ represents the observations of hourly electricity generation (MWh) of the turbines $i = 1, 2, ..50$ in $j = 1, 2, .., 8753$ h collected throughout 2016 at the respective hydroelectric plant. Thus, the arrangement of the dataset used can be demonstrated by the matrix $\mathbf{X}$ of Eq. 1.

$$\mathbf{X} = [X_{i,j}]_{50 \times 8753} = \begin{bmatrix} X_{1,1} & X_{1,2} & \cdots & X_{1,8753} \\ X_{2,1} & X_{2,2} & \cdots & X_{2,8753} \\ \vdots & \vdots & \ddots & \vdots \\ X_{50,1} & X_{50,2} & \cdots & X_{50,8753} \end{bmatrix} \tag{1}$$

Then, for each of the vectors, boxplots were constructed and the main descriptive measures were calculated (average, standard deviation (SD), coefficient of variation (CV), minimum, maximum, range value, and total energy generation (Total)) for the 50 turbines.

According to the authors [4–18], from the X matrix, an appropriate distance measure is chosen, thus creating the Manhattan distance matrix, also known as the absolute distance matrix. This is the distance between any two elements related to the energy generation data of the X_{il} and X_{ik} plant turbines with $l \neq k$ and $i = \{1, 2, .., 50\}$, can be defined by Eq. 2.

$$D = D_{50 \times 50} = d(X_{il}, X_{ik}) = \sum_{i=1}^{50} \mid X_{il} - X_{ik} \mid \qquad (2)$$

Subsequently, the average linkage grouping method was used together with the distance matrix created, with the purpose of creating electric energy generation groups, from the turbines of the hydroelectric plant. In this method, the criterion for calculating the distance between a newly formed group with other pre-existing groups is given by the average of all distances between objects in the two groups. In this way, if there is a fusion of the C_r group with C_s both with n_r and n_s turbines of the hydroelectric plant, and the distance between this group for a pre-existing group C_t with n_t turbines will be established by Eq. 3.

$$d\left[(C_r, C_s), C_t\right] = \frac{1}{n_r + n_s + n_t} \left[\sum_{i \text{ in } r} \sum_{k \text{ in } t} d_{ik} + \sum_{j \text{ in } s} \sum_{k \text{ in } t} d_{jk}\right] \qquad (3)$$

This identity represents the average of all the distances between the turbines of the groups (C_r, C_s) with those of the C_t group.

The representation of the clustering of turbines was given by the construction of a dendrogram, which corresponds to a hierarchical structure, known as a tree diagram, which displays the groups formed by clusters of turbines at each step in their similarity levels. Where the similarity level is generally measured along a vertical/horizontal axis and the different turbine observations will be listed along the horizontal/vertical axis.

The determination of the number of groups, or cut-off point on the similarity axis, will be done through the application of Mojena's method [19], which is based on the relative size of the fusion levels (distances) of the dendrogram used. And the principle is chosen following the method that should be developed, then the inequality of this method (Eq. 4).

$$\alpha_j > \theta_k \qquad (4)$$

where α_j is the distance value of the melting level corresponding to the steps $j = \{1, 2, ..., g - 1\}$ and θ_k represents the cut-off reference value, given by:

$$\theta_k = \bar{\alpha} + k\hat{\sigma}_\alpha \qquad (5)$$

On what:

- $\bar{\alpha}$ is the average of the values of α;
- $\hat{\sigma}_\alpha$ is the standard deviation of the values of α;
- k is a constant suggested by Milligan and Cooper [20]. Its value is $k = 1.25$ and is adopted as a stopping rule in defining the number of groups.

In this way, one has to:

$$\bar{\alpha} = \frac{1}{g-1} \sum_{j=1}^{n-1} \alpha_j$$

$$\hat{\sigma}_\alpha = \sqrt{\frac{\sum_{j=1}^{g-1} \alpha_j^2 - \frac{1}{g-1} \sum_{j=1}^{n-1} \alpha_j}{g-2}}$$

After obtaining the groups and the appropriate dendrogram structure, the cophenetic correlation coefficient was calculated, which quantifies the similarity of the dendrogram distance matrix (cophenetic matrix) compared to the original distance matrix used by the Manhattan distance. The value of the coefficient is inversely proportional to the distortion caused by the clustering.

According to the authors [8,11,16,18], the expression of the cophenetic correlation coefficient will be:

$$r_{cophenetic} = \frac{\sum_{i=1}^{n-1} \sum_{j=i+1}^{n} (C_{ij} - \bar{C})(D_{ij} - \bar{D})}{\sqrt{\left(\sum_{i=1}^{n-1} \sum_{j=i+1}^{n} (C_{ij} - \bar{C})\right)^2 \cdot \left(\sum_{i=1}^{n-1} \sum_{j=i+1}^{n} (D_{ij} - \bar{D})\right)^2}} \tag{6}$$

where:

$$\bar{C} = \frac{2}{n(n-1)} \sum_{i=1}^{n-1} \sum_{j=i+1}^{n} C_{ij}$$

$$\bar{D} = \frac{2}{n(n-1)} \sum_{i=1}^{n-1} \sum_{j=i+1}^{n} D_{ij}$$

On what:

- C_{ij} and the value of the distance between individuals i and j in the cophenetic matrix;
- D_{ij} and the value of the distance between the same individuals in the original distance matrix;
- n is the dimension of the matrix.

From the calculation of the cophenetic correlation coefficient $r_{cophenetic}$, the validity of its value can be tested by applying a classical hypothesis test, given by:

$$H_0 : \rho_{cophenetic} = 0$$

or

$$H_1 : \rho_{cophenetic} > 0$$

Which is given by:

$$\rho_{cophenetic} = \sum_{i=1}^{n-1} \sum_{j=i+1}^{n} (C_{ij} - \bar{C})(D_{ij} - \bar{D}) \qquad (7)$$

Later, it was tested another test for the cophenetic correlation coefficient $r_{cophenetic}$, known as randomization of Mantel [21], which is a test based on randomization in the distribution of two involvement separation matrices from one of the two involvement matrices in the study.

The implementation of this set of chained multivariate analysis statistical techniques took place with the aid of the software R [22].

3   Results and Discussion

From the data collected and referring to the variables under study, the descriptive behavior of the time series of daily vectors of electric energy generation of 50 turbines of the Santo Antônio hydroelectric plant was evaluated, containing each of the vectors 8,753 hourly observations in measured MWh from the 1st to the 24th hour, during the year 2016 from January 1st to December 30th. Figure 1 represents the descriptive behavior of the time series involved.

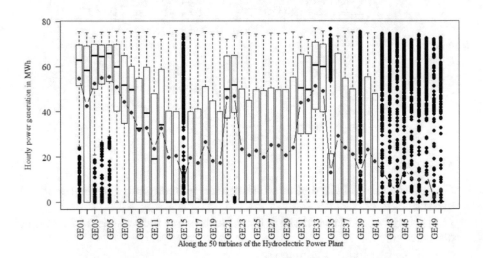

Fig. 1. Boxplots with the averages of electricity generation of the 50 turbines of the Santo Antônio hydroelectric plant in the year 2016.

Table 1. Detailing of the main descriptive measures referring to the time series of hourly energy generation of the 50 turbines in MWh in the year 2016.

Turbines	Averages	SD	CV	Minimum	Maximum	Range	Total
GE01	54.64	22.08	40.42	0.00	75.35	75.35	478,300.80
GE02	42.60	29.96	70.32	0.00	74.96	74.96	372,890.92
GE03	52.47	25.31	48.24	0.00	75.17	75.17	459,239.40
GE04	54.99	21.98	39.98	0.00	75.17	75.17	481,340.56
GE05	55.29	22.62	40.91	0.00	75.18	75.18	483,914.71
GE06	50.99	23.44	45.97	0.00	75.62	75.62	446,294.56
GE07	44.32	25.31	57.10	0.00	75.13	75.13	387,923.30
GE08	39.70	26.21	66.00	0.00	75.61	75.61	347,531.92
GE09	32.00	25.32	79.13	0.00	75.13	75.13	280,058.41
GE10	32.97	27.30	82.81	0.00	75.38	75.38	288,596.87
GE11	23.67	25.07	105.93	0.00	73.22	73.22	207,179.06
GE12	32.68	25.58	78.27	0.00	72.15	72.15	286,083.52
GE13	19.71	25.21	127.90	0.00	74.48	74.48	172,495.78
GE14	20.37	24.12	118.40	0.00	75.78	75.78	178,336.96
GE15	10.15	20.64	203.38	0.00	74.34	74.34	88,855.58
GE16	19.51	23.83	122.11	0.00	74.79	74.79	170,808.21
GE17	17.39	25.34	145.70	0.00	74.17	74.17	152,215.21
GE18	26.61	28.27	106.22	0.00	75.50	75.50	232,960.73
GE19	18.33	25.30	138.00	0.00	74.24	74.24	160,447.07
GE20	17.31	25.30	146.15	0.00	74.45	74.45	151,492.43
GE21	46.20	22.68	49.10	0.00	72.11	72.11	404,356.29
GE22	46.82	22.68	48.42	0.00	73.63	73.63	409,899.36
GE23	23.38	26.91	115.06	0.00	75.00	75.00	204,680.63
GE24	20.79	25.31	121.69	0.00	75.01	75.01	182,012.54
GE25	22.75	26.39	115.99	0.00	74.32	74.32	199,128.14
GF26	19.82	25.60	129.17	0.00	73.62	73.62	173,486.58
GE27	25.20	27.74	110.08	0.00	74.85	74.85	220,596.66
GE28	24.89	27.39	110.51	0.00	74.44	74.44	217,842.80
GE29	20.72	26.73	129.00	0.00	74.81	74.81	181,369.15
GE30	24.01	28.93	120.51	0.00	75.27	75.27	210,189.39
GE31	43.94	25.60	58.27	0.00	72.93	72.93	384,564.02
GE32	45.03	23.50	52.18	0.00	71.79	71.79	394,167.16
GE33	51.28	22.65	44.16	0.00	77.03	77.03	448,818.94
GE34	49.01	24.55	50.09	0.00	75.61	75.61	428,894.04
GE35	12.96	22.74	175.49	0.00	76.78	76.78	113,437.79
GE36	29.19	31.82	109.04	0.00	73.49	73.49	255,490.56
GE37	24.10	29.07	120.63	0.00	75.53	75.53	210,968.74
GE38	21.18	28.24	133.38	0.00	75.18	75.18	185,349.19
GE39	12.93	24.99	193.21	0.00	75.35	75.35	113,195.74
GE40	23.21	29.75	128.18	0.00	74.68	74.68	203,132.62
GE41	17.89	28.81	160.99	0.00	74.96	74.96	156,631.62
GE42	13.61	26.99	198.26	0.00	74.51	74.51	119,140.42
GE43	8.23	22.50	273.49	0.00	74.46	74.46	72,011.88
GE44	4.49	17.18	382.72	0.00	74.21	74.21	39,291.26
GE45	14.84	27.09	182.51	0.00	71.67	71.67	129,904.25
GE46	10.55	24.29	230.20	0.00	71.91	71.91	92,338.76
GE47	9.70	22.47	231.60	0.00	74.12	74.12	84,928.63
GE48	11.88	25.30	212.96	0.00	72.60	72.60	103,979.87
GE49	2.21	11.84	536.73	0.00	72.10	72.10	19,304.19
GE50	5.41	18.17	336.08	0.00	72.72	72.72	47,318.65

Figure 1 shows the behavior of the distributions of hourly electricity generation along with the average of energy generation over the 50 turbines in 2016. Turbines $GE05$ and $GE50$ have the highest and lowest average. Table 1 reveals the detailed descriptive behavior of the electricity generation of the 50 turbines of the hydroelectric plant.

It is observed that the turbines have the highest and lowest average, as turbines $GE49$ and $GE15$ are larger, while turbines larger in this energy and $GE49$ indicate the highest and lowest generation of electricity in this hydroelectric plant.

The ideal configuration, which best suited the theory used and the proposed objectives, was the application of the Manhattan absolute distance, together with the average linkage method as a grouping technique and cut-off point by the Mojena method in the value of 7,092.37 for the electrical energy generations of the 50 turbines of the plant. Figure 2 demonstrates the structure of cluster formation.

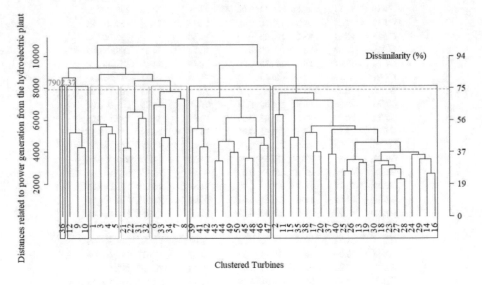

Fig. 2. Dendrogram for the formation of electricity generation clusters from the data of the turbines of the Santo Antônio hydroelectric plant in the year 2016.

The clustering technique used indicated the formation of 7 clusters of turbines named $G01$, $G02$, $G03$, $G04$, $G05$, $G06$ and $G07$. Table 2 shows the formation of the 7 groups with the details of their respective turbines.

Table 2. Identification of groups of hourly power generation turbines in MWh in the year 2016.

Groups	Group of Turbines	Quantity
G01	36	1
G02	12; 9; 10	3
G03	1; 3; 4; 5	4
G04	21; 22; 31; 32	4
G05	6; 33; 34; 7;8	5
G06	39; 41; 42; 43; 44; 49; 50; 45; 48; 46; 47	11
G07	2; 11; 15; 35; 38; 17; 20; 37; 40; 25; 26; 13; 19; 30; 18; 23; 27; 28; 24; 29; 14; 16	22

The cophenetic correlation coefficient calculated for the average binding method combined with the absolute distance was $r_{cophenetic} = 0.89$ with p-value = 2.20E-16, generated by a simple Pearson correlation test. The value of the cophenetic correlation coefficient suggests a good clustering structure of the plant's turbines. However, the Mantel test was also carried out with 1,000 randomizations in order to further validate the structure of formation of the groups, and the value of the statistic $Z_{calculated} = 1.06E+06$ and the $p-value = 9.99E - 04$ indicated a good structuring of the formed groups, in these randomizations.

Table 3, on the other hand, indicate the descriptive behavior of the electric power generation groups at the Santo Antônio plant.

Table 3. Detailing of the main descriptive measures relative to the hourly power generation series of the turbine groups in MWh in the year 2016.

Turbines	Averages	SD	CV	Minimum	Maximum	Range	Total
G01	29.19	31.83	109.04	0.00	73.49	73.49	255,490.56
G02	97.65	63.95	65.49	0.00	213.63	213.63	854,738.80
G03	217.39	58.44	26.88	0.00	299.04	299.04	1,902,795
G04	181.99	65.82	36.16	0.00	286.62	286.62	1,592,987
G05	235.30	75.56	32.11	0.00	378.75	378.75	2,059,553
G06	111.74	127.76	114.34	0.00	663.82	663.82	978,045.27
G07	478.68	411.20	85.90	0.00	1,336.82	1,336.82	4,189,876

Groups $G01$ and $G07$ have groups containing 01 and 22 turbines, and are also the ones that generate the smallest and largest average and total amounts of electricity generation at the plant. Figure 3 presents the behavior of the detailed distributions and profiles of each of the electric power generation groups with their averages, generated by the technique applied in the present research.

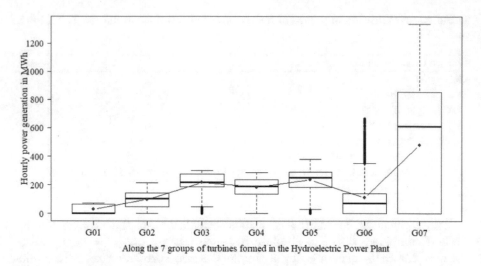

Along the 7 groups of turbines formed in the Hydroelectric Power Plant

Fig. 3. Boxplots with the averages of electricity generation of the groups of turbines of the Santo Antônio hydroelectric plant in the year 2016.

It is verified that the groups with the highest and lowest averages, standard deviation (SD) and total electricity production are $G01$ and $G07$, and also that the $G03$, $G04$ and $G05$ have values close to means, standard deviation (SD), and also that $G03$, $G04$ and $G05$ have values close to the means, standard deviations (SD), coefficients of variation (CV) and total electricity generation, which makes the boxplots of these clusters have similarity, indicating that their distributions have a certain similarity in this plant.

4   Conclusions

The cluster analysis used in this work indicated that the groups with the highest and lowest mean, standard deviation, and a total of electric energy production are the $G01$ and $G07$, which is an expected fact because they are the groups with less and more turbines grouped together. And also for these same measures, there is an increasing ordering of groups from $G01$ to $G07$, and there are some similarities between groups $G03$ and $G04$, in terms of their variations. This methodology will be able to contribute as another tool for better monitoring of the electric energy generation of the Santo Antônio hydroelectric plant and other plants in Brazil and the world, through the replication of the same method for different years, evaluating the potentials and bottlenecks of each group and its turbines.

Acknowledgments. Thanks go to God first, and then to the Coordination for the Improvement of Higher Education Personnel (CAPES) in Brazil and to the postgraduate program in Experimental and Agronomic Statistics at the State University of São Paulo (USP/ESALQ) campus from Piracicaba-SP and also the University of the State of Mato Grosso (UNEMAT-FACET-Electrical Engineering) campus of Sinop-MT, for all the support to carry out this research. The ideas and opinions expressed herein are those of the authors alone, and endorsement by the authors' institution is not intended and should not be inferred.

References

1. Goldemberg, J., Lucon, O.: Energia e meio ambiente no Brasil. Estudos avançados **21**, 7–20 (2007)
2. Passos, F.F.: Análise temporal da série de consumo residencial de energia elétrica no Brasil no período de,: a 2012, p. 2015. Universidade Federal de Alfenas, Minas Gerais, Brasil, Monografia (Bacharel em Ciências Econômicas)-Instituto de Ciências Sociais Aplicadas (1963)
3. Bermann, C.: Identification of common molecular subsequences.Energia no Brasil, Para que? Para quem?: crise e alternativa para um país sustentável. Editora Livraria da Física, Brasil, (2002)
4. Mahalanobis, P.C.: On the generalized distance in statistics. Proc. National Inst. Sci. India **12**, 49–55 (1936)
5. Everitt, B.S.: Unresolved problems in cluster analysis. Biometrics, 169–181 (1979)
6. Punj, G., Stewart, D.W.: Cluster analysis in marketing research: Review and suggestions for applications. J. Mark. Res. **20**, 134–148 (1983)
7. Dunn, C.: Applied Multivariate Statistical Analysis. Taylor & Francis (1989)
8. Bussab, W. O., Miazaki, E.S., Andrade, D.F.: Introdução à análise de agrupamentos. ABE, 1–105 (1990)
9. Diniz, C.A., Louzada, N.F.: Data Mining: Uma Introdução. 14º Simpósio Nacional de Probabilidade e Estatística (SINAPE/ABE). Caxambu, 1–122 (2000)
10. Mingoti, S.A.: Análise de Dados Através de Métodos Estatísticos Multivariados: Uma abordagem aplicada. 1º ed. Belo Horizonte: UFMG (2005)
11. Albuquerque, M.A.: Estabilidade em análise de agrupamento (cluster analysis). Biometry Masters Thesis. Recife: Universidade Federal Rural de Pernambuco-UFRPE (2005)
12. Manly, B.F.J., Alberto, J.A.N.: Métodos estatísticos multivariados: uma introdução. Bookman Editora (2008)
13. Hair, J.F., Anderson, R.E., Tatham, R.L., Black, W.C.: Multivariate data analysis, 7th edn. Pretince Hall, Upper Saddle River, NJ (2009)
14. Everitt, B., Hothorn, T.: An Introduction to Applied Multivariate Analysis with R. Springer Science & Business Media (2011)
15. Ferreira, D.F.: Estatística multivariada. Editora UFLA-Lavras-MG (2012)
16. Silva, A.R.: Métodos de agrupamento: avaliação e aplicação ao estudo de divergência genética em acessos de alho. Dissertação de Mestrado em Biometria da Universidade Federal de Viçosa-MG (UFV) (2012)
17. Johnson, R.A., Wichern, D.W.: Applied multivariate statistical analysis. Duxbury (2015)
18. Silva, A.R.: Métodos de análise multivariada em R. Piracicaba-SP, FEALQ (2016)
19. Mojena, R.: Hierarchical grouping methods and stopping rules: an evaluation. Comput. J. **20**, 353–359 (1977)
20. Milligan, G.W., Cooper, M.C.: An examination of procedures for determining the number of clusters in a data set. Psychometrika **50**, 159–179 (1985)

21. Mantel, N.: The detection of disease clustering and a generalized regression app-roach. Can. Res. **27**, 209–220 (1967)
22. R Core. Team: R: A Language and Environment for Statistical Computing. R Foundation for Statistical Computing, Vienna, Austria (2022). https://www.R-project.org/

Changes in Salivary pII After Application of Xylitol Toothpaste Using a Digital pH Meter: A Pilot Study

Tania Carola Padilla-Cáceres[1]([⊠]) [iD], Luz Marina Caballero-Apaza[1] [iD],
Vilma Mamani-Cori[1] [iD], Sheyla Lenna Cervantes-Alagón[1] [iD],
and Paula Olenska Catacora-Padilla[2] [iD]

[1] Universidad Nacional del Altiplano, Puno, Peru
tpadilla@unap.edu.pe
[2] Universidad Autónoma de Barcelona, Barcelona, Spain

Abstract. The fixed orthodontic treatment produces an accumulation of bacterial plaque in patients, which produces changes in the pH of saliva. The purpose of the study considered evaluating changes in saliva pH after the application of a commercial dentifrice with xylitol and cetylpyridinium chloride in a group of teenagers from Puno with fixed orthodontic appliances. A single-blind quasi-experimental study was performed. The sample was made of 34 patients of both sexes, with fixed orthodontic appliances who met the established criteria, all were instructed in a brushing technique and randomly assigned to one of two groups: experimental group, with 17 patients who used toothpaste with xylitol plus cetylpyridinium chloride, and control group, with 17 patients who used conventional fluoride toothpaste. A saliva sample was taken from both groups at the beginning of the study and at 3 and 5 weeks to assess the pH. The T-Student test found that salivary pH increased in patients who used toothpaste with xylitol plus cetylpyridinium chloride, reaching 7.45 in the fifth week with a statistically significant difference (<0.0001). We conclude that toothpaste with xylitol and cetylpyridinium chloride improves salivary pH concerning the use of conventional toothpaste.

Keywords: Fixed orthodontics · toothpaste · xylitol · fluoride · salivary pH

1 Introduction

Dental malocclusions are prevalent diseases of the oral cavity, which is why orthodontic treatment is becoming more and more frequent. Treatment aids can accumulate bacterial plaque and these can constitute areas of low salivary flow, and produce side effects such as white spots, dental caries lesions [1] and even periodontitis [2].

Better hygiene in these patients is achieved with complementary dental products, specially designed toothbrushes, dental floss, and mouth rinses, but oral hygiene is not always adequate, and there is less natural cleaning action of saliva [3].

The quantity and quality of saliva play a major role in the balance of the process between demineralization and remineralization of enamel in a cariogenic environment, fixed orthodontics produces greater plaque retention [4].

This accumulation of plaque during orthodontic treatment can induce alterations in buffering capacity [5], pH acidity [6], and saliva flow rate [7, 8].

Salivary pH can be assessed with an instrument that measures the activity of hydrogen ions, indicating their acidity or alkalinity, which is expressed as pH; the digital pH meter is safer than test strips [9].

A toothpaste that contains fluoride as the main component is a preventive measure for caries in patients with orthodontic treatment, its regular application during oral hygiene will depend on each patient. It has been shown that xylitol reduces the levels of *Streptococcus mutans* in bacterial plaque and saliva [10] due to the interruption of energy production processes and cell death [11].

Cetylpyridinium chloride is an antiseptic quaternary ammonium compound, which is often a component of toothpaste and rinses, it has a high affinity for gram-positive bacteria such as *Streptococcus mutan*. In dental plaque, it prevents cell aggregation and the maturation of dental biofilm and has the ability to adhere to buccal surfaces, although its substantivity is limited [12].

The aim of the study was to estimate changes in salivary pH after the application of toothpaste with xylitol and cetylpyridinium chloride in teenagers with fixed orthodontic appliances, using a digital pH meter.

2 Methodology

The study had a quasi-experimental design of single blinding with an experimental group and a control group carried out in a private dental clinic in Puno city. 17 participants were considered for each group, who met sample selection criteria such as patients with orthodontic treatment, with permanent dentition, with vestibular fixed appliances, with metal brackets, conventional archwires and who had given their written consent to participate in the study. Patient data were handled anonymously. Patients with a history of recent treatment for systemic diseases, patients who presented enamel hypoplasia, patients with antibiotic treatment or local antiseptics in the three weeks prior to taking the sample, or those who had received treatment with antibiotics were excluded. All subjects were instructed in a brushing technique and randomly assigned to one of two groups. On the day of the sample collection, it was instructed not to brush their teeth or eat food for 30 min. To guarantee the frequency of dental brushing in patients, telephone monitoring was carried out.

2.1 Obtaining the Pastes

It was obtained as commercial products, which were part of the following groups:

- Experimental Group: Paste 1 (xylitol and cetylpyridinium chloride);
- Control Group: Paste 2 (conventional fluoride toothpaste).

2.2 Pretest

Salivary pH Test. Equipment calibration: The EZ-9901 digital pH meter was subjected to acid and alkaline concentrations with pH 7 and 4.5 in the laboratory.

pH Measurement. Wait at least 2 h after ingesting these foods or beverages (excluding water) before testing.

Once the equipment is calibrated, the measurement is taken in saliva stimulated with chewing stimulated with paraffin in a beaker diluted in 50 ml of purified distilled water so that there is a better distribution of hydrogen ions, the cathode of the digital pH meter is placed in the glass containing the two components and wait 2 min for the result to be standardized [5, 13].

2.3 Treatment

Conventional fluoride toothpaste and cetylpyridinium chloride plus xylitol toothpaste were delivered to participants according to the study group. Participants were instructed in the brushing technique and were instructed to brush their teeth 3 times a day; monitoring for brushing compliance was done by telephone. Salivary tests were done 3 and 5 weeks after applying the paste.

2.4 Post-test

Salivary pH tests were performed 3 and 5 weeks after applying the pastes, with the same procedure as above.

2.5 Data Analysis

Data analysis was performed with descriptive statistics, and categorical data were analyzed using Student's t-test. The significance threshold was $P < 0.001$.

Statistical Hypothesis:

$$H0 : \mu1 \geq \mu2 \, vs \, H1 : \mu1 < \mu2$$

where: $\mu1$: mean PH level in the saliva after applying the toothpaste with xylitol and cetylpyridinium chloride.

And:

$$H0 : \mu1 \geq \mu2 \, vs \, H1 : \mu1 < \mu2$$

where: $\mu1$: mean PH level in saliva prior to application of conventional toothpaste; $\mu2$: mean of the PH level in the saliva after 3 and 5 weeks of the application of the conventional dentifrice.

3 Result

In relation to the effect of toothpaste with xylitol and cetylpyridinium chloride on salivary pH, we observed that there is an increase in pH from 5.65 to 6.56 in the third week and to 7.45 in the fifth week of use. This increase in pH value was statistically significant (P < 0.001), as shown in Table 1.

In relation to the effect of conventional toothpaste with fluoride only on the saliva pH, it is observed that this increases, as the conventional toothpaste is used, from 5.55 to 6.15 in the third week and 6.88 in the fifth week of use. This increase in pH value was statistically significant (P < 0.001), as shown in Table 2.

Table 1. Effect of toothpaste with xylitol and cetylpyridinium chloride on salivary pH.

Statistical of the test of "t"	Pretest pH before use of the paste	pH in the 3rd week of use	pH in the 5th week of use
Mean	5.65	6.56	7.45
SD	±0.12	±0.16	±0.17
LB	5.59	6.48	7.36
UB	5.71	6.65	7.54
T calculated	186.61	165.47	173.99
P	<0.0001	<0.0001	<0.0001

SD = standard deviation; LB = lower bounds; UB = upper bounds

Table 2. Effect of conventional fluoride toothpaste on salivary pH.

Statistical of the test of "t"	Pretest pH before use of the paste	pH in the 3rd week of use	pH in the 5th week of use
Mean	5.55	6.15	6.88
SD	±0.19	±0.36	±0.18
LB	5.45	6.05	6.78
UB	5.65	6.25	6.97
T calculated	117	129.65	152.15
P	<0.0001	<0.0001	<0.0001

SD = standard deviation; LB = lower bounds; UB = upper bounds

The best effect on salivary pH (Fig. 1), occurs in the fifth week of using toothpaste with xylitol plus cetylpyridinium chloride in relation to the use of conventional toothpaste with fluoride, with a statistically significant difference of 7.45 compared to 6.88 respectively (P < 0.001).

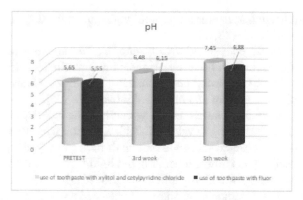

Fig. 1. Significant difference between the use of toothpaste with xylitol plus cetylpyridinium chloride in relation to the use of conventional toothpaste with fluoride.

4 Discussion

Orthodontic treatment using fixed appliances prevents adequate oral brushing in patients, so there is a greater chance of retaining dental biofilm, which produces changes in the pH of saliva and the count of bacteria [14]. Due to this situation, these patients are considered a risk group for the establishment of dental caries and periodontal disease [15]. Controlling dental plaque efficiently during treatment with fixed orthodontic appliances is an important condition for oral health care, if these measures are neglected, the damage can be considerable and the benefits of orthodontic treatment are debatable [16].

Studies show that patients with fixed orthodontic appliances have a higher salivary count of *Streptococcus mutans* than those without orthodontic appliances [17], including high values of *Lactobacillus spp* [18] and these high levels of bacteria may remain even after fixed orthodontic appliances have been removed [19].

In these patients with fixed orthodontic treatment, changes in the characteristics of the saliva can also be found; thus, we have a decrease in the amount of saliva during orthodontic treatment [14]. This decrease in saliva puts the patient at risk for a higher incidence of caries than those who do not wear orthodontic appliances [17].

The decrease in salivary pH values has been reported immediately after having applied fixed appliances, attributing these results to exposure to 37% phosphoric acid, returning the pH value to normal at 6 weeks [5], however, other researchers report a significant increase in salivary pH a few weeks after exposure to fixed orthodontic appliances [8, 18].

The results of this study showed an increase in pH values as toothpaste with xylitol and cetylpyridinium chloride was used, results that coincide with those reported by other authors, who refer to a significant increase in values of pH after the use of xylitol having as a vehicle a chewing gum [20, 21]; as well as a chewable tablet with xylitol [22].

This is due to the fact that xylitol, by reducing the levels of Streptococcus mutans in plaque and saliva, interrupts energy production processes, favoring a useless energy cycle and inducing cell death, thus reducing the adhesion of these bacteria to the enamel surface of the teeth and thus decreases its acid production potential, which produces an increase in saliva pH levels [23, 24].

Xylitol increases the concentrations of ammonia and amino acids and decreases the production of lactic acid in bacterial plaque, thus neutralizing acids and promoting neutral conditions in the oral cavity; and promotes an ecological change and this results in a less cariogenic environment and increased salivary pH [25].

In this study, as the toothpaste containing cetylpyridinium chloride was used, the salivary pH improved, increasing its values, and this is due to the fact that cetylpyridinium chloride is a positively charged molecule that binds to negatively charged bacteria and its antimicrobial activity is known, degrading the lipid bilayer of the cell, interrupting the control of membrane permeability and leading to leakage of cell content. Likewise, it inhibits the action of extracellular enzymes that synthesize a polysaccharide from sucrose, which is important for the development of dental caries [26]. Oral products containing cetylpyridinium chloride limit biofilm formation and bacterial adhesion to the tooth, helping to prevent oral diseases such as gingivitis, periodontitis, and dental caries [27].

The results of this study also showed increased salivary pH levels in the control group as a conventional fluoride toothpaste was used, and this is because fluoride reduces the amount of *Streptococcus mutans* and *lactobacilli* in plaque, because it inhibits the metabolism of carbohydrates and therefore the production of acids, therefore the concentration of fluoride affects the salivary pH and when the concentration of fluoride is high the pH is also high [28].

5 Conclusions

In both groups there were changes in salivary pH, the highest values were in the group that used toothpaste with xylitol and *cetylpyridinium* chloride, the difference being statistically significant. The frequency of brushing and care will help prevent carious lesions in patients with fixed orthodontics.

The limitation of this study lies in the short-term design. Additional studies with longer follow-up periods and with study designs that consider a control group are required, and using other commercial pastes that contain in their composition other alternatives for the control of bacterial plaque and *Streptococcus mutan*.

References

1. Mei, L., Chieng, J., Wong, C., Benic, G., Farella, M.: Factors affecting dental biofilm in patients wearing fixed orthodontic appliances. Prog. Orthod. **18**(1), 1–6 (2017). https://doi.org/10.1186/s40510-016-0158-5
2. Gorbunkova, A., Pagni, G., Brizhak, A., Farronato, G., Rasperini, G.: Impact of orthodontic treatment on periodontal tissues: a narrative review of multidisciplinary literature. Int. J. Dent. **2016** (2016)
3. Alshahrani, I., Hameed, M.S., Syed, S., Amanullah, M., Togoo, R.A., Kaleem, S.: Changes in essential salivary parameters in patients undergoing fixed orthodontic treatment: A longitudinal study. Niger. J. Clin. Pr. **22**, 707–712 (2019)

4. Negrete, J.C.M., Iano, Y., Negrete, P.D.M., Vaz, G.C., de Oliveira, G.G.: Sentiment analysis in the ecuadorian presidential election. In: Iano, Y., Saotome, O., Kemper Vásquez, G.L., Cotrim Pezzuto, C., Arthur, R., Gomes de Oliveira, G. (eds.) Proceedings of the 7th Brazilian Technology Symposium (BTSym 2021). BTSym 2021. Smart Innovation, Systems and Technologies, vol. 207, pp. 25–34. Springer, Cham (2023). https://doi.org/10.1007/978-3-031-044 35-9_3

5. Zogakis, I.P., Koren, E., Gorelik, S., Ginsburg, I., Shalish, M.: Effect of fixed orthodontic appliances on nonmicrobial salivary parameters. Angle Orthod. **88**, 806–811 (2018)

6. Teixeira, H.S., Kaulfuss, S.M.O., Ribeiro, J.S., Pereira, B.D.R., Brancher, J.A., Camargo, E.S.: Calcium, amylase, glucose, total protein concentrations, flow rate, pH and buffering capacity of saliva in patients undergoing orthodontic treatment with fixed appliances. Dental Press J. Orthod. **17**, 157–161 (2012)

7. Al-Haifi, H.A.A., Ishaq, R.A.A., Al-Hammadi, M.S.A.: Salivary pH changes under the effect of stainless steel versus elastomeric ligatures in fixed orthodontic patients: a single-center, randomized controlled clinical trial. BMC Oral Health **21**, 1–7 (2021)

8. Peros, K., Mestrovic, S., Anic-Milosevic, S., Slaj, M.: Salivary microbial and nonmicrobial parameters in children with fixed orthodontic appliances. Angle Orthod. **81**, 901–906 (2011)

9. Tenuta, L.M.A., Fernandez, C.E., Brandão, A.C.S., Cury, J.A.: Titratable acidity of beverages influences salivary pH recovery. Braz. Oral Res. **29**, 1–6 (2015)

10. Subramaniam, P., Nandan, N.: Effect of xylitol, sodium fluoride and triclosan containing mouth rinse on Streptococcus mutans. Contemp. Clin. Dent. **2**, 287 (2011)

11. Thiagarajan, Y., de Oliveira, G.G., Iano, Y., Vaz, G.C.: Identification and analysis of bacterial species present in cow dung fed microbial fuel cell. In: Iano, Y., Saotome, O., Kemper Vásquez, G.L., Cotrim Pezzuto, C., Arthur, R., Gomes de Oliveira, G. (eds.) Proceedings of the 7th Brazilian Technology Symposium (BTSym 2021). BTSym 2021. Smart Innovation, Systems and Technologies, vol. 207, pp. 16–24. Springer, Cham (2023). https://doi.org/10.1007/978-3-031-04435-9_2

12. Williams, M.I.: The antibacterial and antiplaque effectiveness of mouthwashes containing cetylpyridinium chloride with and without alcohol in improving gingival health. J. Clin. Dent. **22**, 179 (2011)

13. Zanarini, M., Pazzi, E., Bonetti, S., Ruggeri, O., Bonetti, G.A., Prati, C.: In vitro evaluation of the effects of a fluoride-releasing composite on enamel demineralization around brackets. Prog. Orthod. **13**, 10–16 (2012)

14. Arab, S., Malekshah, S.N., Mehrizi, E.A., Khanghah, A.E., Naseh, R., Imani, M.M.: Effect of fixed orthodontic treatment on salivary flow, pH and microbial count. J. Dent. (Tehran) **13**, 18 (2016)

15. Baumgartner, S., Menghini, G., Imfeld, T.: The prevalence of approximal caries in patients after fixed orthodontic treatment and in untreated subjects (2013)

16. Shimpo, Y., et al.: Effects of the dental caries preventive procedure on the white spot lesions during orthodontic treatment—an open label randomized controlled trial. J. Clin. Med. **11**, 854 (2022)

17. Moussa, S.A., Gameil Gobran, H., Salem, M.A., Barkat, I.F.: Dental biofilm and saliva biochemical composition changes in young orthodontic patients. J. Dent. Oral. Disord. Ther. **5**, 1–5 (2017)

18. Maret, D., et al.: Effect of fixed orthodontic appliances on salivary microbial parameters at 6 months: a controlled observational study. J. Appl. Oral Sci. **22**, 38–43 (2014)

19. Jung, W.-S., Kim, H., Park, S.-Y., Cho, E.-J., Ahn, S.-J.: Quantitative analysis of changes in salivary mutans streptococci after orthodontic treatment. Am. J. Orthod. Dentofac. Orthop. **145**, 603–609 (2014)

20. Padminee, K., Poorni, S., Diana, D., Duraivel, D., Srinivasan, M.R.: Effectiveness of casein phosphopeptide-amorphous calcium phosphate and xylitol chewing gums on salivary pH, buffer capacity, and Streptococcus mutans levels: an interventional study. Indian J. Dent. Res. **29**, 616 (2018)
21. Shinde, M.R., Winnier, J.: Effects of stevia and xylitol chewing gums on salivary flow rate, pH, and taste acceptance. J. Dent. Res. Rev. **7**, 50 (2020)
22. Minango, P., Iano, Y., Chuma, E.L., Vaz, G.C., de Oliveira, G.G., Minango, J.: Revision of the 5G concept rollout and its application in smart cities: a study case in South America. In: Iano, Y., Saotome, O., Kemper Vásquez, G.L., Cotrim Pezzuto, C., Arthur, R., Gomes de Oliveira, G. (eds.) Proceedings of the 7th Brazilian Technology Symposium (BTSym 2021). BTSym 2021. Smart Innovation, Systems and Technologies, vol. 207, pp. 229–238. Springer, Cham. https://doi.org/10.1007/978-3-031-04435-9_21
23. Koşar, S., Çokakoğlu, S., Kaleli, İ: Effects of xylitol impregnated toothbrushes on periodontal status and microbial flora in orthodontic patients. Angle Orthod. **90**, 837–843 (2020)
24. Padilla-Cáceres, T.C., et al.: Efecto de una pasta dental con xilitol sobre Streptcococcos mutans en pacientes con ortodoncia fija. Vive Rev. Salud. **5**, 245–256 (2022)
25. Thiagarajan, Y., et al.: Design and fabrication of human-powered vehicle-a measure for healthy living. In: Iano, Y., Saotome, O., Kemper Vásquez, G.L., Cotrim Pezzuto, C., Arthur, R., Gomes de Oliveira, G. (eds.) Proceedings of the 7th Brazilian Technology Symposium (BTSym 2021). BTSym 2021. Smart Innovation, Systems and Technologies, vol. 207, pp. 1–15. Springer, Cham. https://doi.org/10.1007/978-3-031-04435-9_1
26. Yeon, L.S., Young, L.S.: Susceptibility of oral streptococci to chlorhexidine and cetylpyridinium chloride. Biocontrol Sci. **24**, 13–21 (2019)
27. Demanboro, A.C., Bianchini, D., Iano, Y., de Oliveira, G.G., Vaz, G.C.: 6G Networks: An Innovative Approach, but with Many Challenges and Paradigms, in the Development of Platforms and Services in the Near Future. In: Brazilian Technology Symposium. pp. 172–187. Springer (2023)
28. Gavic, L., Gorseta, K., Borzabadi-Farahani, A., Tadin, A., Glavina, D.: Influence of toothpaste pH on its capacity to prevent enamel demineralization. Contemp. Clin. Dent. **9**, 554 (2018)

PID Controller Optimized Based on PSO for Trajectory Tracking of Free-Floating Satellite Robotic Manipulator

Ali Alouache[(✉)] [ID]

Centre des Techniques Spatiales, Algerian Space Agency, Arzew, Oran, Algeria
aalouache@outlook.com

Abstract. This paper deals with trajectory tracking of a free-floating Satellite robotic manipulator (FFSRM) under the problem of communication failure (CF) for space applications. Communication in robotic systems may fail very often due to noises, external disturbances, and errors in the sensors. In the event of CF, the samples of the reference trajectory are missing, which would cause the failure of the robot to accomplish the tracking process. For this purpose, the control strategy that is proposed in this paper consists mainly of two parts. First, the conventional Proportional Integral Derivative (PID) controller is optimized based on Particle Swarm Optimization (PSO) algorithm in order to adjust the torque of the FFSRM with a view to make the tracking error attains the minimum possible between the reference and the actual trajectory of the FFSRM. Second, a polynomial fitting algorithm is applied to estimate the reference trajectory to overcome the CF events. Finally, a Matlab example is conducted to validate the effectiveness of the proposed control approach in comparison with the conventional PID controller and PID optimized by Genetic Algorithms (GA).

Keywords: Free-Floating Satellite Robotic Manipulator · Trajectory Tracking · Communication Failure

Nomenclature

FFSRM:	Free-Floating Satellite Robotic Manipulator
CF:	Communication Failure
PID:	Proportional Integral Derivative
PSO:	Particle Swarm Optimization
GA:	Genetic Algorithms
CMAC:	Cerebellum Model Articulation Controller
DEM:	Dynamically Equivalent Manipulator
FORAC:	Fractional Order Resolved Acceleration Control
RAC:	Resolved Acceleration Control
MAS:	Multi Agent System
B_0:	Base of the Satellite
C_0:	Centroid of the base

© The Author(s), under exclusive license to Springer Nature Switzerland AG 2023
Y. Iano et al. (Eds.): BTSym 2022, SIST 353, pp. 83–93, 2023.
https://doi.org/10.1007/978-3-031-31007-2_8

m_0:	Mass of the base
B_i:	i^{th} link
C_i:	Centroid of the link
m_i:	Mass of the link
a_i:	Scalar from the ith joint to the centroid of the next link
b_i:	Scalar from the ith centroid of the link to the joint of the next link
r_i:	Position vector
I_i:	Moment of inertia
K:	Kinetic energy
U:	Potential energy
E_T:	Total energy
$M(q)$:	Inertia matrix
$B(q, \dot{q})$:	Vector of coriolis and centrifugal forces
q:	Joint position
$\dot{q}$:	Velocity vector
$\ddot{q}$:	Acceleration vector
τ:	Torque control input

1 Introduction

Recently, the study of free-floating Satellite robotic (FFSRM) manipulators has become a challenging topic due to the recent achievements in the space industry [1]. Many research works have focused on the study of kinematics, dynamics, and trajectory tracking control of FFSRM because its base is floating in space in order to perform various space missions [2–4]. The conventional PID controller has been adopted so far for the control of FFSRM because of its simplicity and design ease [5–7]. However, the PID controller requires an accurate system model to adjust its parameters. The previous works that applied PID controller for the FFSRM considered that the dynamic model of the manipulator is known exactly and the conditions are not changing. However, in space applications, the conditions of operations might vary due to gravity changes, noises, external disturbances, and the Satellite base that is floating in space. Hence, it is very difficult to achieve optimal tracking performance by using only the PID controller for space applications. In order to overcome the limitations of PID controllers, there have been many works that proposed computational intelligence methods to be used with the PID controller for the FFSRM control. For instance, [8] proposed a fuzzy PID controller by the fusion of a PID controller with a fuzzy controller and demonstrated its effectiveness in various gravity areas compared with a PID controller. [9] proposed an adaptive fuzzy CMAC PID controller and demonstrated its effectiveness in comparison with a PID controller. [10] used the DEM technique to simplify the model of the FFSRM and controlled it based on an adaptive sliding mode PID controller. [11] proposed a CMAC approach for compensating the uncertainties with H_∞ method to deal with the disturbance-based DEM model. Ref. [12] proposed the FORAC approach to control FFSRM with system uncertainty and compared its effectiveness with traditional RAC that is based on a PID controller.

1.1 Related Works

In addition to the problem of deficiency in the PID controller when it is used alone for FFSRM control, communication failure (CF) is another challenging problem in practical applications. Because it is noted that the previous works considered that the FFSRM is receiving the coordinates of the reference trajectory regularly under the assumption of perfect communication. However, in physical applications, it is well known that communication in robotic systems may fail very often due to noises, external disturbances, and errors in the sensors. In the event of CF, the samples of the reference trajectory are missing, which would cause the failure of the robot to accomplish the tracking process. In recent years, there have been some works that proposed different solutions to overcome the CF problem. For example, [13] proposed estimation algorithms to overcome CF in consensus tracking of single and double integrators MAS. [14] proposed least squares algorithm to remedy the CF problem for consensus tracking of single integrator MAS with a time-varying reference state. [15] proposed a PSO algorithm to overcome CF in multiple robots formation control by using $l - \varphi$ controller. [16] proposed GA to optimize the parameters of $l - \varphi$ controller in the formation of multi robots, and applied also GA to overcome CF between the leader and the followers. [17] proposed a polynomial estimation algorithm to deal with CF in distributed formation tracking of multi-robots based on a graph theoretical approach. [18] proposed a GAPID controller for path tracking of an autonomous wheeled mobile robot and applied also GA to overcome CF.

1.2 Motivations and Contribution

Based on this background, it emerges that the CF problem has not been studied yet in the literature for the control of FFSRM. However, CF is still an open issue and seems to be an important problem for space missions. Hence, the major contribution of the present paper is to investigate the CF problem in trajectory tracking of the FFSRM. The control approach that is proposed in this paper consists mainly of two parts. First, the conventional PID controller is optimized based on the PSO algorithm in order to improve its performance in terms of robustness, accuracy, and convergence speed. PSO is an efficient and robust optimization method that has more advantages than the other optimization algorithms [15]. Second, optimization is not going to be used in this paper to estimate the reference trajectory in the case of CF as in [18] because using another optimization process in the control system would increase the computation costs. Instead, the polynomial fitting algorithm of [17] is going to be used in this paper due to its simplicity and effectiveness. Finally, a Matlab example is carried out to show the effectiveness of the proposed control approach. To the best of the author's knowledge, this is the first work that investigates CF for trajectory tracking of the FFSRM.

The remainder of this paper is structured as follows. Section 2 describes the system modeling of the FFSRM. Section 3 discusses in detail the proposed control approach. Section 4 demonstrates the simulation results to validate the proposed algorithms. Section 5 summarizes the main concluding remarks and future works.

2   System Modeling

Let us consider the FFSRM depicted in Fig. 1, which comprises n rigid links that are attached to a Satellite whose base is floating in space.

While the primary core of the manipulator makes a movement, a dynamic force exerts on its base, which makes the base attitude and position transform. Therefore, the dynamic model of the FFSRM is formulated as follows.

The kinetic energy, i.e., K of the FFSRM, can be established as given by (1).

$$K = \frac{1}{2} \sum\nolimits_{i=0}^{n} m_i \dot{r}_i^T \dot{r}_i + \frac{1}{2} \sum\nolimits_{i=0}^{n} I_i \dot{q}_i^T \dot{q}_i \tag{1}$$

The potential energy i.e. U of the FFSRM can be established as given by (2).

$$U = \frac{1}{2} \sum\nolimits_{i=0}^{n} m_i \dot{r}_i^T \dot{r}_i \tag{2}$$

Therefore, the total energy, i.e., E_T of the space manipulator, can be established as given by (3).

$$E_T = K + U \tag{3}$$

Based on the Lagrangian modeling method, the dynamic model of the FFSRM that is derived from (3) is given by (4).

$$M(q)\ddot{q} + B(q, \dot{q})\dot{q} = \tau \tag{4}$$

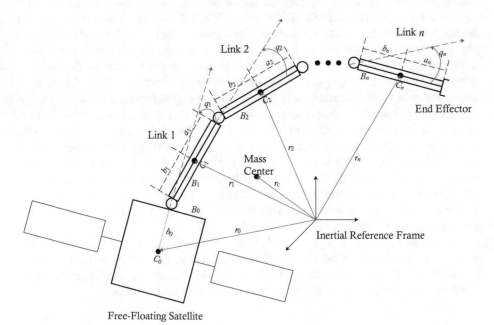

Fig. 1. System modeling of FFSRM

3 Proposed Control Approach

The proposed approach for trajectory tracking of the FFSRM subject to CF is presented in the block diagram of Fig. 2. It comprises mainly the following three steps. First, the formulation of the tracking error function and the equation of the PID controller. Second, optimization of the PID controller by using the PSO algorithm. Third, the application of the polynomial fitting algorithm for estimating of reference path in the case of CF. The algorithm of each step is discussed in detail in the following subsections.

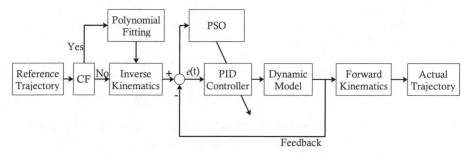

Fig. 2. Block diagram of the proposed control approach

3.1 PID Controller

Let us consider the reference trajectory, i.e., Y^d, then the desired joint position, i.e., q^d, is found by the inverse kinematics of the manipulator. Therefore, the tracking error, i.e., $e(t)$, is defined as given by (5).

$$e(t) = q^d - q \tag{5}$$

The torque of the FFSRM is adjusted based on the PID controller as given by (6).

$$\tau(t) = k_p e(t) + k_i \int e(t)dt + k_d \frac{de(t)}{dt} \tag{6}$$

where k_p, k_i and k_d are non-negative coefficients of the controller that denote respectively proportional, integral, and derivative terms.

3.2 Optimization of PID Controller Based on PSO Algorithm

Let's assume the fitness function J to be the integral square error as given by (7).

$$J = \int_0^\infty [e(t)]^2 dt \tag{7}$$

While $e(t)$ is the tracking error that is given by (5). The best parameters of the PID controller (k_p, k_i, and k_d) correspond to the smallest fitness function calculated based on the PSO algorithm given below.

Initialization
Instruction 1: set all initial positions and velocities
of the particles with random values;
Instruction 2: compute the fitness function of each par-
ticle using (7);
Instruction 3: save each particle position as the best
local position, i.e., $p_b(t)$;
Instruction 4: store the particle position with the best
fitness function as the best global position, i.e., $p_g(t)$;
Search process
Instruction 5: upgrade the velocity vector of each parti-
cle, i.e., $v(t)$, as given by (8);

$$v(t+1) = w.v(t) + c_1 r_1 (p_b(t) - p(t)) + c_2 r_2 (p_g(t) - p(t)) \tag{8}$$

where w is the inertia weight and its value is adjusted between the interval [0.4 0.9]; c_1 and c_2 are constants that are fixed as $c_1 = c_2 = 2$; r_1 and r_2 are two random numbers that are selected between 0 and 1;

Instruction 6: upgrade the position vector $p(t)$ as given
by (9);

$$p(t+1) = p(t) + v(t) \tag{9}$$

Instruction 7: compute again the fitness function for
each particle;
Instruction 8: upgrade the values of the best local position, i.e., $p_b(t)$, and the best global position, i.e.,
$p_g(t)$;
Convergence check
Instruction 9: verify the best fitness function value. If
it still changes extremely in the last iterations, then
return to the search process; otherwise, end optimization;

3.3 Communication Failure

The proposed approach to overcome CF events is described in the flow chart shown in Fig. 3 and is summarized in the following steps [17].

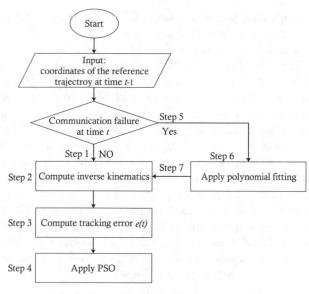

Fig. 3. Proposed approach to overcome CF

Step 1: if communication failure is NO then go to step 2;
Step 2: compute the inverse kinematics;
Step 3: compute the tracking errors using equation (5);
Step 4: apply PSO optimization in order to estimate the best parameters (k_p, k_i, k_d);
Step 5: if communication failure is Yes then go to step 6;
Step 6: apply the polynomial fitting algorithm to estimate the reference trajectory with the reference coordinates that are received up to time $t-1$;
Step 7: back to step 2;

4 Simulation Results

A simulation example is conducted in this section in order to show the effectiveness of the proposed approach for trajectory tracking of the FFSRM subject to CF.

Let us consider a circle reference trajectory of radius $1m$. Hence, $x_r(t) = cos(t)$ and $y_r(t) = sin(t)$ are the coordinates of the reference path along the X-axis and Y-axis, respectively. Let us assume an FFSRM that is composed of two rigid links and its parameters are indicated in Table 1.

Table 1. Parameters of the two link FFSRM.

Link	$a_i(m)$	$b_i(m)$	$m_i(kg)$	$I_i(kg.m^2)$
0	–	0.5	40	6.667
1	0.5	0.5	4	0.333
2	0.5	0.5	3	0.25

The system is simulated with two events of CF and the performance of the proposed PID-PSO controller is compared with the conventional PID and PID-GA controllers.

The results of trajectory tracking of the end effector along the X-axis and Y-axis are depicted in Figs. 4 and 5, respectively. Thus, it can be seen in these figures that the proposed PID-PSO controller is capable to perform robust and precise tracking control of the FFSRM along both axes in comparison with PID and PID-GA controllers. The result of the tracking error is shown in Fig. 6, where it can be seen that the proposed controller is capable to overcome the events of CF by polynomial fitting algorithm since the FFSRM returned quickly for tracking during CF events. The results of trajectory tracking along the X-Y plane based on the three controllers are depicted in Fig. 7, in which the proposed PID-PSO controller is the best, and the CF events are neglected during the tracking process based on the proposed polynomial fitting algorithm.

Finally, it can be concluded from these results that the proposed PID-PSO controller performs the best in terms of robustness and precision for tracking the FFSRM in comparison with PID and PID-GA controllers. Moreover, the system is able to overcome the events of CF based on a polynomial fitting algorithm where there are no effects of the CF events in the trajectory tracking of the FFSRM.

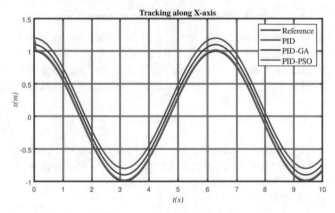

Fig. 4. Trajectory tracking of FFSRM along the X-axis

5   Conclusions

This paper deals with the problem of communication failure (CF) in trajectory tracking of FFSRM. The proposed control approach is composed mainly of two parts. First, the PID controller is optimized by the PSO algorithm in order to adjust the torque of the FFSRM. Second, a polynomial fitting algorithm is adopted to predict the reference path to overcome the CF events.

The simulation results demonstrated the efficiency of the proposed approach in comparison to the previous works about trajectory tracking control of FFSRM. The major advantages of this paper are the followings; (i) the proposed PID-PSO controller gives better results than classical PID and PID-GA controllers; (ii) the proposed polynomial fitting algorithm is capable to overcome CF for trajectory tracking of FFSRM which is very important for practical applications.

In future works, the following tasks are suggested; combining the proposed approach with a potential field to deal with obstacle avoidance; investigation of time delays, uncertainties, and external disturbances in the dynamic model.

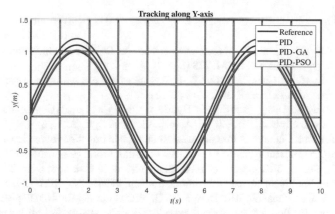

Fig. 5. Trajectory tracking of FFSRM along the Y-axis

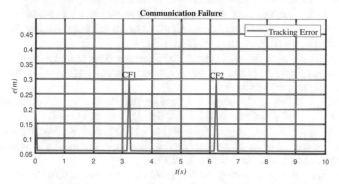

Fig. 6. Tracking error with two events of CF

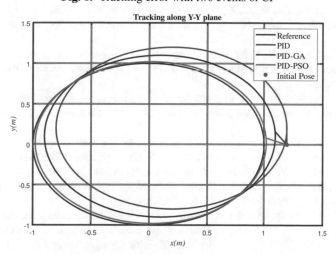

Fig. 7. Trajectory tracking of FFSRM on the X-Y plane

References

1. Papadopoulos, E., Aghili, F., Ma, O., Lampariello, R.: Robotic manipulation and capture in space: A survey. Front. Robot. AI. **228** (2021)
2. Liu, X.-F., Li, H.-Q., Chen, Y.-J., Cai, G.-P.: Dynamics and control of space robot considering joint friction. Acta Astronaut. **111**, 1–18 (2015)
3. Xu, W., Peng, J., Liang, B., Mu, Z.: Hybrid modeling and analysis method for dynamic coupling of space robots. IEEE Trans. Aerosp. Electron. Syst. **52**(1), 85–98 (2016)
4. Wilde, M., Kwok Choon, S., Grompone, A., Romano, M.: Equations of motion of free-floating spacecraft-manipulator systems: an engineer's tutorial. Front. Robot. AI. **5**, 41 (2018)
5. Zheng, C., Su, Y.: PID control of robot manipulators in task space. In: 2010 8th World Congress on Intelligent Control and Automation. pp. 1794–1799. IEEE (2010)
6. Mandava, R.K., Vundavilli, P.R.: Design 4-DOF PID controller for 4-DOF planar and spatial manipulators. In: Proceedings of the International Conference on Robotics Automation and Control and Embedded systems. IEEE, Chennai, India (2015)
7. Mandava, R.K., Vundavalli, P.R.: Design of PID controllers for 4-DOF planar and spatial manipulators. In: 2015 International Conference on Robotics, Automation, Control and Embedded Systems (RACE). pp. 1–6. IEEE (2015)
8. Liu, F.-C., Liang, L.-H., Gao, J.-J.: Fuzzy PID Control of Space Manipulator for Both Ground Alignment and Space Applications. Int. J. Autom. Comput. **11**(4), 353–360 (2014). https://doi.org/10.1007/s11633-014-0800-y
9. Zhang, W., Hu, X., Fang, Y.: Adaptive control for free-floating space flexible robot based on fuzzy CMAC. J. Inf. & COMPUTATIONAL Sci. **11**, 141–149 (2014)
10. Kharabian, B., Bolandi, H., Ehyaei, A.F., Mousavi Mashhadi, S.K., Smailzadeh, S.M.: Adaptive tuning of sliding mode-PID control in free floating space manipulator by sliding cloud theory. Am. J. Mech. Ind. Eng. **2**, 64–71 (2017)
11. Li, L., Chen, Z., Wang, Y., Zhang, X., Wang, N.: Robust task-space tracking for free-floating space manipulators by cerebellar model articulation controller. Assem. Autom. (2019)
12. Shao, X., Sun, G., Yao, W., Li, X., Zhang, O.: Fractional-order resolved acceleration control for free-floating space manipulator with system uncertainty. Aerosp. Sci. Technol. **118**, 107041 (2021)
13. Haoran, L., Qinghe, W., Sabir, D.: Consensus tracking algorithms with estimation for multi-agent system. In: The 27th Chinese Control and Decision Conference (2015 CCDC). pp. 3808–3813 (2015)
14. Alouache, A., Wu, Q.-H.: Consensus based least squares estimation for single-integrator multi-agent systems with a time-varying reference state. J. Electron. Sci. Technol. **18**, 100053 (2020)
15. Rabah, A., Wu, Q.: Communication failure in formation control of multiple robots based on particle swarm optimization algorithm. In: 2015 7th International Conference on Intelligent Human-Machine Systems and Cybernetics. pp. 448–451. IEEE (2015)
16. Alouache, A., Wu, Q.: Tracking Control of Multiple Mobile Robot Trajectory by Genetic Algorithms. Electroteh. Electron. Autom. 65, (2017)
17. Alouache, A., Wu, Q.: Distributed Formation Tracking of Multi Robots with Trajectory Estimation. In: Del Ser, J., Osaba, E., Bilbao, M.N., Sanchez-Medina, J.J., Vecchio, M., Yang, X.-S. (eds.) IDC 2018. SCI, vol. 798, pp. 237–246. Springer, Cham (2018). https://doi.org/10.1007/978-3-319-99626-4_21
18. Alouache, A., Wu, Q.: Genetic algorithms for trajectory tracking of mobile robot based on PID controller. In: 2018 IEEE 14th International Conference on Intelligent Computer Communication and Processing (ICCP). pp. 237–241. IEEE (2018)

Fault Management in Manufacturing Process: Quality Indicators for Short- and Medium-Term Monitoring and Their Interrelationship

Murilo O. Homem[1] (ID), Frederico R. Bettanin[1] (ID), Jorge Moreira de Souza[2] (ID),
Giovanni Moura de Holanda[2] (ID), and Fabrício Cristófani[2](✉) (ID)

[1] Ingeteam Ltda, Campinas, Brazil
{murilo.homem, frederico.bettanin}@ingeteam.com
[2] FITec – Technological Innovations, Campinas, Brazil
{jmdsouza, gholanda, fabriciocristofani}@fitec.org.br

Abstract. One of the first metrics of production quality is the FTQ (First Time Quality) index, which has gained new attention with process control methods driven by Industry 4.0. A manufacturing line with an FTQ below 100% causes the discarding of produced units or rework time, implying higher production costs and negative impacts on quality goals. To guide quality actions, mainly in processes with several incident factors, there is a need for a lower granularity target that allows the definition of correction actions still during production. This paper presents a study on quality indicators that can better represent the performance regarding the occurrence of defective units in the final test process of the equipment assembled by Ingeteam Brasil. The methodological guideline is to assess the effectiveness of using some quality indicators for short- (weekly) and medium-term (monthly) monitoring of the performance of the mentioned process, aiming to identify correlations between them and support faster decisions to reach the desired quality targets. In this sense, a short-term upper control limit is derived for each product based on its behavior during the test process to identify units and failure causes that may compromise the FTQ goal and should be analyzed. To this end a software quality test tool was developed, the Quality Test System (QTS), which records important information about the test process such as required test stations, operators, product serial number, test steps, detected failures, etc. QTS is integrated with the shop floor system integrating production and testing.

Keywords: Failure Management · Statistical Analysis · Process Control · Quality Indicators

1 Introduction

In every manufacturing process, it is essential to control the variation of the produced items together with fault management that acts not only to avoid production waste but also to reduce as much as possible the occurrence of non-conforming products. Fault Management is one of the steps of quality management and is directly linked to the

Y. Iano et al. (Eds.): BTSym 2022, SIST 353, pp. 93–102, 2023.
https://doi.org/10.1007/978-3-031-31007-2_9

increase in productivity [1] and quality assurance of production. In this management field, analytical resources help the production team to act preventively and minimize the number of nonconforming or defective items, avoiding material discard and reducing test and adjustment time.

Quality managers use the information from failure events recorded during the testing stages of a project to correct problems as they arise, improving the process, setting and evaluating targets, identifying points "outside the curve" that need to be improved, and feeding back into the production chain. Such procedures may enable more reliable decision-making and support not only quality managers but also other managers with different roles within the organization, cf. [2]. In this way, it is possible to propose improvement actions even for the previous stages of production.

A dictum of quality is "do it right the first time", established by Philip Crosby in his fundamentals for a zero-defect policy [3]. This goal is measured by the First Time Quality (FTQ) index, which expresses the percentage of defect-free units in relation to the number of units produced. "Zero defect" means FTQ is equal to 100%. Achieving defect-free levels of production is a goal that has driven several efforts in production methods, cf. Six Sigma [4], Lean Manufacturing in Industry 4.0 [5], and Lean Six Sigma [6], and several factors in a production line may directly affect FTQ [7].

The FTQ index below 100% leads to discarded units or rework time, that is, higher production costs. The rework time is a function of the number of failures detected in the units produced, representing more time for corrections and completion of the production lot for delivery to the customer. The Quality Test Index (QTI) represents the ratio between the number of failures detected and the total number of units produced.

Seeking to achieve the FTQ goal, Ingeteam Brasil's quality test management evaluates these two indices monthly to monitor the quality of all products throughout the year. Within the scope of an R&D project carried out in the company to systematize this monitoring and support improvement actions, some important issues were identified:

- The two quality indexes are inversely proportional: an increase in QTI implies a decrease in FTQ. In the year 2021, for all of Ingeteam Brasil's products, this negative correlation is high with a magnitude of 82%.
- The test activities are very dynamic requiring daily corrective actions that are summarized weekly to provide guidelines for the test team.
- The guidelines are based on the failure records showing up the main defects that occurred in the last weeks to warn the testers and the shop floor process.

With those issues in mind a software quality test tool was developed, the Quality Test System (QTS), which records important information about the test process like required test stations, operators, product serial number, test steps, detected failures, number of units tested, etc. QTS interacts with the shop floor system integrating production and testing.

The indexes FTQ and QTI are not suitable for a weekly quality follow-up, since it depends on the number of produced units and a product can take months to have its units finished. The FTQ index has a quantitative goal for total production that also holds for each product as a benchmark during the test process. To this end, an upper control limit for the QTI is derived for each product based on its behavior during the test process to warn an out-of-control number of failures in each week that should be analyzed.

The next section briefly presents the QTS and the steps of the test process. The following section presents the analytical development and real quantitative examples.

2 The Quality Test System (QTS)

The objective of the QTS software is to record all important information during the test process. It reflects the experience of the test managers and fulfills the needs to follow, control, and record the many daily activities. It interacts with the shop floor control system to associate the product identification and the respective units' serial number assigned for the test to assure data integrity along the production.

Each product serial number to be tested must be registered at QTS generally based on the file set automatically made available by the shop floor control. The test team records the details of each failure event such as test stage, failure characteristics, test station, operators, etc. The test process, in turn, has two stages running in sequence. All failures should be cleaned at the first stage providing a zero-defect unit to the next step, the second stage, where the system is tested for all functionalities. Only the remaining failures detected at the second stage are considered in the QTI and FTQ calculation. Figure 1 shows the defect report screen.

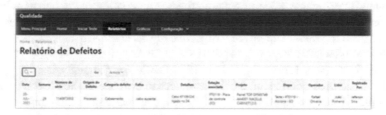

Fig. 1. Defect Report Screen (in Portuguese)

The system QTS also keeps a daily record of the number of units tested (project/serial number). The number of units produced for a project is only accounted for when it is finished.

Test activities are very dynamic, requiring daily corrective actions, and that is why it is proposed a weekly control limit to identify at the second stage the out-of-control units that affect the QTI and FTQ indexes.

To allow key insights into failure behavior, QTS feeds the recorded data into Power BI (Microsoft) tool. QTS/BI is an analytical tool allowing the quality team to go deeper into the failure details as will be shown in the examples.

3 Analytical Development

3.1 Statistical Fault Management

Mechanisms and systems for fault detection and diagnosis in manufacturing processes have been receiving attention and gaining a new level of presence in the industry [8]. In recent years, intelligent systems have made it possible to raise the levels of productivity and resilience of manufacturing processes from the wide availability of data and the ability to process them in real-time [9]. However, these same authors point out that changes in the traditional approaches of operation, analysis, and control are necessary to ensure the performance of these new systems.

Methods used for fault detection and diagnosis can be classified into data-driven, model-based, and knowledge-based approaches [10–12]. In a data-driven approach, decisions are made based on data instead of intuition or even tacit knowledge (cf. [13]). This approach has been widely applied in industrial process monitoring; however, its successful use depends on the analytical models used as well as the quality of historical data [12]. Model-based approaches use the relations among the process variables to determine the faults of a system from the comparison of available system measurements with a priori information generated by the system's mathematical model, while knowledge-based approaches consider a priority the knowledge or rules as well as the process data. The choice of the best approach occurs according to the needs and feasibility of each industry and process being considered.

In manufacturing processes in general, there is a variation in the behavior between the expected results in certain production steps, which must be quantitatively analyzed using statistical methods. The primary objective of this statistical analysis is to provide the means to understand the origins and causes of these variations. Statistical tools such as control charts (see, for example, [14, 15]), Pareto for the analysis of origins and causes [16], and projection using moving averages to evaluate the achievement of goals are examples of methods that, when well applied, can add a lot in this sense.

Models based on moving averages have been used as tools to control manufacturing processes that present autocorrelated variables [17, 18] or as an alternative to control charts in the form of transfer function models [19]. Another approach used for fault management in production systems is the evidence-based method [20], in which there is the involvement of experts and the team responsible for fault control in identifying and solving problems.

3.2 FTQ Control

Ingeteam uses a data-driven approach. The index FTQ is a quantitative goal for total production that also holds for each product as a benchmark during the test process. It measures the zero-defect number of units tested in the second stage and does not consider the failure types of the faulty units. On the other hand, the index QTI is based on the number of failures that remain in the second stage pointing out possible test flaws in the first stage. In the second stage, QTI should be zero and FTQ one. As far as QTI increases, the FTQ decreases implying a negative correlation between the two indexes.

The proposal is to define an upper control limit (UCL) that should be evaluated weekly due to the dynamic characteristics of the test process. The QTS recorded data are the number of tested units including the non-failed ones and the number of failures per failed unit allowing the derivation, namely QTI_i and FTQ_i, defined by Eqs. (1) and (2), as follows.

$$QTI_i = \frac{Number\ of\ failures\ per\ week}{Number\ of\ tested\ units\ per\ week} \tag{1}$$

$$FTQ_i = \frac{Number\ of\ non\ failed\ units\ per\ week}{Number\ of\ tested\ units\ per\ week} \tag{2}$$

$$QTI_i \rightarrow 0 \ as \ FTQ_i \rightarrow 1$$

Quality control takes place using a chart (control chart) where the out-of-control weeks are defined by $QTI_i > UCL$ whose failures should be investigated.

Suppose a sample of (QTI_i, FTQ_i) tuple connected $(0, 1)$ by a straight line as shown in Fig. 2(a).

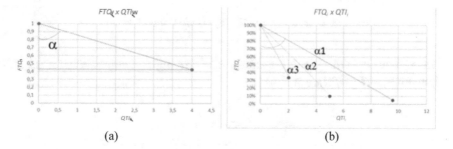

(a)   (b)

Fig. 2. (QTI_i, FTQ_i) tuple relationship

The (QTI_i, FTQ_i) tuple relates with the tangent of α, as expressed by Eq. (3).

$$\tan \alpha_i = \frac{QTI_i}{1 - FTQ_i} \tag{3}$$

Figure 2(b) shows the samples after three weeks of the test progress. The upper limit UCL for each week is determined by Eq. (4), where the mean of the tangents is an estimation of the test process behavior to derive UCL based on the FTQ_{goal} considered as a benchmark for each product for quality control (FTQ is a goal for overall production).

$$\text{Mean}[\tan \alpha_i] = \frac{UCL}{1 - FQT_{goal}} for \ i = 1, 2, \ldots, w \tag{4}$$

The control quality analysis is carried out when $QTI_i > UCL$ for all product serial numbers tested up to week w. The next section shows two real examples to illustrate the modeling proposal.

Examples. The preceding idea is illustrated using the data recorded (test second stage) for products A and B (wind power products) with a test period of 9 and 12 weeks, respectively. Only the weeks such that $QTI_i \neq 0$ is considered. At the end of the product test, considering all weeks observed, the FTQ calculated was 56%.

Product A. Figure 3(a) plots the indexes $FTQ_i \times QTI_i$ recorded along the test weeks, and Fig. 3(b) depicts the control chart.

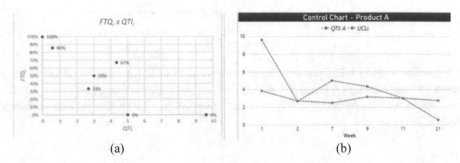

(a)   (b)

Fig. 3. (a) FTQ_i vs. TI_i, (b) QTS/BI Control Chart

Table 1 presents the weekly evaluation of the upper control limit for an FTQ benchmark of 60% ($FTQ_{goal} = 0.6$).

Table 1. Test data: Product A.

Week i	QTI_i A	FTQ_i A	tan α_i	UCL_i
1	9.60	0%	9.6	3.84
2	2.67	33%	4.0	2.72
7	5.00	0%	5.0	2.48
9	4.33	67%	13.0	3.16
11	3.00	50%	6.0	3.01
21	0.57	86%	4.0	2.77

Weekly, the control chart warns the quality team of an out-of-control test behavior requiring additional investigation of failure-prone product units (serial number) and their failures. This is accomplished using the QTS/BI failure analytics pointing out the critical units (serial number) for the out-of-control weeks (1, 7, 9), as illustrated in Fig. 3 (b).

QTS/BI allows a search tree analysis per product displaying the attributes "week/serial number/failure type/failure details", as subtrees as depicted in Fig. 4 for Product A.

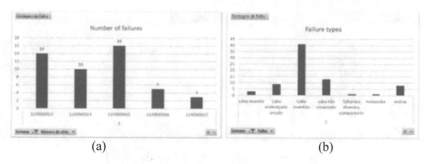

(a)   (b)

Fig. 4. Failure details per serial number, i = 1

Figure 5 shows the QTS failure record (in Portuguese) for unit 1140969015. The critical failure type is the wrong connected cables, whose details are also displayed.

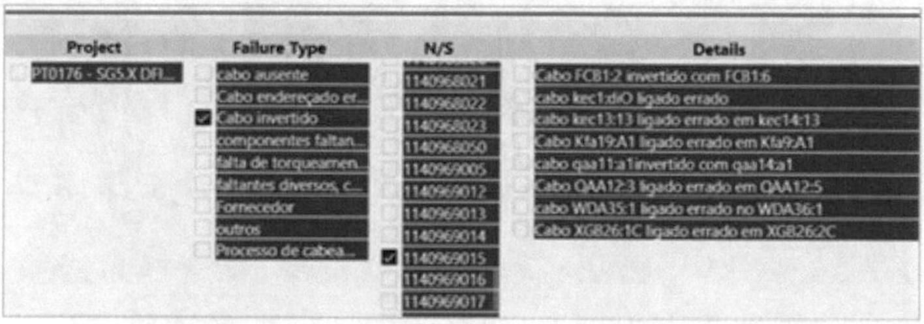

Fig. 5. STQ/BI serial number 1140969015/failure details

Product B. This example depicts the charts as displayed by the QTS/BI tool. At the end of the product test, considering all weeks observed, the FTQ calculated was 53%. Figure 6 depicts the control chart relating product B's QTI_i to its upper limit (UCL_i).

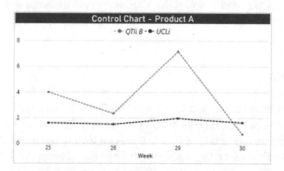

Fig. 6. Control Chart for Product B

As shown for Product A, the tree analysis displaying the attributes "week/serial number/failure type/failure details" is depicted in Fig. 7 for Product B.

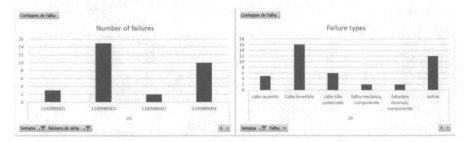

Fig. 7. Failure details per serial number, i = 1

In turn, Fig. 8 shows the QTS failure record (also in Portuguese) for unit 1140989002. In this case, the critical failure type is the inverted cable.

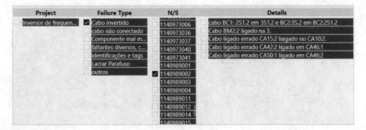

Fig. 8. STQ/BI serial number 1140989002/failure details

These two examples illustrate the modeling proposal for supporting QTS's management, adhering to the particularities of the production testing methodology adopted at Ingeteam Brasil. In this way, it is possible to identify failure-prone product units and point out the critical units. In addition, the approach is shaped to reflect the need of weekly identifying those units that have QTI_i values greater than the UCL threshold in order to guide the subsequent week's schedule. This analytical resource tends to increase the decision-making power of managers and increase the efficiency of the testing process.

4 Conclusions

Quality managers monitor the testing process with the intention of delivering a zero-defect product to the client. To achieve this goal quality, indexes are defined, evaluated, and pursued. They are based on the failure behavior during the process.

Ingeteam Brasil's quality test management has established the First Time Quality (FTQ) index to quantify the percentage of defect-free units in relation to the number of units produced. To tackle the failures when FTQ is less than 100%, the Quality Test Index (QTI) is used to quantify the number of failures.

This paper presents a data-driven methodology to define an upper limit for QTI based on the (QTI, FTQ) tuple. It is a control chart distinguishing the QTI out-of-control points, that is, those ones exceeding the upper limit (UCL). Such a methodology can be applied in any test process aiming at improving the product FTQ, regardless of product type.

For this purpose, Ingeteam and FITec developed a Quality Test System (QTS) software to record all important information during the test process. It implements the methodology to supply the managers with the relevant information to monitor and control the quality during the test activities. The QTS system is already in production.

To implement the methodology, the recorded failure data is accessed by Power BI (a data visualization software developed by Microsoft), which is the tool used by the QTS/BI to provide interactive dashboards with graphics for detailed analysis. In this paper, two real examples of wind power products being tested illustrate the methodology application and the use of QTS/BI.

Acknowledgments. The authors thank the Ministry of Science, Technology, and Innovation for the financial support to this R&D project through the PPB (Basic Productive Process).

References

1. Guelbert, M.: Strategy of process and quality management. IESDE Brazil, Curitiba (2012)
2. Rogošić, A.: Quality cost reporting as a determinant of quality costing maturity. Int. J. Qual. Res. **15** (2021)
3. Crosby, P.B.: Quality is Free: The Art of Making Quality Certain, 1st edn. McGraw-Hill, New York (1979)
4. Midor, K.: Use of Six Sigma in the production process-case study. Syst. Wspomagania w Inżynierii Prod. **6** (2017)
5. Gallo, T., Cagnetti, C., Silvestri, C., Ruggieri, A.: Industry 4.0 tools in lean production: a systematic literature review. Procedia Comput. Sci. **180**, 394–403 (2021)
6. Antony, J., McDermott, O., Powell, D.J., Sony, M.: Mapping the terrain for Lean Six Sigma 4.0. In: Powell, D.J., Alfnes, E., Holmemo, M.D.Q., Reke, E. (eds.) Learning in the Digital Era. IFIP Advances in Information and Communication Technology, vol. 610, pp. 193–204. Springer, Cham (2021). https://doi.org/10.1007/978-3-030-92934-3_20
7. Ou, X., Huang, J., Chang, Q., Hucker, S., Lovasz, J.G.: First time quality diagnostics and improvement through data analysis: a study of a crankshaft line. Procedia Manuf. **49**, 2–8 (2020)
8. Park, Y.-J., Fan, S.-K.S., Hsu, C.-Y.: A review on fault detection and process diagnostics in industrial processes. Processes **8**, 1123 (2020)
9. Kibira, D., Morris, K.C., Kumaraguru, S.: Methods and tools for performance assurance of smart manufacturing systems. J. Res. Natl. Inst. Stand. Technol. **121**, 282 (2016)
10. Vaz, G.C., Iano, Y., de Oliveira, G.G.: IoT - from industries to houses: an overview. In: Iano, Y., Saotome, O., Kemper Vásquez, G.L., Cotrim Pezzuto, C., Arthur, R., Gomes de Oliveira, G. (eds.) Proceedings of the 7th Brazilian Technology Symposium (BTSym 2021). Smart Innovation, Systems and Technologies, vol. 295, pp. 734–741. Springer, Cham (2022). https://doi.org/10.1007/978-3-031-08545-1_73
11. Venkatasubramanian, V., Rengaswamy, R., Kavuri, S.N., Yin, K.: A review of process fault detection and diagnosis: Part III: Process history based methods. Comput. Chem. Eng. **27**, 327–346 (2003)

12. Laouti, N., Sheibat-Othman, N., Othman, S.: Support vector machines for fault detection in wind turbines. IFAC Proc. **44**, 7067–7072 (2011)
13. Holanda, G., de Souza, J.M., Adorni, C.Y.K.O., de Nader, M.V.P.: Tacit knowledge and a multi-method approach in asset management. Logeion Filos. da Informação **8**, 197–212 (2022)
14. Montgomery, D.C., Runger, G.C.: Applied Statistics and Probability for Engineers. Wiley, New York (1999)
15. de Souza, J.M., de Holanda, G.M., Henriques, H.A., Furukawa, R.H.: Modified control charts monitoring long-term semiconductor manufacturing processes. In: Iano, Y., Saotome, O., Kemper, G., Mendes de Seixas, ACl., Gomes de Oliveira, G. (eds.) Proceedings of the 6th Brazilian Technology Symposium (BTSym'20). Smart Innovation, Systems and Technologies, vol. 233, pp. 80–87. Springer, Cham (2021). https://doi.org/10.1007/978-3-030-75680-2_11
16. Carpinetti, L.C.R.: Gestão da qualidade. EDa Atlas SA (2012)
17. Guarnieri, J.P.: Eficiência dos gráficos de controle na detecção de outliers em processos autorregressivos e de médias móveis (2010)
18. Carmona, A.R.R.: Application of statistical process control in an automotive industry. Dissertation (Master), Faculty of Science and Technology, New University of Lisbon (2017)
19. Russo, S., Rodrigues, P.M.M.: Metodologia alternativa às técnicas de gráficos de controle. In: Proceedings of the XXXVII Simpósio Brasileiro de Pesquisa Operacional - SBPO, Gramado – RS (2005)
20. Ferreira, A.P.D.: Gerenciamento de falhas baseada em evidências: proposta de método e protótipo computacional. Thesis (Doctoral), UNISINOS (2020)

Analysis of Electrical Neural Data Using MUSE and EEGLAB

Matheus Ramires Bonfim$^{(\boxtimes)}$ (ID) and Amilton da Costa Lamas (ID)

Pontifícia Universidade Católica de Campinas, Campinas, Brasil
matheus.rb1@puccampinas.edu.br

Abstract. This work consists of the analysis of neural electrophysiological data and proposes the use of a brain signal detection strip, known as MUSE, as a method of capturing the signals that will be analyzed. MUSE is a device that measures brain activity using four electroencephalographic sensors and sends the collected data to an application developed for smartphones. Originally, MUSE was designed and developed as a device for guided meditation, however, the authors of this study have adopted it as a low-cost electroencephalogram device. Although MUSE has far fewer electrodes than a clinical device, both of them share the same principle for data collection. After MUSE generates and collects the neural electrophysiological signals, they will be processed and analyzed with MATLAB software, which will be complemented by the EEGLAB ToolBox, developed by the University of California, in the United States. As result, plots of brain waves will be created to compare their behavior when an individual is at rest or performing meditation.

Keywords: Electroencephalogram · MUSE · MATLAB · EEGLAB · ICA · FIR

1 Introduction

Electroencephalography is a method of electrophysiological monitoring that is used to record the electrical activity of the brain [1]. This is normally a non-invasive method, with electrodes placed on the scalp, although there are some methods used in specific applications that are invasive.

EEG measures voltage fluctuations resulting from ionic currents within neurons in the brain. Its purpose is the evaluation of brain activity, and it is usually indicated by a general practitioner or neurologist for the diagnosis of some diseases or conditions, such as epilepsy and evaluation of sleep disorders, among others. The electroencephalogram can be done in different ways, the main type being in wakefulness, done with the person awake and with the purpose of identifying most brain changes.

The electroencephalogram in sleep, in which it is performed during sleep, its objective is to facilitate the detection of brain changes that may arise during sleep, such as sleep apnea. There is also EEG with brain mapping, in which all brain activity captured by the electrodes is transmitted to a computer, which creates a map capable of making it possible to identify the regions of the brain that are currently active.

© The Author(s), under exclusive license to Springer Nature Switzerland AG 2023
Y. Iano et al. (Eds.): BTSym 2022, SIST 353, pp. 103–117, 2023.
https://doi.org/10.1007/978-3-031-31007-2_10

The EEG signal acquired with a single channel can be used to monitor mental activity [2]. Advances in digital signal processing techniques in recent decades, particularly in time-frequency and non-linear analyses, have provided new methods of accessing the complexity of the EEG signal.

Analysis techniques in the signal frequency domain were applied to the EEG as the event-related potential. These techniques assume that the observed data is stationary over a short period (between 2 and 4 s). The basis of support for this work is based on digital signal processing (DSP). It is possible to say that DSP is distinguished from other areas of computing and engineering solely by the fact that it uses the signal as a data type [3–5].

DSP is the mathematics, algorithm, and computational procedure used to manipulate signals after they have been converted into digital form [6–8]. Brain electrical activity is a signal that is characterized by being periodic with low frequencies (between 0.5 Hz and 40 Hz) [2].

An electroencephalogram (EEG) device is a device used to image the electrical activity of the brain. Different available models of the handset have multiple channels. The signals recorded by the electroencephalograph have different wave patterns [9].

MUSE is a multisensory device in the form of a headband that provides real-time signals about brain activity, heartbeat, breathing, and movement. In this work, the device used is its second generation, known as MUSE2. MUSE2 was originally developed for the acquisition of neurological signals (Mobile Electroencephalography – mEEG) during meditation exercise, but recently it has been used for the acquisition of neurological signals in low-cost research showing results comparable to commercial EEG systems [10], this work uses meditation (its initial proposal) and performs measurements of neurological signs.

2 Objectives

The general objective of this project is the analysis of electrical signals through a low-cost electroencephalogram device known as MUSE2.

This project is also part of the scope of the extension project "PROMOTION OF SAFE AUTONOMY OF THE DISABILITIES" by Amilton da Costa Lamas following the student work plan "Analysis of bioelectrical signals by sensors - Phase 2" whose objective is to develop competence in the analysis of bioelectrical signals as preparation for EEG studies in disabled people with impaired mobility.

The specific objective of this work is the use of digital signal processing and ICA, considering:

- The study of signals generated by the brain in different mental states of the individual, such as at rest or in a state of alert (conscious);
- Carry out a spectral power mapping of the rhythms known as Alpha, Beta, Gamma, Delta, and Theta;
- Comparatively analyze these rhythms, their production, and intensity in different regions of the brain.

Within the scope of the extension project, the objective of this work is also to promote actions for the development of innovative technological solutions, providing opportunities for social entrepreneurship and the sustainability of the population in social fragility in the Metropolitan Region of Campinas.

Among the specific objectives of the extension project, for this work, the following stand out:

1. Develop systems, services, and/or applications, solutions, proofs of concept, and low-cost prototypes that have innovative technological or social aspects, that promote safe and autonomous mobility and the well-being of people with disabilities of any nature and /or elderly.
2. Develop entrepreneurship plans, methods, and processes related to the developments listed in objective (1);
3. Transfer (via the appropriation method) to partner institutions and make the results arising from objectives (1) and (2) available to society in general.

3 Motivation

The Brazilian market has quality commercial electroencephalographs, which meet the required clinical examination standards, but most of them are imported and have a high purchase price [11]. One of the objectives of this work is the analysis and validation of data generated by a low-cost EEG device.

In addition, there are some differences between clinical EEG and the engineering understanding of EEG, physicians are commonly trained to analyze the EEG in the time domain, inspecting the waveforms recorded over the course of an examination. This type of analysis prioritizes the amplitude of the signals and their shape. Its objective is the medical analysis in finding some diseases that can be detected by this type of exam. For engineering, the EEG study is carried out through sequential transforms, based on the analysis of bioelectrical signals in the time and frequency domain, which is divided into five (5) bands, Alpha, Beta, Theta, Delta, and Gamma.

This work focused on considering a qualitative and quantitative analysis of an EEG signal and seeking harmony between the two views, measuring the data in mathematical models.

The construction of this work also improved the knowledge in programming mathematical software such as MATLAB and the development of technical mathematical applications in the processing of medical signals for possible quantification and analysis of the same.

4 Theoretical Foundation

4.1 Electroencephalographic Biopotentials

EEG biopotentials are the result of communication between specialized cells of the Central Nervous System. This communication takes place through networks of neurons, which are cells specialized in the transfer of electrical impulses [11]. The circulating currents through the internal and external conductive volume of the neuronal membranes are characterized by the ability to generate electric potentials and magnetic fields in the scalp [12]. The spontaneous and stimulated electroencephalogram is used in numerous applications, such as monitoring patients in anesthetic procedures, diagnosing encephalopathies, monitoring epilepsy cases, and evaluating peripheral nerve pathways [13].

4.2 Electroencephalogram (EEG)

The Electroencephalogram has several applications, from basic diagnosis for headaches to more specific diagnoses, as well as psychiatric and neurological diseases, the EEG can be described as a bioelectrical sampling of the nerve endings contained in the cranial cavity around the brain [14]. Brain electrical activity is expressed as the potential difference between two electrodes, one located in the cortex region and the other at a neutral reference site.

The EEG signal has frequencies between 0.5 Hz to 40 Hz, has a low amplitude in the region of 50 uV, and can vary between 5 and 300 uV [14]. The Electroencephalogram is the recording of the difference in electric potential between two points located on the scalp of a given individual as a function of time, corresponding to a visualization of the electric fields produced by brain activity. The collection of these powers is done by metallic electrodes arranged in regions of interest. These electrodes are composed of metallic alloys, usually, Silver/Silver Chloride (Ag/AgCl) is used, due to the fact that it has a low half-cell voltage, approaching depolarized electrodes (ideal) in addition to a low acquisition cost [15].

For the acquisition of EEG signals, we follow the international rule of 10–20, where electrodes with diameters of 1 to 3 mm are positioned on the individual's scalp [14]. The waves generated by the electrodes can be characterized by the relationship between the types of activity and frequency, as shown in Table 1 below:

Table 1. Table of Rhythms and Frequencies.

Rhythms (Waves)	Frequencies	Type of activity
Alpha	8–12 Hz	Inhibition control, eye closure, and relaxation state
Beta	18–30 Hz	Alert State (attention)
Theta	4–6 Hz	Relaxation (awake)
Delta	0.5–4 Hz	Deep Sleep, no dreams
Gamma	>30 Hz	Sensory information (sight, hearing, touch), short-term memory (recognition of objects, sounds and sensations)

4.3 MUSE Headband

The MUSE2 [16] is a portable device whose main purpose is guided meditation. However, it can be used as a portable EEG, as it can detect brain signals in the same way as clinical equipment (although on a smaller scale) [17]. One of the objectives of this work is to study the relevance and efficiency of this type of low-cost device as a home EEG.

4.4 MATLAB

MATLAB (short for MATrix LABoratory) is a specialized computer program optimized for scientific and engineering calculations, initially designed for matrix calculations, however, over the years, it has developed into a very flexible system, capable of solving essentially, any technical problem [17].

The program uses a language of the same name, together with a high library of functions [17] and tools developed by third parties and by the company that owns MATLAB, known as ToolBox, these tools further expand the potential of MATLAB.

4.5 EGGLAB Toolbox

This work will be entirely carried out based on the electroencephalogram analyzed through the EEGLAB tool, developed by the University of California. This plugin for MatLab is necessary for the analysis of treatments, since it can convert a .csv spreadsheet into editable graphics in which we can handle the data in the necessary ways.

EEGLAB has an interactive graphical interface, allowing great flexibility. Mainly, it is possible to use high-density analysis processes known as ICA (Independent Component Analysis) [18].

4.6 Digital Signal Processing

A digitized EEG signal is polluted by noise and interference. This signal can be processed by a system that operates as a noise filter, allowing the visualization of the signal without interference and noise.

Signal processing is considered the transformation or manipulation of the information that a signal contains. For example, separating two signals that were previously joined [19]. The difference between continuous and discrete signal processing is that the discrete signal is digitized, that is, composed of a set of consecutive values that were previously sampled or generated by a digital device [20].

There are several applications for digital signal processing, and the focus of this work will be its use in biomedical systems.

4.7 ICA (Independent Component Analysis) and FFT (Fast Fourier Transform)

Within Digital Signal Processing, there are several in which we can analyze our raw signals. For EEG, the following filters are some of the most used for data analysis and cleaning.

Known as Independent Component Analysis, or ICA, became known as a powerful application to remove artifacts generated in EEG [21]. ICA is responsible for decomposing a multi-channel recording (as is the case with the multiple electrodes of an electroencephalogram) into a stronger linear signal [21]. Figure 1 below illustrates in a simplified way the ICA process performed by EEGLAB.

A mathematical model widely used for the characterization of frequencies is the FFT (Fast Fourier Transform), where the correlation between rhythms in different brain states, functions, and pathologies was discovered. With this technique, any periodic signal can be described with the sum of the sinusoidal signals, therefore, the main characteristic used in this work is the Spectral Density (Power Spectral Density – PSD), defined as the transform resulting from the calculation of the autocorrelation function of the signal.

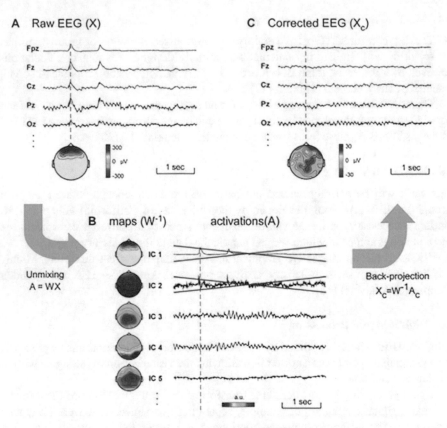

Fig. 1. Representation of an EEG process.

5 Methodology

This work is conducted based on the analysis of an electroencephalogram generated by low-cost equipment, which was designed for guided meditations. However, after tests carried out by a team from the University of San Diego in California, it was concluded that the equipment known as MUSE EEG is suitable for capturing electroencephalogram data, which, depending on its purpose, can be compared directly with data of clinical equipment [10].

The MUSE device, in this case, using the MUSE2, has the following main features:

1. Wireless communication via Bluetooth 2.1;
2. Signal sampling rate between 220 Hz and 500 Hz, reference electrode FPz (CMS) with potential adjustment (DRL);
3. Electrodes in positions TP9, AF7, AF8 and TP10, the electrodes in positions TP9 and TP10 are made of conductive rubber;
4. 3-axis accelerometer; and
5. DRL noise suppression system with 2 uV background (RMS) and a notch filter at 60 Hz. The use of 7 sensors (electrodes) allows the estimation of hemispherical signal asymmetries, facilitating the analysis of signals.

Data were obtained using the commercial system MUSE2 developed by Interaxon INC [16], initially through the MUSE application (version 25.2.518) by Interaxon itself (not used in this work) and, later, through the Mind Monitor application (version 2.2.1 – 2019) developed by James Clutterbuck, both available in app stores. The first analyzes were performed first in the applications and, later, the Matlab software (version 2020) from MathWorks was used with the EEGLAB 2022.1 toolbox [18] developed by Arnaud Delorme [22].

For the acquisition of EEG signals, the 10–20 international system rule is generally followed. Figure 2 below illustrates all points of the system.

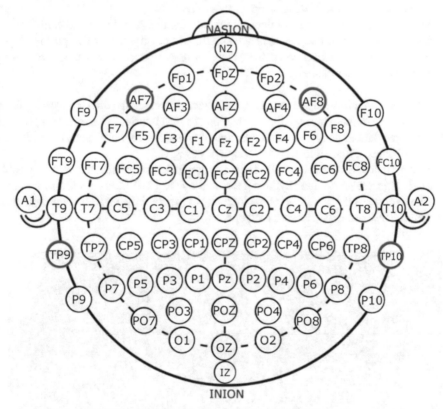

Fig. 2. Rule of the 10–20 International System.

The points circled in blue (AF7, AF8, TP9, and TP10) are the points where the electrodes of the MUSE2 equipment come into contact.

Given the objectives, this work analyzed individuals in meditation and at rest (conscious and alert), the data were recorded through an application known as Mind Monitor, the application is available on the Play Store for cell phones with the Android operating system [23], the readings will be taken in sessions between 5–30 min with some stimuli for detection on the device. The mentioned application, after the end of the session, can generate a spreadsheet in a.csv pattern, which can be read by the EEGLAB Toolbox in MATLAB. Therefore, the first part of the experiment consists of collecting the raw data from the Monitor, after which the data will be sent to a computer where we can start our analysis and filtering through the EEGLAB Toolbox in MATLAB.

We are interested in studying the Delta, Theta, Alpha, Beta, and Gamma bands, where each one reflects different states of the individual's brain. Electroencephalogram signals are always subject to artifacts and noises during their acquisition, the most common ones, such as blinking the eyes, generate the so-called "spikes" in the EEG graph, for this and other types of noise, the toolbox itself will be used so that one can edit the graphics.

Rhythms can be identified as follows:

1. Delta – present intensely during sleep;
2. Theta – associated with deep sleep and visualization;
3. Alpha – rhythm that appears intensely with the individual relaxed and calm;
4. Beta – present when the person is actively thinking or trying to solve problems.
5. Gamma – which occurs when the person is in a higher-order mental process as information consolidation.

After the acquisition of the raw data, the device processes the data, converting them to the frequency domain through the application of a Fast Fourier Transform and presents the processed data already separated into five rhythms, traditionally analyzed in EEGs, and consolidates signals into standard frequency ranges.

Figure 3 below illustrates the Mind Monitor application interface, where it is possible to visualize, in real-time, the rhythms generated by the MUSE2 user's brain. It is also possible to observe the evolution of the intensity of the rhythms in dB in a measurement interval of a few seconds (the so-called epochs).

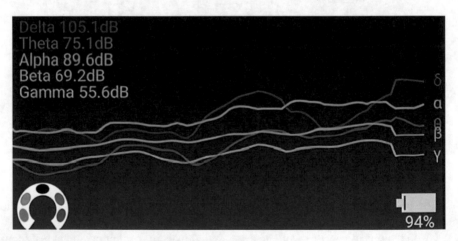

Fig. 3. Mind Monitor Interface.

The raw data obtained were transferred to a computer to allow signal analysis using MATLAB with the EEGLAB toolbox. This toolbox allows a deep analysis of the EEG signal, which was not performed in this project, considering that the objective is a demonstration and familiarization with bioelectrical signals.

Figure 4 below shows the raw data (in μV) after loading the file previously recorded by Mind Monitor and generated by MUSE2 in the MATLAB/EEGLAB environment.

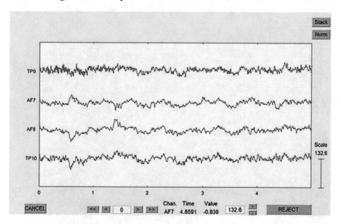

Fig. 4. EEGLAB loaded with the raw data.

In this way, we can summarize the data collection and analysis process as illustrated in Fig. 5 below:

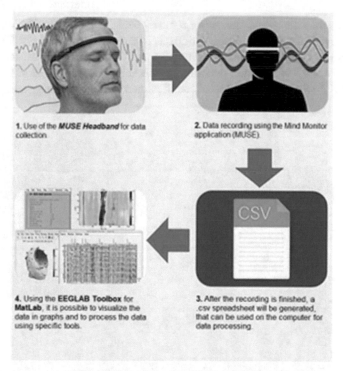

Fig. 5. Summary of the Study Process.

With the data already loaded in EEGLAB, we can perform our first treatment of the data. Figure 6 below shows the EEGLAB tools interface, here the option to create a basic

FIR filter, low pass 0.5 Hz, where everything below this frequency will be removed from the data.

Fig. 6. EEGLAB Tools.

This frequency range was chosen for removal because, as we saw earlier, the lowest frequency wave is the Delta rhythm, which has a lower frequency from 0.5 Hz to 4 Hz.

Once this is done, it remains to manually analyze the state of the data for more accurate removal of artifacts and remaining noise, this is possible in EGGLAB through the tool "Plot > Channel Data (scroll)", as illustrated in Fig. 7.

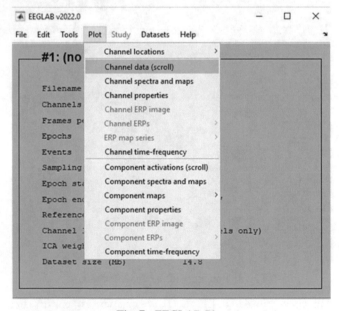

Fig. 7. EEGLAB Plot.

From this moment on, we can start to reject the noise present in the data. Figure 8 below illustrates the result of the previous option, the plotted graph, where one can select and exclude apparent noise.

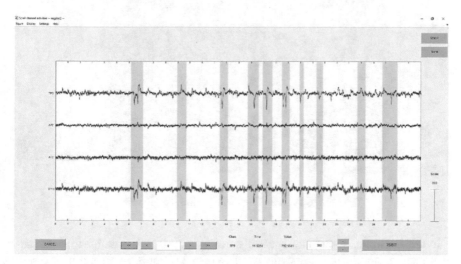

Fig. 8. EEGLAB eegplot() function.

The green bands in Fig. 8 represent the data that were rejected, they are characterized for the most part by "big spikes" in the channels during the plot.

6   Results

With the data treated in the previous steps, we enter the data analysis stage here, through the "Study" tool we can perform our spectral plots per channel.

6.1   Analyzed Channels

The channels that we focus on in this work are the TP10 and AF8 channels, our right brain electrodes, which, both during meditation and relaxation, are placed at a low brain frequency, which allows our analysis in this work.

6.2   AF8 Channel

Figure 9 below shows the AF8 electrode in a comparison between rest and meditation.

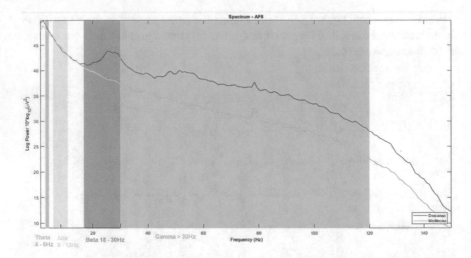

Fig. 9. AF8 Channel Spectral Density.

In this electrode, through the spectral density analysis, it is possible to visualize the growth and predominance, respectively, of Beta and Gamma waves during the resting state compared to the meditation state of this same channel.

6.3   TP10 Channel

Figure 10 below shows the TP10 electrode in a comparison between rest and meditation.

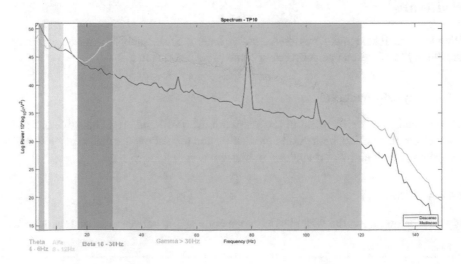

Fig. 10.   Spectral Density of the TP10 Channel.

In this case, through the analysis of the spectral density of the TP10 electrode, we obtain different results, the Theta waves are predominant during the individual's rest in this channel, while the Alpha waves are relatively similar, although they present a growth during meditation. We can also see rapid growth of Beta waves, and soon after rapid growth and predominance of Gamma waves.

7 Final Considerations

EEG signals from the AF8 and TP10 channels of a young adult were analyzed, the relaxation state was carried out in such a way that the individual was sitting, still, at rest, not moving, but actively talking, during his state of meditation, the individual was not interrupted at any time, the individual is someone who regularly performs meditations.

The application of FIR and ICA is extremely important in an EEG analysis. With these tools, it is possible to eliminate a large part of all the noise generated, the EEGLAB tool proved to be extremely practical and effective for the analysis, requiring only the user to filter manually the rest of the noise and artifacts that the tool was not able to remove.

As a result of this study, the Alpha rhythm predominated during meditation in all areas studied, while the predominance of Beta rhythms and Gamma varied between the points studied, showing predominance during rest in the frontal part of the brain and predominance during meditation in the temporal-parietal (TP) part, the other rhythms had little impact during the study.

Acknowledgments. The authors would like to thank volunteer Caissa Silveira Belo Nascimento Roque for collecting the data, which proved to be fundamental for the creation of this project.

The authors would also like to thank the support received from the Pro-Rectory of Extension and Community Affairs at PUC-Campinas.

The author Matheus Ramires Bonfim consents to the use and dissemination of the results of electroencephalography measurements. All procedures performed in studies involving human participants were in accordance with institutional and/or national research committee ethical standards and the 1964 Declaration of Helsinki and its subsequent amendments or comparable ethical standards.

References

1. Ferrero, R., Ferrero, A.R.: Análisis computado del EEG. Ed. por Ferrero, RGA (1995)
2. Costa, E.J.X.: Estudo da atividade elétrica cerebral em humanos e bovinos usando processamento digital de sinais e instrumentação eletrônica (2006)
3. Demanboro, A.C., Bianchini, D., Iano, Y., de Oliveira, G.G., Vaz, G.C.: Regulatory aspects of 5G and perspectives in the scope of scientific and technological policy. In: Iano, Y., Saotome, O., Kemper Vásquez, G.L., Cotrim Pezzuto, C., Arthur, R., Gomes de Oliveira, G. (eds.) Proceedings of the 7th Brazilian Technology Symposium (BTSym 2021). Smart Innovation, Systems and Technologies, vol. 207, pp. 163–171. Springer, Cham (2021). https://doi.org/10.1007/978-3-031-04435-9_16

4. Demanboro, A.C., Bianchini, D., Iano, Y., de Oliveira, G.G., Vaz, G.C.: 6G networks: an innovative approach, but with many challenges and paradigms, in the development of platforms and services in the near future. In: Iano, Y., Saotome, O., Kemper Vásquez, G.L., Cotrim Pezzuto, C., Arthur, R., Gomes de Oliveira, G. (eds.) Proceedings of the 7th Brazilian Technology Symposium (BTSym 2021). Smart Innovation, Systems and Technologies, vol. 207, pp. 172–187. Springer, Cham (2021). https://doi.org/10.1007/978-3-031-04435-9_17
5. Izario, D., Brancalhone, J., Iano, Y., de Oliveira, G.G., Vaz, G.C., Izario, K.: 5G - automation of vertical systems in the industry 4.0. In: Iano, Y., Saotome, O., Kemper Vásquez, G.L., Cotrim Pezzuto, C., Arthur, R., Gomes de Oliveira, G. (eds.) Proceedings of the 7th Brazilian Technology Symposium (BTSym 2021). Smart Innovation, Systems and Technologies, vol. 207, pp. 35–43. Springer, Cham (2023). https://doi.org/10.1007/978-3-031-04435-9_4
6. Vaz, G.C., Iano, Y., de Oliveira, G.G.: IoT-from industries to houses: an overview. In: Iano, Y., Saotome, O., Kemper Vásquez, G.L., Cotrim Pezzuto, C., Arthur, R., Gomes de Oliveira, G. (eds.) Proceedings of the 7th Brazilian Technology Symposium (BTSym 2021). Smart Innovation, Systems and Technologies, vol. 295, pp. 734–741. Springer, Cham (2022). https://doi.org/10.1007/978-3-031-08545-1_73
7. Nishimura, E.H., Iano, Y., de Oliveira, G.G., Vaz, G.C.: Application and requirements of AIoT-enabled industrial control units. In: Iano, Y., Saotome, O., Kemper Vásquez, G.L., Cotrim Pezzuto, C., Arthur, R., Gomes de Oliveira, G. (eds.) Proceedings of the 7th Brazilian Technology Symposium (BTSym 2021). Smart Innovation, Systems and Technologies, vol. 295, pp. 724–733. Springer, Cham (2022). https://doi.org/10.1007/978-3-031-08545-1_72
8. Sampaio, I.A, et al.: The use of the Elman preconditioner in the early iterations of interior point methods. In: Iano, Y., Saotome, O., Kemper Vásquez, G.L., Cotrim Pezzuto, C., Arthur, R., Gomes de Oliveira, G. (eds.) Proceedings of the 7th Brazilian Technology Symposium (BTSym 2021). Smart Innovation, Systems and Technologies, vol. 295, pp. 355–363. Springer, Cham (2022). https://doi.org/10.1007/978-3-031-08545-1_34
9. Pereira, O.F.S.: Análise de Metodologias de Classificação das Rítmicas de Sinais Digitais de Eletroence-falógrafo. Centro Federal de Educação Tecnológica de Minas Gerais (2016). https://docplayer.com.br/158326560-Analise-de-metodologias-de-classificacao-das-ritmicas-de-sinais-digitais-de-eletroencefalografo.html. Accessed 20 Mar 2022
10. Krigolson, O.E., Williams, C.C., Norton, A., Hassall, C.D., Colino, F.L.: Choosing MUSE: validation of a low-cost, portable EEG system for ERP research. Front. Neurosci. **11**, 109 (2017)
11. Otoni, J.D.S.: Desenvolvimento de um aparelho de eletroencefalografia mobile de baixo custo (2019)
12. Speckmann, E.-J.: Introduction of the neurophysiological basis of the EEG and DC potentials. In: Electroencephalography: Basic Principles, Clinical Applications, and Related Fields, pp. 15–26 (1993)
13. Bagnato, S., Boccagni, C., Prestandrea, C., Sant'Angelo, A., Castiglione, A., Galardi, G.: Prognostic value of standard EEG in traumatic and non-traumatic disorders of consciousness following coma. Clin. Neurophysiol. **121**, 274–280 (2010)
14. Cantarelli, T.L., Júnior, J., Júnior, S.L.S.: Fundamentos da medição do eeg: Uma introdução. Semin. ELETRONICA E AUTOMAÇÃO, Ponta Grossa (2016)
15. Neuman, M.R.: Biopotential electrodes. Med. Instrum. Appl. Des. **4**, 189–240 (1998)
16. Muse™ EEG-Powered Meditation & Sleep Headband. https://choosemuse.com/. Accessed 20 Mar 2022
17. Chapman, S.J.: Programação em MATLAB para engenheiros. Pioneira Thomson Learning (2003)
18. EEGLAB. https://sccn.ucsd.edu/eeglab/index.php. Accessed 20 Mar 2022
19. Oppenheim, A.V., Buck, J.R., Schafer, R.W.: Discrete-Time Signal Processing, vol. 2. Prentice Hall, Upper Saddle River (2001)

20. da Rosa, D.L.: Sistema de processamento de sinais biomédicos: filtragem de sinais de eletroencefalograma (2009)
21. Viola, F.C., Debener, S., Thorne, J., Schneider, T.R.: Using ICA for the analysis of multi-channel EEG data. In: Simultaneous EEG and fMRI: Recording, Analysis, and Application: Recording, Analysis and Application, pp. 121–133 (2010)
22. Delorme, A., Makeig, S.: EEGLAB: Una caja de herramientas de código abierto para el análisis de la dinámica de EEG de un solo ensayo, incluido el análisis de componentes independientes. J. Neurosci. Métodos. **134**, 9–21 (2004)
23. Teo, J., Chia, J.T.: EEG-based excitement detection in immersive environments: an improved deep learning approach. In: AIP Conference Proceedings, p. 20145. AIP Publishing LLC (2018)

Classification of Respiratory Sounds Anomalies Using Digital Audio Signal Processing and Artificial Neural Networks

Mauricio Calheiro⑩, Danilo Frazão⑩, and Edgard Silva^(✉) ⑩

Universidade do Estado do Amazonas, Escola Superior de Tecnologia, Manaus, Brazil
{mscl.eng,dsf.eng17,elsilva}@uea.edu.br

Abstract. Respiratory diseases are constantly present among the significant causes of death in Brazil and the world. Pulmonary auscultation is one of the most common exams that can detect this type of disease. In this paper, a machine learning model was developed to classify lung sounds, predicting the presence or absence of adventitious sounds – wheezes and crackles – which can be related to respiratory diseases. The data used were obtained from a dataset distributed free of charge over the internet and due to the variation in some characteristics of the audio signals, signal processing techniques were used to standardize and extract their features (MFCCs and Mel-spectrograms). Those features were used as inputs to a Convolutional Neural Network (CNN) responsible for performing the classification task. The results obtained show that it is possible to perform the classification with precision only for some classes, which indicates that it is necessary to refine the method or data used.

Keywords: Lung sounds · Audio signals · Convolutional Neural Network

1 Introduction

In the last decades (2000 – 2019), respiratory diseases such as Chronic Obstructive Pulmonary Disease (COPD) and lower respiratory infections were among the biggest causes of death in the world. In 2019 alone, the top 10 causes were responsible for more than half of deaths on the planet [1]. These same diseases also appear on a national scale in Brazil [2]. Pulmonary auscultation is one of the most common exams in cases of suspect respiratory diseases because it is quick, non-invasive, and does not require advanced equipment. However, its results are subjective and heavily depend on the examiner's experience and perceptual skills, and therefore subject to errors [3–5].

The main goal of this paper is to detect the presence or absence of crackles and wheezes in respiratory sound recordings. Crackles are discontinuous lung sounds with short duration (less than 100 ms) detected mainly at the anterior and posterior chest wall and the posterior lung base, while wheezes have a relatively longer duration (over 250 ms) and can be detected in most areas of the chest wall. Crackles are related to diseases such as pneumonia and pulmonary fibrosis, while the latter is related to asthma [6–8].

Y. Iano et al. (Eds.): BTSym 2022, SIST 353, pp. 118–124, 2023.
https://doi.org/10.1007/978-3-031-31007-2_11

2 Methodology

The first step of this work was researching relevant material on audio signal processing and sound classification. The result was a collection of books, papers, and video tutorials that were used as references. Then, the data required for the task has been gathered, and, finally, the experimental stage. All experiment has been done using Python 3.9.5 and a few modules, listed in Table 1.

Table 1. Modules used and their versions

Module	Version	Description
Librosa	0.8.1	Modules used for reading audio files, extracting features, exporting new audio, and normalizing amplitudes and sample rates
Soundfile	0.10.3	
Numpy	1.19.5	Modules used for reading CSV files (annotations) and creating data frames (tables) for data analysis and plotting graphs
Pandas	1.2.4	
Matplotlib	3.4.2	
Tensorflow	2.5.0	Modules used for designing the CNN, training, and validating the model
Keras	2.5.0	
Scikit-learn	0.24.2	

Some other auxiliary modules have been used, but they do not impact the development and require no detailed explanation. Newer versions of Python and the modules may have been released, so it is important to note that some aspects may behave differently. To reproduce the experiments, it is recommended to install the same versions listed above or refactor the code to work on the latest versions.

2.1 Understanding the Data

In an ideal scenario, the lung sounds would be recorded and labeled by the authors. However, due to the complexity of this task and resource constraints, mainly time and expertise, the team opted on using existing data, available at https://bhichallenge.med.aut h.gr. The database consists of a total of 5.5 h of recordings containing 6898 respiratory cycles, of which 1864 contain crackles, 886 contain wheezes, and 506 contain both crackles and wheezes, in 920 annotated audio samples from 126 subjects [9]. Other information is available, such as acquisition mode (mono or multichannel) and recording equipment, since four different were used:

- AKG C417L Microphone (AKGC417L),
- 3M Littmann Classic II SE Stethoscope (LittC2SE),
- 3M Littmann 3200 Electronic Stethoscope (Litt3200),
- WelchAllyn Meditron Master Elite Electronic Stethoscope (Meditron)

This is important information because it affects some parameters of the audio files, such as amplitude scale and sample rate.

2.2 Preprocessing Stage

As mentioned previously, the data provided is not ready to be used yet. Due to being captured on different devices, the amplitude scale and sample rate of the recordings had to be normalized. Files with more than one audio channel have turned into single-channel (mono) files.

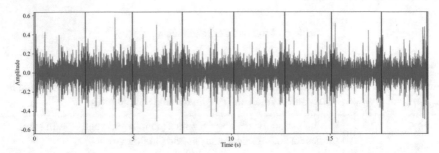

Fig. 1. Waveform of a lung sound recording (blue). Red lines indicate the boundary between respiratory cycles. The horizontal axis is time and the vertical axis is amplitude.

In addition to that, each recording contains many respiratory cycles (delimited by red lines in Fig. 1). The timestamp for the start/end of each cycle as well as the events that are present are annotated in CSV files; an example is provided in Table 2.

Table 2. Dataframe with cycles and events.

	cycle_start	cycle_end	crackle	wheeze
0	0.0000	4.3188	0	0
1	4.3188	7.6336	0	0
2	7.6336	11.0150	0	0
⋮	⋮	⋮	⋮	⋮
7	22.9670	25.6470	0	1
8	25.6470	28.2140	0	1
9	28.2140	29.3600	0	0

Using Librosa and Soundfile, it is possible to generate the audio files for each cycle, but one final issue must be addressed: CNNs require that all inputs have the same shape (dimensions). To attend to this constraint, every file representing the respiratory cycles needs to have the same duration (as well as other properties that have been previously standardized).

According to analysis performed on the 6898 respiratory cycles, the max duration must be between 5 and 6 s. Any audio file with a duration smaller than 6 s has been padded with zeros (equivalent to silence) and the files longer than 6 s have been truncated (cut) to the max duration. Having done that, the preprocessing stage is over, and the data is almost ready to be fed to the CNN.

2.3 Feature Extraction Stage

Once the audio recordings have been preprocessed and split, the final part involving signal processing starts. Since classification will be done in a CNN, it is interesting to have image-like inputs, once these networks are mainly used in image recognition problems [10].

The spectrogram is a two-dimensional representation, of the content of audio signals that aims to show information about the spectrum and how it behaves over time. One of its axes represents time and the other one represents frequency [11]. The MFCC attribute extraction technique consists of windowing the signal, applying the discrete Fourier transform (DFT), obtaining the logarithmic magnitude, applying the Mel-frequency scale, and finally applying the discrete transform of cosine (DCT) [12]. A representation of each feature is shown in Fig. 2.

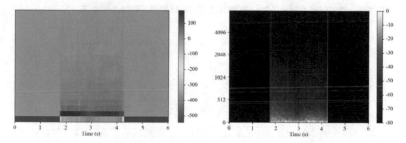

Fig. 2. Visualizing features: MFCCs on the left and spectrograms on the right.

Once again, the Librosa module provides the methods to extract the features needed for this task. A relatively simple method was written to extract both features and store them in arrays.

2.4 Classification Stage

At this point, the inputs are ready to be used in the CNN, which was designed using the Keras module and can be seen in Fig. 3. This stage is mostly experimental and needed to be performed a couple of times to fine-tune the model and achieve better results.

Supervised classification was performed with a split of 75% of the respiratory cycles being used for training and the remaining for validation. The output layer consists of a 4 neurons dense layer with softmax activation, which is used in multiple classes of predictions. The possible classes are:

– Crackle
– Wheeze
– Both (crackle + wheeze)

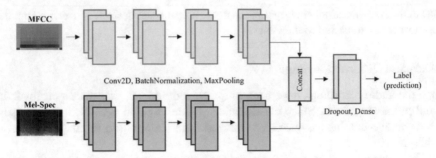

Fig. 3. Representation of the proposed CNN. The orange and magenta groups represent the same groups of layers: Conv2D, BatchNormalization, and MaxPooling.

– Healthy (no crackles or wheezes)

The model has been complied with loss function 'sparse categorial entropy' and ADAM optimizer, and early stopping has been set to stop training if the learning rate stops improving significantly. The learning curve is shown in Fig. 4.

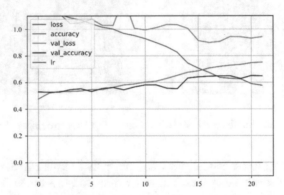

Fig. 4. Learning curve. Note that the model stopped improving just after 20 decades, so the training stopped before the max number of epochs (100).

3   Results and Discussion

After the training was done, the model has been evaluated by its accuracy and F1 score. The scikit-learn module provides good methods to acquire these metrics easily and was used in this task.

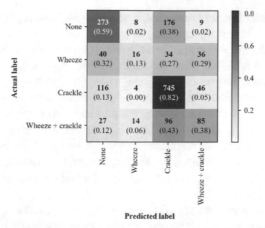

Fig. 5. Confusion matrix showing the prediction results for each class. The values in the main diagonal represent the correct predictions and darker tones correspond to higher accuracy.

As shown in Fig. 5, Crackles have good accuracy (82%), None has about 60% and the other two classes have been predicted poorly. It is expected for the inputs containing both sounds to have lower accuracy, since they could be easily confused with other classes, but the Wheezes label presented an extremely low accuracy (13%).

Table 3. Other metrics for the model.

Class	Precision	Recall	F1-score
None	0.60	0.59	0.59
Wheeze	0.38	0.13	0.19
Crackle	0.71	0.82	0.76
Both	0.48	0.38	0.43

One worth-noting thing is that the classes are unbalanced, that is, some of them have many more samples than others and that could impact the model. Additionally, when dealing with unbalanced data, it is recommended to use F1-score to evaluate the model, as it is a more honest metric for this case. The value of the F1-score can be checked in Table 3 and the overall accuracy is 65%. Considering the values presented, the model needs improvement. It could make correct predictions of crackles since both the accuracy and the F1-score are high for this class but would certainly make bad predictions for audios containing other classes of sounds.

4 Conclusion and Future Works

The task of audio classification using neural networks is challenging. The higher metrics for the "crackles" label show that it is a possible achievement. However, as seen in the results, other classes have not been labeled accordingly. This may happen due to similarities in the signals or unbalanced data, or even due to network structure. The process of designing the CNN is not straightforward and requires an experimental approach for fine-tuning, which is not ideal when deadlines must be respected.

On the other hand, the preprocessing stage has provided the authors with the experience of data manipulation and analysis, as well as the opportunity to apply signal processing knowledge to solve an interesting problem. The original database provides 920 audio recordings and annotation files. The preprocessing stage outputs 6898 new audio files corresponding to the respiratory cycles. Those new files have their parameters normalized and are ready to be used by those replicating the experiments or making new experiments with the same data. Anyone interested could start on the feature extraction stage, saving significant time.

Regarding future works, we suggest the development of a dataset with more samples and better data distribution. This would require a team of experts in many disciplines but would certainly be very useful for the community and could lead to a more precise model. We also suggest experimenting with different features, since audio signals have many other attributes to be explored, as well as using different neural networks that suit those attributes. Additionally, audio classification can be used in other fields. One suggestion that could be explored is identifying bird species in the wild, or even insects on a crop to know how to act properly.

References

1. The top 10 causes of death. https://www.who.int/news-room/fact-sheets/detail/the-top-10-cau ses-of-death. Last accessed 1 Nov 2022
2. Principais causas de morte. https://vital-strategies.l3.ckan.io/pt_BR/querytool/public/princi pais-causas. Last accessed 1 Nov 2022
3. Hafke-Dys, H., Bręborowicz, A., Kleka, P., Kociński, J., Biniakowski, A.: The accuracy of lung auscultation in the practice of physicians and medical students. PLoS ONE **14**, e0220606 (2019)
4. Minango, P., Iano, Y., Chuma, E.L., Vaz, G.C., de Oliveira, G.G., Minango, J.: Revision of the 5G concept rollout and its application in smart cities: a study case in South America. In: Brazilian Technology Symposium, pp. 229–238. Springer (2023)
5. Lustosa, T.C., Iano, Y., Oliveira, G.G. de, Vaz, G.C., Reis, V.S.: Safety management applied to smart cities design. In: Brazilian Technology Symposium, pp. 498–510. Springer (2020)
6. Palaniappan, R., Sundaraj, K., Ahamed, N.U.: Machine learning in lung sound analysis: a systematic review. Biocybern. Biomed. Eng. **33**, 129–135 (2013)
7. Demanboro, A.C., Bianchini, D., Iano, Y., de Oliveira, G.G., Vaz, G.C.: Regulatory aspects of 5G and perspectives in the scope of scientific and technological policy. In: Brazilian Technology Symposium, pp. 163–171. Springer (2023)
8. Izario, D., Brancalhone, J., Iano, Y., de Oliveira, G.G., Vaz, G.C., Izario, K.: 5G-automation of vertical systems in the industry 4.0. In: Brazilian Technology Symposium, pp. 35–43. Springer (2023)
9. ICBHI 2019 Challenge Respiratory Sound Database. https://bhichallenge.med.auth.gr. Last accessed 1 Nov 2022
10. Géron, A.: Mãos à obra: Aprendizado de Máquina com Scikit-Learn & TensorFlow. Alta Books, Rio de Janeiro (2019)
11. Christensen, M.G.: Introduction to Audio Processing. Springer (2019)
12. Rao, K.S., Vuppala, A.K.: Speech Processing in Mobile Environments. Springer (2014)

Design and Simulation of a Test Bench
for Horizontal Axis Wind Turbines

Enzo Giraldo[iD], Juan Matos, Leonardo Vinces[(✉)] [iD], José Oliden[iD],
and Julio Ronceros[iD]

Peruvian University of Applied Sciences, Lima, Peru
{u201613661,u201512831,pcljoli,pcmajron}@upc.edu.pe,
leonardo.vinces@upc.pe

Abstract. Currently, the global energy matrix is governed by the generation of energy with non-renewable resources. The downside of these resources is that they take several thousand years to form and cannot be replaced as quickly as they are used today. Peru, due to its strategic location, is a country with great wind potential. However, it is not used enough due to the lack of laboratory equipment that studies this form of energy generation. The present work consists of the design of a test bench for horizontal axis wind turbines that contains an open circuit wind tunnel to generate a uniform wind flow towards the turbine blades. There are fan blades attached to the shaft of a motor, which generate wind inside the tunnel. This tunnel has a nozzle to stabilize the flow and said basin tunnel with the capacity to generate a wind of up to 16 m/s with a 25 HP motor. There is a logic controller that allows 2 types of operation as required by the user. The following article mainly contains the mechanical design of the structure and geometry of the tunnel, a numerical simulation of the fluid inside the wind tunnel, a simulation of stresses in the structure, and a simulation of the controller for the 2 types of operation.

Keywords: Wind tunnel · Wind turbine · Numerical simulation · Electrical energy

1 Introduction

Currently, the global energy matrix is governed by forms of energy generation with non-renewable resources such as coal, oil, or natural gas. The disadvantage of these resources is that they take several thousand years to form and cannot be replaced as quickly as they are used today [1]. The forms of energy generation mentioned above are based on non-renewable resources, however, energy can be obtained from renewable resources provided by nature. Renewable energies are clean, inexhaustible, and increasingly competitive energy sources [2]. There are different types of renewable energies, such as solar energy, wind energy, hydroelectric energy, sea energy, geothermal energy, etc. Peru is a rich country in renewable resources, and due to its strategic location in an area of high pressure in the South Pacific, during the year, the wind on the coast is very constant, so our country has an excellent wind resource [3]. Wind energy is produced thanks to the kinetic energy obtained from the wind and this is used for different uses that have been changing and evolving throughout history. The first examples of this type of energy were the use of sails on ships to take advantage of the wind, during the seventeenth century BC in Babylon an irrigation system based on windmills was used, but it was not until 1887 in the United States, where Charles Frances Brush invented the first wind turbine for electricity generation [4].

There are not many wind turbine test benches that allow reproducing wind profiles in order to recreate real environmental conditions, the only way to collect data is the traditional way, using wind fields, which must have a specific amount of wind. Sometimes, they are in areas far from cities where the wind is adequate to carry out tests, many times it is necessary to wait for certain hours of the day or wait for the weather conditions to be favorable to carry out data collection. According to the wind map of Peru [5], the places where there are greater wind resources are far from the capital and if it is necessary to carry out studies on the wind farms in these areas, they require transportation and extra time, a price that most times are not willing to accept, so emulators or test benches are necessary for the development of renewable energies.

Bai Yefei designed and implemented a wind turbine test bench, it consisted of a diffuser-shaped wind tunnel and had 5 possible positions to locate the wind turbine. This design was very novel due to the inclusion of 5 possible positions for the wind turbine, however, the wind tunnel with a diffuser was not ideal for analyzing the behavior of the fluid. Chen Liren designed and implemented a straight wind tunnel with the possibility of moving the turbine and placing it in any straight direction to the tunnel. However, the investigation focused on this aspect in its entirety, so it did not present information on the electrical parameters of the wind turbine in operation. Ma Qunjie left aside the wind tunnels and to exert movement on the wind turbine he designed a mechanical arm with 3 jaws that hold the turbine blades and make it rotate at the desired speed.

Various authors create patents and theses on the design of wind tunnels as test benches for wind turbines. However, there are few that present the electrical part of the wind turbine. Companies like Ecosense do focus on obtaining the electrical parameters of the wind turbine, however, they do not present a real wind turbine. This equipment consists of a wind turbine generator and a coupled electric motor that allows movement.

Other companies, such as Electronica Venetta, consider both criteria, the electrical parameters and the inclusion of a wind tunnel. However, the tunnel that the company manufactured does not have an appropriate design to guarantee a stable flow of wind in the blades of the wind turbine. Another important criterion is the inclusion of interactive panels to present the performance data of the wind turbine.

In this project, a design of a wind turbine emulator is proposed to carry out studies of parameters of interest in wind turbines, increase interest in wind energy applications in the energy sector, and gradually reduce the use of fossil fuels. To carry out this design, analysis and study of the main parameters of interest in the study of horizontal axis wind turbines [6] and the calculations necessary to obtain them were carried out. Also, physical and mechanical principles were considered for the design of a wind tunnel and structure capable of supporting all the equipment contained in the project. In order to validate the calculations and design, simulations were carried out with various computer programs and the results will be presented in Sect. 3 [7]. For the generation of wind, the coupling of a fan to the axis of a motor will be used. The wind will be directed to the blades of the wind turbine [8, 9].

2   Description of the Proposed Method

Figure 1 shows the block diagram of the development of the proposed method. It began by designing the geometry of the wind tunnel through which the wind will flow. Due to the circumstances of the pandemic, the numerical simulation of the tunnel wind flow was carried out using the ANSYS software. Then, the TIA PORTAL Siemens software was used to carry out the control systems, since the project has 2 loops. In said loops, the speeds obtained by numerical simulation were used [10, 11]. Finally, validations and conclusions were made.

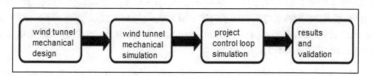

Fig. 1. Block diagram of the process.

2.1   Mechanical Design of the Tunnel

For practical reasons, a 4.5 m long tunnel was chosen, so that the wind can stabilize. It presents circular geometry for better wind flow in an open tunnel [12]. Since commercial wind turbines have a diameter of 1.2 m in the blades, the tunnel has a diameter at the entrance and exit of 1.6 m and 1.4 m, respectively, to cover the entire rotation of the blades. The Venturi effect will be used to increase the speed at the exit by placing a nozzle in the middle of the tunnel. Likewise, it is fulfilled that the inlet and outlet flow rates are the same [13]. This effect presents a behavior explained in Eq. (1) [14].

$$Q_{in} = Q_{out} \tag{1}$$

where Q_{in} is the wind flow at the tunnel entrance (m³/s) and Q_{out} is the wind flow at the tunnel exit (m³/s). The flow rate is equal to the product of the area through which the fluid passes and its velocity. For this, the relation (2) [14] is obtained:

$$A_{in} \times v_{in} = A_{out} \times v_{out} \tag{2}$$

where A_{in} is the tunnel entrance area (m²), v_{in} is the wind speed at the tunnel entrance (m/s), A_{out} is the tunnel exit area (m²), and v_{out} is the wind speed at the tunnel exit (m/s). Under these considerations, the tunnel was designed. The following figure shows the side view to visualize dimensions and geometry. As indicated, the tunnel is reduced in the area for the desired speed increase, dimensions in mm are also shown in Fig. 2.

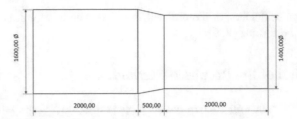

Fig. 2. Wind tunnel dimensions.

2.2 Numerical Simulation of the Wind Tunnel

The ANSYS ICEM program was used to design the simulation mesh, which has the shape of a wind tunnel. Similarly, the ANSYS FLUENT [15] program was used to perform the wind flow simulation. In this process, the following considerations were taken to simulate a wind flow that can closely resemble real values obtained experimentally. The wind speed at the entrance of the tunnel. Each simulation carried out took a different wind speed value between 3 and 18 m/s.

Reynolds Number. It is a dimensionless number used in fluid mechanics and transport phenomena to characterize the motion of a fluid. This is calculated with the following formula [16]:

$$Re = \frac{D \times \rho \times v}{\mu} \tag{3}$$

where Re is Reynolds number, D is the diameter of the pipe (m), v is the velocity of the liquid (m/s), ρ is the density of the fluid (kg/m^3), and μ is the viscosity of the fluid (kg/ms). If Re $\leq$ 2000 the flow is considered laminar. If Re $\geq$ 4000 the flow is considered turbulent.

Wind Turbulence Regime. Because the simulation must be as close as possible to reality, a turbulent wind model must be used, since it is expected to obtain a high Reynolds number. The model used was the K-epsilon.

Intensity of Turbulence. This parameter tells us as a percentage how much turbulence is being generated in the simulation. It is obtained with the following formula [15]:

$$I_t = 0.16 \times Re^{\frac{-1}{8}} \tag{4}$$

where I_t is the turbulence intensity value and Re is the Reynolds number.

With the mentioned parameters, the design of the mesh began. The result is shown in Fig. 3. This shows the final design of the mesh used in the simulation. It presents the same geometry as the chosen wind tunnel. Additionally, a fine adjustment was made in the circular sections, since a turbulent wind model was used.

Subsequently, the simulation was carried out. The example in Fig. 4 was carried out with a wind speed of 6 m/s at the tunnel entrance and the speed vectors with their respective magnitudes can be observed. Similarly, the increase in speed is due to the Venturi effect.

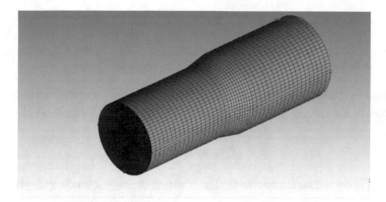

Fig. 3. Mesh used in numerical simulation.

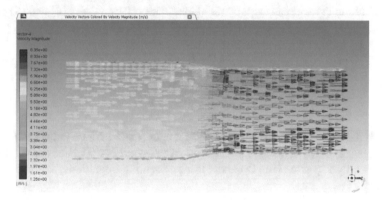

Fig. 4. Wind speed vectors.

2.3 Controller Simulation

In order to obtain the most important operating parameters of the wind turbine, various mathematical formulas were used, and the participating variables are identified below.

Bernoulli's Principle. Bernoulli's principle will be used to obtain the wind speed inside the tunnel. The sensor responsible for obtaining this parameter is the averaging Pitot tube. This is placed inside the wind tunnel and connected to a differential pressure manometer so that a pressure difference is obtained. For that, Eq. (5) [16] will be used.

$$P_1 + e_f.g.h + \frac{e_f.v_1^2}{2} = P_2 + e_f.g.h + \frac{e_f.v_2^2}{2} \tag{5}$$

Simplifications are made, and the relation (6) [17] is obtained

$$v_2 = \sqrt{\frac{2(P1 - P2)}{e_f}} \tag{6}$$

where P_1 is the pressure at the tunnel entrance (Pa), P_2 is the pressure at tunnel exit (Pa), h is the height (m), g is the acceleration of gravity (m/s^2), v_1 is the wind speed at the tunnel entrance (m/s), v_2 is the wind speed (m/s), $P_1 - P_2$ is the differential pressure (Pa), and e_f is the density of the fluid, in this case, the wind (kg/m^3).

Wind Power. The power of airflow is equal to the pressure multiplied by the flow rate. In the case of airflow, the pressure is dynamic and is given by formula (7) [17].

$$P_{Din} = \rho \times \frac{v^2}{2} \tag{7}$$

where p_{din} is the dynamic pressure (Pa), ρ is the air density (kg/m3), and v is the wind speed (m/s).

It is known that the flow rate is the section multiplied by speed, and the section of the wind turbine is the area swept by its blades. The relations (8) [14] and (9) [17] are obtained:

$$Q = A \times v \tag{8}$$

$$Q = \frac{\pi \times d^2}{4} \times v \tag{9}$$

where Q is the flow (m^3/s), d is the section diameter (m), v is the wind speed (m/s), and A is the area (m^2). Therefore, the total power of the wind that reaches the wind turbine will be given by formula (10) [18] and, after performing operations, formula (12) [18] is obtained.

$$P_{wind} = p_{din} \times Q \tag{10}$$

$$P_{wind} = \rho \times \frac{v^2}{2} \times \frac{\pi \times d^2}{4} \times v \tag{11}$$

$$P_{wind} = \frac{v^3 \times \rho \times A}{2} \tag{12}$$

where P_{wind} is the wind power (W), P_{din} is the dynamic pressure (W), ρ is the air density (kg/m^3), A is the wind turbine swept area (m^2), v is the wind speed (m/s), and d is the section diameter (m),

Electrical Power. The power generated by the wind turbine is given by Eq. (13) (Ohm's law):

$$P_{gen} = V \times I \tag{13}$$

where P_{gen} is the generated electric power (W), V is the generated voltage (V), and I is the generated current (A)

Power Coefficient. The power coefficient is the fraction of the total wind power that a given wind turbine transforms into power. It is given by expression (14) [18], which is calculated with the relations (12) [18] and (13):

$$C_p = \frac{P_{gen}}{P_{wind}} \tag{14}$$

where C_p is the power coefficient, P_{gen} is the generated electric power (W), and P_{wind} is the wind power (W). For theoretical reasons, the maximum value of the power coefficient is 0.59, which occurs in an ideal wind turbine. To receive data and operate it with the previously presented formulas, a simulator of the S71200 PLC was used. Within the general program of the project, there are 2 control loops, which are the following:

- Loop 0: This control loop consists of controlling the speed of the motor, since, in this way, the speed of the generated airflow is controlled, and this generates the movement of the wind turbine blades and the generation of electrical power. If the engine speed increases, the energy generated by the wind turbine also increases; and if the speed of the motor decreases, the power generation also decreases. This control loop is considered an open loop (see Fig. 5).

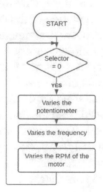

Fig. 5. Control Loop 0 Flow Diagram.

- Loop 1: This control loop consists of regulating the power generated by the wind turbine, that is, the user will enter a power value and the control loop will find the appropriate speed at which the motor will turn and generate a wind flow that impacts with the blades of the wind turbine generates the electrical power established by the user. This control loop is considered a closed loop since it receives feedback to reach the indicated value (see Fig. 6).

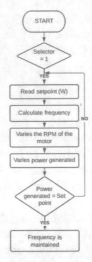

Fig. 6. Control Loop 1 Flow Diagram.

The use of one or the other depends on the value of the "Selector" variable. When said variable has a value of "0", control loop 0 will be used, and, when it has a value of "1", control loop 1 will be used. For the simulation of the control loop "0", the SIM PLC simulator was used. For the simulation of the control loop "1", a connection was made with the Labview software, in order to simulate a plant with a behavior similar to a 600W wind turbine, for this the following software was used: TIA Portal/PLC SIM [19], NI OPC SERVER [20], NetToPLC [21], and Labview [22]. The 2 variables that are connected between the TiaPortal and LabView are the power of the plant and the output value of the PID controller. The plant used for the project has an inherent non-linearity, that is, the linear part can be separated from the non-linear part, and it can be visualized in (15) transfer function with gain 1. The linear model described in the investigation was taken as reference [23], which will be affected by the polynomial equation in (16). Finally, a conventional PID controller was made. The method known as LGR was used. In (17) we can see the PID obtained parameters.

$$H(s) = \frac{1}{12.859s + 1} \tag{15}$$

$$-1.9179x^3 + 30.84x^2 - 57.851x + 11.765 \tag{16}$$

$$Kp = 0.0128, Kd = 0.0381, Ki = 0.0007 \tag{17}$$

Figure 7 shows the graph of the system with the PID parameters obtained previously. However, this obtaining of parameters was carried out for the first-order system, without considering the non-linear part of the plant. To solve this issue, a variation was made in the integration constant until optimal control was reached for the system. The final value used for the integration constant was KI = 0.283. Figure 8 shows the plant designed in LabView, where the input to the system is the PID output and the output is the power generated by the wind turbine.

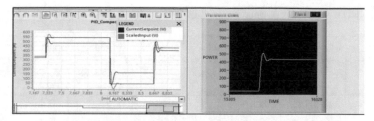

Fig. 7. Simulation without adjusting KI.

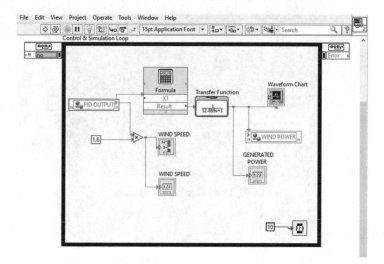

Fig. 8. Plant used in LabView.

3 Results

After the numerical simulation, not only the speed values were obtained, but also the simulation was able to calculate the static and dynamic pressure values at the entrance and exit of the wind tunnel, which were used in the thesis for other calculations such as the required power. by the motor and the static power of the fan. Six data collections were made at different speeds, and these values were ordered in Table 1.

With these data obtained, it can be verified that the generated wind flow will have adequate speeds for the investigation according to the graph of speed vs. generated power of the wind turbine taken from reference [24]. Speeds between 3 and 18 m/s were chosen because they are values with which we can know how much power is being generated and later, these values will be used in the simulation of the controller. LabVIEW software was used to simulate a plant. The results were favorable, a good control could be carried out with the parameters obtained for the PID, in the following image you can see the control both in the PID interface of the TiaPortal and in the behavior of the plant in LabView. The step response is shown with the new integration constant KI. Figure 9 shows the step response of the controller after having tuned the value of the KI parameter to eliminate the overshoot that was generated.

Table 1. Results obtained from the numerical simulation.

Turbulence intensity (%)	Reynolds number	Input speed (m/s)	Output Speed (m/s)	Input static pressure (pa)	Output static pressure (Pa)	Input dynamic pressure (Pa)	Output dynamic pressure (Pa)
3.201	389403.974	3	4.17	4.6	1.54	5.64	8.85
2.790	1168211.02	9	12.60	39.06	−1.17	48.43	87.9
2.617	1947019.87	15	21.10	106.54	−5.36	136.22	248.12
2.558	2336423.84	18	25.30	152.83	−7.62	196.72	357.17

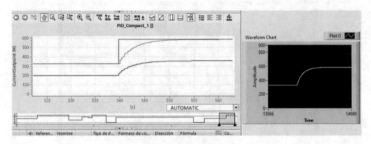

Fig. 9. Loop Control simulation.

4 Conclusions

The simulation served to have a broader panorama of what is happening inside the tunnel when the wind flow is circulating, and thanks to this tool various points of interest can be visualized that can be verified experimentally. It was verified that the proposed design of the wind tunnel will offer us an adequate wind current that is necessary for the development of the project. It was possible to verify that the PID controller, whose parameters were obtained by studying control theory, works correctly. It was found that it is feasible to simulate a plant through communication between PLCSim and Labview. It is expected that the development of this work can promote more research on projects related to wind energy and clean energy sources in general.

Acknowledgments. To the Research Directorate of Universidad Peruana de Ciencias Aplicadas for the support provided in order to develop this research work UPC-EXPOST-2022-2.

References

1. Akella, A.K., Saini, R.P., Sharma, M.P.: Social, economical and environmental impacts of renewable energy systems. Renew. Energy. **34**, 390–396 (2009)
2. Gamio Aita, P.: Energy: a necessary change in Peru (2017)
3. Bhattacharyya, S.C.: Energy access programmes and sustainable development: a critical review and analysis. Energy Sustain. Dev. **16**, 260–271 (2012)

4. Conocemos la primera turbina eólica de la historia. https://ecoinventos.com/primera-turbina-eolica-de-la-historia. Last accessed 4 Nov 2022
5. Atlas Eólico del Perú. https://biblioteca.olade.org/opac-tmpl/Documentos/cg00367.pdf. Last accessed 4 Nov 2022
6. Dekali, Z., Baghli, L., Boumediene, A.: Experimental emulation of a small wind turbine under operating modes using DC motor. In: 2019 4th International Conference on Power Electronics and their Applications (ICPEA), pp. 1–5. IEEE (2019)
7. Quiles, E., Garciia, E., Cervera, J., Vives, J.: Development of a test bench for wind turbine condition monitoring and fault diagnosis. IEEE Lat. Am. Trans. **17**, 907–913 (2019)
8. Maurya, N.K., Maurya, M., Tyagi, A., Dwivedi, S.P.: Design and fabrication of low speed wind tunnel and flow analysis. Int. J. Eng. Technol. **7**, 381–387 (2018)
9. Gregio, R.P., et al.: Energy use in urban areas using neodymium magnets. In: Brazilian Technology Symposium, pp. 988–1005. Springer (2020)
10. Lima, L.B. de, et al.: Mathematical modeling: a conceptual approach of linear algebra as a tool for technological applications. In: Brazilian Technology Symposium, pp. 239–248. Springer (2023)
11. Sampaio, I.A., et al.: The use of the Elman preconditioner in the early iterations of interior point methods. In: Brazilian Technology Symposium, pp. 355–363. Springer (2022)
12. Rohrer, S.: La India María: Mexploitation and the Films of María Elena Velasco. University of Texas Press (2017)
13. Tukimin, A., Zuber, M., Ahmad, K.A.: CFD analysis of flow through Venturi tube and its discharge coefficient. In: IOP Conference Series: Materials Science and Engineering, p. 12062. IOP Publishing (2016)
14. Kefford, B.J., et al.: Salinized rivers: degraded systems or new habitats for salt-tolerant faunas? Biol. Lett. **12**, 20151072 (2016)
15. Rivas, J.R.R., Pimenta, A.P., Salcedo, S.G., Rivas, G.A.R., Suazo, M.C.G.: Study of internal flow of a bipropellant swirl injector of a rocket engine. J. Braz. Soc. Mech. Sci. Eng. **40**(6), 1–16 (2018). https://doi.org/10.1007/s40430-018-1205-6
16. Mott, R.L., Noor, F.M., Aziz, A.A.: Applied fluid mechanics (2006)
17. De las Heras, S.: Engineering Fluid Mechanics, pp. 258–289. Polytechnic University of Catalonia (2012)
18. Eraso-Checa, F., Escobar-Rosero, E., Paz, D.F., Morales, C.: Methodology for the determination of wind characteristics and assessment of wind energy potential in Túquerres Nariño. Rev. Scientífica. 19–31 (2018)
19. SIOS. https://support.industry.siemens.com/cs/document/109761045/descarga-del-simatic-step-7-y-wincc-v15-1-de-prueba-(trial)?dti=0&lc=es-MX. Last accessed 4 Nov 2022
20. NetToPLCsim – Network extension for Plcsim. https://nettoplcsim.sourceforge.net. Last accessed 4 Nov 22
21. OPC Servers Download – NI. https://www.ni.com/es-cr/support/downloads/software-pro ducts/download.opc-servers.html#305861. Last accessed 4 Nov 22
22. LabVIEW Download – NI. https://www.ni.com/es-cr/support/downloads/software-products/download.labview.html#460283. Last accessed 4 Nov 2022
23. Escobar, A., Barrero, L.: Mathematical model of a wind turbin. Electronic Vis. J. Year **3**(1), 48–60 (2009)
24. Feitosa, E., Albiero, A.: Power curves of wind turbines for low wind speed in the generation of electrical energy for family farming Ensaio tractors and agricultural machines, pp. 190–196 (2014)

A CFD Analysis of Water Jet Uniformity Using Oscillating Interior Atomizers for Insulator Cleaning

Josue Anco⬛, Claudia Borda⬛, and Leonardo Vinces$^{(\boxtimes)}$ ⬛

Universidad Peruana de Ciencias Aplicadas, Lima, Peru
{u201420402,u201621551}@upc.edu.pe, leonardo.vinces@upc.pe

Abstract. This article proposes to carry out a CFD analysis of the uniformity of a demineralized water jet through a mechanical design of a fluidic oscillating nozzle for washing insulation chains in high-voltage towers. According to various studies, the atomizers have different spray patterns, for example, full cone, hollow cone, and flat curtain, depending on the need of the project. In this study, the importance of the process lies in achieving the uniformity of the water flow at a distance of 2 to 3 m from the tower and at a pressure of 100 psi in the pipe to guarantee efficient, rapid cleaning and at the same time save money, water, and energy resources, since currently, the insulator cleaning activity could take between 4 h and 2 days, depending on the method to be used. In this sense, comparisons were made, in terms of speed and uniformity, with other structural methods that produce oscillations in the water jets to determine the efficiency of the vibrational structure designed for this study. In this aspect, the fluid mechanic calculations were carried out, as well as the simulation of the design of the new nozzle to obtain a minimum impact speed of 25 m per second. The geometric and mesh designs of the nozzles under study were carried out in the Ansys Spaceclaim and ICEM CFD software. Likewise, the results of the simulations were shown using the ANSYS Fluent software.

Keywords: Nozzle · fluidic oscillators · mechanical design · insulator cleaning · ANSYS Fluent · power lines · electrical insulators

1 Introduction

Electrical insulators are elements intended to be flexible or rigid supports, their main function is to electrically isolate this equipment from the ground [1]. Likewise, insulators suffer damage to their structure due to adverse weather conditions such as corrosion, atmospheric discharge, sulfur, salts in the environment, dust, rain, pollutants such as bird droppings, chemicals in the environment, smog (car emissions), smoke, among others. The failure of these elements in the high-voltage towers would cause current leakage, which would leave a certain area of the population without electricity [2]. In this sense, the vast majority of high-voltage towers are found on the coast of Peru where many of the pollutants mentioned above are found [3]. For this reason, the cleaning of

© The Author(s), under exclusive license to Springer Nature Switzerland AG 2023
Y. Iano et al. (Eds.): BTSym 2022, SIST 353, pp. 136–145, 2023.
https://doi.org/10.1007/978-3-031-31007-2_13

these turns out to be of interest in the maintenance plans of high-tension towers [4]. For example, the company ISA REP, in 2010 conducted a study of contamination of electrical insulators on the coast of Peru, resulting in 69% of polymeric insulators that had failures located less than 25 km from the sea. Among them, eroded and broken insulators with at least 6 months of operation were found, which demonstrates the need to perform frequent maintenance on these elements [4]. However, this activity has been shown to be time-consuming and costly due to the preparation and resources it requires.

Currently, the cleaning of the insulators is carried out through extensive manual maintenance plans in which it is necessary to de-energize the electrical lines. This activity could also be carried out with the line energized [5], and, in this case, it is carried out using trucks that contain an elevator so that an operator can carry out cleaning with a hose [6]. Both alternatives prove to be efficient; however, the first interferes with the electrical continuity distributed to the population and the second technique requires many energy and water resources.

For the cleaning of electrical insulators, a fast and low-cost technique is required, among which, the most important is through robotic systems. However, these technologies have not been adopted for the maintenance of high-voltage towers in Peru and some designs require complex and expensive manufacturing. For this reason, it is necessary to have an optimal hydraulic cleaning system, through the mechanical design of a specialized nozzle to cover the entire range of the isolation chain. Likewise, it produces a uniform jet to comply with a homogeneous cleaning and reduces the use of water and energy resources. For this reason, the necessary studies carried out on the design of nozzles were taken as a reference [7–14].

Kuen S., Ahmad H., Woon J., and Yong S. [15] propose a nozzle design with two feedback channels to ensure mechanically self-sustaining spatial oscillation of the water jet, which generates uniformity at the outlet through the oscillations generated by the internal structure. However, the fluid temporarily oscillates and loses its properties over long distances.

Liao J., Luo X., Wang P., and Zhou Z. [16] propose the use of different sizes of nozzle orifice and air induction to increase the speed of the water jet. However, using an additional fluid does not guarantee uniformity in the cleaning of insulators.

Sarasua J., Ruiz L., Aranzabe E., and Vilas L. [17] present a nozzle model coupled to an ultrasonic generator to obtain vibrations in the fluid, which increases the efficiency of water jet washing. This would not be suitable as it uses additional power for the generator and is used at high pressures.

Si Chen Z. and Deng X. [18] carried out an investigation on a modified cavitation model, for the pulsed jet of self-excited oscillation, through a numerical design using the PISO algorithm and the unstable model of the FLUENT software. This is done in order to maintain a constant speed in the jet coming out of the nozzle.

Fan J., Wang Z., and Chen S. [19] conducted a study on the self-excited oscillation frequency characteristics for a parallel jet nozzle, which was deduced by a single-chamber transfer function in the software Matlab, in this way the frequencies were analyzed, resulting in the pulse frequency of the jet increasing when there are two chambers with rational parameters.

Zhang, S., Fu, B., and Sun, L. [20] study the jet characteristics and pulse mechanism of a self-excited oscillating pulse jet nozzle by analyzing the effects of inlet diameter, cavity, cavity length, wall reflection angle, and self-excited oscillation pulsed jet (SOPJN) inlet pressure over maximum velocity, oscillation frequency, and jet cavitation number, experimentally. With this, it was shown that the key structural parameters influence the SOPJN.

Oz, F. and Kara, K. [21] analyze the oscillation frequency of a jet emitted by a scavenging jet actuator through numerical simulations using a three-dimensional non-stationary Navier-Stokes model with Reynolds averaging (3D-URANS) with Ansys Fluent v17.1. The jet oscillation frequency was predicted by analyzing the velocity time histories at the actuator output. The results obtained show that through this method it is possible to predict all operating conditions and a linear relationship is found between the oscillation frequency of the jet and the Mach number of the outlet nozzle averaged over time.

Han, S.-W., Shin, Y.-S., Kim, H.-C., and Lee, G.-S. [22] study the nozzle design and geometry in a flow model to generate the maximum injection based on the Bosch method. The results show that increasing the diameter of the nozzle orifice provides an increase in mass flow rate and when increasing the elevation of the angle of inclination at the end of the nozzle, the total area of uniformity of the jet increases.

Considering the observations made from the studies shown, this article proposes to design and analyze fluidic nozzle designs for the adequate washing of insulators through water jets, which includes uniformity at the outlet and speed.

2   Description of the Proposed Method

Figure 1 shows the block diagram of the development of the proposed method.

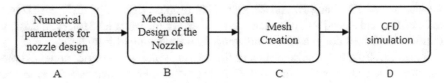

Fig. 1. Block diagram of the process.

2.1   Numerical Parameters for Nozzle Design

For the high-voltage insulation string washing process, the technique that presents the best results in the quality of cleaning, scope, and portability was investigated. In this way, the chosen technique was through high-pressure water jets, which presents pressure parameters in the nozzle of 100 psi for a time of 20 min per isolation chain [23]. From these values, the pressure will be considered for the simulation in the ANSYS FLUENT program, the environment with pressure 0 atm and the range at a distance of 1.5 m from the nozzle outlet. Because it is required to know the spray angle, the maximum washing height, and the speed of reaching the isolation chain.

2.2 Filter Mechanical Design

Calculation of the Thickness of the Nozzle. The dimensions of the nozzle were parameterized with the dimensions of the pipe that will be coupled through an elbow with the following characteristics: inner diameter of 12.42 mm and outer diameter of 15.08 mm with PVC material capable of withstanding up to 150 psi.

Through Barlow's theorem, the thickness is obtained with stainless steel material to withstand higher pressures.

$$e = \frac{P \times D}{2 * \sigma_T} \tag{1}$$

$$\sigma_T = FS * \sigma_f \tag{2}$$

where σ_f is the yield stress of the steel, FS is the reduction factor for stress, and σ_T is the steel working stress.

The reduction factor is 0.6 for typical and normal conditions and 0.72 for non-permanent conditions due to the water hammer, which will be used to open the jet by means of a solenoid valve. In addition, for a yield point of 5000 kg/cm², an internal pressure of 100 psi will be used. Therefore, through 1 and 2 the thickness is:

$$e = 1.3mm \tag{3}$$

Spray Angle Calculation. To calculate the spray angle, it was necessary to analyze the distance from the nozzle to the insulation chain, as well as its dimensions when it is suspended. For this reason, the following is used to find the spray angle.

$$\alpha = 2 * \sin^{-1}\left(\frac{\left(\frac{H}{2} - \frac{h}{2}\right)}{D}\right) \tag{4}$$

where α is the spray angle [°], H is the insulation distance in suspension [mm], h is the nozzle hole distance [mm], and D is the distance between the nozzle and insulator [mm].

$$\alpha = 17.1° \tag{5}$$

Figure 2 was made in Ansys Geometry with the data of the size of the insulator of 45 cm; the distance of the nozzle orifice is 3 mm and finally, the distance from the nozzle to the insulator is 1.5 m.

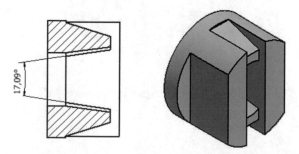

Fig. 2. Spray angle at the end of the nozzle.

2.3 Mesh Creation

- Design of the geometric figure in Ansys SpaceClaim: To obtain a quality mesh that allows obtaining results close to experimental values. It was decided to design the geometric figure in 3D in the Ansys SpaceClaim program, as shown in Fig. 3, which shows the experimental nozzle in 2D of the central section, that is, the mouthpiece split in half to observe the hollow parts of it. Figure 4 shows the 3D design.

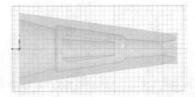

Fig. 3. 2D geometric figure nozzle designed [C]

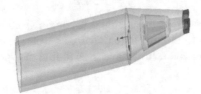

Fig. 4. 3D geometric figure designed nozzle [C]

The nozzles shown in Figs. 5 and 6 are the ones that will be compared in simulation, which is a conventional one with a smaller area [A] and another with an oscillation system [B].

Fig. 5. D geometric figure nozzle model [A]

Fig. 6. D geometric figure nozzle model [B]

Fig. 7. Mesh 3D nozzle model [A]

- Generation and creation of the mesh
- Once the 3D models of the nozzle and its geometries were obtained, it was designed in the same way in the ICEM CFD program to be able to detail the mesh and visualize the phases of the water through the nozzle and outside.

Figure 8 shows the mesh of the conventional model B nozzle, which shows where the fluid will pass through and the quality of the mesh on the nozzle as well as on the outside.

Fig. 8. Mesh 3D nozzle model [B]

Figure 9 has no visible difference from Fig. 7, since it uses the same nozzle casing, but unlike it, it has an oscillating mechanism inside it that can be seen in the following figure.

Fig. 9. Meshed 3D nozzle model [C].

In Fig. 10, for the meshing of the model nozzle, VORFN was used to eliminate the surfaces that coincide with the oscillation mechanism, in such a way that when simulating the fluid it does not cross through that space.

In addition, dimensions of a ratio of 0.01 and a scale of 1.2 were used for the edge of the nozzle.

Fig. 10. D model nozzle phases [C]

• Analysis of meshes in quality (Table 1)

Table 1. Nozzle mesh quality

Nozzle	Quality
A	0.85–0.90
B	0.8–0.85
Designed	0.95–1

2.4   CFD Simulation

We will now define the simulation parameters and analyze which of the 3 nozzles has greater uniformity at the outlet of the water jet and manages to be more efficient with respect to the impact speed with the isolation chain. For this simulation, the ANSYS FLUENT program was used (Figs. 11, 12 and 13).

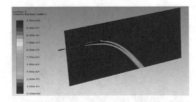

Fig. 11. Uniformity of the water jet in nozzle model [A]

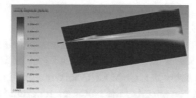

Fig. 12. Uniformity of the water jet in nozzle model [B]

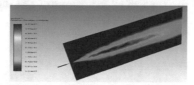

Fig. 13. Uniformity of the water jet in the designed nozzle [C]

In the same way, the following results are displayed regarding the speeds at a distance of 1.5 m (Figs. 14, 15, and 16).

Fig. 14. Speed of the water jet in model nozzle [A]

Fig. 15. Speed of the water jet in nozzle model [B]

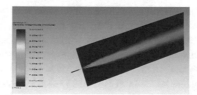

Fig. 16. Water jet speed at designed nozzle [C]

3   Conclusion

With this research, an oscillating mechanical system was developed to achieve uniformity of the water jet at a distance of two meters with an input of 100 psi. By simulating the types of nozzles proposed using the ICEM CFD software, results that differ in the quality of the meshes, uniformity, and speed of the water jet generated by the three nozzles were achieved. In this way, the performance of the mechanical system of the nozzle for the uniformity of the demineralized water jet is demonstrated (Table 2).

Table 2. Results comparison

Nozzle	A	B	C
Mesh quality	0.85–0.90	0.80–0.85	0.95–1
Uniformity	Short	Half	High
Speed	13.4 m/s	20.5 m/s	22 m/s

The results show that the nozzle that includes the oscillating interior (nozzle C) presents higher quality in the creation of the mesh, and its uniformity and speed in the jet at a distance of 1.5 m is higher than nozzles A and B.

Acknowledgments. To the Research Directorate of Universidad Peruana de Ciencias Aplicadas for the support provided in order to develop this research work UPC-EXPOST-2022-2.

References

1. Aisladores Eléctricos: Reseña Histórica by CITE Energía – Issuu, https://issuu.com/citeen ergia/docs/ing._alonso_portella_retuerto. Last accessed 17 June 2021
2. Pacheco, C.S.: Modelo de mantenimiento para aisladores contaminados en la línea 220 kv Cóndores-Parinacota (2018)
3. Map of Electric Power Transmission Lines 2018. http://www.minem.gob.pe/minem/archivos/Anexo_4_Map_of_Electric_Power_Transmission_Lines_2018.pdf. Last accessed 7 May 2021
4. Companies – REP. www.aai.com.pe. Last accessed 7 May 2021
5. Uriarte, H.: Influence of the use of preventive maintenance with the method of Hydrowashing in medium voltage distribution networks, 10 Kv, of the transformation substation Huaca del Sol - Trujillo [Thesis to obtain the professional title of electrical mechanical engineer]. Cesar Vallejo University (2018). https://repositorio.ucv.edu.pe/bitstream/handle/20.500.12692/26324/uriarte_mh.pdf?sequence=1&isAllowed=y. Last accessed 7 May 2021
6. IEEE Guide for Cleaning Insulators. In: IEEE Std 957-2005 (Revision of IEEE Std 957-1995). IEEE (2005)
7. Cáceres, D., Dominguez, M., Vinces, L., Ronceros, J.: Design of a parabolic solar collector for the drying of Spirulina and Cushuro microalgae. In: 2021 IEEE XXVIII International Conference on Electronics, Electrical Engineering and Computing (INTERCON), pp. 1–4. IEEE (2021)

8. Padilla, C., Vivanco, A., Vinces, L., Klusmann, M.: Design of a multi-hole cylindrical extruder, driven by a linear actuator and used for the formation of bakery dough. In: 2020 IEEE XXVII International Conference on Electronics, Electrical Engineering and Computing (INTERCON), pp. 1–4. IEEE (2020)
9. Siegle, A.R., Iano, Y., de Oliveira, G.G., Vaz, G.C.: Proposal of mathematical models for a continuous flow electric heater. In: Brazilian Technology Symposium, pp. 213–228. Springer (2023)
10. Farfan, G.A.P., Verastegui, F.M.N., Ramos, L.N.V., Martínez, J.F.O.: Design of a system for the external washing and winding of fire hoses composed of a polyester and rubber jacket. In: 2020 IEEE XXVII International Conference on Electronics, Electrical Engineering and Computing (INTERCON), pp. 1–4. IEEE (2020)
11. Thiagarajan, Y., Pasupulati, B., de Oliveira, G.G., Iano, Y., Vaz, G.C.: A simple approach for short-term hydrothermal self scheduling for generation companies in restructured power system. In: Brazilian Technology Symposium, pp. 396–414. Springer (2022)
12. Loayza, J.C., Ronceros, J., Vinces, L.: A thermal analysis of the internal flow in 2 helical coils for the delignification process of sugar cane bagasse using superheated steam. In: Brazilian Technology Symposium, pp. 461–469. Springer (2022)
13. del Riego, D.G., Gómez, G., Vinces, L.: An optimal blade design for mini wind generators mountable on the spoiler of a vehicle. In: Brazilian Technology Symposium, pp. 536–544. Springer (2022)
14. Lima, L.B. de, et al.: Mathematical modeling: a conceptual approach of linear algebra as a tool for technological applications. In: Brazilian Technology Symposium, pp. 239–248. Springer (2023)
15. Kim, S.K., Ahmad, H., Moon, J.W., Jung, S.Y.: Nozzle with a feedback channel for agricultural drones. Appl. Sci. **11**, 2138 (2021)
16. Liao, J., et al.: Analysis of the influence of different parameters on droplet characteristics and droplet size classification categories for air induction nozzle. Agronomy **10**, 256 (2020)
17. Miranda, J.A.S., Ruiz-Rubio, L., Aranzabe Basterrechea, E., Vilas-Vilela, J.L.: Non-immersion ultrasonic cleaning: an efficient green process for large surfaces with low water consumption. Processes. **9** 585 (2021)
18. Wang, Z., Chen, S., Deng, X.: Research on modified cavitation model for self-excited oscillation pulsed jet nozzle. In: 2017 International Conference on Mechanical, System and Control Engineering (ICMSC). pp. 90–95. IEEE (2017)
19. Jiarong, F., Zhaohui, W., Si, C.: Self-excited oscillation frequency characteristics of a paralleled pulsed jet nozzle. Energy Procedia. **141**, 619–624 (2017)
20. Zhang, S., Fu, B., Sun, L.: Investigation of the jet characteristics and pulse mechanism of self-excited oscillating pulsed jet nozzle. Processes. **9**, 1423 (2021)
21. Oz, F., Kara, K.: Jet oscillation frequency characterization of a sweeping jet actuator. Fluids **5**, 72 (2020)
22. Han, S.-W., Shin, Y.-S., Kim, H.-C., Lee, G.-S.: Study on the common rail type injector nozzle design based on the nozzle flow model. Appl. Sci. **10**, 549 (2020)
23. Lara, J.M.: Diseño y Plan de Mantenimiento de una Línea Eléctrica de Alta Tensión con un Tramo Aéreo y Otro Subterráneo. University of Zaragoza (2020). https://zaguan.unizar.es/record/107314/files/TAZ-PFC-2021-005.pdf. Last accessed 7 May 2021

Batzbot: A Creativity Tool for Disabled Children

Daniel Duzzi Paulo⬤ and Amilton da Costa Lamas(✉)⬤

Pontifícia Universidade Católica de Campinas, Campinas, Brazil
daniel@puccampinas.edu.br

Abstract. The development of playful tools to promote cognition and allow artistic progress may contribute to disabled children's rehabilitation, especially those with cerebral palsy. The use of this type of tool may help children express emotions, especially those that are difficult to talk about. Playful tools can also induce the discovery of new capabilities otherwise unknown as well. Arts may reduce anxiety and depression and improve memory and reasoning. This work reports on the idealization, development, and the very first use of a cabled remote-controlled robot that assists children with cerebral palsy rehabilitation through drawing practice. The device was developed in an intensive collaboration method between the university team and the therapists of the partner organization. It consists of three modules that comply with functional and non-functional requirements. The requirements were defined by the therapists of a partner institution. The proof of concept is now under testing, to validate and identify other functionalities to be included in an upcoming version.

Keywords: Arts · Creativity robot · Cerebral palsy · Rehabilitation

1 Introduction

The rehabilitation challenges of disabled children are quite big, there are so many different disabilities and tools that it is difficult to select the most appropriate solution for a specific treatment. Simultaneously the available tools/solutions are very expensive and often enough one must import them from overseas in order to offer the best rehabilitation treatment. This imposes strong access limitations on professionals in third-world countries. Specialized institutions are constantly searching for new solutions and innovative technical approaches to succeed in making available specific and multidisciplinary rehabilitation therapy routines. This is especially true if they aim in providing tailored assistance adapted to each child's specific needs. This work presents a proof of concept (POC) of an assistive robot aimed at promoting the physical rehabilitation of children with cerebral palsy (CP) through artistic activities. The solution was developed during a university extension project at Pontifícia Universidade Católica de Campinas (PUC-Campinas). It is expected that its usage may reduce the difficulty in drawing and painting and, at the same time, promote physical rehabilitation [1–6].

Y. Iano et al. (Eds.): BTSym 2022, SIST 353, pp. 146–153, 2023.
https://doi.org/10.1007/978-3-031-31007-2_14

1.1 Background

Cerebral Palsy is a congenital disorder of movement, muscle tone, or posture. It occurs due to abnormal brain development, often before birth, most likely due to poor cerebral oxygenation. Symptoms include exaggerated reflexes, flexible or rigid limbs, and involuntary movements. They occur in early childhood [7, 8]. The rehabilitation process may include a series of muscle and posture exercises under the guidance of a team of several professionals with different specialties. It can be performed autonomously or with minimum supervision. The rehabilitation success depends on a set of stimuli that encourages the patient to increase performance while recognizing how important the recovery is for their own well-being [9]. Involving children with CP in artistic activities is important for developing self-expression and may reduce depression and anxiety. Artistic engagement may increase cognitive capabilities as well as memory and reasoning [10]. Play with arts is a form to express feelings often hard to talk about. Special needs children may have a much deeper need and difficulty expressing feelings like fear, shame, anger, and outrage. This is a common social situation in times when bullying is very much present. Having access to tools that allows the children to be creative and joyful may help them learn to communicate such a type of feelings in a healthy way. If the children have speech difficulty, as often happens in the case of cerebral palsy, art may be a very powerful tool to express emotions and overcome social discrimination. If the young can realize that art is a form of communication, they may increase their self-esteem and get around difficulties [11].

1.2 University Extension Project

The mission of PUC-Campinas is to generate, structure, and socialize the academic knowledge produced within its bounds. It docs that through research, schooling, and extension programs. This tripodal structure is mandatory for a student's education of excellence. Formal education includes professional and holistic aspects of a human being while feeding back the incentives of society. In this way, PUC-Campinas contributes expressively to social justice and solidarity [12]. The university has improved its extension programs by offering options of 24- or 10-h time so that the professor can work 40 h a week job. Extension projects rely on establishing partnerships with external institutions which have synergy with the university's goals. These partnerships make possible activities for hundreds of undergraduate and even graduate students to participate in outside experiences. Extension projects enrich the undergraduate experience by bringing the opportunity to work outside the university, explore different contexts, and have hands-on experience with actual social problems. This adds an even deeper contribution to formal education. On the other hand, the partner institutions benefit from the absorption of academic technical and non-technical knowledge brought up by the university team. This process is based on highly frequent meetings, called conversation rounds, where knowledge exchange takes place. Some of this knowledge comes from common day-to-day activities of the partner's team and some from the undergraduate student and professors that participate in the project. The conversation rounds are an excellent method to promote the convergency between the university ideas and the social needs experienced by the partner institutions.

This dialogic process allows the university group to learn, with outside people which have different academic and non-academic backgrounds, about how to endure and overcome the existing social challenges. The conversation rounds are very useful to adjust the project's goals and pace. Through this knowledge appropriation, the university team can easily adapt its mindset and therefore perform adjustments on the solution so that it will properly answer the social demand in a way to promote the community's independence and autonomy without disrupting the local culture. The interactivity, resulting from a virtuous information exchange cycle, allows the community to have a better understanding of its needs and challenges, therefore clarifying the way to find the most appropriate answer to the social demands. All the project participants benefit from the use of such a collaborative method in the sense that the boundary conditions and requirements are commonly understood. Strictly following this process assures that the final solution will efficiently attend to all the commonly identified requirements.

2 Methodology

University extension interventions at PUC-Campinas are characterized by a large diversity of partner institutions from different social segments. This guarantees that the program will cover a large spectrum of interests, synergic to the university goals. The method is sustained by two major pillars: 1) the building of partnerships with well know specialized institutions/businesses, which are representative of the social segment of interest, and 2) the application of a widely used complex software development method adapted for the social intervention process.

2.1 Partnership with Specialized Institutions/Business

The first step in the social intervention process is to build a formal partnership with well-known social institutions that work on the project subject. The selection follows a series of procedures established by the Pro Reitoria de Extensão e Assuntos Comunitários (PROEXT) of PUC-Campinas. PROEXT has defined several boundary conditions that range from juridical contours to the social impact of the institution's results/projects. This action tries to confirm that the intended partner institution is reliable and performs good social work. Furthermore, these steps also indicate how much synergy exists between the project and the potential partners' goals and social target market. Public and private enterprises/associations are equally considered. This work was performed in conjunction with Therapies Serviços de Fisioterapia e Terapia Ocupacional LTDA (Therapies). Therapies is an intensive care rehabilitation clinic that aims on providing the best and more advanced treatments for the physical rehabilitation of children with CP. Therapies it is also world widely known for its success in treating children with severe physical limitations. Its multidisciplinary professional team employs holistic treatments so that all the patients' needs are properly attended to. These characteristics also contribute to the proposition of high-quality solutions.

2.2 Social Intervention Method

The conception, development, validation, and delivery of the assistive robot POC presented in this work is based on three columns: 1) Knowledge appropriation: where both teams freely discuss and exchange perceptions, ideas, and propositions about the needs and the solution to be proposed. This column certifies that the target market, the physical therapists from the partner institution, actively and intensively participates in every single step of the project execution; 2) POC development: follows the guidelines of the former Rational Unified Process (RUP) based on micro cycles. The IBM RUP [13] is widely employed in the development of complex software solutions and has been greatly simplified to be used for a very small development team for this work. All the developments were carried out on the PUC-Campinas premises and later validated at Therapies; 3) Cultural material production: consists of preparing support materials for the POC use and later, independent, replication. Most often is made of audio, image, and video productions for easy access and understanding. Care is taken to the use of proper language so that non-engineers can understand the instructions.

In summary, the applied methodology consists of a series of short cycled meetings (conversation rounds) which are highly interactive, characterizing an intensely collaborative process. The social intervention method is also based on the execution of three models: 1) Knowledge Appropriation Model; 2) POC Development Model; and 3) Cultural Material Production Model. A complete description of the former two models can be found in the article Sistema Autônomo para Travessia de Deficientes Visuais of Mário Joaquim de Lemes Neto [14]. The Cultural Material Production Model is fully described in the paper Projeto Final e Extensão – Compartilhando Estratégias e Resultados de Engenharia Elétrica, written by Freitas et al. [15].

3   Results and Discussion

3.1   Functional and Non-functional Requirements

Therapies patients are mostly children with CP which have no visual impairment but have severe motor limitations. After several conversation rounds, the project team decided to develop a POC of an assistive robot to promote the motor and cognitive development of children with CP. The assistive robot would help the Therapies patients with drawing and painting, contributing to the patients' self-expression as previously mentioned.

Some of the functional and non-functional requirements agreed upon are, the system should: 1) allow the therapist to give optical and audio feedback upon task completion; 2) allow free or guided interaction so that the patient can define challenges by himself or have them defined by the therapist; 3) allow the therapist to choose the type and intensity of the feedback (always positive); 4) have a recognizable shape, preferably of an animal; 5) allow the patient to freely draw any desirable figure; 6) have controllable speed response; and 7) allow the patient to decide whether or not draw during POC motion.

3.2   System Architecture

The POCs name, Batzbot, refers to the Maia deities Hun Batz, and its twin brother Hun Chouen. According to the Maia folklore, they were elder sons of Hun Hunahpu. They became deities associated with the arts. There are legends reporting that they were trapped in a tree where they assumed a monkey appearance to return to the ground. Therefore, the robot was conceived with the appearance of a monkey. Batzbot is a cabled remote-controlled robot with the purpose of promoting the creative capabilities of children with CP through art expression. The solution is composed of three modules: A) robot, B) user control, and C) therapist control. Figure 1 shows the electrical architecture.

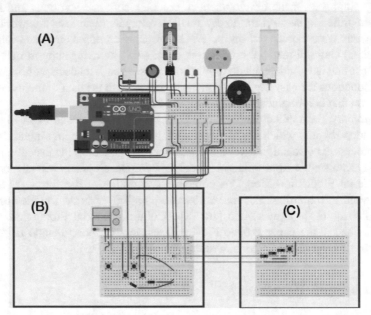

Fig. 1. Electrical architecture schematics.

3.3 The Assistive Robot

The Therapies team drew the first free sketch of the robot, as shown in Fig. 2. Although not quite a monkey yet, it already has the form of a small animal, which may evoke children's empathy.

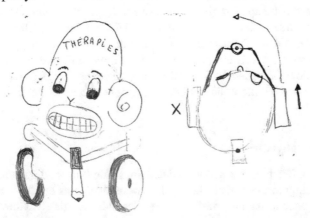

Fig. 2. Batzbot first sketch drawn by the Therapies team. Note the drawing arm in front.

After a few turns of conversation rounds, the development team started to build the robot using a metal chassis, with a couple of wheels that would accommodate the robot body. The robot has a small arm, made on a 3D printer, that hosts a marker pen, for example. The wheel traction and all electronics needed for arms control (up and down movements) are inside the robot's body. The eyes are made with two green LEDs. The inside buzzer and the windmill at the top of the robot's hat have their control electronics hosted inside the body as well. Finally, the tail at the back of the robot is used to adjust its speed response to patient control. Figure 3 shows the first version of the POC.

Fig. 3. First version of the POC.

3.4 User Control

The user control allows the children with PC to drive the robot around and to move the drawing arm up and down. This control is based on assistive technology using large switches and a joystick for motion in the X-Y directions. The joystick can be replaced by four push-button switches for use by children with more severe motor disabilities. An independent switch controls the drawing arm movements.

3.5 Therapist Control

The therapist uses a separate control to send positive feedback when a child completes a given task. There are three types of feedback that can be combined in any order: 1) spin the cap windmill, 2) activate the buzzer, and 3) light the eyes up (green LEDs). Each type of feedback is selected by a set of on-off switches, activated by a separate push button. This allows the therapist to select any combination of feedback signals they wish.

The complete system, made by the three modules is shown in Fig. 4, i.e., the Batzbot (A), user control (B), which has the independent arm switch to control the writing arm (shown with a pen marker), and the therapist controller (C).

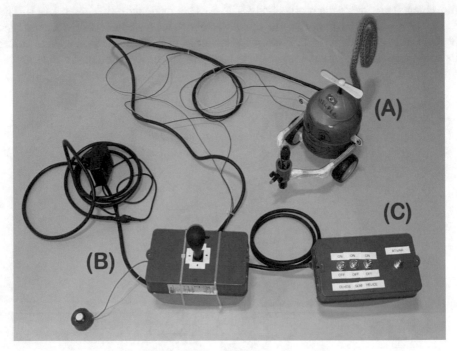

Fig. 4. The complete Batzbot system.

A new version is now being tested and validated at Therapies.

4   Conclusion

The development of an assistive drawing robot (Batzbot) was successively concluded and demonstrated. The robot is now undergoing validation testing at the partner institution (Therapies). It is expected several improvement suggestions to be included in the next version. A group of therapists of the university team is developing a rehabilitation program to be soon delivered to Therapies. A second version with wireless controls is under development and should be soon delivered.

Acknowledgments. The university team would like to thank PUC-Campinas PROEXT for the financial support and Therapies Serviços de Fisioterapia e Terapia Ocupacional LTDA for the partnership.

References

1. Demanboro, A.C., Bianchini, D., Iano, Y., de Oliveira, G.G., Vaz, G.C.: Regulatory aspects of 5G and perspectives in the scope of scientific and technological policy. In: Brazilian Technology Symposium, pp. 163–171. Springer (2023)
2. Demanboro, A.C., Bianchini, D., Iano, Y., de Oliveira, G.G., Vaz, G.C.: 6G networks: an innovative approach, but with many challenges and paradigms, in the development of platforms and services in the near future. In: Brazilian Technology Symposium, pp. 172–187. Springer (2023)
3. Izario, D., Brancalhone, J., Iano, Y., de Oliveira, G.G., Vaz, G.C., Izario, K.: 5G-automation of vertical systems in the industry 4.0. In: Brazilian Technology Symposium, pp. 35–43. Springer (2023)
4. Vaz, G.C., Iano, Y., de Oliveira, G.G.: IoT-from industries to houses: an overview. In: Brazilian Technology Symposium, pp. 734–741. Springer (2022)
5. Nishimura, E.H., Iano, Y., de Oliveira, G.G., Vaz, G.C.: Application and requirements of AIoT-enabled industrial control units. In: Brazilian Technology Symposium, pp. 724–733. Springer (2022)
6. Sampaio, I.A., et al.: The use of the Elman preconditioner in the early iterations of interior point methods. In: Brazilian Technology Symposium, pp. 355–363. Springer (2022)
7. Haenggeli, C., Suter-Stricker, S.: Freeman, M., Steven, J.B. (eds.) Cerebral palsy. A complete guide for caregiving (2007)
8. Caricchio, M.B.M.: Tratar brincando: o lúdico como recurso da fisioterapia pediátrica no Brasil. Rev. Eletron. Atual. Sau. **6**, 43–57 (2017)
9. Lamb, V.: Teaching motor skills to children with cerebral palsy and similar movement disorders: a guide for parents and professionals. Pediatr. Phys. Ther. **19**, 340–341 (2007)
10. Warmbrodt, R.: Engaging in the arts for children with cerebral palsy, cerebral palsy guidance. https://www.cerebralpalsyguidance.com/cerebral-palsy/living/engaging-arts/. Last accessed 22 Sep 2022
11. Mak, H.W., Fancourt, D.: Arts engagement and self-esteem in children: results from a propensity score matching analysis. Ann. N. Y. Acad. Sci. **1449**, 36–45 (2019)
12. PUC-CAMPINAS. Pontifícia Universidade Católica de Campinas. Missão da Universidade. https://www.puc-campinas.edu.br/institucional/reitoria/. Last accessed: 22 Sep 2022
13. IBM. Rational software. https://www01.ibm.com/software/br/rational/ (2014). Last accessed 22 Sep 2022
14. Neto, M.J.L., Lamas, A.C.: Sistema autônomo para travessia de deficientes visuais em semáforos, VI jornada de extensión universitária del mercosur, Tandil. 24-27 de abril 2018 ISBN: 978-950-658-448-1. http://extension.uniccn.edu.ar/jem/Libro_JEM_2018.pdf (2018). Last accessed 22 Sep 2022
15. Freitas, D.E., et al.: Projeto final e extensão-compartilhando estratégias e resultados de engenharia elétrica-anais do 45o congresso brasileiro de educação em engenharia – cobenge 2017. Available at: http://www.abenge.org.br/cobenge/legado/arquivos/2/LivroSD2017.pdf. Last accessed 22 Sep 2022

An Algorithm for the Reconstruction of 4 ECG Lead Signals Based on the Attention Mechanism

Kevin Picón, Juan Rodriguez, Rodrigo Salazar-Gamarra, Manuel Márquez, and Guillermo Kemper(✉)

Universidad Peruana de Ciencias Aplicadas, Lima, Peru
{u201611243,u201726246,pcodrsal,pcelmmar}@upc.edu.pe,
guillermo.kemper@upc.pe

Abstract. This work proposes an algorithm to reconstruct 4 precordial electrocardiogram (ECG) lead signals. Standard cardiovascular disease (CVD) monitoring and detection uses all 12 available ECG leads. However, this number of leads implies a certain complexity of the equipment in terms of size, weight, and power consumption. Computational algorithms aimed at reducing the number of required leads for CVD detection help lower the time consumption and errors due to needing many signal acquisition cables. In this work, an LSTM sequence-to-sequence (Seq2Seq) neural network model with attention takes only 4 ECG leads (I, II, V2, and V5) and outputs the mentioned precordial leads. This proposal contributes to making ECG signal acquisitions easier and more accessible by requiring fewer cables and thus facilitating its use by people with little training. The model achieved a maximum average Pearson correlation coefficient of 0.9707 for all leads. It was validated using the PTB Diagnostic ECG Database.

Keywords: ECG leads · Attention mechanism · LSTM · Reconstruction

1 Introduction

The electrocardiogram (ECG) is a standard technique used by cardiologists to diagnose different cardiovascular diseases (CVD) using electrical information from the heart. An ECG is constituted of 12 leads: 3 bipolar leads in the limbs (I, II, III), 3 augmented leads computed from the previously stated ones (aVR, aVL, aVF), and 6 precordial (chest) leads (V1, V2, V3, V4, V5, and V6). Normally, all 12 leads need to be obtained using multiple electrodes, so the time required to prepare a patient for an ECG may be long. Thus, there are multiple attempts to use fewer leads and reconstruct the missing ones from the acquired ones.

For example, [1] proposes using the average of the outputs of multiple feedforward multilayer neural networks to reconstruct precordial leads V1, V3, V4, V5, and V6. The algorithm achieves correlation coefficients of 0.97, 0.96, 0.88, 0.91, and 0.93, respectively, when comparing the real signals with the reconstructed signals.

Other works use neural network architectures specifically designed to handle time series, such as long-short-term memory (LSTM) [2] or focus time-delay (FTDNN) neural networks [3]. The work at [2] uses stacked bidirectional LSTMs, achieving a promising artifact noise reduction but a maximum correlation coefficient of 0.84. On the other hand, the work at [3] uses an FTDNN and achieves average correlation coefficients ranging from 0.8609 to 0.9678. This work omitted samples to compute the final correlation coefficient, labeling them as "outliers"; this might bias the work's results. Additionally, the reconstructed V4 lead has the lowest correlation, such as in [1]. The reconstruction of the V4 lead is improved by using convolutional neural networks in [4]. The network takes leads I, II, and V2 as input and achieves a correlation coefficient of 0.9380 for the reconstructed V4 lead.

Although the presented works are successful in reconstructing ECG leads from a reduced number of them, the correlation coefficients are not yet similar between the reconstructed leads. Thus, this work proposes using a Seq2Seq LSTM model with attention, such that the attention mechanism can compute the best weights for the Seq2Seq output for each input. This architecture has been proven useful in time series prediction applications, such as in finance [5], environmental monitoring [6], or renewable energy [7]. The work in [5] presents an LSTM with attention and achieves better performance than only using an LSTM. At [6], a Seq2Seq LSTM with attention models surface water runoff and performs better than traditional regression models. Finally, [7] successfully predicts wind power levels using a Seq2Seq LSTM with a single attention layer.

The proposed algorithm achieves a maximum average correlation of 0.9707 for leads V1, V3, V4, and V6. The individual maximum correlations when using 20 sample inputs are 0.9739, 0.9774, 0.9688, and 0.9655, respectively. Moreover, using 200 sample inputs results in a correlation of 0.9704, which implies no relationship between a larger input size and a better correlation coefficient. The following sections describe the algorithm and the results.

2 Description of the Proposed Equipment

Figure 1 shows the block diagram of the proposed system. The first step consists of database preparation. Here, incomplete measurements were excluded, signal noise was filtered out and then signals were normalized. Next, the pre-processed samples were separated into a training and a validation subset [8–11]. Finally, these samples were used to train a neural network. The network's architecture is detailed in a later section.

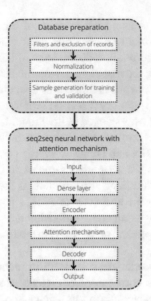

Fig. 1. Block diagram of the proposed system.

2.1 Database Preparation

This work uses the PTB (Pysikalisch-Technische Bundesanstalt) ECG diagnostics database, from Physiobank [12], which is aimed at research uses. All records were taken from healthy patients and patients diagnosed by cardiology at the Benjamin Franklin university hospital in Berlin, Germany. The database has a total of 549 ECG records from 290 patients; each record has the 12 standard leads and 3 Frank leads (vx, vy, and vz), the latter of which will not be used in this work. Table 1 shows a summary of the records in the database.

Record Filtering and Exclusion. The diagram in Fig. 2 shows the procedure to prepare the records from the database. First, all derivations without diagnosis data are discarded. Next, the signals are filtered with a band-pass filter from 0.67 Hz to 150 Hz with zero phase distortion [13], according to the recommendations by the American Heart Association (AHA). The signals have a sampling rate of 1000 Hz but are downsampled to 500 Hz such as to reduce computational load; this sampling rate is in the range recommended by the AHA. Then, records with baseline deviations, artifacts, and noise after filtering are excluded. Moreover, records with not enough registers for dividing into training and validation are also excluded. These records are labeled as "Others" in the Diagnostic column in Table 1.

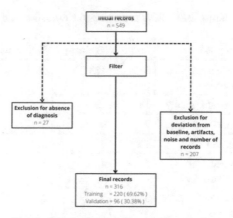

Fig. 2. Block diagram for record exclusion.

Table 1. ECG recordings summary.

Diagnostic	Number of records
Myocardial infarction	368
Healthy control	80
Arrhythmia	16
Branch block	17
Myocarditis	4
Myocardiopathy	17
Myocardial hypertrophy	7
Valvular heart disease	6
Others	7
No information	27
Total	**549**

The exclusion process resulted in 316 records which were divided into 69.62% for training and 30.38% for validation. Table 2 presents a summary of records after exclusions.

Data Normalization. Data normalization consists in taking the maximum and minimum per derivation, per record, and applying the following equation:

$$X_{nor} = \frac{X - X_{min}}{X_{max} - X_{min}} \tag{1}$$

where X is the value to be normalized and X_{nor} is the normalized value.

Table 2. Summary of ECG recordings for validation and training.

Diagnostic	Total	Training	Validation
Myocardial infarction	219	153	66
Myocardiopathy	18	12	6
Branch block	9	6	3
Arrhythmia	10	7	3
Myocardial hypertrophy	6	4	2
Valvular heart disease	5	3	2
Myocarditis	4	3	1
Healthy	45	32	13
Total	**316**	**220**	**96**
Percentage total	**100%**	**69.62%**	**30.38%**

Training and Validation Sample Generation. Figure 3 shows the sample generation procedure. Each input sample consists of a 4 x N matrix, where N is the input sequence length, for each of the 4 input leads. The output is an N-size vector. Thus, there is a model for each reconstructed derivation. Different input sequence lengths are evaluated. Single sample displacement is applied to extract each N-sample long input sequence from the complete ECG lead.

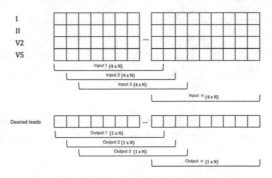

Fig. 3. Training sample generation scheme.

2.2   Seq2Seq Model with Attention

Figure 4 shows the proposed architecture. A 4 x N input enters a fully-connected ("Dense") network, which attempts to compress the information into an N-size vector. This is the input to the Seq2Seq encoder. The encoder holds the LSTM neuron states

in C_t and the neuron hidden states in $\overline{h}_s$. The encoder's output is connected to the attention mechanism. An alignment vector is computed from the encoder neuron states C_t,
the encoder's hidden states $\overline{h}_s$ and the decoder's hidden states h_t [5]:

$$\alpha_{ts} = \frac{\exp\left(score\left(h_t, \overline{h}_s\right)\right)}{\sum_{s'=1}^{s} score\left(h_t, \overline{h}_{s'}\right)} \tag{2}$$

The score function may be computed in 3 different ways [5]:

$$score\left(h_t, \overline{h}_s\right) = \begin{cases} h_t^{\mathsf{T}}\overline{h}_s & (dot) \\ h_t^{\mathsf{T}}W_a\overline{h}_s & (general) \\ W_a\left[h_t; \overline{h}_s\right] & (concat) \end{cases} \tag{3}$$

This work uses the dot function, which calculates the dot product of the encoder and
decoder hidden states. This function has low computational complexity and does not
have any trainable parameters.

The alignment vector and the encoder hidden states are used to compute a context
vector [5]:

$$c_t = \sum_s \alpha_{ts}\overline{h}_s \tag{4}$$

Finally, the attention weight vector a_t is computed [5] according to:

$$a_t = \tanh(W_c[c_t; \ h_t]) \tag{5}$$

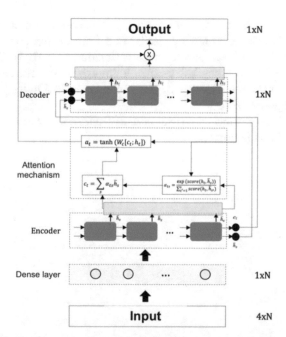

Fig. 4. Seq2Seq neural network model with an attention mechanism.

where W_c are the trainable parameters in the attention mechanism. This attention vector is multiplied by the decoder hidden state vector to obtain the desired ECG lead sequence.

The fully-connected ("Dense") network uses 20 layers. This number of layers was chosen experimentally. Fewer layers resulted in model underfitting, while more layers increased the training time and resulted in model overfitting.

3   Results

As mentioned in Subsect. 2.1., different input sequence sizes (N) were tested. Table 3 shows the results of these experiments, which were evaluated using the Pearson correlation coefficient.

Table 3. Comparison result for correlation according to input sequence size

Lead	Correlation coefficient by input sequence size						
	10	20	40	60	80	100	200
V1	0.9234	0.9739	0.9629	0.9721	0.9735	0.9724	0.9712
V3	0.9524	0.9747	0.9709	0.9601	0.9712	0.9624	0.9789
V4	0.9223	0.9688	0.9732	0.9517	0.9325	0.9523	0.9625
V6	0.8721	0.9655	0.9645	0.9753	0.9619	0.9701	0.9691
Average	0.9176	0.9707	0.9679	0.9648	0.9598	0.9643	0.9704

An input sequence size of 20 resulted in the best correlation coefficient, with an average of 0.9707. This result is very similar to the correlation obtained by using an input sequence size of 200 samples (average correlation of 0.9704). This implies that a larger sequence size has a negligible effect in improving the correlation coefficient. Nonetheless, the smallest sequence size (10 samples) resulted in the worst correlation coefficient (average of 0.9176).

Figures 5, 6, 7 and 8 show some examples of lead reconstructions using the model with a 20-sample input sequence.

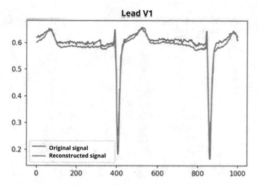

Fig. 5. Original and reconstructed V1 lead

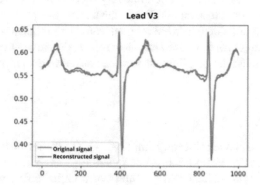

Fig. 6. Original and reconstructed V3 lead

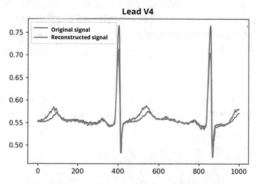

Fig. 7. Original and reconstructed V4 lead

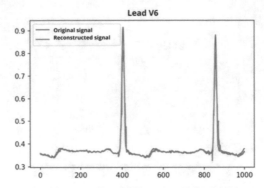

Fig. 8. Original and reconstructed V6 lead

Although the figures illustrate a qualitatively successful lead reconstruction, some reconstruction limitations are apparent. For instance, the QRS peaks in the reconstructed leads are consistently smaller than in the original leads. This might be due to an amplitude variation that is too quick for the LSTM model to follow. Future works will aim to mitigate this limitation, although the amplitude error does not have a significant impact on the diagnosis.

4 Conclusions

The attention mechanism significantly improves ECG lead reconstruction. The model achieves a maximum 0.9797 correlation coefficient for leads V1, V3, V4, and V6, when using a 20-sample input sequence size. Moreover, no relationship was found between the sequence size and the correlation coefficient. A larger, 200-sample input sequence size resulted in an average correlation coefficient of 0.9704, which is very close to the 20-sample input sequence model. Finally, the worst performance corresponded to using 10 samples in the input sequence, achieving a correlation coefficient of 0.9176.

Future works will seek to improve the correlation coefficients in order to achieve a more accurate lead estimation; additionally, they will aim to integrate the algorithm into an electronic device capable of accurately measuring ECG leads that will serve as inputs to the developed neural network model.

Acknowledgments. The authors would like to thank the Dirección de Investigacion of Universidad Peruana de Ciencias Aplicadas for funding and logistical support with Code UPC-D-2022-2.

References

1. Atoui, H., Fayn, J., Rubel, P.: A novel neural-network model for deriving standard 12-lead ECGs from serial three-lead ECGs: application to self-care. IEEE Trans. Inf. Technol. Biomed. **14**, 883–890 (2010)
2. Zou, J., Zhang, Q., Frick, K.: Intelligent mobile electrocardiogram monitor-empowered personalized cardiac big data. In: 2020 11th IEEE Annual Ubiquitous Computing, Electronics & Mobile Communication Conference (UEMCON), pp. 280–284. IEEE (2020)

3. Smith, G.H., Van den Heever, D.J., Swart, W.: The reconstruction of a 12-lead electrocardio-gram from a reduced lead set using a focus time-delay neural network. Acta Cardiol. Sin. **37**, 47 (2021)
4. Wang, L., Zhou, W., Xing, Y., Liu, N., Movahedipour, M., Zhou, X.-G.: A novel method based on convolutional neural networks for deriving standard 12-lead ECG from serial 3-lead ECG. Front. Inf. Technol. Electron. Eng. **20**(3), 405–413 (2019)
5. Zhang, X., Liang, X., Zhiyuli, A., Zhang, S., Xu, R., Wu, B.: AT-LSTM: an attention-based LSTM model for financial time series prediction. In: IOP Conference Series: Materials Science and Engineering, p. 52037. IOP Publishing (2019)
6. Xiang, Z., Yan, J., Demir, I.: A rainfall-runoff model with LSTM-based sequence-to-sequence learning. Water Resour. Res. **56**, e2019WR025326 (2020)
7. Zhang, Y., Li, Y., Zhang, G.: Short-term wind power forecasting approach based on Seq2Seq model using NWP data. Energy **213**, 118371 (2020)
8. Lima, L.B. de, et al..: Mathematical modeling: a conceptual approach of linear algebra as a tool for technological applications. In: Brazilian Technology Symposium, pp. 239–248. Springer (2023)
9. Neto, A.B., et al.: The BFS method in a cloud environment for analyzing distributed energy resource management systems. In: Brazilian Technology Symposium, pp. 349–362. Springer (2023)
10. Bonello, D.K., Iano, Y., Neto, U.B., de Oliveira, G.G., Vaz, G.C.: A study about automated optical inspection: inspection algorithms applied in flexible manufacturing printed circuit board cells using the mahalanobis distance method 1. In: Brazilian Technology Symposium, pp. 198–212. Springer (2023)
11. Chuma, E.L., Iano, Y., Roger, L.L.B., De Oliveira, G.G., Vaz, G.C.: Novelty sensor for detection of wear particles in oil using integrated microwave metamaterial resonators with neodymium magnets. IEEE Sens. J. **22**, 10508–10514 (2022)
12. Goldberger, A.L., et al.: Physiobank, physiotoolkit, and physionet: components of a new research resource for complex physiologic signals. Circulation **101**, e215–e220 (2000)
13. Kligfield, P., et al.: Recommendations for the standardization and interpretation of the elec-trocardiogram: part I: the electrocardiogram and its technology a scientific statement from the American heart association electrocardiography and arrhythmias committee, council on clinical cardiology; the American college of cardiology foundation; and the heart rhythm soci-ety endorsed by the International society for computerized electrocardiology. J. Am. Coll. Cardiol. **49**, 1109–1127 (2007)

Design of a Mobile App for Measuring the Ultraviolet Index in Real-Time

Ciro William Taipe Huaman[1](✉) (iD), Madelaine Huánuco Calsín[2] (iD),
Olivia Magaly Luque Vilca[1] (iD), Lucio Ticona Carrizales[1] (iD),
and Eva Genoveva Mendoza Mamani[2] (iD)

[1] Universidad Nacional de Juliaca, Juliaca, Peru
{c.taipe,oluque,l.ticonac}@unaj.edu.pe
[2] Universidad Nacional del Altiplano, Puno, Peru
emendoza@unap.edu.pe

Abstract. The objective of this research was to develop a mobile application to estimate the ultraviolet index values in real-time using a cellphone. For which an application is developed in Android Studio considering data obtained from the environment by the cellphone light sensor and adjustment equations between global solar radiation and ultraviolet index. The correlation and standard error statistics were considered for the validation of the measurements and a UV meter GD-UV06, to compare the measurements in real-time. Results were obtained for eight days during the year 2021, considering the four seasons of the year in the region of Puno. A data correlation of 0.99 was obtained between the data estimated by the cellphone with respect to the data measured by the UV meter GD-UV06 and a maximum average standard error of 0.521. Concluding that it is possible to estimate UV index values by using a cellphone and mobile App in real-time.

Keywords: Mobile app · Ultraviolet index · Light sensor · Cellphone · Solar radiation

1 Introduction

Currently, the information on ultraviolet (UV) index values is obtained from databases provided on the web, such as the one provided by the National Service of Meteorology and Hydrology of Peru SENAMHI, which are daily average values for large regions, which differ from the estimated values in real-time, due to the characteristics of the place, the type of weather that is present. The other way to obtain UV index values is in mobile applications that provide data from web databases, they are also average estimated values that differ from real-time measurements because these values are estimated for large areas and do not consider the cloudiness that may occur on-site. There are also applications that rely on the cellphone camera instead of databases, i.e., only on the information provided by the image information, which cannot estimate the UV index values, when these images are not taken in the proper way [1].

There are also applications based on the use of the cellphone light sensor, which, to estimate the value of the UV index, uses a proportionality factor with the global

Y. Iano et al. (Eds.): BTSym 2022, SIST 353, pp. 164–173, 2023.
https://doi.org/10.1007/978-3-031-31007-2_16

solar radiation, which makes the estimation of the UV index difficult [2] because this proportionality is for daily average values of the UV index, which differs from those estimated in real-time, considering that the intensity of solar radiation varies during the day. The other way to obtain it is through measuring instruments such as spectroradiometers and portable UV index measuring instruments, whose result is extremely accurate, the drawback is that citizens do not have access to the use of these instruments.

Solar UV radiation has harmful effects on the health of human beings. In the skin, UV radiation causes premature aging, allergic-type reactions, such as photokeratitis [3], and skin cancer [4]. In the eyes, it causes cataracts [5] and affects the immune system [6]. The most common effect of overexposure to solar radiation is sunburn or erythema, which appears 10–16 h after sun exposure [7]. However, the exposure is not in its full magnitude detrimental, since it is related to vitamin D [8]. Effects in nature, such as in agriculture and aquatic life, occur in plants and fish [9–11]. It is also relevant for the conservation and durability of materials such as plastics and paint [12, 13].

Cellphones, especially smartphones are developing rapidly in recent years and are becoming the central communication and computing devices in people's daily life. Along with the development of cellphones, the development of mobile applications has also gained much popularity due to their convenience [14, 15]. Buller et al. [16] state that mobile smartphones are rapidly emerging as an effective means of communication. Using mobile applications, they can access remote databases, track time and location, and integrate user input to provide personal health information.

Ananno [2] developed an application based on the ambient light sensor of the cellphone to estimate the ultraviolet index. Based on the properties of the light sensor, the deficiency found is with respect to the quadratic adjustment to estimate the ultraviolet index. Mei [1] uses the camera properties of the cellphone to estimate the ultraviolet index The error is when inadequately taking pictures. Also, Morelli [17] develops a mobile application based on satellite data to estimate the ultraviolet index, but the estimated data based on satellite data differ from the point measurements. Buller [18] developed a mobile application to inform about the dangers of overexposure to ultraviolet index levels. Brinker [19] developed a photoaging application to prevent skin cancer in order to raise awareness among the population. Salvadori [20] compared six mobile applications to measure the ultraviolet index and concluded that only one application can predict with more than 70% accuracy, and all the others are below 30%.

Oliveira [21] proposes an improved design of a Spectrophone, which consists of a module for absorption and emission of radiation, these data are processed by a mobile application that has the function of an interface. Fahrni [22] implements Sundroid, which measures ultraviolet radiation using a body unit that communicates with the cellphone to perform data processing and then notify the user about the amount of ultraviolet radiation received. Meng [23] offers a simple real-time method to measure the ultraviolet index through smartphones, which uses an ultraviolet index measuring card to measure in real-time. The analysis is performed by the mobile application, and the shortcoming of this work is that they are dependent on an external agent to the cellphone.

Therefore, the objective is to implement a mobile app to estimate in real-time the reliable values of the ultraviolet index, for which the mobile app will be developed for the estimation of ultraviolet index values in real-time and then the validation of the ultraviolet index values calculated by the mobile app with measurements of a portable instrument will be performed. This UV index level information will allow the Smartphone user to take precautions regarding prolonged exposure to solar radiation in order to contribute to the prevention of diseases caused by overexposure to prolonged solar radiation.

2   Materials and Methodology

2.1   Cellphone

It has been used Huawei P40 Lite cellphone [24] with an Android 10 system, EMUI 10 manufacturer interface and sensors Accelerometer, Compass, Gyroscope, Fingerprint reader on the side, Ambient light, and Proximity. The ambient light sensor is used in this research. The cellphone is shown in Fig. 1. For the development of the mobile App, Android Studio software is used.

Fig. 1. Huawei P40 Lite Cellphone

2.2   UV Index Measuring Instrument

UV meter GD-UV06 [25], which is used to measure the UV index in real-time and thus perform validation of the measured values by mobile App, has been used. The UV meter is shown in Fig. 2 which has a keychain presentation, which facilitates its use.

2.3   Solar Radiation Calculation by Light Sensor

The onboard light sensor of most smart devices typically uses the TRD277XX series of ambient light sensor hardware. These sensors are calibrated to measure the light intensity of surfaces for ambient luminance sources [26, 27]. The ambient light sensor can give an accurate measurement of solar irradiance in lux. The conventional unit for solar irradiance is Watts per square meter. Therefore, we convert the unit to lux using Eq. 1, since there is no direct relationship between these two units [2]. The unit of lux used in Eq. 1 is the Watt per square meter.

$$I_{lux} = K_m \int I_{watt} V(\lambda) \, d\lambda \tag{1}$$

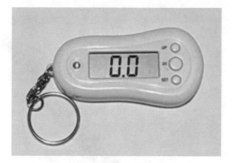

Fig. 2. GD-UV06 UV Meter

where I_{lux} is the solar irradiance in lux units, I_{watt} is the corresponding solar irradiance in Watt unit, $V(\lambda)$ is the visual response function normalized to a peak value, and K_m is the luminous efficacy, which serves as the scaling factor that carries the value and the appropriate units for $V(\lambda)$. For photonic response function, K_m is 683 lm/watt, corresponding to the peak value of $V(\lambda)$ at a wavelength of 555 nm considering sunlight as monochromatic for simplicity [2].

$$I_{watt} = \frac{I_{lux}}{K_m} \tag{2}$$

Using the appropriate values for $K_m = 120$, the solar irradiance in Watts per square meter is calculated.

According to Iqbal [28], visible light at ground level with the sun at its zenith is 44% of the global solar radiation incident on the earth's surface.

2.4 UV Index Determination

There is no simple relationship between the UV index and solar radiation intensity. However, the UV index is more widely accepted and used clinically. We modified our algorithm to give the output of solar radiation intensity in terms of UV index and from the data obtained from the weather forecast of the Puno region for 8 clear days considering the four seasons of the year shown in Fig. 3, we fit a polynomial regression model to convert solar radiation intensity in terms of UV index using the following Eq. 3.

The equation relating these two quantities is:

$$I = 0.07646 - 0.00202R + 0.0000149757R^2 \tag{3}$$

where I is the estimated UV index, R is the solar radiation, the regression model has a correlation coefficient of 0.9925.

2.5 UV Index Estimation Process Flow Chart

Figure 4 shows the flow chart of the ultraviolet index calculation process. In the process we initialize the application, access permission is given to the ambient light sensor of

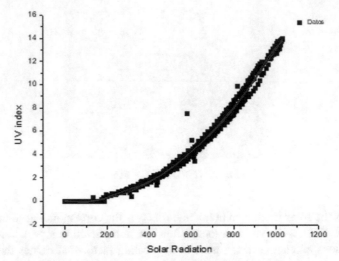

Fig. 3. Ratio of UV Index and Solar Radiation

the cellphone. Ambient light sensor process, light intensity is measured in units of lux, and conversion to Watts per square meter is done by Eq. (2). Estimation process of the ultraviolet index, the calculation of the ultraviolet index is carried out using Eq. (3). Screen printing process, the result of the estimation of the ultraviolet index is displayed on the screen of the device.

Fig. 4. UV Index Calculation Flowchart

2.6 Evaluation Statistics

The mean standard error (RMSE), the mean bias error (MBE), also called bias or deviation, the coefficient of determination (R2) and the correlation coefficient (r) were used to measure the linear relationship between the values measured by the station with respect to those obtained by the models [29–31]. They are given by the following equations:

$$RMSE = \left[\frac{\sum_{i=1}^{n} (I_{mi} - I_{si})^2}{n} \right]^{1/2} \tag{4}$$

$$MBE = \frac{\sum_{i=1}^{n} (I_{mi} - I_{si})}{n} \tag{5}$$

$$R^2 = \frac{\left[\sum_{i=1}^{n} (I - \bar{I}_{mi})(I_{si} - \bar{I}_{si}) \right]^2}{\left[\sum_{i=1}^{n} (I_{mi} - \bar{I}_{mi})^2 \right] \left[\sum_{i=1}^{n} (I_{si} - \bar{I}_{si})^2 \right]} \tag{6}$$

$$r = \sqrt{R^2} \tag{7}$$

where: I_{mi} is the data measured by UV GD-UV06, I_{si} is the data obtained by the mobile App, $\bar{I}_{mi}$ is the average of the data measured by UV GD-UV06, $\bar{I}_{si}$ is the average of the data obtained by the mobile App, and n is the total number of observations [32].

3 Experimental Results

The mobile App has been developed in Android Studio, considering the data measured by the ambient light sensor of the cellphone and Eqs. 2 and 3 to perform the calculation of the UV index, then the application displays on screen the results as shown in Fig. 5. After performing the calculations, the application displays on the screen the UV index.

To perform the measurements with the cellphone and the mobile App, the cellphone must be placed with the screen horizontally in a place where there are no obstacles that distort the sunlight.

The estimation of UV index values in real-time by means of UV meter GD-UV06 and mobile App application on a Huawei P40 cellphone, which is shown in Fig. 6, has been performed for a clear day on October 15, 2021.

Figure 7 shows the results of the UV index measurement with the cellphone and the GD-UV06 UV meter at one-hour intervals for October 15, 2021, in Puno, Peru, the date is considered because it was a clear day without clouds.

The results in Fig. 7 show that the maximum value for the cellphone is 14.8 and a value of 13.7 for the UV meter. It is observed that extreme values of UV index are found in the period from 10:00 am to 1:00 pm which requires protection to avoid exposure to sunlight during that period, consider using a shirt, sunscreen, and hat, to avoid sunburn caused by the sun's rays [18] and avoid skin burns [19].

Fig. 5. UV index measurement per application

Fig. 6. Real-time UV Index Measurement

Table 1 shows statistical results with Eqs. 4–7 for six different dates during the year 2021 for the city of Puno considering the four seasons of the year. The results show a correlation coefficient of greater than 0.99 between the data measured by the cellphone and the UV meter and a standard error of less than 0.521. These results are in agreement with Ananno et al. [2], who achieved an accuracy of 95.03% in the estimation of the UV index by cellphone using an ambient light sensor, and Mei et al. [1], who achieves an estimation of the UV index with a maximum of 3% standard deviation by cellphone using data obtained from the cellphone camera.

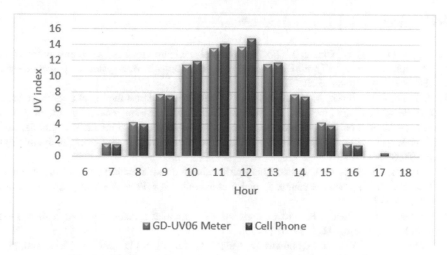

Fig. 7. Cellphone UV Index Measurement and GD-UV06 Meter

Table 1. UV Index Measurement Statistics.

Dates	RMSE	MBE	R^2	r
07/02/2021	0.343	0.038	0.997	0.998
17/04/2021	0.365	0.030	0.995	0.997
14/06/2021	0.091	0.007	0.999	0.999
16/08/2021	0.521	0.284	0.993	0.996
15/10/2021	0.417	0.136	0.996	0.998
01/12/2021	0.409	0.107	0.997	0.998

4   Conclusion

A mobile App developed in Android Studio was implemented to measure the UV index using the ambient light sensor of the Huawei P40 lite cellphone in real-time, with a maximum average standard error of 0.521 and a correlation coefficient greater than 0.99 for the city of Puno with respect to the measurement of the cellphone and the GD-UV06 UV meter, for clear days. The limitation of the application is that the cellphone has to be in a horizontal position without any obstacle that distorts the sunlight, and Eq. 3 is a Statistical adjustment that may vary according to the data considered. In future works, a theoretical model should be considered to correct the measurement of the ultraviolet index.

References

1. Mei, B., Cheng, W., Cheng, X.: Fog computing based ultraviolet radiation measurement via smartphones. In: 2015 Third IEEE Workshop on Hot Topics in Web Systems and Technologies (HotWeb), pp. 79–84. IEEE (2015)
2. Ananno, A.A., Akash, A.A., Rahman, A.: Development and prototyping of an android based mobile application to measure UV intensity in real time development and prototyping of an android based mobile application to measure UV intensity in real time. In: International Conference on Engineering Research and Education School of Applied sciences & Technology, SUST, Sylhet (2018)
3. Sordo, C., Gutiérrez, C.: Cáncer de piel y radiación solar: experiencia peruana en la prevención y detección temprana del cáncer de piel y melanoma. Rev. Peru. Med. Exp. Salud Publica. **30**, 113–117 (2013)
4. Gallagher, R.P., Lee, T.K.: Adverse effects of ultraviolet radiation: a brief review. Prog. Biophys. Mol. Biol. **92**, 119–131 (2006)
5. Lonsberry, B., Wyles, E., Goodwin, D., Casser, L., Lingel, N.: Diseases of the Cornea, Fifth edn. Elsevier Inc. (2008)
6. Norval, M.: The effect of ultraviolet radiation on human viral infections. Photochem. Photobiol. **82**, 1495–1504 (2006)
7. Torres, O., et al.: Aerosols and surface UV products from Ozone Monitoring Instrument observations: an overview. J. Geophys. Res. **112**, D24S47 (2007). https://doi.org/10.1029/2007JD008809
8. Fioletov, V.E., McArthur, L.J.B., Mathews, T.W., Marrett, L.: On the relationship between erythemal and vitamin D action spectrum weighted ultraviolet radiation. J. Photochem. Photobiol. B Biol. **95**, 9–16 (2009)
9. Sweet, M., Kirkham, N., Bendall, M., Currey, L., Bythell, J., Heupel, M.: Evidence of melanoma in wild marine fish populations. PLoS ONE **7**, e41989 (2012)
10. Kunz, B.A., Cahill, D.M., Mohr, P.G., Osmond, M.J., Vonarx, E.J.: Plant responses to UV radiation and links to pathogen resistance. Int. Rev. Cytol. **255**, 1–40 (2006)
11. Zhang, L., Allen, L.H., Jr., Vaughan, M.M., Hauser, B.A., Boote, K.J.: Solar ultraviolet radiation exclusion increases soybean internode lengths and plant height. Agric. For. Meteorol. **184**, 170–178 (2014)
12. Johnson, B.W., McIntyre, R.: Analysis of test methods for UV durability predictions of polymer coatings. Prog. Org. Coatings. **27**, 95–106 (1996)
13. Mouillet, V., Farcas, F., Besson, S.: Ageing by UV radiation of an elastomer modified bitumen. Fuel **87**, 2408–2419 (2008)
14. Seeger, C., Buchmann, A., Van Laerhoven, K.: myHealthAssistant: a phone-based body sensor network that captures the wearer's exercises throughout the day. In: 6th International ICST Conference on Body Area Networks (2012)
15. Lane, N.D., Miluzzo, E., Lu, H., Peebles, D., Choudhury, T., Campbell, A.T.: A survey of mobile phone sensing. IEEE Commun. Mag. **48**, 140–150 (2010)
16. Buller, D.B., et al.: Smartphone mobile application delivering personalized, real-time sun protection advice: a randomized clinical trial. JAMA Dermatol. **151**, 497–504 (2015)
17. Morelli, M., Masini, A., Simeone, E., Khazova, M.: Validation and in vivo assessment of an innovative satellite-based solar UV dosimeter for a mobile app dedicated to skin health. Photochem. Photobiol. Sci. **15**, 1170–1175 (2016)
18. Buller, D.B., Berwick, M., Shane, J., Kane, I., Lantz, K., Buller, M.K.: User-centered development of a smart phone mobile application delivering personalized real-time advice on sun protection. Trans. Behav. Med. **3**(3), 326–334 (2013)

19. Brinker, T.J., et al.: A skin cancer prevention facial-aging mobile app for secondary schools in Brazil: appearance-focused interventional study. JMIR mHealth uHealth. **6**, e9794 (2018)
20. Salvadori, G., Leccese, F., Lista, D., Burattini, C., Bisegna, F.: Use of smartphone apps to monitor human exposure to solar radiation: comparison between predicted and measured UV index values. Environ. Res. **183**, 109274 (2020)
21. de Oliveira, H.J.S., et al.: A handheld smartphone-controlled spectrophotometer based on hue to wavelength conversion for molecular absorption and emission measurements. Sens. Actuators B Chem. **238**, 1084–1091 (2017)
22. Fahrni, T., Kuhn, M., Sommer, P., Wattenhofer, R., Welten, S.: Sundroid: Solar radiation awareness with smartphones. In: Proceedings of the 13th international conference on Ubiquitous computing, pp. 365–374 (2011)
23. Meng, Q., Fang, L., Han, T., Huang, S., Xie, S.: A photochromic UVI indication card and the colorimetric analysis system built on smartphones. Sens. Actuators B Chem. **228**, 144–150 (2016)
24. Huawei P40 Lite – Principales características y rendimiento. https://www.movilzona.es/mov iles/huawei/huawei-p40-lite/. Last accessed 24 Aug 2022
25. Aliexpress UV detector UV detector GD-UV06. https://irecommend.ru/content/brelok-dlya-tekh-kto-ne-khochet-sgoret-na-solntse. Last accessed 24 Aug 2022
26. Chuma, E.L., Iano, Y., Roger, L.L.B., De Oliveira, G.G., Vaz, G.C.: Novelty sensor for detection of wear particles in oil using integrated microwave metamaterial resonators with neodymium magnets. IEEE Sens. J. **22**, 10508–10514 (2022)
27. Vaz, G.C., Iano, Y., de Oliveira, G.G.: IoT-from industries to houses: an overview. In: Brazilian Technology Symposium, pp. 734–741. Springer (2022). https://doi.org/10.1007/978-3-031-08545-1_73
28. Iqbal, M.: An Introduction to Solar Radiation. Elsevier (2012)
29. Blal, M., et al.: A prediction models for estimating global solar radiation and evaluation meteorological effect on solar radiation potential under several weather conditions at the surface of Adrar environment. Measurement **152**, 107348 (2020)
30. Lima, L.B. de, et al.: Mathematical modeling: a conceptual approach of linear algebra as a tool for technological applications. In: Brazilian Technology Symposium, pp. 239–248. Springer (2023). https://doi.org/10.1007/978-3-031-04435-9_22
31. Santos, P.A., et al.: Analysis of the relationship between maturity indicators using the multivariate linear regression: a case study in the Brazilian cities. In: Xu, Z., Alrabaee, S., Loyola-González, O., Zhang, X., Cahyani, N.D.W., Ab Rahman, N.H. (eds.) CSIA 2022. LNDECT, vol. 125, pp. 203–210. Springer, Cham (2022). https://doi.org/10.1007/978-3-030-97874-7_26
32. Tabari, H.: Evaluation of reference crop evapotranspiration equations in various climates. Water Resour. Manag. **24**, 2311–2337 (2010)

An Overview of P4-Based Load Balancing Mechanism in SDN

Alex Midwar Rodriguez Ruelas[1]([✉]) [iD], Jeanette Quiñones Ccorimanya[1] [iD],
and Marco Antonio Quispe Barra[2] [iD]

[1] State University of Campinas, Campinas, Brazil
alex.rodriguez@ieee.org, jeanetqc@decom.fee.unicamp.br
[2] Universidad Nacional del Altiplano, Puno, Peru
mbarra@unap.edu.pe

Abstract. The growth of network traffic due to emerging technologies, such as 5G, Cloud Computing, Big Data, Network Function Virtualization (NFV), and the Internet of Things (IoT), allows an increase in connections for users and electronic devices to data centers. As a consequence, this evolution affects the quality of service and the availability of data center resources and services for users, due to bottlenecks created when servers do not respond with suitable speed to user requests. In this paper, four load-balancing mechanisms (connection hashing, random, round-robin, and weighted round-robin) that use the P4 programming language are proposed. Currently, network infrastructures and computing systems rely heavily on load balancing to allocate resources among multiple systems. The load balancing methods herein discussed are stateful, which means that P4 switches store information locally to perform load balancing. Some methods, such as round robin and weighted round robin, use active polling to obtain network performance indicators.

Keywords: Software-Defined Networking · Programmable data plane · P4 · Load balancing

1 Introduction

The growth of network traffic due to different emerging technologies [1], in particular, 5G, Cloud Computing, Big Data, Network Function Virtualization (NFV), and the Internet of Things (IoT), is affecting the quality of services, the availability of bandwidth and is creating bottlenecks by not responding with the same speed to user requests on the servers. Then, with the continued advancement of science and technology, various solutions and technologies have been proposed to solve all these problems. Among the proposed solutions [2], we can mention the SDN (Software-Defined Network) with the OpenFlow protocol, which reduced network complexity based on the division of the control plane and data plane, getting programmable switches in the data plane and centralizing intelligence in the control plane as a software outside of the switches.

The programmable switch (devices) [2, 3] is an evolution of OpenFlow protocol, allowing engineers and researchers to develop, test, and deploy software that

© The Author(s), under exclusive license to Springer Nature Switzerland AG 2023
Y. Iano et al. (Eds.): BTSym 2022, SIST 353, pp. 174–179, 2023.
https://doi.org/10.1007/978-3-031-31007-2_17

defines the behavior of how packets are processed in much less time. The Programming Protocol-independent Packet Processors (P4) language [2] is the de facto standard for describing forwarding behavior. P4 programmable switches have eliminated the previously-reserved entrance barrier for network providers.

We can now increase the capability of networking devices because of the development of data plane programming in recent years [4]. For instance, they are able to do computations at line speed in the data plane. This computational approach enables the implementation of load-balancing mechanisms in P4 switches. Currently, network infrastructures and computer systems depend heavily on load balancing, which allocates resources among several systems. By dispersing the burden, load balancing seeks to maximize resource utilization, provides the quickest reaction time, and minimizes overloads [5]. Therefore, this paper describes four load-balancing mechanisms implemented in the P4 language (connection hash, random, round-robin, and weighted round-robin).

The remaining sections of this essay are organized as follows. Background information can be found in Sect. 2. The load-balancing study methodology and design are covered in Sect. 3. Finally, Sect. 4 presents the conclusion and future prospects.

2 Background

A language called P4 (Programming protocol-independent packet processors) [3] was created to modify how SDN switches, or forwarding devices, send packets. P4 language [6] is used in conjunction with SDN control protocols like OpenFlow to program the packet handlers independent of protocols. The number of header formats supported by OpenFlow, which has gone from 12 to approximately 50 in the previous several years, is explicitly stated in its current implementation. Despite a large rise in the number of supported protocols, some processing bottlenecks still need to be fixed due to a lack of flexibility in usage. P4 switches are flexible enough to be modified by a parser, allowing them to forward packets in accordance with any protocol. Three advantages over OpenFlow were intended for P4 [7]: Field reconfigurability, protocol independence, and target independence. A P4 switch compiler automatically converts a P4 program into the machine code that the intended hardware needs.

Figure 1 illustrates how custom headers, custom tables, and match-actions at a pipeline ingress or egress phases can specify how packets are parsed, treated, and sent back into the network (custom deparser, add, or remove headers) [8]. Multiple memory blocks [2, 7, 9], such as Ternary Content Addressable Memory (TCAM) tables and Static Random-Access Memory (SRAM) blocks, as well as Arithmetic Logic Units (ALUs), are present in a single match-action stage. The action units are the ALUs, and the memory blocks are utilized for matching. Stateful objects [1] stored in the SRAM, including registers, counters, and meters, can be used to provide additional action logic. We can create our own third-party external functions (also known as externs) that can be integrated into the data plane, describe how to count for packets and bytes, and define network meters. Packets may also be treated differently in queues and given a specific priority depending on the P4 programmable hardware.

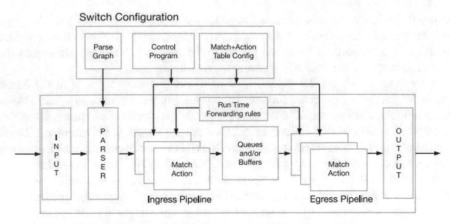

Fig. 1. Abstract forwarding structure for the P4 switch [5, 6]

3   Load Balancing Using P4 Switch

In this paper, we are going to focus on presenting codes written in P4 Language for implementing various types of load balancers for P4 switches. The load balancers simulation scenarios are composed of a P4 switch, an outward virtual server IP (Virtual IP), and 2 web servers [4, 10]. The implementation scenario can be seen in Fig. 2.

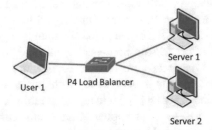

Fig. 2.   General topology of Load Balancer

3.1   Connection Hash Load Balancer for P4 Switch

The connection hash load balancer algorithm is described step by step in [4, 10]. The hash algorithm generates hash values for the n servers in the backend stack using five tuples from the IP and TCP header. The tuples are the source IP, destination IP, source port, destination port, and protocol value.

When a user sends a request to the server, the hash algorithm from five-tuple returns a value that chooses the connection to a server and answers the user's query, the pseudocode for implementing the hash algorithm in P4 language is shown in Fig. 3. Refer to [4, 10] for the whole code and a model of this load balancer.

```
action set_ecmp_select(bit<8> ecmp base, bit<8> ecmp_count) {
    hash(meta.mymetadata.ecmp_select, HashAlgorithm.crc16, (bit<14>)ecmp_base,
        {hdr.ipv4.srcAddr,hdr.ipv4.dstAddr,hdr.ipv4.protocol,hdr.tcp.srcPort,hdr.tcp.dstPort},
        (bit<28>)ecmp_count);
    meta.mymetadata.ecmp_select = meta.mymetadata.ecmp_select + 14w1;
}
```

Fig. 3. P4 code for Connection Hash Load Balancer

3.2 Random Load Balancer

An algorithm for randomized load-balancing [4, 10] uses a random number generator to distribute requests to servers randomly. In contrast to the connection hash load balancer, the random load balancer chooses the server using a random number generator. Pseudocode for implementing the random algorithm in the P4 language is shown in Fig. 4. Refer to [4, 10] for the whole code and a model of this load balancer.

```
action set_ecmp_select() {
    hash(meta.mymetadata.flowlet_map_index, HashAlgorithm.crc16, (bit<13>)0, { hdr.ipv4.srcAddr, hdr.ipv4.dstAddr, hdr.ipv4.protocol,
hdr.tcp.srcPort, hdr.tcp.dstPort }, (bit<26>)8192);
    meta.mymetadata.flowlet_select = (bit<2>)meta.random;
    flowlet_select.write((bit<32>)meta.mymetadata.flowlet_map_index, meta.mymetadata.flowlet_select);
    flowlet_select.read(meta.mymetadata.flowlet_select, (bit<32>)meta.mymetadata.flowlet_map_index);
}
```

Fig. 4. P4 Code for Random Load Balancer

3.3 Round Robin Load Balancer

For the round-robin (RR) load balancer, The "myselect" and "flowlet_select" objects are used to store the indexes for the round-robin load-balancing method [4, 10], which routes client requests to various servers based on a rotating list. Incoming requests are routed by the load balancer, which keeps a list of available servers. The first request is sent to the first server, the second to the second server, and so forth. The load balancer loops back to the beginning and restarts on the first server when it reaches the end of the list. Pseudocode for implementing the round-robin algorithm in the P4 language is shown in Fig. 5. Refer to [4, 10] for the whole code and a model of this load balancer.

```
action set_ecmp_select() {
    modify_field_with_hash_based_offset(mymetadata.flowlet_map_index, 0, my_map_hash, 8192);
    register_read(mymetadata.flowlet_select, flowlet_select, mymetadata.flowlet_map_index);
    register_read(mymetadata.myselect, myselect, 0);
    add_to_field(mymetadata.myselect, 1);
    modify_field(mymetadata.flowlet_select, mymetadata.myselect);
    add_to_field(mymetadata.flowlet_select, 1);
    register_write(myselect, 0, mymetadata.myselect);
    register_write(flowlet_select, mymetadata.flowlet_map_index, mymetadata.flowlet_select);
}
```

Fig. 5. P4 Code for Round Robin Load Balancer

3.4   Weighted Round Robin Load Balancer

This method [4, 10] distributes requests sequentially based on the weights given to each server. The weighted round-robin (WRR) load balancing algorithm is an improved variant of the round-robin method. Based on the weighted score of the servers, it distributes incoming requests. The weight may be an integer that represents the server's specifications or processing power. This enables the algorithm to take server specs into account while allocating traffic. Pseudocode for implementing the weighted round-robin algorithm in the P4 language is shown in Fig. 6. Refer to [4, 10] for the whole code and a model of this load balancer.

```
action set_ecmp_select() {
    hash(meta.mymetadata.flowlet_map_index, HashAlgorithm.crc16, (bit<13>)0, { hdr.ipv4.srcAddr, hdr.ipv4.dstAddr, hdr.ipv4.protocol,
hdr.tcp.srcPort, hdr.tcp.dstPort }, (bit<26>)8192);
    flowlet_select.read(meta.mymetadata.flowlet_select, (bit<32>)meta.mymetadata.flowlet_map_index);
    myselect.read(meta.mymetadata.myselect, (bit<32>)0);
    meta.mymetadata.myselect = meta.mymetadata.myselect + 2w1;
    meta.mymetadata.flowlet_select = (bit<3>)meta.mymetadata.myselect;
    myselect.write((bit<32>)0, (bit<2>)meta.mymetadata.myselect);
    flowlet_select.write((bit<32>)meta.mymetadata.flowlet_map_index, (bit<3>)meta.mymetadata.flowlet_select);
}
action rewrite() {
    myselect.write((bit<32>)0, 0);
}
```

Fig. 6.   P4 code for Weighted Round Robin Load Balancer

4   Conclusion

This work studies a P4 switch with four alternative load-balancing algorithms. These implementations show that a load balancer can operate without needing a controller for P4 switches thanks to the stateful objects of the P4 language, including registers, counters, and meters. The P4 load balancer has the benefit of separating data packets and health checks into separate pipelines, allowing for the integration of health checks without raising the data plane overhead.

As part of future work, we can expect network programming to evolve rapidly over the years. Therefore, contribute to the design of future computer architectures to make them more flexible and programmable.

References

1. Kaur, S., Kumar, K., Aggarwal, N.: A review on P4-programmable data planes: architecture, research efforts, and future directions. Comput. Commun. **170**, 109–129 (2021)
2. Vaz, G.C., Iano, Y., de Oliveira, G.G.: IoT - from industries to houses: an overview BT. In: Iano, Y., Saotome, O., Kemper Vásquez, G.L., Cotrim Pezzuto, C., Arthur, R., Gomes de Oliveira, G. (eds.) Proceedings of the 7th Brazilian Technology Symposium (BTSym'21), pp. 734–741. Springer International Publishing, Cham (2022)
3. Bosshart, P., et al.: P4: Programming protocol-independent packet processors. ACM SIG-COMM Comput. Commun. Rev. **44**(3), 87–95 (2014)

4. Kulkarni, M., Goswami, B., Paulose, J.: P4 based load balancing strategies for large scale software-defined networks. In: 2022 Second International Conference on Advances in Electrical, Computing, Communication and Sustainable Technologies (ICAECT), pp. 1–7. IEEE (2022)

5. Nishimura, E.H., Iano, Y., de Oliveira, G.G., Vaz, G.C.: Application and requirements of AIoT-enabled industrial control units BT. In: Iano, Y., Saotome, O., Kemper Vásquez, G.L., Cotrim Pezzuto, C., Arthur, R., Gomes de Oliveira, G. (eds.) Proceedings of the 7th Brazilian Technology Symposium (BTSym'21), pp. 724–733. Springer International Publishing, Cham (2022)

6. Hsu, S.J., Ke, C.H., Chen, Y.S., Hung, C.F., Lo, Y.W.: Design and performance evaluation of a P4 based load balancer. In: 2019 8th International Conference on Innovation, Communication and Engineering (ICICE), pp. 149–152. IEEE (2019)

7. AlSabeh, A., Khoury, J., Kfoury, E., Crichigno, J., Bou-Harb, E.: A survey on security applications of P4 programmable switches and a STRIDE-based vulnerability assessment. Comput. Netw. **207**, 108800 (2022)

8. Thiagarajan, Y., et al.: Design and fabrication of human-powered vehicle - a measure for healthy living BT. In: Iano, Y., Saotome, O., Kemper Vásquez, G.L., Cotrim Pezzuto, C., Arthur, R., Gomes de Oliveira, G, (eds,) Proceedings of the 7th Brazilian Technology Symposium (BTSym'21), pp. 1–15. Springer International Publishing, Cham (2023)

9. Michel, O., Bifulco, R., Retvari, G., Schmid, S.: The programmable data plane: abstractions, architectures, algorithms, and applications. ACM Comput. Surv. (CSUR) **54**(4), 1–36 (2021)

10. Ke, C.H., Hsu, S.J.: Load balancing using P4 in software-defined networks. J. Internet Technol. **21**(6), 1671–1679 (2020)

Construction of a Low-Cost Solar Air Collector Prototype for Heating Andean Houses

Grover Marín Mamani[1](✉) ⓘ, Esteban Marín Paucara[1](✉) ⓘ,
José Alberto Llanos Condori[1](✉) ⓘ, Vitaliano Enríquez Mamani[2](✉) ⓘ,
and Néstor Bolívar Espinoza[2](✉) ⓘ

[1] Universidad Nacional del Altiplano, Puno, Peru
{gmarin,emarin,jllanos}@unap.edu.pe
[2] Universidad Nacional de Juliaca, Juliaca, Peru
{v.enriquezm,nbolivar}@unaj.edu.pe

Abstract. Solar energy is crucial to reduce the carbon footprint and combat the consequences of climate change in the ecosystems of the Andes, and the cold is a product of this phenomenon, the buildings are not conditioned to combat this effect by its technological and constructive precariousness. The objective was to develop a low-cost solar air collector prototype to increase the interior temperature of rural buildings in the high Andean climates of the Peruvian Andes. Two prototypes of similar structural characteristics (three chambers) were built, the solar air collector for heating 1 (SAHC1) adopted as thermal storage the chillihua type ichu located in its chamber 1, the solar air collector for heating 2 (SAHC2) without thermal storage. The final cost of each prototype is $28.22, in addition, the thermal behavior of both prototypes has been compared, which shows no significant differences, however, the temperature of SAHC1 is 46.87 ± 4.21 °C and SAHC2 is 44.81 ± 2.80 °C in the morning, in the afternoon the temperature of SAHC1 is 53.09 ± 4.06 °C and 46.50 ± 2.07 °C in SAHC2. The horizontal and vertical hot air flow performance is the same in both collectors.

Keywords: Ichu · Passive heating · Solar collector · Solar energy

1 Introduction

Climate change issues have become significant challenges for sustainable growth [1]. The energy sector is key in climate change mitigation and emission reduction [2, 3]. Solar energy has a greater potential than all other renewable energy sources [4–7]. Efficient utilization of solar energy is a significant challenge as the global energy demand is increasing dramatically [8–10]. Much of the energy is for indoor space heating in winter [11, 12]. Applications such as indoor space heating in buildings are frequent uses of solar energy [13]. Solar heating systems can be passive or active depending on how they can store excess energy [4, 13, 14]. Solar air collectors as a passive technology are widely used with different variations in their structure and guarantee constant hot

© The Author(s), under exclusive license to Springer Nature Switzerland AG 2023
Y. Iano et al. (Eds.): BTSym 2022, SIST 353, pp. 180–188, 2023.
https://doi.org/10.1007/978-3-031-31007-2_18

ait flow rates [15], besides, being low-cost solar thermal collectors that represent one of the most used technologies for heat production from renewable sources [16]. The solar collector collects solar radiation, transferring solar energy to a fluid or gas, and transforming it into thermal energy [17, 18].

Solar radiation in the high Andean regions of the Andes is the highest on Earth [19]. 84.64% of the territory of the Puno region is located in the Peruvian Andes, at an altitude ranging from 3800 m.a.s.l. to more than 4800 m.a.s.l. [20]. The ambient temperature is 6 °C in the high Andean zone and below 0 °C in the snowy zone, and the relative humidity ranges from 30% to 50%, with average annual sunshine hours of 8 to 10 h [21]. Due to climate change in this region, the National Meteorological and Hydrological Service of Peru has reported that in areas above 2500 m.a.s.l., the nighttime temperature is 0 °C and in areas above 4000 m.a.s.l. and above, the temperature ranges from 0 °C to −20 °C [22]. In addition, according to the Peruvian Institute of Economics, the Puno region is the poorest in Peru, with a total poverty rate of 42.6% [23]. These homes are precarious and lack basic services, with only one room and a kitchen [24, 25], and these conditions predispose their users to respiratory diseases in children and the elderly. The precarious economic and living conditions of rural housing users call for low-cost solar heating systems that contribute to the Peruvian government's efforts to reduce the high impact of the cold in high Andean areas [26].

2   Collector Design

Initially, the design criteria were determined. The first criterion was materials (abundant in the region and easy to obtain), where wood, plywood, expanded polystyrene, and low-density polyethylene sheets were chosen. The second criterion was workability (easy construction, low cost of materials and labor). The third criterion is mobility (dismountable and lightweight). The average volume of a rural room is 10 m^3, for the design we chose an outlet diameter of 1.5″ and a velocity of 1 m/s to obtain an airflow of 4,104 m3/h, with a two-hour renovation and 10% error. To calculate the real volume of the solar air heating collectors (SAHC), it is necessary to anchor a vertex at the origin of the three-dimensional rectangular coordinate system, the SAHC cover is also contained in the plane as Eq. 1, and the base, which is made up of the insulating material, contained between the plane as Eq. 2, the volume of the solar collector is V_{inside}, the volume of energy stored in the three sections V1, V2, and V3 is 0.661 m^3.

$$z = f_1(x, y) = 0.3 \, \text{m} \tag{1}$$

$$z = f_2(x, y) = 0.0414 \, \text{m} \tag{2}$$

The construction is shown in Fig. 1, both SAHC prototypes are the same to determine the operation and their thermal performance.

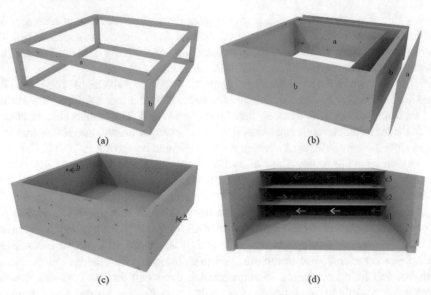

Fig. 1. Modular construction of a solar air heating collector.

Figure 1a shows the structure in the shape of a parallelepiped with a square base 1.00 m long and wide, with a height of 0.30 m, three 1.5″ wooden strips were used for $3.87, and the horizontal bars (a) were joined to the vertical bars (b) using nail-reinforced sockets for $0.64. In Fig. 1b, the structure was reinforced with sides with two sheets of plywood for $12.37 (a) and a 1.5″ expanded polystyrene sheet as a core for $3.09 (b), the base has the same composition with a black paint coating for $2.58, with a thickness of 0.0414 m. In Fig. 1c, the airflow circulation is by gravity, the air inlet is through the circular perforation (a) of 1.5″ Ø, and the outlet is 1″ Ø (b). In Fig. 1d, the main chamber has been divided into three (thermal storage c1, heater c2, and air cushion c3) with three low-density polyethylene sheets of 2 mm, which have perforations of 2″ Ø (b and c) with a value of $3.09, the arrows show the operation and distribution of air between the chambers, the module construction has a cost of $28.22. The characteristics of the modules built for the experimentation are coded in SAHC1 and SAHC2, the difference between the modules is in the chamber 1 (c1) for SAHC1 with thermal storage of ichu (*Stipa ichu*), which has thermal properties of millinery used in many Latin American cultures [27], and SAHC2 without thermal storage with black paint on the bottom of the chamber. Temperature, humidity, and flow rate values were monitored. DTH22 sensors located in the center of gravity of the chambers c1, c2, and c3 were used as seen in Fig. 2a, connected to an Arduino mega 2560 [28], UNI-T UT363BT anemometer [29], located in (a) and (d) as seen in Fig. 2b, was used to measure the inlet and outlet flow velocity of SAHC1 and 2.

For the monitoring of the indicators of interest, the SAHC1 and SAHC2 were exposed to real conditions (natural environment) for the entire month of June 2021 reported by the National Meteorology and Hydrology Service from Peru, in the facilities of the National University of Juliaca located at an altitude of 3830 m.a.s.l. The collection period is

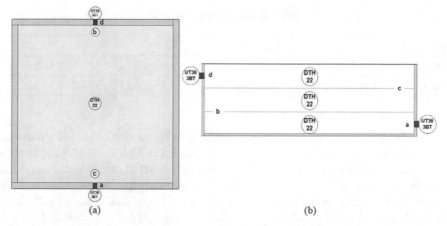

Fig. 2. Location of sensors and measuring instruments, A plan view, and B sectional view.

30 min per indicator, registering 1440 for each sensor. For the analysis the data have been divided into four timeframes; morning (p1) groups data from 6:00 to 12:00 h, afternoon (p2) from 12:00 to 19:00 h, night (p3) from 19:00 to 00:00 h and dawn (p4) from 00:00 to 6:00 h.

The analysis of the data obtained for SAHC1 (with ichu heat store, chilihua type, the cannulas arranged in the direction of airflow with a weight of 4 kg) and SAHC2 (without heat store, with the base painted black) is descriptive for the grouping p1, p2, p3, and p4, then the data were re-grouped by the hours of sun exposure which was called heating (ca) composed by p1 + p2 and by cooling (en) composed by p3 + p4, estimating the measures of central tendency of the temperature and humidity of c1, c2, and c3 (chambers) of both prototypes. In addition, the descriptive of the inlet and outlet airflow velocities were estimated for the calculation of the flow rate and the hot air renewal time. The horizontal and vertical thermal behavior of chambers c1, c2, and c3 of the prototypes was also modeled. The comparison of means for temperature and humidity of the heating (ca) and cooling (en) data does not meet the normality assumption; therefore, the non-parametric Mann Witney U test was chosen.

3 Experimental Results

The descriptive analysis shows that the SAHC1 prototype has better thermal performance on p1 (morning), p2 (afternoon), and p4 (early morning) as shown in Table 1. The average mean difference is 3.14 °C, this is due to the presence of the chillihua type ichu in c1 (chamber 1, thermal storage), in SAHC1 the thermal difference in p2 (afternoon) is higher than SAHC2 by 6.59 °C, and the ichu by its structure contains non-fibrous and tubular scabrous sheaths, which allows maintaining the temperature concentrated for a longer time.

Table 1. Temperature behavior

Prototype	p1	p2	p3	p4
SAHC1	46.87 ± 4.21	53.09 ± 4.06	2.90 ± 0.18	−1.99 ± 0.20
SAHC2	44.81 ± 2 .80	46.50 ± 2.07	3.23 ± 0.13	−2.77 ± 0.12

The Peruvian National Building Regulations, in its standard EM. 110 norm indicates that the variables of thermal comfort for housing in high Andean zones is 18 °C temperature and 50% relative humidity, the prototype SAHC1, and SAHC2 exceed the normative value by 28.87 °C and 26.81 °C in the morning (p1, heating period), in the afternoon (p2, storage period) SAHC1 exceeds by 35.09 °C and SAHC2 by 28.50 °C, this result is particular SAHC1 has a difference in favor of 6.59 °C. This is due to the ichu chillihua type.

Table 2. Humidity behavior

Prototype	p1	p2	p3	p4
SAHC1	13.07 ± 1.15	11.31 ± 1.16	14.94 ± 1.80	14.42 ± 1.59
SAHC2	15.07 ± 0.38	12.46 ± 0.24	8.50 ± 0.008	17.787 ± 0.20

However, humidity has a different behavior as the SAHC2 prototype has a better mean difference at p1 (morning), p2 (afternoon), and p4 (early morning) as seen in Table 2. The average difference is 2.17%.

The temperature analysis of SAHC1 and SAHC2 shows that in (p3) evening and (p4) early morning, the temperature is below the 18 °C normative value of environmental comfort in Peru, due to the extreme environmental conditions of the −10 °C outdoor environment zone, in this timeframe the performance of both prototypes shows deficiencies due to their solar dependence. However, the performance in p1 (morning) and p2 (afternoon) is good, as shown in Fig. 3.

Figure 3 shows the results of the thermal behavior of SAHC2 on p1, showing symmetrical quartiles, in this case, the temperature has homogeneous heating compared to SAHC1. In p2 SAHC1 has more symmetrical quartiles, and the temperature is preserved longer because of the chilligua type ichu compared to SAHC2. In addition, in the period of solar radiation (p1 and p2) SAHC2 has a higher median than SAHC1, which also has a higher dispersion. In both prototypes, it can be seen that the normative value is in the second quartile below the median.

The horizontal performance in hours of solar radiation in the morning and afternoon (p1 and p2) of the interior of the storage, heating, and air cushion chambers (c1, c2, and c3) of both prototypes (SAHC1 and SAHC2) shows an equal performance and no significant difference is shown. The inlet of the cold air is through (a) registering an average flow velocity of 0.9 m/s with an inlet temperature of 10 °C, the heating flow goes in a horizontal direction to (b) inlet of c2 (heating chamber) in this path c1 takes

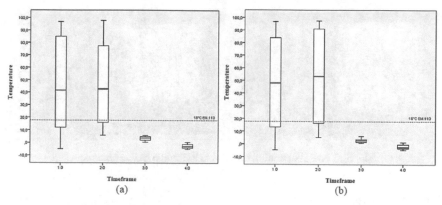

Fig. 3. Thermal behavior of SAHC1 (A) and SAHC2 (B).

approximately 25 min to renew its volume dispersing throughout the chamber with reaching a temperature of 44.32 °C for SAHC1 and 42.44 °C for SAHC2 at the opening of c2, as shown in Fig. 4a. In c2 the flow direction is reversed with direction from (b) to (c) which is the opening of c3, the volume renewal of this chamber is approximately 6 min reaching temperatures of 50.10 °C for SAHC1 and 45.77 °C in SAHC2, as seen in Fig. 4h. In the same way in c3, the flow direction is from (c) to (d) the hot air outlet of both collectors has an average velocity of 1 m/s and temperature of 55 °C for SAHC1 and 49 °C in SAHC2, as shown in Fig. 4c, the heating of the collector is gradual per chamber guaranteeing high outlet temperatures in the timeframe of solar radiation.

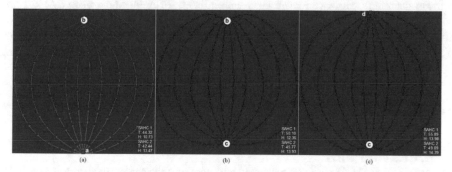

Fig. 4. Horizontal operation of SAHC1 and SAHC2 chambers.

The vertical operation of both collectors is by gravity, the cold air entering the first chamber with a flow rate of 0. 027 m³/min, exits to c2 with an increased flow rate due to the opening between c1 and c2 which has a larger diameter than the collector inlet, in addition, the air inside c1 is progressively heated in a maximum time of 24 min and 26 s, in c2 the hot air flow rate is 109 m³/min with a renewal time of 6 min and 6 s, in c3 the hot air flow rate is 0.030 m³/min and a renewal time of 22 min, as seen in Fig. 5. Both solar collectors are heated in the same way, however, SAHC1 shows a better capture of solar radiation.

Fig. 5. Vertical operation of the SAHC1 and SAHC2 chambers.

4 Conclusion

The construction of the prototypes required 6 h of work, which is a constructive advantage over other similar technologies, the SAHC1 has a weight of 24 kg and the SAHC2 of 21 kg, in addition, the structure is removable in small pieces, it is also easy to move, repair and maintain, it has also shown great resistance to weathering by adding varnish in the finish. The thermal performance of the SAHC1 and SAHC2 prototypes in the morning and afternoon is very good, ensuring a temperature exchange above 18 °C until 19:00 h; however, at night and in the early morning hours, the temperature drops below the EM 110 standard. The SAHC1 has shown a better performance than the SAHC2, due to the chillihua type ichu installed in the thermal storage chamber. The operation of the three chambers (thermal storage, heater, and airbag) in the design helps to increase the internal flow velocity, ensuring high outlet temperatures due to the pressure built up in these chambers. However, there are no significant differences between SAHC1 and SAHC2. Therefore, we will continue to study the thermal storage properties of woody natural resources and face-change materials existing in the Peruvian Andes, in addition to adapting technological systems that allow extending the period of operation during the cold and snowy seasons.

References

1. Vickers, N.J.: Animal communication: when i'm calling you, will you answer too? Curr. Biol. **27**, R713–R715 (2017)
2. Ornetti, P., et al.: Clinical effectiveness and safety of a distraction-rotation knee brace for medial knee osteoarthritis. Ann. Phys. Rehabil. Med. **58**, 126–131 (2015)
3. Barbosa, J., Dias, L.P., Simoes, S.G., Seixas, J.: When is the sun going to shine for the Brazilian energy sector? a story of how modelling affects solar electricity. Renew. Energy. **162**, 1684–1702 (2020)
4. Murugan, M., et al.: An overview on energy and exergy analysis of solar thermal collectors with passive performance enhancers. Alexandria Eng. J. **61**, 8123–8147 (2022)
5. Kumar, N., Gupta, S.K.: Progress and application of phase change material in solar thermal energy: an overview. Mater. Today Proc. **44**, 271–281 (2021)
6. Singh, D.B., Mahajan, A., Devli, D., Bharti, K., Kandari, S., Mittal, G.: A mini review on solar energy based pumping system for irrigation. Mater. Today Proc. **43**, 417–425 (2021)

7. da Silva Neto, D.T., et al.: Proposal MPPT algorithm using the kalman filter. In: Iano, Y., et al. (eds.) Proceedings of the 7th Brazilian Technology Symposium (BTSym'21): Emerging Trends in Systems Engineering Mathematics and Physical Sciences, Volume 2, pp. 750–759. Springer International Publishing, Cham (2022). https://doi.org/10.1007/978-3-031-08545-1_75

8. Roy, J.S., Morency, S., Dugas, G., Messaddeq, Y.: Development of an extremely concentrated solar energy delivery system using silica optical fiber bundle for deployment of solar energy: daylighting to photocatalytic wastewater treatment. Sol. Energy. **214**, 93–100 (2021)

9. Schuetz, P., et al.: Automated modelling of residential buildings and heating systems based on smart grid monitoring data. Energy Build. **229**, 110453 (2020)

10. Ooi, K.B., Noguchi, M., Chau, H.W.: Sustainable heating or cooling and ventilation of affordable zero-energy housing. Procedia Eng. **205**, 1294–1301 (2017)

11. Oñate, W., Catota, A., Simbaña, J., Caiza, G.: Implementation of a control system in a dual axis cylindrical-parabolic solar tracking system. In: Iano, Y., Saotome, O., Kemper, G., de Seixas, A.C.M., de Oliveira, G.G. (eds.) BTSym 2020. SIST, vol. 233, pp. 957–967. Springer, Cham (2021). https://doi.org/10.1007/978-3-030-75680-2_104

12. Dong, J., Li, Y., Zhang, W., Zhang, L., Lin, Y.: Impact of residential building heating on natural gas consumption in the south of China: taking Wuhan city as example. Energy Built Environ. **1**, 376–384 (2020)

13. Qiu, G., Yu, S., Cai, W.: A novel heating strategy and its optimization of a solar heating system for a commercial building in term of economy. Energy **221**, 119773 (2021)

14. Bravo Hidalgo, D.: A survey of materials for solar thermal energy storage. Ingeniería. **23**, 144–165 (2018)

15. Shemelin, V., Matuska, T.: Unglazed solar thermal collector for building facades. Energy Rep. **8**, 605–617 (2022)

16. Koulibaly, A., González, J.J.: Modelling of a solar collector for air heating. Ingeniería Energética **36**(3), 292–302 (2015). http://scielo.sld.cu/scielo.php?script=sci_arttext&pid=S1815-59012015000300007&lng=es&tlng=en

17. Ricci, M., Bocci, E., Michelangeli, E., Micangeli, A., Villarini, M., Naso, V.: Experimental tests of solar collectors prototypes systems. Energy Procedia **82**, 744–751 (2015)

18. Siegle, A.R., Iano, Y., de Oliveira, G.G., Vaz, G.C.: Proposal of mathematical models for a continuous flow electric heater. In: Brazilian Technology Symposium, pp. 213–228. Springer (2023)

19. Chand, S., Chand, P., Ghritlahre, H.K.: Thermal performance enhancement of solar air heater using louvered fins collector. Sol. Energy. **239**, 10–24 (2022)

20. Vargo, L.J., Galewsky, J., Rupper, S., Ward, D.J.: Sensitivity of glaciation in the arid subtropical Andes to changes in temperature, precipitation, and solar radiation. Glob. Planet. Change. **163**, 86–96 (2018)

21. Perú – inei:: Puno: Resultados Definitivos de los Censos Nacionales 2017. https://www.inei.gob.pe/media/MenuRecursivo/publicaciones_digitales/Est/Lib1563/. Accessed: 18 Nov 2022

22. Em.110 Confort Térmico y lumínico con Eficiencia Energética. https://www.gob.pe/institucion/munisantamariadelmar/informes-publicaciones/2619729-em-110-confort-termico-y-luminico-con-eficiencia-energetica. Accessed: 18 Nov 2022

23. Datos/Datos Hidrometeorológicos. https://www.senamhi.gob.pe/?&p=estaciones. Accessed: 18 Nov 2022

24. Ipe: Evolución de la Pobreza Regional 2004–2021: Tablero interactivo: IPE. https://www.ipe.org.pe/portal/evolucion-de-la-pobreza-regional-2004-2021/ (2022). Accessed: 18 Nov 2022

25. Chavarria, D., Ramos, R., Raymundo, C.: Development of a hybrid heating system based on geothermal–photovoltaic energy to reduce the impact of frosts on inhabitants of rural areas in the ring of fire, southern Peru. In: Iano, Y., Arthur, R., Saotome, O., Estrela, V.V., Loschi, H.J. (eds.) BTSym 2018. SIST, vol. 140, pp. 131–139. Springer, Cham (2019). https://doi.org/10.1007/978-3-030-16053-1_12

26. Santos, P.A., et al.: Analysis of the relationship between maturity indicators using the multivariate linear regression: a case study in the Brazilian cities. In: Xu, Z., Alrabaee, S., Loyola-González, O., Zhang, X., Cahyani, N.D.W., Ab Rahman, N.H. (eds.) CSIA 2022. LNDECT, vol. 125, pp. 203–210. Springer, Cham (2022). https://doi.org/10.1007/978-3-030-97874-7_26

27. Piñas, J.M., Lira, L., Horn, M., Solis, J.L., Gómez, M.M.: Influence of Stipa ichu on the thermal and mechanical properties of adobe as a biocomposite material. J. Phys.: Conf. Series **1433**, 12003 (2020)

28. Mamani, G.M., Vilca, R.A.L., Carreon, C.A.H., Calderón, R.A.B.: Construcción de termohigrómetro prototipo con base datalogger en placa Arduino para interior de edificaciones. Rev. Campus. **22**, 171–178 (2018)

29. Zhang, Y., et al.: An ultra-durable windmill-like hybrid nanogenerator for steady and efficient harvesting of low-speed wind energy. Nano-Micro Lett. **12**, 1–11 (2020)

Automatic Extraction of Metadata Based on Natural Language Processing for Research Documents in Institutional Repositories

Alain Paul Herrera-Urtiaga[1,2](✉) [ID], Fred Torres-Cruz[1,2] [ID],
Charles Ignacio Mendoza-Mollocondo[1] [ID], Juan-Reynaldo Paredes-Quispe[1] [ID],
and Edwin Wilber Chambi-Mamani[2] [ID]

[1] Computer Science Research Institute, Universidad Nacional del Altiplano de Puno, Puno, Peru
aherrera@unap.edu.pe
[2] Electronic Engineering, Universidad Nacional del Altiplano de Puno, Puno, Peru

Abstract. The Institutional Repositories allow to organize, preserve, and disseminate scientific and academic production of an institution. Metadata are data about other data, which help identify, recover, and preserve the information of the research documents produced by the Universidad Nacional del Altiplano. The extraction of metadata is a time-consuming process in the treatment of research documents, and there may be a risk of introducing erroneous information. The purpose of this research is to optimize the extraction of metadata on 380 research documents, which is a necessary process for their preservation, Therefore, an algorithm was developed to allow the automatic extraction of metadata using natural language processing (NLP) techniques for Institutional Repositories (E-MeRI), to which the linear algorithmic complexity $O(n)$ was determined, and at the same time, the level of accuracy was determined between 96% and 99% of correct results based on the metrics Precision and Recall. Finally (E-MeRI) proved to be efficient compared to other extractor tools with 50 test documents.

Keywords: Algorithms · Automatic extraction · Metadata · Natural language processing · Tool

1 Introduction

The availability of large, accessible, and diverse electronic document repositories on the web is increasing rapidly. Much of this information is in the form of unstructured text, which makes it difficult to consult the information, but there are now more structured ways of accessing information. In this sense, four fundamental concepts emerge: learning objects, metadata, standards, and institutional repositories. The uses of metadata have become popular due to the emergence of digital resources and electronic information resources. Institutional repositories are electronic archives of the scientific output of an institution, which are stored in a digital format, where they are searchable and retrievable

Y. Iano et al. (Eds.): BTSym 2022, SIST 353, pp. 189–197, 2023.
https://doi.org/10.1007/978-3-031-31007-2_19

to disseminate the scholarly and scientific resources of an institution [1]. Repositories are means that allow us to import, identify, store, preserve, retrieve, and export a set of digital objects, usually from a web page [2]. Institutional Repositories aim to store all the scientific and academic production, for which it is necessary the process of metadata extraction, which is responsible for obtaining the attributes that identify each document [3]. This is a process that is normally performed manually by the personnel in charge of extracting the metadata, which requires time and may take some time depending on the number of research documents from which the metadata will be extracted.

Metadata extraction is responsible for obtaining the attributes or tags that identify each research document [4]. This metadata allows the retrieval, search, authentication, and evaluation of a resource within an institutional repository. The reliable information of these metadata is crucial for the organization of data since this process is necessary within an Institutional Repository, unfortunately, there are not many tools that allow the extraction of reliable and quality metadata about research documents such as thesis, monographs, and academic papers, among others. The main objective of this work is to perform automatic metadata extraction based on natural language processing (NLP) on research documents that are stored in Institutional Repositories, for which (E-MeRI) has been implemented.

2   Background

2.1   Institutional Repositories in Peru

The Law that regulates the National Digital Repository of Science, Technology, and Innovation of open access, approved in March 2013, makes it mandatory in our country to publish the results of all scientific research financed with public funds, which must be made available in open access digital repositories [5]. The objective of the ALICIA National Repository is to form an interoperable network of institutional repositories, based on the establishment of policies, standards, and protocols for the exchange of information common to all members of the Network [6].

2.2   Metadata

The first meaning of the word metadata, which is currently the most frequent, was "data about data". According to [7], metadata is defined as follows: Metadata (pronounced the same way) is data that describes other data, it is information that describes the content of a file or object. Metadata is often used to index information in a database to easily locate a document, file, or object.

2.3   Metadata Extraction

Metadata extraction has become an open and difficult-to-solve problem, due to the variety of resource types, the different file formats used, and the lack or diversity of file structure. This problem has been partially addressed in [8], where some systems dedicated to the automatic extraction of educational metadata from learning objects were analyzed, which although relevant, are not implemented or are not available as free tools. This, added to the standardization of metadata and the rise of institutional repositories and open access to knowledge that was glimpsed and described above, results in the necessary foundation to understand the real importance of the development of new algorithms for automatic extraction in institutional repositories.

KEA Automatic Keyphrase Extraction. KEA [9] is the JAVA implementation of the KEA algorithm developed in [10], where it is presented the tool which automatically extracts key phrases from the full text about the document to be analyzed, the set of all selected phrases in a document in which they are identified by making use of rudimentary lexical processing.

ParsCit. It is an open-source tool that allows the analysis of bibliographic references. ParsCit performs the analysis by examining each reference and identifying each field that composes it. It consists of two tasks for the extraction of references, preprocessing and postprocessing [11].

Mr. Dlib. It is a digital library that facilitates access to a large number of full-text articles and their metadata in XML and JSON format through a RESTful web service [12]. In its beta stage of development, its functionalities are used by third parties and allow the extraction of Title and Authors [13].

2.4 Natural Language Processing

Natural language is the language that humans use to communicate with each other. Natural Language Processing (NLP) deals with the computational processing of natural language and its application to solve engineering problems. At the same time, it involves a transformation to a formal representation, manipulates this representation, and finally, if necessary, converts the results back to natural language [14–16].

2.5 Regular Expressions

A regular expression serves as a descriptor of a language. Formally, the goal of regular expressions is to represent all possible languages defined over an alphabet, based on a set of primitive languages, and composition operators [17]. Regular expressions make it possible to display regular languages, both because of their ability to specify them by means of a reduced number of operators and because of their practical applications in the construction of lexical analyzers. Every finite language is regular, and by Kleene's theorem, every regular language can be represented by finite-state automata. In formal language theory, according to the hierarchy of [18], it is classified as type 3 grammars, the subset with the lowest expressivity.

In Python, the regular expression operation is included in the re.py module, where one can create a string for matching with combinations of letters of the alphabet, digits, or special symbols representing sets. In conclusion, the search is performed with the re.search or re.match methods on a defined expression, where you can tag and sort matched text fragments using the directive [19].

3 Materials and Methods

The methodology for this work is based on the development of an algorithm for the automatic extraction of metadata (E-MeRI), on a population that was formed by all the research documents published in the Institutional Repository of the Universidad Nacional del Altiplano in the year 2021. The sample design used in the research work was non-probabilistic, using convenience sampling. This type of sampling is characterized by obtaining accessible representative samples, therefore, it was considered as a sample of the research documents that were published in the undergraduate and graduate collections in the Institutional Repository during the period of July and December 2021, this in order to obtain better automatic learning, resulting in 380 documents for E-MeRI, and 50 for the comparison of algorithms. The research design used is the experimental design and the level is quasi-experimental with pre-test and post-test with a single group. The Python programming language was used to develop the algorithm, since it has libraries that allow the linguistic analysis of documents and natural language processing. The platform used for text analysis was the Natural Language Toolkit (NLTK). The algorithm was started by loading the research document from which the meta-data would be extracted, which was received in PDF format. To perform the analysis of the document, it must be in text format, so it was converted from PDF to text using the PyPDF2 library, which allows the management of PDFs such as extracting information from a document, dividing documents by pages, merging several documents into a single one, among other actions. After obtaining the text, we proceeded with the cleaning, which means converting the raw text into a list of words and saving it again, for which the document was divided by blank spaces, new lines, tabs, and line breaks. Then punctuation was removed from each word by using regular expressions to select punctuation characters with a constant named string.punctuation and replacing them with nothing.

For better processing of the text, each word in the document was converted from uppercase to lowercase. Once the text was normalized, NLTK was used to split strings into tokens with the word_tokenize function. With the document tokenized, text processing was made easier by filtering the tokens of interest for document metadata extraction. For the implementation of the development of the automatic metadata extraction algorithm, the process of sending research documents to the repository was restructured (see Fig. 1).

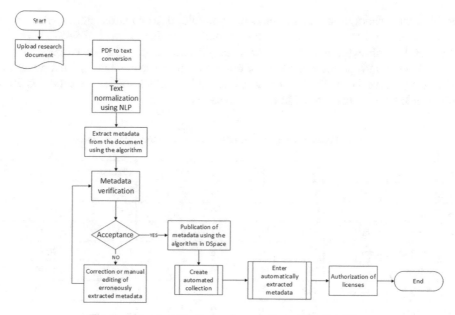

Fig. 1. Flowchart for the implementation of the algorithm

4 Results

The results of this work are presented below. To determine the level of accuracy of the algorithm, the Precision and Recall metrics [20] shown in Eqs. 1 and 2 were used on 380 research documents in PDF format, which were processed by the algorithm

$$Precision = \frac{TP}{TP + FP} \qquad (1)$$

$$Recall = \frac{TP}{TP + FN} \qquad (2)$$

The metrics used are classified into four categories: TP (true positive), which represents the so-called true positive values, i.e. those values that were identified by the algorithm as the corresponding metadata, and in fact are; TN (true negative), which are the metadata that could not be extracted and do not really appear in the document either; FP (false positive), which represents the so-called false positive values, i.e. they are the values identified by the algorithm as metadata, but they are not the correct ones; finally, FN (false negative), which represents the so-called false negative values, i.e. those values that the algorithm did not identify as the corresponding metadata, but should be considered correct.

Table 1 shows the results of the precision and coverage of each of the metadata extracted from the 380 documents processed, showing the performance of the algorithm: it achieved a precision of 0.99 for the summary, which means that it obtained 99% of correct results in the extraction of the metadata. A precision of 0.98 for titles, type of document to be published, institution granting the academic degree (faculties), professional school, name of master's or doctorate, denomination, and level of education, which indicates that the extracted metadata obtained a level of 98% of correct matches. Regarding the extraction of the metadata author and field of study, they reached a precision of 0.97, so there is a 97% of correct coincidences. Finally, with a precision of 0.96 for the metadata publication date and subject, which implies that there is 96% of correct results in the extraction of both metadata.

Table 1. Precision and Recall results for each metadata extracted

Metadata	TP	TN	FP	FN	Precision	Recall
Title	368	0	9	3	0.98	0.99
Author	359	0	10	11	0.97	0.97
Date of publication	349	10	12	9	0.96	0.97
Type of publication	366	0	8	6	0.98	0.98
Publisher	368	0	9	3	0.98	0.99
Thesis degree grantor	372	0	6	2	0.98	0.99
Thesis degree name	366	0	7	7	0.98	0.98
Level of education	368	0	6	6	0.98	0.98
Field of study	342	18	10	10	0.97	0.97
Subject	338	16	13	13	0.96	0.96
Abstract	370	0	5	5	0.99	0.99

The analysis of the complexity of the algorithm on the process of automatic extraction of metadata using the Big O notation was performed. For the automatic extraction of metadata, a main module is used by means of a function that receives as parameters the documents in PDF format. It starts with the reading of the document, where natural language processing is used to convert the text into a list of words that receive a process in order to normalize the text of the document, these lines of code are executed only once, which is equivalent to $O(1)$. Then the normalized text is sent to the different functions that aim to extract the different metadata from the document, each of these functions contains four cycles to iterate on the tokens within the normalized text, which will perform a matching, so the lines of code within the functions iterate n times, which is equivalent to $O(n)$, for each of the functions as shown in Fig. 2.

By summing all the calculations, simplifying them, and obtaining the most representative value, it is determined that the complexity of the algorithm for the automatic extraction of metadata from research documents is linear $O(n)$. Therefore, the algorithm execution time will depend on the number of tokens obtained from the normalized text by natural language processing of each document, as shown in Eq. 3.

$$O(G) = 8 + 9(O(n)) \tag{3}$$

```
def extractMetadata(document):
  mydocument=open(document,mode="rb")            #(1)
  converttotext=pdftotext.PDF(mydocument)     #(1)
  # split words by space
  words = converttotext.split()                  #(1)
  #prepare regex for character filtering
  re_punc = re.compile('[%s]' % re.escape(string.punctuation))  #(1)
  #convert to lowercase
  words = [word.lower() for word in words]  #(1)
  #remove punctuation from each word
  stripped = [re_punc.sub('', w) for w in words]   #(1)
  text=stripped       #(1)
  tokens=nltk.word_tokenize(text) #(1)
  textDocument=nltk.Text(tokens)  #(1)
  #Metadata to extract
  _metadataName=getFirstLastName(textDocument)   #O(n)
  _metadataTitle=getTitle(textDocument)    #O(n)
  _metadataDegreeName=getDegreeName(textDocument) #O(n)
  _metadataDegreeGrantor=getDegreeGrantor(textDocument)    #O(n)
  _metadataDegreeDiscipline=getDegreeDiscipline(textDocument)   #O(n)
  _metadataDescriptionUri=getDescriptionUri(textDocument)   #O(n)
  _metadataDate=getDate(textDocument)    #O(n)
  _metadataSubject=getSubject(textDocument)   #O(n)
  _metadataAbstract=getAbstract(textDocument)   #O(n)
```

Fig. 2. Algorithmic complexity for automatic extraction of metadata

In order to evaluate the efficiency of the algorithm for automatic metadata extraction, a comparison was made with the Keyphrase extraction algorithm (KEA) [9], Mr.Dlib [12], ParsCit [11], and the proposed algorithm, because these tools allow integration with other development projects such as institutional repositories, digital libraries, among others, through modules, which were implemented for comparative purposes. For comparison purposes, metadata extraction was performed on 50 documents from the Institutional Repository of the Universidad Nacional del Altiplano with the aforementioned tools. The initial size was reduced due to the limitations of the execution of the algorithms and with the purpose of having a unanimous criterion for their evaluation. The purpose of the comparison was to evaluate the results obtained by extracting the metadata: author's full name, title, date of publication, type of document, institution granting the academic degree, professional school, name of the master's or doctoral degree, title, level of education, field of study, subject, and summary. At the same time, we proceeded to record and analyze the average response time in minutes to extract the metadata and the amount of metadata extracted.

Table 2 shows that the KEA, Mr.Dlib, and ParsCit tools partially extract the metadata, which are author, title, and abstract, unlike the algorithm that extracts all metadata. In terms of extraction time, the tools take more time compared to the automatic metadata extraction algorithm proposed in this research.

Table 2. Comparison in quantity and time of extracted metadata with other extractor tools.

Metadata	KEA Time: 00:39:49	Mr.Dlib Time: 00:31:65	ParsCit Time: 00:38:74	E-MeRI Time: 00:12:88
Title	30	24	25	50
Author	27	33	31	50
Date of publication	-	-	-	46
Type of publication	-	-	-	49
Publisher	-	-	-	50
Thesis degree grantor	-	-	-	49
Thesis degree name	-	-	-	50
Level of education	-	-	-	44
Field of study	-	-	-	39
Subject	25	11	23	50

5 Conclusions

Natural language processing (NLP) allowed the development of the automatic metadata extraction algorithm using the NLTK library of the Python programming language normalizing the text and making use of regular expressions to search for patterns and identify parts of the text that helped to obtain the metadata to extract, also the efficiency of the proposed E-MeRI algorithm was evaluated, obtaining a linear algorithmic complexity $O(n)$, which proved to extract more metadata from research documents and to be much faster compared to other extracting tools. The E-MeRI algorithm was based on natural language processing (NLP) for automatic metadata extraction and obtained an accuracy level between 96% to 99% of correct results, which indicates that the algorithm is efficient for the extraction of metadata in the research documents of the Institutional Repository of the Universidad Nacional del Altiplano. The algorithm developed allowed the automatic extraction of metadata on research documents in editable PDF format, so it is necessary to use other techniques or models for better extraction, such as autoregressive language models, Optical Character Recognition (OCR) techniques, and unstructured texts.

References

1. Rivera Gómez, A.C.: Creación de un repositorio digital con la producción intelectual de la Dra. María Eugenia Bozzoli Vargas, en el laboratorio de etnología de la Universidad de Costa Rica (2009)

2. Bustos-González, A., Porcel, A.: Directrices para la creación de repositorios institucionales en universidades y organizaciones de educación su-perior. Alfa Network Babel Library (2007)
3. Texier, J., De Giusti, M., Oviedo, N.F., Villarreal, G.L., Lira, A.J.: El Uso de Repositorios y su Importancia para la Educación en Ingeniería. In: WEEF 2012-Foro Mundial de Educación en Ingeniería-World Engineering Education Forum (2012)
4. Senso, J.A., de la Rosa Piñero, A.: El concepto de metadato: algo más que descripción de recursos electrónicos. Ciência da Informação. **32**, 95–106 (2003)
5. Congreso de la República del Perú: Ley 30035: La Ley que regula el Re-positorio Nacional Digital de Ciencia, Tecnología e Innovación de acce-so abierto. Diario El Peruano (2013)
6. Directrices para el procesamiento de información en los repositorios institucionales | Repositorio CONCYTEC. http://repositorio.concytec.gob.pe/handle/20.500.12390/2165. Last accessed 19 Nov 2022
7. Leite, F.C.L.: Como gerenciar e ampliar a visibilidade da informação científica brasileira: repositórios institucionais de acesso aberto. Instituto Brasileiro de Informação em Ciência e Tecnologia (2009)
8. Pire, T., Deco, C., Casali, A., Espinasse, B.: Extracción automática de metadatos de objetos de aprendizaje: un estudio comparativo. In: VI Congreso de Tecnología en Educación y Educación en Tecnología (2011)
9. Kea: http://community.nzdl.org/kea/. Last accessed 19 Nov 2022
10. Witten, I.H., Paynter, G.W., Frank, E., Gutwin, C., Nevill-Manning, C.G.: KEA: Practical automatic keyphrase extraction. In: Proceedings of the fourth ACM conference on Digital libraries. pp. 254–255 (1999)
11. Ramakrishnan, C., Patnia, A., Hovy, E., Burns, G.A.P.C.: Layout-aware text extraction from full-text PDF of scientific articles. Source Code Biol. Med. **7**, 1–10 (2012)
12. Mr. DLib: http://mr-dlib.org/. Last accessed 19 Nov 2022
13. Beel, J., Gipp, B., Langer, S., Genzmehr, M., Wilde, E., Nürnberger, A., Pitman, J.: Introducing Mr. DLib, a machine-readable digital library. In: Proceedings of the 11th annual international ACM/IEEE joint conference on Digital libraries. pp. 463–464 (2011)
14. Ghosh, S., Gunning, D.: Natural Language Processing Fundamentals: Build intelligent applications that can interpret the human language to deliver impactful results. Packt Publishing Ltd. (2019)
15. Negrete, J.C.M., Iano, Y., Negrete, P.D.M., Vaz, G.C., de Oliveira, G.G.: Sentiment analysis in the ecuadorian presidential election. In: Brazilian Technology Symposium, pp. 25–34. Springer (2023)
16. Negrete, J.C.M., Iano, Y., Negrete, P.D.M., Vaz, G.C., de Oliveira, G.G.: Sentiment and emotions analysis of tweets during the second round of 2021 ecuadorian presidential election. In: Brazilian Technology Symposium, pp. 257–268. Springer (2023)
17. Alfonseca Cubero, E.-A.: Teoría de autómatas y lenguajes formales (2007)
18. Chomsky, N.: Language and other cognitive systems. What is special about language. Lang. Learn. Dev. **7**, 263–278 (2011)
19. Pan, Y.: Extracción de información de sentencias judiciales (2020)
20. Metrics and scoring: Quantifying the quality of predictions. https://scikit-learn.org/stable/modules/model_evaluation.html. Last accessed 19 Nov 2022

A Hybrid Algorithm for the Optimization of the TDoA Localization Method in IoT Devices

Euler Apaza Medina$^{(\boxtimes)}$ (iD), Fredy Vilca Aliaga (iD), José Cruz (iD),
and Marco Ramos González (iD)

Universidad Nacional del Altiplano, Puno, Peru
euler.apaza@unap.pe, {josecruz,marcoramos}@unap.edu.pe

Abstract. In smart environments, depending on the type of service, Internet of Things (IoT) applications will need to know their geolocation in order to operate. Currently, the most widely used geolocation systems are the Global navigation satellite systems, such as Global Positioning System (GPS). However, these cannot be efficiently implemented in IoT systems due to high implementation costs and high power consumption. On the other hand, network-based localization methods have been studied in the literature, one of them is the Time Difference of Arrival (TDoA), which calculates the position using measurements of signal propagation times. In this work, a hybrid algorithm is proposed to improve the precision of the TDoA method, the proposed algorithm is based on the combination of the Chan and the Taylor series linearization algorithms. To obtain propagation times, a simulation tool based on the COST259 channel model was implemented. The performance of the proposed algorithm was evaluated in four scenarios: typical urban, dense urban, rugged terrain, and rural area. The results show that the proposed algorithm is on average 33.4% more accurate compared to the Chan algorithm.

Keywords: IoT · Localization · TDoA · Hybrid algorithm · COST259

1 Introduction

In the Internet of Things (IoT) systems, a large number of intelligent objects send information from the environment to a cloud system for processing [1, 2]. Depending on the type of service, various IoT applications will need to know the location of the device [3]. According to [4], accuracy and power consumption are two important features to consider in localization systems.

The most widely used localization systems are based on Global Navigation Satellite Systems (GNSS), such as GPS. However, using a GPS in each device would increase the cost of production and energy consumption, being inefficient in IoT systems [2, 3, 5]. Localization methods without the use of GPS have been studied in the literature. In [3], a classification of localization systems for IoT systems is presented. Some network-based methods are: Received Signal Strength Indicator (RSSI), Angle of Arrival (AoA), Time of Arrival (ToA), and Time Difference of Arrival (TDoA) [3, 6].

© The Author(s), under exclusive license to Springer Nature Switzerland AG 2023
Y. Iano et al. (Eds.): BTSym 2022, SIST 353, pp. 198–210, 2023.
https://doi.org/10.1007/978-3-031-31007-2_20

An advantage of the TDoA method is that it does not require the devices to be synchronized with the network. Two algorithms that compute position using the TDoA method are the Chan algorithm and the Taylor series linearization algorithm. However, in urban environments, due to the existence of buildings, trees, and other structures, most of the time the device to be located does not have a line of sight with the base station, this means that the signal propagation has multiple paths, which reduces the quality of the signal and introduces delays in its propagation, it generates errors in the precision of localization [7–10].

In this work, we propose a hybrid algorithm in order to improve the accuracy of the TDoA method, this proposed algorithm is based on the combination of the Chan and Taylor series linearization algorithms. To perform the simulations, we implement a simulation tool based on the COST259 channel model.

The rest of this paper is organized as follows. Section 2 presents the TDoA method and the Chan and Taylor series linearization algorithms. Section 3 describes the proposed algorithm. Section 4 presents the simulation tool and the parameters used. Section 5 shows the results obtained. The paper finally concludes with Sect. 6.

2   Time Difference of Arrival (TDoA)

This system is based on measurements of the arrival time difference of a signal received at different base stations. In this way, the TDoA method has the advantage that it does not need to know the exact moment in which the device to be located responds to the request sent by the base station. If two base stations receive a signal emitted from the device, the two received versions of that signal will be correlated to estimate the time difference of arrival between these two base stations. This difference in time of arrival between the two bases projects a hyperbola that has them as foci. Having similar measurements from another base station, another hyperbola can be generated, and the intersection of these hyperbolas is the result of the location of the device.

In TDoA-based localization methods, also known as hyperbolic methods, the measurements are obtained to establish the difference in the distances between the device to be located and two base stations [11, 12].

Considering, $\tau_{i,j}$ as the TDoA parameter measured between the device and two base stations i and j, the difference in the distances is:

$$d_{i,j} = c\tau_{i,j} = c(t_i - t_j) = d_i - d_j \qquad (1)$$

where t_i and d_i are respectively the time of arrival (ToA) and the distance relative to the i-th base station. The TDoA measurement generates as a locus of the terminal position $x = (x, y)$ a hyperbola with the foci at the two base stations. Being defined by the following equation in two-dimensional (2-D).

$$d_{i,j} = \sqrt{(x - x_i)^2 + (y - y_i)^2} - \sqrt{(x - x_j)^2 + (y - y_j)^2} \qquad (2)$$

where (x_i, y_i), indicates the coordinates of the i-th base station. To determine the position of the device in the 2-D plane, at least three base stations are necessary to obtain two independent TDoA hyperbolas. The geometric intersection between the two resulting hyperbolas determines the position of the mobile device, as shown in Fig. 1.

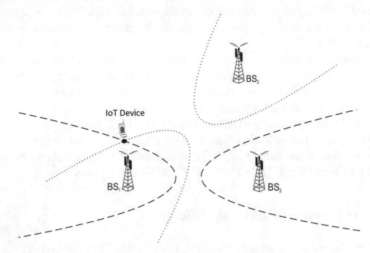

Fig. 1. Calculation of position using TDoA measurements.

In solving the geometric equations of the TDoA method, there is a wide possibility that ambiguous solutions are presented. To solve this problem, some algorithms were proposed in the literature, the most outstanding, according to their performance and computational complexity to calculate the position are the Chan algorithm [13] and the Taylor series linearization algorithm [14].

2.1 The Chan Algorithm

An optimal performance algorithm is the algorithm proposed by Y. T. Chan [13], which presents different solutions depending on the number of base stations used in the calculation. For the case of three base stations, where there are two TDoA measurements, the algorithm calculates the position of the mobile (x, y) in terms of d_1 (distance between base station 1 and the device).

The squared distance between the device and the i-th base station is given by:

$$d_i^2 = (X_i - x)^2 + (Y_i - y)^2 = K_i - 2X_i x - 2Y_i y + x^2 + y^2 \quad i = 2, 3, \ldots M \quad (3)$$

where:

$$K_i = (X_i)^2 + (Y_i)^2 \quad (4)$$

Given that: $d_{i1} = c\tau_{i1} = d_i - d_1$, we have:

$$d_{i1} + d_1 = d_i \quad (5)$$

Squaring Eq. (5) gives the equality:

$$d_{i1}^2 + 2d_{i1}d_1 + d_1^2 = K_i - 2X_i x - 2Y_i y + x^2 + y^2 \tag{6}$$

Making $i = 1$ in (3) and subtracting from (6) we have:

$$d_{i1}^2 + 2d_{i1}d_1 = K_i - K_1 - 2X_{i1}x - 2Y_{i1}y \quad i = 2, 3, ...M \tag{7}$$

where: $X_{i1} = X_i - X_1$ and $Y_{i1} = Y_i - Y_1$.

For three base stations we have:

$$d_{21}^2 + 2d_{21}d_1 = K_2 - K_1 - 2X_{21}x - 2Y_{21}y \tag{8}$$

$$d_{31}^2 + 2d_{31}d_1 = K_3 - K_1 - 2X_{31}x - 2Y_{31}y \tag{9}$$

The values of x and y can be solved in terms of d_1:

$$\begin{bmatrix} x \\ y \end{bmatrix} = - \begin{bmatrix} x_{21} & y_{21} \\ x_{31} & y_{31} \end{bmatrix}^{-1} \left\{ \begin{bmatrix} d_{21} \\ d_{31} \end{bmatrix} d_1 + \frac{1}{2} \begin{bmatrix} d_{21}^2 - K_2 + K_1 \\ d_{31}^2 - K_3 + K_1 \end{bmatrix} \right\} \tag{10}$$

Substituting this result in (3) for $i = 1$ results in a quadratic equation in d_1. By obtaining the positive root of this equation and substituting it in (10), it is possible to find the position of the device.

2.2 The Taylor Series Linearization Algorithm

This algorithm considers the expansion of hyperbolic equations in series [12, 14], this allows the transformation of the original nonlinear problem into a linear problem to obtain a solution using least squares. Knowing the TDoA measurements and choosing an initial approximation for the position of the device, the deviation of the position calculation is given by:

$$\begin{bmatrix} \Delta_x \\ \Delta_y \end{bmatrix} = \left(G_t^T Q^{-1} G_t \right)^{-1} G_t^T Q^{-1} h_t \tag{11}$$

where:

$$h_t = \begin{bmatrix} d_{21} - \left(\tilde{R}_2 - \tilde{R}_1 \right) \\ d_{31} - \left(\tilde{R}_3 - \tilde{R}_1 \right) \\ . \\ . \\ d_{M1} - \left(\tilde{R}_M - \tilde{R}_1 \right) \end{bmatrix} \tag{12}$$

$$d_{i1} = \sqrt{(X_i - x)^2 + (Y_i - y)^2} - \sqrt{(X_1 - x)^2 + (Y_1 - y)^2} \tag{13}$$

$$G_t = \begin{bmatrix} (X_1 - x)/\tilde{R}_1 - (X_2 - x)/\tilde{R}_2 & (Y_1 - y)/\tilde{R}_1 - (Y_2 - y)/\tilde{R}_2 \\ (X_1 - x)/\tilde{R}_1 - (X_3 - x)/\tilde{R}_3 & (Y_1 - y)/\tilde{R}_1 - (Y_3 - y)/\tilde{R}_3 \\ \cdot & \cdot \\ \cdot & \cdot \\ (X_1 - x)/\tilde{R}_1 - (X_M - x)/\tilde{R}_M & (Y_1 - y)/\tilde{R}_1 - (Y_M - y)/\tilde{R}_M \end{bmatrix} \tag{14}$$

Q is the covariance matrix of the TDoA measures. The values of $\tilde{R}_i, i = 1, \ldots M$ are given by:

$$\tilde{R}_i = \sqrt{(X_i - x_0)^2 + (Y_i - y_0)^2} \tag{15}$$

where (x_0, y_0) is the first iteration of the initial position estimate of the device. In subsequent iterations, the values of x_0 and y_0 are updated with $(x_0 + \Delta_x)$ and $(y_0 + \Delta_y)$ using the values of (Δ_x, Δ_y) obtained in the previous iteration.

3   The Proposed Algorithm

A characteristic of the Chan algorithm is that it has a low computational cost and low processing time. On the other hand, the Taylor series linearization algorithm allows better precision, but it depends on an input value that would be an approximate position coordinate for the calculation through iterations, if that input value is random or is distant from the real position, the algorithm will need a greater number of iterations for the estimation, which means more processing time and higher energy consumption.

In this work, a hybrid algorithm is proposed, we use the Chan algorithm to obtain a quick estimate of the device position, then that Chan estimate is used as input (initial approximation) of the Taylor series linearization algorithm, as can be seen in Fig. 2.

The initial approximation that results from the Chan algorithm will reduce the number of iterations that the Taylor series linearization algorithm needs to calculate the position of the device. In this way, the precision is increased, and in addition, the processing time and the computational cost should be reduced.

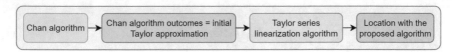

Fig. 2. Proposed Algorithm

4   Simulation Tools and Parameters

In order to obtain the propagation times of the signal between a base station and the device to be located, the COST259 channel model was used, which allows for simulating the time in which a signal propagates over a certain distance according to the type of scenario. These propagation times are then used to calculate the TDoA values that are needed to estimate the position of the IoT device. Thus, we implement in Matlab software a simulation tool with a graphical environment that uses the COST259 channel model based on [15] and the Chan and Taylor series linearization algorithms.

4.1 COST259 Channel Model

The COST-259 DCM channel model (Directional Channel Model) [16], based on statistical calculations allows simulation systems that require space-time processing. This channel model uses parameters such as:

- Operating frequency in Hz;
- Position vector (x, y) of the IoT device in reference to the position (0, 0) where the base station is located;
- IoT device and base station antenna heights;
- Type of network: Macro, micro, and pico;
- Type of scenario: Typical urban (TU), Dense Urban (DU), Rough Terrain (RT), Rural Area (RA).

  - TU: areas that are composed of residential houses, gardens, and parks.
  - DU: areas that are made up of tall buildings and blocks of commercial buildings.
  - RT: areas composed of hills, valleys, and mountains.
  - RA: areas with few buildings, open fields, flat land, etc.

4.2 Implemented Simulation Tool

Figure 3 shows the graphical tool developed in Matlab software. In this tool is possible to configure parameters such as the localization algorithm, the operating frequency, the type of scenario, and the simulation coordinates. As a result, this tool shows the estimated coordinates of the proposed algorithm and the precision errors.

In this tool, we need to enter a coordinate to be simulated, then the tool determines the type of scenario and the three closest base stations to the position of the IoT device. Using the COST259 channel model, measurements are made of the time it takes for the signal to travel the distance from the IoT device to each of the three base stations.

To calculate each arrival time, the multipath effect is considered, in this way the signal received at a base station will be composed of a set of signal versions sent by the IoT device, each signal version that travels different paths due to bounces with dispersion have a different time and power than the other versions. To solve the multipath effect, a relationship between time versions and their respective power levels is made, obtaining an average of all the signals received by the base station; this average time is considered as arrival time.

These three times of arrival measurements are subtracted from each other, in such a way that it is possible to find the TDoA measurements. Finally, the TDoA measurements are used in the localization algorithms.

Figures 4 and 5 show simulations of the COST259 channel model to obtain propagation times at 850 MHz and 1900 MHz frequencies for a TU scenario. The x-axis represents the distance between the device and the base station, and the y-axis represents the signal propagation time. The graphs show the ideal propagation time and the simulated propagation time in a TU scenario.

Fig. 3. Simulation Tool

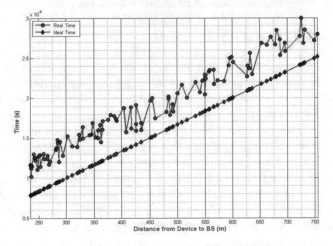

Fig. 4. Propagation times for TU – 850 MHz

4.3 Simulation Parameters

In this paper, the four simulation scenarios defined in [16] are considered (TU, DU, RT, and RA).

The frequencies used in the simulations are divided into two groups: 850 MHz and 1900 MHz, we chose these two groups of frequencies because they are low-frequency bands, in whose adjacent frequencies communication systems for IoT using technologies such as LoRa, 4G, 5G could be implemented in the future.

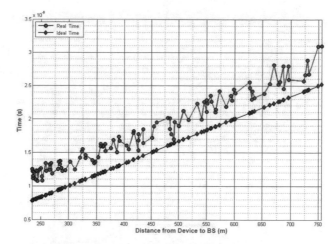

Fig. 5. Propagation times for TU – 1900 MHz

Sample Determination. The sample size was determined using Eq. 16. For a degree of confidence z = 1.96, assumed error e = 0.05, positive variability p = 0.5, and negative variability q = 0.5, the sample size is 384. These samples were classified for the four simulation scenarios.

$$n_0 = \left(\frac{z}{e}\right)^2 pq \tag{16}$$

4.4 Accuracy Measurement in Localization Systems

To determine the accuracy of the location algorithms, the real coordinates of the device are compared with the coordinates estimated by the simulated algorithms. In this work, the RMS error (Root Mean Square Error – RMSE) was used, defined by Eq. 17.

$$RMSE = \sqrt{E[(x - \hat{x})^2 + (y - \hat{y})^2]} \tag{17}$$

where (x, y) is the real position and $(\hat{x}, \hat{y})$ is the estimated position.

5 Results

Figures 6, 7, 8 and 9 show the simulations in all the scenarios (TU, DU, RT, and RA) at 850 MHz frequency, where the x-axis represents each simulated sample, and the y-axis shows the RMS errors at each point for the Chan and the proposed algorithms.

Figures 10, 11, 12 and 13 show the simulations in all the scenarios for the 1900 MHz frequency, where the x-axis represents each simulated sample, and the y-axis shows the RMS errors at each point for the Chan and the proposed algorithms.

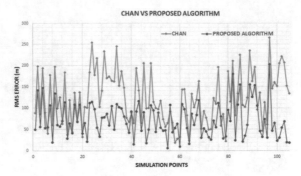

Fig. 6. Position error(m) for TU – 850 MHz

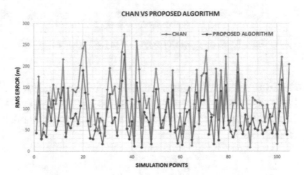

Fig. 7. Position error(m) for DU – 850 MHz

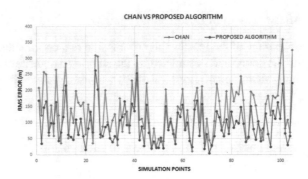

Fig. 8. Position error(m) for RT – 850 MHz

A summary of the results obtained from the simulations is shown in Figs. 14 and 15. Each figure is composed of four groups of bars that represent the type of simulated scenario (TU, DU, RT, and RA). In each group of bars, for example, for TU the bar on the left represents the RMS error of the Chan algorithm, and the bar on the right represents the RMS error of the proposed algorithm. It can be seen that the proposed algorithm has a smaller RMS error compared to the Chan algorithm.

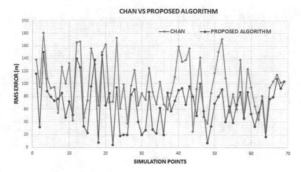

Fig. 9. Position error(m) for RA – 850 MHz

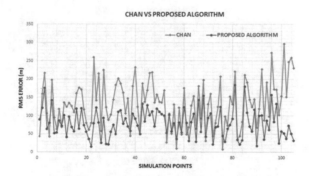

Fig. 10. Position error(m) for TU – 1900 MHz

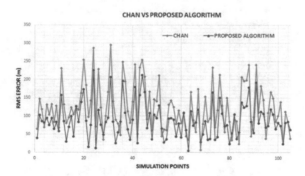

Fig. 11. Position error(m) for DU – 1900 MHz

Table 1 shows the RMS localization errors in the four defined scenarios. These values were obtained from the simulations of Figs. 6, 7, 8, 9, 10, 11, 12 and 13.

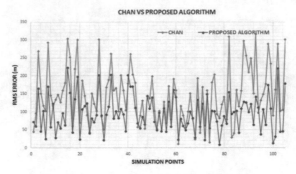

Fig. 12. Position error(m) for RT – 1900 MHz

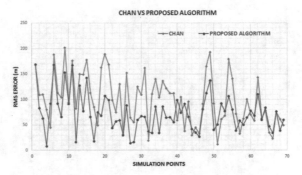

Fig. 13. Position error(m) for RA – 1900 MHz

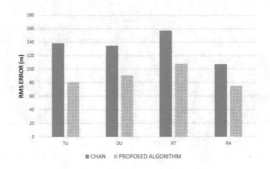

Fig. 14. RMS errors at 850 MHz

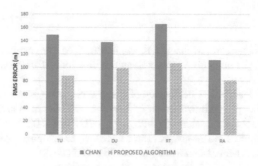

Fig. 15. RMS errors at 1900 MHz

Table 1. RMS errors (m), according to the type of scenario and frequency.

Scenarios	Error at 850 MHz		Error at 1900 MHz	
	Chan algorithm	Proposed algorithm	Chan algorithm	Proposed algorithm
Typical Urban (TU)	137.98	81.01	148.67	87.64
Dense Urban (DU)	134.52	90.98	137.77	98.86
Rugged Terrain (RT)	156.99	107.74	165.20	106.61
Rural Area (RA)	107.01	75.41	111.51	81.01

The results in the four scenarios show that the proposed algorithm increases the precision in the estimation of the localization using TDoA measurements. On average, the proposed algorithm is 33.4% more accurate than the Chan algorithm.

6   Conclusions

A problem in location systems occurs when there is no line of sight between the base station and the device, due to the adverse environment, the same signal can travel different paths, with different distances at different times, thus presenting errors in the estimation of the position of the IoT device.

In this work, an algorithm based on the hybrid use of the Chan algorithm and the Taylor series linearization algorithm was proposed to improve the accuracy of the TDoA method. To measure the performance of the proposed algorithm, a graphic simulation tool was implemented in Matlab based on the COST259 channel model and the proposed hybrid algorithm. The results showed that the proposed algorithm reduces the location error by an average of 33.4% compared to the Chan algorithm. In future work, the study of localization methods in indoor environments is recommended.

References

1. Al-Fuqaha, A., Guizani, M., Mohammadi, M., Aledhari, M., Ayyash, M.: Internet of things: a survey on enabling technologies, protocols, and applications. IEEE Commun. Surv. Tutorials **17**, 2347–2376 (2015)
2. Akbari, M., Hamidzadeh, J.: Localization of internet of things (IoT) with evolutionary calculations and grasshopper optimization algorithms. In: 2020 6th Iranian Conference on Signal Processing and Intelligent Systems (ICSPIS), pp. 1–7. IEEE (2020)
3. Khelifi, F., Bradai, A., Benslimane, A., Rawat, P., Atri, M.: A survey of localization systems in internet of things. Mob. Networks Appl. **24**, 761–785 (2019)
4. Wang, T., Xiong, H., Ding, H., Zheng, L.: A hybrid localization algorithm based on TOF and TDOA for asynchronous wireless sensor networks. IEEE Access **7**, 158981–158988 (2019)
5. Ghany, A.A., Uguen, B., Lemur, D.: A parametric TDoA technique in the IoT localization context. In: 2019 16th Workshop on Positioning, Navigation and Communications (WPNC).,pp. 1–6. IEEE (2019)
6. Drane, C., Macnaughtan, M., Scott, C.: Positioning GSM telephones. IEEE Commun. Mag. **36**, 46–54 (1998)
7. Vaz, G.C., Iano, Y., de Oliveira, G.G.: IoT-from industries to houses: an overview. In: Brazilian Technology Symposium, pp. 734–741. Springer (2022)
8. Nishimura, E.H., Iano, Y., de Oliveira, G.G., Vaz, G.C.: Application and requirements of AIoT-enabled industrial control units. In: Brazilian Technology Symposium, pp. 724–733. Springer (2022)
9. Bacega, P.R. de O., Iano, Y., Carvalho, B.C.S. de, Vaz, G.C., Oliveira, G.G. de, Chuma, E.L.: Study about the applicability of low latency in HAS transmission systems. In: Brazilian Technology Symposium, pp. 73–87. Springer (2023)
10. Lustosa, T.C., Iano, Y., Oliveira, G.G. de, Vaz, G.C., Reis, V.S.: Safety management applied to smart cities design. In: Brazilian Technology Symposium, pp. 498–510. Springer (2020)
11. Spirito, M.A.: Accuracy of hyperbolic mobile station location in cellular networks. Electron. Lett. **37**, 708–710 (2001)
12. da Costa, R.B.F.: Estudo e Simulação de Métodos de Localização de Terminais Móveis (2003)
13. Chan, Y.T., Ho, K.C.: A simple and efficient estimator for hyperbolic location. IEEE Trans. signal Process. **42**, 1905–1915 (1994)
14. Torrieri, D.J.: Statistical theory of passive location systems. IEEE Trans. Aerosp. Electron. Syst. **AES-20**, 183–198 (1984)
15. Castilho, S.D.: Ferramenta de simulação computacional de canal de propagação em ambiente celular baseado em modelos geométricos estatísticos (2006)
16. Correia, L.M.: Wireless Flexible Personalized Communications. John Wiley & Sons, Inc. (2001)

Appraisal of a Rural Mobile Telephony Service Propagation Model

Guido Humberto Cayo-Cabrera[1]([✉]) [ID], Teobaldo Raul Basurco-Chambilla[1] [ID],
Oscar J. M. Peña Cáceres[2] [ID], Elmer A. Chunga Zapata[2] [ID], and Fred Torres-Cruz[3] [ID]

[1] Facultad de Ingeniería de Mecánica Eléctrica, Electrónica y Sistemas, Universidad Nacional del Altiplano de Puno, Puno, Peru
{ghcc_telematic,trbasurco}@unap.edu.pe
[2] Facultad de Ingeniería de Sistemas, Universidad Cesar Vallejo, Piura, Peru
ojpenac@ucvvirtual.edu.pe, echunga@ucv.edu.pe
[3] Facultad de Ingeniería Estadística e Informática, Universidad Nacional del Altiplano de Puno, Puno, Peru
ftorres@unap.edu.pe

Abstract. Currently, telephone operators in the city of Puno have coverage in rural areas of Puno. For the evaluation of the coverage service, the rural area of Llachon has been considered as a reference, where tourism is projected to reach an average of 36,672 visitors. The objective was to evaluate the 3G-4G mobile service using the Hata propagation model. For this purpose, the behavior and fixation of the application were used by means of linear regression. Measurements were performed using a spectrum analyzer and various applications in the 700 MHz and 900 MHz UHF bands, centralizing the frequencies in the B28 and B8 bands, respectively. Statistical correlation adjustments of the measurements were made during the day in winter and autumn seasons at temperatures from -12 °C to 16 °C, obtaining acceptable power levels in the mobile devices of -58 dBm to -95 dBm according to the recommendations of the regulation organism: OSIPTEL-Peru. The quality of coverage and voice service is seriously affected by latency and signal fading, especially internet service.

Keywords: Rural mobile telephony · Hata propagation model · UHF band

1 Introduction

The modeling of the telecommunication channels represents the distance-dependent attenuation between the transmitter and receiver. The propagation calculation determines a measurable and statistically processed behavior according to the spectrum data of the mobile telephone operator. The research orients the analysis of electromagnetic wave propagation to the Llachón - Capachica - Puno town center. In this sense, it is necessary to analyze the behavior of the operators for the indicated area, the most pertinent to the Hata propagation model.

© The Author(s), under exclusive license to Springer Nature Switzerland AG 2023
Y. Iano et al. (Eds.): BTSym 2022, SIST 353, pp. 211–222, 2023.
https://doi.org/10.1007/978-3-031-31007-2_21

According to [1], the path propagation losses using the simplified empirical loss method depend on fewer variables than the traditionally used models, and from the data collected in the field, they present a better performance for the 2.13 GHz frequency, referring that for their analysis they apply 4G LTE propagation models: Xia-Bertoni, and Walfisch-Bertoni. However, these models are applicable to dense urban and semi-urban areas [2–4].

However, it is necessary to consider, according to [5], that "one way to check the efficiency of an experimental model of radio propagation is with the adjustment of the data of the mathematical expression with respect to the logarithmic model of path loss, taking as a reference the distance to determine the possible attenuations and loss factors that may occur in the variation of the signal power," and use in its analysis the technique of restricted nonlinear regression. But this analysis can be very well analyzed considering the behavior of radio propagation coverage of the model proposed by the 3GPP for an urban environment in an LTE network using conventional antenna systems and adaptive antenna systems as well as it indicates [6].

[7] analyzes the statistical adjustment of the scenario of the city of Cali, by means of the Okumura-Hata, Stanford University Interim (SUI), and Walfisch-Bertoni models, using measurements. For the simulation of the intervening systems, the software Xirio: Tool for the planning of mobile cellular communications networks could be very well applied [8].

Now, [9] mentions that "empirical propagation models are widely used to calculate path losses in a wireless channel in different types of scenarios, and their results are taken into account when selecting the location of base stations and planning their coverage area". A trend is to consider the development of an indispensable tool for the planning of LTE mobile systems; because with the use of GIS geographic information systems, the information referred to as a base mapping of specific areas is available and it is possible to create cartography for the management and analysis of radio communications systems [10].

Finally, in [11], the authors evaluate the performance of each of the implemented radio resource planners and determine the impact of the techniques on the throughput that can be achieved in an LTE network. However, values at the WLAN network level should be developed using a semi-empirical model for the prediction of propagation loss in indoor environments, using received power measurements, performed for the case where the signals are presented for the case of two commercial buildings [12].

2   Hata Model (Okumura-Hata)

It consists of a set of equations that allows for estimating propagation losses in different types of areas (urban, semi-urban, and rural) [13]. It is an empirical formulation of the propagation loss data provided by Okumura, and is valid in the VHF and UHF frequency range, from 150 MHz to 1500 MHz [14].

The urban area corresponds to large cities with tall buildings and houses with 2 or more stories, or where there is a large concentration of houses.

$$L_{50}(urban) = 69.55 + 26.16\,log(f_c) - 13.82\,log(h_{te}) - \alpha(h_{re}) + (44.9 \atop -6.55log(h_{te}))log(d)} \tag{1}$$

Taking into account:

$$150\,\text{MHz} < f_c < 1500\,\text{MHz}$$
$$30\,\text{m} < h_{te} < 200\,\text{m}$$
$$1\,\text{m} < h_{re} < 10\,\text{m}$$

where:

- f_c: Carrier frequency [MHz].
- h_{te}: Height of the transmitting antenna [m], ranging from 30 to 200 m.
- h_{re}: Height of the receiving antenna [m], ranging from 1 to 10 m.
- $\alpha(h_{te})$: Correction factor for the effective height of the mobile antenna that is a function of the type of service area.
- d: Distance between transmitter and receiver [km].

For small and medium-sized cities:

$$a(h_{re}) = (1.1\log(f_c) - 0.7)h_{re} - 1.56\log(f_c) - 0.8)\,\text{dB} \tag{2}$$

For large cities:

$$a(h_{re}) = (8.29\log(1.54h_{re}))^2 - 1.1\,\text{dB for} f_c < 300\,\text{MHz} \tag{3}$$

$$a(h_{re}) = 3.2(\log(11.75h_{re}))^2 - 4.97\,\text{dB for} f_c > 300\,\text{MHz} \tag{4}$$

Suburban area:

$$L(dB) = L_{50}(urbano) - 2\left[log\frac{f_c}{28}\right]^2 - 5.4 \tag{5}$$

Rural area:

$$L(dB) = L_{50}(urbano) - 4.78(\log(f_c))^2 + 18.33\log(f_c) - 40.94 \tag{6}$$

3   Mobile Telephony

It is a telecommunication service that aims to provide a communication channel between different users, through the use of terminals within a defined area, being able to maintain an established communication, although one or both communicators are moving [15]. The frequency bands allocated to the Mobile Telephony services and the general technical standards for the use of the radio-electric spectrum are detailed in the National Frequency Allocation Plan (PNAF) and are presented in summary form (see Table 1).

Table 1. Table of bands allocated to mobile communications services in Peru [16]

Operator	2G GPRS, EDGE	3G HSDPA, H, H+, 3G+, 3.5G	4G 4G+, 4.5g, LTE, LTE-A, LTE Advanced
Claro	1900 MHz (B2)	850 MHz (B5)	1900 MHz (B2) 700 MHz (B28) 2600 MHz (B7) OLO
Movistar	850 MHz (B5)	1900 MHz (B2)	1700/2100 MHz AWS.1 (B4) 700 MHz (B28)
Entel	1900 MHz (B2)	1900 MHz (B2)	1700/2100 MHz AWS.1 (B4) 700 MHz (B28) Home internet 2300 MHz (B40)
Bitel	–	1900 MHz (B2) 900 MHz (B8)	900 MHz (B8) 2600 MHz (B7)

As search criteria, the following descriptors were included: "radio spectrum", "radio spectrum measurement", "radio spectrum evaluation", and "radio spectrum occupation". These descriptors were combined in various ways at the time of scanning in order to broaden the search criteria. (see Table 2).

Table 2. Table of distribution of mobile lines by modality and operator (Quarter "B") [17]

Modality	America MovilPeru S.A.C.	Entel Peru S.A.	Telefonica Peru S.A.A.	Viettel Peru S.A.C.	Guinea Mobile S.A.C.	Incacel Mobile S.A.
Contract	4364445	2875161	4778119	1775819		
Prepaid	7392870	5190582	8545256	4903979	1630	16752
Sub-Total	11757315	8065743	13323375	6679798	1630	16752

Total of mobile lines = 39844613

4   Geographical Location of the Analysis Points

The points to be linked are located within the Puno-Llachon route, according to the results obtained in the field study (see Table 3 and Fig. 1).

These points made it possible to determine the referential distance of the system measurement to support the propagation model (referential point - see Table 4 and Fig. 2).

Table 3. Geographical location of the points in the rural area.

Measurement points	Latitude (°)	Length (°)	Altitude (m)
PLlach-1	−15.722858	−69.762222	3878
PLlach-2	−15.726221	−69.777687	3880
PLlach-3	−15.726463	−69.775265	3871
PLlach-4	−15.727218	−69.772616	3853
PLlach-5	−15.728217	−69.770194	3846
PLlach-6	−15.727442	−69.769169	3868
PLlach-7	−15.726907	−69.767685	3874
PLlach-8	−15.727049	−69.76627	3870
PLlach-9	−15.726165	−69.764167	3883
PLlach-10	−15.726153	−69.762222	3881

Fig. 1. Location distribution of the points considered in the analysis.

Table 4. Location of reference tie points [18].

Station	Geographic Coordinates		Altitude
	Latitude	Longitude	(m.a.s.l.)
Puno referential	15°50′33.79″S	70°01′18.84″ W	3962.0
Llachon repeater	15°43′22.17″ S	69°47′10.11″ W	3919.7

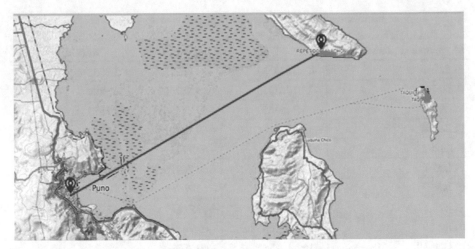

Fig. 2. Reference location of the link to CP Llachon.

5   Equipment Used for Measurements

5.1   Spectrum Analyzer

2.7 GHz spectrum analyzer. Model: GW INSTEK GSP-827. Voltage (Volts) 100–240 V. Other variables (Accuracy, Phase, Frequency, Operating Speed, among others). Frequency: 13M, 15.36M, 15.4M, 19.2M. Overload protection: +30DBM, ±25VDC. Impedance: 50 ohms (see Fig. 3).

Fig. 3. Spectrum analyzer GSP-827.

6   Results and Discussion

6.1   Measurements of Points in the Rural Mobile Telephone Reference Zone

For the measurements, tests were performed considering tower heights of approximately 30 m, the measurement equipment at a height of 1.5 m, a 3 dB correction factor, and 700 MHz and 900 MHz frequencies. In the analysis, Mobile Telephony Companies operating in the UHF band have been considered as MPC (mobile phone companies), but the authors will use the acronyms that are commonly used in Spanish: ETMs. Table 5 shows the power levels from 53 dBm to −101 dBm for ETM-1, from −63 dBm to −104 dBm for ETM-2, and from −59 dBm to −121 dBm for ETM-3. According to [19], the quality of service (QoS) coverage indicator is defined as the percentage of signal level measurements greater than or equal to the signal strength value −95 dBm (see Table 5).

Table 5. Power level measurement at the analysis points - Llachon area.

Measurement points	GEOGRAPHICAL POSITION		Altitude (m.a.s.l.)	RSSI (dBm)		
	Latitude (°)	Length (°)		ETM-1	ETM-2	ETM-3
PLlach-1	−15.722858	−69.762222	3878	−53	−63	−59
PLlach-2	−15.726221	−69.777687	3880	−55	−68	−61
PLlach-3	−15.726463	−69.775265	3871	−57	−72	−66
PLlach-4	−15.727218	−69.772616	3853	−61	−75	−78
PLlach-5	−15.728217	−69.770194	3846	−68	−81	−89
PLlach-6	−15.727442	−69.769169	3868	−75	−85	−95
PLlach-7	−15.726907	−69.767685	3874	−83	−89	−107
PLlach-8	−15.727049	−69.766270	3870	−86	−94	−112
PLlach-9	−15.726165	−69.764167	3883	−90	−101	−116
PLlach-10	−15.726153	−69.762222	3881	−101	−104	−121

Table 6 shows the general parameters of the operator, such as EARFCN, indicating the number of channels of the carries in LTE, RSSNR the average signal-to-noise ratio, considering the Frequency Division Duplexing mode, LTE type, bands B28 (700 MHz), B8 (900 MHz), PCI Physical Cell Identifier, etc.

Table 7 and Table 8 specify the system losses for bands B28 and B8. Figures 4 and 5 show the behavior of the linear regression of the reference distances considered from the transmitter to the measurement points for the B28 and B8 UHF bands of the mobile telephone companies. The general equation of the resulting dependent lines is represented in Figs. 4 and 5). According to the figure, the signal level attenuation is higher in bands B8 and B28.

Table 6. Power measurements at the analysis points

	ETM-1	ETM-2	ETM-3
Operator	716 10	716 06	716 15
Type	LTE	LTE	LTE
Duplex Mode	FDD	FDD	FDD
TAC	54601	5183	42401
CI	224674:252	775012:88	330105:1
PCI	103	98	246
EARFCN	9435	9585	3750
BAND	B28	B28	B8
FREQUENCY (MHz)	700 APT	700 APT	900 GSM
RSRQ (dB) average	−7−−12	−6−−10	−10−−19
RSSNR (dB) average	60−140	30−222	−72−238
TA	14	6	15
Wind Speed	0.36−1.43	0.36−1.43	0.36−1.43

Table 7. Losses applying propagation model for B28 band, Considering hte = 30 m, hre = 1.5 m, alpha = 3 dB.

D (Km)	Lrural (dB)	Hata Model (dBm)	PpromETMs (dBm)	PpromHata-ETMs (dBm)
1	93.08249	−58.08249	−58	−58.041245
2	103.686228	−68.686228	−61.5	−65.093114
3	109.889017	−74.889017	−64.5	−69.6945085
4	114.289966	−79.289966	−68	−73.644983
5	117.703608	−82.703608	−74.5	−78.601804
6	120.492756	−85.492756	−80	−82.746378
7	122.850947	−87.850947	−86	−86.9254735
8	124.893705	−89.893705	−90	−89.9468525
9	126.695545	−91.695545	−95.5	−93.5977725
10	128.307346	−93.307346	−102.5	−97.903673

Table 8. Losses applying propagation model for band B8, Considering hte = 30 m, hre = 1.5 m, alpha = 3 dB.

D (Km)	Lrural (dB)	Hata Model (dBm)	PpromETMs (dBm)	PpromHata-ETMs (dBm)
1	94.9127502	−59.9127502	−59	−59.4563751
2	105.516488	−70.516488	−61	−65.758244
3	111.719278	−76.719278	−66	−71.359639
4	116.120227	−81.120227	−78	−79.5601135
5	119.533868	−84.533868	−89	−86.766934
6	122.323016	−87.323016	−95	−91.161508
7	124.681207	−89.681207	−107	−98.3406035
8	126.723965	−91.723965	−112	−101.8619825
9	128.525805	−93.525805	−116	−104.7629025
10	130.137606	−95.137606	−121	−108.068803

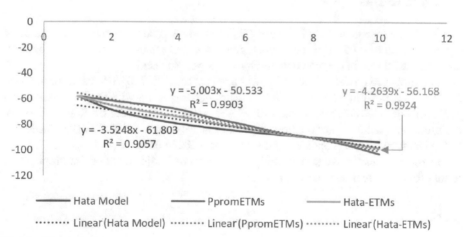

Fig. 4. Dependent linear regression of model for the rural area B28-700 MHz/Transmitter Power of 35 dBm.

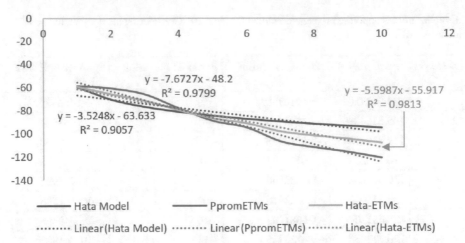

Fig. 5. Dependent linear regression of model for the rural area B8-900 MHz/Transmitter Power of 35 dBm.

7 Conclusions

The service coverage quality indicator (SQC) must be greater or equal to the value of signal strength of −95 dBm [19], which guarantees the establishment of calls made by users of the service in the area covered by the population center.

The proposed model adjusts the power levels in the B28-700 MHz band for the rural area of Llachon from −58.04 to −97.90 dBm, in comparison with the Hata model that proposes power levels from −58.08 to −93.31 dBm; while, in the B8-900 MHz band, the proposed model adjusts the power levels from −59.46 to −108.07 dBm, compared to the Hata model that proposes from −59.91 to −95.14 dBm.

In future research, we aim to analyze the statistical adjustment of the propagation model for rural areas considering rain and hail.

References

1. Vidal-Beltrán, S., Degollado-Rea, E.A., López-Bonilla, J.L.: Simplified propagation model for LTE in the frequency of 2.1 GHz. Universidad de la Salle Bajío – México (2017). http://www.scielo.org.mx/pdf/ns/v9n19/2007-0705-ns-9-19-00083.pdf. Accessed 19 Nov 2022
2. Minango, P., Iano, Y., Chuma, E.L., Vaz, G.C., de Oliveira, G.G., Minango, J.: Revision of the 5G concept rollout and its application in smart cities: a study case in South America. In: Iano, Y., Saotome, O., Kemper Vásquez, G.L., Cotrim Pezzuto, C., Arthur, R., Gomes de Oliveira, G. (eds.) Brazilian Technology Symposium, pp. 229–238. Springer, Cham (2023). https://doi.org/10.1007/978-3-031-04435-9_21
3. Demanboro, A.C., Bianchini, D., Iano, Y., de Oliveira, G.G., Vaz, G.C.: Regulatory aspects of 5G and perspectives in the scope of scientific and technological policy. In: Iano, Y., Saotome, O., Kemper Vásquez, G.L., Cotrim Pezzuto, C., Arthur, R., Gomes de Oliveira, G. (eds.) Brazilian Technology Symposium, pp. 163–171. Springer, Cham (2023). https://doi.org/10.1007/978-3-031-04435-9_16

4. Demanboro, A.C., Bianchini, D., Iano, Y., de Oliveira, G.G., Vaz, G.C.: 6G Networks: an innovative approach, but with many challenges and paradigms, in the Development of Platforms and Services in the Near Future. In: Iano, Y., Saotome, O., Kemper Vásquez, G.L., Cotrim Pezzuto, C., Arthur, R., Gomes de Oliveira, G. (eds.) Brazilian Technology Symposium, pp. 172–187. Springer, Cham (2023). https://doi.org/10.1007/978-3-031-04435-9_17
5. Rubio, J.E.H., Rozo, W.V.: Setting and checking of an experimental model radio propagation in semi urban outdoor environments for wireless systems in the 2.4 Ghz Frequency band. Rev. Colomb. Tecnol. Av. Univ. Pamplona 2, 51–58 (2014). https://ojs.unipamplona.edu.co/ojsviceinves/index.php/rcta/article/view/1205/1295. Accessed 19 Nov 2022
6. Peña, J.E.A.: Simulación de Cobertura del Modelo de Radio Propagación 3GPP para un Entorno Urbano en una Red 4G – LTE. Ing. Telecomunicaciones, Fund. Univ. Autónoma Colomb. 15, 33–40 (2013). https://www.researchgate.net/publication/327146961_Simula cion_de_cobertura_del_modelo_de_radio_propagacion_3GPP_para_un_entorno_urbano_ en_una_red_4G_-_LTE/fulltext/5b7cbe24a6fdcc5f8b5b05d7/Simulacion-de-cobertura-del-modelo-de-radio-propagacion-3GPP-para. Accessed 19 Nov 2022
7. Navarro, A., Andredy, C.: Ajuste estadístico de modelos de propagación de señal usando medidas de la ciudad de Cali. Ingenium - Grup. Investig. i2t, Univ. Icesi, Cali - Colomb. 6, 11–18 (2012). https://repository.usc.edu.co/bitstream/handle/20.500.12421/702/Ajusteest adísticodemodelosdepropagacióndeseñal.pdf?sequence=1&isAllowed=y. Accessed 19 Nov 2022
8. Rodríguez, J.D., Bautista, J.C., Sotomonte, L.: Xirio: Herramienta para la planeación de redes de comunicaciones móviles celulares. Universidad Distrital Francisco José de Caldas, Bogotá, Colombia, 32 (2018). https://repository.udistrital.edu.co/bitstream/handle/11349/13741/Rod riguezMeloJuanDavid2018.pdf?sequence=1&isAllowed=y. Accessed 19 Nov 2022
9. Barrios-Ulloa, A.R.: Comparison of radio wave propagations models of a wireless channel in the urban environment of the city of Barranquilla. J. Comput. Electron. Sci. Theory Appl. 2, 31 (2021)
10. Piedra, A.C.: Redes Móviles LTE: Herramienta de Planificación basada en Sistemas de Información Geográfica. Universidad del Azuay (2013). https://dspace.uazuay.edu.ec/bitstream/datos/2563/1/09751.pdf. Accessed 19 Nov 2022
11. Quintero-Flórez, V.M., Hernández-Bonilla, C.M., Giraldo-Medina, D., Uribe-Ante, D.F.: Modelado y simulación de planificadores de recursos radio para una red LTE. Ing. y Tecnol. - Unilibre - Cali 12, 230–245 (2016). https://revistas.unilibre.edu.co/index.php/cntram ado/article/view/5062. Accessed 19 Nov 2022
12. Torres, J.M., Pinto-Mangones, A., Macea, M.R., Pérez-García, N.A., Rujano, L.M.: Modelo para la estimación de las pérdidas de propagación en redes wlan operando en 2,4 ghz y 5,8 ghz, para ambientes interiores de edificios comerciales. Universidad, Cienc. y Tecnol. 20, 42–53 (2016). http://ve.scielo.org/pdf/uct/v20n78/art04.pdf. Accessed 19 Nov 2022
13. Hata, M.: Fórmula empírica para la pérdida de propagación en servicios de radio móviles terrestres. https://1library.co/article/f%C3%B3rmula-emp%C3%ADrica-p%C3%A9rdidas-propagaci%C3%B3n-servicios-radiom%C3%B3viles-terrestres.lq51jd3y. Accessed 19 Nov 2022
14. Okumura, Y.: Field strength and its variability in VHF and UHF land-mobile radio service. Rev. Electr. Commun. Lab. 16, 825–873 (1968)
15. Mellado Ochoa, A.L.: Análisis sobre la necesidad de regular la calidad del servicio de telefonía móvil en el Perú. Pontif. Univ. Católica del Perú (2013). https://tesis.pucp.edu.pe/repositorio/bitstream/handle/20.500.12404/1755/MELLADO_OCHOA_ABEL_ANA LISIS_NECESIDAD.PDF?sequence=1&isAllowed=y. Accessed 19 Nov 2022

16. More, J., Argandoña, D.: Estado del espectro radioeléctrico en el Perú y recomendaciones para promover su uso en nuevas tecnologías. Organismo Supervisor de Inversión Privada en Telecomunicaciones (Perú) (2020). https://www.osiptel.gob.pe/media/g4zh4gcn/dt-43-estado-espectro-radioelectrico-peru.pdf. Accessed 19 Nov 2022
17. OSIPTEL: Tráfico Originado Local por Modalidad y Operador. Organismo Supervisor de Inversión Privada en Telecomunicaciones (Perú) (2020). https://repositorio.osiptel.gob.pe/handle/20.500.12630/150?show=full. Accessed 19 Nov 2022
18. Google Earth. https://www.google.com/intl/es/earth/. Accessed 19 Nov 2022
19. Señal Osiptel. https://serviciosweb.osiptel.gob.pe/CoberturaMovil/. Accessed 19 Nov 2022

Sensitivity of the Response of Hysteretic Models and Plasticity Models of a Slender Shear Wall to 8 Levels of Seismic Intensities in Rigid Soil

Arias Rosas⬡, Solórzano Pacori⬡, and Moreno Sánchez$^{(\boxtimes)}$ ⬡

Universidad Peruana de Ciencias Aplicadas, Lima, Peru
{u201819314,u201621657,pccijmor}@upc.edu.pe

Abstract. In this article, the sensitivity of computational models of plasticity and hysteresis of slender shear walls at 8 levels of seismic intensity will be evaluated. Slender-reinforced concrete shear walls are structural elements used in buildings to provide lateral stiffness and resistance against seismic and wind actions, so this study was carried out in order to indicate the variability of the error of selecting a poorly calibrated model with respect to a well-calibrated one in the face of greater seismic intensity. The use of computational models when they are not adjusted to the calibration in slender shear walls can give us incorrect results of up to 17.61% in terms of resistance and up to 44.91% in terms of displacement. Therefore, based on the achieved results, it is possible to see that the biggest errors that can be made when choosing a poorly calibrated model of a slender shear wall are in terms of displacements.

Keywords: Plasticity models · Hysteresis · Calibrations · Seismic performance · Uniform seismic hazard

1 Introduction

1.1 Problem

Slender-reinforced concrete shear walls are structural elements used in buildings to provide lateral stiffness and resistance against seismic and wind actions. During a nonlinear structural analysis, due to the inelastic behavior of its materials, the question arises as to which hysteretic model, together with which computational plasticity model, is the most appropriate to represent its real performance. The choice of a bad computational model could lead to variable errors according to the seismic intensity of demand.

1.2 State of the Art

To start with the nonlinear dynamic analysis, the Peruvian Standard E-030 [1], ASCE 41-17 [2], and FEMA P-58-1 [3] point out that the behavior of the structural elements must be adjusted to the laboratory tests in terms of creep, resistance degradation, stiffness degradation and narrowing of the hysteretic bonds. Therefore, the calibration process

© The Author(s), under exclusive license to Springer Nature Switzerland AG 2023
Y. Iano et al. (Eds.): BTSym 2022, SIST 353, pp. 223–234, 2023.
https://doi.org/10.1007/978-3-031-31007-2_22

consists of replicating, using available analysis tools (software or computational codes), the elastic stiffness, the cracked stiffness, the stiffness after creep, the resistance, and the dissipated energy of the monotonic or cyclic tests [4].

In addition, it is interesting to analyze the importance of the calibration process with the sensitivity of the response of computational models to incremental dynamic analysis. Regarding this, FEMA P-58-1 [3] indicates a methodology based on uniform hazard spectra to build 8 seismic intensity levels needed for incremental analysis; and, in this way, it allows the selection of records to no longer be a complex task [4].

Fiber-like plasticity models are commonly used in slender walls, where the cross-section is discretized into various fibers of concrete and steel. With appropriate inelastic axial stress-strain characteristics of the material, fiber models can capture with reasonable accuracy the variation in axial and flexural stiffness due to concrete cracking and steel creep. One limitation, however, is the assumption that planar sections remain planar, thus not capturing shear effects associated with bending and warping torsion. These effects can be significant in non-flat wall configurations [5–7].

1.3 Proposal

Based on existing tests on slender shear walls, the sensitivity of the response (displacements, accelerations, and base shears) to 8 levels of seismic intensity is analyzed.

The computational models include fiber-type and layer-type plasticity models, and Concrete and Pivot-type hysteretic models for concrete. All of these are duly detailed in the CSI manual [8]. Then, based on indicators such as dissipated energy and resistance, well-calibrated and poorly calibrated models of each type of plasticity are selected, highlighting the benefits and deficiencies of each one. A random location is determined on the Peruvian coast with the rigid ground. Subsequently, the selected computational models are subjected to 8 levels of seismic intensity according to uniform hazard spectra, a methodology that is indicated in FEMA P-58-1 [3]. Finally, the sensitivity of the response and error variation are analyzed. It is important to highlight that the reason for selecting a rigid soil is to reconcile the uniform hazard spectra made in Peru, which were obtained in the same type of soil.

1.4 Contribution

The sensitivity of the response of hysteretic models and plasticity models of a slender shear wall to 8 levels of seismic intensities in rigid soils is provided. This is in order to represent the variation of the error due to the increase in the seismic intensity of a poorly calibrated model compared to a well-calibrated one.

2 Materials and Methods

2.1 Materials or Tools

Regarding the slender shear wall, the test of the WSH6 wall carried out in the investigation is required [9].

The computational models are elaborated in the ETABS structural software with the constitutive, plasticity, and hysteretic models available by the program.

As for the rules that regulate the proposed procedure, they are mentioned below: FEMA P-58-1 [3] and ASCE 41-17 [2]. Also, the SENCICO computer program is used [10] to obtain the Peruvian uniform hazard spectra and apply the methodology outlined in [3].

2.2 Methodology

Test Characteristics. The test carried out on the slender shear wall WSH6 in the investigation is extracted [9] as shown in Fig. 1. Regarding the materials, the concrete presents an expected f_c' of 45.6 MPa and an elastic modulus equal to 36.9 GPa, the steel presents an expected f_y of 580 MPa and an expected f_u of 695 MPa. In addition, to simulate its belonging to a real building, an axial load of 1476 kN is assigned to it.

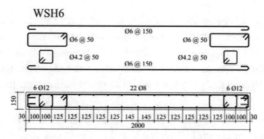

Fig. 1. Reinforcement in the plastic zone of the WSH6 wall. All dimensions are in mm [9].

Creation of Computational Models. In both the fiber-type and layer-type plasticity models, the constitutive models for concrete and steel are Mander and Simple (with strain hardening), respectively.

Fiber-Type Plasticity Models. In particular, for the fiber-type plasticity, it was found that 5 horizontal divisions constitute an acceptable approximation to the strength and ductility of the test. Although a greater discretization would be closer to the maximum basal shear of the test, it would present an early degradation of the resistance. Then, the following cyclical models are proposed with the same calibration displacements:

- Model 1: Wall with 5 horizontal divisions, with fiber-type plasticity, with Concrete-type hysteresis for concrete and subjected to the cyclic load of the test.
- Model 2: Wall with 5 horizontal divisions, with fiber-type plasticity, with Concrete-type hysteresis with degradation factor f = 1 for concrete and subjected to the cyclic load of the test.
- Model 3: Wall with 5 horizontal divisions, with fiber-type plasticity, with Pivot-type hysteresis for the concrete and subjected to the cyclic load of the test.

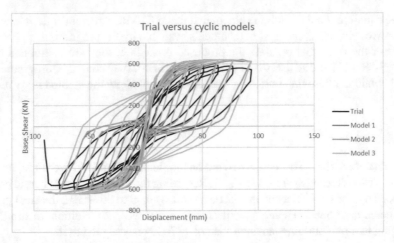

Fig. 2. Trial versus cyclic models

Layer-Type Plasticity Models. In particular, for the plasticity type layer, it was found that 3 horizontal divisions constitute an acceptable approximation to the strength and ductility of the test. Although a greater discretization would be closer to the maximum basal shear of the test, it would present an early degradation of the resistance. Then, the following cyclical models are proposed with the same calibration displacements:

- Model 4: Wall with 3 horizontal divisions, with layer-type plasticity, with Concrete-type hysteresis for the concrete and subjected to the cyclic load of the test.
- Model 5: Wall with 3 horizontal divisions, with layer-type plasticity, with Concrete-type hysteresis with degradation factor $f = 1$ for concrete and subjected to the cyclic load of the test.
- Model 6: Wall with 3 horizontal divisions, with layer-type plasticity, with Pivot-type hysteresis for the concrete and subjected to the cyclic load of the test.

Designation of Well and Poorly Calibrated Models in Fiber-Type Plasticity Models. Among the cyclical models 1, 2, and 3, the well and poorly-calibrated models are defined. Based on the accumulated energy dissipation, Table 1 and Fig. 2 show that model 1 has the lowest average error (29.16%). Regarding the evaluation of resistance, model 3 presents the least error (6.96%); however, it does not constitute a well-calibrated model due to the considerable error it presents in energy dissipation (78.27%). Therefore, models 1 and 3 represent the well and poorly-calibrated models, respectively.

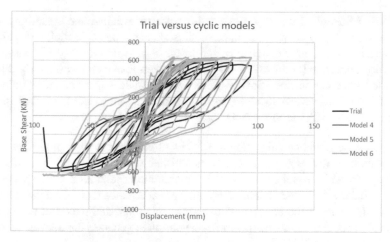

Fig. 3. Trial versus cyclic models

Table 1. Maximum shear error and accumulated dissipated energy of the cyclic models.

	Maximum shear	Error	Accumulated dissipated energy (kN.mm)	Error
Test	599.036		212 786	
Model 1	642.250	7.21%	274 839	29.16%
Model 2	642.862	7.32%	282 682	32.85%
Model 3	640.740	6.96%	379 329	78.27%

Designation of Well and Poorly Calibrated Models in Layer-Type Plasticity Models.
Among the cyclical models 4, 5, and 6, the well and poorly-calibrated models are defined.
Based on the accumulated energy dissipation, Table 2 and Fig. 3 show that model 4 has the
lowest average error (11.49%). Regarding the evaluation of resistance, model 6 presents
the least error (6.59%); however, it does not constitute a well-calibrated model due to
the considerable error it presents in energy dissipation (57.81%). Therefore, models 4
and 6 represent the well and poorly-calibrated models, respectively.

Table 2. Maximum shear error and accumulated dissipated energy of the cyclic models.

	Maximum shear	Error	Accumulated dissipated energy (KN.mm)	Error
Test	599.036		212 786	
Model 4	725.819	21.16%	237 606	11.66%
Model 5	737.702	23.15%	244 327	14.82%
Model 6	638.497	6.59%	338 759	59.20%

Creation of Seismic Intensity Levels. In order to evaluate the sensitivity of the response, the well and poorly-calibrated models of each type of plasticity are subjected to an incremental dynamic analysis with 8 levels of seismic intensity according to the methodology described in FEMA P-58-1 [3]. The Peruvian coast with the rigid ground is indicated as a location, specifically in Lima with latitude $-12.1°$ and longitude $-77°$. In general, uniform hazard spectra (Uniform Hazard Seismic-UHS) of each intensity level are obtained with the SENCICO computer program [10].

Based on the fundamental period of 0.235 s of the shear wall, a minimum spectral acceleration level (Sa) equal to 0.05 g is established with a mean annual frequency of exceedance (MAFE) equal to 0.763, and a maximum acceleration level spectral (Sa) equal to 1.728 g with a mean annual frequency of exceedance (MAFE) equal to 0.0002. Then the MAFE logarithmic curve, between the minimum and maximum elevation, is discretized in equal intervals of spectral acceleration to generate the 8 levels of seismic intensity, as shown in Table 3.

With the inverse of the MAFE, the return time and the uniform hazard spectra are calculated in SENCICO [10]. The generated spectra are shown in Fig. 4.

Table 3. Seismic Intensities

	Sa (g)	MAFE	T return (years)	PGA (g)
Min	0.050	0.76294		
e1	0.155	0.13987	7.15	0.0884
e2	0.365	0.02504	39.94	0.1975
e3	0.574	0.00778	128.58	0.3066
e4	0.784	0.03086	324.01	0.4134
e5	0.994	0.00153	654.94	0.5109
e6	1.204	0.00079	1269.33	0.6116
e7	1.414	0.00041	2470.74	0.7297
e8	1.623	0.00023	4385.11	0.8360
e9	1.728	0.00020		

Eight earthquakes are selected and, therefore, 16 seismic records (N-S and E-W components) with similar characteristics: accelerographic stations in rigid soils, interface earthquakes, and high-frequency earthquakes. The minimum limit of 11 records required by ASCE 41-17 [2] is taken into account to perform a dynamic nonlinear analysis.

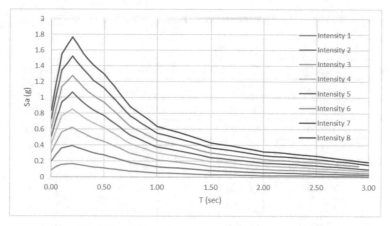

Fig. 4. Uniform hazard spectra for seismic intensity levels.

We proceed with the scaling of the corrected records to the objective uniform hazard spectrum of a given intensity by means of the Al Atik-Abrahamson numerical algorithm [11] present in the SeismoMatch program. It is enough to ensure scaling to the target spectrum between the intervals of $0.2T = 0.047$ s and $1.5T = 0.3525$ s as indicated by the NTP-E030 [1].

3 Results

As a result of non-linear time-history analysis, the maximum values of displacements, accelerations, and basal shears of the slender shear wall are extracted from the 16 seismic records of each of the 8 seismic intensities; then, the arithmetic average is chosen as the representative value of each variable. This is done for the poorly calibrated and well-calibrated models of each type of plasticity, and the representative values of displacements, accelerations, and basal shears of each intensity are obtained. In this way, when comparing them, the error percentages are obtained, as shown in Table 4 for the fiber-type plasticity model and in Table 5 for the layer-type plasticity model. Additionally, Table 6 compares the two types of plasticity.

3.1 In the Fiber-Like Plasticity Model

Error percentages are shown, both numerically (Table 4) and graphically (Fig. 5), for each intensity level.

Table 4. Error percentages

Intensity	PGA (g)	Error (%)		
		Displacement	Acceleration	Base shear
1	0.0884	2.35%	1.20%	1.91%
2	0.1975	33.95%	9.44%	10.40%
3	0.3066	44.91%	15.53%	16.60%
4	0.4134	29.05%	8.18%	6.75%
5	0.5109	32.49%	3.09%	3.39%
6	0.6116	24.66%	5.17%	1.95%
7	0.7297	25.07%	5.04%	1.65%
8	0.836	22.02%	4.92%	1.17%

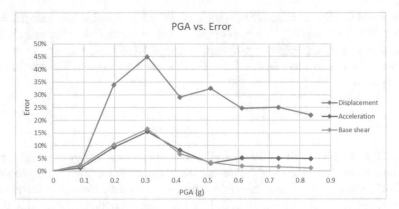

Fig. 5. PGA vs. Error

3.2 In the Layer-Type Plasticity Model

The error percentages are shown, both numerically (Table 5) and graphically (Fig. 6), for each level of intensity.

Table 5. Error percentages

| | | Error (%) | | |
Intensity	PGA (g)	Displacement	Acceleration	Base shear
1	0.0884	0.34%	0.15%	0.28%
2	0.1975	27.79%	6.37%	6.04%
3	0.3066	33.24%	10.50%	11.76%
4	0.4134	24.53%	10.81%	15.93%
5	0.5109	28.01%	10.41%	11.91%
6	0.6116	23.79%	5.71%	4.85%
7	0.7297	16.04%	7.06%	9.20%
8	0.836	10.32%	8.52%	17.61%

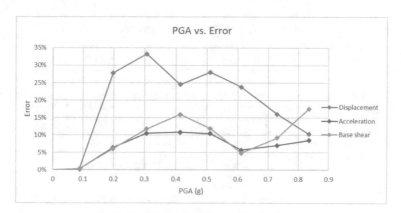

Fig. 6. PGA vs Error

3.3 Comparisons Between Fiber and Layer

The following percentage variations of the layer-type plasticity model with respect to the fiber-type plasticity model are established, as shown in Table 6 and Fig. 7.

Table 6. Layer/Fiber percentage variation

Intensity	PGA (g)	Layer/Fiber percentage variation (%)		
		Displacement	Acceleration	Base shear
1	0.0884	1.63%	2.13%	3.64%
2	0.1975	13.30%	2.81%	4.58%
3	0.3066	23.13%	6.76%	2.50%
4	0.4134	14.40%	0.38%	13.65%
5	0.5109	15.87%	3.69%	19.91%
6	0.6116	16.15%	0.77%	23.39%
7	0.7297	20.05%	1.93%	30.24%
8	0.836	17.73%	2.45%	45.56%

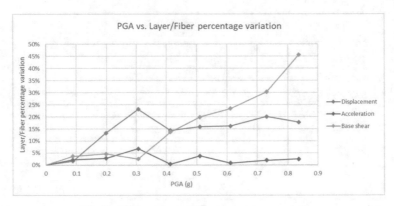

Fig. 7. PGA vs. Layer/Fiber percentage variation

4   Analysis and Interpretation of Results

If a poorly calibrated fiber-type plasticity model is used, there is a maximum error of 44.91% in displacement, 15.53% in acceleration, and 16.60% in base shear. These maximum errors occur at intensity 3 with a PGA of 0.3066 g, as shown in Table 4 and Fig. 5. If, on the contrary, a poorly calibrated layer-type plasticity model is used, a maximum error is presented of 33.24% in displacement at intensity 3 with a PGA of 0.3066 g, 10.81% in acceleration at intensity 4 with a PGA of 0.4134 g, and 17.61% in base shear at intensity 8 with a PGA of 0.836 g, as shown in Table 5 and Fig. 6. Then, whether fiber-type or layer-type plasticity models are used, if a poorly calibrated model is chosen, the largest error will be produced by displacement and the smallest errors by resistance and acceleration.

The layer model, by presenting a lower displacement and a higher basal shear than the fiber model, constitutes a more rigid model and, therefore, less conservative than the fiber model. If the latter is chosen as the appropriate type of plasticity, the choice of a layer plasticity model presents a maximum error of 23.13% in displacement at intensity 3 with a PGA of 0.3066 g, 6.76% in acceleration at the same previous intensity and 45.56% in resistance at intensity 8 with a PGA of 0.836 g, as shown in Table 6 and Fig. 7.

In addition, in the adjustment of the models to the test in terms of energy dissipation, the fiber type model presents a greater error (29.16%) than the layer type model (11.66%); while in the adjustment in terms of maximum base shear, the layer type model presents the greatest error (21.16%) than the fiber type model (7.21%).

5   Conclusions

Calibrations are essential in the inelastic analysis of slender shear walls Poorly calibrated computational models on slender shear walls give incorrect results of up to 17.61% in resistance and up to 44.91% in displacement.

The process of adjusting the computational models to the test can produce improvements in some characteristics to the detriment of others. For this reason, it is up to the engineer to find a balance between dissipated energy, resistance, and stiffness.

In addition, the possibility of using two types of plasticity is provided. If energy dissipation is given more importance than resistance, a layer-type plasticity model would be ideal. If, on the other hand, maximum base shear is a more important criterion than energy dissipation, a fiber-type plasticity model should be used.

Also, whether with fiber-type or layer-type plasticity, well-calibrated models use a Concrete-type hysteresis type for concrete, while poorly-calibrated models use a Pivot-type hysteresis type. Therefore, with the results shown, the concrete type better represents the seismic performance of a slender shear wall.

Finally, in a future line of research, it would be convenient to evaluate the sensitivity of the response of the hysteretic and plasticity models of a slender shear wall in soft soils with the purpose of evaluating, also, the soil-structure interaction.

References

1. SENCICO: Norma E.030 Diseño Sismorresistente. Servicio Nacional de Capacitación para la Industria de la Construcción (2020). https://www.gob.pe/institucion/sencico/informes-pub licaciones/887225-normas-del-reglamento-nacional-de-edificaciones-rne. Accessed 25 Nov 2022
2. ASCE: Seismic evaluation and retrofit of existing buildings. American Society of Civil Engineers (2014). https://ascelibrary.org/doi/abs/https://doi.org/10.1061/978078441 4859. Accessed 25 Nov 2022
3. FEMA: FEMA P-581: Seismic Performance Assessment of Buildings, Volume 1 - Methodology, Second Edition. Federal Emergency Management Agency (2019). https://www.atc ouncil.org/docman/fema/246-fema-p-58-1-seismic-performance-assessment-of-buildings-volume-1-methodology-second-edition?category_access=1. Accessed 25 Nov 2022
4. Villacorta, A., ADGAVI and Associates SAC: El Analisis no Lineal Dinamico y su Aplicación en la Simulación de Respuestas Estructurales. https://www.udocz.com/apuntes/19976/el-ana lisis-no-lineal-dinamico-y-su-aplicacion-en-la-simulacion-de-respuestas-estructurales-por--adolfo-galvez-villacorta--msc--1. Accessed 25 Nov 2022

5. Deierlein, G.G., Reinhorn, A.M., Willford, M.R.: Nonlinear structural analysis for seismic design. NEHRP Seism. Des. Tech. Br. **4**, 1–36 (2010)
6. de Oliveira, G.G., Iano, Y., Vaz, G.C., Chuma, E.L., Negrete, P.D.M., Negrete, J.C.M.: Structural analysis of bridges and viaducts using the IoT concept. An approach on dom pedro highway (Campinas-Brazil). In: Iano, Y., Saotome, O., Kemper Vásquez, G.L., Cotrim Pezzuto, C., Arthur, R., Gomes de Oliveira, G. (eds.) Brazilian Technology Symposium, pp. 108–119. Springer, Cham (2022). https://doi.org/10.1007/978-3-031-08545-1_10
7. de Oliveira, G.G., Iano, Y., Vaz, G.C., Chuma, E.L., Negrete, P.D.M., Negrete, J.C.M.: Prop walls: a contextualization of the theme in a case study in the city of Campinas (Brazil). In: Iano, Y., Saotome, O., Kemper Vásquez, G.L., Cotrim Pezzuto, C., Arthur, R., Gomes de Oliveira, G. (eds.) Brazilian Technology Symposium, pp. 128–139. Springer, Cham (2022). https://doi.org/10.1007/978-3-031-08545-1_12
8. CSI: CSI Analysis Reference Manual for SAP2000, ETABS, SAFE and CSiBridge. Computers & Structures Inc. (2016). https://docs.csiamerica.com/manuals/sap2000/CSiRefer.pdf. Accessed 25 Nov 2022
9. Dazio, A., Beyer, K., Bachmann, H.: Quasi-static cyclic tests and plastic hinge analysis of RC structural walls. Eng. Struct. **31**, 1556–1571 (2009)
10. SENCICO: Servicio Web de Consultas para la Determinación del Peligro Sísmico en el Territorio Nacional. Servicio Nacional de Capacitación para la Industria de la Construcción (2022). https://www.gob.pe/institucion/sencico/informes-publicaciones/2869566-servicio-web-de-consultas-para-la-determinacion-del-peligro-sismico-en-el-territorio-nacional. Accessed 25 Nov 2022
11. Al Atik, L., Abrahamson, N.: An improved method for nonstationary spectral matching. Earthq. spectra. **26**, 601–617 (2010)

Industry 4.0 and Its Impact on Innovation Projects in Steelworks

Ernandes Scopel[1] , Wandercleiton Cardoso[2]([envelope]) , André Luiz Caulit Silva[3] ,
Marcelo Margon[4] , Danyelle Santos Ribeiro[5] , Thiago Augusto Pires Machado[1] ,
and André Itman Filho[1]

[1] Instituto Federal do Espirito Santo, Vitoria, Brazil
[2] Università degli Studi di Genova, Genoa, Italy
wandercleiton.cardoso@dicca.unige.it
[3] Fucape Business School, Vitoria, Brazil
[4] Pontifícia Universidade Católica, Belo Horizonte, Brazil
[5] Università Degli Studi Niccolò Cusano, Rome, Italy

Abstract. It is clear that the dynamic demands of steel consumers, combined with
fierce competition in the market, are increasingly forcing steel mills to improve
their ability to adapt to such changes in scenarios, as it is a global phenomenon.
The steel industry is of undeniable importance, not only because its products are
widely used, but also because it is an energy-intensive industry and one of the
main sources of greenhouse gases. Although Industry 4.0 in particular entails a
radical change in the way factories currently operate, we have seen innovative
outcomes occur in both processes and products. The former are usually protected
by trade secrets or know-how, while the latter is eventually patented. An important
point to consider is that the Brazilian steel industry has a larger share of foreign
investment. In conclusion, it was found that further research on this topic is needed
to better understand the process of business model innovation and the archetypes
resulting from the adoption of Industry 4.0 in the Brazilian steel world.

Keywords: Industry 4.0 · Innovation · Steel industry

1 Introduction

The steel industry is of undeniable importance, not only because its products are widely
used, but also because it is an energy-intensive industry and one of the main sources of
greenhouse gases. Brazil is the eighth-largest producer of steel. It accounts for 2% of
global production [1, 2].

The main competitive advantage of the Brazilian iron and steel sector is the country's
wealth of high-quality iron ore reserves. Brazil is responsible for 21% of global iron ore
production and 24% of global iron ore exports [1, 2].

Steel is produced in Brazil in three main types of metallurgical plants: (a) integrated
plants, which carry out the processes of iron ore reduction, steelmaking, smelting, and
forming; (b) semi-integrated plants, which use pig iron and sponge iron from other

plants or recycled metals for the processes of steelmaking, casting, and forming; (c) plants owned by independent producers, which produce only hot metal [1–3].

Not only in the steel industry, but also in other industries, innovation has become a key activity that cannot only affect the viability of a company, but also trigger social and economic change. The ability to innovate is critical to maintaining competitive advantage [2–4].

Innovation is critical to the survival of modern businesses. Although companies often perceive innovation as inherently positive for organizations, the relationship between innovation and performance is still an open question [1, 3, 5].

Industry 4.0 is a high-tech strategy that represents the fourth industrial revolution after mechanization, electrification, and computerization. Industry 4.0 describes the increasing digitalization and automation of the production environment and the creation of digital value chains that enable communication between products, their environment, and business partners [1–3, 6].

The aim of this paper is to give a brief and systematic account of the evolution of the steel industry in Brazil in terms of innovation projects, focusing on the impact caused by the principles of Industry 4.0 (Fourth Industrial Revolution) and the consideration of the principles of business sustainability.

2 Brazilian Steel Plant

Brazil began the 20th century with a steel sector of very little practical importance. As early as 1910, the debate on the national steel problem took shape within the framework of some projects that linked the country's steel production to the projects that had been created at the time for the export of iron ore from the Minas Gerais iron ore zone.

In April 1941, on the initiative of the Getúlio Vargas government, Companhia Siderúrgica Nacional (CSN) was founded in Volta Redonda, Rio de Janeiro, the first integrated Brazilian steel plant.

Regarding serving the steel market, several companies such as Gerdau (1901, year of foundation) in the south of the country, Cosipa (1953), in the state of São Paulo, Belgo-Mineira (1921), Acesita (1944) and Usiminas (1952), in the state of Minas Gerais, and Companhia Siderúrgica Tubarão, CST, (1976) in the state of Espírito Santo were founded and are still operating in the country [7–10].

The main competitive advantage of the Brazilian steel industry is the country's wealth of high-quality iron ore reserves. With an installed production capacity of 41.0 million tonnes in 2007, Brazil ranked 12th among exporting countries with 33.78 million tonnes (in 2016). According to the World Trade Organisation (WTO) annual report, Brazil dropped from 26th to 27th place among the world's largest exporters in 2018 [5, 7, 9, 11].

The steel industry is of great importance for the processing industry, for its share of GDP, and job creation. According to Instituto Aço Brasil (2018), crude steel production in the Brazilian steel industry reached 34.4 million tonnes in 2017, a growth of 9.9% compared to 2016. The production of steel products (flat and long rolled products, slabs, ingots, blooms, and billets) reached 36.1 million tonnes in the same year [5, 7, 9, 11, 12].

The country's coke-integrated plants account for about 70–75% of Brazil's steel production. Figure 1 shows the main processes in integrated plants.

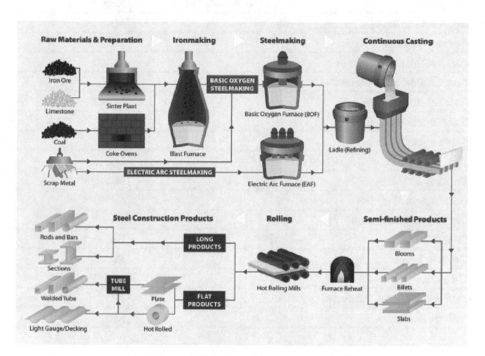

Fig. 1. Process flowchart of integrated steel mills.

The steel industry (steel made from an iron-carbon alloy, in which the second element (carbon) enters the composition with a share of 0.008%C to 2.14%C) in Brazil has the characteristics of an oligopoly, in which a few companies operate and, above all, hold most of the production in the sector [5, 7, 9, 11–14].

According to a 2019 report by Instituto Aço Brasil, the number of relevant steel parks in Brazil totals 32 plants, ranking Brazil 9th in the world in terms of steel production. Table 1 shows the main steel companies reported by Instituto Aço Brasil [7, 15].

Brazil has a large steel industry on its territory, with the technological capacity to supply the local and international markets with different types of steel products. Despite the increase in production, the average utilization of installed capacity in the Brazilian steel industry is still low. In 2017, the steel industry worldwide recovered from a recovery that had started the previous year [5, 7, 9, 11–16].

According to the World Steel Association (WSA), global steel production grew by 5.5% in 2017, with all regions performing well. ArcelorMittal, the world's largest steel producer, forecast that the global steel market would grow between 1.5% and 2.5% in 2018 [5, 7, 9, 11–17].

Table 1. Main steel mills in Brazil.

Companies	Number of installations	Region
Aço Verde do Brasil	01	MA
Aperam South America	01	MG
ArcelorMittal Aços Longos	03	MG/SP
ArcelorMittal Sul Fluminense	02	RJ
ArcelorMittal Tubarão	02	ES/SC
Siderúrgica Nacional	01	RJ
Siderúrgica do Pecém	01	CE
Gerdau Açominas	01	MG
Gerdau Aços Longos	09	Several regions
Gerdau Aços Especiais	03	SP/RS
Siderúrgica Norte Brasil	01	PA
SIMEC	02	ES/SP
Ternium Brasil	01	RJ
Usiminas	02	MG/SP
Vallourec Soluções Tubulares	01	MG
Villares Metals	01	SP

3   Industry 4.0: Concepts and Principles

This is not the first time academia has debated how digital technologies are reshaping the manufacturing industry. In the late 1950s, debates focused on how computer-integrated manufacturing (CIM) enables companies to improve their manufacturing processes [18].

In the following, turn briefly to Industry 4.0, an important current debate on how new digital technologies will change manufacturing. The term is mainly used in European countries such as Germany, the UK, and Italy, but also beyond, e.g. in South Korea [1–4, 6, 8, 19].

The implementation of Industry 4.0 in the Brazilian scenario brings challenges such as (i) the development of strategic policies and government incentives; (ii) the meeting of entrepreneurs and managers with a proactive attitude; and (iii) the technological development and training of professionals close to the industry [20–24].

Artificial intelligence, used for example in planning driverless vehicle routes in factories and warehouses, leads to time and cost savings in supply chain management (SCM). Furthermore, applied to Big Data, it shortens the processing time of complex tasks and increases the reliability of analyses [20–24].

Functional nanomaterials and nanosensors can also be used in quality control in production to enable more efficient management, or they allow the production of advanced robots that cooperate with occupational safety [20–24].

Maintenance drones in production areas or their use in inventorying stock and delivering spare parts, at any time of the day or night, in any terrain, and any weather, are other applications that are becoming routine in smart factories. The improvement of these technologies improves the productive environment and generates input for the emergence of other new technologies [19–25].

Usually, two promises are made to companies in debates about Industry 4.0. First, companies can significantly increase their productivity, flexibility, and efficiency. Cyber-physical systems are considered an enabling technology that allows for numerous innovative applications and also the innovation of a company's business model [26].

Cyber-physical systems refer to technical systems that are integrated into larger systems such as devices, buildings, infrastructure, and production facilities. Cyber-physical systems capture, shop, and interpret data from the environment and respond to signals from the environment. Unlike other technologies, cyber-physical systems regulate themselves as they are able to communicate with both human actors and other devices both locally and globally [26, 27].

This new approach leads to industrial value creation that is not only automatic, mainly within individual factories, but also networked between objects, products, and people, based on the concept of the Internet of Things. Industry 4.0 thus has to do with the networking of various functions within the supply chain, which is also based on the use of artificial intelligence [26–28].

4 Innovation Processes in the Main Brazilian Steel Mills

The term business model is widely known and very present in business and innovation research. Although the research community emphasizes that there is no universally accepted definition of a business model, interpretations of the term are increasingly converging toward its conceptualization as a sum of complementary elements that primarily create, capture, and offer value [25–29].

A business model innovation stands for "innovations that are designed for, new to, and non-trivial to the key elements of a company's business model and/or the architecture that connects these elements". This definition implies that senior management plays an essential role in shaping business model innovation [30].

It also signals that a business model innovation entails new tasks that go beyond small adjustments to the business environment, such as variations in the value proposition through products adapted to the market. In contrast, a business model innovation attracts new customers who are not satisfied with or do not have access to current solutions [31–33].

As for the concept of innovation, the Austrian economist Joseph Alois Schumpeter already spoke about innovation and its importance at the beginning of the 20th century. He talked about innovation and its meaning in the early twentieth century. Innovation arises from a number of different combinations of resources, which can arise in five different ways: The introduction of a new good, the introduction of a new production method, the development of new markets, new sources of raw materials, and new industrial organization [31–33].

5   Final Considerations

From the systematic review of the literature, it can be concluded that the scientific research question and objectives have been achieved. We expanded our understanding of the impact of Industry 4.0 on innovation projects in the main steel mills studied and found that the Brazilian steel industry needs to intensify its innovation projects through the Industry 4.0 approach.

In the sectors where economies of scale play a major role, as noted throughout the bibliographic research, we found that industries producing consumer durables, such as the steel industry, stand out.

The intensity of innovation efforts is considerable, considering that most technological inputs are internally generated. In the case of "steel", the scenario reviewed contrasts the high intensity of investment in internal and external innovation, i.e., internal efforts are used in the plant itself and external when the initiatives are acquired by the plant through market practices or at the periphery of the plant.

Innovative outcomes occur in both processes and products. The former are usually protected by trade secrets or know-how, while the latter is eventually leased out. An important point to consider is that the steel industry has a larger share of foreign investment.

It is a fact that Industry 4.0 is having a major positive impact on the functional configuration of Brazil's main steel mills. It is believed that the replacement of labor with new technologies will have an impact on improving quality, speed, and performance in production, results that in some cases may go far beyond human skills, i.e., a new professional profile will be required, as Industry 4.0 means, in particular, a fundamental change in the way the factory floor currently functions.

It has also been observed that the factories with a greater technological content tend to have a greater impact on their innovation projects and therefore have the greatest technological opportunities to report. It is a fact that the factories that have achieved the most results are also the ones that give importance to a greater number of learning and knowledge variables.

AcelorMittal Tubarão (ES), for example, has set up a research center for product development. The plant focused on eliminating bottlenecks, simplifying processes and reducing costs in the value chain to enable greater agility, productivity, and competitiveness, i.e., proactive measures that qualified the product portfolio.

The analysis of the main innovation projects in the main Brazilian steel mills, which emerges from the sectoral analysis of this study, also confirms the limitations of the Brazilian industry in terms of innovation project performance compared to other countries. It has been observed with great intensity that the main Brazilian steel mills are making large and significant investments in environmental protection, taking into account the Triple Bottom Line oriented concepts.

The results of the sustainability reports show that increasing the use of charcoal in pig iron production from 23.0% to 32.5% can reduce total CO_2 emissions by 11.3% by 2050 while introducing the best available technologies and disruptive technologies in new steel mills can reduce CO_2 emissions by 15.6%. If both effects are taken into account, the CO_2 reduction potential would reach 23.2% in 2050.

The statements on innovation capacity were obtained from the sustainability reports of the main steel mills studied and from the results of a study of the steel industry developed as part of the Directory of Private Research in Brazil (DPP), a project that collects information on the innovation strategies of Brazilian companies on a broad basis.

In order to extend the assessment to the entire Brazilian steel industry, a larger sample of mills would be required, including all steel mills, as the problem discussed has several other facets that warrant conducting a future study.

Future research could reveal which factors are responsible for the transition from an innovation policy to a wide-ranging innovation discourse.

References

1. Dallasega, P., Rauch, E., Linder, C.: Industry 4.0 as an enabler of proximity for construction supply chains: a systematic literature review. Comput. Ind. **99**, 205–225 (2018)
2. Iannino, V., Denker, J., Colla, V.: An application-oriented cyber-physical production optimisation system architecture for the steel industry. IFAC-PapersOnLine **55**, 60–65 (2022)
3. Guo, D., Ling, S., Rong, Y., Huang, G.Q.: Towards synchronization-oriented manufacturing planning and control for Industry 4.0 and beyond. IFAC-PapersOnLine **55**, 163–168 (2022)
4. Song, X.: Parameterized fragility analysis of steel frame structure subjected to blast loads using Bayesian logistic regression method. Struct. Saf. **87**, 102000 (2020)
5. Cardoso, W., Di Felice, R.: A novel committee machine to predict the quantity of impurities in hot metal produced in blast furnace. Comput. Chem. Eng. **163**, 107814 (2022)
6. Klingenberg, C.O., Borges, M.A.V., do Vale Antunes, J.A. Jr.: Industry 4.0: what makes it a revolution? A historical framework to understand the phenomenon. Technol. Soc. **70**, 102009 (2022)
7. Cardoso, W., Barros, D., Baptista, R., di Felice, R.: Mathematical modelling to control the chemical composition of blast furnace slag using artificial neural networks and empirical correlation. IOP Conf. Ser. Mater. Sci. Eng. **1203**, 32096 (2021)
8. Beham, A., Raggl, S., Hauder, V.A., Karder, J., Wagner, S., Affenzeller, M.: Performance, quality, and control in steel logistics 4.0. Procedia Manuf. **42**, 429–433 (2020)
9. Cardoso, W., di Felice, R., Baptista, R.C.: A critical overview of development and innovations in biogas upgrading BT. Presented at the Proceedings of the 7th Brazilian Technology Symposium (BTSym 2021) (2022)
10. Hermann, M., Pentek, T., Otto, B.: Design principles for industrie 4.0 scenarios. In: 2016 49th Hawaii International Conference on System Sciences (HICSS), pp. 3928–3937. IEEE (2016)
11. Cardoso, W., di Felice, R., Baptista, R.C.: Artificial neural network-based committee machine for predicting the slag quality of a blast furnace fed with metallurgical coke. In: Iano, Y., Saotome, O., Kemper Vásquez, G.L., Cotrim Pezzuto, C., Arthur, R., Gomes de Oliveira, G. (eds.) Brazilian Technology Symposium, pp. 66–73. Springer, Cham (2022). https://doi.org/10.1007/978-3-031-08545-1_6
12. Itman Filho, A., Cardoso, W.D.S., Gontijo, L.C., Silva, R.V.D., Casteletti, L.C.: Austenitic-ferritic stainless steel containing niobium. Rem. Rev. Esc. Minas. **66**, 467–471 (2013)
13. Garvey, A., Norman, J.B., Barrett, J.: Technology and material efficiency scenarios for net zero emissions in the UK steel sector. J. Clean. Prod. **333**, 130216 (2022)
14. Yu, X., Tan, C.: China's pathway to carbon neutrality for the iron and steel industry. Glob. Environ. Chang. **76**, 102574 (2022)

15. Rad, F.F., et al.: Industry 4.0 and supply chain performance: a systematic literature review of the benefits, challenges, and critical success factors of 11 core technologies. Ind. Mark. Manag. **105**, 268–293 (2022)
16. Cardoso, W., di Felice, R., Baptista, R.C.: Artificial neural network for predicting silicon content in the hot metal produced in a blast furnace fueled by metallurgical coke. Mater. Res. **25** (2022)
17. Goschin, T., Vogel, M., Flassig, R.: Energy technologies for decarbonizing the steel processing industry–a numerical study. IFAC-PapersOnLine. **55**, 1–5 (2022)
18. Cardoso, W., Felice, R.D., Baptista, R.C., Machado, T.A.P., Galdino, A.G.D.S.: Evaluation of the use of blast furnace slag as an additive in mortars. REM-Int. Eng. J. **75**, 215–224 (2022)
19. Kim, D.-Y., Kumar, V., Kumar, U.: Relationship between quality management practices and innovation. J. Oper. Manag. **30**, 295–315 (2012)
20. Cardoso, W., Di Felice, R., Baptista, R.C.: Artificial neural networks for modelling and controlling the variables of a blast furnace. In: 2021 IEEE 6th International Forum on Research and Technology for Society and Industry (RTSI), pp. 148–152. IEEE (2021)
21. Pourmehdi, M., Paydar, M.M., Ghadimi, P., Azadnia, A.H.: Analysis and evaluation of challenges in the integration of Industry 4.0 and sustainable steel reverse logistics network. Comput. Ind. Eng. **163**, 107808 (2022)
22. Nishimura, E.H., Iano, Y., de Oliveira, G.G., Vaz, G.C.: Application and requirements of AIoT-enabled industrial control units. In: Iano, Y., Saotome, O., Kemper Vásquez, G.L., Cotrim Pezzuto, C., Arthur, R., Gomes de Oliveira, G. (eds.) Brazilian Technology Symposium, pp. 724–733. Springer, Cham (2022). https://doi.org/10.1007/978-3-031-08545-1_72
23. Izario, D., Brancalhone, J., Iano, Y., de Oliveira, G.G., Vaz, G.C., Izario, K.: 5G-automation of vertical systems in the industry 4.0. In: Iano, Y., Saotome, O., Kemper Vásquez, G.L., Cotrim Pezzuto, C., Arthur, R., Gomes de Oliveira, G. (eds.) Brazilian Technology Symposium, pp. 35–43. Springer, Cham (2023). https://doi.org/10.1007/978-3-031-04435-9_4
24. Vaz, G.C., Iano, Y., de Oliveira, G.G.: IoT-from industries to houses: an overview. In: Iano, Y., Saotome, O., Kemper Vásquez, G.L., Cotrim Pezzuto, C., Arthur, R., Gomes de Oliveira, G. (eds.) Brazilian Technology Symposium, pp. 734–741. Springer, Cham (2022). https://doi.org/10.1007/978-3-031-08545-1_73
25. Cardoso, W., Di Felice, R., Baptista, R.C.: Mathematical modeling of a solid oxide fuel cell operating on biogas. Bull. Electr. Eng. Informatics. **10**, 2929–2942 (2021)
26. Mazzoleni, M., et al.: A fuzzy logic-based approach for fault diagnosis and condition monitoring of industry 4.0 manufacturing processes. Eng. Appl. Artif. Intell. **115**, 105317 (2022)
27. Cardoso, W., di Felice, R., Baptista, R.: Mathematical modelling to predict fuel consumption in a blast furnace using artificial neural networks. In: García Márquez, F.P. (ed.) Integrated Emerging Methods of Artificial Intelligence & Cloud Computing, pp. 1–10. Springer, Cham (2022). https://doi.org/10.1007/978-3-030-92905-3_1
28. Itman Filho, A., Silva, R.V., Cardoso, W.D.S., Casteletti, L.C.: Effect of niobium in the phase transformation and corrosion resistance of one austenitic-ferritic stainless steel. Mater. Res. **17**, 801–806 (2014)
29. Cardoso, W., et al.: Modeling of artificial neural networks for silicon prediction in the cast iron production process. IAES Int. J. Artif. Intell. (IJ-AI) **11**(2), 530 (2022). https://doi.org/10.11591/ijai.v11.i2.pp530-538
30. Satyro, W.C., et al.: Industry 4.0 implementation: the relevance of sustainability and the potential social impact in a developing country. J. Clean. Prod. **337**, 130456 (2022)
31. Cardoso, W., di Felice, R.: Prediction of silicon content in the hot metal using Bayesian networks and probabilistic reasoning. Int. J. Adv. Intell. Informatics. **7**, 268–281 (2021)

32. Rajab, S., Afy-Shararah, M., Salonitis, K.: Using Industry 4.0 capabilities for identifying and eliminating lean wastes. Procedia CIRP **107**, 21–27 (2022)
33. Cardoso, W., Machado, T.A.P., Baptista, R.C., de S Galdino, A.G., Pinto, F.A.M., de Souza Luz, T.: Industrial technological process for welding AISI 301 stainless steel: focus on microstructural control. In: Iano, Y., Saotome, O., Kemper Vásquez, G.L., Cotrim Pezzuto, C., Arthur, R., Gomes de Oliveira, G. (eds.) Brazilian Technology Symposium, pp. 34–41. Springer, Cham (2022). https://doi.org/10.1007/978-3-031-08545-1_3

The Method of Ontological Designing of the Risk Concept in the Normative Regulation

Nikolai I. Plotnikov[✉] [ID]

Scientific Research Project, Civil Aviation Institute «AviaManager», 630078 Novosibirsk, Russian Federation
am@aviam.org

Abstract. The existing normative definition of risk, based on probability theory, is a particular definition of risks and does not correspond to the variety of measures for calculating life risks. This paper presents a method of ontologically designing a new description of the concept in terms of hazard and outcome. The hazard measure absorbs a wide class of soft measures. The measure of the magnitude of the outcome combines the concepts of damages. The aim of the work is the development of normative models and definitions of risks necessary for the formation of standards for the regulation and management of life risks. To achieve the goal, the following tasks were performed. An analysis and assessment of the consistency of existing risk research approaches, a study of the linguistic sources of the term risk, and an analysis of the psychometric paradigm of risk perception were compiled. The method of ontological designing is applied and establishes a sequence of analysis and information modeling for identifying the characteristics of objects necessary for life risk management.

Keywords: Ontological designing · Regulatory model · Risk estimation · Risk quantification · Hazard · Outcome · Risk Matrix

1 Introduction

There are numerous concepts of risk in scientific studies of the risks of vital activity. There are three approaches to studying the subject of risk: the measurement of risk, the socio-cultural evaluation, and the psychometric evaluation. Risk measurement focuses on how to transform data on damage, casualties, and financial losses, and how risk is influenced. The socio-cultural evaluation looks at the impact of group and cultural variables on risk. Risk psychometry establishes the emotive responses of people to risk situations that form risk judgment (Fig. 1).

The problems of the subject of the risk concept are as follows: a) the unclear origin of the term "risk", b) numerous incompatible classifications and definitions of risks, c) groundlessness of the concept of risk measurement, d) groundlessness of risk identification through uncertainty, e) groundlessness of risk identification as a negative consequence through a combination probability and damage. The concept of risk measurement and the regulatory standards [1, Error! Reference source not found.] is defined as: risk

© The Author(s), under exclusive license to Springer Nature Switzerland AG 2023
Y. Iano et al. (Eds.): BTSym 2022, SIST 353, pp. 244–267, 2023.
https://doi.org/10.1007/978-3-031-31007-2_24

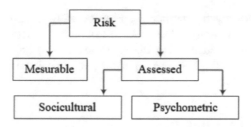

Fig. 1. Risk classification

(a) is the product of multiplication (b) the probability, and (c) the consequences (impact, damage) of an event (Eq. 1).

$$R = P \cdot D(Risk = Probability \times Damage) \qquad (1)$$

The scientific validity of the formula raises many questions: (1) Risk constitutes any content of human life and nature, where outcomes coexist that can be assessed as neutral, negative, and positive. However, the risk in the formula is determined only in the negative understanding of the consequences as damage. (2) Risk contains the expectation of an event in the form of probability, and probabilistic measures are used for the calculation. (3) Events take place in time. The frequency of events is set as an average per unit of time, usually a year. This calculation is mathematically incorrect, especially with the uneven distribution of events throughout the year. (4) The quantification ratio of consequences and likelihood is reduced to the mathematical multiplication. However, it is impossible to perform a calculation using this formula since the variable consequences also have a probabilistic random nature. The ratio can be summative, multiplicative, unspecified, or non-linear. In any case, calculating risks through the product of consequence and probability can be a particular option. So, the problem of the normative description and standards of risks used by the world community is as follows: why in the formula only probability is used, and no other measures, damage, not positive and neutral outcomes, multiplication, and no others ratio? The scientific basis for the risk formula remains debatable and controversial. This paper has an accent on the development of the regulatory standards of risk management [2, 4].

The aim of the work is the development of normative models and definitions of risks necessary for the formation of standards for the regulation and management of life risks. To achieve the goal, the following tasks were performed. An analysis and assessment of the consistency of existing risk research approaches, a study of the linguistic sources of the term risk, and an analysis of the psychometric paradigm of risk perception were compiled. A three-component model of uncertainty is proposed, and an experiment is carried out to substantiate the possibility of calculating risks through uncertainty. A method for multivariate risk assessment has been compiled. Risk definitions and a new regulatory model have been developed, creating a new basis for risk management.

The method of ontological designing (MOD) in this paper is considered a scientific approach to reducing the uncertainty in the description of complex structural objects and events [5]. The basis of the method postulates the thesis that in order to control any object, it is necessary to identify its purpose through terms and definitions. Definitions set the features necessary for modeling and calculating the properties of an object, which is a condition of control. The method establishes a sequence of analysis and information modeling for identifying the characteristics of objects necessary for life risk management. The method offers a linguistic and logical approach for modeling the example of aviation safety.

2   Analysis of Risk Concept

2.1   Linguistic Sources

Dictionary descriptions provide the following risk information: chance, likelihood, possibility, danger, gamble, hazard, peril, speculation, uncertainty, venture [6]; to risk-forge: to indulge in luck, in the wrong deed, at random [7], the possibility of danger, failure [8]; possible danger, acting at random in the hope of a happy accident [9]; a situational characteristic of activity, consisting in the uncertainty of its outcome and possible adverse consequences in case of failure [10]. Risk: Greek ($\rho\iota\zeta\alpha$, riza) - root, base, foot of a mountain; Spanish (risco) rock, reef, reef; French (risquer) - maneuver between rocks, take risks. In European languages from the 15th century (risicum) gets the legal meaning of "losses" in maritime trade; Arab. (rischio) and (riezgo) "in search of prosperity". Much earlier, the concept of risk was set forth in Arnaud-Nicole's Logic or the Art of Thinking, 1662: "Fear of harm ought to be proportional not merely to the gravity of the harm, but also the probability of the event" (Antoine Arnauld et Pierre Nicole (1662), *La Logique, ou l'art de penser*) [Error! Reference source not found.]. Let us pay attention to the keywords: "event", "harm", "proportionality", and "probability": the word "risk" is missing. In general, the origin of the term "risk" remains undetermined.

2.2   Psychometric Paradigm

The psychometric paradigm (PP) studies the issues of subjectivity in the definition of randomness and the consequences of an event. Otherwise, how people perceive, endure, and agree to various risks. C. Starr, 1969 is considered to be the author of the concept [11]. Since then, numerous assessments have been performed and psychometric classifications have been developed. Established risk assessments based on judgments: a) voluntariness and controllability; b) benefits from activities associated with risk; c) the number of victims in a normal and emergency year; d) the number of victims in a given risk relative to victims for other reasons. Revealed ten risk perception factors: dread, control, nature vs. man-made, choice, children, novelty, publicity, propinquity, risk-benefit tradeoff, and trust [Error! Reference source not found.]. It is studied where the risk involved the actions of others, and how people assess the risk will be significantly affected by the extent to which one trusts the other party or parties involved.

   In [13], a comparative psychometry of the risks of nuclear energy and X-ray radiation was performed on a seven-point scale of values according to nine antonymous concepts: voluntary - involuntary, chronic - catastrophic, ordinary - threatening, non-fatal - fatal, unexpressed - pronounced, immediate - delayed, known to science - unknown to science, uncontrolled - controlled, new - old. The new, the threatening, the unknown, the

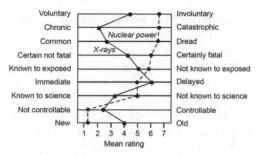

Fig. 2. Psychometric comparison of risks of the same nature

involuntary, the uncontrollable, and the fatal are perceived in the maximum risk values (Fig. 2).

In [15] the space of psychometric assessment, the perception of 81 types of risks was assessed, two-dimensional diagram of the space of risk perception was compiled, which is derived in terms of the "unknown risk – dread risk" pair (Fig. 3).

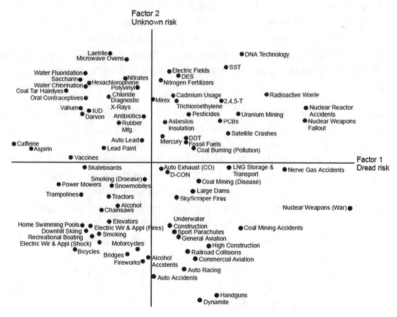

Fig. 3. Psychometric assessment of 81 types of risks

The polar relations of the couple are structured by 15 concepts, 10 of which explain the dread risk, and five concepts explain the known risk. The effect of "social amplification" was established: 1) the strongest connection with the victim of the event, then 2) the responsibility of the company that created the event, 3) the department, industry, 4) state, government, and the international community. The effect of social strengthening is greater, the greater the uncertainty and the threat with catastrophic consequences.

The work [16] presents the regression analysis of risk psychometry of various technologies done in the work [Error! Reference source not found.]. According to surveys of 294 respondents, the rank relationship of 18 technologies was revealed on a seven-point plus-minus scale. The values of the assessments were compiled in the regression of five independent variables, which were also ranked: risk, benefit, voluntariness, the possibility of protection, and substitutability of technology. The model fits the data ratio with a mean proportion of the independent variable of 0.407. The weight of the standardized regression shows that risk is the most important variable, and benefit is next in importance. Other variables have marginal and complementary values.

Subjective Risk Perception. The subjective risk perception is carried out through the work of the mode of emotional irrational response and the mode of rational reasoning. The emotional response of genetic, natural, and social experience forms an immediate command for behavior, how to act in a risky situation. It has been established that in the event of a conflict with the rational beginning of the assessment of harm-gain, emotion prevails [17]. Research by neurophysiologists proves that both modes work together and synchronously for decision-making and action. A logical reasonable analytical conclusion cannot effectively take place without the effect of emotional mode [19]. When evaluating events of extreme and rare risks, respondents exaggerate the magnitude of their impact [20], and in repeated experiments of the same events, they underestimate them [21]. In general, it was concluded that exaggeration should be expected in the perception of rare risks. Another conclusion is the observation of (1) the prevalence of behavior to eliminate the risk that has arisen, but (2) the lack of behavior to prevent such events [22].

The subjective perception of risk assessment is confirmed by the statistics of a decrease in commercial load due to passenger refusals to fly on flights that have been involved in accidents. Numerous reports of an "inner voice" of danger have been established in people with the greatest sensitivity who have escaped death: a non-drinking passenger gets drunk before a flight and is not allowed on the plane; another did not take off due to a fever or was stuck in a traffic jam on the way to the airport. Many similar cases have been established when a person evaluates danger and risk based on subjective perception. Absence, suspension, and refusals from emergency flights, according to various sources, is from four to 15 percent of the reduction in commercial airline load [23, Error! Reference source not found.].

To model risks, the consistency of the concept out of risk measurability through uncertainty and experiments are carried out. A multivariate risk assessment method is proposed, and a normative risk model is developed.

2.3 Assessing the Consistency of Risk Measurability Through Uncertainty

The concept of uncertainty (U) is considered to establish a relationship between uncertainty and risk in order to check the possibility of quantification - numerical estimates of uncertainty and risk. Consider certainty - the opposite concept of uncertainty. The ontological law of certainty is formulated: every side of the world accessible to sensory or rational contemplation is something that is different, special than everything else, excluding everything else.

In logic, "certainty is a condition of knowledge and thinking, based on the laws of identity, contradiction and exclusion of the third" [24, p. 68]. If logical laws are not observed, the opposite concept is called uncertainty. A negation is called a contradictory opposite if the content of one excludes some of the features of the other without replacing it with anything. The law of exclusion of the middle is valid only for contradictory opposition with clarity of content. Thus, uncertainties appear for cases of a) contradictory opposition according to the logical law of negation, and b) the law of exclusion of the third. Negation is called the opposite if the content of one excludes some of the features of the other, with the replacement of some of the features or an incompatible positive feature. Example. On the pre-landing straight, the pilot's decision "to land or not to land" requires the crew to evaluate the landing configuration and accurately indicate the decision height (DHL), upon reaching which it is necessary to act: to land or go around.

In this paper classification and definitions of uncertainty are compiled, partially similar to [26]. Uncertainty is classified into three types: (U_o) objective ontological uncertainty, as a mediated limited existence of the subject; (U_e) subjective epistemological uncertainty as the degree of reliable scientific knowledge; (U_m) moral uncertainty as free will, (lat. *Liberum arbitrium*), the ability of a person to make a choice of action (Fig. 4).

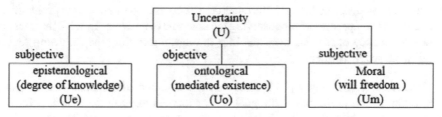

Fig. 4. Uncertainty classification

Definition 1. Epistemological uncertainty (U_e) as a degree of reliable scientific knowledge is a subjective lack of certainty of the subject due to limited knowledge about the existing state, situation, and future possible outcomes and consequences of decisions and actions that need to be done in the present.

Definition 2. Ontological uncertainty (U_o) is the objective impossibility of decisions and actions that need to be done in the present time due to the mediated limited existence of the subject.

Definition 3. Moral uncertainty (U_m) is a subjective plausible choice of the subject of decisions and actions that need to be done in the present tense, based on free will in the modalities "I want", "I can", and "I must".

The uncertainty of knowledge has been known since ancient times in philosophical doctrine and is presented as follows (Table 1):

Table 1. Four levels of knowledge uncertainty

Knowledge	Concept	Judgment
Unconscious ignorance	Ignorance	"I don't know that I don't know"
Conscious ignorance	Incompetence	"I know that I know"
Conscious knowledge	Competence	"I know that I don't know" (Socrates)
Unconscious knowledge	Mastery	"I don't know what I know"

Next, experiments are performed on the content of the uncertainties U_e and U_o, except for the uncertainty U_m due to the extreme complexity of this concept.

2.4   Risk Quantification Experiments Through Uncertainty

In game theory, uncertainty, risk, and the outcome of events appear in fuzzy measures. A bet in tossing a coin has the simplest rule, the outcome is evaluated by the probability measure $p(Ex) = 0.5$. The game of throwing a dice-hexahedron can have several rules and the outcome is estimated as $p(Ex) = 1/6$. Card games contain even more knowledge of the rules and techniques. Accordingly, the uncertainty becomes greater, and the probabilistic measures are less appropriate for observing the outcome of an event. To solve the question of the consistency of the risk measurability through uncertainty the following mental experiments are performed.

Experiment 1 (Urn) Object (O) is a closed urn that can contain items. The subject is assigned an action prescription: the goal (G) of interaction with the object; achieving the goal is associated with risk $R = [0;1]$ and uncertainty $U = [0;1]$. The activity event is evaluated by a number. Modeling the uncertainty of the form U_e is carried out by the fact that the target action is prescribed to the subject without knowing the conditions of the contents of the urn. Modeling of the uncertainty of the form U_o is carried out by the objective impossibility or limitation of the subject to perform the target action. Here, visual contact with the items in the urn is limited, so it is not possible to essentially ascertain the color of the item. Important conditions: (1) the modeling of the uncertainty U_o is carried out jointly and simultaneously with the uncertainty U_e, in a particular case, one can denote the conjunction $U_e \cap U_o$, although their relationship requires additional study; (2) the subject performs each experience discretely, "as if for the first time", without taking into account the knowledge and information obtained from other experiences. This seems to be important since it is possible to complicate the connections, which is still undesirable at this level of the experiment; (3) the uncertainty U_m in this experiment has not yet been modeled due to the particular complexity of this concept. The purpose of the experiment: a) to establish what is the subject of risk in the event; b) how risk is related to uncertainty. Let us do experiments.

1. The goal is not set, there is no description of the object. The uncertainties of the two types are the same: $U_e = U_e \cap U_o = 1$, $R = 0$;

2. There are no items in the urn. The goal is to get items. Uncertainty is estimated for $U_e = 1$, while the maximum risk is $R = 1$. For $U_e \cap U_o = 0$, since the subject knows that there are no objects in the urn and the instruction to "get an object" in an empty urn does not constitute uncertainty.

3. There are items in the urn. The goal is to get items. Uncertainty for $U_e = 1$, the risk is maximum $R = 1$. For $U_e \cap U_o = 0$, no risk $R = 0$.

4. There are black and white balls in the urn, the goal is to get one white ball. The instruction of the action contains the information "white ball", but the subject does not know what objects and what color are in the urn. Therefore, the uncertainty for $U_e > 0$, and the risk of the action will be $R = 0.5$. For the type of uncertainty $U_e \cap U_o = 0, 5$, since the subject knows that there are balls of two colors in the urn, but in essence (ontologically) is limited to eliminate the uncertainty. The risk is $R = 0.5$. Similar risks are estimated in other experiments.

5. An urn contains five white and five black balls. Get the white ball. For $U_e > 0$, risk $R = 0.5$. For $U_e \cap U_o = 0.5$, risk $R = 0.5$.

6. An urn contains nine black balls and one white ball. Get the black ball. Since the degree of objective ignorance of the object by the subject is higher, the uncertainty for $U_e \gg 0$, the risk $R = 0.9$. For $U_e \cap U_o = 0.9$, risk $R = 0.9$.

7. An urn contains nine white balls and one black ball. Get the black ball. Also for $U_e \gg 0$, risk $R = 0.1$. For $U_e \cap U_o = 0.1$, risk $R = 0.1$ (Table 2).

Table 2. Experiment of the possibility of calculating risks through uncertainty (G - goal, U - uncertainty, R - risk)

Experiment	G	U		R
1. There is an urn	not assigned	U_e	1	0
		$U_e \cap U_o$	1	0
2. There are no items in the urn	to get subject	U_e	1	1
		$U_e \cap U_o$	0	0
3. There are items in the urn	to get subject	U_e	1	0
		$U_e \cap U_o$	0	0
4. There are black and white balls in the urn	to get white ball	U_e	>0	0,5
		$U_e \cap U_o$	0,5	0,5
5. There are 5 black and 5 white balls in the urn	to get white ball	U_e	>0	0,5
		$U_e \cap U_o$	0,5	0,5
6. There are 9 black and 1 white balls in the urn	to get black ball	U_e	>>0	0,9
		$U_e \cap U_o$	0,9	0,9
7. There are 1 black and 9 white balls in the urn	to get black ball	U_e	>>0	0,1
		$U_e \cap U_o$	0,1	0,1

The purpose of the activity creates complex structures of actions and uncertainty and is the cause and measure of risk. The general condition of the experiment is written in Eq. 2.

$$R = \mu U(O, G) \tag{2}$$

where the calculated measure of uncertainty μU is made up of the content of the object of activity and the prescription of the goal (O, G).

Numerical estimates of uncertainty and risk are carried out here on the basis of simple expert judgments. We find that in each experiment there are dependences of U and R on the given goal. Let us continue the risk quantification experiment to explore the possibility of calculations through the outcome of an event in the following content.

Experiment 2 (Hunting). The purpose of the experiment is to establish how event structure is related to risk and outcome. Purpose of the hunt: the hunter (H) kills the beast (B). Let us compose the structure of the event, where the objects H and B can be in different states: "alive", "wounded", or "killed" (Table 3).

Table 3. Hunt Event

Objects		State		
		alive	wounded	dead
		a	b	C
Hunter	1	**1a**	1b	1c
Beast	2	2a	2b	**2c**

The normal meaning of human hunting as prey or leisure presupposes the outcome of the event when the hunter is alive and the beast is killed: E |(1, 2c) → Ex, cells of object states in Table 3. If the imperative of survival of both the hunter and the beast is added to the meaning, then the outcomes can be both negative and positive at the same time. For example, a hunter brings prey after being wounded by a slain beast. The goal has been achieved and there is damage. The outcome may be such that the hunter could die, and the beast may be wounded or unharmed. The combinatorics of the event is done. Alphabet: outcome $[Ex^+]$ absolutely positive, Ex^+ positive, $\tilde{Ex}$ fuzzy, Ex^- negative. To designate a risk, let us introduce the values: numbers and the symbol (~) an undetermined risk (Table 4).

The number of options can be much larger. The first three options make up the meaning of hunting as a means of obtaining food or leisure, the six following as an imperative of survival, which is identical to war. We find that even for the simplest event structure it is extremely difficult to quantify outcome and risk. For a more accurate calculation of risk in each variant or thought experiment, additional conditions and information are suggested and required.

So, the subject of risk is the fuzzy observable uncertainty of the outcome of an expedient activity. To calculate the risk, descriptions of the subject in a structured formalized

Table 4. Combinatorics of the Hunt event

Option	Conditions	Outcome	Risk
1a | 2a	E | (1a, 2c)	Ex^-	~
1a | 2b	E | (1a, 2c)	$\tilde{E}x$	~
1a | 2c	E | (1a, 2c)	$[Ex^+]$	~
1b | 2a	E | (1b, 2c)	Ex^-	<1
1b | 2b	E | (1b, 2c)	$\tilde{E}x$	0,5–1
1b | 2c	E | (1b, 2c)	Ex^+	>0,5
1c | 2a	E | (1c, 2c)	Ex^-	1
1c | 2b	E | (1c, 2c)	Ex^-	1
1c | 2b	E | (1c, 2c)	$\tilde{E}x$	1

presentation are required. In experimental risk modeling, we find that there is uncertainty without risk and there is no risk without uncertainty. Solving the problem of calculating risk through uncertainty is impossible without defining the goal. Expedient activity is a prerequisite for the presence of risk. Uncertainty is the existence of possibility. Risk is observed as a set of possibilities with outcomes in fuzzy measures of real events. Uncertainty can be identified with fuzzy measures, in a particular case with probability. This measure in each experiment is mentally correlated with the value of the goal being set. In complex structures, correlation events and the combination of measure and result can be difficult to define.

2.5 Multivariate Risk Assessment

Initial Data. The study of psychometric risk perception contains assessment data of 30 risk objects activity or technology [16]. Respondents were experts, and three social groups: active club members, college students, and league of women voters were asked the question: "how safe is safe enough"? Subsequently, annual mortality statistics were included in the list of objects of risk to study the relationship between risk perception and statistics. It is the availability of statistical data that is of interest to the calculations and calculations performed. The task is to establish correlations of three different data: (1) statistics, (2) expertise, and (3) psychometric risk perception. For some of the 30 risk objects, statistical data are not available. The characteristics of the general population, the statistical sample, the method of examination, and the processing of the results are unknown.

The data were revised by the author of this work as follows. The data are ranked in five columns of the table: The absolute data of the statistics of risk objects are ranked with the addition of the "rank" value. For risk objects where there are no statistical data, a conditional rank is set equal to the expert risk rank (bold type). The list of risk objects for annual mortality data is divided with the addition of a column into three groups of risk objects: "high", "medium", and "low". The statistics of high-risk objects have 331,000 annual losses and a share of 95 percent. The medium risk group is 17,000 losses and about five percent. The low-risk activity group is 1000 losses and about half a percent. Expert ranking largely coincides with statistical ranking. This can be interpreted in two ways: experts know or use statistical data, or experts know a reality close to statistics. Psychometric data of the three social groups have a significant spread of estimates between groups. This can probably be explained by the random selection of respondents with different education, social maturity, and culture (Table 5).

2.6 Generalization of the Risk Uncertainty Concept

Frank Knight (1885–1972) distinguished risk and uncertainty (1921): "Uncertainty must be taken in a sense radically distinct from the familiar notion of risk, from which it has never been properly separated. The essential fact is that 'risk' means in some cases a quantity susceptible to measurement, while at other times it is something distinctly not of this character; and there are far-reaching and crucial differences in the bearings of the phenomena depending on which of the two is really present and operating. It will appear that a measurable uncertainty, or 'risk' proper, as we shall use the term, is so far different from an unmeasurable one that it is not in effect an uncertainty at all" [27].

Russian philosopher-theologian P.A. Florensky (1882–1937) described the mutual dependence of two fuzzy quantities as follows [28, pp 420–424]. "Every judgment and every conclusion in the field of historical sciences is a judgment with a coefficient of probability, a spectrum of degrees of firmness of our faith or our disbelief in a hypothesis. So, when examining a monument, we have in mind it itself, as a certain value α, and its authenticity - never, however, absolute, but always only more or less probable - degree of authenticity, degree of probability, measured by a certain coefficient ρ. But neither α nor ρ are given to us separately, because we cannot judge either the value of a work, completely abstracted from the question of its origin, or its origin, regardless of value. These quantities ρ and α are always given to us in real life together, in the form of a product $\rho\alpha$, which is called "mathematical expectation"; the expression $\rho\alpha$ or P and should be the subject of examination of any conscious criticism; an attempt to find out the value of ρ and α separately is a naive dream about the impossible, and even unnecessary. For us, what is important is that for which the product P is significant (Table 6).

The value of P is determined either by the significance of ρ or by the significance of α, or by both. At the same time, ρ is always a positive, proper fraction, that is, greater than zero and less than one because the case of the possible authenticity of a well-known creation is never excluded and the possibility of its inauthenticity is never excluded. As for α, it extends from $-\infty$ to $+\infty$ (Eq. 3).

$$(0 < \rho < 1) \text{ and } (-\infty < \alpha < +\infty). \tag{3}$$

It is possible that in other cases, instead of the value of α, Bernoulli should be taken or, if we consider it insufficiently accurate, some other function $\varphi(\alpha)$, such that instead of the "mathematical expectation" P, we get the "moral expectation" (Eq. 4).

$$Q = \rho\varphi(\alpha) \text{ or } Q'' = 0(\rho\alpha) \tag{4}$$

But, one way or another, however, it is clear that with a very large α, i.e. with a very valuable monument, even a small probability of its authenticity can still save a

Table 5. Multivariate risk assessment method (statistics groups: 1–5 - high, 8–15 - medium, 16–30 – low)

Activities or technology	Statistics		Expertise	Psychometrics		
	Quantity	Rank	Experts	Club	Students	League
1. Smoking	150000	1	2	4	3	4
2. Alcohol	100000	2	3	6	7	5
3. Vehicles	50000	3	1	2	5	3
4. Weapon	17000	4	4	3	2	1
5. Electricity	14000	5	9	18	19	19
6. Motorcycles	3000	6	6	5	6	2
7. Swimming	3000	6	10	19	30	17
8. Surgery	2800	7	5	10	11	9
9. Medical x-ray	2300	8	7	22	17	24
10. Pesticides	-	8	8	9	4	15
11. Railways	1950	9	11	24	23	29
12. Private aviation	1300	10	12	7	15	11
13. Major constrution	1100	11	13	12	14	13
14. Bicycle	1000	12	15	16	24	14
15. Hunting	800	13	23	13	18	10
16. Food preservatives	-	14	14	25	12	28
17. Home appliances	200	14	22	29	27	27
18. Work as a firefighter	195	15	18	11	10	6
19. Work in the police	160	16	17	8	8	7
20. Contraceptives	150	17	19	20	9	22
21. Commercial aviation	130	18	16	17	16	18
22. Nuclear danger	100	19	20	1	1	8
23. Mountaineering	30	20	29	15	22	12
24. Food coloring	-	21	21	26	20	30
25. Football	23	21	27	23	26	21
26. Alpine skiing	18	22	30	21	25	16
27. Vaccinations	10	23	25	30	29	29
28. Antibiotics	-	24	24	28	21	26
29. Spray cans	-	26	26	14	13	23
30. Mowers	-	28	28	27	28	25

Table 6. Probability qualifiers according to P.A. Florensky

$+\infty$	absolutely yes $\rightarrow$ probably $\rightarrow$ definitely yes $\rightarrow$ definitely $\rightarrow$ no doubt $\rightarrow$ definitely yes $\rightarrow$ **YES** $\rightarrow$ obviously yes $\rightarrow$ apparently yes $\rightarrow$ probably yes $\rightarrow$ seems yes $\rightarrow$ possibly yes $\rightarrow$ maybe yes $\rightarrow$ probably yes $\rightarrow$ likely yes
0	don't know; but god knows; yes and no; and so and so
$-\infty$	probably not $\leftarrow$ like not $\leftarrow$ maybe not $\leftarrow$ possibly not $\leftarrow$ seems not $\leftarrow$ probably not $\leftarrow$ apparently not $\leftarrow$ obviously not $\leftarrow$ **NO** $\leftarrow$ definitely $\leftarrow$ without a doubt $\leftarrow$ certainly not $\leftarrow$ probably $\leftarrow$ certainly not $\leftarrow$ absolutely not

significant mathematical P or moral Q or Q^ "waiting for him" [28, p 424]. So, we see that the value of some value of the object $\propto$ and the randomness of the event ρ have fuzziness in different areas of definition $(0 < \rho < 1)$ and $(-\infty <\propto< +\infty)$. D. Bernoulli: "The value of moral expectation and possible increments α, β, γ... of value (a) is measured by Eq. 5.

$$h = (a + \alpha)(a + \beta)^q (a + \gamma)^r \ldots a \tag{5}$$

where ρ, q, r are the probabilities of obtaining these increments." [28, p 612].

The above-presented experiments as well the statements of well-known scientists F. Knight and P. Florensky 100 years ago correspond to the conclusion that the problem of identifying the subject of risk and methods for calculating risk states remains fuzzy. The question of the consistency of the left and right limits of the two domains of definition by P.A. Florensky is not considered here, which would further complicate the logical conclusions. Accordingly, the method of joint calculation of the expression $\rho\alpha$ or P remains unknown. The author of this paper sees the solution to the problem in the risk identification approach proposed below, the derivation of definitions, and the development of regulatory models for risk management.

3 Regulatory Risk Modeling

The task of regulatory risk management is: observation of an event, risk identification, risk assessment, decision, risk control, and impact on the event. Based on the identification, an assessment of the magnitude of the risk and the preparation of solutions are carried out: risk aversion, risk acceptance, and risk reduction (Fig. 5).

Risk identification is the most important basis for regulatory risk management and the main objective of this work, which is described below. The presentation uses the materials of the author's work [29].

3.1 Identification of the Risk Subject

The subject of risk comes down to understanding the uncertainty of a random event: an "event" (E), which leads to an outcome (exodus) (Ex) and is represented by a set: a) a combination of a fuzzy measure of what (how often and when) can happen, b) the magnitude of the impact of what (good, neutral, bad and how much) might happen.

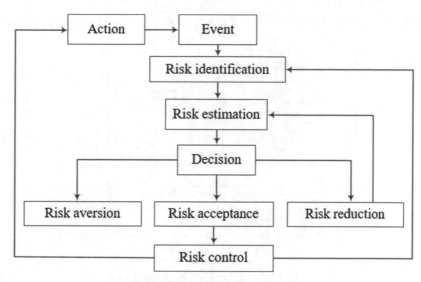

Fig. 5. Regulatory risk modeling task

The measure of randomness (hazard) (H) of an outcome is denoted here as a fuzzy measure of the first kind $\tilde{\mu}_1 ExH$. The measure of the magnitude of an outcome (magnitude) (M) is denoted as a fuzzy measure of the second kind $\tilde{\mu}_2 Ex^{\pm}M$. These measures are by nature very different kinds of measures. The task of identifying the subject of risk is to observe the measure of the randomness of the event and the measure of the magnitude of the outcome. The need for observation (measurement, evaluation) of risk lies in the search for the possibility of assigning numbers to the outcomes of events: from fuzziness to acceptable clarity, from the evaluation (qualification) to calculation (quantification). Risk $(\overset{\leftrightarrow}{R})$ can be written as Eq. 6.

$$\overset{\leftrightarrow}{R} : \{\tilde{\mu}_1 Ex H\}, \{\tilde{\mu}_2 Ex^{\pm}M\} \tag{6}$$

The uncertainty of the measure of the hazard of an event is related to the uncertainty of the measure of the magnitude of the outcome. In the formula, it is necessary to disclose the content of three elements: 1 - the hazard of the outcome, 2 - the magnitude of the outcome, 3 - the ratio (1) and (2), which is indicated by a comma (Fig. 6).

Qualification of the Measure of Hazard of the Outcome $\{\tilde{\mu}_1 Ex H\}$**.** Estimation of the hazard of an event is carried out in the elements of the measure: the frequency of events of this kind in the areas of definition [uncertainty, certainty], [fuzziness, clarity], [discreteness, continuity]. Depending on the established assessments, the selection of the method and measures of calculation is carried out: plausibility, possibility, probability, trust, and necessity [29]. The result of the qualification of the measure of the randomness of the outcome is the numerical estimates of the values, the achieved formalization, suitable for subsequent calculation, and risk quantification.

Qualification of the Measure of the Magnitude of the Outcome $\{\tilde{\mu}_2 Ex^{\pm}M\}$**.** The event is a set, it has the value of the magnitude of the outcomes, which are evaluated as

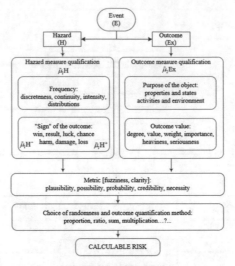

Fig. 6. Model of the risk subject calculation

positive, negative, or neutral. The evaluation of the magnitude of the outcome of an event is carried out in terms of: positive concepts (result, gain, luck), and/or negative concepts (harm, damage, loss), both, with the appropriate degrees (value, weight, importance, severity, and seriousness). The result of the qualification of the measure of the magnitude of the outcome is numerical estimates of the values, the achieved formalization, suitable for subsequent calculation, and risk quantification.

Risk Quantification. Quantification consists in establishing a method for calculating risk: the ratio of the measure of the hazard of the outcome and the measure of the magnitude of the outcome. The ratios for discrete events are determined by the sum (Eq. 7), multiplication (Eq. 8), and continuous (Eq. 9) functions.

$$\overleftrightarrow{R}_i = \sum_{i=1} \left\{ \tilde{\mu}_1 H, \ \tilde{\mu}_2 Ex^{\pm} \right\} \tag{7}$$

$$\overleftrightarrow{R}_i = \prod_{i=1} \left\{ \tilde{\mu}_1 H, \ \tilde{\mu}_2 Ex^{\pm} \right\} \tag{8}$$

$$\overleftrightarrow{R}_i = \int \left\{ \tilde{\mu}_1 H, \ \tilde{\mu}_2 Ex^{\pm} \right\} \tag{9}$$

where $\overleftrightarrow{R}_i$ is a particular version of the risk calculation method.

In statistical decision theory, the risk function of a statistical sample (δ) with respect to the parameter (θ),) of the calculated observable is defined as the expected value of the outcome function $\overleftrightarrow{R}$ (Eq. 10):

$$\overleftrightarrow{R}\langle \theta, \delta \rangle = \int Ex\langle \theta, \delta \rangle f(X | \theta) dx \tag{10}$$

The presented risk quantification formulas are staging for the task of calculating activity risks. In the proposed normative model, the subject of risk differs from known analogs by the fundamental difference between the measure of hazard and the measure of the magnitude of the outcome of an event in various elements of evaluations and calculations.

3.2   Derivation of Risk Definition

The model of the risk subject provides an opportunity to overcome the above problems of known standards and allows formulating a new definition of risk.

Definition 4. The risk ($\overleftrightarrow{R}$) is defined as the aggregate of the observation of the measure of the hazard of the outcome and the measure of the magnitude of the outcome of the event of expedient activity in the conditions of a given habitat and destination environment of the activity.

The differences between this definition from the known definition [1, Error! Reference source not found.] are: a) "the aggregate" instead of multiplication; b) "observation" instead of measurement; c) "outcome" instead of consequences (damage); d) "hazard" instead of probability, revealed in the choice of fuzzy measures: likelihood, possibility, probability, confidence, necessity; e) "magnitude of the outcome" (instead of damage), disclosed in the nature of the event "where the scales will tip" for a positive or negative outcome with a distinction in the properties of events in the calculation of magnitude; f) "expedient activity"; g) "habitat", given or artificially created; h) "destination environment of the activity", chosen or specified. The meaning of the content items (f–g) is that without the existence of expediency and the environment of life, the subject of risk does not exist.

In the proposed definition of risk, the replacement of the concept of probability with the broader concept of hazard is based on the following. The classical definition of probability considers random events with a stable frequency, which fall into a finite number of equally probable cases. Of these, one event is defined as real, probable (clear, explicit by faith) out of many possible ones. The classical definition of probability is often inapplicable in solving natural science and economic problems since events break up into an infinite number of possible incompatible cases. Then it is not the probability that is determined, but only its existence is postulated and a method for approximate determination is indicated, which is called statistical [30]. The solution to this problem is considered in limit theorems, by testing hypotheses about the parameters of distributions, in the theory of estimates by the maximum likelihood method [31]. Replacing the concept of damage with the concept of the magnitude of the outcome is based on the practical use of various tools for evaluating events - "heat maps" and risk matrices. They present positive (green), transitional (yellow), and red (negative) assessments of the states of objects.

3.3   Regulatory Risk Model Development

The development of a normative regulatory model of life risk is presented as the following formal structure of space. The following regulatory concepts, definitions, and symbols of risk in the model are introduced: levels (L), which indicate the measure of risk; ranges, which denote normalized subspaces of the model; areas that are made up of two or more ranges; digital indication (1, …, 15) of the points of intersection of the lines of the normalized structure of the model; a color indication of the heatmaps "green - yellow - red". A new risk arises when choosing a new niche of activity, for example, space exploration. In the regulatory model the following definitions of risk levels are introduced: zero → minimum → nominal → limit.

Definition 5. Zero risk level L_0 [1 – 11]. A risk equal to zero is a hypothetical risk since any activity contains a risk greater than zero.

Definition 6. Minimum risk level L_{nom} [3 – 13]. A risk greater than zero, at the value of which it is possible to observe it for the calculation and regulation of activities.

Definition 7. Nominal risk level L_{nom} [3 – 13]. Risk, above the value of which active regulation of activities is carried out.

Definition 8. The level of marginal risk L_{lim} [4 – 14]. Risk, above the value of which the activity is impossible and unacceptable.

Ranges. The following definitions of activity ranges are introduced (Fig. 7).

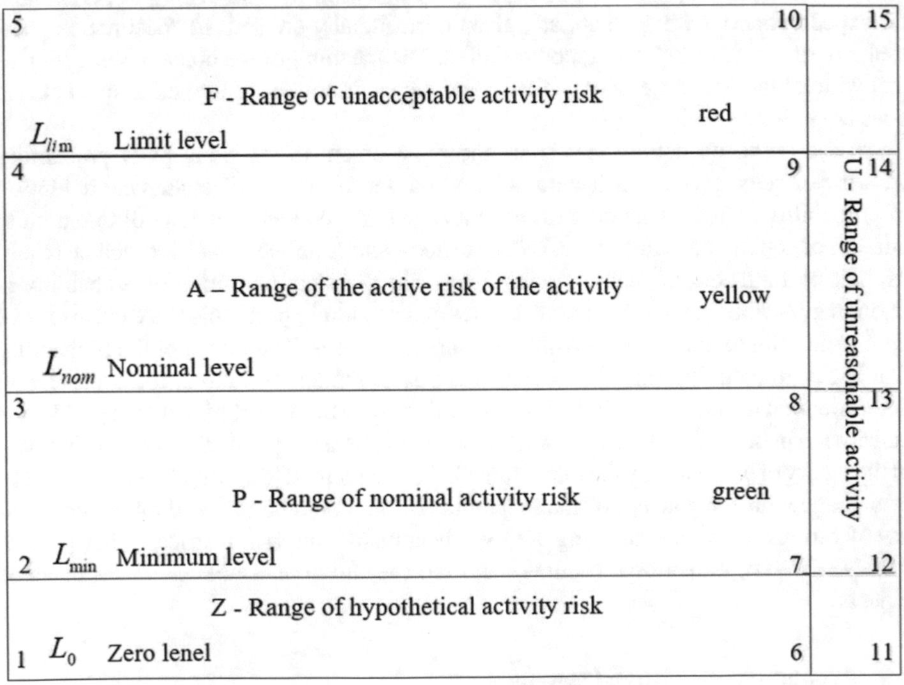

5	10	15
F - Range of unacceptable activity risk	red	
$L_{li m}$ Limit level		
4	9	14
A – Range of the active risk of the activity	yellow	
L_{nom} Nominal level		
3	8	13
P - Range of nominal activity risk	green	
2 L_{min} Minimum level	7	12
Z - Range of hypothetical activity risk		
1 L_0 Zero lenel	6	11

U - Range of unreasonable activity

Fig. 7. Regulatory life risk model

Definition 9. Range of unacceptable activity risk (F). [4 - 14 - 15 - 5]; the risk is impossible, not corresponding to the resource states of the activity. This may include undeveloped activities such as interplanetary flights.

Definition 10. Range of inappropriate activities (U): [6 - 10 - 15 - 11]; the risk in this range is resource untenable, leads to unacceptable results; subsequently recognized as erroneous; previously expedient activity, for example, primitive forms of labor.

Definition 11. Range of active risk of the activity (A): [3 - 4 - 14 - 13], limited by the normative and limiting levels of risk; includes part of the subspace U.

Definition 12. Range of nominal activity risk (P): [3 - 4 - 9 - 8], limited to the minimum and regulatory levels of risk and includes most of the almost low-risk activities.

Definition 13. Range of active risk of expedient activity (E): [3 - 4 - 9 - 8], includes new spaces of vital activity; except for part of the subspace U (Eq. 11).

$$E = A \backslash U \tag{11}$$

Definition 14. Range of nominal risk of expedient activity (C): [2 - 3 - 8 - 7] (Eq. 12):

$$C = P \backslash U \tag{12}$$

Definition 15. Range of hypothetical activity risk (Z): [1 - 2 - 12 - 11], risk area from minimal to zero.

Areas. The following definitions of areas of activity are introduced:

Definition 16. Area of acceptable activity risk (D): [2 - 4 - 14 - 12] is limited by the minimum and marginal risk levels and includes active and nominal activity risk ranges, including part of the subspace U (Eq. 13).

$$D = A \cup P \tag{13}$$

Definition 17. Area of acceptable risk of expedient activity (X): [2 - 4 - 9 - 7] includes the ranges of active nominal accepted risk (Eq. 14).

$$X = E \cap C = (A \backslash U) \cap (P \backslash U) \tag{14}$$

Definition 18. Area of inappropriate activity (N): [1 - 2 - 7 - 10 - 15 - 11] can be singled out as a theoretical area and considered as not appropriate to meet the needs, meanings, and values (Eq. 15).

$$N = (Z \backslash U) \cap (F \backslash U) \cap U \tag{15}$$

New risks arise when creating objects for the protection of existence and habitat. For example, the exit from the natural habitat to the cities, where there are many new risks.

There are networks of risks, generations, and eras of risks. Then the risk can be defined as Eq. 16.

$$\overleftrightarrow{R} = \overleftrightarrow{R} : \{\tilde{\mu}_1 Ex\, H\}\left(\frac{V_R}{\{\tilde{\mu}_2\, Ex^{\pm}M\}}\right) \qquad (16)$$

where V_R- the value of the resources involved in the activities.

Risk management of this model corresponds to soft computing methods, using heatmaps corresponding to the areas: F - red, A - yellow, and P - green [2]. The developed regulatory model fully reveals the structure, volume, and content of the above definition of risk, which is the logical basis for the formation of standards for regulating life risks.

3.4   Risk Modeling by the Method of Statistical Transport Ranking

Motivation to satisfy needs is as irrational as the previously presented results of subjective perception of risks. Below is a quantitative assessment of identifying the motivation to reimburse resources for different products and services [32] (Table 7).

Table 7. Motivation needs

For the best quality	agree to overpay	of consonants are ready to overpay
Car	90% consumers	36% of the cost
Detergents	96% consumers	55% of the cost
Shoes	97% consumers	135% of the cost
TV	94% consumers	66% of the cost
Furniture	96% consumers	74% of the cost
Flight safety	67% consumers	30% of the cost

The data presented is striking in that household products appear to be significantly preferable to flight safety. The reason can be explained as follows. The use of material objects is carried out physically, while safety is perceived by consciousness. It demonstrates the well-known thesis of marketing theory: "products are consumed, services are experienced." The second reason may be the distorted information of consumers about certain services. Example: "Air transport continues to be the safest mode of transport, however, this fact is not a reason for complacency" (Executive letter from the top management of ICAO, IATA, IFALPA) [33, p 3]. Most often it is argued that traveling by car is much more dangerous than flying by plane. This statement is based on the number of accidents relative to travel distance.

Movement Motivation. Movement, as a reason for the behavior of a person and social groups, contains several variables and selection criteria when making a decision. Let us compose a model: mode of movement (M), distances (S) km, time (T) ours, movement frequency (F) per year, cost (C) in conventional units (c.u. [0 ÷ 100]. Additional criteria are implied: accessibility, convenience, and freedom to choose the mode of movement. There is no statistical data for the task. Numerical values are evaluated expertly and, with available statistics, can be adjusted (Table 8).

Table 8. Movement choice motivation

Mode	S km / T, ours				F	C
	> 1000	100–1000	10–100	< 10		
Aircraft	2	1			4	100
Sea	50	20			1	50
Train	20	10	2		10	30
Car	10	5	1		100	20
Bus		10	1		100	10
River		20	10		10	10
Bicycle			10	1	1000	-
On foot				1	10000	-

The motivation of the decision is associated with a combinatorial choice of options movement and is lined up in a tuple (Eq. 17).

$$\text{Choice} : (M)|\ \underline{def}\ \{S \cdot T \cdot F \cdot C\}\mu R \rightarrow \text{Decision} \qquad (17)$$

where (M) is the choice of the mode and is determined by the combinatorics of the components, (·) is the sign denoting the complex connection of the components, and μR is the subjective assessment of the risk measure.

The movement choice motivation model is used in the method presented below.

The Method of Statistical Transport Ranking. Ranging by one indicator from a set of indicators is called ranking. The method shows the possibility of quantitative calculations of risks. To perform an analysis of the comparative risks of modes of transport, data from the State Statistics Committee of the Russian Federation (1992–1998) were used. Indicators for five modes of transport: road, air, rail, sea, and river. The original table [4] contains the following indicators: A - the volume of passenger traffic, million people; B - passenger turnover, billion passenger kilometers (pkm); C - the number of deaths, people; D - the number of deaths per 1 million people transported; D - the number of deaths per 100 million pkm. The risks were calculated by comparing the parameters: a) the number of deaths, people; b) the number of deaths per 1 million transported; c) the number of deaths per 100 million pkm. The mean values ($\overline{X}$) are derived. The ranking ($R_{D_i}^j$) of the j-th mode of transport was compiled by the i-th indicator (Eq. 18):

$$R_{D_i}^j = minN_i^j (i, \dots, n) \qquad (18)$$

where $N_i^j (i, \ldots, n)$ is the natural number of the j-th mode of transport according to the i-th indicator (Table 9):

Table 9. Statistical ranking of transport risks

Mode	Ri	Indicators and Parameters	X̄	Ra·	Rb	Rc
Road	a	The number of deaths	32598,71	1		
	b	The number of deaths per 1 million transported	0,81		3	
	c	Number of deaths per 100 million pkm	13,27			1
Air	a	The number of deaths	178,86	2		
	b	The number of deaths per 1 million transported	5,10		1	
	c	Number of deaths per 100 million pkm	0,24			4
Rail	a	The number of deaths	10,86	3		
	b	The number of deaths per 1 million transported	0,01		5	
	c	Number of deaths per 100 million pkm	0,01			5
Sea	a	The number of deaths	5,43	5		
	b	The number of deaths per 1 million transported	1,12		2	
	c	Number of deaths per 100 million pkm	2,41			2
River	a	The number of deaths	9,71	4		
	b	The number of deaths per 1 million transported	0,34		4	
	c	Number of deaths per 100 million pkm	0,80			3

Known claims that flying by plane is many times safer than traveling by car are based on the absolute number of victims and the number of victims per distance parameter: passenger-kilometers, pkm (passenger-miles, pm). The performed calculations show that the number of deaths in air transportation rank is second. The number of deaths per one million passengers the rank is first. The number of deaths per 100 million pkm rank is fourth. It remains to be clarified which indicators and parameters of statistical analysis can be recognized as scientifically substantiated as the main ones.

In economic science, it is known that the most important macroeconomic indicator of the level of development of the country is the mobility of the population: the number of movements, trips, and flights. The primary motivation for movement is the motivation of the individual. The motivation of the consumer is contained in the reason for the trip, the assessment of risks, the assessment of the advantages of modes of movement, and costs. Costs and benefits by mode of transport are relatively easy to assess (see frequencies of car trips, Table 8). The reason for travel and risk assessment are complex and are the main factors in the decision to travel, as the statistics show. Consequently, the highest frequency of trips by car is a combination of risk assessment and trip motivation, despite the absolute highest rates of losses and damages. When compared by the number of movements by car and by plane, the risk turns out to be approximately equal: one or two insured events per million trips there and back. Therefore, the most reasonable indicator is the ratio of damage to the total amount of work performed in the appropriate units of calculation: the number of victims per the number of people transported. Another important indicator of safety calculation is a measure of damage per flight.

4 Conclusion

Risk is a human instinct that unconsciously influences actions and behavior. According to the Russian philosopher P.A. Kropotkin, "… a person has a desire for the most intense, that is, enhanced and diverse life, for expansion beyond the field of self-preservation." [34, p 250]. Analysis of the subject of risk shows that the origin of the term remains unidentified, and the concept of risk is abstract. Therefore, psychometric paradigm research is dominant. The identification of the subject of risk has two keywords: hazard and outcome, which greatly expand the understanding of risk. The problem of identifying the subject of risk and methods for calculating risk states remains fuzzy. The solution to the problem in the risk identification approach proposed the derivation of definitions and the development of regulatory models for risk management.

The definition proposed in this paper reveals the content and scope of the concept of risk. The result is the development of a new normative model of risks in the metric of space by levels, and ranges with appropriate definitions; new definitions have been introduced: risk as a combination of a measure of hazard and a measure of the outcome of an event, risk qualification, risk quantification; the possibility of calculations outside the domain of definition [probability, consequence] is substantiated. The most acceptable approach for calculating risks is the method of soft computing risk matrices [2].

References

1. Annex 19 to the Convention on International Civil Aviation. Safety Management, Second ed., ICAO, p. 46 (2016)
2. Oliveira, G.G.D., Iano, Y., Vaz, G.C., Chuma, E.L., Arthur, R.: Intelligent transportation: application of deep learning techniques in the search for a sustainable environment. In: Proceedings of the 2022 5th International Conference on Big Data and Internet of Things, pp. 7–12 (2022)
3. Plotnikov, N.I.: Soft computing method in events risks matrices. In: Iano, Y., Saotome, O., Kemper, G., Mendes de Seixas, A.C., Gomes de Oliveira, G. (eds.) BTSym 2020. SIST, vol. 233, pp. 578–588. Springer, Cham (2021). https://doi.org/10.1007/978-3-030-75680-2_64
4. Plotnikov, N.I.: Transport complex safety resources. AviaManager, Novosibirsk, p. 286 (2013) (in Russian). http://www.aviam.org/images/sampledata/book/2015_tcsr.pdf
5. Plotnikov, N.I.: Methods of resource modeling of organizational objects. In: Kwasiborska, A., Skorupski, J., Yatskiv, I. (eds.) ATE 2020. LNITI, pp. 116–130. Springer, Cham (2021). https://doi.org/10.1007/978-3-030-70924-2_10
6. The Oxford Minireference Thesaurus by Alan Spooner, p. 617. Clarendon Press, Oxford (1997)
7. Dal, V.I.: Explanatory dictionary of the living Great Russian language. Rus. Lang. Media Moscow **1**, 699. **2**, 779. **3**, 555. **4**, p. 683 (2005). (in Russian)
8. Ozhegov, S.I., Shvedova, N.Y.: Explanatory dictionary of the Russian language, p. 944. LLC ITI Technologies, Moscow (2003). (in Russian)

9. Ushakov, D.N.: Explanatory dictionary of the Russian language. Moscow **1**, 1562, **2**, 1040, **3**, 1424, **4**, 1502 (1935–1940). (in Russian)
10. Yaroshevsky, M.G.: Psychology. Dictionary, p. 494. Politizdat. Moscow (1990). (in Russian)
11. de Oliveira, G.G., Iano, Y., Vaz, G.C., Chuma, E.L., Gregio, R.P., Akkari, A.C.S.: Analysis of the ergonomic concept of public transportation in the city of campinas (Brazil). In: Stanton, N. (ed.) AHFE 2021. LNNS, vol. 270, pp. 453–459. Springer, Cham (2021). https://doi.org/10.1007/978-3-030-80012-3_52
12. Starr, C.: Societal benefit versus technological risk. Science **165**, 1232–1248 (1969). https://doi.org/10.1126/science.165.3899.1232
13. Chuma, E.L., Iano, Y., Roger, L.L.B., De Oliveira, G.G., Vaz, G.C.: Novelty sensor for detection of wear particles in oil using integrated microwave metamaterial resonators with neodymium magnets. IEEE Sens. J. (2022)
14. Fischhoff, B., Slovic, P., Lichtenstein, S., Read, S., Combs, B.: How safe is safe enough? A psychometric study of attitudes towards technological risks and benefits. Policy Sci. **9**, 127–152 (1978)
15. Slovic, P., Fischhoff, B., Lichtenstein, S.: Rating the Risks. Environ. Sci. Policy Sustain. Dev. **21**(3), 14–39 (1979)
16. Sjöberg, L.: Risk perception is not what it seems: the psychometric paradigm revisited. In: Andersson K. (ed), Stockholm VALDOR Conference, pp. 14–29 (2003)
17. de Oliveira, G.G., Iano, Y., Vaz, G.C., Chuma, E.L., Negrete, P.D.M., Negrete, J.C.M.: Structural analysis of bridges and viaducts using the IoT concept. An approach on dom pedro highway (Campinas-Brazil). In: Iano, Y., Saotome, O., Kemper Vásquez, G.L., Cotrim Pezzuto, C., Arthur, R., Gomes de Oliveira, G. (eds.) Brazilian Technology Symposium, pp. 108–119. Springer, Cham (2022). https://doi.org/10.1007/978-3-031-08545-1_10
18. Loewenstein, G.F., Weber, E.U., Hsee, C.K., Welch, E.: Risk as feelings. Psychol Bull **127**(2), 267–286 (2001)
19. Damasio, A.R.: Descartes' Error: Emotion, Reason, and the Human Brain. Avon, New York (1994)
20. Kahneman, D., Tversky, A.: Prospect theory: an analysis of decision under risk. Econometrica **47**(2), 263–291 (1979)
21. Erev, I.: Signal detection by human observers: A cutoff reinforcement learning model of categorization decisions under uncertainty. Psychol. Rev. **105**, 280–298 (1998)
22. Weber, E.U.: Perception and expectation of climate change: precondition for economic and technological adaptation. Psycholog. Perspect. Environ. Ethical Issues Manag., 314–341 (1997)
23. Zhigora, D.: Riddles of air crashes, p. 512. Literature, Minsk (1998). (in Russian)
24. Izario, D., Brancalhone, J., Iano, Y., de Oliveira, G.G., Vaz, G.C., Izario, K.: 5G-Automation of Vertical Systems in the Industry 4.0. In: Iano, Y., Saotome, O., Kemper Vásquez, G.L., Cotrim Pezzuto, C., Arthur, R., Gomes de Oliveira, G. (eds.) Brazilian Technology Symposium, pp. 35–43. Springer, Cham (2023). https://doi.org/10.1007/978-3-031-04435-9_4
25. Lossky, N.O.: Logic. Obelisk, Berlin, p. 168 (1923) (in Russian)
26. Lindley, D.V.: Understanding Uncertainty, Wiley-Interscience (eds), p. 272 (2006) https://en.wikipedia.org/wiki/Dennis_Lindley
27. https://en.wikipedia.org/wiki/Knightian_uncertainty
28. Florensky, P.A.: Pillar and Ground of Truth. Experience of Orthodox Theodicy, p. 640. Act, Moscow (2003). (in Russian)
29. Plotnikov, N.I.: The development of the subject domain observation complex for management purposes. In: 2018 XIV International Scientific-Technical Conference on Actual Problems of Electronics Instrument Engineering (APEIE), vol. 1, part 1, pp. 268–272 (2018). https://doi.org/10.1109/apeie.2018.8545868

30. Karasev, A I : Probability Theory and Mathematical Statistics, p. 279. Statistics, Moscow (1979). (in Russian)
31. Pugachev, V.S.: Probability Theory and Mathematical Statistics, p. 496. Nauka, Moscow (1979). (in Russian)
32. Moeller, K.: Quality: Seminar-Training. Time Manager International, Denmark (1990) https://www.tacktmiglobal.com/
33. Fatigue risk management system (FRMS): Implementation guide for operators, ICAO, p. 150 (2011)
34. Kropotkin, P.A.: Ethics. Selected #orks, p. 496. Politizdat, Moscow (1991). (in Russian)

Ontological Foundations of Safety Theory in Air Transport Regulation

Nikolai I. Plotnikov[✉] (iD)

Scientific Research Project Civil, Aviation Institute «AviaManager», 630078 Novosibirsk,
Russian Federation
am@aviam.org

Abstract. The safety of technosphere activity presupposes the existence of scientific grounds for research and development of an intellectual product in the form of technical regulation standards. The problem of identification of the subject and definitions of aviation safety notes contradictions and inconsistencies in the terms and definitions of existing practiced standards. Until now the global aviation community has been searching for acceptable definitions of safety in aviation, which is confirmed by constant amendments to the standards. The task of establishing the terminology of the subject area is the formation of a normative conceptual base that is consistent with the theory and meets the requirements of practice. A technical term is a word or phrase that accurately and unambiguously denotes a concept used in science and technology. The solution to the terminological problem is possible through the reduction of the meanings of the linguistic units of the word and the definition of the term. The method of ontological designing in this paper is considered a scientific approach to reducing the uncertainty in the description of complex structural objects and events. The method establishes a sequence of analysis and information modeling for identifying the characteristics of objects necessary for life safety management.

Keywords: Ontological designing · Logical analysis · Air transport ·
Regulation · Flight safety · Aviation security · And Safety definitions

1 Introduction

Socrates: *"Dangerous is what generates fear, safe, on the contrary, does not generate it. Fear, in turn, is generated not by emerging and not cash troubles, but by expected ones: after all, fear is the expectation of an impending disaster."* PLATON, Laches. [1, p 290].

At the Pan American Convention on Air Navigation, Havana in 1928, the term "safety" was not yet included in aviation dictionaries [2]. "The fundamental problem is the gap between the practice of the safety of society and an adequate theory of safety that would explain the meaning and essence of safety" [3]. The safety of technosphere activity presupposes the existence of scientific grounds for research and development of an intellectual product in the form of technical regulation standards. Standards, in particular, in industry and transport, are compiled as a set of developments of concepts, terms,

Y. Iano et al. (Eds.): BTSym 2022, SIST 353, pp. 268–287, 2023.
https://doi.org/10.1007/978-3-031-31007-2_25

definitions, and the establishment of quantitative indicators of permissible activity limits. The concept of safety (security) as a kind of "freedom from danger" characterizes a non-existent and never-realizable state. The concept of safety means a calm state of a person's spirit and protection from danger and corresponds to many identical words: reliability, efficiency, quality, calmness, stability, perfection, impeccability, development, peace, prosperity, independence, and integrity. In the technical field, the understanding of danger is accepted in the definitions of various states of danger: incident, accident, and catastrophe. An incident is an event that characterizes the deterioration of the state of safety. An accident is an event of a violation of the state of safety. A catastrophe is an event of complete destruction of the state of safety. "*Catastrophes are abrupt changes that occur as a sudden response of the system to a smooth change in external conditions*" [**Error! Reference source not found.**, p 3].

Standardization and regulation start with definitions. Until now the global aviation community has been searching for acceptable definitions of safety in aviation, which is confirmed by constant amendments to the standards [4–9]. Classifications and definitions of safety in various industries are not coordinated and do not have a single basis [10]. The mutual contradiction of concepts, definitions, and terms of technogenic activity is reflected in the legislation on technical regulation, which provides for more than a dozen types of safety. The safety of interaction with the natural environment is mixed with man-made types of interaction. The classification problem makes it difficult to consciously observe and regulate life safety.

Definitions of aviation safety were formed in terms of "safety", "flight safety" (FS), and "aviation security" (AS). "Safety is the state in which risks associated with aviation activities, related to, or in direct support of the operation of aircraft, are reduced and controlled to an acceptable level" [8, 9]. "Security safeguards civil aviation against acts of unlawful interference. This objective is achieved by a combination of measures and human and material resources" [**Error! Reference source not found.**]. Example: "Hazard is a condition or an object with the potential to cause or contribute to an aircraft incident or accident" [8, 9]. Every word raises questions. The word "hazard" means fuzzy event, neither positive nor negative; "condition or an object" are totally different things. "Safety risk. The predicted probability and severity of the consequences or outcomes of a hazard" [8, 9]. The combination of two concepts "safety" and "risk" in the collocation of two words is not justified in any way. The scientific basis for the risk formula remains debatable and controversial [11]. It is logically impossible to explain many terms in standards: "risk factor", "dangerous actions", "gaps in management levels", "protection barriers", and "prevention barriers" schemes and models: SHELL, HFACS ("Swiss cheese"). These models do not explain the object's formal relationships in the subject of safety and do not give the possibility of compiling algorithms for control purposes.

This paper postulates the thesis that the cause of the problems is the lack of humanitarian research and the development of standards. The paper provides a logical and linguistic analysis in natural language (NL) regarding the concept of safety and security. The performed analysis reveals the structure of the problems of modern international safety standards and allows introducing new grounds for research and development.

The task of establishing the terminology of the subject area is the formation of a normative conceptual base that is consistent with the theory and meets the requirements of practice. A technical term is a word or phrase that accurately and unambiguously denotes a concept used in science and technology. The solution to the terminological problem is possible through the reduction of the meanings of the linguistic units of the word and the definition of the term. The subject of danger is considered as the relationship of concepts in the grammatical structure of the language. The language exists in theoretical textbooks, dictionaries, and practical representations. Textbook academic publications fix new norms for the development of the grammar of the language. The practical existence of language is carried out in a variety of written and oral speech. Between the textbook and practical contours of the language, there is an environment consisting of a thesaurus from fundamental dictionaries of the language to special terminological publications and standards. The interaction of the theoretical (T), vocabulary (V), and practical (P) sides is the essence of the development of the language in time (t) and is represented by a tuple of changes (Eq. 1).

$$\sum : \{T(t0), V(t0), P(t0)\} \rightarrow f\{T(t1), V(t1), P(t1)\} \tag{1}$$

where $(t_0 - t_1)$ is a time interval, (f) is a function of the problem of NL development.

The task is to create a new ontological structure of concepts related to the safety category. Dictionary and grammatical features, the order of interrelation of the main grammatical classes of the language of the linguistic cluster of safety are investigated. A semantic cluster and relations of concepts are being built. Characteristics of grammatical classes show the connections of word classes, their motivations, meanings, and features. The structure of the concepts of the subject of danger shows the relationship of words in NL and allows the derivation of definitions. A dictionary of basic terms and the basis of the subject of danger has been compiled. The general solution of the problem is considered as a formalization of the NL means for describing the technosphere activity.

The method of ontological designing (MOD) in this paper is considered a scientific approach to reducing the uncertainty in the description of complex structural objects and events [12]. The basis of the method postulates the thesis that, in order to control any object, it is necessary to identify its purpose through terms and definitions. Definitions set the features necessary for modeling and calculating the properties of an object, which is a condition of control. The method establishes a sequence of analysis and information modeling for identifying the characteristics of objects necessary for life safety management. The method offers a linguistic and logical approach for modeling and deriving definitions of concepts in the example of aviation safety.

2 Analysis of Safety Theory and Terminology

2.1 Linguistic Vocabulary Analysis

Language manifests itself in "thinking and action" [**Error! Reference source not found.**]. The grammar of the language is organized by word formation, morphology, and syntax. Word formation studies the interdependent formation of words, called motivation. In morphology, grammar classes are organized as parts of speech. In this paper, on the basis of modern language grammar [13–16], lexico-grammatical classes of words associated with the concept of safety are studied. Forms of thinking (thought forms) appear in the language as concepts. The concept names the limit of the comprehended essence as a generic concept. In development, generic concepts become specific and form words. The word is the basic shortest unit of the language, expressing in its composition the concept of an object, a process, phenomena of reality, their properties, and relations between them. The word exists in the language as a set of word forms. "The word form is one of the manifestations of the types of the existence of the word. The minimum significant part, isolated in the composition of a word form, is called a morph" [15, pp 123-124]. The relations of words are also connected with each other by a dependence called motivation and are represented by lexical and grammatical categories. One of the words connected by the relation of motivation is motivating, the other is motivated or derivative, formally more complex [15, p 133].

The vocabulary cluster of the concept of danger in explanatory dictionaries proposes the following content. "Danger: crisis, distress, hazard, insecurity, jeopardy, menace, peril, pitfall, trouble, uncertainty" [17]. Dictionaries [18–20] summarize the content: the threat of bad, misfortune; dangerous condition; loss: deprivation, death, drop, destroy, ruin, kill, take away life; damage: waste, diminishment; threat: intimidation, fright, promise of harm, evil; possible danger, expressed in any form the intention to cause physical, material or other harm to public or personal interests; threat: to threaten, to intimidate, to intimidate. In general, danger is understood as evil, harm, loss, decline, damage, loss, and deprivation.

The dictionary safety cluster of explanatory dictionaries has the following content: "safe: non-dangerous, non-threatening, not able to cause harm or harm; harmless, safe, faithful, reliable. "Safety: no danger; safety, reliability" [**Error! Reference source not found.**]. "Safety: a state in which danger is not threatened, there is protection from danger. Safe: not threatening danger, protecting from danger" [18]. "Safe: defended, foolproof, guarded, immune, impregnable, invulnerable, protected, secured, shielded. Safety: cover, immunity, invulnerability, protection, security, shelter" [17]. In [21] the concept of safety is described as follows. "Hazard (H) is defined as a series of circumstances that can cause injury or death. Risk (R) is considered as insecurity from harm or loss, as the probability of a hazardous event occurring. Danger (D) is defined as a combination of chance and risk: $D = f(H, R)$. Threat (T) is defined as the exposure to harm or the potential impact on the state of being protected."

Vocabulary and lexico-grammatical analyses increase the volume of concepts, but it is not possible to structure the content of dictionaries more strictly in the normative meanings of terms. As a rule, undertaken searches and analyses of vocabulary contents are unproductive. Vocabulary analysis does not bring the structure of the words of NL into the classification of generic relations, which is necessary for the derivation of terms and definitions.

2.2 Logical Analysis of the Theory of the Concept

In this paper, the understanding of the theory of the concept as a direction of logic is outlined. "A term whose meaning is established by means of a definition is called a concept" [22, p 60]. In logic, rules and requirements are established for the volume and content, types and relationships of concepts, and the conclusions of definitions of concepts. Generic relations are especially difficult to sum up with regard to the most abstract concepts, called categories, which cannot be generalized, such as essence, quality, quantity, relation, and thing. A logical assessment of the concepts is compiled, which makes it possible to establish their generic relations and definitions. "Language cannot keep up with the variety of types of consciousness, and therefore the same term has many different meanings, which can only be established from the contexts of speech" [22, p 91].

A judgment consists of a representation and a concept. Representations have unclear content and indistinct volumes of knowledge. "Representation is a thought about an object, containing in itself any features distinguished in it (sides of the object). A concept is a thought about an object that contains only those distinct features that form a whole that serves as the basis for a system of consequences" [22, p 85]. "The clarity and distinctness of a concept is the precise dissected knowledge of its content and scope. The dismemberment of this knowledge is expressed in the ability to give a definition of the concept, as regards its content, and to divide the concept, as regards its volume" [22, p 116] (Fig. 1).

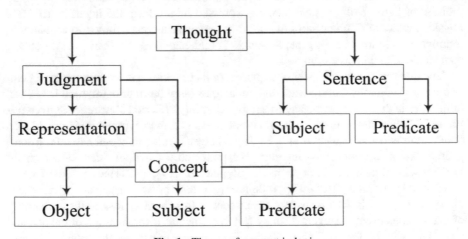

Fig. 1. Theory of concept in logic

Logical Classification of Concepts. "Concepts: specific (primary, derivative), non-specific (not defined through others)" [22, p 60]. "The set of individual concepts (or individual representations) denoting these objects is called the volume of the concept. The totality of features conceivable in the concept, identical in all individuals of the class, is called the content of the general concept" [22, p. 92]. Examples: a) the scope of the concept of "flight" includes a set of single concepts "aircraft", "bird"; b) the concept of the class "flight" contains signs of movement in three-dimensional space for all objects: aircraft, birds. The volume and content of the concept are inversely related: enriching the content, reducing the volume, and vice versa. The law works for concordant concepts when the attribute is characteristic of a part of the scope of the original concept, and for concepts related by generic relations.

Types of Concepts by Volume. A single concept contains one object or element: "Antarctica" or "Delta Airlines". Single concepts and representations have no volume since they mean one object, and not a class of objects. Single concepts have content because they have at least one attribute. The general concept contains several or many items: "factory" or "country". General concepts can be registering and infinite. In registering concepts, a set of elements can be taken into account and can be fixed: "flight". In infinite concepts, the set of elements is not limited, cannot be counted, and has an infinite scope: "aviation".

Types of Concepts by Content. According to the content, four pairs of concepts are distinguished. Abstract object denotes an abstract-ideal being, the signs of an object form an independent object of thinking, a thought without the presence of an object: "risk" and "security". A specific concept denotes a real object: "airplane" and "person" (a set of countable real objects). Concepts are generalized or limited. General concepts can be both concrete and abstract. For example, the concept of "pilot" is general and concrete, and the concept of "piloting" is general and abstract. Concepts are called positive in the presence of the properties of the object, and negative - in the absence of the properties of the object: "danger" - "safety". In coexisting concepts, objects have conceived that name the existence of another: "pilot" - "aircraft". In independent concepts, objects are thought of separately: "city" and "forest". A collective concept consists of a limiting set of homogeneous objects as a whole: "fleet" and "crew". Non-collective concepts denote an uncountable single object: "sky", "safety", or a countable unity of heterogeneous objects - "aviation".

Logical Relations of Concepts. The logical relations between the concepts of the subject under study have corresponding ontological relations between classes or classes and individuals. The most important relationships are the degree of kinship between the contents and volumes of concepts. The absence of kinship means that objects do not have relationships or connections and exist separately. They are called irrelevant concepts, for example, the concepts of "aircraft - shovel" do not have relationships. If in the signs of the volume of objects there is a connection, the basis for relations, then the concepts are called correlative: "aviation - flight" or "flight - safety". "In comparison, concepts are divided into two classes: agreeable and disagreeable (opposite). Disagreeable concepts are called, in the content of which there are signs incompatible with each other. Opposite concepts are distinguished as contradictory concepts: "human" and "non-human", and opposing concepts: "dangerous" and "safe". "Agreeable are called concepts in the context of which there are no signs that, having different content at the same time, should be attributed to the subject in the same respect" [22, pp 108-109]. Between the content of agreed concepts, there are relations according to the degree of kinship of identity, subordination, cosubordination, crossing of part of the volumes, or at least one sign, at one point.

Establishing the Basis of Division. The logical analysis begins with the division of a generic concept. The division of concepts into types is carried out by classes. "A set of single objects, designated by a general concept, is called a class." "The sign, according to the modifications of which the concept is divided into types, is called the basis of division (*fundamentum divisionis*) [22, p 132]. "A sign is any distinct side of an object" [22, p 94]. "Division is a logical operation by means of which the volume of a divisible concept (set) is distributed into a number of subsets using the chosen division base. If with the help of the definition of the concept its content is revealed, then with the help of the division of the concept its volume is revealed. The sign by which the division of the volume of the concept is made is called the basis of division. The subsets into which the volume of the concept is divided are called members of the division. A divisible concept is a generic one, and its division members are species of a given genus, subordinate to each other, i.e., not intersecting in their scope (having no common members)" [22, p 46]. The relationship in volume between concepts is expressed using Euler circles (L. Euler, 1707–1783) (Fig. 2).

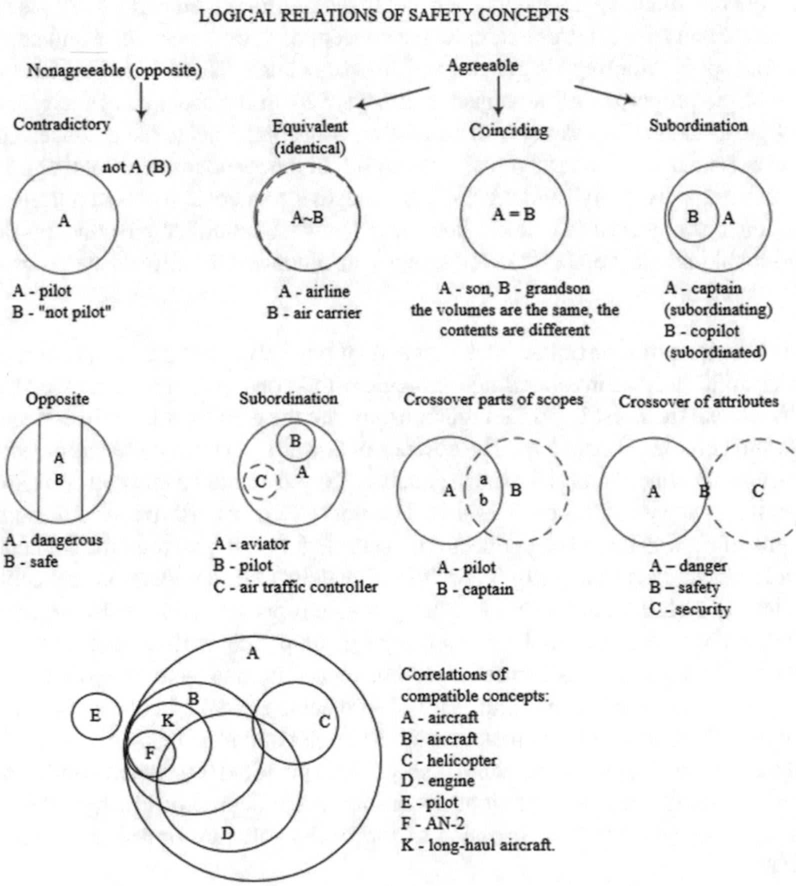

Fig. 2. Logical relationships of safety concepts

2.3 Methodological Requirements for Defining Concepts

The meaning of the definitions of concepts lies in the fact that they are the ultimate language form for the subsequent regulation of activities. "The definition of a concept is a judgment that establishes the content of the concept by indicating a set of features that are necessary and sufficient to distinguish the object or class of objects denoted by the concept from all other objects" [22, p 116]. The way to give definitions is the establishment of the nearest generic concept and specific distinguishing features. "The establishment of a definition is an act that aims to find the content of the concept and thus open the concept, to have in the mind both its content and volume in a distinct and clear form" [22, p 131]. In the logical literature [22-**Error! Reference source not found.**], methodological requirements and formal rules for defining concepts have been developed:

1. Strict definition. "Terms are signs from which statements are built. Definition - the establishment of a subject by a term with meaning." [23, pp 52, 59].
2. Definition through the nearest genus and specific difference: the generic concept is combined with the specific concept. The concept whose content is to be disclosed is called the defined concept (definended) (Dfd), and the concept by which it is defined is called the defining concept (definiended) (Dfn). The correct definition establishes the relation of equality (equivalence) between them: Dfd ≡ Dfn [24]. Examples: "aircraft flight", "bird flight", "flight of thought".
3. Nominal definition: "a definition expressing a prescription or requirement, how the introduced concept should be used, to what objects it should be applied" [**Error! Reference source not found.**].
4. Genetic definition: tells the origin of the subject and the way it was formed. Example: snow is one of the four states of water at a temperature below zero degrees.
5. Definability: the defining concept should be more known than the defined one.
6. Specificity: the abstract concept is determined by the concrete, and not vice versa.
7. Proportionality: the scope of the defining and the defined concepts should be comparable in size.
8. Openness: do not use the word itself to define it, otherwise the definition is considered tautological. An example of a tautology: "a value is everything that can be increased and decreased."
9. Non-negativity: the definition indicates the sign of what the object is, and not what it is not.
10. Explicative (explanatory) definition: the meaning of the original concept is revealed by synonyms or other words.

Explicative definitions are the weakest definition mode. The following should be considered as additional methodological requirements. That is the knowledge of the subject area by the researcher, who solves the problem of defining concepts. The knowledge of the subject makes it possible to establish the basis and signs of the generic division of difficult, especially abstract concepts, called categories. Grammatical analysis of NL units that describe the subject area of the study. Identification of motivation and relations of concepts, on the basis of which definitions are derived.

3 Ontological Design of the Concepts of the Safety

3.1 Logical Derivation of Danger Concept

To solve the problem, the order of interconnection of the main grammatical classes of the language of the studied linguistic cluster of the concepts of danger is established. Based on the theoretical norms of grammar, the characteristics of the main classes of the language are compiled [13–16]. In accordance with the norms of word formation in adjective-verb pairs, a verb is recognized as motivated. In the pairs "verb - noun" and "adjective - noun", the noun is recognized as motivated. The vector of motivation according to the norms of relations is directed from the adverb to the adjective, the verb, and the noun. A word-building chain of single-root words is built, which are in a relationship of sequential motivation, where the motivating word is indicated by an arrow. The top (source word) is an unmotivated word with "zero" motivation [15, p 134] (Table 1).

Table 1. Characteristics of grammar classes (M – motivation)

Classes	Word	M	Has meaning	Is called
Adverb	Dangerously	0	Non-procedural and procedural signs and properties	Signs as circumstances, nature of intensity, degree of comparison, mode of action
Adjective	Dangerous	↑	Non-procedural features	Signs as properties and qualities of objectivity
Verb	Be dangerous	↑	Procedural features	Signs as processes, actions, and states
Noun	Danger	↑	Objectivity	Material and non-material substances of procedural and non-procedural signs, qualities, properties, actions, and states

Relationships of words form word-building chains with relationships of motivation. That is defined root morphs and built a semantic cluster consisting of two opposite contours of danger and safety. The construction can be extended by more detailed word-building chains. Further formalization is achieved when drawing up relationships of concepts included in the subject of safety. For the purposes of this paper, the minimum cluster size is presented in Fig. 3.

This analysis is necessary to draw up the logical relationships between the studied concepts of safety and danger. Structuring a vocabulary cluster based on word motivation links creates the initial formalized content of the subject area of any activity or subject of knowledge. Danger is a concept that has the meaning of an abstract negative state and names the signs and properties of the object of possible negative outcomes of an activity. The danger relation is a description of the role of the entities involved in the activity.

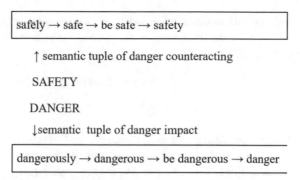

Fig. 3. Semantic cluster of the concept of danger

Since the adjective "dangerous" has the meaning of a non-procedural attribute, and the noun "danger" names a non-procedural state, they are abstract and establish potential relations between objects and negative outcomes of an activity.

The establishment of observable relations of objects of danger in the problem of the NL is solved by replacing the word "danger" with the word "threat", a noun motivated by the verb threaten. The word "threat" has the meaning of the subjectivity of object relations and names the signs and properties of negative outcomes of an activity. The establishment of object relations is called a pair of active and passive participles "threatening – threatened". An active participle means an action presented as a characterizing feature that is active in the action being performed. Passive participle means a sign presented as a characterizing sign, passive in the action being tested [15, p 665]. An antonymous pair of the concept of danger should be considered participles of safety "protecting - protected". The above is represented by a diagram (Fig. 4).

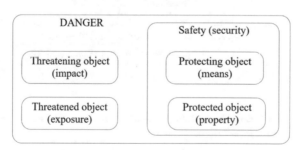

Fig. 4. Danger space terms relations

Logical Derivation of Definitions. The term (statement) of the subject "danger" [D] constitutes the semantic space of objects (Eq. 2).

$$[D] : \leftarrow \{[d_1] \cdot [d_2]\} \tag{2}$$

Which have signs (characterized) denoted by each of the terms: $[d_1]$- threatening object that has the characteristics of a subject of threat and names the property of possible damage (harm, loss) to the threatened object; $[d_2]$ - threatened object that has signs of exposure (vulnerability) to a threat and names the property of possible damage from the impact of a threatening object.

The subject term "safety" [S] constitutes the semantic space of objects (Eq. 3).

$$[S] :\leftarrow \{[s_1] \cdot [s_2]\} \tag{3}$$

Which have features denoted by each of the terms: $[s_1]$ - protecting object that has features of protection (means) from possible damage from the impact of a threatening object; $[s_2]$ - protected object that has the property of counteracting and absorbing possible damage from the impact of a threatening object.

The universal danger space decomposes into a direct sum of subspaces (Eq. 4).

$$D = d_1 \oplus d_2 \oplus s_1 \oplus s_2 \tag{4}$$

where $(d_1 \cdot d_2 \cdot s_1 \cdot s_2)$ is the item denoted by each of the terms.

Objects enter into safety relationships that name the roles of participants as the parties involved in the activity. "It is safety relations that can be the subject of research, and from the position of relations, it is possible to make a description of the subject area of research" [3, p 100]. The concept of "relation" is the main category of the subject of danger (Table 2).

Table 2. Glossary of basic terms

Concepts		Objects	Relations
Danger	d_1	Threatening	[1] impact
	d_2	Threatened	[2] exposure
Safety (security)	s_1	Protecting	[3] protection
	s_2	Protected	[4] protectability

Definition 1. Danger is defined as the impact of a threatening object of possible damage and exposure to a threatened object.

Definition 2. Safety (security) is defined as the protection and protectability of an object in sufficient and necessary protective measures.

Definition 3. Safety (security) management is defined as the management of the properties of the object being protected and as the management of the means of protection.

Discussion. Thus, it is obtained logically justified the concepts of danger and safety. In the absence of a threatening object and/or threatened object relations [1–4] are absent: there is no danger, there is no need for safety. There is just safe activity. Safety (security) is necessary for the space of relations [3, 4] only for the threatened object [2]. Safety management is using means of protection: [3] blocking threats: barrier, border, fencing, defense, prevention; counteraction, action towards, resistance, confrontation; the capture of the forces of a threatening object and their use against the object; [4] creation of a resource (object property) that exceeds or compensates for the magnitude of impacts and susceptibility to threats. Let's explain with examples.

Example 1: Straight Razor. A razor in the hands of a child becomes a threatening object to health and life. The ratio of the impact of the threat entails the ratio of exposure to the threat, the child becomes a threatened object. The relationship of safety is created by the following measures of communication between the threatened object and protection: a) teaching the rules and skills of safe use of a razor; b) restriction of admission and access to the use of a razor by everyone who does not know the rules and does not know how to use a razor; c) changing the properties of an object - the invention of blades for a safety razor; d) exclusion the object; e) replacement of an object with an electric razor.

Example 2: "Ice". Ice coverage of the road and danger to any vehicles. Without establishing a relationship with each specific vehicle, the danger property is unknown. Let car A has "winter" tires that prevent slipping, and car B has not. The object of danger has the property of a threat to car B through the relation of the impact of the threat, which becomes a threatened object through the relation of exposure to the threat. Protected car A has the property due to the protective means of protecting "winter" tires through the relation of counteracting the threat. The ratio of protection against the threat of an accident for car B is created by: a) dumping sand on the road surface; b) cessation of movement; c) canceling the trip. The main resource of the object's security relationship is its purpose or nominal safety (security) - the property of absorbing the impact of a threat and compensated damage.

This presentation demonstrates the possibility of a formalized representation of NL in thinking and action in the studied subject area of activity. The grounds for the object of danger are of fundamental importance for the subsequent development of definitions, which are methods for calculating the states of objects for control purposes.

4   Safety Model Development

4.1   Solution of the Problem of the Aviation Safety Definitions

ICAO Flight Safety Definition. The international community has adopted several successively adjusted definitions long period to date: 1. "Safety. The state in which risks associated with aviation activities, related to, or in direct support of the operation of aircraft, are reduced and controlled to an acceptable level [7–9]. 2. Acceptable level of safety performance (ALoSP). The minimum level of the safety performance of civil aviation in a state, as defined in its state safety program, or of a service provider, as defined in its safety management system, expressed in terms of safety performance targets and safety performance indicators." [7, 8].

ICAO Aviation Security Definition. The common concept of "unlawful interference" in the documents [**Error! Reference source not found.**, 8, 9] is established as a kind of generic concept of "Aviation security": 1. a set of measures, as well as human and material resources, designed to protect civil aviation from acts of unlawful interference; 2. a state of protection of aviation from illegal interference in activities in the field of aviation. The concept of "act of unlawful interference" (AUI) means unlawful actions, including terrorist acts, which may threaten the security of the transport complex. AUI is defined as "acts or attempts to commit acts that endanger the safety of civil aviation and air transport".

The definition of aviation security (AS) consists of two paragraphs, the contents of which are identical in meaning and practically come down to protection from AUI. The concept of "aviation" is a concept of an incomparably larger scope than the concept of AUI. AUI is aimed at flight operations, as well as terms of airport infrastructure. The largest part of all aviation processes, in particular in the aircraft industry, cannot be the object of AUI. Thus, the convolution of the concepts AS to AUI has no theoretical and logical foundations.

These descriptions, according to the author, are problematic and require research. Developments of the standard [**Error! Reference source not found.**] were proposed in the paper [26]. In the present work, the development and derivation of aviation safety definitions are carried out. The definitions are formed in the concept of an acceptable level of flight safety risks. The introduction of this concept responds to the use of an approach based on indicators, levels, and security requirements. Indicators are a measure of the results achieved in flight safety. At present, four main and four additional indicators have been adopted, which show the extent of the damage that has already occurred. The level is understood as the achieved state, calculated as a set of indicators. Requirements are established to achieve appropriate safety performance and target levels of flight safety. They include operating procedures, facilities, systems, and programs for which indicators are set. We consider the purposes in the parameters or states of security, reliability, and risk. The totality of these three most important concepts currently constitutes a shortage of modern developments and a serious theoretical problem. Let the set of business functions of an air carrier be described by a linear function (Eq. 5).

$$W(w_1 x_1, w_2 x_2, \ldots, w_i x_i, \ldots, w_n x_n) \tag{5}$$

where w_i and x_i are the function and input variables of the i-th business structure.

Acceptable and predetermined levels of flight safety are identical to the goals and objectives of the overall activity of the airline. The level can be calculated by the natural number $\overline{L}$ The established number of indicators is also calculated by a clear value of performances $\overline{P}$. Requirements $\tilde{R}$ are fuzzy values, recommendations for the development of security programs, and the sole responsibility of air carriers (Eq. 6).

$$\overline{P}\left\{\tilde{R}(W)\right\} :\to \overline{L} \tag{6}$$

This expression prescribes the achievement of the safety level of a process flight operation through the observation of all processes and functions, that is, the observation and achievement of the individual through the general. The air carrier needs to solve the problem: to structure business functions in such a way that any set of them can definitely be reduced to indicators and levels of safety. The totality of the problems of identifying the subject of safety in aviation, conceptual descriptions, definitions, and terms is the lack of theoretical developments, the result of which is the normative fuzziness of safety standards. The objective of this work is to identify the subject of aviation safety by logical analysis and establishing definitions of the key concepts of aviation safety: safety, aviation, and flight.

4.2 Development of Aviation Safety Definitions

Evaluation of concepts is carried out in the following sequence: a) evaluation of the type of concept in terms of volume and b) establishment of the basis for its division, c) content and presence of signs, d) establishment of relations between concepts. The initial meaning of the concept is associated with the task of the study: the subject of safety in aviation. Therefore, each concept has a meaning: "aviation" is a field of technosphere activity, "flight" is the physical flight of an aircraft, and "safety" is a set of measures for the physical protection of processes in aviation and flights. Further, formal-logical assessments of concepts are carried out and characteristics of species are compiled in terms of volume, content, and relationships. The development of definitions is carried out in pairs of concepts "subordinating - subordinated". (Table 3).

Table 3. Logical characteristics of concepts

Concepts	Volume	Content	Relationship
Aviation	General infinite	Concrete positive independent non-collective	Consonant correlated
Safety	General infinite	Abstract negative independent non-collective	Consonant correlated
Flight	Total registering	Concrete positive independent non-collective	Consonant correlated

The bases for dividing volumes for each of the defined concepts are established. According to concept theory, danger and safety are seen as inconsistent opposite concepts. The concept of "safety" has a sign of consistency between the concepts of "danger" and "security" (Fig. 5).

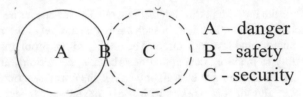

Fig. 5. Crossing concepts on one basis (at one point)

Aviation, (lat. *avis* – bird), implies the movement of an object (bird) in the air space, that is, flight. The synonymy of the pair "aviation - flight" makes it difficult to define the concepts of "aviation safety" and "flight safety". The following combinations of the concepts of safety "subordinating - subordinated" are compiled: {aviation, flight}, {safety, flight}, {aviation, safety}. We will understand the entry in curly brackets as follows: a) the previous concept is generic, and the subsequent concept is specific in volume; notation separated by commas means an unknown connection of concepts that should be established. The ratios of the volumes of compatible subordinate concepts are presented in the form of circles. Each of the generic concepts will be subjected to the ultimate division before reaching the name of the next specific concept. We observe the division rules established in logic: continuity, incompatibility of class types, coincidence of class volumes and the sum of types, and the presence of a basis (sign) of division. The basis for the division of the generic concept will establish the process of organizing production: the sequence of creating the means of production and their use.

The first division of the generic concept of "aviation" (A) gives two specific concepts in special terms: (A) "aviation" (O) "operation". The aviaindustry is divided into (A1) design, (A2) engineering, and (A3) production (manufacturing) of aircraft. The operation is divided into (O1) transportation (air operations of the airline) and other functions (O2... n) infrastructure (air navigation, airports, etc.). Since the goal is to establish a connection between the concept of aviation and the concept of flight, in this classification the subsequent division of classes, except for the class "transportation" is omitted. The activities of an airline in air transportation are structured: flight operations (O1F); other functions depending on the strategy and organizational design: administration, personnel management, aircraft maintenance and repair, commerce, service, finance (O2... m). The content is presented in a diagram (Fig. 6).

The operations of the flight complex (FC) consist of flight operations (O1FO) - "flight" and other functions (O2F... k). The production organization process will compose a flight resource tuple (FRT) (Eq. 7).

$$(FRT) \sum : (O1FO) \in (O1F) \in (O1) \in (O) \in (AN) \tag{7}$$

In this expression, the created resource is "flight", the concept of which has the greatest content in the aviation (aerospace) industry.

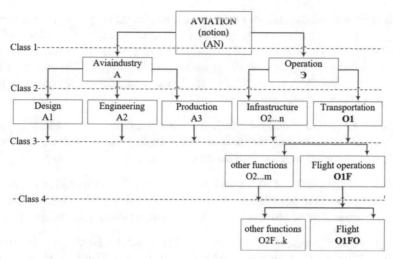

Fig. 6. Model of safety aviation notion

4.3 Derivation of Definitions

Relations of Concepts {Aviation, Flight}. To derive the definition of "flight" in aviation, let us establish the content of the relation of the pair of concepts {aviation, flight}. According to the law of the inverse relationship "volume - content" of generic relations, the content of the species-subordinated concept "flight" includes all the features of each of the subordinate generic concepts of a larger tuple of resources (Fig. 7).

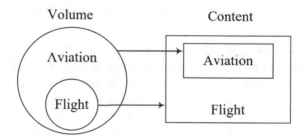

Fig. 7. Correlation of volumes and contents of concepts {aviation, flight}

To distinguish from the volumes of the content of concepts, they are represented by rectangles. Using the rules and requirements definitions are derived. The defining concepts will be all the features of the concepts of the sequence "flight → aviation" with the addition of attributes in turn.

Definition 4. Flight is the operations of the aircraft crew in the process of flight operations transportation.

This definition corresponds to the accepted basis for flight operations transportation (see Fig. 6). For comparison, let us present the following known definition: "Flight is a controlled process of movement of an object in a gaseous medium either by using jet propulsion or other propulsion means or without it (by inertia)". The basis (content of features) of this definition is compiled on the basis of features of the content in natural scientific, physical and technical terms.

Relations of Concepts {Safety, Flight}. To derive a definition, let us establish the content of the relation of the pair of concepts {safety, flight}. The content of the concept of "safety" includes features of each of the concepts of the exploitation tuple.

Definition 5. Flight safety (FS) is a parameter of the quality (property) of flights, showing the ratio of positive outcomes of flights performed to negative outcomes of flights in the chosen typology of observation (measurement, evaluation, calculation).

The principal differences between this definition and the existing regulatory definitions are as follows. The definition establishes the concept - a flight, the state of which is prescribed to be observed through the relationship of the outcomes of an activity (Fig. 8).

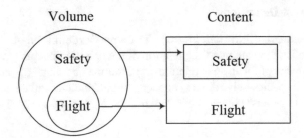

Fig. 8. Correlation of volumes and contents of concepts {safety, flight}

Consequences of applying the definition: a) the term "flight" strictly refers to the operations of flight operations and does not correspond to the concepts of a larger scope of the content of the activities; b) normative monitoring of outcomes in structured business processes is observed; c) it is not allowed to mix the concepts of safety with the concepts of dependability, risk and inexplicable phrases such as "safety risk". Accordingly, the inverse ratio of negative to positive outcomes of flights performed is a definition of flight danger (FD). These grounds are specified by a previously presented expression (Eq. 6) and are written in Eq. 8.

$$\overline{p_i}\left\{\overline{r_i}\left(\sum\nolimits_{i=1}^{n} W\right)\right\} :\to \overline{l_i} \equiv \left[\underline{\underline{\text{def}}} FS\right] \tag{8}$$

Unlike the specific definition of the concept of flight described above, the concept of safety is abstract, which creates additional difficulties in dividing its volume. The content of the concept of FS includes only signs of contours and tuples of operation (see Fig. 6). The volume of the concept of "aviation" does not correlate with the class of aviaindustry, where the content of the concepts of technical objects is formed in the theory of dependability,

Relations of Concepts [Aviation, Security]. The content of the concept of "aviation" includes features of each of the concepts of safety (security) of the operation tuple. The number of features of the content of the concept of "aviation" is much greater than the number of features of the content of the concept of safety (Fig. 9).

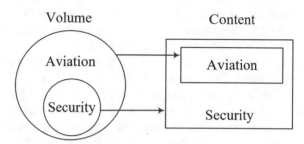

Fig. 9. Correlation of volumes and contents of concepts {aviation, security}

Definition 6. Aviation security (AS) - the state of security of operational processes and procedures for organizing aviation operation transportation.

In this definition, the content of the concept of aviation security, as well as in the definition of the concept of FS, does not correlate with the class of aircraft engineering and the class of operation includes only signs of the concepts of aviation operation transportation.

The model of safety aviation notion establishes scientifically reasonable definitions of safety. Aviation security processes and procedures in structured content may include: a) flight security; c) protection of civil aviation from AUI; c...i) any other definitions of the concepts of operation processes. In a particular case, two concepts: "security of flights" as flight operations, and "protection against AUI" in flight can be considered equivalent, coinciding. The concept of AS can also be used as a generic concept, structured into classes [AS: civil aviation, military aviation, industrial aviation, general aviation], each of which is defined in the processes of security.

5   Conclusion

"When the order was established, the names appeared. Since names have arisen, one must know the limit of their use. Knowing the limit allows you to get rid of the danger" Lao Tzu [28, p 194].

The subject of danger is a set incomparably greater than the subject of safety (security). The subject of safety is a subset, part of the subject of danger. The subject of danger is connected by the relations of objects of the subject area involved in the activity. Dangers "naturally exist", they are mostly unknown, rediscovered, or created in technosphere activities. Dangers can be observed (measured and evaluated) only when object relations are established. It has been established that in the semantic cluster of the subject of danger, the primary feature is called the adverb dangerously and the adjective dangerous. Based on the attribute, the properties, processes, and states of the object are identified. In the semantic pair "dangerous - safe", the word "dangerous" refers to the set of states of the object, and the word "safe" refers to the only state of the object - the absence of signs of danger (zero). The concept of safety has the meaning of security and names the properties and states of objects that are in security relations. The concept of security is semantically equivalent to the concept of safety in only one sense - the absence of danger. Securities are objects of natural origin and are also created artificially. Securities respond to manifested, newly discovered dangers.

The significance of the results lies in the development of the most important definitions based on this approach. Developments of the standard [**Error! Reference source not found.**] in the field of AS were proposed in the paper [26]. The practical significance lies in the creation of logically sound developments of technical standards for the safety of technosphere activities. The study and modeling of the subject of danger in the category of relations: the impact of a threat, exposure to a threat, counteraction to a threat, and protection against a threat allows the conclusion of logically justified definitions of danger and safety (security). The universal basis for the definitions is the process of organizing the production of aviation: aircraft manufacturing (aviaindustry) and aircraft operation. This basis obliges the need to apply the term "safety" only to the processes and procedures of the operational component in aviation.

References

1. Platon: Apology of Socrates, Crito, Ion, Protagoras. Thought, Moscow, p. 864 (1999) (in Russian)
2. Akimov, V.A., Vladimirov, V.I. Izmalkov, В.И.: Disasters and safety. Delovoi Express, Moscow, p. 387 (2006) (in Russian)
3. Nikanorov, S.P.: Safety research. Concept, Moscow, p. 624 (1998) (in Russian)
4. Nishimura, E.H., Iano, Y., de Oliveira, G.G., Vaz, G.C.: Application and Requirements of AIoT-Enabled Industrial Control Units. In: Brazilian Technology Symposium. pp. 724–733. Springer (2022)
5. GOST R ISO/IEC 31010 - 2011 Risk management. Risk assessment methods. Publishing house of standards, Moscow, p. 71 (2011) (in Russian)
6. Lima, L.B. de, Iano, Y., Oliveira, G.G. de, Vaz, G.C., Almeida, A.D. de, Motta, G.B., Villaça, G.M., Schwarz, M.O., Noritomi, P.Y.: Mathematical Modeling: A Conceptual Approach of Linear Algebra as a Tool for Technological Applications. In: Brazilian Technology Symposium. pp. 239–248. Springer (2023)
7. Doc 10004 Global Aviation Safety Plan 2020–2022, ICAO Draft, p. 137 (2022)
8. ICAO Safety Management Manual (Doc 9859) AN/474, Fourth Edition. Canada, p. 182 (2018)
9. Annex 19 to the Convention on International Civil Aviation. Safety Management, Second ed., ICAO, p. 46 (2016)
10. Plotnikov, N.I.: Transport complex safety resources. AviaManager, Novosibirsk, p. 286 (2013) (in Russian) load: http://www.aviam.org/images/sampledata/book/2015_tcsr.pdf
11. Plotnikov, N.I.: Soft Computing Method in Events Risks Matrices. In: Iano, Y., Saotome, O., Kemper, G., Mendes de Seixas, A.C., Gomes de Oliveira, G. (eds.) BTSym 2020. SIST, vol. 233, pp. 578–588. Springer, Cham (2021). https://doi.org/10.1007/978-3-030-75680-2_64

12. Plotnikov, N.I.: Methods of Resource Modeling of Organizational Objects. In: Kwasiborska, A., Skorupski, J., Yatskiv, I. (eds.) ATE 2020. LNITI, pp. 116–130. Springer, Cham (2021). https://doi.org/10.1007/978-3-030-70924-2_10
13. Demanboro, A.C., Bianchini, D., Iano, Y., de Oliveira, G.G., Vaz, G.C.: 6G Networks: An Innovative Approach, but with Many Challenges and Paradigms, in the Development of Platforms and Services in the Near Future. In: Brazilian Technology Symposium. pp. 172–187. Springer (2023)
14. Demidov, D.V.: Theoretical English Grammar: the manual for part-time students of higher educational institutions. Luhansk Taras Shevchenko National University, Luhansk, p. 121 (2014)
15. Russian grammar (in 2 volumes). Nauka, Moscow. vol. 1, p. 784 (1980) (in Russian)
16. Kachalova, K.N., Izrailevich, E.E.: Practical grammar of the English language. Vneshtogizdat, Moscow. p. 720 (1959) (in Russian)
17. The Oxford Minireference Thesaurus by Alan Spooner. Clarendon Press, Oxford, p. 617 (1997)
18. Siegle, A.R., Iano, Y., de Oliveira, G.G., Vaz, G.C.: Proposal of Mathematical Models for a Continuous Flow Electric Heater. In: Brazilian Technology Symposium. pp. 213–228. Springer (2023)
19. Ozhegov, S.I.: Shvedova, N.Y. Explanatory dictionary of the Russian language. LLC ITI Technologies, Moscow, p. 944 (2003) (in Russian)
20. Ushakov, D.N.: Explanatory dictionary of the Russian language. Moscow: vol. 1, p. 1562, vol. 2, p. 1040, vol. 3, p. 1424, vol. 4, p. 1502 (1935–1940) (in Russian)
21. Salvendy, G., Karwowski, W.: Handbook of Human Factors and Ergonomics, 5th Edition. Wiley, Hoboken, New Jersey. p. 1600 (2021)
22. Lossky, N.O.: Logic. Obelisk, Berlin, p. 168 (1923) (in Russian)
23. Zinoviev, A.A.: The logic of science. Thought, Moscow, p. 279 (1971)
24. Getmanova, A.D.: Logic textbook, second ed. Vlados, Moscow, p. 303 (1995) (in Russian)
25. Goncharov, S.S., Ershov, Y.L., Samokhvalov K.F.: Introduction to the logic and methodology of science. Interpraks, Moscow, p. 256 (1994) (in Russian)
26. Demanboro, A.C., Bianchini, D., Iano, Y., de Oliveira, G.G., Vaz, G.C.: Regulatory Aspects of 5G and Perspectives in the Scope of Scientific and Technological Policy. In: Brazilian Technology Symposium. pp. 163–171. Springer (2023)
27. Plotnikov, N.I.: The Method of Ontological Design of Safeguarding International Civil Aviation Against Acts of Unlawful Interference. In: Iano, Y., Saotome, O., Kemper, G., Mendes de Seixas, A.C., Gomes de Oliveira, G. (eds.) BTSym 2020. SIST, vol. 233, pp. 317–333. Springer, Cham (2021). https://doi.org/10.1007/978-3-030-75680-2_36
28. Klir, J. G.: Architecture of systems problem solving. Radio and Communication, Moscow, p. 544 (1990) (in Russian)

Petrological Retrospective and Technological Potentials of Magnetite Nanolites in Volcanic Glasses

Augusto Gonçalves Nobre[1,2]([✉]) [iD] and Fábio Ramos Dias de Andrade[1] [iD]

[1] Institute of Geosciences, University of São Paulo, São Paulo, Brazil
{augusto.goncalves,dias}@usp.br
[2] Center for Natural and Exact Sciences, Federal University of Santa Maria, Santa Maria, Brazil

Abstract. Magnetite is a mineral known since Ancient Greece and has a scientific interest because it behaves like a natural magnet. Magnetite nanolites found in volcanic glasses have been studied in volcanology and experimental petrology due to their potential to contribute to explosive eruptions. Synthetic magnetite nanoparticles have a wide range of morphologies and technological applications and have been produced by several routes. The main problems associated with the use of synthetic magnetite nanoparticles are their high susceptibility to oxidation when exposed to the atmosphere and their tendency to clump together when not anchored to a substrate. On the other hand, the magnetite nanolites of volcanic glasses are naturally coated and anchored by volcanic glasses, being stabilized inside the rocks. Despite not having the main threats of synthetic nanoparticles, magnetite nanolites currently have uses restricted to the areas of waste control and inertization. In this way, research into the applications of magnetite nanolites in volcanic glasses is encouraged beyond the fields of volcanology, as there is a dormant potential for the high-tech industry.

Keywords: Magnetic crystals · Mineral nanotechnology · Magma rheology

1 Introduction

Although nanomaterials are ubiquitous in nature, it was only with the characterization and controlled manipulation of nanomaterials that mankind could make purposeful and systematic use of their properties [1].

Nanotechnology refers to the development of devices, machines, products, and processes, based on components (individual or in blocks) made up of nanomaterials, which are those materials that have at least one dimension in the order of size between 1 and 100 nm [2]. Mineral nanotechnology focuses on the use of natural solids (rocks, minerals, mineraloids - or non-minerals) in nanotechnology through simple beneficiation processes [3].

Graphene, an emblematic nanomaterial, was synthesized in laboratory and had its properties characterized [4], and eventually, its natural analog was found in a geological context [5]. Minerals that occur as nanoparticles, such as magnetite, have been studied

Y. Iano et al. (Eds.): BTSym 2022, SIST 353, pp. 288–295, 2023.
https://doi.org/10.1007/978-3-031-31007-2_26

due to their potential for unprecedented properties when compared to the conventional properties of the same minerals in larger particles [6].

Magnetite (Fe_3O_4) is known since Ancient Greece and is a natural magnet [7]. Magnetite on a nanometric scale (nanolite) has been described in volcanic glasses, and its crystallization has relevant rheological consequences in erupting magmas.

The literature points out several devices that use nanometric magnetite and their potential in nanoscience for the coming decades. This work reviews the implications of the presence of nanomagnetite in volcanic glasses and discusses the potential use of this mineral resource as raw material for nanotechnology.

2 Bulk Magnetite

Magnetite was described by the Greek philosopher Thales in 600 BC, who identified its magnetic properties, but it was only in the Middle Ages that its mineralogical description began with the letter of Petrus Peregrinus in 1269 AD [8] and later in the Renaissance with the work *De Magnet* by William Gilbert written in Latin in 1600 AD [9].

One of the most accepted hypotheses of the magnetite name refers to the Magnesia region, in Thessaly, the Greece region referenced by Wilhelm Karl von Haidinger in 1845. Gilbert studied magnetite varieties and verified the existence of one magnetite type that has an important external magnetic field, unlike most specimens that required an external magnetic field induction to become magnets, and that was called lodestone.

This nomenclature comes from the English 'lode' with the now-obsolete meaning of 'path' or 'journey', a reference to the use of this variety of magnetite in navigational compasses. The nomenclature discussion became blurred from the 19th century onwards, when geologists began to name all mineral varieties of iron oxide attracted by permanent pocket magnets as magnetite [7]. Today, the nomenclature is no longer blurred and magnetite is considered a double oxide of Fe^{2+} and Fe^{3+}, with a spinel-like structure.

The crystal structure of magnetite and, consequently, the understanding of the origin of its magnetic properties began in 1915 with Bragg's studies on spinel group crystals [10]. Natural magnetism is responsible for most technological and industrial uses of mineral and synthetic magnetite [11].

3 Magnetite Nanolites in Volcanic Glasses

Schillinger and Veblen [12] were pioneers in describing volcanic glass shards with superparamagnetism in the Turkana basin, northern Kenya. The authors identified cubic magnetite crystals with dimensions from 20 to 100 Å via transmission electron microscopy (TEM) and interpreted the precipitation of magnetite as a syn-eruptional process in which the dark color of volcanic glasses with felsic composition is given by these fine crystals' dispersion.

The term "nanolite" was given by Sharp et al. [13] referring to pyroxenes (ortho- and clinopyroxene), plagioclase, and magnetite occurring in crystals smaller than 0.6 μm identified via TEM in rhyolitic glasses from the Ben Lomond lava dome, New Zealand. The authors interpreted the origin of nanolites as a result of post-eruption crystallization, associated with the devolatilization of rhyolitic magma.

Raman spectroscopy has become fundamental for nanolites detection in volcanic rocks, at a cost and analysis time much lower than TEM, in addition to being non-destructive and not requiring sample preparation [14–16]. The association between the magnetite nanolites crystallization and the water loss in magmas implies an important increase of viscosity, which results in a change in the flows behavior and eruptive style and may be responsible for explosive eruptions whose initial analyses were carried out on glasses and explosive products of volcanism from the Pantelleria island in Italy [17]. Di Genova et al. [18] present a proposal to estimate the water content in volcanic glasses, using Raman spectroscopy. The work points out that the presence of nanolites can generate underestimation in the water content in natural glasses.

Although degassing is the main cause of explosive volcanic eruptions, viscosity is critical to controlling the escape of volatiles and switching between effusive and explosive behavior. "Temperature and composition control the melt viscosity, but crystallization above a critical volume (>30 volume %) can lock up the magma, triggering an explosion" [19]. However, a small volume of nanocrystals can cause a relevant increase in magma viscosity and above the critical value required for explosive eruption, even for low-viscosity melts [19].

The numerical model and experimental procedures that provide the link confirmation between nanolites crystallization and the increase in the explosiveness of volcanic eruptions were presented by Cáceres et al. [20]. In this work, the authors argue that the degassing of magmatic water normally involves nucleation and bubble growth, which drive magma ascent. Crystals suspended in magma can influence both nucleation and bubble growth, however, the action of crystals may be different depending on their size. Micrometer to centimeter-sized crystals can cause heterogeneous nucleation of bubbles and facilitate bubble coalescence. On the other hand, nanolites can be efficient sites for bubble nucleation, promoting an increase in bubbles' number and also in their growth rate. In this way, nanolites can generate an increased propensity for explosive eruptions [21].

The rhyolitic pink pumice released by the deep-sea eruption of Havre volcano in New Zealand in 2012 was studied by Knafelc et al. [22], who pointed out that the pink color of the rock was due to the content of magnetite nanolites oxidized to hematite at high temperatures in air conditions, which indicates that despite being a short-lived event, it had a very relevant explosive intensity that made it possible for the hot pyroclasts to be launched into the atmosphere. This model challenges previously existing depth models for explosive eruptions in underwater environments and suggests that magnetite nanolites may be drivers of this type of volcanic activity.

Other volcanic events in Italy [23, 24], Japan [25–27], and Peru [28] have sparked interest in the investigation of nanolites in addition to experimental petrology studies [29, 30], demonstrating the broad discussion underway in the scientific community.

4   Technological Potentials of Magnetite Nanolites

Nanomagnetite used in technological applications is synthetic and its synthesis includes top-down (physical procedures) and bottom-up (chemical and biological) methods in addition to microfluidics and recycled iron-based unconventional methods [31].

On average, magnetite nanoparticles, at certain temperatures, have zero magnetization, however, their magnetic susceptibility is very high in this state, allowing them to be easily magnetized by an external magnetic field [32]. These properties make magnetite nanoparticles suitable for a wide range of applications, such as magnetic resonance imaging contrast agents [33], magnetic fluids [34], hyperthermia therapy [35], bio-sensing and diagnosis [36], drug delivery [37], cancer treatment [38], data storage [39], catalysis [40], magnetic paints [41], microelectronics [42, 43], high-density magnetic recording [44], magnetic refrigeration [45], batteries [46, 47], and sorbents for pollutants removal [48].

Magnetite nanoparticles do not depend exclusively on their magnetic properties to be of technological interest, since they are non-toxic to humans, biocompatible and biodegradable, have chemical, physical and colloidal stability, easy dispersibility, antimicrobial properties, and can be chemically functionalized [49].

Magnetite nanoparticles, as well as many other natural or synthetic nanomaterials, tend to agglomerate after their production/obtaining and need to be anchored for technological proposals. At the same time, these nanoparticles are not stable to atmospheric exposure, having a great tendency to oxidize to maghemite, requiring coating to be used in environments exposed to air [50].

Although incipient, the first uses of volcanic glasses with the presence of magnetite nanolites acting for technological purposes have been reported in the literature. So far, the main uses are associated with the inertization and isolation of effluents and residues [51]. The process is based on the great capacity of nanomagnetite from basaltic rocks to host potentially toxic heavy metals, such as Cr or Ba, when exposed to phosphate-rich effluents and residues that are also inertized after thermal treatment. The products of these treatments can compose glass and glass ceramics with potential applications in the construction industry [52].

5 Discussion

Magmatic provinces, bearing acidic volcanic glasses (with dacitic or rhyolitic composition), such as the Paraná state, in southern Brazil, have rocks with stabilized magnetite nanolites for more than a hundred million years [53]. Weathering can produce and stabilize magnetite nanolites through biological activity [54]. However, so far natural magnetite nanoparticles remain with their technological potential low explored.

Nanometric magnetite in shapes such as cubes, rods, disks, tubes, plates, hexagons, octahedrons, truncated octahedrons, tetrahedrons, octopods, tetrapods, rings, flowers, and concaves, in solid, hollow, or porous forms [23] has been widely synthesized for diverse applications [55, 56]. Synthetic production becomes progressively faster, cheaper, and more efficient, which makes it easier for current technological uses to be substantially based on the use of synthetic nanometric magnetite.

It is notable that the current uses of volcanic glass magnetite nanolites for technological applications are fundamentally for massive and robust uses, with large masses of material with low processing and little entry into the high technology field.

Studies of magnetite nanolites are on the rise given their application in the fields of volcanology and experimental petrology, but the potential for refined applications is still dormant.

As magnetite nanolites are encapsulated by volcanic glasses, they are automatically anchored, giving stability, and coated, which protects them against oxidation. In this way, natural nanomagnetite has the potential for technological use, as they are naturally protected against the greatest threats to synthetic magnetite nanoparticles.

6 Conclusion

The scientific literature shows that magnetite nanolites in volcanic glasses may trigger explosive eruptions.

Synthetic magnetite nanoparticles are widely used in medical and biomedical applications, magnetic fluids, inks, energy generation and storage, data storage, electronics, and environment fields, being easily synthesized, manipulated, and functionalized.

Although in an initial state, there are uses of volcanic magnetite nanolites in control and inertization of waste and effluents, capable of generating inert materials that can be used in civil construction.

In this way, it is possible to conclude that the magnetite nanolites of volcanic glasses have an application potential still little explored, but interesting, because they are stable and coated by the glass that prevents their degradation and agglutination, which are the main challenges of the field of synthetic magnetite nanoparticles.

References

1. Vance, M., E, Kuiken T, Vejerano EP, McGinnis SP, Hochella Jr MF, Rejeski D. et al.: Nanotechnology in the real world: Redeveloping the nanomaterial consumer products inventory. Beilstein J. Nanotechnol. **6**, 1178–1769 (2015)
2. Hochella, M.F., Spencer, M.G., Jones, K.L.: Nanotechnology: nature's gift or scientists' brainchild? Environ. Sci. Nano. **2**, 114–119 (2015)
3. Augusto Gonçalves Nobre, José Armando Espinosa Martínez, Odila Florêncio,: Mineral Nanotechnology in Circular Economy. In: Yuzo Iano, Osamu Saotome, Guillermo Kemper, Ana Claudia Mendes de Seixas, Gabriel Gomes de Oliveira, (ed.) BTSym 2020. SIST, vol. 233, pp. 220–226. Springer, Cham (2021). https://doi.org/10.1007/978-3-030-75680-2_26
4. Hersam, M.C., et al.: Nanoscience and technology: a collection of reviews from nature journals. Technology **158**, 165 (2009)
5. Nobre, A.G., Martínez, J.A.E., Terence, M.C., Florêncio, O.: A ação de zonas de cisalhamento na disponibilização natural de nanoplaquetas de grafita: o exemplo dos metadolomitos do Grupo Itaiacoca e dos xistos do Grupo Dom Silvério. Brazilian J. Anim. Environ. Res. **3**, 3108–3118 (2020)
6. Nobre, A.G., da Silva, L.P.N., de Andrade, F.R.D.: Graphene geology and the fourth industrial revolution. In: Yuzo, I., (eds.) Proceedings of the 7th Brazilian Technology Symposium (BTSym'21): Emerging Trends in Human Smart and Sustainable Future of Cities (Volume 1), pp. 342–348. Springer International Publishing, Cham (2023). https://doi.org/10.1007/978-3-031-04435-9_34
7. Mills, A.A.: The lodestone: History, physics, and formation. Ann. Sci. **61**, 273–319 (2004)
8. Sparavigna, A.C.: Petrus Peregrinus of Maricourt and the Medieval Magnetism. arXiv Prepr. arXiv1512.02634 (2015)
9. Lindsay, R.B.: William Gilbert and Magnetism in 1600. Am. J. Phys. **8**, 271–282 (1940)

10. Fleet, M.E.: The structure of magnetite. Acta Crystallogr. Sect. B Struct. Crystallogr. Cryst. Chem. **37**, 917–920 (1981)
11. Nadoll, P., Angerer, T., Mauk, J.L., French, D., Walshe, J.: Ore Geology Reviews. Ore Geol. Rev. **61**, 1–32 (2014)
12. Schlinger, C.M., Smith, R.M., Veblen, D.R.: Geologic origin of magnetic volcanic glasses in the KBS tuff. Geology **14**, 959–962 (1986)
13. Sharp, T.G., Stevenson, R.J., Dingwell, D.B.: Microlites and" nanolites" in rhyolitic glass: microstructural and chemical characterization. Bull. Volcanol. **57**, 631–640 (1996)
14. Giordano, D., et al.: A calibrated database of Raman spectra for natural silicate glasses: implications for modelling melt physical properties. J. Raman Spectrosc. **51**, 1822–1838 (2020)
15. González-García, D., Giordano, D., Russell, J.K., Dingwell, D.B.: A Raman spectroscopic tool to estimate chemical composition of natural volcanic glasses. Chem. Geol. **556**, 119819 (2020)
16. González-García, D., et al.: Retrieving dissolved H2O content from micro-Raman spectroscopy on nanolitized silicic glasses: application to volcanic products of the Paraná magmatic province, Brazil. Chem. Geol. **567**, 120058 (2021)
17. Di Genova, D., Caracciolo, A., Kolzenburg, S.: Measuring the degree of "nanotilization" of volcanic glasses: Understanding syn-eruptive processes recorded in melt inclusions. Lithos **318**, 209–218 (2018)
18. Di Genova, D., Sicola, S., Romano, C., Vona, A., Fanara, S., Spina, L.: Effect of iron and nanolites on Raman spectra of volcanic glasses: a reassessment of existing strategies to estimate the water content. Chem. Geol. **475**, 76–86 (2017)
19. Di Genova, D., et al.: In situ observation of nanolite growth in volcanic melt: A driving force for explosive eruptions. Sci. Adv. **6**, eabb0413 (2020)
20. Cáceres, F., et al.: Can nanolites enhance eruption explosivity? Geology **48**, 997–1001 (2020)
21. Cáceres, F., et al.: From melt to crystals: the effects of cooling on FeTi oxide nanolites crystallisation and melt polymerisation at oxidising conditions. Chem. Geol. **563**, 120057 (2021)
22. Knafelc, J., et al.: Havre 2012 pink pumice is evidence of a short-lived, deep-sea, magnetite nanolite-driven explosive eruption. Commun. Earth Environ. **3**, 1–11 (2022)
23. Allabar, A., Salis Gross, E., Nowak, M.: The effect of initial H2O concentration on decompression-induced phase separation and degassing of hydrous phonolitic melt. Contrib. to Mineral. Petrol. **175**, 1–19 (2020)
24. Vigliotti, L., Bilardello, D., Winkler, A., Del Carlo, P.: Rock magnetic fingerprint of Mt Etna volcanic ash. Geophys. J. Int. **231**, 749–769 (2022)
25. Mujin, M., Nakamura, M., Miyake, A.: Eruption style and crystal size distributions: Crystallization of groundmass nanolites in the 2011 Shinmoedake eruption. Am. Mineral. **102**, 2367–2380 (2017)
26. Matsumoto, K., Geshi, N.: Shallow crystallization of eruptive magma inferred from volcanic ash microtextures: a case study of the 2018 eruption of Shinmoedake volcano. Japan. Bull. Volcanol. **83**, 1–14 (2021)
27. Yoshida, K., et al.: Variety of the drift pumice clasts from the 2021 Fukutoku-Oka-no-Ba eruption. Japan. Isl. Arc. **31**, e12441 (2022)
28. Samaniego, P., et al.: Linking magmatic processes and magma chemistry during the postglacial to recent explosive eruptions of Ubinas volcano (southern Peru). J. Volcanol. Geotherm. Res. **407**, 107095 (2020)
29. Pistone, M., Formo, E., Whittington, A.G., Herbst, T., Cottrell, E.: Direct nanoscale observations of degassing-induced crystallisation in felsic magmas. Contrib. Miner. Petrol. **177**(3), 1–21 (2022). https://doi.org/10.1007/s00410-022-01900-1

30. Kennedy, E., Sari, B., Scott, M.C.: Chemical and structural alterations in the amorphous structure of obsidian due to nanolites. Microsc. Microanal. **28**, 289–295 (2022)
31. Niculescu, A.-G., Chircov, C., Grumezescu, A.M.: Magnetite nanoparticles: Synthesis methods–A comparative review. Methods. (2021)
32. Israel, L.L., Galstyan, A., Holler, E., Ljubimova, J.Y.: Magnetic iron oxide nanoparticles for imaging, targeting and treatment of primary and metastatic tumors of the brain. J. Control. Release. **320**, 45–62 (2020)
33. Soleymani, M., et al.: Effects of multiple injections on the efficacy and cytotoxicity of folate-targeted magnetite nanoparticles as theranostic agents for MRI detection and magnetic hyperthermia therapy of tumor cells. Sci. Rep. **10**, 1–14 (2020)
34. Gu, T., Zhang, Y., Khan, S.A., Hatton, T.A.: Continuous flow synthesis of superparamagnetic nanoparticles in reverse miniemulsion systems. Colloid Interface Sci. Commun. **28**, 1–4 (2019)
35. Chircov, C., Grumezescu, A.M., Holban, A.M.: Magnetic particles for advanced molecular diagnosis. Materials (Basel). 12, 2158 (2019)
36. Ficai, D., et al.: Antibiofilm coatings based on PLGA and nanostructured cefepime-functionalized magnetite. Nanomaterials **8**, 633 (2018)
37. Sirivat, A., Paradee, N.: Facile synthesis of gelatin-coated Fe_3O_4 nanoparticle: Effect of pH in single-step co-precipitation for cancer drug loading. Mater. Des. **181**, 107942 (2019)
38. Gajare, S.P., et al.: Nano-magnetic Copper Complexes as Double-Edged Sword against MCF-7 Breast Cancer Cells. ChemistrySelect. **7**, e202103818 (2022)
39. Gao, G., et al.: Shape-controlled synthesis and magnetic properties of monodisperse Fe_3O_4 nanocubes. Cryst. Growth Des. **10**, 2888–2894 (2010)
40. Amendola, V., Riello, P., Meneghetti, M.: Magnetic nanoparticles of iron carbide, iron oxide, iron@ iron oxide, and metal iron synthesized by laser ablation in organic solvents. J. Phys. Chem. C. **115**, 5140–5146 (2011)
41. Kolchanov, D.S., et al.: V: Sol–gel magnetite inks for inkjet printing. J. Mater. Chem. C. **7**, 6426–6432 (2019)
42. Osouli-Bostanabad, K., Hosseinzade, E., Kianvash, A., Entezami, A.: Modified nano-magnetite coated carbon fibers magnetic and microwave properties. Appl. Surf. Sci. **356**, 1086–1095 (2015)
43. Chuma, E.L., Iano, Y., Roger, L.L.B., De Oliveira, G.G., Vaz, G.C.: Novelty sensor for detection of wear particles in oil using integrated microwave metamaterial resonators with neodymium magnets. IEEE Sens. J. (2022)
44. De Queiroz, D.F., de Camargo, E.R., Martines, M.A.U.: Synthesis and characterization of magnetic nanoparticles of cobalt ferrite coated with silica. Biointerface Res. Appl. Chem. **10**, 4908–4913 (2020)
45. Tong, S., Quinto, C.A., Zhang, L., Mohindra, P., Bao, G.: Size-dependent heating of magnetic iron oxide nanoparticles. ACS Nano **11**, 6808–6816 (2017)
46. Li, J., et al.: Selective synthesis of magnetite nanospheres with controllable morphologies on CNTs and application to lithium-Ion batteries. Phys. status solidi. **216**, 1800924 (2019)
47. Roger Prior Gregio, Yuzo Iano, Lia Toledo Moreira Mota, Gabriel Caumo Vaz, Gabriel Gomes Oliveira, Diego Arturo Pajuelo Castro, Carolina Fernandes Frangeto,: Energy Use in Urban Areas Using Neodymium Magnets. In: Yuzo Iano, Osamu Saotome, Guillermo Kemper, Ana Claudia Mendes de Seixas, Gabriel Gomes de Oliveira, (ed.) BTSym 2020. SIST, vol. 233, pp. 988–1005. Springer, Cham (2021). https://doi.org/10.1007/978-3-030-75680-2_107
48. Mashkoor, F., Nasar, A.: Carbon nanotube-based adsorbents for the removal of dyes from waters: a review. Environ. Chem. Lett. **18**, 605–629 (2020)
49. Novoselova, L.Y.: Nanoscale magnetite: new synthesis approach, structure and properties. Appl. Surf. Sci. **539**, 148275 (2021)

50. Wallyn, J., Anton, N., Vandamme, T.F.: Synthesis, principles, and properties of magnetite nanoparticles for in vivo imaging applications—a review. Pharmaceutics. **11**, 601 (2019)
51. Tarrago, M., Garcia-Valles, M., Martínez, S., Neuville, D.R.: Phosphorus solubility in basaltic glass: limitations for phosphorus immobilization in glass and glass-ceramics. J. Environ. Manage. **220**, 54–64 (2018)
52. Tarragó, M., Esteves, H., Garcia-Valles, M., Martínez, S., Neuville, D.R.: Effect of Ca in P-doped basaltic glass-ceramics: application to waste inertization. Mater. Lett. **220**, 266–268 (2018)
53. de Andrade, F.R.D., Polo, L.A., de Assis Janasi, V., de Souza Carvalho, F.M.: Volcanic glass in Cretaceous dacites and rhyolites of the Paraná Magmatic Province, southern Brazil: Characterization and quantification by XRD-Rietveld. J. Volcanol. Geotherm. Res. **355**, 219–231 (2018)
54. Bortnikov, N.S., Novikov, V.M., Zhukhlistov, A.P., Boeva, N.M., Soboleva, S. V, Zhegallo, E.A.: Biogenic nanomagnetite in cuirass of the bauxite-bearing crust of weathering in basalt from South Vietnam. In: Doklady Earth Sciences, pp. 754–757. Pleiades Publishing, Ltd.(Плеадес Паблишинг, Лтд) (2013)
55. Xie, W., et al.: Shape-, size-and structure-controlled synthesis and biocompatibility of iron oxide nanoparticles for magnetic theranostics. Theranostics. **8**, 3284 (2018)
56. Design strategies for shape-controlled magnetic iron oxide nanoparticles: Roca, A.G., Gutiérrez, L., Gavilán, H., Brollo, M.E.F., Veintemillas-Verdaguer, S., del Puerto Morales, M. Adv. Drug Deliv. Rev. **138**, 68–104 (2019)

Application of Industrial Inspection of Metal Parts by CNN

Leandro de Sousa Silva$^{(\boxtimes)}$ ⓘ, Leandro Ronchini Ximenes ⓘ, and Rangel Arthur ⓘ

School of Technology, State University of Campinas, Limeira, Brazil
1191138@dac.unicamp.br, {leandro,rangel}@ft.unicamp.br

Abstract. With the increase of information generated in manufacturing and the demand for speed in obtaining information from the productive processes derived from the concept of Industry 4.0, some application niches have been standing out among researchers. Image classification using CNN and deep learning is a very researched topic. The application of deep learning techniques when there are few samples has proved to be a challenge to overcome. For this study, a simulation of a dynamic manufacturing process was performed where a machine may be able to produce two different parts and a need to classify these images using low-cost equipment. A dataset with a limited number of images (249 images), organized in training and validation directories, containing subdirectories divided between images conform and anomaly image, with an industrial bias. Four CNN classifier models were used and their individual performances were compared, using accuracy and loss from model training and validation as the main metrics. The CNN models developed obtained an accuracy of 92% using only one convolutional layer.

Keywords: Deep Learning · CNN with few samples · Industry 4.0

1 Introduction

Technological innovation has always been one of the main parameters of highlighting companies [1]. Vision systems have become a strong ally for companies to adapt to the quality controls of their products or services [2], increasingly stricter.

The computer vision systems usually employed in industries are composed of a camera, specifically designed lights, and a trigger sensor, which informs the position of the product so that the camera can photograph the image and make its analysis [3, 4]. Despite the great evolution of these systems, and due to the technological evolution of industries, there is a great demand for information and process data captured by the sensors, generating a large volume of information to be processed.

New vision systems based on machine learning and deep learning are gaining more and more notoriety in industrial applications, and meeting the demand of working with a huge volume of collected data. But this technology upgrade faces some operational and technological barriers, such as the fear of the management and technical staff of the companies because it is a new technology [5]. Many companies also face Internet vulnerability, fear of cyber-attacks, and even overloaded or deficient ethernet networks [6, 7]. With the popularization of the industry 4.0 concept, which has Big-Data and IoT as its driving forces, other technologies have been following the requirements of this concept [8–10]. Machine learning, and deep learning, are very powerful tools for realizing the implementation of Industry 4.0 [11–13]. CNN networks are becoming increasingly popular in the context of vision systems for image classification [14, 15].

The objective of this study is to develop a deep learning training model for the classification of diversified images in the industrial context, by simulating a dynamic production in which the same equipment can classify images of different items in "real-time", and can be applied to existing low-cost equipment [16].

A comparison of four CNN-based image classifier models was performed and compared to a dataset with few samples and two different types of images with industrial bias. With the results obtained in the study, it will be possible to capture the necessary information to develop a robust image classifier system for low-cost industrial applications.

2 Methodology

Four different CNN (Convolutional Neural Network) models were defined to perform a direct comparison of the performance of each model's accuracy when applied to three different databases.

The model parameters of all CNNs remained unchanged, except for image size, where the pre-trained models require specific sizes. All images were submitted to the same number of training epochs with the same batch size as we can see in the main training parameters of the CNN models in Table 1.

Table 1. List of parameters used to train the CNNs

Parameters	Value	Comments
Image_width	160	Width of the image
Image_height	160	Height of the image
Image_color_channel	3	Core layers
Image_color_channel_size	255	The maximum intensity of variation of pixels
Image_size	160 x 160	Size of the image
Image_shape	(160 x 160) x 3	Shape of the image
Batch_size	10	Number of images used
Epochs	100	Period number of training
Learning_rate	0.0001	Learning rate of training

2.1 CNN Models Used

For this comparison, four types of models were developed, where the main characteristics that differentiate them are the number of hidden layers applied on the same dataset.

The general architecture used can be seen below in Fig. 1.

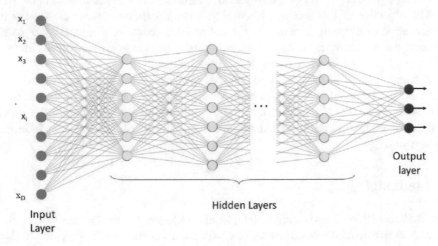

Fig. 1. Neural network architecture

The pre-trained models chosen for the test are renowned and used for mobile applications due to their small size (between 14 and 23 MB) [17] and their performance applied to various operating systems, which can be a great advantage in industrial applications, such as industrial computers, or development boards like Raspberry or Jetson. The pre-trained models were assigned using the weights pre-set with the dataset ImageNet, which has more than 14 million images subdivided into 1000 different categories [18].

CNN Model 1. The first CNN model is the most basic one used to generate a reference point for comparison with the other models. It contains only one convolutional layer and other basic layers. The CNN for model 1 is composed of an initial layer to adjust the image to the dimensions needed to train the model, a second convolution layer, composed of a 3 x 3 kernel, which scans all pixels of the image 16 times and has a ReLU activation function, where it has a variance with a minimum threshold of 0. The max pooling layer is responsible for reducing information losses due to image com-pression after the convolution layer. Table 2, shown below, displays a summary of model 1 used in all datasets.

CNN Model 2. The developed CNN model 2 is similar to model 1 but contains more convolution layers (5 layers) and max pooling as we can see in Table 2.

CNN Model 3. For the developed CNN model 3, a pre-trained model with other images was used. This technique is frequently used in other image classification applications. The model selected was the "MobileNetV2" [19], which was developed preferably for mobile applications, where it is necessary to optimize the processing as much as possible due to the limitations of mobile-type hardware. The pre-trained model was selected because of its amount of training parameters of 3.5 million and its low file size of 14 MB [17].

CNN Model 4. For the developed CNN model 4, a pre-trained model with other images was also used. The model selected was "NASNetMobile" [20], which was also developed preferably for mobile applications. The pre-trained model was selected because of its amount of training parameters of 5.3 million and its low file size of 23 MB.

Table 2 shows the summary of all the models used, and their respective parameters for training and validating the CNN models.

Table 2. Parameters of the CNN models used

Model	Total Params	Trainable Params	Non-trainable Params
Model 1	13,107,905	13,107,905	0
Model 2	1,884,449	1,884,449	0
Model 3	2,259,265	1,281	2,257,984
Model 4	5,327,717	1,001	5,326,716

For better equalization of the models, a "Dropout" layer was added, which randomly deactivates 20% of the neurons in order to not create a bias in training or validation, due to the differences in samples.

2.2 Datasets Used

The choice of datasets was defined by simulating a dynamic manufacturing industry, where the same production line can produce several different parts, as is one of the concepts of industry 4.0, in the case of the study carried out, they were parts of a centrifugal pump rotor and washers.

Three datasets were used to compare the effectiveness of each model. For the comparison, four types of models were developed, where the main characteristics that differentiate them are the amounts of hidden layers applied [21].

The datasets were manipulated in order to contain the same number of samples in all existing directories as can be seen in Fig. 2, thus allowing an analysis of the application of each model using few samples for training and validation.

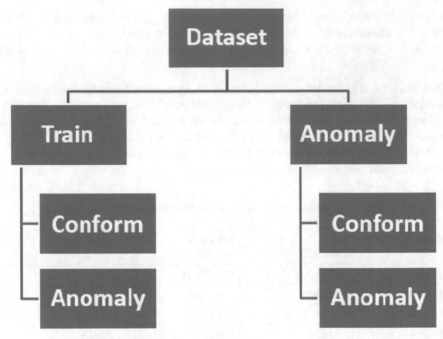

Fig. 2. Structure of all datasets used

- Datasets are classified as:
- Dataset - 01: Obtained through Kaggle® datasets [22], the dataset was manipulated in order to equalize the number of samples in all directories as shown in Fig. 2 above. For a better understanding, Fig. 3 below is a random image of the samples contained in the datasets.
- Dataset – 02: Obtained through Kaggle® datasets [23], the dataset was manipulated in order to equalize the number of samples in all directories. The washer's images were chosen due to the geometric similarity with the parts of dataset 01 (centrifugal pumps rotor), and with the difference between the anomalies of the parts considered defective.
- Dataset – 03: A homogeneous blend was made between datasets 01 and 02, keeping the same amount of samples in all directories in order to merge all samples. This dataset can simulate a dynamic production.

The example of the samples of each dataset (01/02/03) can be seen in Fig. 3.

2.3 Evaluation Metrics

The evaluation metrics focused on training and validation accuracy and losses, as this is an intuitive metric to track model performance

$$Accuracy = \frac{TP + TN}{TP + TN + FP + FN} \tag{1}$$

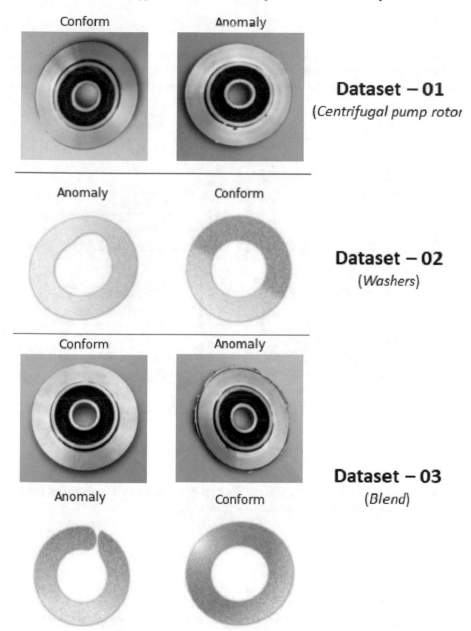

Fig. 3. Illustrative picture of the datasets used.

where TP = True positive, TN = True negative, FP = False positive, and FN = False negative.

The accuracy-based metric is usually the initial parameter for model performance evaluation, where we can adjust the parameters before generating more complete data.

3   Results

The results obtained from training and validation of the four models applied to dataset 03 are shown in Fig. 4. Only results based on dataset 03 (Blend) will be displayed, because it is the dataset that blends the other two, generating a more diverse dataset.

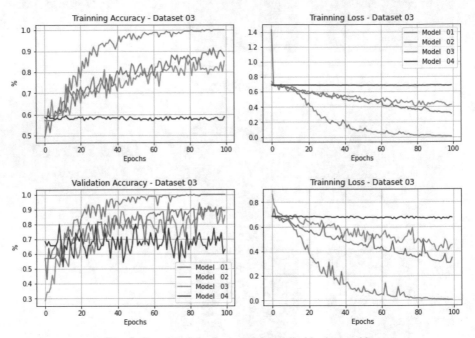

Fig. 4. Results of the four models applied in dataset 03

We can list the models in order from the best performing to the worst performing when comparing accuracy and loss metrics as follows.

1. CNN model – 2
2. CNN model – 1
3. CNN model – 3
4. CNN model – 4

Table 3 shows a summary of the performance of the programs applied to dataset 03.

As observed in Fig. 4 and Table 3, model 2 obtained a maximum accuracy of 100% for training and validation, a minimum loss percentage of 5.25% for training, and 4.25% for validation.

Table 3. Summary of tests applied to dataset 03

Model	Training		Validation	
	Max Accuracy	Min Loss	Max Accuracy	Min Loss
CNN model 1	91.42%	30.68%	92.00%	30.43%
CNN model 2	**100%**	**5.35%**	**100%**	**4.25%**
CNN model 3	86.85%	40.50%	94.28%	39.85%
CNN model 4	59.43%	67.84%	80.00%	66.12%

4 Conclusion

With the analysis of the results, it is possible to identify that the models that did not use transfer learning and were developed manually obtained a better performance when compared to those that used pre-trained models, even though they had more layers and training parameters using various images.

The pre-trained models, models 3 and 4, performed worse than models 1 and 2. This was due to the low epoch interactions, which for this study was limited to 100, a batch size of only 10 samples per interaction, and a dataset limited to 249 samples mixed and subdivided into training sets with 175 samples, and the validation set with 74 samples, as shown in Fig. 3.

These conditions severely limited the performance of all models, especially the pre-trained models that typically use many samples and many interactions for processing and feature extraction for training. Due to these conditions, models 1 and 2 excelled with the low number of samples available for training and validation.

Model 2 stabilized accuracy at 100% after 91 interactions, the other models did not stabilize accuracy, but model 1 had the second-best performance, followed by models 3 and 4.

The study restricted the analysis to the accuracy and loss metrics only and did not take into consideration other metrics such as the confusion matrix, AUC curve, and ROC, which can help in the construction of the models [24, 25].

References

1. Kotler, P., Bes, F.T., Szlak, C.: A bíblia da inovação. 1st edn. Lua de Papel. São Paulo (2011)
2. Benoit, B.: Introdução aos sensores de visão: o caso da automação com visão industrial. https://inovasense.pt/wp-content/uploads/2021/03/Intro_Sensores_Visao.pdf, Accessed Nov 22 2022
3. Rudek, M., Coelho, L.S., Junior, O.C.: Visão computacional aplicada a sistemas produtivos: fundamentos e estudo de caso. https://abepro.org.br/biblioteca/enegep2001_tr10_0917.pdf, Accessed Nov 22 2022last
4. Weeks, A.R.: Fundamentals of Electronic Image Processing. 1st edn. Spie Press Book (1996)
5. Costa, F.O.: Barreiras para a implementação da Indústria 4.0: uma revisão bibliométrica e sistêmica. https://repositorio.ufsc.br/bitstream/handle/123456789/210227/TCC_20201_Fra ncineDeOliveiraCosta.pdf?sequence=1&isAllowed=y, Accessed Nov 22 2022

6. Pacchini, A.P.T., da Silva Santos, J.C., Logiudice, R., Lucato, W.C.: Indústria 4.0: barreiras para implantação na indústria brasileira. Exacta. **18**, 278–292 (2020)

7. Izario, D., et al.: 5G-Automation of Vertical Systems in the Industry 4.0. In: Brazilian Technology Symposium. pp. 35–43. Springer (2023). https://doi.org/10.1007/978-3-031-044 35-9_4

8. Indústria 4.0: guia prático sobre o que é, conceitos e tecnologias - Indústria: Tendências, Oportunidades e Soluções - Siemens Brasil, https://new.siemens.com/br/pt/empresa/stories/ industria/industria-4-0.html, Accessed Nov 22 2022

9. Vaz, G.C., Iano, Y., de Oliveira, G.G.: IoT-From Industries to Houses: An Overview. In: Brazilian Technology Symposium, pp. 734–741. Springer (2022). https://doi.org/10.1007/ 978-3-031-08545-1_73

10. Nishimura, E.H., Iano, Y., de Oliveira, G.G., Vaz, G.C.: Application and Requirements of AIoT-Enabled Industrial Control Units. In: Brazilian Technology Symposium, pp. 724–733. Springer (2022). https://doi.org/10.1007/978-3-031-08545-1_72

11. Dalzochio, J., et al.: Machine learning and reasoning for predictive maintenance in Industry 4.0: Current status and challenges. Comput. Ind. **123**, 103298 (2020)

12. Kunst, R., Avila, L., Binotto, A., Pignaton, E., Bampi, S., Rochol, J.: Improving devices communication in Industry 4.0 wireless networks. Eng. Appl. Artif. Intell. **83**, 1–12 (2019)

13. Bonello, D.K., Iano, Y., Neto, U.B., Gomes, G., de Oliveira, G., Vaz, C.: A Study about Automated Optical Inspection: Inspection Algorithms Applied in Flexible Manufacturing Printed Circuit Board Cells Using the Mahalanobis Distance Method 1. In: Iano, Y., Saotome, O., Vásquez, G.L.K., Pezzuto, C.C., Arthur, R., Gomes, G., de Oliveira, (eds.) Proceedings of the 7th Brazilian Technology Symposium (BTSym'21): Emerging Trends in Human Smart and Sustainable Future of Cities (Volume 1), pp. 198–212. Springer International Publishing, Cham (2023). https://doi.org/10.1007/978-3-031-04435-9_19

14. Algan, G., Ulusoy, I.: Image classification with deep learning in the presence of noisy labels: a survey. Knowl.-Based Syst. **215**, 106771 (2021)

15. Wang, W., Liang, D., Chen, Q., Iwamoto, Y., Han, X.-H., Zhang, Q., Hongjie, Hu., Lin, L., Chen, Y.-W.: Medical image classification using deep learning. In: Chen, Y.-W., Jain, L.C. (eds.) Deep Learning in Healthcare: Paradigms and Applications, pp. 33–51. Springer International Publishing, Cham (2020). https://doi.org/10.1007/978-3-030-32606-7_3

16. Kölsch, A., Afzal, M.Z., Ebbecke, M., Liwicki, M.: Real-time document image classification using deep CNN and extreme learning machines. In: 2017 14th IAPR international conference on document analysis and recognition (ICDAR), pp. 1318–1323. IEEE (2017)

17. Keras Applications, https://keras.io/api/applications/, Accessed Nov 22 2022

18. ImageNet, https://www.image-net.org/, Accessed Nov 22 2022

19. Howard, A.G., et al.: Mobilenets: Efficient convolutional neural networks for mobile vision applications. arXiv Prepr. arXiv1704.04861 (2017)

20. Zoph, B., Vasudevan, V., Shlens, J., Le, Q. V: Learning transferable architectures for scalable image recognition. In: Proceedings of the IEEE Conference on Computer Vision And Pattern Recognition, pp. 8697–8710 (2018)

21. Ahmad, T., et al.: Variable Few Shot Class Incremental and Open World Learning. In: Proceedings of the IEEE/CVF Conference on Computer Vision and Pattern Recognition, pp. 3688–3699 (2022)

22. casting_product_image_data | Kaggle, https://www.kaggle.com/datasets/gyanshashwat1611/ casting-product-image-data, last Accessed Nov 22 2022

23. Simplified washers for anomaly detection | Kaggle, https://www.kaggle.com/datasets/577 f789c117d111c296e1c63421f16e8acddd7666211b5858fc56a8253514e85, Accessed Nov 22 2022

24. Narkhode, S.: Understanding auc-roc curve. Towar. Data Sci. **26**, 220–227 (2018)
25. Fusco, R., et al.: Radiomics and artificial intelligence analysis with textural metrics extracted by contrast-enhanced mammography in the breast lesions classification. Diagnostics. **11**, 815 (2021)

Security in Smart Home Using Blockchain

Gabriel Gomes de Oliveira$^{(\boxtimes)}$![iD], Lucas Alves Rodrigues de Sá ![iD], Yuzo Iano ![iD], and Gabriel Caumo Vaz ![iD]

School of Electrical and Computer Engineering, State University of Campinas, Campinas, Brazil
oliveiragomesgabriel@ieee.org, {1226526,g226919}@dac.unicamp.br, yuzo@unicamp.br

Abstract. The interest in smart homes has grown exponentially in the last few years. A topic that has been treated with great attention is the security of the data generated by the Internet of Things Devices (IoTDs) within the smart home. Methods and architectures for the scenario of smart homes have also been researched as smart homes become more popular. Since IoTDs generate sensitive data about the smart home environment, data security and privacy are key points for smart homes to continue getting popular. Blockchain is a technology that offers security and privacy naturally due to its decentralized aspects and the high level of interaction between the blockchain's members and the manner that data is stored in hashed blocks. A smart contract is a computer code that runs inside the blockchain to provide authentication for the blockchain's members. The combination of blockchain and smart contracts provides the management of smart devices in a manner that their data is handled securely and protected from unauthorized parties. A smart home network architecture based on blockchain and smart contracts is proposed to simplify the way to manage smart devices and assign security to their data.

Keywords: Internet of Things · Smart cities · Smart homes · Smart devices · Security

1 Introduction

Internet of Things Devices (IoTDs) are becoming more common and increasingly revolutionizing the way of thinking and building technologies. They can be defined as any hardware that can collect data from the physical world, such as temperature, size, and speed, and share this data with the internet [1].

In the current plurality of applications, IoTDs integrate centralized architectures where they are managed by users that are all connected to a single controller that receives user's requests like access, monitoring, and control over the IoTDs. Security and authentication methods are a step more to be added to these applications to have resistance against attackers and non-authorized parts [2].

© The Author(s), under exclusive license to Springer Nature Switzerland AG 2023
Y. Iano et al. (Eds.): BTSym 2022, SIST 353, pp. 306–313, 2023.
https://doi.org/10.1007/978-3-031-31007-2_28

IoTDs have resource constraints concerning the processing power required by the security and authentication methods, and this is being noticed as an important point of improvement in the current architectures [2].

A smart home is a kind of application that is directly affected by the lack of security and authentication of resource-constrained IoTDs that are used to automate tasks or monitor the home. In this article, an architecture based on blockchain and smart contracts is proposed for a smart home scenario. Blockchain can be conceptualized as a decentralized database introduced in 2009 by Satoshi Nakamoto in bitcoin cryptocurrency. A smart contract is defined as a script stored in the blockchain that executes instructions in a distributed manner across all contract participants [3].

2   Technological Background

The work [4] presents the concept of Internet of Things (IoT), security limitations of IoTDs, the concept of blockchain, and how to analyze whether an IoT application would be benefited or not from blockchain implementation.

In this work, an architecture for a smart home based on blockchain and smart contracts is proposed. Before we go over the proposed architecture let us discuss what is exactly smart homes and smart contracts.

A smart home is a home equipped with IoTDs, including a smart thermostat, smart lamps, IP cameras, and several other smart devices [5]. In a smart home, residents can access data produced by IoTDs and monitor and control them remotely once all IoTDs and users are connected over the internet. There are many ways to establish the interactions between IoTDs and users, many architectures are proposed for this, the most common ones suggest the usage of a centralized manager that takes control of the whole application and a central database where the data produced by the IoTDs are stored and then accessed by the users. In Fig. 1, the current most common architecture for smart homes is presented.

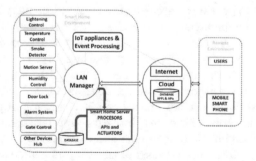

Fig. 1. Most common architecture for current smart home

Smart contracts are sets of conditions and business rules that must be met before a transaction is executed on a blockchain network, technically speaking, it is computer code that can be self-maintained and self-executed [6]. Figure 2 illustrates how a smart contract implemented in the blockchain acts during the transaction validation process.

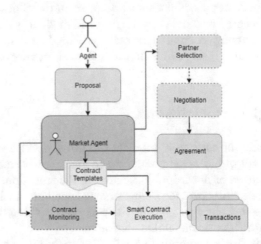

Fig. 2. Deployment of smart contracts in the blockchain

3   Methodology

In smart homes, several IoTDs need to be well managed to guarantee that the data generated by them are visible and accessible only to the residents of the smart home.

This work aims to provide an architecture for smart homes where data security, data privacy, and the management of IoTDs can be reached. The motivation for this work is explained by the fact that the lack of security and privacy in smart homes directly affects the security, privacy, and comfort of smart home residents.

Several articles, theses, and books were collected to support this research. The article [7], whose author proposes a distributed and safe architecture for smart homes based on blockchain, based the investigation of possible proposals for improvements in terms of security, integrity, and data management. Figure 3 shows the designed architecture for smart home scenarios.

Basically, this architecture consists of three layers named smart houses, P2P network, and cloud storage. Each layer is separately described below to better understand how the architecture works.

1. The smart home layer is composed of (I) IoTDs, such as smart freezers, TV, thermostat, presence sensors, light sensors, monitoring cameras, curtains,

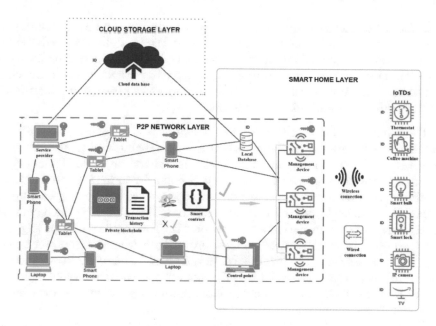

Fig. 3. Blockchain and smart contract-based architecture for smart homes

locks, coffee machines, etc.; (II) IoTD management devices, such as Raspberry Pi, which are responsible to manage the resource-restricted IoTDs in a wired or wireless way; (III) a local database for storage of all data generated by the IoTDs as a backup drive (whenever a transaction is validated in the architecture, the data requested by the transaction must be stored in the sub-local designated for each IoTD in the local database); and (IV) a control point that can be considered as the entry gate of the proposed architecture, through the control point a private blockchain and a smart contract must be developed. All IoTDs in the smart home must be added to the architecture and configured, and all users (P2P network nodes) must be added to the blockchain by a genesis transaction. For each P2P network integrant, it is given a private key [8] that defines the level of access, control, and monitoring over the IoTDs and their data.

2. In the P2P layer, devices such as laptops, tablets, smartphones, service providers devices, control points, management hardware cloud, and local databases are nodes of a private blockchain that registers in a decentralized and immutable way all transactions that happen within the P2P layer. In the private blockchain, a smart contract is executed by all nodes so that control, access, and monitoring transactions are validated at the time they occur and the private key of each P2P layer's nodes is authenticated at the time the nodes perform a transaction.

3. In the cloud storage layer, any reliable cloud database can be selected to store all data generated by the IoTDs. Similarly, in the local database, whenever a transaction is validated by the smart contract, the data requested by the transaction must be stored in the sub-local designated for each IoTD in the cloud database. In addition, the cloud database works as a server that makes stored data available to authorized requesters.

The interaction between the aforementioned layers is only possible through a transaction, they are extremely important for the dynamic and robustness of the proposed architecture. First, without a previous transaction, no IoTD can be controlled, monitored, or have its data accessed. Second, for an IoTD to be controlled, monitored, or have its data accessed the smart contract that is triggered by the previously performed transaction must verify in its terms whether the requesters' private keys have the authorization to perform the transaction that has triggered it. In the positive case, the transaction is approved to do what the requester intends to do and it is stored in the blockchain. In the negative case, a message must be printed to every node in the chain that the requester has no permission to perform that type of transaction, and no controlling, monitoring, or data access transactions should be carried out.

To illustrate how the 3 layers are involved with each other when a transaction is carried out by a node of the P2P layer, the flowchart shown in Fig. 4 was created.

4   Evaluation and Analysis

The performance of the proposed architecture was evaluated analytically against some security and privacy attacks. In this context, we consider that attacks are promoted by adversaries capable of preventing communication between the layers of the architecture, creating false transactions and deleting transactions within the blockchain, adding non-authorized nodes in the P2P layer, adding non-authorized IoTDs in the smart home layer, and even deleting or change data in both local and cloud storage [9]. In the proposed architecture, an adversary can be a node of the P2P layer, an IOTD, or even the cloud and local database. Below, there is a list of some blockchain common attacks that might occur against the proposed architecture [10] and how the proposed architecture reacts to them.

- Denial of Service (DOS): In DOS attacks, the adversary tries to prevent the user from accessing a service or data for a particular application. In the proposed architecture, an adversary can promote this attack, making fake transactions. As it is proposed with the sharing of private keys for each node of the P2P layer for the validation process, only transactions of authentic nodes are validated.
- Modification Attack: To carry out this attack, the adversary tries to compromise the security of the database by changing or deleting a user's data. The proposed architecture shows resistance to this attack because the autonomy of deleting data on the databases should not be granted by the control point to any node of the P2P layer, i.e., the smart contract should not approve any data change and the data storage should only be granted to the management hardware.

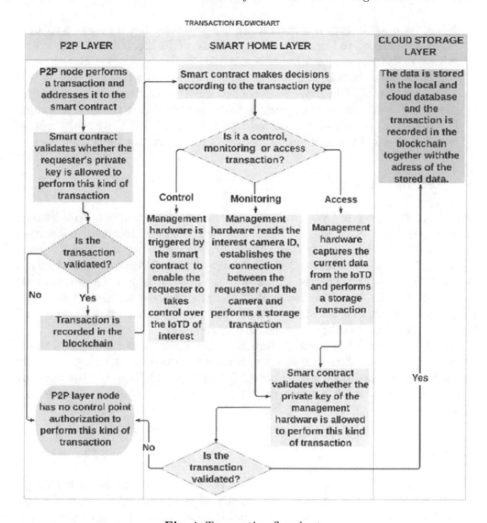

Fig. 4. Transaction flowchart

- Linking attack: In this attack, the adversary tracks all transactions carried out by a common private key's node in order to find out who is the requester in the real world. This attack seeks to violate privacy. The proposed architecture, by using a private blockchain, keeps nodes of the P2P layer anonymous from adversaries that do not participate in the blockchain.
- Dropping Attack: To carry out this attack, the adversary needs to take control over a group of nodes of a given blockchain. The attacked nodes start to reject all transactions, not validating them, thus disrupting the flow of the blockchain. In the proposed architecture, validations are not performed through the P2P layer's nodes by themselves, validations are performed automatically by the smart contract.

- Miner Attack: To carry out this attack, the adversary needs to take control of blockchain miners to record false transactions on the blockchain. There are no miners in the proposed architecture.
- Authentication Attack: This attack happens when an adversary tries to add a new node in the P2P layer to carry out all types of transactions. The proposed architecture shows resistance to this attack because a genesis transaction is required for a node to be inserted into the blockchain. The smart contract must allow only the control point to carry a genesis transaction out.

5   Related Works

In [5,11], and [12] it is proposed a hierarchical architecture compounded of a smart home layer, a P2P layer, and a cloud storage layer. The architecture is managed by three different blockchains that add privacy, security, and robustness against several attacks. The author suggests the usage of three blockchains and does not propose the use of any consensus algorithm like PoW. It is proposed instead that each blockchain has a transaction storage acceptance policy, which is observed by a mining hardware that has a list of blockchain nodes' public or private keys, used to give permissions to the nodes according to the policy.

In [13], it is proposed an architecture for smart homes known as domotic, which is basically an automatic management of resources (temperature, energy, etc.) and the deployment of artificial intelligence (AI) techniques for the prediction and resolution of failures. In this manner, domotic automatically adapts to the behavior of users.

6   Conclusion

The proposed architecture presents a decentralized way of IoTDs data management. In addition, the security and privacy that are essential points for IoT development in smart home scenarios are increased thanks to the adaptation of blockchain and smart contracts. Positive gains in terms of comfort, tranquility, and primarily security and privacy of data are reachable.

The main differential of the proposed architecture to the others cited in topic 5 of this work is that it executes a smart contract within a single private block-chain, which makes it simpler than the other state-of-the-art smart home architectures. Other features such as resistance to attacks, privacy, and security levels are maintained since blockchain is used. In addition, the proposed architecture is capable of allowing low processing power IoTDs to be involved in a safe and private environment, empowering them to interact with physical and cyber environments safely and reliably.

References

1. Vaz, G.C., Iano, Y., de Oliveira, G.G.: IoT-From Industries to Houses: An Overview. In: Brazilian Technology Symposium, pp. 734–741. Springer (2022). https://doi.org/10.1007/978-3-031-08545-1_73

2. Nishimura, E.H., Iano, Y., de Oliveira, G.G., Vaz, G.C.: Application and Requirements of AIoT-Enabled Industrial Control Units. In: Brazilian Technology Symposium, pp. 724–733. Springer (2022). https://doi.org/10.1007/978-3-031-08545-1_72

3. Ferreira, E., Albuquerque, C., Rocha, A., Chicarino, V.R., L.: Uso de Blockchain para Privacidade e Segurança em Internet das Coisas. In: Minicursos do XVII Simpósio Brasileiro em Segurança da Informação e de Sistemas Computacionais - SBSeg2017. Sociedade Brasileira de Computação - SBC, Rio de Janeiro (2017)

4. de Sá, L.A.R., Iano, Y., Gomes de Oliveira, G., Pajuelo, D., Borges Monteiro, A.C., Padilha França, R.: An insight into applications of internet of things security from a blockchain perspective. In: Iano, Y., Arthur, R., Saotome, O., Kemper, G., Padilha França, R. (eds.) BTSym 2019. SIST, vol. 201, pp. 143–152. Springer, Cham (2021). https://doi.org/10.1007/978-3-030-57548-9_13

5. Dorri, A., Kanhere, S.S., Jurdak, R.: Blockchain in internet of things: challenges and solutions. arXiv Prepr. arXiv1608.05187. (2016)

6. Karafiloski, E., Mishev, A.: Blockchain solutions for big data challenges: A literature review. In: IEEE EUROCON 2017–17th International Conference on Smart Technologies, pp. 763–768. IEEE (2017)

7. Dorri, A., Kanhere, S.S., Jurdak, R.: Towards an optimized blockchain for IoT. In: 2017 IEEE/ACM Second International Conference on Internet-of-Things Design and Implementation (IoTDI), pp. 173–178. IEEE (2017)

8. Buchmann, J.A.: Introduction to Cryptography, 2nd edn. Springer, New York (2004)

9. Lima, L.B. de, Iano, Y., Noritomi, P.Y., Oliveira, G.G. de, Vaz, G.C.: Data Security, Privacy, and Regulatory Issues: A Conceptual Approach to Digital Transformation to Smart Cities. In: Brazilian Technology Symposium. pp. 256–263. Springer (2022). https://doi.org/10.1007/978-3-031-08545-1_24

10. Lee, H.: Home IoT resistance: extended privacy and vulnerability perspective. Telemat. Informatics. 49, 101377 (2020)

11. Davidso, M., Mustard, S.: Will blockchain technology disrupt the ICS world?. https://www.isa.org/intech-home/2017/november-december/features/will-blockchain-technology-disrupt-the-ics-world, Accessed 17 Oct 2022

12. Bagchi, R.: Using blockchain technology and smart contracts for access management in IoT devices. University of Helsinki (2017). https://helda.helsinki.fi/bitstream/handle/10138/228832/blockchain_thesis_RupshaBagchi.pdf Accessed 17 Oct 2022

13. What Are the Key Requirements of IoT Security? — Thales, https://www.thalesesecurity.com/faq/internet-things-iot/what-are-key-requirements-iot-security Accessed 17 Oct 2022

Emerging Trends in Human Smart and Sustainable Future of Cities

Pregnant Women Diabetic Prediction Using 1D-Convolutional Neural Network and SMOTE Procedure

Suja A. Alex[1]([⊠]) [iD], Gabriel Gomes de Oliveira[2] [iD], and Yuzo Iano[2] [iD]

[1] Department of Information Technology, St. Xaviers Catholic College of Engineering, Chunkankadai, India
suja@sxcce.edu.in
[2] School of Electrical and Computer Engineering, State University of Campinas, Campinas, Brazil
oliveiragomesgabriel@ieee.org, yuzo@unicamp.br

Abstract. Diabetes Mellitus is a durable (chronic) disease that augments blood glucose levels. The diabetic patient's blood glucose level is constantly monitored to permit them to enjoy a superior life. Diabetic classification is a difficult issue in the real world because an inherent class imbalance is the most noticeable hurdle to designing a successful classifier. There are a variety of ways to manage unbalanced data prior to categorization. Synthetic Minority Over-sampling Technique (SMOTE), employing a one-dimensional Convolutional Network (1DCNN) for diabetes forecast, is the proposed approach. Classification is handled via the so-called SMOTE-based 1DCNN or SMOTE + 1DCNN. The accuracy of a proposed model is evaluated against the Pima Indian Diabetes Dataset about ancestry girls. The fallouts show better improvement concerning classification accuracy than employing other machine learning baseline methods together with SMOTE. Widely recognized metrics, such as accuracy, recall, and precision were used to assess the models and it made possible the comparison among them.

Keywords: Diabetic disease · Pima dataset · Class imbalance · SMOTE · 1D-Convolutional Neural Network

1 Introduction

Diabetes Mellitus (DM) continues to be a chronic (long-term) condition that engenders hyperglycemia or raised-up blood glucose levels, conducting to several problems. As per a recent study, the number of diabetics will turn up to 642 million by 2040 globally, with one-tenth of the global population impaired by this disorder. Several organs, counting kidneys, nerves, eyes, heart, and blood vessels, are susceptible to long-term damage and malfunction due to diabetes [1, 2]. This disease may appear as types 1 and 2. Type 1 patients are often younger, with the majority being less than 30 years of age.

© The Author(s), under exclusive license to Springer Nature Switzerland AG 2023
Y. Iano et al. (Eds.): BTSym 2022, SIST 353, pp. 317–328, 2023.
https://doi.org/10.1007/978-3-031-31007-2_29

One can point to the Pima pregnant women from Arizona among manifold vulnerable populations. Health records about Indian (Native American) females of this ancestry under the age of 21 have helped assemble a dataset that gathers info about diabetic girls of such a heritage. From now on, this text will refer to this repository as the Pima dataset (for short). This Indian ethnic group has suffered several lifestyle changes due to the dams' constructions for rerouting water to more densely inhabited settlements. As a byproduct, the Pima Indians lost vital hydrological supplies and abandoned their original agrarian lifestyle.

Recurrent urination and augmented thirst are commonplace clinical signs of hyperglycemia [3]. Predictive classification has enticed a lot of buzz in fostering medical diagnostics to empower patients. Throughout the preceding years, Artificial Intelligence (AI), i.e., Machine Learning (ML), and especially Computational Intelligence (CI) techniques have provided good accuracy in healthcare data classification [4–7]. The classification stage can learn predicting if a person is diabetic or not, influencing the diagnosis of diabetes. Occasionally, diabetes data may display skewness, i.e., curve distortion or asymmetry that deviates it from a symmetrical normal or bell-shaped distribution to the right or the left (skewed curve). Sampling strategies aid in balancing datasets. Oversampling is a strategy for transforming unbalanced datasets into balanced ones for the classification procedure. Hence, before classification, it is necessary to preprocess the dataset. The information preprocessing building block takes charge of the Synthetic Minority Over-sampling Technique (SMOTE) to yield oversampling in which synthetic samples are formed for the minority class.

As a rule, the SMOTE will bring about indispensable synthetic samples to balance impeccably the majority and minority categories. Nonetheless, due to the latest healthcare data analysis progresses, Imbalanced Data Classification (IDC) has gained traction academically. It is necessary to mitigate the diabetic IDC issue and bring out a classification to obtain the maximum classification accuracy results. Over other ML models, deep learning components perform well when classifying healthcare data. This work used a one-dimensional Convolutional Network (1DCNN) for diabetic forecasting along with the SMOTE scheme. Thus, it is deemed as SMOTE + 1DCNN. This arrangement can transform the earliest (raw) information into a data vector whose entries facilitate human diagnosis reliant on activity and vital signs recognition. [8]. The SMOTE + 1DCNN contains two steps in this work. The IDC is dealt with in the earliest module via SMOTE, and diabetes is detected in the second stage exploiting a 1DCNN classifier.

The contributions of this investigation are twofold [6–13]: (i) trying to improve the Pima people's overall lifestyle while increasing prepartum and post-partum quality of life (QoL) and (ii) devising an AI structure to diagnose DM fast and remotely.

This paper is structured as follows. Section 2 describes Materials and Methods, which discusses Dataset details and the proposed SMOTE + 1DCNN Architecture. Section 3 describes the Experimental Results and Discussion. The conclusions are drawn in Sect. 4.

2 Materials and Methods

Due to its snowballing prevalence, DM hurts the general public with many complications [14]. Contemporarily, several research pieces have predicted diabetes. Most diabetic prediction questions are solved with shallow Machine Learning (ML) models and regression approaches [15]. Parashar et al. utilized Linear Discriminant Analysis (LDA) working with a Support Vector Machine (SVM) for diabetes classification, with an accuracy of 77.6%.

Nonetheless, the Pima dataset gathers ancestry diabetic girls' info encompassing unbalanced classes. Several preprocessing tasks were accomplished in order to create a balanced dataset. The traditional techniques of handling class imbalance, such as Random Over-Sampling (ROS), in addition to Random Under-Sampling (RUS), generate samples until the class is balanced [16]. Likewise, the Random Under-Sampling approach removes important data. As a result, Chawla et al. presented SMOTE [15], a strategy that integrates this issue and tackles the over-fitting problem. SMOTE is an over-sampling strategy that engenders synthetic samples from minority groups. It determines linear interpolations for generating a new minority sample using any of the K-Nearest Neighbours (KNN) of each minority sample. Because the Pima dataset is the least skewed, it performs well [17]. Many scholars have utilized Artificial Neural Networks (ANNs) to predict DM [18]. In recent years, SMOTE using ML tactics has become a widely held exploratory topic for DM prediction. Convolutional Neural Networks (CNN), Recurrent Neural Networks (RNN), and other variants utilization becoming widely offered [19]. The 1DCNN has accomplished tasks like foot type classification [14], electronic fault diagnosis [20], and mental imagery classification [21] utilizing sensor-enabled footwear, among other tasks. The SMOTE + 1DCNN workflow emerges in Fig. 1.

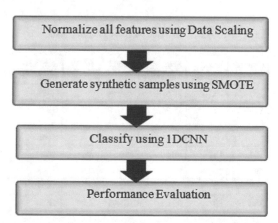

Fig. 1. SMOTE + 1DCNN workflow shows the sequence of steps involved in diabetic prediction

2.1 Dataset

The Kaggle Platform hosts the Pima databank thanks to the National Institute of Diabetes and Digestive and Kidney Diseases (NIDDK) from India [4]. It helps diagnose pregnant women and uncover whether or not they have DM. Altogether, the Pima information partakes a total of 9 traits considered paramount to predicting DM. In addition to pregnancy, other eight diverse relevant predictive features follow:

1. Number of times gestation occurred,
2. Basal plasma glucose at 2 h following a test to evaluate the oral glucose tolerance,
3. Minimum arterial pressure,
4. Skinfold thickness around triceps,
5. 2-h insulin level in serum,
6. Body Mass Index (BMI),
7. Time of life (age), and
8. Diabetes pedigree function.

The Pima dataset has 768 instances and eight dimensions, such as Pregnancies, Glucose, BloodPressure, SkinThickness, Insulin, BMI, DiabetiesPedigreeFunction, and Age. The binary class labels are stored in the Outcome attribute. Table 1 shows the statistics of the Pima dataset in terms of mean, standard deviation, minimum, maximum, 25th percentile, 50th percentile, and 75th percentile. The dimensions SkinThickness and Insulin have missing values and these missing values are replaced by zeros. Likewise, the histogram in Fig. 2 allows one to visualize the relations between a single parameter and the outcome. The correlation between variables and the confusion matrix stem from the Pearson Correlation coefficient. Figure 3 illustrates the correlation analysis.

Table 1. Statistics of the Pima Dataset.

Statistics	Pregnancies	Glucose	Blood Pressure	Skin Thickness	Insulin	BMI	Diabetes-PedigreeFunction	Age	Outcome
Mean	3.845	120.894	69.105	20.536	79.799	31.992	0.471	33.24	0.348
Standard Deviation	3.369	31.972	19.355	15.952	115.244	7.884	0.331	11.76	0.476
Minimum	0	0	0	0	0	0	0.078	21	0
Maximum	17	199	122	99	846	67.1	2.42	81	1
25%	1	99	62	0	0	27.3	0.243	24	0
50%	3	117	72	23	30.5	32	0.372	29	0
75%	6	140.25	80	32	127.25	36.6	0.626	41	1

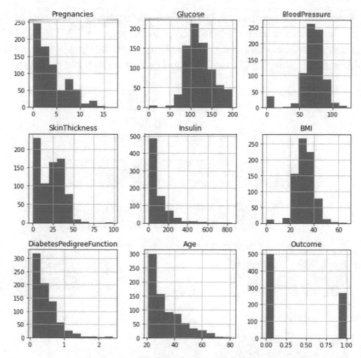

Fig. 2. Relationship between every single variable and the corresponding outcome

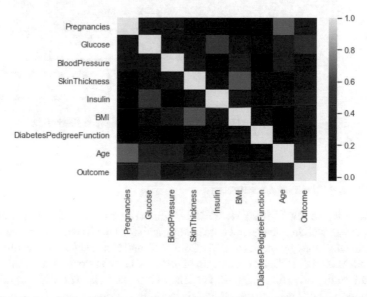

Fig. 3. Correlation Analysis Corresponding to the 9-entry Feature Vector for the Pima Dataset

Figure 4 confirms strong linear relationships among these traits. Age and pregnancies, in particular, have a reasonable positive linear association. BMI and SkinThickness have a similar positive linear association. Although the correlation between glu-cose and insulin is theoretically low, 0.58 is near 0.6 and can be considered moderate.

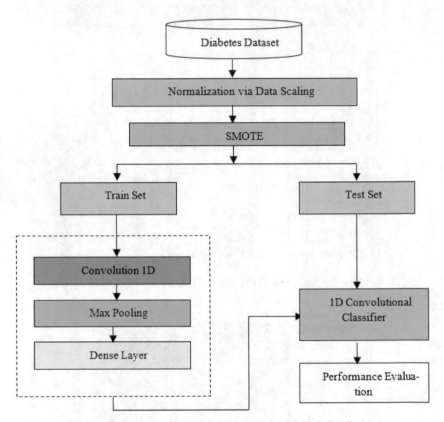

Fig. 4. SMOTE + 1DCNN Architecture for Diabetic Prediction

2.2 SMOTE + 1DCNN Architecture

This section pictures the SMOTE + 1DCNN, which relies on deep learning architecture and can perform well in unbalanced data categorization. This framework betters diabetic classification accuracy by means of a 1D Convolutional Neural Network as illustrated in Fig. 5. The SMOTE + 1DCNN is made up of 45 2 × 2 kernel filters. Three configurations of CNN are built with 16 kernels, 45 kernels, and 64 kernels. The CNN configuration with 45 kernels yields good results than other configurations.

The activation function takes on a ReLU, with a subsequent max-pooling layer. Finally, the concluding layer is a fully connected dense layer. It performs prediction of whether there exists diabetes or not. During the experiment, the diabetic dataset was put into Jupyter Notebook using Python 3.6, a model was developed, and the proposed classifier's prediction accuracy was evaluated.

Data Scaling. The diabetic data is scaled using a standard scaler [22] to guarantee a fair comparison, i.e., normalization. Each input variable is scaled individualistically by deducting the mean and dividing by the standard deviation. One of the key advantages of adopting standard scaling is that it helps increase convergence ability much better than other strategies. By taking the mean out and scaling the variance to 1, the standard scalar technique [22] normalizes each function. Because the mean and variance aid in normalizing values with manifold benefits, including linearity, reversibility, simplicity, as well as extreme scalability. Hence, all attributes range from zero to one, which facilitates analyses and comparisons. Thus, data scaling homogenizes all the parameters' depictions. After scaling, the data are divided into training (70%) and testing (30%) datasets.

SMOTE. There are 268 positive class samples and 500 negative class samples in the pima dataset. The classifier's sensitivity in detecting diabetes cases will be a desirable feature. In this paper, the smote oversampling scheme assists in solving a problem with two classes. Table 2 shows the original diabetic dataset. The imbalance issue in the dataset was handled by smote algorithm. Table 3 shows the results of diabetic instance count before and after applying smote.

Table 2. Dataset Distribution.

Dataset	Majority Class	Minority Class
Pima	500	268

1DCNN. The 1dcnn accomplishes 1d convolution utilizing the samples. It also extracts features that represent the input data's internal pattern automatically. The network involves a single one-dimensional convolutional layer tailed by a pooling layer in addition to a fully linked multi-layer perceptron for classification. The convolutional layer encompasses filters, each one with a $k \times k$ kernel. The convolutional layer makes use of relu the activation, which max $(0, x)$ applies to each relu input described by x. These filters yield feature maps from the one-dimensional input. The 1dcnn executes convolutions to obtain one-dimensional features [23]. Each kernel over a specific vicinity on the feature map gives specific characteristics. This weight-sharing tactic lessens the total of trainable parameters to preserve competitive performance. The 1d-convolution layer formula is below.

$$Ijl = fi = 1MIil - 1.Kijl + bjl \tag{1}$$

where k is the total amount of convolution kernels, the kernel size is j, M alludes to the channel input whose number is I_i^{l-1}, f symbolizes the activation function coupled with a kernel bias b, and (.) denotes the convolution operator.

After the convolution, the max-pooling layer is used to progressively shrink the feature maps' spatial sizes. The pooling layer is supplied with the convolution layer output. The next layer performs a sampling operation. In this case, each function map applies to the max-pooling process. This creates the most important characteristics (here, the selection of features with the highest values). The finishing network block contains fully-connected dense layers. The prediction of the instances is performed as per the sigmoid activation function in the last output layer.

Optimization of SMOTE + 1DCNN Parameters The SMOTE + 1DCNN framework takes an input vector of 32 samples per batch. The adam optimizer [24] trains the network and has in recent times appeared in most academic papers as the *de facto* optimizer because its convergence supersedes other adaptive approaches. Adam amalgamates pluses from stochastic gradient descent (sgd) extensions like the root mean square propagation (rmsprop) together with the adaptive gradient algorithm (adagrad). The network training happened with a learning rate of 0.3 besides randomly choosing weights and biases from a uniform distribution range (–0.01, 0.01). Further, the optimal parameters for the neural network were chosen from trial-and-error experimentation. The elected hyper-parameters emerge in Table 3.

Table 3. Optimal Parameters for SMOTE + 1DCNN.

Layers	Parameters
1DCNN Layer	Kernel size = 2
	Number of filters = 45
	Activation function = ReLu
	Strides = 2
Max-pooling Layer	Size = 2
	Strides = 2
Flatten Layer	-
Dense Layer	Number of neurons in dense layers (hidden) = 128
	Activation Function = Sigmoid
	Number of neurons in dense layers (output) = 12
	Activation Function = Sigmoid

Table 4. SMOTE Results.

	Before SMOTE	After SMOTE
Positive Values	34.69%	50.0%
Negative Values	65.30%	50.0%

3 Experimental Results and Discussion

The section describes the experimental part of diabetes classification on the Pima dataset. The class distribution imbalanced dataset contains eight numeric features and a class label (0 or 1). The value '0' indicates that the patient has no diabetes, and '1' means that the patient is diabetic. The experiments were carried out on a desktop with an Intel Core i5 processor running at 3.6 GHz and 8 GB of RAM running Windows 10. The coding is written in Python in the Jupyter Notebook environment on the Anaconda3 edition. When using deep learning algorithms to analyze diabetes, classification accuracy is often chosen as a success predictor. To evaluate the model's accuracy, many metrics can be used, such as accuracy, precision, and recall [25].

The accuracy is measured by the fraction of correctly classified instances to the total instances Table 4. The accuracy is given as follows:

$$Accuracy = \frac{TP + TN}{TP + TN + FP + FN} \tag{2}$$

Table 5. Analysis of SMOTE-based Classifiers.

Classifier	Accuracy	Precision	Recall
SMOTE + Logstic Regression	70.129	56.338	72.727
SMOTE + Gaussian Naïve Bayes	74.025	60.563	78.181
SMOTE + SVM	68.831	54.794	72.727
SMOTE + KNN	68.831	55.932	60.0
SMOTE + X Gradient Boosting	72.077	58.333	76.363
SMOTE + 1DCNN	82.543	78.514	82.142

Recall measures the fraction of positive instances that are classified correctly. It is presented as follows:

$$Recall = \frac{TP}{TP + TN} \tag{3}$$

Table 5 compares the SMOTE + 1DCNN to a collection of existing ML algorithms based on Accuracy, Precision, and Recall as their main evaluation metrics at SMOTE + 1DCNN do better than other classifiers. While SMOTE-Logistic Regression has an accuracy of 70.1%. SMOTE-Gaussian Naive Bayes displays an accuracy rate of 74%, and SMOTE-SVM awards an accuracy rate of 68.8%. SMOTE-KNN, SMOTE-XGBoosting, and SMOTE + 1DCNN have maximum accuracies of 68.8%, 72%, and 82.5% respectively. Based on Precision, SMOTE-Logistic Regression shows 56.3%, SMOTE-Gaussian Naive Bayes shows 60.5%, and SMOTE-SVM shows 54.7%. Precision is the ratio of correctly classified positive observations to all the expected positive instances.

$$Precision = \frac{TP}{TP + FP} \tag{4}$$

SMOTE-KNN demonstrates 55.9%, SMOTE-XGBoosting displays 58.3%, and SMOTE + 1DCNN shows 78.5%. When comparing the values based on precision, it is clear that SMOTE + 1DCNN is more precise than other classifiers. Based on the recall parameter, SMOTE-Logistic Regression shows 72.7%, SMOTE-Gaussian Naive Bayes shows 78.1%, SMOTE-SVM shows 72.7%, SMOTE-KNN shows 60%, SMOTE-XGBoosting shows 76.3%, and SMOTE + 1DCNN shows 82.1%. SMOTE + 1DCNN has a high-recall value of 82.1%. Hence, SMOTE + 1DCNN is performing the best in the context of accuracy, precision, and recall.

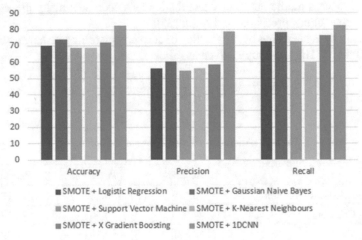

Fig. 5. Accuracy, Precision, Recall Analysis

Table 5 plots a graph with metrics, and percentages of performance on the x-axis and y-axis respectively. Precision, recall, and accuracy are the three measures taken in Fig. 5 for analysis. As mentioned before, SMOTE + 1DCNN shows superior performance compared to other baseline algorithms.

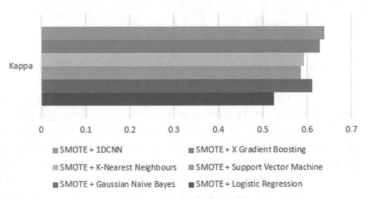

Fig. 6. Kappa Analysis

Cohen's Kappa statistic measures how much the prediction approves with true class.

Kappa Coefficient quantifies the inter-rater reliability and intra-rater reliability for all class labels. Figure 6 shows that SMOTE + Logistic Regression (LR) yields Kappa of 0.526, SMOTE + Gaussian Naive Bayes (GNB) shows 0.611, SMOTE + SVM shows 0.585, SMOTE + KNN shows 0.593, SMOTE + XGBoost shows 0.628, and SMOTE + 1DCNN shows 0.639. In terms of Kappa, SMOTE + 1DCNN led to better results than the other baseline classifiers.

K-fold cross-validation is popularly used in classification tasks in which the dataset is divided into different folds of train and test sets. 10-fold cross-validation is also conducted over the Pima dataset. However, it produced results that are not satisfactory since the size of the dataset is small.

4   Conclusion

This work has proposed the SMOTE + 1DCNN architecture and has used the Pima dataset as a case test. The SMOTE handles the class imbalance issue, and the 1DCNN is in charge of classification. This whole framework enhanced the predictive accuracy of diabetic prognosis compared to other AI models combined with SMOTE by removing class imbalance. The performed analysis shows that the SMOTE + 1DCNN model suits diabetic prediction regarding the accuracy, recall, and precision evaluation metrics. In future work, this work can be extended to deep 1DCNN layers to improve prediction accuracy. This work does not predict the type of diabetes. Hence, future work will seek to indicate the type of diabetes with good accuracy.

References

1. Krasteva, A., Panov, V., Krasteva, A., Kisselova, A., Krastev, Z.: Oral cavity and systemic diseases—diabetes mellitus. Biotechnol. Biotechnol. Equip. **25**, 2183–2186 (2011)
2. Iancu, I., Mota, M., Iancu, E.: Method for the analysing of blood glucose dynamics in diabetes mellitus patients. In: 2008 IEEE international conference on automation, quality and testing, robotics. pp. 60–65. IEEE (2008)
3. Monteiro, A.C.B., França, R.P., Estrela, V. V, Razmjooy, N., Iano, Y., Negrete, P.D.M.: Meta-heuristics applied to blood image analysis. In: Metaheuristics and Optimization in Computer and Electrical Engineering. pp. 117–135. Springer (2021). https://doi.org/10.1007/978-3-030-56689-0
4. Dwivedi, A.K.: Analysis of computational intelligence techniques for diabetes mellitus prediction. Neural Comput. Appl. **30**(12), 3837–3845 (2017). https://doi.org/10.1007/s00521-017-2969-9
5. Dwivedi, A.K., Chouhan, U.: Comparative study of machine learning techniques for genome scale discrimination of recombinant HIV-1 strains. J. Med. Imaging Heal. Informatics. **6**, 425–430 (2016)
6. Deshpande, A., Estrela, V.V., Patavardhan, P.: The DCT-CNN-ResNet50 architecture to classify brain tumors with super-resolution, convolutional neural network, and the ResNet50. Neurosci. Informatics. **1**, 100013 (2021)
7. Deshpande, A., Razmjooy, N., Estrela, V.V.: Introduction to Computational Intelligence and Super-Resolution. In: Deshpande, A., Estrela, V.V., Razmjooy, N. (eds.) Computational Intelligence Methods for Super-Resolution in Image Processing Applications, pp. 3–23. Springer, Cham (2021). https://doi.org/10.1007/978-3-030-67921-7_1

8. Lee, S.-M., Yoon, S.M., Cho, H.: Human activity recognition from accelerometer data using Convolutional Neural Network. In: 2017 IEEE International Conference on Big Data and Smart Computing (bigcomp), pp. 131–134. IEEE (2017)

9. Khelassi, A., Estrela, V.V.: Advances in Multidisciplinary Medical Technologies– Engineering, Modeling and Findings

10. Alex, S.A.: Novel Applications of Neuralink in HealthCare-An Exploratory Study

11. Alex, S.A., Ghosh, U., Mohammad, N.: Weather Prediction from Imbalanced Data Stream using 1D-Convolutional Neural Network. In: 2022 10th International Conference on Emerging Trends in Engineering and Technology-Signal and Information Processing (ICETET-SIP-22). pp. 1–6. IEEE (2022)

12. Alex, S.A., Nayahi, J.J.V., Shine, H., Gopirekha, V.: Deep convolutional neural network for diabetes mellitus prediction. Neural Comput. Appl. **34**(2), 1319–1327 (2021). https://doi.org/10.1007/s00521-021-06431-7

13. Alex, S.A., Jhanjhi, N.Z., Humayun, M., Ibrahim, A.O., Abulfaraj, A.W.: Deep LSTM Model for Diabetes Prediction with Class Balancing by SMOTE. Electronics **11**, 2737 (2022)

14. Negrete, J.C.M., Iano, Y., Negrete, P.D.M., Vaz, G.C., de Oliveira, G.G.: Sentiment and Emotions Analysis of Tweets During the Second Round of 2021 Ecuadorian Presidential Election. In: Brazilian Technology Symposium, pp. 257–268. Springer (2023)

15. Ding, L., McDonald, D.J.: Predicting phenotypes from microarrays using amplified, initially marginal, eigenvector regression. Bioinformatics **33**, i350–i358 (2017)

16. Chawla, N.V., Bowyer, K.W., Hall, L.O., Kegelmeyer, W.P.: SMOTE: synthetic minority over-sampling technique. J. Artif. Intell. Res. **16**, 321–357 (2002)

17. Pradhan, M., Sahu, R.K.: Predict the onset of diabetes disease using Artificial Neural Network (ANN). Int. J. Comput. Sci. Emerg. Technol. (E-ISSN 2044–6004). **2**, 303–311 (2011)

18. Larabi-Marie-Sainte, S., Aburahmah, L., Almohaini, R., Saba, T.: Current techniques for diabetes prediction: review and case study. Appl. Sci. **9**, 4604 (2019)

19. Negrete, J.C.M., Iano, Y., Negrete, P.D.M., Vaz, G.C., de Oliveira, G.G.: Sentiment Analysis in the Ecuadorian Presidential Election. In: Brazilian Technology Symposium, pp. 25–34. Springer (2023)

20. Thiagarajan, Y., Palanivel, G., Soubache, I.D., de Oliveira, G.G., Iano, Y., Vaz, G.C., Monga, H.: Design and Fabrication of Human-Powered Vehicle-A Measure for Healthy Living. In: Brazilian Technology Symposium, pp. 1–15. Springer (2023)

21. Izzuddin, T.A., Safri, N.M., Othman, M.A.: Mental imagery classification using one-dimensional convolutional neural network for target selection in single-channel BCI-controlled mobile robot. Neural Comput. Appl. **33**(11), 6233–6246 (2020). https://doi.org/10.1007/s00521-020-05393-6

22. Ferreira, P., Le, D.C., Zincir-Heywood, N.: Exploring feature normalization and temporal information for machine learning based insider threat detection. In: 2019 15th International Conference on Network and Service Management (CNSM). pp. 1–7. IEEE (2019)

23. Eren, L., Ince, T., Kiranyaz, S.: A generic intelligent bearing fault diagnosis system using compact adaptive 1D CNN classifier. J. Signal Process. Syst. **91**, 179–189 (2019)

24. Kingma, D.P., Ba, J.: Adam: A method for stochastic optimization. arXiv Prepr. arXiv1412.6980. (2014)

25. Tong, H., Liu, B., Wang, S.: Software defect prediction using stacked denoising autoencoders and two-stage ensemble learning. Inf. Softw. Technol. **96**, 94–111 (2018)

New Technological Waves Emerging in Digital Transformation: Internet of Things IoT/IoE, 5G/6G Mobile Networks and Industries 4.0/5.0

José Roberto Emiliano Leite[1]([✉]) [iD], Edson Luiz Ursini[1] [iD],
Adão Maciel Monteiro Chmielewski[2] [iD], and Antônio José Dias da Silva[2] [iD]

[1] School of Technology, State University of Campinas, Limeira, Brazil
joserobertoemilianoleite@gmail.com, ursini2@unicamp.br
[2] University Santa Ursula, Rio de Janeiro, Brazil
adao.maciel@usu.edu.br

Abstract. The Internet has established itself as a "Network of Networks" and a globalized communication tool, initially enabling the connection between people themselves and between people and computers (machines). The cheapness and reduction in the size of Internet access components made it possible for simpler equipment and devices of our daily lives to also access the global network, thus creating the Internet of Things (IoT), which aims to interconnect devices/objects/things of everyday use. Intelligence and automation result from the additions of processing, memory, and communication in the objects involved and the use of access by Mobile Networks, AdHoc, and RFID. The 5G Mobile Network evolved to serve as the basis of IoT communication, due to its characteristics of Massive Use, Broadband, Low Latency (Delay), and high demand for better quality service. Aspects of architectures, multiple access techniques, and emerging technologies (massive MIMO, software-defined networking, mm-Wave) are presented historically, including 1G/2G/3G/4G/5G Mobile Networks up to the future 6G Network. Industry 4.0 is known as the fourth industrial revolution, in which we will have billions of people connected by mobile devices, with processing power, storage resources, connectivity, and access to knowledge without limits. This new wave of technology, which will include several areas: Artificial Intelligence (AI), Advanced Robotics, Internet of Things (IoT), Autonomous Vehicles, Big Data, Cloud Storage, Virtual Reality (VR)/Augmented Reality (AR), Cyber-Physical Systems, Digital Security, and 3D Printing, among others, has been increasingly incorporated by large companies as a new trend of digital transformation, enabling more security and productivity.

Keywords: Internet of Things (IoT) · Mobile Networks (1G/2G/3G/4G/5G/6G) · Indistries 4.0/5.0

1 Introduction

The Internet was created in the 1960s with the aim of linking academic and research environments. With its growth, the Internet was expanded to the business and commercial

Y. Iano et al. (Eds.): BTSym 2022, SIST 353, pp. 329–339, 2023.
https://doi.org/10.1007/978-3-031-31007-2_30

areas, increasing its use even more with the emergence of the web search form (WWW) and social networks. Currently, it is impossible to imagine our life without the use of the Internet and social and commercial networks [1].

The Internet evolved into the Internet of Things (IoT) connecting everyday devices [2] (TV, refrigerator, stove, air conditioning, residential alarms, lamps, cameras, automobiles, and hospital devices), thus executing communication between things/objects/ devices, enabling greater automation of our daily lives, through the use of cellular access. The IoT is evolving towards the interconnection of all things: IoE (Internet of Everything). It also enables digital transformation and increased intelligence in various sectors of the economy: Smart Grid (Electric Sector), Smart Homes/Buildings/Cities, Industry, Health, Leisure and Commercial Automation (wholesale and retail), Connected Farms, and Recovery of Disasters, among others. The 5G Mobile Network [3–7] serves as IoT communication due to its Massive Use, Quality, Broadband, and Low Latency (Delay) characteristics. The Covid-19 pandemic has increased the use of digital technologies, due to the need to continue to solve the same everyday problems from home. The process of using the technologies was accelerated due to the need, giving them greater visibility.

Historically, at the beginning of the 18th century in Great Britain [8–10], the first industrial revolution began, with the emergence of the steam engine, which was widely used for the automation of textile production: manufacturers were replaced by industries. The second industrial revolution, on the other hand, began in the second half of the 19th century, with electricity playing a fundamental role in the changes, with homes benefiting, in addition to machines and engines presenting increasingly reduced dimensions, enabling the production line of cars. The Third Industrial Revolution began in the mid-20th century, thanks to the invention of the transistor, which boosted electronics with faster and more stable circuits and small components, being responsible for the modernization of its factories, becoming dominated by Programmable Logic Controllers (PLCs). Then comes the introduction of information technology in manufacturing processes. The computer appears in the manufacturing process for supervision and control, in addition to the first communication systems [11, 12].

Currently, we have the fourth industrial revolution, or Industry 4.0, which began to spread in the second decade of the 21st century, with the digital revolution, that is, the Internet is much more mobile and global, and the integration of smaller and more powerful sensors, machine learning and artificial intelligence (AI) supported by massively networked communication and intercommunication requirements, established globally. As a consequence, a new paradigm in the organization of work and leisure emerges, questioning the traditional view and generating degrees of complexity and interconnection between sectors [13]. This article presents the characteristics of these 3 emerging technological waves in Digital Transformation with their main architectures, technologies, and applications: IoT/IoE(Everything) [1, 2], 5G/6G Mobile Networks [3–7], and Industries 4.0/5.0(Humanized) [8, 9], including but not limited to Virtual Reality (VR) and Augmented Reality (AR), software-defined networking (SDN) and Network Function Virtualization (NFV), Digital Twin, and Quality of Experience (QoE).

2 IoT Architectures, Models, Protocols, Technologies, and Applications

The IoT Architecture chose open, simple, cheap, and consecrated technologies, such as Ethernet, Wi-Fi, Ad-Hoc, ZigBee, Bluetooth, RFID (Radio-Frequency Identification), WSS (Wireless Signal Solutions), 5G/6G Mobile Networks, and sensors. Of course, wired solutions like Ethernet Wired can also be used. The IoT Architecture selected other established Architectures such as TCP/IP and SOA (Service Oriented Architecture). The IoT Architecture separates Communication into the following Layers: Sensor and Network Connectivity; Gateways and Networks; Network and Information Security Management Services, and Applications; alongside LTE (4G) there is currently the 5G Mobile Network and, in the future, 6G. The IoT made it possible to create applications for direct use in society and the World Economy, such as Environmental, Energy (Smart Grid), Transport, Health, Retail/Wholesale, Production Chain, Monitoring of People's Health (Healthcare), and Security (Smart Home, Building, City), among others. The IoT Reference Model according to the ITU-T, ISO, and IEC Telecommunications understanding also follows the layered model (Application, Service and Application Support, Network, and Device). Like all ITU-T reference models, it has 2 columns referring to Network and Security Management, columns that have functionality spread across all layers of the model. The IoT Communication Model was based on the ISO OSI (Open System Interconnection) Model. The main focus is the information exchanged ("Data") between the object and the application.

Most of the protocols used in the IoT and the WEB have taken advantage of the TCP/IP Architecture, already widely used internationally. IoT has selected several technologies already internationally standardized and used in Residential and Business environments. With the new waves, LTE (4G), 5G, and 6G Mobile Networks will be widely used. Most technologies are radio and wireless (Radio Access Technologies), that is, using the IEEE 802.11, IEEE 802.15, and IEEE 802.16 standards, for reasons of flexibility and range.

2.1 Most Widely Used Applications in the IoT

The IoT has selected several applications in different Sectors of the World Economy [2]: Client and Residence (comfort and convenience); Buildings (commercial and institutional); Industry (automation); Health Care; energy, water, gas, and telecom; Market (wholesale and retail); Transport; Public Security and "Information and Communication Technologies (ICTs)".

Smart Home aims to offer home automation using Smartphone or Tablet for remote access, such as turning lights on and off, knowing the lifetime of lamps, opening and closing doors and gates, turning TV/Air-Conditioning on and off, generating and sending the list of groceries missing from the fridge to the supermarket, receive information via SMART TV and Videos, etc.

Smart Building aims at automation in a building, making it 'green' in terms of electricity, water, solar heating, battery systems, etc. High-consumption equipment (air-conditioning and lighting) can be dynamically adjusted according to the temperature/humidity/light inside and outside the building. Battery Systems may be supervised to anticipate replacement in case of a future failure.

Smart Cities deals with the exchange of information between cars, cellphones, buildings, and traffic lights, aiming to improve the traffic and flow of cars in a city. Smart City covers the following areas: health of buildings and bridges structures; garbage monitoring; air quality monitoring; noise monitoring; traffic congestion monitoring; energy consumption in the city; smart parking; smart traffic lights; automation and health in public buildings. The ITS (Intelligent Transportation System) is a functional part of the Smart City on roads.

Smart Grid (Energy) takes care of the automation of the electric sector, aiming to place smart readers (smart meters) in homes that pass consumption information directly to the supplying companies, which use the grid itself to manage their equipment and faults. It uses a specific network for the electrical sector with PLC (Power Line Communication) technology, for reasons of reliability and response time. Its main components are generation; streaming; distribution automation; electric cars and electric energy management in the residence.

Healthcare (Remote Medical Assistance) enables remote monitoring and follow-up of patients in their homes, by collecting information from sensors (on the patient) of temperature/blood pressure/heart-rate/glucose level/oxygenation level, environmental sensors presence/temperature/pressure/movement, RFID badges for patients, nurses, caregivers, employees, medicines, and equipment, among others, i.e., information that is sent to the cloud and accessed by doctors and hospitals. The doctor will be able to access them through his Smartphone and request that the patient is transferred to the hospital in case of dangerous values in his vital signs. This application enables a new business model for health plans, in which the patient only goes to the hospital in serious situations.

Smart Manufacturing (Industry) is responsible for the control and automation of real manufacturing processes (Industry 4.0) on industrial devices (lathes, presses, numerical controllers, Programmable Logic Controllers (PLCs), robots), requiring short reaction times (real-time), with little delay and jitter, and little amount of data produced. Adapters, bridges, and gateways are necessary due to the large number of islands (applications) existing with proprietary protocols.

Smart Farming or Connected Farm automates the farm, through its interconnection with the global world. It enables the interconnection of tractors, harvesters, drones, farm headquarters, cooperatives, agricultural entities, and spray planes. Employees and animals are identified using RFID tags. It is necessary to install a Radio Base Station on the farm, allowing the interconnection of these different parts, which makes it possible to build an online farm. This application is of great importance for Brazil as it is a heavily agricultural and livestock country.

Other applications are emerging in various sectors of the economy, such as transport, logistics, commercial automation (wholesale and retail), disaster recovery (natural or not), and dam safety.

3 Evolution of Mobile Networks: 1G/2G/3G/4G/5G/6G

The development of mobile communication was necessary to support and enable increases in the number of users, mobility, coverage, data rate, spectral efficiency, and delay reduction, among others [3–7]. Historically, in the 1980s, the 1G network (Fig. 1) was launched to provide voice calls over analog signals. In the 1990s, the 2G network began to provide voice services through digital signals and new short message services (SMS); the intermediate 2.5G version offered e-mail and WEB services. In the 2000s, the 3G network initiated video telephony, mobile tv, and video conferencing, with the emergence of smartphones and mobile broadband.

Historically Circuit Switching (CS) is used in 1G and 2G networks while Circuit Switching (CS) together with Packet Switching (PS) is used in 2.5 and 3G networks (Fig. 1) [3]. In the 2010s, the 4G network offers high data rate applications, e.g. HDTV, cloud computing, video game, etc. In the 2020s, the 5G network started offering services that enable the deployment of the Internet of Things: Smart city, Massive Broadband, Virtual Reality (VR), Augmented Reality (AR), Device to Device Communication (D2D), Vehicular AdHoc Networks (VANETs), etc. The IoT Communication Base includes Massive Use, Broadband, and Low Latency (Delay), in addition to the use of small antennas and a 10-fold increase in the current band. Packet Switching (PS) was used for all services, including voice and video, on 4G and 5G networks. There was an increase in access speed: 1G (2.4 kbps), 2G (64 kbps), 3G (2000 kbps), 4G (100 Mbps), and 5G (>1 Gbps). The 6G network is expected to offer peak data rates from 10 Gbps to 1 Tbps [7] with the Radio Base Station installed next to the Communication Satellite in space. In the terrestrial optical network, the switching method will become Optical Switching (OS), as well as all the Network Intelligence will be executed by the Optical Network to be more efficient.

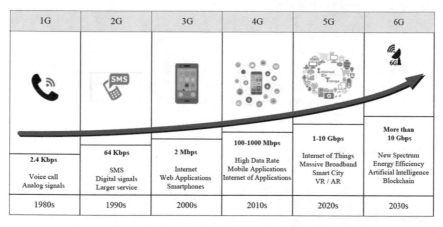

1G	2G	3G	4G	5G	6G
					More than 10 Gbps
			100-1000 Mbps	1-10 Gbps	
2.4 Kbps	64 Kbps	2 Mbps	High Data Rate	Internet of Things	New Spectrum
			Mobile Applications	Massive Broadband	Energy Efficiency
Voice call	SMS	Internet	Internet of Applications	Smart City	Artificial Intelligence
Analog signals	Digital signals	Web Applications		VR / AR	Blockchain
	Larger service	Smartphones			
1980s	1990s	2000s	2010s	2020s	2030s

Fig. 1. The evolution of Mobile Networks, adapted from [3].

- 1G

  - Standards: AMPS, NMT, TACS.
  - Applications: Voice call with analog signals.
  - Technical multiple-access resources: FDMA.
  - Physical method: Frequency.
  - Duplexing Techniques: FDD.
  - Switching Techniques: CS.

- 2G

  - Standards: GSM, IS-54, IS-95.
  - Applications: Voice services with analog signals and SMS. From 2.5G, email and web browsing.
  - Technical multiple-access resources: TDMA.
  - Physical method: Time Slots.
  - Duplexing Techniques: FDD.
  - Switching Techniques: CS. From 2.5G, CS & PS.

- 3G

  - Standards: WCDMA, CDMA2000.
  - Applications: Mobile TV, De-telephony, and Videoconferencing.
  - Technical multiple-access resources: CDMA.
  - Physical method: Time Slots and PN codes.
  - Duplexing Techniques: FDD\TDD.
  - Switching Techniques: CS & PS.

- 4G

  - Standards: LTE.
  - Applications: High data rate applications: HDTV, Cloud Computing.
  - Technical multiple-access resources: OFDMA.
  - Physical method: Time\Frequency.
  - Duplexing Techniques: FDD\TDD.
  - Switching Techniques: PS.

- 5G

  - Standards: NR.
  - Applications: IoT, Massive Broadband, Smart Cities, VR, AR.
  - Technical multiple-access resources: OFDMA.
  - Physical method: Time\Frequency.
  - Duplexing Techniques: FDD\TDD.
  - Switching Techniques: PS.

The 5G Mobile Network enabled the following technologies:

- Network Ultra Densification (Multi-Radio Access Technology): massive addition of small base stations;
- Massive MIMO and New Radio Access Techniques;
- Software Defined Networks (SDN) and Network Functions Virtualization (VNF);
- Spectrum expansion (centimeter and millimeter waves);
- Big Data and mobile cloud computing;
- Green Communications;
- Scalable Internet of Things (autonomous cars, home appliances, telemedicine, agriculture, and education, among others);
- 4G legacy support;
- Device to Device connectivity with high mobility (D2D).

The following 5G communication services are offered: 1) Interpersonal (Internet): eMBB (enhanced Mobile Broadband): Data + Voice + Video; 2) URLLC (Ultra-Reliable and Low Latency Communications) Critical: Autonomous Cars, drones, robotics, industrial control; 3) Between Machines: mMTC (Massive Machine Type of Communications). The 6G Mobile Networks are already being studied in China for the use of Radio Base Stations in the communication satellite itself in space. The Digital Twin, along with Artificial Intelligence (AI) and Machine Learning, will be essential for 6G; the real system will have a digital twin that quickly evaluates the real parameters and provides the solution to be applied to the real system in near-real time. The following technologies are considered drivers for 6G: Virtual Reality, Robotics, and Autonomous Systems, Brain/Computer Interactions, Blockchain, Big Data, Analytics, Distributed Cloud, QoE, Virtual Assistants, and Distributed Accounting (BDLT).

4 Concept and Definitions of Industry 4.0

Industry 4.0 or Fourth Industrial Revolution encompasses technologies for automation and data exchange within a manufacturing environment, focusing on improving the efficiency and productivity of processes [9, 14]. It uses Cyber-Physical Systems, the Internet of Things, and Cloud Computing technologies. Industry 4.0 enables the vision and execution of Smart Factories with modular structures, cyber-physical systems monitoring physical processes, creating a virtual copy of the physical world, and making decentralized decisions. With the IoT, cyber-physical systems communicate and cooperate with humans in real time and through cloud computing, both internal and intra-organizational services are offered and used by participants in the value chain.

These new technologies bring countless opportunities to add value to customers and increase the productivity of processes, but without the proper focus, they can waste large investments, with few results. The term "Industry 4.0" originated in a strategic high-tech project of the German Government that promotes the computerization of manufacturing and data integration.

Industry 4.0 has a greater capacity for integration and connectivity between people, machines, and factories, due to the emergence of advanced materials, which allow the development of new sensors, faster processing technology, advanced production networks, computer-controlled production devices, computers, and some cases already automated with autonomous robots, allowing an interaction between the real and the virtual, through technologies [5], such as Artificial Intelligence (AI), Advanced Robotics, Internet of Things (IoT), Autonomous Vehicles, Big Data, Cloud Storage, Augmented Reality, Cyber-Physical Systems (CPS), Digital Security, and 3D Printing. The evolution of Industry 4.0 is open, as it is emerging and expanding, making predicting the future much more difficult.

The fourth industrial revolution is characterized by a set of technologies that allow the fusion of the physical, digital, and biological worlds (Fig. 2), described below.

Autonomous or Advanced Robots perform activities and accomplish objectives without navigation or human intervention. Industry 4.0 also can "learn alone" and reshape its strategy, according to the environment they are in. In addition, they can interact with other machines and perform tasks faster and safer, resulting in reduced costs and increased productivity.

Big Data must be able to handle a large volume of data and is used to define a large set of IT tools that allow the capture, analysis, and cataloging of data in real-time [14]. It is based on 5 principles: volume, variety, speed, veracity, and value.

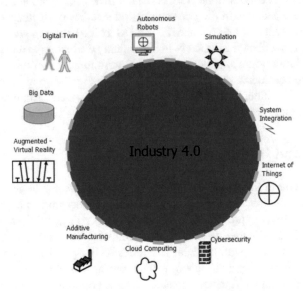

Fig. 2. Industry 4.0 Technologies, adapted from [4].

Cloud Computing or Storage is not a place, but a method of managing IT resources that replaces local machines and private data centers with a virtual infrastructure. In this model, users access virtual computing, networking, and storage resources made available online by a remote provider. These resources can be provisioned instantly. It allows the user to use hardware, operating system, communications systems, and application software from the cloud itself, without having to buy them, using them as a "service".

Augmented Reality (AR) and Virtual Reality (VR) are technologies that allow the virtual world to be mixed with the real, enabling greater interaction and opening a new dimension in the way we perform tasks or even those that we assign to machines.

3D Printing, also known as rapid prototyping, is a form of additive manufacturing technology where a three-dimensional model is created by successive layers of material. It does not require the use of molds and allows the production of shapes that are not viable in other production methods.

Cybersecurity is the practice that protects computers and servers, mobile devices, electronic systems, networks, and data from malicious attacks. It is also called information technology security or electronic information security.

Internet of Things (IoT) is an extension of the current Internet that makes it possible for everyday objects, whatever they may be, but which have computational and communication capabilities, to connect to the Internet, making it possible, in the first place, to remotely control the objects and, second, that the objects themselves be used as service providers.

Systems Integration aims to connect the different areas of industry and extract data and information that will be used to carry out continuous improvements in the entire production process and related support areas. Integration can be horizontal, which refers to IT systems and flows in the supply/value chain, including the various processes that pass through it, or it can be vertical, in which it allows all levels of the factory to be connected, from the factory to executives.

Simulation is the virtual reproduction of complex development and manufacturing environments and processes in factories. It is a practice that enables the digital and faithful reproduction of the operation of industrial plants, covering equipment, Digital Twin operational functions, and employees, with the objective of better monitoring them, foreseeing difficulties, and improving production.

Application of Artificial Intelligence using Neural Networks in Pattern Recognition: The objective of the project [11] was to develop software that can identify objects through pattern recognition algorithms using Neural Networks. For this, it is necessary to read the image from a webcam, convert the RGB bitmap (red, green, blue) into grayscale, apply filters so that it is only in black and white and finally carry out measurements. Some of the parameters that were measured are square area, centroid, shape, perimeter, and the color of the object. This data must feed the neural network machine learning to take place. Then the program can recognize objects and qualify them.

Industry 5.0 is about adding the human touch to the innovations that Industry 4.0 has brought to light: automation and efficiency; humanization, innovation, and human creative potential are of equal value in the process. Industry 5.0 is characterized by the union of machines and human beings, with the ultimate goal of adding value to production and creating customized products capable of meeting the specific needs of customers. This contributes to the quality of life not only of workers, who start to act more "lightly" on the factory floor but of society as a whole.

5   Final Considerations

The IoT enables a digital transformation, connecting devices, increasing business value, redefining organizations, and generating a huge amount of opportunities. Undoubtedly, this is a new technological wave, creating a new frontier of the connected world with people, computers, devices (objects/things), environments, and virtual objects, all connected and capable of interacting with each other.

5G Mobile Networks are coming to serve as the basis of IoT communication due to their Massive Use, Broadband, and Low Latency (Delay) characteristics. It is already being implemented worldwide, with a tendency to increase its use with cheaper smartphones due to the increase in users. It brings new features such as D2D (Device to Device) that provide communication between smartphones, independent of base stations.

In Industry 4.0, the digital connection with the advancement of software intelligence is changing society, due to its scope and speed. It is a paradigm shift that causes a new way of living. This technology has been increasingly incorporated by large companies, as a new trend to be explored, enabling more security and productivity. These new technological waves generate many opportunities for specification and development, and new job opportunities for new generations, thus requiring their training and education at universities and technical schools. IoT Evolutions to IoE, Mobile Networks 5G to 6G, and Industry 4.0 to 5.0 are already taking place.

References

1. Leite, J.R.E.: Modelagem e simulação de redes IoT, AdHoc e RFID. Universidade Estadual de Campinas (2019). https://hdl.handle.net/20.500.12733/1638028, Accessed Dec 2 2022
2. Emiliano Leite, J.R., Martins, P.S., Ursini, E.L.: Internet of Things: An Overview of Architecture, Models, Technologies, Protocols and Applications. In: Iano, Y., Arthur, R., Saotome, O., Estrela, V.V., Loschi, H.J. (eds.) BTSym 2017, pp. 75–85. Springer, Cham (2019). https://doi.org/10.1007/978-3-319-93112-8_8
3. Shah, A.F.M.S.: A survey from 1G to 5G including the advent of 6G: architectures, multiple access techniques, and emerging technologies. In: 2022 IEEE 12th Annual Computing and Communication Workshop and Conference (CCWC). pp. 1117–1123. IEEE (2022)
4. Demanboro, A.C., Bianchini, D., Iano, Y., Gomes, G., de Oliveira, G., Vaz, C.: Regulatory Aspects of 5G and Perspectives in the Scope of Scientific and Technological Policy. In: Iano, Y., Saotome, O., Vásquez, G.L.K., Pezzuto, C.C., Arthur, R., Gomes, G., de Oliveira, (eds.) Proceedings of the 7th Brazilian Technology Symposium (BTSym'21): Emerging Trends in Human Smart and Sustainable Future of Cities (Volume 1), pp. 163–171. Springer International Publishing, Cham (2023). https://doi.org/10.1007/978-3-031-04435-9_16
5. Minango, P., Iano, Y., Chuma, E.L., Vaz, G.C., Gomes, G., de Oliveira, J., Minango,: Revision of the 5G Concept Rollout and Its Application in Smart Cities: A Study Case in South America. In: Iano, Y., Saotome, O., Vásquez, G.L.K., Pezzuto, C.C., Arthur, R., Gomes, G., de Oliveira, (eds.) Proceedings of the 7th Brazilian Technology Symposium (BTSym'21): Emerging Trends in Human Smart and Sustainable Future of Cities (Volume 1), pp. 229–238. Springer International Publishing, Cham (2023). https://doi.org/10.1007/978-3-031-04435-9_21
6. Izario, D., Brancalhone, J., Iano, Y., Gomes, G., de Oliveira, G., Vaz, C., Izario, K.: 5G - Automation of Vertical Systems in the Industry 4.0. In: Iano, Y., Saotome, O., Vásquez, G.L.K., Pezzuto, C.C., Arthur, R., Gomes, G., de Oliveira, (eds.) Proceedings of the 7th Brazilian Technology Symposium (BTSym'21): Emerging Trends in Human Smart and Sustainable Future of Cities (Volume 1), pp. 35–43. Springer International Publishing, Cham (2023). https://doi.org/10.1007/978-3-031-04435-9_4

7. Hassebo, A.: The Road to 6G, Vision, Drivers, Trends, and Challenges. In: 2022 IEEE 12th Annual Computing and Communication Workshop and Conference (CCWC). pp. 1112–1116. IEEE (2022)
8. Demanboro, A.C., Bianchini, D., Iano, Y., de Oliveira, G.G., Vaz, G.C.: 6G Networks: An Innovative Approach, but with Many Challenges and Paradigms, in the Development of Platforms and Services in the Near Future. In: Brazilian Technology Symposium. pp. 172–187. Springer (2023). https://doi.org/10.1007/978-3-031-04435-9_17
9. Chimielewski, A.M.M., da Silva, A.J.D., Leite, J.R.E.: Indústria 4.0: Revolução e Impacto no Mundo Moderno. Projectus. 5, 1–12 (2020)
10. Vaz, G.C., Iano, Y., Gomes, G., de Oliveira,: IoT - From Industries to Houses: An Overview. In: Iano, Y., Saotome, O., Vásquez, G.L.K., Pezzuto, C.C., Arthur, R., Gomes, G., de Oliveira, (eds.) Proceedings of the 7th Brazilian Technology Symposium (BTSym'21): Emerging Trends in Systems Engineering Mathematics and Physical Sciences, Volume 2, pp. 734–741. Springer International Publishing, Cham (2022). https://doi.org/10.1007/978-3-031-08545-1_73
11. Figueiredo, V.: Identificador visual automático para sistema de manufatura (2019). https://revistas.unisuam.edu.br/Findex.php/projectus/article/download/709/485/&usg=AOvVaw2YccbbkDQ-oY2932-7BsOW, Accessed Dec 2 2022
12. Branco, A.L. Revoluções Industriais: Primeira, segunda e terceira revoluções. https://educacao.uol.com.br/disciplinas/geografia/revolucoes-industriais-primeira-segunda-e-terceira-revolucoes.htm, Accessed Dec 02 2022
13. Schwab, K.: A quarta revolução industrial. 1st edn. Edipro (2019)
14. Big Data 101: Unstructured Data Analytics, https://www.intel.com/content/dam/www/public/us/en/documents/solution-briefs/big-data-101-brief.pdf, Accessed Dec 02 2022

A Rational Interpretation of Laboratory Direct Shear Test Results for Soils

Samuel Laura Huanca[1]([envelope]) [iD], Julio Cesar Laura Huanca[2] [iD],
and Russel Allidren Lozada Vilca[2] [iD]

[1] Universidad Privada del Norte, Cajamarca, Peru
samuel.laura@upn.pe
[2] Universidad Nacional de Juliaca, Juliaca, Peru
{jc.laura,ralozadav.doc}@unaj.edu.pe

Abstract. An important property of soils is the shear strength, which guarantees the stability of geotechnical structures. This property is represented by two parameters: internal friction angle and cohesion, obtained from shear testing in the field and laboratory. The direct shear test is the most popular and intensively used for determining shear strength parameters. The aim of this paper is to present a rational procedure to interpret the results of the laboratory direct shear test for defining the strength parameters of soils. Two series of direct shear tests under consolidated and drained conditions (ASTM D3080) were carried out with samples of a wet well-graded sand (SW) compacted to a dense state, from Cutimbo's bank of aggregates, and saturated soft clay (CL and CH), from lacustrine deposits of Puno city. The procedure was applied to the results, for two soils, and the strength parameters were determined considering typical response curves and validity ranges of normal stresses for application purposes. Calculated strength parameters values were consistent with reported values in several publications and reduces the uncertainty of the reported values from direct shear tests.

Keywords: Shear strength · Direct shear testing · Interpretation procedure · Strength parameters

1 Introduction

Shear strength is one of the most important properties of soils [1–7] because the safety of any geotechnical structure (foundations, embankments, retaining structures, dams, slopes, among others) mainly depends on this soil property [2, 3, 6, 8, 9]. This property allows the soil to resist sliding across the internal surfaces of a soil mass [3, 5, 6]. The failure (or slide) of the soil mass occurs as a result of the mobilization of the maximum shear stress that it can support, so understanding shear strength is essential to understand part of the behavior of soils [2, 3, 6, 10–12].

The parameters that define the soil strength can be obtained by various methods, including field and laboratory tests [2, 9, 13, 14]. In the laboratory, the direct shear test is the most popular and intensively used test by engineers in different works to determine the shear strength parameters of soils, mainly due to its speed of execution and low cost [3, 5, 12, 15, 16].

The aim of this study is to present a rational procedure to interpret the results of the laboratory direct shear test and define the shear strength parameters of soils. The described procedure is applied to the results obtained from laboratory tests, carried out according to standardized procedures, and then compared with reported values taken from the available bibliographic references.

2 Shear Strength of Soils

To adequately interpret the shear strength of soil, based on the results of direct shear tests, a failure criterion must be considered [5, 9, 17, 18]. The Mohr-Coulomb law of failure is the criterion commonly used for interpreting the results of laboratory strength tests [2, 3, 10–12, 14], and the expression of the shear strength τ_f can be expressed, with modern symbols, by the following equation [19]:

$$\tau_f = c + \sigma' \tan\phi \tag{1}$$

where σ' is the effective normal stress on the analyzed plane, c is the cohesion, and ϕ is the angle of internal friction or, simply, the friction angle of the soil, the last two are "constant" for a soil [3, 5, 6, 8].

This equation defines a linear failure envelope and allows us to evaluate that for shear stress, on a certain plane less than τ_f, the deformations will be limited, but if these shear stresses reach the value of the resistance τ_f, the shear deformations will be unlimited, indicating shear failure [3, 5, 10, 12, 14]. The cohesion, c, indicates that even when the normal stress is zero, certain shear stress is needed to produce a shear failure [5, 10].

For soils, Eq. 1 must be expressed in terms of effective stresses, because the stresses that act in the contacts between the solid particles determine an eventual landslide. For this reason, soil properties are denoted as c' and ϕ', to highlight that these magnitudes refer to effective stresses [2, 3, 5, 6, 8].

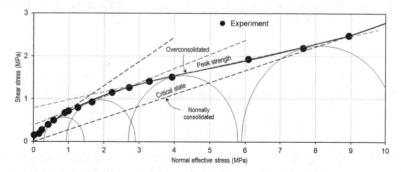

Fig. 1. Shear strength envelopes of undisturbed London clay in the $\sigma' - \tau$ plane [10, 20].

Typical experimental results for the shear strength of soils plotted in the $\sigma' - \tau$ space in Fig. 1, for a very large range of stresses, show that the failure envelope of an overconsolidated clay, the same as in dense sand, initially has a curved shape until it reaches the condition of normally consolidated, or a critical state strength [9, 10, 16].

To apply the Mohr-Coulomb criterion (Eq. 1) we must consider that the range of stresses applied to the soil mass, due to the applied loads from the engineering works is small. For common applications, the estimated stress ranges are below 1 MPa, for which the Mohr-Coulomb criterion is fully applicable, as shown in Fig. 1 [10, 21].

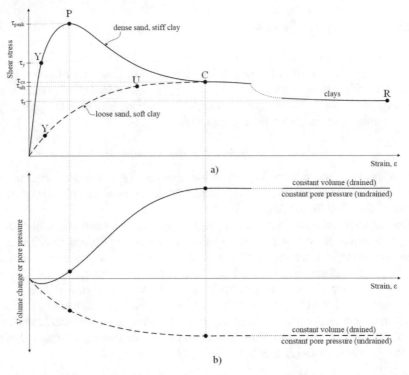

Fig. 2. Types of soil response, defined by: a) plot of shear stress-strain; b) plot of volume change or pore pressure–strain [14, 17, 18].

The behavior of soils can be observed through their stress-strain curves, in which different points can be recognized at which a soil can be considered to have failed. Figure 2 shows stress-strain curves for dense, loose, normally consolidated and overconsolidated soils, showing the points at which the soil fails, which define different criteria that can be adopted [3, 5, 6, 9, 18], which can be:

1. **Yield (Y):** Although it is not the maximum shear stress available for the soil, it represents the point where the curve ceases to have elastic behavior to experience elastoplastic behavior. Beyond this point, higher stresses will cause deformations, and ground movements are considered a failure [18].
2. **Peak shear strength (P):** Corresponds to the maximum shear stress that the soil can support, commonly present in dense sands and rigid or overconsolidated clays.

It can be dangerous to rely on this value because the soil rapidly loses strength if it deforms beyond this point [17, 18].

3. **Ultimate strength (U):** For loose sands and soft clays, can increase the stress, due to soil hardening, to the ultimate shear stress. The ultimate strength value is usually limited to shear (horizontal) strain between 10% and 20% [17, 18], related to the behavior of the soil structure.

4. **Critical state strength (C):** Sometimes can also be called ultimate strength. It is the shear stress for when the soil reaches a constant volume state (due to dilatancy or compression) or constant pore pressure [18], continuing the soil shear. It is sometimes called constant volume strength.

5. **Residual strength (R):** Sometimes it is also known as ultimate strength. It occurs after considerable deformation, on the slip surface, and is the lowest value of strength that the soil can support. This strength is very important in the analysis of the reactivation of old landslides [18].

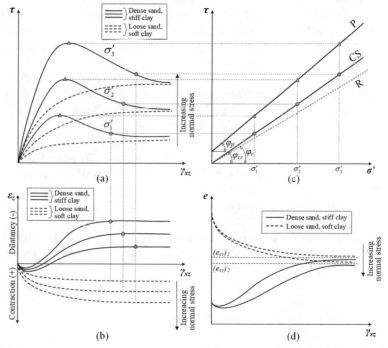

Fig. 3. Typical curves on the effect of increasing normal stress in soil behavior against shear stress [9, 20, 22].

Figure 2 shows typical curves, for single normal stress, for two large groups of soils. In a series of three or more direct shear tests with different applied normal stresses, different typical behavior curves will be produced, as shown in Fig. 3 [9, 22]. As a result of the repetition of the direct shear test procedure, the results are taken into diagrams shear stress – horizontal or shear strain (Fig. 3a) and volumetric strain – horizontal strain (Fig. 3b). Depending on the adopted criterion to define the shear strength of soil, the corresponding pairs (σ', τ) are transferred to the normal stress – shear stress plane (Fig. 3c) that allows a plot of corresponding failure envelope (P – Peak strength, CS – Strength at a critical state, R – Residual strength). The volumetric deformation - horizontal deformation diagram allows us to observe the variation of the soil void ratio (Fig. 3d), and it can also be verified that the critical void ratio is dependent on the magnitude of the normal effective stress [9, 23, 24].

3   Materials and Methods

For this study, a qualitative and quantitative analysis of the rational procedure for interpreting the results of direct shear tests under consolidated and drained conditions is carried out, to determine the parameters of the shear strength of soils.

Results of direct shear tests of two typical soils of Puno city are considered for the application of the interpretation procedure proposed in this paper. One soil is a clean well-graded sand (SW) compacted to a dense state, from Cutimbo's bank of aggregates normally used in works in this city. The other soil is a soft clay of medium to high plasticity (CL and CH) with the presence of organic material, characteristic of the lacustrine zone of this city.

The procedure described below is based on the approaches proposed by Morilla [25]. Then, the rational procedure proposed, for the interpretation of results of direct shear tests, assumes that to obtain the values of shear strength parameters (ϕ' and c') the soil already has these 'true' values, therefore we must follow:

1. Carry out a series of three or more direct shear tests with the same soil sample, in each test: shear stresses (τ), horizontal deformations (δ_h), and vertical deformations (δ_v) must be measured for each normal stress: $\sigma'_1 < \sigma'_2 < \sigma'_3 < \ldots < \sigma'_n$.
2. Plot the results of readings in two graphs: horizontal strain (by shear) versus shear stress ($\epsilon_h - \tau$) and horizontal strain versus volumetric strain ($\epsilon_h - \epsilon_v$).
3. Determine the type of response or failure criterion is considered to determine the corresponding parameters, according to Fig. 2. The adopted criterion must be indicated when submitting the final results.
4. Determine the pairs (σ', τ) for each test, determining the shear stresses according to the type of response determined.
5. Write Eq. 1 for each test performed, in an equation system, as follows:

   - Eq. 1 (specimen 1): $\tau_1 = c' + \sigma'_1 \tan \phi'$
   - Eq. 2 (specimen 2): $\tau_2 = c' + \sigma'_2 \tan \phi'$
   - Eq. 3 (specimen 3): $\tau_3 = c' + \sigma'_3 \tan \phi'$
   - Equation n (specimen n): $\tau_n = c' + \sigma'_n \tan \phi'$

6. Determine various values for the angle of friction (ϕ') and cohesion (c'), corresponding to the combination of each pair of the last equation system.

7. If the test was carried out following the standardized procedure (ASTM D3080), the results of ϕ' and c', from each pair of equations, must be very close so that finally a statistical procedure can be carried out (average, regression, etc.) to determine their final values. In addition, graphs $\epsilon_h - \tau$ and $\epsilon_h - \epsilon_v$ of the same soil should be observed, which should indicate a similar typical behavior, according to what is shown in Figs. 2 and 3.

8. Finally, in a checking way, the values obtained for the resistance parameters (ϕ' and c') must be compared with those typical values reported in the literature.

4 Results and Discussion

Figure 4 shows direct shear test results of wet dense sand ($\gamma = 18.3\,\text{kN/m}^3$) and a saturated soft clay ($\gamma = 14.5\,\text{kN/m}^3$), performed in a 60 mm × 60 mm shear box and a specimen of 30 mm and 20 mm thickness respectively. The dense sand was subjected to six different normal stresses, with two values above the common (13.6; 27.2; 54.5; 109.0; 163.4, and 217.9 kPa), and shear stresses in peak and critical state were identified, according to the behavior of this type of soil. On the other hand, the soft clay was subjected to four normal stresses within the common range (13.6; 27.2; 54.5, and 109.0 kPa) and ultimate shear stresses were identified for a horizontal strain of 15% (3 mm). This completes the first three steps of the procedure described above.

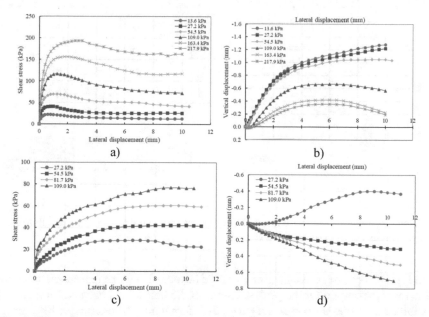

Fig. 4. Direct shear test results: wet dense sand (a and b), and saturated soft clay (c and d).

Then, in step 4, the pairs (σ', τ) are identified and determined for the adopted criteria that were indicated for each type of soil. In Table 1 and Fig. 5, it can be seen that for dense sand, six pairs (σ', τ_p) were determined for peak strengths, corresponding to the six tests carried out, and four pairs (σ', τ_{cs}) for strengths in a critical state, which correspond to the last four tests that show the trend to constant volume, while the first two tests continue with the increase in the volume of the test specimen. On the other hand, Table 1 and Fig. 5 show that four pairs (σ', τ_{max}) and four pairs (σ', τ_{ult}) corresponding to the four tests performed were determined for soft clay.

Table 1. Pairs of points (σ', τ) from failure criteria for wet dense sand and saturated soft clay.

Normal stress (σ')	Wet dense sand		Saturated soft clay	
	Peak shear stress (τ_p)	Critical state shear stress (τ_{cs})	Maximum shear stress (τ_{max})	Ultimate shear stress (τ_{ult})
kPa	kPa	kPa	kPa	kPa
13.6	22.0	-	28.4	23.9
27.2	40.8	-	42.3	32.5
54.5	69.2	44.1	60.6	46.3
109.0	116.4	84.1	76.9	57.3
163.4	156.2	128.4	—	—
217.9	193.7	170.6	—	—

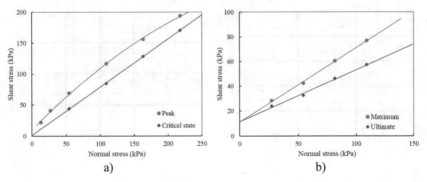

Fig. 5. Shear strength envelopes obtained by regression (commonly), according to failure criteria for a) wet dense sand and b) saturated soft clay.

In Fig. 5a, it can be seen that an error would be made if a linear regression of the pairs (σ', τ_p) was performed for the peak strengths of the dense sand because, in reality, the peak failure envelope is a non-linear curve, therefore it must be interpreted by segments, in which the Mohr-Coulomb failure criterion is valid, which in this case can be: 25–125 kPa and 100–225 kPa. On the other hand, the critical state failure envelope shows the existence of cohesion, which does not correspond to the critical state failure criterion in which the cohesion must be zero.

In the case of soft clay, Fig. 5b shows that both maximum strength and ultimate strength envelopes apparently can be obtained by linear regression, obtaining values of shear strength parameters without qualitative analysis of the tests, which also leads to a wrong interpretation.

Thus, for results shown in Table 1, the equations for each pair of values for each soil can be written, considering as an example of criteria the peak strength for wet dense sand and ultimate strength for saturated soft clay. Then, according to step 6 described above, the values of ϕ' and c' are calculated for each combination of the equations.

According to step 7 of the procedure described above, the results obtained are analyzed. For wet dense sand, the first segment of normal stresses between 25 and 125 kPa, the valid results to determine the values of ϕ' and c' are those corresponding to specimens 2, 3, and 4, with the corresponding combinations of equations. For this stress range, Fig. 6a shows that the values obtained are relatively close, noting that the combination of 1 and 2 shows high values of the angle of friction and low of cohesion, therefore the result of a resulting weighted average is $\phi_p' = 42.7°$ and $c_p' = 17.2\,kPa$. In this case, the result is practically the same as that which would be obtained through a linear regression with $R2 = 0.9978$ (42.5° and 17.2 kPa), due to the good quality of the procedure performed and the results obtained from the direct shear test.

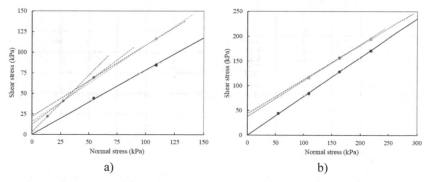

Fig. 6. Trend lines of combinations of direct shear test results for wet dense sand: a) normal stress between 25 and 125 kPa, and b) normal stress between 100 and 225 kPa.

Proceeding in the same way for the interval between 100 and 225 kPa, for the combinations related to specimens 4, 5, and 6, values of the shear strength parameters of $\phi_p' = 35.4°$ and $c_p' = 39.6\,kPa$ are obtained (see Fig. 6b). Again, the results are practically the same as those obtained by linear regression with $R2 = 0.9996$ (35.4° and 39.4 kPa). The results obtained for wet dense sand correspond to reported values in the bibliography [2, 9, 25–27] for shear strength parameters in sands.

For soft clay, considering that the test was carried out for common normal stresses, a linear failure envelope must be considered, for which the pairs (σ', τ) for maximum and ultimate strengths must correspond to a straight line. Figure 7 shows the combinations that can be obtained from the specimens subjected to testing. In Figs. 4c and 4d, it can be seen that specimen 1 should be discarded because it does not correspond to the results of the rest of the test specimens since it shows a peak resistance and volume increase (dilatancy) that does not correspond to soft clay. Therefore, for this case, the combinations related to specimens 2, 3, and 4 must be considered. Thus, the ultimate strength parameters are determined to be $\phi'_{ult} = 24.5°$ and $c'_{ult} = 8.4\,\text{kPa}$, results are practically the same as those obtained from linear regression with $R2 = 0.9959$ (24.5° and 8.1 kPa), which is due to the good quality of the tests carried out, except with specimen 1. These values of drained shear strength parameters for soft clay are consistent with those reported by various authors [2, 9, 26].

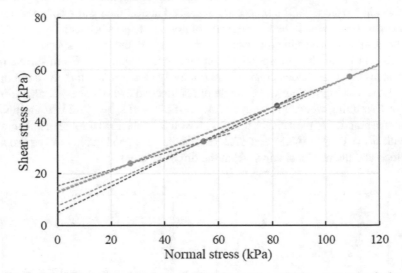

Fig. 7. Trend lines of combinations of direct shear test results for saturated soft clay.

5   Conclusion

The procedure to interpret the results of the direct shear test (in drained consolidated condition) was presented and explained, with considerations previously established by various authors. The results of direct shear tests carried out with samples of wet dense sand and saturated soft clay, characteristic of the city of Puno in Peru, were interpreted. The results obtained, with the criteria adopted and the observation of the response curves of the soils, were consistent with the values reported in the available bibliography. Therefore, the proposed procedure allows obtaining results that reduce the uncertainty of the reported values, selecting the valid results (points or specimens) and the validity ranges for the determined parameters for application purposes. In the future, similar procedures must be carried out with other laboratory tests such as triaxial compression, carried out in accordance with the corresponding standards.

References

1. Lambe, T.W., Whitman, R.V: Soil mechanics. John Wiley & Sons (1991)

2. Jiménez, S.J.A., De Justo, J.L.: Geotecnia y Cimientos. 2da. Edici. Madrid, España: Editorial Rueda. Developments in Geotechnical Engineering **66**, 466 (1975)
3. Jewell, R.A., Wroth, C.P.: Direct shear tests on reinforced sand. Geotechnique **37**, 53–68 (1987)
4. de Oliveira, G.G., Iano, Y., Vaz, G.C., Chuma, E.L., Negrete, P.D.M., Negrete, J.C.M.: Prop Walls: A Contextualization of the theme in a case study in the city of campinas (Brazil) BT - In: Proceedings of the 7th Brazilian Technology Symposium (BTSym'21). Presented at the (2022)
5. Taylor, D.W.: Fundamentals of soil mechanics. LWW (1948)
6. Terzaghi, K., Peck, R.B., Mesri, G.: Soil mechanics in engineering practice. John Wiley & Sons (1996)
7. de Oliveira, G.G., Iano, Y., Vaz, G.C., Chuma, E.L., Negrete, P.D.M., Negrete, J.C.M.: Structural analysis of bridges and viaducts using the IoT concept. an approach on dom pedro highway (Campinas-Brazil). In: Brazilian Technology Symposium, pp. 108–119. Springer (2022)
8. Alonso, E.: Las catástrofes y el progreso de la geotecnia: discurso del académico Excmo. Sr. D. Eduardo Alonso Pérez de Ágreda, leído en la sesión inaugural del año académico el día 18 de enero de 2005. Real Academia de Ingeniería (2005)
9. Budhu, M.: Soil Mechanics and Foundations. 3 edn. New York: John Wiley & Sons, Inc.; (2010)
10. Bishop, A.W.: The strength of soils as engineering materials. Geotechnique **16**, 91–130 (1966)
11. Minango, P., Iano, Y., Chuma, E.L., Vaz, G.C., de Oliveira, G.G., Minango, J.: Revision of the 5G concept rollout and its application in smart cities: a study case in South America. In: Brazilian Technology Symposium, pp. 229–238. Springer (2023)
12. Terzaghi, K., Peck, R.B.: Mecánica de suelos; en la ingeniería práctica (1978)
13. Bishop, A.W., Bjerrum, L.: The relevance of the triaxial test to the solution of stability problems. Publ, Nor. Geotech. Inst (1960)
14. Witlow, R.: Basic Soil Mechanics. In: Bishop, A.W., Henkel, D.J., (ed.) 1995 The measurement of soil properties in the triaxial test. Longman Group Limited, London (1962)
15. Ziaie Moayed, R., Alibolandi, M., Alizadeh, A.: Specimen size effects on direct shear test of silty sands. Int. J. Geotech. Eng. **11**, 198–205 (2017)
16. Nguyen, G.: Consideration of specimens shear area changes during direct shear test of soils and its effects on a size of spread foundation. International Multidisciplinary Science GeoConference SGEM, vol. 2. p. 203 (2015)
17. Witlow, R.: Basic Soil Mechanics. Longman Group Limited, London (1995)
18. Chuma, E.L., Iano, Y., Roger, L.L.B., De Oliveira, G.G., Vaz, G.C.: Novelty sensor for detection of wear particles in oil using integrated microwave metamaterial resonators with neodymium magnets. IEEE Sens. J. (2022)
19. Bardet, J.-P.: Experimental soil mechanics. Prentice Hall (1997)
20. Thiel, R.: Designer's Forum-A technical note regarding interpretation of cohesion (or adhesion) and friction angle in direct shear tests. In: Geosynthetics, p. 10 (2009)
21. Abt, S.R., Hamilton, G.B., Watson, C.C., Smith, J.B.: AB Chance company. the chance: Large woody debris jams, channel hydraulics and habitat for. Geophys. Monogr. **89**, 151–164 (1996)
22. Bol E, İspıroğlu M. Determination of the shearing rate in drained direct shear test. In: 4th International Symposium on Innovative Technologies in Engineering and Science, Antalya, Turkey, pp. 977–85 (2016)
23. Atkinson, J.H., Bransby, P.L.: The mechanics of soils: an introduction to critical state soil mechanics (1978)
24. Wood, D.M.: Soil mechanics: a one-dimensional introduction. Cambridge University Press (2009)

25. Morilla, I.: Interpretación de los ensayos geotécnicos en suelos (2012)
26. Look, B.G.: Handbook of geotechnical investigation and design tables. Taylor & Francis (2007)
27. Peck, R.B., Hanson, W.E., Thornburn, T.H.: Foundation engineering. John Wiley & Sons (1991)

Substitution of Wheat Flour for Sweet Potato, Oca, and Pea Flour in a Sponge Cake: Sensory Acceptability and Nutritional Composition

Bregette Avila Zavaleta[1] , Wendy Geraldine Pereda Calderón[1] ,
Meliza Lindsay Rojas[2](✉) , and Cesia Elizabeth Boñón Silva[1]

[1] Escuela de Ingeniería Agroindustrial, Universidad Privada del Norte (UPN), Trujillo, Peru
cesia.bonon@upn.edu.pe
[2] Dirección de Investigación, Innovación y Responsabilidad Social, Universidad
Privada del Norte, Trujillo, Peru
meliza.rojas@upn.edu.pe

Abstract. The objective of this research was to evaluate the effect of the partial substitution of wheat flour for sweet potato, oca, and pea flour on the sensory acceptability and nutritional compounds of a sponge cake. It used the methodology of a simplex mixture design with an expanded centroid, which consisted of 10 treatments, evaluating sensory attributes of appearance, smell, taste, and texture by untrained consumers using a 9-point structured hedonic scale. The data were processed by performing an analysis of variance and a Tukey test at a 95% confidence level to estimate significant differences among treatments and using a grade 2 polynomial mathematical modeling for sensory acceptability. As result, the treatment that allowed obtaining optimal average values for all the sensory attributes evaluated was treatment T1 (20% potato sweet flour substitution), which showed a content of carbohydrates (66%), crude fiber (1.63%), fats (6.10%), and proteins (2.48%). Finally, the flour substitution effect made the product acceptable to consumers with a nutritional improvement under the criteria of the Peruvian technical standard for baking.

Keywords: Sweet potato · *Oxalis tuberosa* · pea flour · sensory acceptability · nutritional composition

1 Introduction

Currently, the study of food processing has been increasing, and it is important to know how foods influence health. The consumption of wheat flour-based products such as bakery products, cakes, pastries, cookies, and extruded products, among others, has increased in recent years [1–3]. The food should be more nutritious and provide health benefits, thus helping to improve their quality of life. Also, they must be palatable to consumers and accepted by them [2].

Consequently, over time, wheat flour has been partially substituted in different formulations of products such as energy bars, bread, biscuits, pasta, and cakes, among others. Different authors partially substituted wheat flour, e.g., Morais et al. [4] elaborated cookies with purple sweet potato flour at 15.5% and kale flour at 24%, obtaining a product with 61% carbohydrates. Similarly, Garcia et al. [5] made cakes with 52% quinoa flour, 22% dry pea, 25% dry carrot, and 1% of tocote.

Wheat flour has adequate compounds (protein-gluten) to form a strong and resistant dough. However, wheat-based products are nutritionally unbalanced, due to their low content of dietary fiber, and the low biological value of its protein associated with the low content of lysine [6, 7]. In this regard, cereals, legumes, tubers, and roots are potential substitutes for wheat flour.

Sweet potato, oca, and pea flour serve as potential substitutes for wheat flour, since the proximal analysis of these, shows that the protein content is 2.1%, 8.76%, and 19.9% respectively and carbohydrates are 85.15%, 88.37%, and 70. 13% respectively; compared with wheat flour which has 9.86% of protein and 75.93% of carbohydrates [8]. Based on this, the objective of this research is to evaluate the effect of the partial substitution of wheat flour for sweet potato, oca, and pea flour on the sensory acceptability and nutritional compounds of a sponge cake, which represents an alternative to improve the nutritional content cake-type baked products.

2 Material and Methods

2.1 Raw Material and Obtention of Substitute Flours

Raw yellow oca (*Oxalis tuberosa*) and pre-roasted pea flour were acquired from the district of Usquil (Otuzco, La Libertad, Peru). The raw sweet potato was acquired from the district of Moche (Trujillo, La Libertad, Peru). First, sweet potato and oca (10 kg of each one), were washed and peeled. Then, they were cut and rinsed three times to remove oxidative substances., they were drained and then spread on stainless steel trays covered with a fine mesh without touching the product, and the products were sun-dried. The dry products were ground and sieved to obtain homogeneous flours (1 kg of sweet potato flour and 1.88 kg of oca flour). Finally, the flours were packaged in hermetic bags for sponge cake elaboration.

2.2 Formulations and Experimental Design

The research was developed following the methodology of a Simplex Tertiary Mixture Design with an extended centroid [9], which consisted of 10 treatments including 3 central points (see Table 1), where 20% of the wheat flour was substituted individually or by a mixture of sweet potato, oca, and pea flours, according to the proportions shown in Table 1.

Table 1. Simplex mixture design with expanded centroid

Treatments	Wheat	Sweet potato	Oca	Pea	Sensory attributes
Control	100%	0.0%	0.0%	0.0%	Y_0
T1	80%	20.0%	0.0%	0.0%	Y_1
T2	80%	0.0%	20.0%	0.0%	Y_2
T3	80%	0.0%	0.0%	20.0%	Y_3
T4	80%	10.0%	10.0%	0.0%	Y_4
T5	80%	10.0%	0.0%	10.0%	Y_5
T6	80%	0.0%	10.0%	10.0%	Y_6
T7	80%	6.7%	6.7%	6.7%	Y_7
T8	80%	13.3%	3.3%	3.3%	Y_8
T9	80%	3.3%	13.3%	3.3%	Y_9
T10	80%	3.3%	3.3%	13.3%	Y_{10}

2.3 Sponge Cake Elaboration

The "Control" cake was made only with wheat flour, and for the other treatments, T1 to T10, sweet potato, oca, and pea flours were used with different concentrations according to Table 1. In the first stage, the substitute flours were weighed (sweet potato, oca, and pea), wheat flour (Nicolini pastry flour), eggs, baking powder, cornstarch, white sugar, orange essence, and vanilla. After all the dry products were mixed homogeneously, the sugar was beaten with the eggs for 6 min, then all the dry mixture was added little by little until completely incorporated, and finally, the orange and vanilla essence was added.

The oven was preheated to 230 °C for 10 min, while a rectangular mold was greased with margarine and special greaseproof paper then the sponge cake mixture was placed with help of a rubber spatula. Finally, it is taken to the oven for 15 min. After the baking time, it was left to cool for about 10 min, then the sponge cakes were unmolded, cut, and packaged. Figure 1 shows an example of the sponge cakes obtained for each formulation, which were packaged and coded for subsequent sensorial analysis.

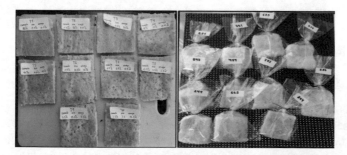

Fig. 1. Samples of sponge cakes obtained with each of the formulations showed in Table 1.

2.4   Evaluation of Sensory Attributes

The cake samples were directed at a population with an age range from 10 to 35 years old. The sample used for the sensory evaluation was determined by non-probabilistic sampling, taking 30 untrained consumers for the sensory tests according to the methodology of Watts et al. [10]. To obtain the data, the consumers tasted the coded samples of prepared sponge cake, which were monadic and sequentially presented. Consumers gave their judgment by evaluating the sensory attributes (appearance, smell, taste, and texture) by using a structured 9-point hedonic scale (ranging from 1 - I dislike it very much to 9 - I like it very much).

2.5   Nutritional Composition Evaluation

The formulations T1, T2, and T3, which were the most acceptable by the consumers, were nutritionally analyzed. For this, different types of standard methodologies were used, such as the methodology of the Official Association of Chemical Analysts (AOAC) and the different methods of the Peruvian Technical Standard (N.T.P).

Carbohydrate content was used by the modified Feh-ling method (AOAC 974.06 18 TH). 2005 Edition. Likewise, the crude fiber content was determined following the method of N.T.P 205.003/79 (Rev. 2016). The fat content was determined following the method of N.T.P 205.006:1980 (Rev. 2011). The protein content was determined according to the Kjeldahl N.T.P 205.005/79 (Rev. 2018) method. The energy content was calculated considering the contribution of carbohydrates (4 kcal/g), proteins (4 kcal/g), and fats (9 kcal/g), according to NTE INEN 1334–2:2011 established by the Ecuadorian Technical Standard [11].

2.6   Statistical Analysis

To analyze the results of the sensory attributes, the non-parametric analysis of variance was applied using the Kruskal-Wallis test at a 95% confidence interval using IBM SPSS Statistics v.23 (IBM Corporation, USA) software [12]. The 3-factor simplex mixture design with expanded centroid analysis was performed using the Statistica v.7 (StatSoft. Inc, USA) software, at a 95% confidence interval. Initially, the quality of fit and significance of the linear and quadratic models to the results of sensory attributes were verified, later optimization was performed through the desirability function.

3   Results and Discussion

3.1   Evaluation of Sensory Attributes

Figure 2 shows labels in red (a, b, and c), which indicate that when the letters are different, there is a significant difference between the formulations for each attribute. On the contrary, if they have the same letter there is no difference between the attributes. Therefore, for the appearance attribute, there is no difference between all the treatments, i.e., there is no influence of the substitutions. Meanwhile, for the smell attribute, samples T1, T2, and T3 were different from the Control, however, samples T4, T5, T6, T7, T8,

T9, and T10 were statistically similar among themselves and with the other treatments including the control. Also, for the taste attribute, it was observed that treatments T1, T2, T3, T6, and T10 did not differ from each other, but did differ from the control sample. Finally, for the texture attribute, treatments T1, T2, T3, and T6 show significant differences with the control sample, while for samples T1, T2, T4, T5, T6, T7, T8, and T10 there are no significant differences among them. This shows that, compared to the control, the individual substitution of each of the flours has a perceptible sensory effect on appearance, smell, taste, and texture.

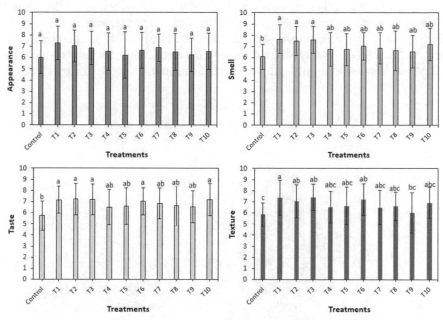

Fig. 2. Sensory evaluation results for attributes of appearance, smell, taste, and texture. Average ± standard deviation. Different letters (labels in red) mean a significant difference (p ≤ 0.05) between formulations medians by the Kruskal-Wallis test.

3.2 Simplex Mixture Design Results and Optimization

The linear and quadratic models were fitted to the experimental data of the sensory attributes of appearance, smell, taste, and texture. Table 2 shows the values obtained of the p-value and the fit coefficient R^2. It is observed that the fit value was better for the quadratic model, although it was only significant (p = 0.05) for the smell attribute. The contour surface graphs obtained with the quadratic model for each attribute showed that the highest values for each attribute tend to be found in the individual values of the factors, that is, with the substitution of wheat flour for the other individual ingredients (only sweet potato or oca, or pea flour).

Since there was a significant effect of the quadratic model only for the smell attribute, the response surface graph for this attribute is shown in Fig. 3, as well as the equation

Table 2. ANOVA results and fit criteria of linear and quadratic models for each attribute.

Model	Appearance		Smell		Taste		Texture	
	p-value	R^2	p-value	R^2	p-value	R^2	p-value	R^2
Linear	0.85	0.04	0.85	0.04	0.90	0.03	0.61	0.13
Quadratic	0.26	0.61	0.05	0.84	0.08	0.79	0.12	0.77

of the quadratic model (1) with the respective resulting coefficients, which describes the results of the smell attribute based on the individual effects and interaction of the factors, where sp: sweet potato, o: oca and p: pea. It is important to mention that the optimization for the smell attribute was carried out through the desirability function, where the use of 20% pea flour is the optimal value to obtain a maximum score in this attribute.

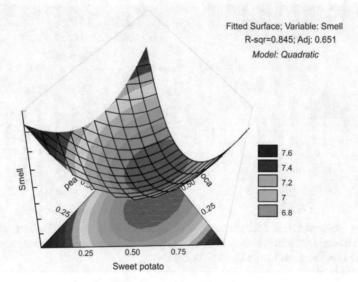

Fig. 3. Response surface of the quadratic model obtained for the sensory attribute of smell.

$$Smell = 7.61 * \%sp + 7.41 * \%o + 7.67 * \%p - 3.36 * \%sp * \%o - 3.24 * \%sp * \%p - 1.76 * \%o * \%p \tag{1}$$

Additionally, the average value of all sensory attributes was analyzed, obtaining a global value (GA). In this case, the linear ($p = 0.89$) and quadratic ($p = 0.06$) models were not significant. However, the quadratic model showed a better fit ($R^2 = 0.82$), after evaluating the significance of the individual and interaction effects of the factors, non-significant effects (pea*oca interaction) were disregarded. Subsequently, the effects on global acceptability were analyzed again considering only the significant effects of the factors, thus obtaining that the quadratic model was significant ($p = 0.03$) with an

R^2 of 0.76. Therefore, Fig. 4 shows the contour graph and the mathematical model (2) that describes the GA values based on the significant individual and interaction effects of the factors.

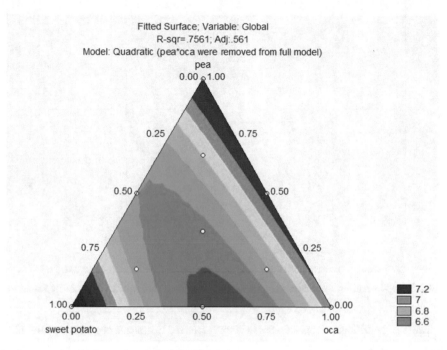

Fig. 4. Contour surface obtained by fitting the quadratic model, for the global average of sensory attributes (GA).

$$GA = 0.370 * \%sp + 0.349 * \%o + 0.359 * \%p - 0.007 * \%sp * \%o - 0.007 * \%sp * \%p \qquad (2)$$

Finally, the global average of sensory attributes (GA) was optimized using the desirability function (see Fig. 5), obtaining that for an optimal GA value, only sweet potato flour should be used. This means that, to obtain an optimal average score for all sensory attributes, it is sufficient to substitute wheat flour for 20% sweet potato flour.

3.3 Nutritional Compounds Evaluation

The protein content for the control treatments, sweet potato 20% (T1) and oca 20% (T2), was low since their composition is rich in carbohydrates and fiber compared to T3 (pea 20%) which had 3.60% of protein (Table 3). This makes sense since pea flour has a high protein content of 19.9% compared to oca flour 8.76% and sweet potato 2.1% [9]. Garcia et al. [5] elaborated cakes with a substitution of 52% of quinoa, 22% of dry pea, 25% of dry carrot, and 1% sweet potato obtaining cakes with 11.3% of protein. The protein content is higher in the cakes, due to the additional contribution of quinoa and pea flour.

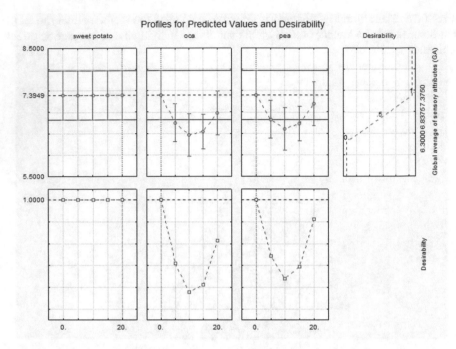

Fig. 5. Optimization results for the value of GA obtained through the desirability function.

Table 3. Nutritional composition of the most preferred treatments compared to Control.

Nutritional composition (x 100g)	Control	T1	T2	T3
Protein (g)	2.80	2.48	2.40	3.60
Fat (g)	6.96	6.10	6.81	6.97
Carbohydrates (g)	63.15	66.00	59.28	63.12
Crude fibre (g)	1.68	1.63	1.75	1.66
Energy (kcal)	326.44	328.82	308.01	329.61

Therefore, the use of substitute flours with a high protein index will result in a product with high protein content.

Regarding fat content, treatments T1 and T2 contain less fat content. This is related to the composition of the flours used. Reyes et al. [8] indicate that the fat values for sweet potato flour are 0.9%, oca flour (1.62%), and pea flour (2.4%). Garcia et al. [5] made cakes with 52% quinoa flour, 22% dry pea, 25% dry carrot, and 1% sweet potato flour substitutions, obtaining a fat content of 7.5%. However, the fat values here obtained are lower due to the low-fat content present in sweet potato and oca flour. In addition, it is important to consider that the lower the fat content, the longer the shelf life [13].

The carbohydrate content obtained for all treatments was similar to those reported by Pereira et al. [4] who elaborated cookies with a substitution of purple sweet potato flour at 15.5% and kale flour at 13% and 24%, thus obtaining a carbohydrate value of 61% and 59%, respectively. Similarly, García et al. [5] formulated cakes with 52% quinoa flour substitution, 22% dry pea, 25% dry carrot, and 1% of corn, obtaining a product with a carbohydrate content of 56.8%. The high carbohydrate content in tubers and roots (such as oca, sweet potato, potato, etc.) comes from starch, with the predominant fraction in tubers ranging from 56% to 84% [14].

The highest crude fiber content was present in T2 (1.75%). It is stated that the higher the fiber content, the lower the glycemic index (GI). It is worth mentioning that wheat flour has a GI of 70, sweet potato flour 48, and pea flour 35, this shows the speed at which the digestive system converts carbohydrates and makes them reach the bloodstream in the glucose form. In addition, this also depends on the heat processes used to obtain the flours: the higher the cooking, the higher the glycemic index [15, 16]. Therefore, in addition to fiber content, several elements and factors influence the digestibility of foods that should be better explored.

In terms of energy content, it was in the range of 329.61 to 308.01 kcal/100g, being the lowest for T2 treatment. This is due to its lower protein and carbohydrate content. However, if compared with other analogous industrial and commercial bakery products, they are even more caloric. For example, energy values of 399.7 kcal/100 g in "Chocman (Costa)". Similarly, 442, 331.76, and 391.43 kcal/100g are found in "Magdalenas", "Bimbo orange cake (Bimbo)" and "vanilla and orange cakes (PYC)" respectively, as can be seen, these products are even more caloric than the product elaborated in this research.

4   Conclusions

The effect of substitution of wheat flour with sweet potato, oca, and pea flours had a significant effect on sensory acceptability in terms of smell, taste, and texture attributes. Compared to the Control, the treatments with the highest acceptability were those of independent substitution with 20% of each flour T1 (sweet potato), T2 (oca), and T3 (pea), with average acceptability values of 7.38, 7.21, and 7.36, respectively. It was also determined that the quadratic model was the one that presented the best fit for all sensory attributes, presenting a significant effect for the smell attribute and that the optimization only for this attribute was the use of 20% pea flour. Additionally, the global average value of all sensory attributes was analyzed and optimized, where it was determined that it is sufficient to replace wheat flour with sweet potato flour at 20% to obtain an optimal average value for all sensory attributes. Finally, for the three best formulations, their nutritional composition was affected by the substitution of wheat flour. It is important to mention that there are very few studies on flours from Andean tubers and legumes such as oca and yellow pea flour; therefore, it is recommended to develop research on these raw materials, taking advantage of the nutritional benefits to be used in different bakery products.

References

1. Chavan, J.K., Kadam, S.S., Reddy, N.R.: Nutritional enrichment of bakery products by supplementation with nonwheat flours. Crit. Rev. Food Sci. Nutr. **33**, 189–226 (1993)
2. Negrete, J.C.M., Iano, Y., Negrete, P.D.M., Vaz, G.C., de Oliveira, G.G.: Sentiment Analysis in the Ecuadorian Presidential Election. In: Brazilian Technology Symposium, pp. 25–34. Springer (2023)
3. Jerome, R.E., Singh, S.K., Dwivedi, M.: Process analytical technology for bakery industry: A review. J. Food Process Eng. **42**, e13143 (2019)
4. Morais, C.P., et al.: Nutritional, Antioxidant and Sensory Evaluation of Calcium-high Content Cookies Prepared with Purple Sweet Potato (Ipomoea Batatas L.) and Kale (Brassica Oleracea Var. Acephala) Flours. J. Culin. Sci. Technol. **19**, 373–389 (2021)
5. García-Ruiz, A., et al.: Guayusa (Ilex guayusa L.) new tea: phenolic and carotenoid composition and antioxidant capacity. J. Sci. Food Agric. **97**, 3929–3936 (2017)
6. Wieser, H., Koehler, P., Scherf, K.A.: Chemistry of wheat gluten proteins: Qualitative composition. Cereal Chem
7. Flores, R.V.: Harina para bizcochos. Ing. Ind. 163–175 (2007)
8. Reyes García, M., Gómez-Sánchez Prieto, I., Espinoza Barrientos, C.: Tablas peruanas de composición de alimentos. Instituto Nacional de Salud (2017)
9. Thiagarajan, Y., de Oliveira, G.G., Iano, Y., Vaz, G.C.: Identification and Analysis of Bacterial Species Present in Cow Dung Fed Microbial Fuel Cell. In: Brazilian Technology Symposium, pp. 16–24. Springer (2023)
10. Watts, B.M., Ylimaki, G.L., Jeffery, L.E., Elías, L.G.: Métodos sensoriales básicos para la evaluación de alimentos (G. Croome, Ed.) Ottawa, Canadá: Centro Internacional de Investigaciones para el desarrollo (1992)
11. de Normalización, I.E.: Rotulado de productos alimenticios para consumo humano. Rotulado Nutr. requisitos. Quito, Ecuador (2011)
12. IBM SPSS Statistics. Software estadístico (20 de octubre de 2022). https://www.ibm.com/pe-es/products/spss-statistics
13. Quintero, J.N., Turbay, S., Gómez, B., Velásquez, C.M.: Contenido de grasa saturada y trans en panes de panaderías de la ciudad de Medellín. Colombia. Rev. Chil. Nutr. **47**, 200–208 (2020)
14. Vargas-Aguilar, P., Hernández-Villalobos, D.: Harinas y almidones de yuca, ñame, camote y ñampí: propiedades funcionales y posibles aplicaciones en la industria alimentaria. Rev. Tecnol. en Marcha. **26**, ág-37 (2013)
15. Vidal, A.R., Zaucedo-Zuñiga, A.L., de Lorena Ramos-García, M.: Propiedades nutrimentales del camote (Ipomoea batatas L.) y sus beneficios en la salud humana. Rev. Iberoam. Tecnol. Postcosecha. 19 (2018)
16. Barrio, R. y Enes, P.: Tablas Lácteos, Cereales y Tubérculos, Legumbres y Frutos Secos. Segunda Edición (2020)

Optimal Charging Coordination of Electric Vehicles Using the Teaching-Learning-Based Optimization Algorithm

Euler B. P. Santos⬥ and Carlos A. Castro(✉)⬥

Pontifical Catholic University of Campinas, Campinas, Brazil
euler.bps2@puccampinas.edu.br, ccastro@puc-campinas.edu.br

Abstract. The automotive market is moving fast toward electrification. Changes in the consumer's consciousness, government policies, and regulations have been driving consumers' acceptance, and consequently the growth of electric vehicle sales. The existing barriers to such sales expansion tend to disappear with time, and it is expected that electric vehicles represent more than 30% of world sales by 2030. The participation by regions, however, should vary from country to country, and one of the main reasons is the insufficient charging infrastructure. The additional electricity demand and the unpredictable behavior of electric vehicle owners will significantly impact the electric energy distribution systems, with consequent instabilities and faults. This research work proposes a solution based on the metaheuristic Teaching-Learning-Based Optimization (TLBO) for the optimal charging of groups of electric vehicles. The proposed method aims to deliver the maximum energy possible to the batteries without violating the limits and constraints of the electric system. The TLBO is an efficient algorithm, which requires few parameters, and shows excellent exploration and exploitation characteristics. Simulation results will be shown for different charging situations and the good-quality results provided by TLBO will be discussed.

Keywords: Electric vehicles · charging · TLBO

1 Introduction

A wide and efficient transportation system is crucial for the organization of modern society. Currently, this system is driven mostly by conventional vehicles powered by internal combustion engines (ICEs). As of 2018, transport accounted for 24% of the CO_2 emissions from energy [1]. Still, according to [1], electrification technologies (including the use of hydrogen) applied to transportation systems could potentially provide significant decarbonization within decades. It is worth mentioning some important initiatives to urge governments to declare a climate emergency [2, 3] which would allow those governments to take decisive actions toward the planet's decarbonization.

Electric vehicle (EV) production has been increasing in the last few years, mostly driven by government incentives and regulations that aim to reduce pollutant emissions and greenhouse effect gases. In 2019, EV sales represented about 3% of the world market, and the expectation is that this share would reach 32% by 2030 [4]. This evolution will occur at variable paces in different regions. For instance, the EV sales share in China will be close to 50%, while in the US they will not surpass 30%, as shown in Fig. 1.

Outlook for EV market share by major region

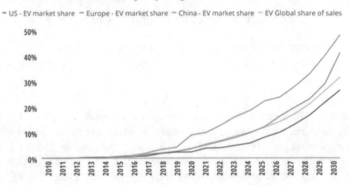

Fig. 1. Participation of EV sales in the market [4].

A successful transportation electrification transition must overcome some crucial barriers, namely, the high prices of EVs, their low autonomy as compared to ICE-based vehicles, and an insufficient number of charging stations (CSs).

EV owners will charge their vehicles in dedicated CSs located at parking lots, shopping facilities, and mainly in their homes. As far as the public CSs, appropriately located CSs should meet the consumers' needs by avoiding unnecessary trips and allowing the battery to be recharged before its minimum charge is reached. By plugging their EVs into a CS, the owners expect that the vehicles' batteries be fully charged. Moreover, the charging process would be as fast as possible.

The authors in [5] evaluated actual data from more than 76 thousand EVs in Beijing, China, for one month. Most users charge their vehicles at night. Users in transit during daylight look for parking lots and specific CSs to charge their vehicles when the state of charge (SOC) is in the range of 20–90%.

Since CSs are supplied by the electrical energy distribution networks, which may impose some limitations on the charging process, optimal coordination is needed. Poor or non-existent coordination may significantly affect the distribution system operation, by increasing power losses and impacting the quality of the service. According to [6], power losses and voltage drops may reach respectively 6% and 10.3% at peak hours, assuming a 30% EV penetration.

In [7], it is shown that the impact of EVs on household consumption is limited, however, the distribution system demand peaks are considerable. A 50% EV penetration would result in a significant increase in the demand peak, as shown in Fig. 2.

Currently, most electrical networks are not prepared to handle this additional demand. The authors of [8] observed that non-coordinated EV charging may cause overloads in electrical network equipment. These overloads reduce equipment's useful lives, leading to precocious equipment replacements.

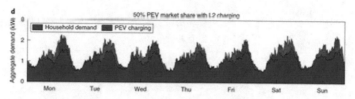

Fig. 2. Per-household average residential electricity demand for an aggregate of 200 sampled households [7].

In [9], a second-order, conic programming method was proposed for the EV coordinated charging process. CSs were connected to the IEEE 32- and 136-bus test distribution systems. The goal was to maximize the EVs' SOC and minimize the charging times. The authors show that non-coordinated charging may lead to distribution system violations, while coordinated charging do not, however, the charging process takes longer.

The EV charging process, especially considering a high EV penetration, cannot be ignored. Non-coordinated charging processes may affect their quality and efficiency as seen from both network and consumers' standpoints.

This work aims to contribute to the development of an efficient charging process, by proposing an optimal, coordinated EV charging procedure that, at the same time, guarantees the fastest charging of all EVs plugged into a CS, and respects the electrical network constraints. To reach this goal, an optimization model is proposed and solved by using the metaheuristics Teaching-Learning Based Optimization (TLBO) [10]. TLBO is an efficient and easy-to-implement metaheuristic, which does not require problem-dependent parameters.

Simulation results will be shown using small-sized cases, to show the effectiveness of the proposed procedure, as well as large ones, to show its efficiency and robustness.

2 Mathematical Model

Consider that a certain number of EVs are connected to a CS. In its turn, the CS is connected to the electric power grid through a distribution transformer, as depicted in Fig. 3. It is assumed that a measuring device is installed and sends information about the transformer's loading to a control circuit, which takes this information as well as information about the vehicles' SOC and coordinates the energy delivered to the EVs within a predetermined time period. The objectives are twofold: (1) the SOC of each EV is the highest possible, and (2) the charging of each EV is as fast as possible.

The proposed mathematical model, based on [9], is

$$\min f = \sum_{v=1}^{NV} \left(SOC_v^{max} - SOC_{v,T} \right)^2 - \sum_{t=1}^{T} \sum_{v=1}^{NV} x_{v,t} \cdot 2^{(T-t)} \tag{1}$$

$$\text{subject } to\, P_{d,t} \geq \sum_{v=1}^{NV} P_v \cdot x_{v,t},\; t = 1, \ldots, T \tag{2}$$

$$SOC_{v,t} = SOC_{v,0} + \eta \cdot \Delta t \cdot P_v \cdot x_{v,t},\; v = 1, \ldots, NV, t = 1 \tag{3}$$

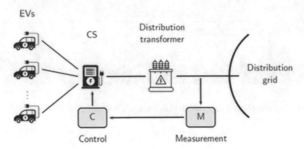

Fig. 3. Illustration of the problem.

$$SOC_{v,t} = SOC_{v,(t-1)} + \eta \cdot \Delta t \cdot P_v \cdot x_{v,t} - \beta \cdot SOC_{v,t}, \ v = 1, \ldots, NV, t = 2, \ldots, T \tag{4}$$

$$SOC_{v,0} \leq SOC_{v,t} \leq SOC_v^{max}, \ v = 1, \ldots, NV \tag{5}$$

$$0 \leq x_{v,t} \leq 1 \tag{6}$$

Equation (1) refers to the objective function, where NV is the number of EVs, SOC_v^{max} is the maximum state of charge of EV v, so, it corresponds to the capacity of its battery. $SOC_{v,T}$ is the state of charge of EV v at time instant T (end of the time period). $x_{v,t}$ is the parcel of P_v (charging capacity of the battery of EV v) delivered to EV v at time period t. The first term of the right-hand side is intended to charge the EVs' batteries the most possible, while the second term forces the charging process to be as fast as possible. Matrix x contains the decision variables of the problem, and its elements are within the range [0, 1], as defined by Eq. (6). Equation (2) guarantees that the power delivered to all batteries does not exceed the transformer capacity $P_{d,t}$ for each time period t. Equations (3) and (4) establish a link between two consecutive time periods, considering the charging capacity of each battery (P_v), the charging efficiency of the battery (η), and the battery self-discharge rate (β). Finally, Eq. (5) establishes the limits on the states of charge of the EVs.

3   Teaching-Learning-Based Optimization

Problems (1)-(6) can be solved by either conventional programming methods or meta-heuristics. In this paper, the solution is obtained by the population-based metaheuristic Teaching-Learning-Based Optimization (TLBO), which was originally proposed by Rao, Savsani, and Vakharia [11]. TLBO is intended to find the optima of continuous functions and was inspired by the relationship dynamics in the classroom.

TLBO, as several other metaheuristics proposed in the literature, presents the ability to solve nonconvex, non-differentiable problems. Those kinds of problems can potentially pose numerical difficulties to conventional mathematical programming methods.

In TLBO the population corresponds to the class members. Each student represents a candidate solution to the optimization problem, that is, a set of decision variables. Students' grades correspond to the fitness function. In the case of a minimization problem, the fitness of each individual is the inverse of his/her grade.

The algorithm is divided into two phases, namely the Teacher phase and the Student phase. In the Teacher phase, the teacher attempts to pass his/her knowledge to the students, while in the Student phase the students share their knowledge among themselves.

Different from other existing metaheuristics in the literature, TLBO does not require problem-dependent parameters to be tuned, which is an important advantage of the method. For instance, Particle Swarm Optimization (PSO) [12] requires the tuning of inertia weight factors and acceleration constants. Also, the Firefly Algorithm (FA) [13] requires the adjustment of the light absorption and the attractiveness coefficients. The Genetic Algorithm (GA) requires the tuning of the mutation rate, the crossover probability, and the selection method [11]. TLBO does not require any such problem-specific parameters to be tuned [14] other than the population size and the number of iterations [10], which is a very interesting feature and makes its implementation much simpler.

TLBO has many advantages in addition to the need for a few parameters [14]. It is also a simple algorithm, easy to understand, computationally fast, provides high accuracy, and has good convergence ability. Moreover, TLBO is flexible, allowing the implementation of variations and improvements. The literature shows that TLBO has been used for solving several power-system-related problems, such as optimal capacitor placement in distribution systems [15], and distribution systems reconfiguration [16], among others.

Consider that the array X contains the decision variables of an optimization problem. Each individual X_i is associated with a value of the objective function, say F_i. Also, consider that (a) X_m is the mean value of all decision variables, and (b) individual X_T is elected as the teacher since it bears the best value of the objective function, F_T.

In the Teacher phase, all students are moved toward the teacher according to

$$X_i^{new} = X_i^{current} + r \cdot [X_T - (T_F \cdot X_m)], \tag{7}$$

where r is a random scalar in the range [0, 1], and the teaching factor T_F can be either 1 or 2, chosen randomly. The new individual replaces the current one if its objective function value shows improvement.

In the Student phase, a pair of students X_i and X_j is chosen arbitrarily and X_i moves according to

$$\begin{cases} X_i^{new} = X_i + r_i \cdot \left(X_i - X_j\right), \text{if} F_i < F_j \\ X_i^{new} = X_i + r_i \cdot \left(X_j - X_i\right), \text{otherwise.} \end{cases} \tag{8}$$

X_i^{new} replaces X_i in case its objective function value shows improvement. The algorithm for TLBO is described below, where the population size is N_p.

Algorithm - TLBO
1. Generate the initial population $X_i, i = 1, ..., N_p$.

Teacher phase
2. Compute the mean individual $X_m = mean(X)$.
3. Choose the Teacher X_T.
4. Compute direction $\Delta = r \cdot (X_T - T_F \cdot X_m)$, where r is a random number in the range $[0,1]$ and T_F is the teaching factor, randomly chosen as either 1 or 2.
5. For each individual i, do
    a. Obtain new individual $X_i^{new} = X_i^{current} + \Delta, i = 1, ..., N_p$.
    b. If $X_i^{current}$ is better than X_i^{new}, maintain $X_i^{current}$ in the population, else, do $X_i^{current} \leftarrow X_i^{new}$.

Student phase
6. For each individual $X_i, i = 1, ..., N_p$, do
    a. Choose an individual X_j randomly.
    b. If individual X_i is better than X_j, then do $Best = X_i$ and $Worst = X_j$. Else do $Best = X_j$ and $Worst = X_i$.
    c. Compute $\Delta = Best - Worst$.
    d. Obtain a new individual $X_i^{new} = X_i + r \cdot \Delta$.
    e. If X_i is better than X_i^{new}, maintain X_i in the population, else, do $X_i \leftarrow X_i^{new}$.
7. If the stopping criterion was met, stop. Else, go back to step 2.

4 Simulation Results

The proposed method for solving problems (1)-(6) through the TLBO algorithm was implemented using GNU Octave 7.2.0 [17], in a laptop with an i5 processor and 8GB RAM. A total of three simulation cases are shown to evaluate the performance of TLBO and the quality of the results.

Table 1 shows the parameters associated with each simulation. All parameters were defined in Sects. 2 and 3. Without loss of generality, the batteries are considered 100% efficient and do not self-discharge. A maximum of 1,000 iterations was set to allow a full appreciation of the evolution of the iterative process.

4.1 Case 1

In this simulation case, the power available from the transformer P_d is less than the total power charging capacities of the batteries (150 kW). The simulation results are summarized in Fig. 4. Figures 4(a)–4(c) show that the vehicles' batteries are fully charged by time period 4. Figure 4(d) shows the evolution of the objective function along the iterations. The high values at the first iterations indicate that some constraints are violated. Afterward, TLBO converges quickly. Figure 4(e) shows a closer view of the evolution of the objective function. It is clear that 1,000 iterations are not necessary for obtaining very good quality solutions.

Table 1. Parameters for the three simulation cases.

Parameter	Case 1	Case 2	Case 3
NV	3	3	3
T	10	10	10
P_d	70	20	70
P_v	[50 50 50]	[50 50 50]	[10 5 30]
η	1	1	1
β	0	0	0
SOC_0	[15 16 25]	[80 10 10]	[80 10]
SOC^{max}	[100 100 100]	[100 100 100]	[100 100 100]
N_p	70	70	70
It_{max}	1,000	1,000	1,000

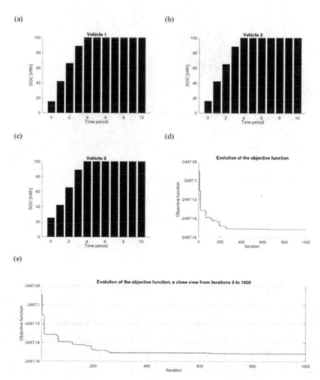

Fig. 4. Simulation results for Case 1.

4.2   Case 2

In this case, the availability of the transformer decreased from 70 kW to 20 kW. Also, two vehicles present low initial SOCs, while the third one has a high SOC from start. Figure 5 shows the simulation results. The limitation in the availability of the supplying transformer implies a longer time for the batteries to fully charge.

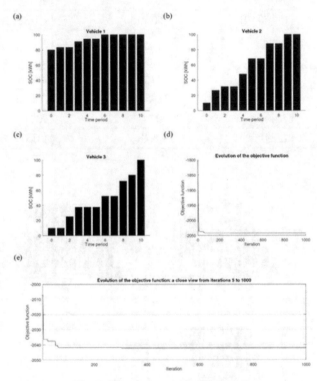

Fig. 5. Simulation results for Case 2.

4.3   Case 3

In this case, the transformer's availability (70 kW) is larger than the total charging capacity of the batteries (45 kW altogether). Once more, two vehicles present low initial SOCs, while the third one has a high SOC from start. Also, the batteries have different charging power capacities. Figure 6 shows the simulation results. The batteries from vehicles 1 and 3 end up fully charged, however, the charging rates are different. Note that vehicle 1 is fully charged before vehicle 3. Also, vehicle 2 has a small charging power capacity, so its final SOC is around 60%.

The computational times for the three cases were 124, 132, and 131 s, respectively. Note that the program was implemented in an interpreted language and that 1,000 iterations were run for each case. Considering also that, according to Figs. 4–6, all cases converged after less than half the number of iterations, the performance of the proposed method was very good regarding its computational speed.

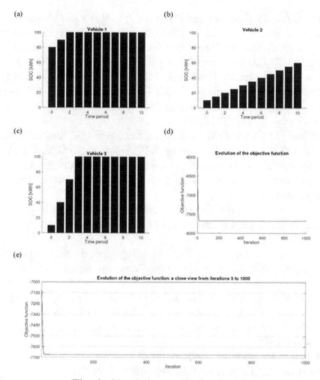

Fig. 6. Simulation results for Case 3.

5 Conclusion

The availability of charging stations is crucial to push forward the adoption of electric vehicles. Additionally, appropriate coordination of the charging processes can potentially increase the confidence of consumers. In this paper, optimal coordination of EVs' charging processes was proposed. The resulting optimization model was solved by the metaheuristic Teaching-Learning-Based Optimization. This metaheuristic showed to be easy to implement and efficient. The simulation results showed that optimal coordination can minimize the non-delivered energy to the EVs' batteries as well as the charging time. In this research, the focus was on the optimal charging coordination itself, and a constraint was added to guarantee that the charging process does not cause any violation in the distribution grid.

References

1. Ritchie H.: Cars, planes, trains: where do CO2 emissions from transport come from? (2020) https://ourworldindata.org/co2-emissions-from-transport. (Accessed 12 Jul 2022)
2. The Climate Mobilization: Our leaders are asleep at the wheel (2022) https://www.theclimatemobilization.org/climate-emergency/. (Accessed 12 Jul 2022)
3. Climate Emergency Declaration (2022). https://climateemergencydeclaration.org/. (Accessed 22 Jul 2022)

4. Quak, E.: The Covid-19 pandemic and the future of Global Value Chains (GVCs) (2020)
5. Sun, M., Shao, C., Zhuge, C., Wang, P., Yang, X., Wang, S.: Uncovering travel and charging patterns of private electric vehicles with trajectory data: evidence and policy implications. Transportation , 1–31 (2021). https://doi.org/10.1007/s11116-021-10216-1
6. Clement-Nyns, K., Haesen, E., Driesen, J.: The impact of charging plug-in hybrid electric vehicles on a residential distribution grid. IEEE Trans. power Syst. **25**, 371–380 (2009)
7. Muratori, M.: Impact of uncoordinated plug-in electric vehicle charging on residential power demand. Nat. Energy. **3**, 193–201 (2018)
8. Verzijlbergh, R.A., Grond, M.O.W., Lukszo, Z., Slootweg, J.G., Ilic, M.D.: Network impacts and cost savings of controlled EV charging. IEEE Trans. Smart Grid. **3**, 1203–1212 (2012)
9. Sá, S.M., Pereira, M.D.I., Franco, J.F.: Linear programming applied to the EV coordinated charging in distribution networks. In: Brazilian Congress on Automatics (CBA), pp. 1–8 (2020) [In Portuguese]
10. Rao, R.V., Savsani, V.J., Vakharia, D.P.: Teaching–learning-based optimization: an optimization method for continuous non-linear large scale problems. Inf. Sci. (Ny) **183**, 1–15 (2012)
11. Rao, R.V., Savsani, V.J., Vakharia, D.P.: Teaching–learning-based optimization: a novel method for constrained mechanical design optimization problems. Comput. Des. **43**, 303–315 (2011)
12. Gaing, Z.-L.: Particle swarm optimization to solving the economic dispatch considering the generator constraints. IEEE Trans. power Syst. **18**, 1187–1195 (2003)
13. Yang, X.-S.: Firefly algorithm, stochastic test functions and design optimisation. arXiv Prepr. arXiv1003.1409 (2010)
14. Xue, R., Wu, Z.: A survey of application and classification on teaching-learning-based optimization algorithm. IEEE Access. **8**, 1062–1079 (2020)
15. Sultana, S., Roy, P.K.: Optimal capacitor placement in radial distribution systems using teaching learning based optimization. Int. J. Electr. Power Energy Syst. **54**, 387–398 (2014)
16. Kumar, D., Gupta, V.K.: Optimal reconfiguration of primary power distribution system using modified Teaching learning based optimization algorithm. In: 2016 IEEE 1st International Conference on Power Electronics, Intelligent Control and Energy Systems (ICPEICES), pp. 1–5. IEEE (2016)
17. Eaton, J.W., Bateman, D., Hauberg, S.: GNU Octave version 3.0. 1 manual: a high-level interactive language for numerical computations. SoHo Books (2007)

Evaluation of a Double Combustion Stove with Solid Biomass in the High Andean Zone of Puno - Peru

A. Holguino Huarza$^{(\boxtimes)}$ ⓘ and V. Román Salinas ⓘ

Universidad Nacional del Altiplano, Puno, Peru
aholguinohh1@gmail.com

Abstract. In the high Andean areas of the Puno region, accessibility to conventional energy is limited. For this reason, biomass provides the necessary energy for cooking through direct combustion, using the traditional stove (TS), which generates polluting emissions and causes health problems for the people who use these stoves. This article shows the results of the evaluation of the thermal efficiency in the transfer of energy and the generation of carbon dioxide (CO_2) during the combustion of solid biomass in the proposed improved stove (PIS). The natural draft PIS with double combustion was designed, with 2 kW of power output, for solid fuels composed of dry llama manure (DLM), dried beef manure (DCM), and dry firewood (DF) or dry wood residues. To evaluate the performance of the PIS, the boiling water test (BWT) was used. Based on BWT, a reduction of 19.4% in fuel consumption was estimated for the PIS concerning TS. In conclusion, the PIS performed better than the TS with a 17.06% reduction in CO_2 emission. The thermal efficiency of the PIS indicated an increase of 7.5% concerning the thermal efficiency of the TS.

Keywords: Double Combustion Stove · Thermal Efficiency · Solid Biomass

1 Introduction

Due to the inaccessibility of conventional energy, the inhabitants of the high Andean areas of Peru use biomass to cook their food. According to [1], in Asia, Africa, and America, more than three million people cook with biomass; therefore, the adoption of cleaner cooking technologies that can reduce the emission of air pollutants in the home is needed.

Improved stoves that use solid biomass are designed to improve the efficiency of energy transfer and reduce the emission of pollutants into the living space. The adoption and impact of improved stoves that burn biomass were acceptable, but the use of traditional stoves persisted in more than half of the houses [1], generating atmospheric air pollution and consuming more solid biomass.

The combustion of solid biomass is one of the largest sources of carbon emissions, which pollute the environment and affect health [2]. Combustion is a process of oxidation of biomass components at high temperatures in the presence of necessary oxygen, during

© The Author(s), under exclusive license to Springer Nature Switzerland AG 2023
Y. Iano et al. (Eds.): BTSym 2022, SIST 353, pp. 371–381, 2023.
https://doi.org/10.1007/978-3-031-31007-2_34

this process heat, carbon dioxide, water, and ash are released. People who use stoves with solid biomass have health problems, whose origin is indoor air pollution due to incomplete combustion of biomass through TS, which causes the death of more than 1.45 million people each year. Long-term and short-term exposure to these emissions is associated with a higher risk of contracting respiratory and cardiovascular diseases, lung cancer, and having a weakened immune system, especially in women and children, since they are the ones who use the stove in the most developing countries [3]. In addition, the production and combustion of charcoal are responsible for very high greenhouse gas emissions per unit of energy [4]. The inefficient burning of biomass leads to a higher level of domestic air pollution, the concentration of smoke due to poor combustion that pollutes domestic air, is strongly related to the type of roof of the house and the existing ventilation inside the house [5]. Likewise, stoves that gasify fuel are attractive due to their potential to reduce environmental pollution [6].

Biomass energy is one of the first sources of energy for humanity, especially in rural areas, where it is often the only accessible and affordable source of energy. The transformation of biomass energy into heat energy takes place during combustion, this being a process of oxidation of biomass components at high temperatures in the presence of necessary oxygen, during combustion heat is released, as well as carbon dioxide, water, and ash. In the process of photosynthesis, biomass absorbs the same amount of carbon dioxide during plant growth and emits it during combustion. Therefore, biomass helps to recycle atmospheric carbon dioxide and decreases the greenhouse effect [7]. According to [8], the annual use of biomass energy currently represents approximately 8 to 14% of the world's energy consumption. Therefore, interventions in improved clean cookstove solutions with high energy efficiency, low specific fuel consumption, and reduced emissions characteristics are important renewable energy technology with far-reaching environmental and health benefits both locally and globally [9]. According to [10], the main greenhouse gases that result from the combustion of solid biomass, other than carbon dioxide, have a potential global warming effect. However, the negative impact of using the biomass stove is usually considered carbon neutral, as the carbon emitted from biomass combustion does not contribute to climate change and the net emissions from biomass burning are zero. On the other hand, the use of cow manure as fuel will reduce pollution and environmental degradation, by minimizing the waste of manure in livestock and agricultural production [11].

2 Materials and Methods

The proposed improved stove (PIS) represented in the diagram (see Fig. 1a), was designed for a power output of 2 kW based on the local needs and habits of a typical family in the rural household [12]. The PIS in the solid biomass combustion process has an adequate performance (see Fig. 1b).

The amount of energy supplied by the fuel fed to the stove allows calculating the rate of fuel consumption using Eq. (1).

$$FCR = \frac{Q_{out}}{CV_b \times \eta_b} \tag{1}$$

where Q_{out} represents the power output, CV_b is the calorific value of the biomass and η_b is the efficiency of the stove.

Table 1. Required parameters and assumptions for the design of the PIS.

Description	Symbol	Value	Authors/Remark
Energy demand (kW)	$\dot{Q}_{out}$	2	[13]
The efficiency of the cookstove (%)	η	25	[12]
Calorific value of firewood (MJ/kg)	CV	19.2	[14]
Eucalyptus calorific value (MJ/kg)	CV	21.8	[15]
Beef manure (MJ/kg)	CV	15.21	[16]
Density air (kg/m^3)	ρ_{air}	1.29	Assumed
Bulk density of biomass (kg/m^3)	ρ_b	450–850	[12]
Superficial velocity (m/s)	u_s	0.05	[17]
Specific gasification rate (kg/m^2.h)	SGR	100	[18]

2.1 Reactor Dimension Design

The diameter of the reactor has been determined by Eq. (2).

$$D = \sqrt{\frac{1.27 \times FCR}{SGR}} \tag{2}$$

where SGR is the specific gasification rate.

The height of the reactor, measured from the height of the weight supports and the height of the vessel supports, is represented by Eq. (3).

$$H_t = \frac{SGR \times T}{\rho_{max}} \tag{3}$$

where $\rho_{max} = 850\,\text{kg/m}^3$ represents the maximum fuel density.

Considering that the reactor is fed from the bottom. The lower height of the reactor measured from the weight supports to the intermediate grid, is represented by Eq. (4).

$$H_b = \frac{SGR \times T}{\rho_{min}} \tag{4}$$

where $\rho_{min} = 450\,\text{kg/m}^3$ is the minimum density of the fuel; while $T = 1.5\text{h}$ represent the work factor of the PIS.

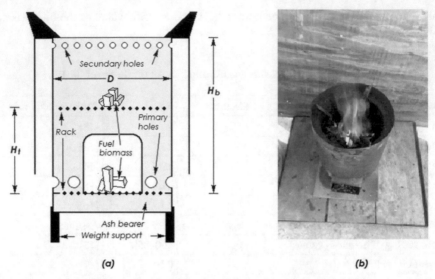

Fig. 1. Diagram of the PIS, (b) Photograph of the evaluated PIS

2.2 Primary Air Requirement for Gasification

Many improved stoves are equipped with fans called forced drafts, to create high-velocity jets of air, a proper mixture of air with fuel, which improves combustion efficiency and heat transfer to the cooking vessel. According to [19], forced draft in stoves supplies enough air for proper mixing, therefore complete combustion with very low emissions is possible [19].

According to [17], the primary air is the main responsible for gasification. Therefore, the fuel combustion rate is 1.5 times; while for secondary air it is 4.5 times. These primary and secondary air requirements are represented by Eqs. (5) and (6) respectively.

$$P_a = 1.5 \times FCR \tag{5}$$

$$S_a = 4.5 \times FCR \tag{6}$$

According to [12], the total area of the holes for the primary air flow is determined by Eq. (7)

$$A_p = \frac{P_a}{\rho_a \times u_p} \tag{7}$$

where the superficial air velocity is $u_p = 0.05$ m/s [17].

In the primary combustion stage, the airflow must be homogeneous through the bed, therefore small openings were made to complete the remaining area, determined by Eq. (8).

$$A_r = A_p - A_{inlet} \tag{8}$$

2.3 Secondary Air Requirement

The secondary airflow to the stove is also uniform, through an opening whose area is determined by Eq. (9).

$$A_s = \frac{S_a}{\rho_a \times u_s}$$ (9)

According to [17], the airflow in this part must be 20 times greater than the surface speed, that is $20u_p = 1$ m/s.

The holes for the secondary air flow must be made 2 cm below the top of the stove [12].

The parameters that characterize the design of the PIS which are represented in Table 2, are determined by the corresponding equations and with the data represented in Table 1.

Table 2. Parameters that characterize the PIS.

Description	Symbol	Value
Energy demand (kW)	$\dot{Q}_{out}$	2
Fuel consumption rate (kg/h)	FCR	1.89
Reactor diameter (m)	D	0.16
Top reactor height (m)	H_t	0.17
Bottom reactor height (m)	H_b	0.33
Primary window opening (cm^2)	A_P	97
Secondary window opening (cm^2)	A_s	14.5

2.4 Determination of Thermal Efficiency

For the quantification of the thermal efficiency of the PIS, it was carried out by means of the BWT, for which the masses of the water, of the solid biomasses necessary to reach the boiling of the water, and that of the aluminum container were determined. Subsequently, the PIS was turned on and the water temperature readings were taken periodically with a frequency of 0.2 Hz until the water reached the local boiling temperature of approximately 87.7 °C. The thermal efficiency was calculated using the principle of conservation of energy.

The heat used and energy produced were determined with Eqs. (10) and (11) respectively.

$$Q_{out} = \left(m_v \times c_{pv} + m_w \times c_{pw}\right)(t_2 - t_1)$$ (10)

$$Q_{in} = (m_b \times CV_b)$$ (11)

Therefore, the thermal efficiency of the PIS has been determined by Eq. (12).

$$\eta = \frac{Q_{out}}{Q_{in}} \qquad (12)$$

where m_v is the mass of the aluminum container, m_w is the mass of water, c_{pv} is the specific heat of aluminum, c_{pw} is the specific heat of water, t_1 is the initial temperature of the water, t_2 is the final temperature or local boiling temperature of the water, m_b is the mass of biomass, and CV_b is the heating value or higher heating value of biomass.

2.5 CO2 Emission Control Procedure

To sample the emission of CO2 during combustion, a quantifier inserted in the chimney was used, and the surrounding hood, whose geometric shape is an inverted circular cone, was placed on the PIS. The smoke escapes into the environment through the chimney located at the top of the hood or the apex of the cone. While for the traditional stove (TS), the CO2 quantifier was installed in the upper part of the exterior wall of a kitchen, through which the smoke emanates into the surrounding environment.

2.6 Procedure for Evaluating the Efficiency of the Stove

The thermal efficiency of the PIS has been evaluated with BWT, through the comparison with the thermal efficiency of the TS, using DLM, DCM, and DF, as fuels commonly used in the high Andean rural area of Puno.

According to [20], solid biomass consisting of dry manure, whose energy density varies from 13 to 19 MJ kg^{-1}, can be burned directly as an alternative substitute for firewood. Therefore, for the combustion of the different types of biomasses, the stove was heated with 300 g of firewood, and subsequently, the necessary amount of dry fuel was used to boil 2.5 L of water.

3 Results and Discussion

3.1 Thermal Efficiency of the PIS Concerning TS

When DCM was used as fuel, during simultaneous combustion in the PIS and TS, various comparison parameters have been determined that are related to the efficiency of both stoves, these are shown in Table 3.

Fuel consumption in the PIS has been 19.4% less than in the TS (see Table 3); however, in investigations carried out by [21], the improved biomass stove, where its fuel consumption was 1.3 times higher, found that the thermal efficiency was 35%. Regarding the useful energy that heated the water, in the PIS it has been registered as 47.9% greater than in TS. The PIS has higher thermal efficiency than the TS by 83.3%. For a global comparison, the efficiency of the PIS is 7.5% higher than the efficiency of the TS (see Table 3). According to [22], the thermal efficiency of traditional stoves in China was generally less than 10%, but after improvement, the thermal efficiency of most improved stoves is around 20%. According to [23], thermal insulation of the

Table 3. Combustion of DCM in the PIS and TS.

Description	PIS	TS
Cow manure (kg)	0.25	0.31
Combustion time (min)	20.8	21.7
Fuel energy (MJ)	3.8	4.7
Useful energy (kJ)	625.4	422.8
Stove efficiency (%)	16.5	9
Firepower (kW)	3.04	3.6
Fuel consumption rate (kg/h)	0.72	0.86

stove with insulating material can reduce biomass consumption and smoke emissions and increase thermal efficiency compared to traditional stoves. The PIS has been built with metallic material and without external insulation, so the efficiencies found have been lower than those obtained by other researchers.

During the combustion process in the PIS than the TS, the heat transfer to the water contained in the aluminum pot is greater, because the temperature range is greater (see Fig. 2). This is consistent with the useful energy captured by both stoves, as indicated in Table 3.

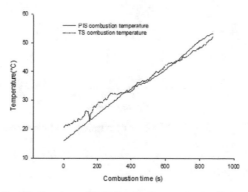

Fig. 2. Combustion of DCM to heat water in the PIS and TS

On the other hand, the combustion of DLM, DCM, and DF was carried out in the PIS, to be evaluated using the BWT, obtaining the values of the parameters shown in Table 4, which evaluate the thermal efficiency of the stove for the three solid bio-masses mentioned.

The amount of fuel needed to bring 2.5 L of water to a boil are very similar. For the energy delivered by the fuel for the boiling of water, it is greater by 18.2% for the combustion of DF concerning DLM and it is also greater by 41.3% for the combustion of DF concerning DCM (see Table 4). The thermal efficiency of the PIS is higher for DCM combustion by 43.5% and 20.4% concerning DF and DLM, respectively (see

Table 4. Specification of BWT through the combustion of solid biomass in the PIS.

Descripción	DF	DLM	DCM
Fuel needed to boil water (kg)	0.34	0.36	0.3
Combustion time (min)	8.25	16.3	13.2
Energy delivered by the fuel (MJ)	6.5	5.5	4.6
Useful energy (kJ)	750.3	749.3	753.5
Stove efficiency (%)	11.5	13.7	16.5
Power delivered to the water (kW)	1.5	0.76	0.95

Table 4). Also, Table 4 shows that the power delivered by the combustion of DF is higher concerning DCM and DLM by 57.9% and 97.4% respectively. This situation is consistent with what is shown graphically (see Fig. 3), where a greater slope is observed for the combustion of DF, which represents better firepower provided by the combustion of DF concerning the combustion of DCM and DLM Respectively.

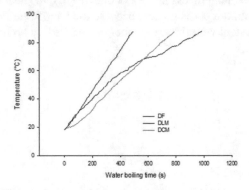

Fig. 3. Boiling of water by burning solid biomass.

3.2   CO2 Concentration

Using the flue gas analyzer, gas samples were taken directly from the center of the stack cross-section to measure CO_2 concentrations, the results of which are represented in the bar graph (see Fig. 4).

The smoke emitted by the combustion of DF through the PIS has a content of 15% less CO_2 than in the TS. While for DCM combustion it is 17.06% less (see Fig. 4).

The injection of secondary air in the combustion reduces the massive emissions of particulate matter, carbon monoxide, and black carbon by at least 90% concerning a traditional stove fire [24]. According to [25], the efficiency increases, while the CO_2 emission decreases with altitude, and the duration of the WBT is shorter for the hot test than for the cold test. This suggests that the use of stoves is recommended in higher altitude Andean areas; it also agrees with the PIS that it is best combusted with the biomass used when it had been previously lit with materials such as wax or kerosene.

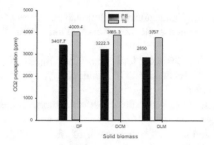

Fig. 4. Average value of CO2 in the combustion of DF and DCM with the PIS and TS.

High moisture and ash content in biomass fuels can cause ignition and combustion problems [7]. Likewise, the PIS CO2 emissions are within an acceptable range; however, refueling during operation caused transient increases in CO2 emissions. Therefore, gradual feeding is suggested. In the TS, on the other hand, even though refueling is also gradual, smoke emission is due to lower efficiency and poor combustion, represented by a difference of at least 17%.

4 Conclusions

During DCM combustion, the PIS efficiency is 7.5% higher than the TS efficiency. Concerning the combustion of DCM, DLM, and DF through the PIS, the fuel that causes the best thermal efficiency is DCM, being higher by 5 and 2.8% compared to the combustion of DF and DLM respectively (see Fig. 4). In the smoke emitted during the combustion of both DF and DCM, the propagation of CO2 increased by more than 17.7% with the PIS and by more than 20.6% with the TS, respectively (see Fig. 4).

Improved stoves such as the PIS have greater thermal efficiency, which is why they allow lower specific fuel consumption and emissions are reduced. Both factors are very important in renewable energy technology with far-reaching environmental and health benefits both locally and globally. Fuels derived or similar to DF are those cause greater efficiency of the PIS, allowing less time for the boiling of water (see Fig. 3).

References

1. Díaz-Vásquez, M.A., Díaz-Manchay, R.J., León-Jiménez, F.E., Thompson, L.M., Troncoso, K., Failoc-Rojas, V.E.: Adoption and impact of improved cookstoves in Lambayeque, Peru, 2017. Glob. Health Promot. **27**, 123–130 (2020)
2. Kaur-Sidhu, M., Ravindra, K., Mor, S., John, S.: Emission factors and global warming potential of various solid biomass fuel-cook stove combinations. Atmos. Pollut. Res. **11**, 252–260 (2020)
3. Patel, M., et al.: Effect of exposure to biomass smoke from cooking fuel types and eye disorders in women from hilly and plain regions of Nepal. Br. J. Ophthalmol. **106**, 141–148 (2022)
4. Maes, W.H., Verbist, B.: Increasing the sustainability of household cooking in developing countries: policy implications. Renew. Sustain. Energy Rev. **16**, 4204–4221 (2012)

5. Fandiño-Del-Rio, M., et al.: Household air pollution exposure and associations with household characteristics among biomass cookstove users in Puno. Peru. Environ. Res. **191**, 110028 (2020)
6. Torres-Rojas, D., Deng, L., Shannon, L., Fisher, E.M., Joseph, S., Lehmann, J.: Carbon and nitrogen emissions rates and heat transfer of an indirect pyrolysis biomass cookstove. Biomass Bioenerg. **127**, 105279 (2019)
7. Demirbas, A.: Combustion characteristics of different biomass fuels. Prog. energy Combust. Sci. **30**, 219–230 (2004)
8. Liu, Y., Shen, Y.: Modelling and optimisation of biomass injection in ironmaking blast furnaces. Prog. Energy Combust. Sci. **87**, 100952 (2021)
9. Boafo-Mensah, G., Darkwa, K.M., Laryea, G.: Effect of combustion chamber material on the performance of an improved biomass cookstove. Case Stud. Therm. Eng. **21**, 100688 (2020)
10. Ravindra, K., et al.: Real-time monitoring of air pollutants in seven cities of North India during crop residue burning and their relationship with meteorology and transboundary movement of air. Sci. Total Environ. **690**, 717–729 (2019)
11. Hamid, N.A., Muaddah, H.A., Afandy, M.D.N.: Biomass Briqmure: BBQ Briquettes fuel source from cow manure. In: First International Conference on Science, Technology, Engineering and Industrial Revolution (ICSTEIR 2020), pp. 457–460. Atlantis Press (2021)
12. Gupta, A., Mulukutla, A.N.V., Gautam, S., TaneKhan, W., Waghmare, S.S., Labhasetwar, N.K.: Development of a practical evaluation approach of a typical biomass cookstove. Environ. Technol. Innov. **17**, 100613 (2020)
13. Arora, P., Das, P., Jain, S., Kishore, V.V.N.: A laboratory based comparative study of Indian biomass cookstove testing protocol and Water Boiling Test. Energy Sustain. Dev. **21**, 81–88 (2014)
14. Quiroga, G., Castrillón, L., Fernández-Nava, Y., Marañón, E.: Physico-chemical analysis and calorific values of poultry manure. Waste Manag. **30**, 880–884 (2010)
15. Chen, W.-H., Peng, J., Bi, X.T.: A state-of-the-art review of biomass torrefaction, densification and applications. Renew. Sustain. Energy Rev. **44**, 847–866 (2015)
16. Shen, X., Huang, G., Yang, Z., Han, L.: Compositional characteristics and energy potential of Chinese animal manure by type and as a whole. Appl. Energy. **160**, 108–119 (2015)
17. Mukunda, H., S., D., Paul, P., N K S, R., Yagnaraman, M., Kumar, D., Deogaonkar, M.: Gasifier stoves: Science, technology and field outreach. Curr. Sci. **98**, 627–638 (2010)
18. Chopra, S., Jain, A.: A review of fixed bed gasification systems for biomass (2007)
19. Samal, C., Mishra, P.C., Das, D.: Design modifications and performance of biomass cookstoves-A review. In: AIP Conference Proceedings, p. 20002. AIP Publishing LLC (2020)
20. Guo, M., Li, H., Baldwin, B., Morrison, J.: Thermochemical processing of animal manure for bioenergy and biochar. Anim. Manure Prod. Charact. Environ. Concerns, Manag. **67**, 255–274 (2020)
21. Rasoulkhani, M., Ebrahimi-Nik, M., Abbaspour-Fard, M.H., Rohani, A.: Comparative evaluation of the performance of an improved biomass cook stove and the traditional stoves of Iran. Sustain. Environ. Res. **28**, 438–443 (2018)
22. Shen, G.: Quantification of emission reduction potentials of primary air pollutants from residential solid fuel combustion by adopting cleaner fuels in China. J. Environ. Sci. **37**, 1–7 (2015)
23. Okino, J., Komakech, A.J., Wanyama, J., Ssegane, H., Olomo, E., Omara, T.: Performance characteristics of a cooking stove improved with sawdust as an insulation material. J. Renew. Energy 2021 (2021)

24. Caubel, J.J., Rapp, V.H., Chen, S.S., Gadgil, A.J.: Practical design considerations for secondary air injection in wood-burning cookstoves: An experimental study. Dev. Eng. **5**, 100049 (2020)
25. Pérez-Bayer, J.F., Graciano-Bustamante, D.S., Gómez-Betancur, J.A.: Caracterización energética y emisiones de una estufa de cocción ecoeficiente con biomasa a diferentes altitudes. Ing. Mecánica. **16**, 227–237 (2013)

Characterization of the Bones of Different Bovine Breeds Based on the Microarchitecture of the Bone Tissue

Rogério Erbereli[1]([⊠]) [iD], Italo Leite de Camargo[2] [iD], Cintia Righetti Marcondes[3] [iD],
Rymer Ramiz Tullio[3] [iD], Carlos Alberto Fortulan[1] [iD],
and João Manoel Domingos de Almeida Rollo[4] [iD]

[1] Mechanical Engineering Department, São Carlos School of Engineering,
University of São Paulo, São Carlos, Brazil
rogerio.erbereli@usp.br
[2] Federal Institute of Education, Science, and Technology of São Paulo, São Paulo,
Itaquaquecetuba, Brazil
[3] Brazilian Agricultural Research Corporation, Livestock Southeast, São Carlos, Brazil
[4] Materials Engineering Department, São Carlos School of Engineering,
University of São Paulo, São Carlos, Brazil

Abstract. This work deals with the characterization of bone based on the microarchitecture of this tissue, aiming to provide data for the manufacture of xenogenic or biomimetic biomaterials. To carry out the studies animals of the Canchim and Nellore bovine breeds of precise and controlled origin were selected, all having the same biological and biomechanical processes from birth to slaughter that occurred before adulthood. Metatarsal bone samples were prepared and characterized by scanning electron microscopy and optical and energy dispersive spectroscopy. Subsequently, their microhardness, elastic modulus, and resistance to plastic deformation by nanoindentation were analyzed. Finally, the crystal structure of dry bone metatarsals was characterized by X-ray diffraction, obtaining grid, crystal size, and micro-formation by the Rietveld refinement method. The results showed that the bones of the two races showed differences not only visually, in the microscope images, but also statistically in the modulus of elasticity, crystallite size, and Knoop microhardness. However, they presented statistical similarities in hardnesses, calcium and phosphorus ratio, and microstructure (micro deformation and parameters of the network). From the results presented, it can be concluded that despite the breeds having the same breeding protocol, the bones presented some differences in their characterization, and, consequently, the manufacture of biomaterials from these bones must follow different protocols.

Keywords: Crystal structure · Hardness · Hydroxyapatite · Microarchitecture · X-ray diffractions

1 Introduction

Hydroxyapatite from bovine is similar to human cancellous bone in its crystalline and morphologic structure and has been used as a biocompatible bone graft, a type of

© The Author(s), under exclusive license to Springer Nature Switzerland AG 2023
Y. Iano et al. (Eds.): BTSym 2022, SIST 353, pp. 382–390, 2023.
https://doi.org/10.1007/978-3-031-31007-2_35

xenograft [1–4]. This topic has gained even more importance with the recent fabrication of personalized scaffolds for bone repair by 3d printing (additive manufacturing) using hydroxyapatite of bovine origin [5]. It has been accepted as safe material with osteoconductive properties, and still from a renewable source. Mechanical properties and structural parameters involving the crystalline structure of biological (in vivo) hydroxyapatite crystals from cortical bones of bovines of the same breed provide information on hydroxyapatite crystals. It can be used as a bone quality indicator based on microarchitecture [6, 7]. Materials for biomedical applications are constantly subjected to mechanical stresses, and thus they must have parameters such as tensile, compressive, shear, and flexural strength reliably determined [8].

Bone tissues also have the function of being a reservoir of calcium, phosphate, and other ions, storing or releasing them in a controlled manner to maintain the concentration of these important ions in body fluids [9, 10]. The maintenance of the living bone is dependent on the remodeling and regeneration of bone tissue and this is not only a biological process but also electrical, biochemical, and mechanical [11].

Research related to large animals shows a connection between bone quality and bone mineral density (BMD), that is, an evaluation occurs through the relationship of bone mass and volume. Radiographic densitometry is a valid technique for local evaluation of bone in vivo and it is highly correlated with bone ashes and bone minerals [12]; expressing the amount of mineral bone, equivalent in density, in millimeters of aluminum. Although BDM is a key factor to estimate the mechanical strength and fracture risk of the bone, this characterization does not satisfactorily predict the risk of osteoporotic fracture [13–16]. The selection of oxen and their bones for use as a bone graft follows protocols defined by the health agencies of each country that are governed by tracking food, pathology, and treatments. However, there are no specifications on race, age, and other characteristics and the question remains: what implications may arise from this additional control?

This study, in the character of originality, to clarify these inquisitions, aims to characterize the metatarsal bones of different bovine breeds (Canchim and Nelore), fully tracked, through the analysis of the bone microarchitecture as a complementary alternative analysis than the traditional BMD in the radiographic image. In addition, the paper presents bone microarchitecture views by Light Microscopy (LM) and Electronic Scan Microscopy (SEM) complemented by the bone modulus of elasticity, microhardness (Vickers/Knoop), and Vickers nano hardness performed at dry cortical bones.

2 Materials and Methods

2.1 Ethical Aspects and Conditions of Handling

The study followed procedures established and approved by research protocol PRT 05/2015 of the Ethics Committee on Animal Use of Brazilian Agricultural Research Corporation (EMBRAPA) Livestock Southeast, the project being classified as an experiment that causes little or no discomfort or stress to the animal.

The animals came from the Southeast Livestock Research Center of the EMBRAPA, located in the city of São Carlos - SP, at Fazenda Canchim. In this study, the animals remained in the pasture for approximately 20 months; and then they were confined to the GrowSafe® system (a system that measures, without interruption, all the food consumed by cattle 24 h a day). The breeding, nutrition, handling, animal welfare, and slaughtering process are in accordance with: Normative Instruction No. 46, of October 6, 2011; Normative Instruction No. 3, of January 17, 2000, and Normative Instruction. No. 56, of November 6, 2008, respectively [17–19].

2.2 Pre-selection of Samples and Description for Samples

Twenty cattle were selected, and ten of each breed were studied (Canchim and Nelore). The left posterior metatarsal bones of the animals were chosen because they are the ones that carry the greatest mechanical load, and thus represent strong bone remodeling activity, besides maintaining the standardization of the samples. In the preparation and characterization of the samples, the steps according to Fig. 1 were followed.

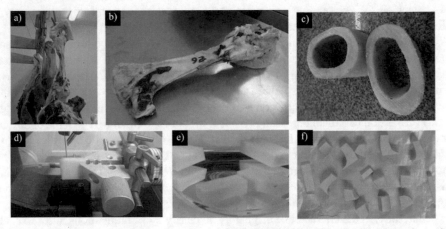

Fig. 1. Sample processing flow, a) section of the leg; b) origin identification, cleaning with mechanical deboning of metatarsal bone; c) samples collected in ring format, d) specimens obtained by cutting the ring-shaped samples; e) specimens boil at 100 °C for 5 min in hydrogen peroxide (100 volumes) for degradation of the organic part and decontaminated in Milli-Q water at room temperature; f) The specimens were kept in an oven at 100 °C for 24 h.

2.3 Light Microscopy and Electronic Scan Microscopy

The images of LM (LEICA microscope, model Leitz DM-RX) were captured with the program Motic Images Version Plus 2.0; and the SEM (FEI - equipped with an electron source called Field Emission Gum). The samples were analyzed longitudinally, according to the direction of higher loads in the animal metatarsal bones, which is the axial direction of the bone.

2.4 Modulus of Elasticity

The nanoindentation (Inspect F-50 microscope) was obtained from 20 indentations in different regions of the samples for each of the bovine breeds. Thus, the modulus of elasticity, microhardness, and nano hardness were measured. The fact that the animals were slaughtered at 24 months, at the puberty-adult limit, resulted in incomplete mineralization and a decrease in mechanical properties values [20].

2.5 Nano Hardness Vickers and Microhardness Vickers and Knoop

The Vickers nano hardness (LEICA VMHT MOT microdurometer) was obtained through 20 indentations performed in different regions of the samples of each breed. Vickers and Knoop microhardness (LEICA VMHT MOT microdurometer) were obtained through 20 indentations, a load of 200 gr at 15 s. This test was also carried out in different regions of the Canchim and Nelore breeds.

2.6 Analysis by Dispersive Energy Spectroscopy – Ca/P Relationship

EDX analysis (Shimadzu, EDX720, Japan) was performed three times for each bone sample, obtaining a total of 60 trials, 30 for the Canchim breed and another 30 for the Nelore breed.

2.7 X-RAY Diffractograms and Rietveld Refinement Method – Network Parameter, Crystal Size, and Microdeformations

X-ray diffraction (Shimadzu, model XRD7000, Japan) was performed from the powder of bones, in the 2θ range from $10°$ to $80°$ at $2°$ per minute. Network crystallite parameters and crystalline micro deformations were obtained by the Rietveld refinement method implemented with the General Structure Analysis System (GSAS) program and, through EXPGUI (graphic interface). For each bone sample, three tests were performed, getting a total of 60 diffractograms, 30 Canchim breed and other 30 for the Nelore breed.

Once the refinement sequence was performed, it was possible to obtain the image of the relationship between the original diffractogram and the refracted (liveplot function). The lstview function allowed us to verify the convergence of the refinement, and to obtain all the necessary parameters for the calculation of micro deformations, size of crystallite, and network parameters.

2.8 Statistics

Statistical analysis was performed using the Microsoft® Excel® 2019 MSO program (version 2202 Build), with the help of the Real Statistics package. First, a descriptive analysis of the data was performed, obtaining means, deviation patterns, medians, and minimum and maximum values. Then, tests based on Shapiro-Wilk were performed to verify normality [21]. The samples that presented normal distribution were tested by the t-test. In addition, the homogeneity of the normal distribution was verified by Levene´s test. The p-values of the samples that showed homogeneity were verified via the t-test considering two independent samples with equal variances, while the p-values of the samples that did not show homogeneity were obtained considering two independent samples with unequal variances. On the other hand, the groups that did not present normality in their distribution were tested via the Mann-Whitney Test for Two Independent Samples. The application of all tests followed a confidence interval of 95%.

3   Results

3.1   Light Microscopy and Electronic Scan Microscopy

The LM images of specimens are represented in Fig. 2.

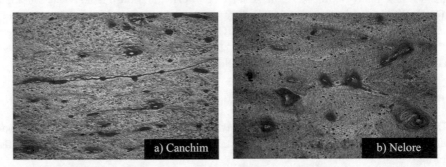

Fig. 2. Metatarsal bones, a) Canchim breed and b) Nelore breed.

SEM images performed on the cortical part of the metatarsal bone exhibit similar characteristics between breeds, as shown in Fig. 3, with the presence of Havers channels, osteocytes (lamellae), and cracks inherent to the formation of bovine bone. They are detailed in the image on the right side.

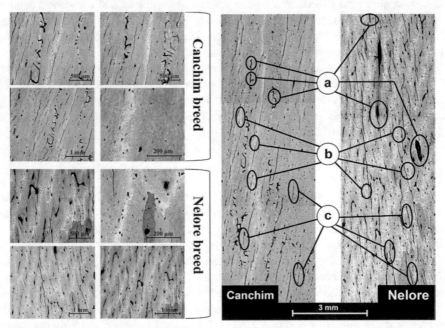

Fig. 3. SEM images from the longitudinal region of Canchim and Nelore highlighting Havers channels (a), gaps occupied by osteocytes (b), and cracks (c).

3.2 Modulus of Elasticity; Nanohardness Vickers; Microhardness Vickers and Knoop; Analysis by EDS - Ca/P Relationship; Network Parameters (a, b, and c); Crystallite Size and Microdeformation

The results of the parameters studied are presented in Table 1. Both breeds presented statistical similarity in most of the considered parameters, with the exception of modulus of elasticity, microhardness Knoop, and crystallite size.

Table 1. Results of similarities or not of the studied parameters.

Parameter studied	Breeds	Average ± Standard deviation	Normality p-value	p – value*	Groups similar
Modulus of elasticity (GPa)	Canchim	16.52 ± 2.42	0.0634	0.0469	No
	Nelore	14.55 ± 1.56	0.7728		
Nano hardness Vickers (HV)	Canchim	65.95 ± 10.52	0.2109	0.548	Yes
	Nelore	63.64 ± 5.45	0.5493		
Microhardness Vickers (HV)	Canchim	48.23 ± 2.12	0.8635	0.8101	Yes
	Nelore	48.51 ± 2.95	0.3766		
Microhardness Knoop (HK)	Canchim	34.78 ± 1.91	0.1806	0.0355	No
	Nelore	36.35 ± 1.72	0.0391		
Relationship Ca/P	Canchim	2.35 ± 0.03	0.9363	0.2950	Yes
	Nelore	2.33 ± 0.03	0.4240		
Network parameter a (Å)	Canchim	9.44 ± 0.02	0.0139	0.3150	Yes
	Nelore	9.43 ± 0.01	0.0003		
Network parameter b (Å)	Canchim	9.44 ± 0.02	0.0139	0.3150	Yes
	Nelore	9.43 ± 0.01	0.0048		
Network parameter c (Å)	Canchim	6.90 ± 0.02	0.0147	0.0630	Yes
	Nelore	6.88 + 0.01	0.0009		
Crystallite Size (Å)	Canchim	66.49 ± 6.09	0.4791	0.0051	No
	Nelore	58.35 ± 2.50	0.4205		
Microdeformation (Å)	Canchim	0.0014 ± 0.0002	0.3215	0.8054	Yes
	Nelore	0.0014 ± 0.0002	0.0591		

* p-value relative to t-tests for parametric (homogeneous or not) or Mann-Whitney tests for non-parametric.

4 Discussion

SEM images showed similar characteristics between breeds, such as the presence of Havers canals, osteocytes (lamellae), and fissures inherent to bovine bone formation, however, it was possible to observe in the LM images that the Canchim breed has a more marbled appearance and more structure refined than the Nellore breed.

The images obtained by SEM also allow the verification of several spots, such characteristics represent the different crystallographic directions (positions of deposition) of the HA, from the images it is possible to verify the Havers system (as mentioned above), with the regions comprised between the channels of Havers and the lacunae (lamellae), which provide strength to the bones.

Considering the X-ray analysis, after the execution of the Rietveld refinement method and the statistical treatment of the data, the micro deformation and the parameters of the network showed similarity. On the other hand, the crystallite size did not show similarity, indicating that the microstructure between samples of different races may present significant change. The calcium and phosphorus ratio of the two races did not show statistical similarity, and both had values much higher than those of human bones (2.02 ± 0.11) [22]). It is an indicator of greater human rigidity and is consistent with greater dynamic activity imposed on human bone.

The modulus of elasticity is a measure of the stiffness of the material [23], and the two races studied in this work showed statistically different values for this property, as well as the case of Knoop microhardness, while the measures of nano and micro-hardness Vickers, showed statistical similarity. Although many studies related to these two parameters are available in the literature for human and bovine bones, a possible comparison of the values obtained is very difficult due to variations in obtaining data such as selected bone, direction, and location of measurements [24–28].

In addition to this wide range of parameters, it is important to emphasize that this work was carried out with bone samples from bovines that have not yet reached bone maturation, which causes a significant difference in bone properties, so the bone remodeling that occurs in adulthood may be the motivation of comparative studies with bones without complete maturation.

5   Conclusions

This original study compares bones of two races by methods that go beyond the traditional BMD, analyzing bone microstructures, calcium and phosphorus ratio, modulus of elasticity, and hardness. In this study, the strict control of biological and biochemical processes from birth to slaughter at 24 months, before entering adulthood, provided samples that did not undergo bone remodeling, without microarchitectures changes that would have occurred with hydroxyapatite substitutions and deficiencies, indicating no significant change in bone quality [22, 29, 30]. The bones of the two breeds showed Havers channels, osteocytes (lamellae), and cracks inherent to the formation of bovine bone. However, the Canchim breed presented a more marbled aspect and refined structure than the breed Nelore. Moreover, the difference in crystallite size parameter may indicate differences in the microstructure between samples of different races.

This unprecedented experimental route applied to the evaluation and comparison of bovine bones of different breeds found statistical differences in crystallite size (which directly influences bone microarchitecture), elastic modulus, and Knoop microhardness. Thus, despite the current regulations do not distinguish bovine breeds in the production of bone extraction biomaterials, it is important to emphasize that their products may present significant differences, and their final product may present distinct characteristics.

Conflict of Interest and Acknowledgment. The authors declare no conflicts of interest and the present work was carried out with the support of the Coordination of Improvement of Superior - Brazil (CAPES) - Financing Code 001.

References

1. Kattimani, V.S., Kondaka, S., Lingamaneni, K.P.: Hydroxyapatite—Past, present, and future in bone regeneration. Bone Tissue Regen. Insights. 7, BTRI-S36138 (2016)
2. Rahman, S.U.: Hydroxyapatite and tissue engineering. In: Handbook of Ionic Substituted Hydroxyapatites, pp. 383–400. Elsevier (2020)
3. Thiagarajan, Y., de Oliveira, G.G., Iano, Y., Vaz, G.C.: Identification and analysis of bacterial species present in cow dung fed microbial fuel cell. In: Brazilian Technology Symposium, pp. 16–24. Springer (2023). https://doi.org/10.1007/978-3-031-04435-9_2
4. Roseti, L., et al.: Scaffolds for bone tissue engineering: state of the art and new perspectives. Mater. Sci. Eng. C. **78**, 1246–1262 (2017)
5. Erbereli, R., de Camargo, I.L., Morais, M.M., Fortulan, C.A.: 3D printing of trabecular bone-mimetic structures by vat photopolymerization of bovine hydroxyapatite as a potential candidate for scaffolds. J. Braz. Soc. Mech. Sci. Eng. **44**(5), 1–9 (2022). https://doi.org/10.1007/s40430-022-03468-0
6. Pramanik, S., Ataollahi, F., Pingguan-Murphy, B., Oshkour, A.A., Osman, N.A.A.: In vitro study of surface modified poly(ethylene glycol)-impregnated sintered bovine bone scaffolds on human fibroblast cells. Sci. Rep. **5**, 9806 (2015)
7. Pramanik, S., Pingguan, B., Cho, J., Osman, N.A.A.: Design and development of potential tissue engineering scaffolds from structurally different longitudinal parts of a bovine-femur. Sci. Rep. **4**, 1–10 (2014)
8. Braga, F.J.C.: Materiais aplicados à medicina e odontologia-físico-química e resposta biológica (2015)
9. Farokhi, M., Mottaghitalab, F., Shokrgozar, M.A., Ou, K.-L., Mao, C., Hosseinkhani, H.: Importance of dual delivery systems for bone tissue engineering. J. Control. Release. **225**, 152–169 (2016)
10. Burr, D.B.: Bone morphology and organization. In: Basic and applied bone biology. pp. 3–26. Elsevier (2019)
11. Paiva, K.B.S., Granjeiro, J.M.: Bone tissue remodeling and development: focus on matrix metalloproteinase functions. Arch. Biochem. Biophys. **561**, 74–87 (2014)
12. Abdalla, R., Omar, A., Eid, K.: Detecting demineralization of enamel and cementum after gamma irradiation using radiographic densitometry. Radiat. Environ. Biophys. **57**(3), 293–299 (2018). https://doi.org/10.1007/s00411-018-0749-2
13. Shanmuganantha, L., Baharudin, A., Sulong, A.B., Shamsudin, R., Ng, M.H.: Prospect of metal ceramic (Titanium-Wollastonite) composite as permanent bone implants: a narrative review. Materials (Basel). **14**, 277 (2021)
14. Pérez-Sáez, M.J., Prieto-Alhambra, D., Díez-Pérez, A., Pascual, J.: Advances in the evaluation of bone health in kidney transplant patients. Nefrol. (English Ed.) **38**, 27–33 (2018)
15. Baldini, M., et al.: Bone quality in beta-thalassemia intermedia: relationships with bone quantity and endocrine and hematologic variables. Ann. Hematol. **96**(6), 995–1003 (2017). https://doi.org/10.1007/s00277-017-2959-0
16. Rossini, M., et al.: Guidelines for the diagnosis, prevention and management of osteoporosis. Reumatismo **68**, 1–39 (2016)

17. Brasil, instrução normativa no 3, de 17 de janeiro de 2000 o secretario de defesa agropecuária do ministério da agricultura, pecuária e abastecimento, no uso da atribuição que lhe confere o art. 83, inciso IV, do Regimento Interno da Secretaria, aprovado pela Por, pp. 3–10 (2000). http://www.agricultura.gov.br/assuntos/sustentabilidade/bem-estar-animal/arquivos/arquivos-legislacao/in-03-de-2000.pdf

18. Brasil, Instrução normativa N°56 de 6 de Novembro de 2008, Diário Of. Da União, Brasília, DF, 6 Nov. 2008, pp. 6–7 (2008)

19. Brasil, Instrução Normativa no 46, de 6 de outubro de 2011. Regulamento Técnico para os Sistemas Orgânicos de Produção Animal e Vegetal., Diário Of. Da União, Brasília, DF, 7 out. 2011. Seção 1, pp. 4–12 (2011)

20. Arabnejad, S., Johnston, R.B., Pura, J.A., Singh, B., Tanzer, M., Pasini, D.: High-strength porous biomaterials for bone replacement: A strategy to assess the interplay between cell morphology, mechanical properties, bone ingrowth and manufacturing constraints. Acta Biomater. 30, 345–356 (2016)

21. Das, K.R., Imon, A.: A brief review of tests for normality. Am. J. Theor. Appl. Stat. 5, 5–12 (2016)

22. Fishlock, A., Patel, N.: Paget's disease of bone. Orthop. Trauma 32, 245–252 (2018)

23. Scott-Baumann, A.: The modulus of elasticity. Francosphères. 7, 147–163 (2018)

24. Isaza, S.J.: Characterization of the mechanical and morphological properties of cortical bones by nanoindentation and Atomic Force Microscopy (2014)

25. Mayya, A., Banerjee, A., Rajesh, R.: Haversian microstructure in bovine femoral cortices: an adaptation for improved compressive strength. Mater. Sci. Eng. C. 59, 454–463 (2016)

26. Helgasson, B., Perilli, E., Schileo, E., Taddei, F., Brynjolfsson, S., Viceconti, M.: Mathematical relationships between bone density and material properties: A literature review. Clin. Biomech. 23, 135–146 (2008)

27. Wang, X.J., Chen, X.B., Hodgson, P.D., Wen, C.E.: Elastic modulus and hardness of cortical and trabecular bovine bone measured by nanoindentation. Trans. Nonferrous Met. Soc. China 16, s744–s748 (2006)

28. Qu, H., Fu, H., Han, Z., Sun, Y.: Biomaterials for bone tissue engineering scaffolds: A review. RSC Adv. 9, 26252–26262 (2019)

29. Rollo, J.M.D. de A., Boffa, R.S., Cesar, R., Schwab, D.C., Leivas, T.P.: Assessment of trabecular bones microarchitectures and crystal structure of hydroxyapatite in bone osteoporosis with application of the Rietveld method. Procedia Eng. 110, 8–14 (2015)

30. Ramesh, S., et al.: Characterization of biogenic hydroxyapatite derived from animal bones for biomedical applications. Ceram. Int. 44, 10525–10530 (2018)

Long-Range Network (LoRa) Behavior in the Amazon Region in a Fluvial Environment

Danilo Frazào[ID], Diana Martins[ID], and Edgard Silva[✉][ID]

Escola Superior de Tecnologia, Universidade do Estado do Amazonas,
Manaus, Brazil
{dsf.eng17,ddom.snf21,elsilva}@uea.edu.br

Abstract. LoRa is a long-range, low-power network that transmits information via radio waves (wireless). They were developed for the Internet of Things with applications in essential services such as Smart Cities. Cities with this feature have several wireless sensors (WSN) to extract data and provide services that contribute to a better quality of life for citizens. This article presents a characterization study of this technology in a river region of the Amazon rainforest in Brazil, navigating a river called Rio Negro near the city of Manaus. The transmitter will be in a boat with variable positions related to the receiver, which will be at a fixed point on the riverbank. The Sect. 1 is the introduction, the Sect. 2 makes a brief description of the LoRa network is made, and, in the Sect. 3, the physical layer is addressed. In the Sect. 4, a description of the methodology of this article is made and finally, the results obtained and the conclusion are verified.

Keywords: LoRa · Smart Cities · Rio Negro · IoT

1 Introduction

This work aims to characterize LoRa network transmissions in a fluvial environment on the Rio Negro, in the Amazon region, near the city of Manaus. For this purpose, it is implementing a testbed with temperature and humidity sensors, and a GPS module in the transmitter and receiver to verify the capacity of the network [1,2]. The transmitter is on a moving boat, sailing down the river, moving away from and approaching the receiver that will be standing on the shore.

Cities that use wireless sensor networks (WSN) and other elements of the Internet of Things to extract data and provide services that contribute to a better quality of life for citizens are called Smart Cities [3,4]. The public administration uses this data to reduce costs and increase its efficiency [5]. But these sensors can also be used within river regions that bathe a city, falling within the scope of the subject of Smart Cities [6]. In the Amazon environment, in river regions, studies on the performance of LoRa technology have not yet been carried out.

Y. Iano et al. (Eds.): BTSym 2022, SIST 353, pp. 391–398, 2023.
https://doi.org/10.1007/978-3-031-31007-2_36

Due to the climatic characteristics of this region, which differ from other parts of the world, it is interesting to collect data from packets transmitted by this technology for analyses and conclusions.

2 What Is LoRa

The name LoRa comes from the abbreviation of the words "long" and "range". And it is a modulation technology from Semtech for low-power wide area networks (LPWANs). Devices based on this technology have batteries that can last up to 10 years, as they require little energy. In addition, it allows demodulating signals better than if using FSK and exceeds the range of transmissions via Wi-Fi, Bluetooth, and cellular. The range can reach a few kilometers in urban areas and in rural areas of 10–15 km [7].

The physical layer and devices based on this technology are capable of converting data into radio frequency (RF) signals that are sent and received over the air, using spread spectrum chirp communications and frequency bands licensed for use by ANATEL. Which is the 900 MHz band with a width of 26 MHz, it goes from 902 to 928 MHz. The advantage of using *chirp* technology is that it is very resistant to interference in adverse [7] radio frequency environments. When we just say the name "LoRa", we are referring to this physical layer.

LoRaWAN is the logical layer that uses the physical layer described in the previous paragraph and refers to the asynchronous network software protocol. It is managed by a non-profit association called the LoRa Alliance [8]. With it, one can create large-scale networks that are ideal for cheaper projects and longer-lasting batteries. It is perfect for networks that require long-range communication, and low power consumption and that work with a small amount of data (usually sensors) [7].

3 The LoRa Physical Layer

3.1 Overview

LoRa modulation is not fully open as it is a proprietary technology of Semtech. This section presents an analysis of the parts of LoRa that are open. A radio modulation technique called Spread Spectrum Chirp (CSS) is used by this layer. It uses the sets of unlicensed bands internationally reserved for Industrial, scientific, and medical development, which is the frequency band with the acronym ISM (*Industrial, Scientific, and Medical*). Depending on the location in which it is being used, it operates in the ISM bands of 433–868 or 915 MHz [9]. The frequency of 915 MHz is the one used in this work.

This modulation is immune to the Doppler shift equivalent to a frequency shift. Because the frequency shifts between the receiver and transmitter are easily eliminated in the decoder due to the linearity of the chirp pulses. LoRa receivers can block received frequency chirps and offer a sensitivity of the order of −130 dBm [9].

3.2   Physical Layer Parameters

Several parameters are available for configuring LoRa modulation, but here are the three most used: Bandwidth (BW), Spread Factor (SF), and Code Rate (CR). These parameters influence its decoding ease, its resistance to interference noise, and its effective bit rate [9].

The spreading factor (SF) defines the number of bits each symbol contains. A hop when decoded represents a symbol. The relationship 2^{SF} represents the number of possible values a symbol can have. Values for this factor are between 7 and 12. The higher the value of this parameter, the higher the signal-to-noise ratio (SNR), improving sensitivity and range. However, this causes the baud rate to halve increasing packet transmission time and consuming more power [9]. Figure 1 displays three frequency spreading factors as a function of time.

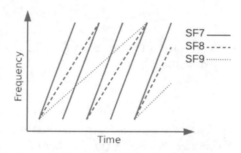

Fig. 1. Variation of symbol duration as a function of mirroring factor [10].

Bandwidth (BW) is shown on the vertical axis of the graph in Fig. 2, which is the interval between the maximum and minimum frequency that the spectrum can traverse. Upon reaching the maximum frequency, an instantaneous jump occurs directly to the minimum frequency. In the same figure, the ordinate axis is the frequency variation and the abscissa axis is the time. The position of this jump across the bandwidth is what encodes the signal into a symbol (group of bits). Chirp is a type of spread spectrum modulation technique, which can increase (upchirp) or decrease (downchirp) its frequency. So, a LoRa symbol has 2^{SF} possible values, which cover the entire frequency band and start with a series of ascending chirps. Since there are 2^{SF} possibilities for chirps for a symbol, a symbol can encode SF bits of information. The values 125, 250, and 500 kHz are the available options for configuring this parameter. The lower the bandwidth, the longer time in the air and consequently lower data rate, but with higher sensitivity due to additional noise integration [9].

Another parameter available in LoRa technology is the code rate (CR). It includes a progressive error correction code that is responsible for performing a direct correction on each data transmission. It is represented mathematically in Eq. 1, where $n \in \{1, 2, 3, 4\}$. It can take the values of 4/5, 4/6, 4/7, or 4/8. The 4/5 code rate increases the useful bitrate according to Eq. 3 and increases the

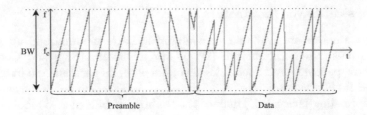

Fig. 2. Frequency variation over time of a sample signal emitted by a LoRa transceiver. The center frequency of the channel is f_c and the bandwidth is BW [9].

transmission time. But it is less tolerant to interference than a signal transmitted with the code rate of 4/8 [9].

$$CR = \frac{4}{4 + n} \tag{1}$$

Equation 2 relates the duration of a symbol (T_S) in the air, in seconds, to the bandwidth and spread factor [9].

$$T_S = \frac{2^{SF}}{BW} \tag{2}$$

Equation 3 and Eq. 4 allow us to calculate the useful bitrate (R_b) given in bits/second, where SF directly represents the number of bits and T_S, as already mentioned, is in seconds [9].

$$R_b = \frac{SF}{T_S} \times CR \tag{3}$$

$$R_b = SF \times \frac{BW}{2^{SF}} \times CR \tag{4}$$

4   Methodology

4.1   Transceiver

This device will transmit every 1 s in ESP32 programming. The data to be sent by the transmitter are *Counter, GPS Time, Latitude, Longitude, and Altitude.* The counter is an integer variable that starts at zero and is added by one for each transmission performed. Latitude and longitude are returned in degrees and decimals of the degree. The altitude is returned in meters. In total, we have a data structure of size 19 bytes to be transmitted. The two devices (transmitter and receiver) will be configured with a code rate (CR) of 4/5, bandwidth (BW) of 125 MHz, spread factor (SF) of 7 to 12, and radio frequency of 915 MHz Through the GPS, the transmitter provides the latitude and longitude coordinates to calculate the distance to the receiver. The main materials used are ESP32 LoRa v2, Steelbras AP3900 Antenna, and GPS Neo-6M v2.

4.2   Receiver

The data to be received is the same data that will be sent by the transmitter, already mentioned in Sect. 4.1. The receiver will be connected to the cell phone through a Bluetooth application developed especially for this project. Since it will be at a fixed point, the location coordinates are manually entered into the application by the user. So, in total ten variables will be displayed on the application screen: *Local Time (GMT-4), RSSI, Packet Size, Spread Factor, Latitude, Longitude, and data received by the transmitter minus altitude.* All this information mentioned above will be stored in the cell phone's database and, subsequently, exported to a .txt file to be imported into a data analysis program. Using the "Counter" variable, a survey must be made of how many packets were lost and how many were successfully received. The receiver has the same settings configured on the transmitter for transmission and reception synchronization.

The antennas that came with the two microcontrollers (ESP32 LoRa v2) had a maximum range of only 350 m. It was noticed that it was necessary to acquire other antennas with a much greater range. So, the Steelbras AP3900 antenna, with an expected maximum range of 6.5 km, was selected to replace the antenna that came with the microcontroller kit. The main materials used are ESP32, LoRa v2, and Steelbras AP3900 Antenna.

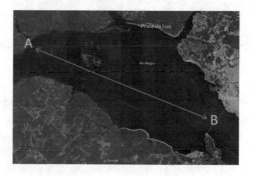

Fig. 3. Map of the trajectory traveled by the transmitter

4.3   Testbed

The trajectory that the transmitter traveled is represented on the map in Fig. 3: from point A, at Praia do Tupé, to point B, near the Ponte do Rio Negro. The receiver was fixed (stopped) at point A. The transmitter was in motion, being transported by a boat from point A to point B and returning from point B to point A. It performed this trajectory six times at each spreading factor (SF) from 7 to 12. The distance between the two points, which form a straight line, is around 20 km.

5   Results

The graph in Fig. 4 shows the packet delivery rate for each of the six spreading factors, which are the packets that were successfully delivered. According to the theory, as the spreading factor increases, this rate should increase. But for this experiment, this did not happen in practice. Supposedly because the transmitter was moving; in spreading factors 7 and 8, the weather was very rainy; the transmitter was traveling in a fluvial environment with different humidity and temperature. In article [9], this experiment was carried out with the devices completely stopped. In that case, the result of the graph was in agreement with the theory.

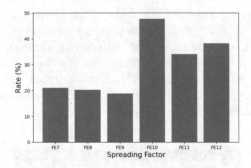

Fig. 4. Package delivery fee (percent). These are the packages that were successfully delivered.

The graph in Fig. 5 resulted in a decreasing exponential function where $f(x) = a^x$ e $0 < a < 1$, that is, the base "a" is a number greater than zero and less than one. RSSI is a function of distance in meters. As the transmitter moves away from the receiver, the strength of the received signal is reduced. The five factors remaining spreading had the same behavior as this graph.

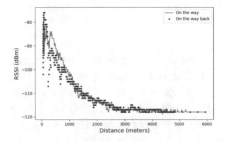

Fig. 5. Spread Factor 7 on the round trip and on the way back

Equation 3 shows that the useful bitrate (bits/s) is reduced while the spreading factor increases. But these parameters also influence the receiver's sensitivity. An increase in the spreading factor increases this sensitivity [9], which makes the transmission reach greater distances. We can realize that this event happens very clearly in the histogram of Fig. 6, except for the spreading factor 9, which must be neglected. This graph shows the maximum distance range of successfully received packets. The spreading factor 12 had the greatest range among them, reaching a distance of 9.7 km, and the 7 achieved a mark of 5.9 km.

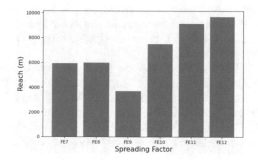

Fig. 6. Maximum range of received packets in meters

6   Conclusion

The experiments done at fixed points, without any movement, worked very well in the article [9], according to the theory. But in this article, the analysis of the data that were collected in a fluvial environment on the river Rio Negro, with the transmitter on the boat moving and the receiver stopped on the shore did not occur as expected in the plot of the graph in Fig. 4. Many possible variations may have occurred to have had this unexpected result. On the day that the data from the first spreading factors of 7 and 8 were collected, it was raining heavily. And the rain causes a degradation of the signal, affecting relatively the transmission of radio waves. The spreading factor that had a higher rate of delivery rate of successfully received packages was number 10. It was expected that the spreading factor of value 12 would be the most successful since it is the one with the best coverage. The other graphics came very close to expectations. In the one in Fig. 6, the transmission reached greater distances as the spreading factor increased, as well as in the one in Fig. 5, which has already been explained in the previous session.

Acknowledgments. This study was financed in part by Fundação de Amparo ã Pesquisa do Estado do Amazonas - FAPEAM. The foundation provide fellowship to the first Author, Danilo Frazão, and provide fellowship to the second Author, Diana Martins.

References

1. Lustosa, T.C., Iano, Y., de Oliveira, G.G., Vaz, G.C., Reis, V.S.: Safety management applied to smart cities design. In: Iano, Y., Saotome, O., Kemper, G., Mendes de Seixas, A.C., Gomes de Oliveira, G. (eds.) BTSym 2020. SIST, vol. 233, pp. 498–510. Springer, Cham (2021). https://doi.org/10.1007/978-3-030-75680-2_55
2. Bacega, P.R. de O., et al.: Study About the Applicability of Low Latency in HAS Transmission Systems. In: Brazilian Technology Symposium. pp. 73–87. Springer (2023). https://doi.org/10.1007/978-3-031-04435-9_7
3. Demanboro, A.C., Bianchini, D., Iano, Y., de Oliveira, G.G., Vaz, G.C.: 6G Networks: An Innovative Approach, but with Many Challenges and Paradigms, in the Development of Platforms and Services in the Near Future. In: Brazilian Technology Symposium. pp. 172–187. Springer (2023). https://doi.org/10.1007/978-3-031-04435-9_17
4. Demanboro, A.C., Bianchini, D., Iano, Y., de Oliveira, G.G., Vaz, G.C.: Regulatory Aspects of 5G and Perspectives in the Scope of Scientific and Technological Policy. In: Brazilian Technology Symposium. pp. 163–171. Springer (2023). https://doi.org/10.1007/978-3-031-04435-9_16
5. Garcia-Font, V., Garrigues, C., Rifà-Pous, H.: A comparative study of anomaly detection techniques for smart city wireless sensor networks. Sensors **16**(6), 868 (2016)
6. Guibene, W., Nowack, J., Chalikias, N., Fitzgibbon, K., Kelly, M., Prendergast, D.: Evaluation of LPWAN Technologies for Smart Cities: River Monitoring Use-Case. In: 2017 IEEE Wireless Communications and Networking Conference Workshops (WCNCW), pp. 1–5 (2017)
7. Portal do Desenvolvedor LoRa (Semtech), https://lora-developers.semtech.com/, Accessed 20 Sep 2021
8. Site oficial de LoRa Alliance, https://lora-alliance.org/ Accessed 20 Sep 2021
9. Augustin, A., Yi, J., Clausen, T., Townsley, W.M.: A study of LoRa: long range & low power networks for the internet of things. Sensors **16**(9), 1466 (2016)
10. Bedaque, D.: Testes de Desempenho de Enlaces Ponto a Ponto da Tecnologia LoRa. Instituto Federal de Santa Catarina (Campus São José) - Engenharia de Telecomunicações (2016). https://wiki.sj.ifsc.edu.br/images/3/37/TCC290_Danilo_Bedaque.pdf Accessed 20 Sep 2021

Water-Resistant Characteristics
of Ch'ampa Type Earth Block Masonry

Yasmani Vitulas Quille[(⊠)] [iD]

Departamento de Ingeniería Civil, Universidad Nacional del Altiplano de Puno,
Puno, Peru
yvitulas@unap.edu.pe

Abstract. At present, in the Peruvian Andes there is a need for houses that can withstand inclement weather, especially rainfall, so, because of this need, it has been identified a traditional construction system with a very unique architecture called *Putuco*, which uses a single type of material extracted from natural terrain called *Ch'ampa*. Therefore, the objective of this research is to study and analyze the water resistance of this traditional building block, obtaining a permeability coefficient between 7.77×10^{-7} and 3.80×10^{-6} cm/s, which indicates that the block is practically impermeable and comparable to modern prefabricated materials, in the SAET erosion tests the level is low or null due to the roots that it has as internal reinforcement, which provides both stability and resistance to permanent humidity, providing an adequate resistant characteristic and compensated with the low cost and recyclability of this construction material. These results differentiate it from other traditional earth construction materials and it is also environmentally friendly.

Keywords: Ancestral · Blocks of natural grass · Ch'ampa · Cultural identification · Putuco · Vernacular · Water-resistant block

1 Introduction

It is necessary to consider that ecotechnology is a methodology that is being studied the harmonious relationship between the environment without neglecting the social and economic values. Among the most used materials in the world, we can mention *adobe* and *tapia* as part of a constructive tradition. If we include the studies of a little-studied material such as *Ch'ampa*, we can formulate the bases of the study of constructive *ethnoengineering* or *ethnodesign*.

In recent years, the interest in earth-based materials for sustainable construction has solved economic and ecological problems as they are abundant and recyclable [1], despite being the oldest building material in the world. Approximately 50% of the population in developing countries are rural and at least 20% of urban populations live in earthen constructions [2]. Despite its properties, lack of recognition, loss of knowledge, and lack of international standardization [3]. However, the use of traditional building materials can generate solutions to many of the current problems of energy and functionality in rural housing constructions that, by

© The Author(s), under exclusive license to Springer Nature Switzerland AG 2023
Y. Iano et al. (Eds.): BTSym 2022, SIST 353, pp. 399–408, 2023.
https://doi.org/10.1007/978-3-031-31007-2_37

their nature, cannot access modern materials because they are inaccessible and very expensive, in addition to reducing the energy required to manufacture these products, the energy required for construction and transportation needs [4–11].

Ch'ampa is a material predominantly used by the *Colla* culture of the Peruvian and Bolivian highlands. It is extracted directly from the earth [12], although there is a lot of research on traditional adobe as ancestral knowledge of Colombia [13], cultural heritage of Najran [14], traditional architecture of Spain [15], and even Europe [16] and Africa [17]. Many standards have been generated for earth blocks as construction units [18], thermal comfort standards in Libya [19], and even comparative studies between thermal and resistant aspects of earth building blocks [20,21], in addition to their mechanical behavior [22], among others. However, contradictorily, no study addresses the *Ch'ampa* as traditional material and this contribution attempts to fill a gap in science that deserves to be deepened, presenting preliminary results as part of a traditional and cultural revaluation where the resistant capacity to prolonged exposure to water of the *Ch'ampa* as earth block masonry is shown.

2   Weather-Resistant Dwellings

2.1   Construction Typology Called *Putuco*

The construction typology of the *Putucos* is a traditional construction system that is developed based on empirical knowledge, with a quadrangular base and pyramidal elevation at half height, concluding with a truncated cone-shaped circular half dome, and its most important characteristic is that its construction is based on a single material called *Ch'ampa* [23].

2.2   Earthen Block Masonry Called *Ch'ampa*

It is a traditional construction material that, unlike *adobe* and *tapial*, is manufactured based on prismatic blocks extracted directly from the natural soil, considering that it has a reticular system of intertwined roots that serve as a binder and give these particular properties to this atypical and not very widespread construction material [24].

Its extraction procedure (see Fig. 1) depends on the area of location and adequate identification of the terrain, which has certain characteristics such as the presence of roots of *Ch'iji* or *Quemello* plants, granulometry, and limits of consistency of the material based on 61–63% silt, 19–22% clay, and 5–9% sand [24] as part of its internal structure, which is also the characteristic of the natural soil of extraction, so it is variable.

3   Permeability at Constant Load

The permeability tests with constant load ($mx.6$ kg/cm^2), also known as tests for measuring the hydraulic conductivity of saturated porous materials using a

Fig. 1. Extraction of the *Ch'ampa* samples using the same artisanal criteria of the study area.

flexible wall permeameter, were developed based on the standards NTP 339.156 and ASTM D5084-10, in the laboratories of the PUCP (see Fig. 2) and by courtesy of M.Sc. Andrea Gamio.

This test is performed to determine whether the soil is permeable or impermeable, using Darcy's law.

Fig. 2. Molding of samples P-1 and P-2 for permeability test.

Table 1 shows the results for specimens P-1 and P-2. In the case of P-1, the dimensions of the specimen were $h = 8.56$ cm and $\emptyset = 5$ cm, and, for P-2, the dimensions of the specimen were $h = 9.06$ cm and $\emptyset = 5$ cm, both exposed at a temperature of $T = 20\,^{\circ}\mathrm{C}$. In addition, there was a variation in the moisture percentage of humidity between the initial and final values of 24.61% (34.82%– 10.21%) for P-1 and 28.86% (35.06%–6.20%) for P-2. It can also be observed that the porosity percentage is maintained at 47.80% for P-1 and 48.00% for P-2. This gives a permeability coefficient of $K_{20} = 7.77 \times 10^{-7}$ cm/s for P-1 and $K_{20} = 3.80 \times 10^{-6}$ cm/s for P-2, which implies that it is practically an impervious material.

3.1 Discussion of Results

According to the results obtained and the SUCS classification, the *Ch'ampa* material is identified as an ML soil, which is a semi-impermeable or practically impermeable soil, and, according to the ASTM classification, the degree

Table 1. Permeability test results.

Specimen Characteristics	Test tube P1		Test tube P2	
	Initial	Final	Initial	Final
Diameter (cm)	5.00	5.00	5.00	5.00
Height (cm)	8.56	8.56	9.06	9.06
Specific gravity of solids Gs	2.63		2.63	
Moisture $w\%$	10.21%	34.82%	6.20%	35.06%
Saturation $Sr\%$	29.30%	100.00%	17.70%	100.00%
Void ratio e	0.92	0.92	0.92	0.92
Porosity $n\%$	47.80%	47.80%	48.0%	48.0%
Density γ (g/cm^3)	1.51	1.85	1.45	1.85
Dry density γ (g/cm^3)	1.37	1.37	1.37	1.37
Type of specimen	Unaltered		Unaltered	
Applied pressure (kg/cm^2)	0.75		0.50	
Confined pressure σ 3 kg/cm^2	1.50		1.50	
Hydraulic gradient i	87.62		55.19	
Permeability coefficient K_{20}	7.77×10^{-7} cm/s		3.80×10^{-6} cm/s	

of permeability is very low with a value of "k", which represents the hydraulic conductivity or permeability coefficient, close to 8×10^{-7} cm/s, considering that values lower than 1×10^{-7} cm/s are practically impermeable soils, a fundamental characteristic of clays.

Permeability depends, among other things, on the particle size and pore continuity of a sample, the presence of cracks and discontinuities of the block, and the void ratio of the soil, i.e., the larger the size the greater the number of voids [25]. These values are highly variable and can be classified according to the recommendations of Angelone et al. [26] and Fierro et al. [27]. If the value of k (cm/s) is between 10^{-6} and 10^{-7}, the drainage is practically impermeable, and the landfill use is good.

According to the recommendations of the Soil Conservation Service of the United States, permeability or hydraulic conductivity, depending on the type of material and its permeability characteristics, are classified as shown in Table 2.

4   Wear Resistance

4.1   Suction

The measurement of the water absorption rate of a masonry block in a given area is an important property because, if it is too high, it will produce possible cracks in these blocks. This test is adapted to the numeral 11 of NTP 399. 613, determining the early absorption index of the analyzed block, which is the capacity of the masonry block to absorb water in an area of 200 cm^2 in a standard time of 1 min $\pm$ 1 s, using masonry units dried at room temperature for no less

Table 2. Permeability test results.

Characteristics	k (cm/h)	k (cm/s)	Type of construction material					
			Ch'ampa	Soil clayey	Adobe AC	Tapia	C°	MRD
Impermeable	<0.00036	<1.000 ×10⁻⁷	X				X***	X***
Very slow	<0.1	<2.778 × 10⁻⁵	X	X*			X	
Slow	0.1–0.5	2.778 ×10⁻⁵ 1.389 ×10⁻⁴			X**			
Moderately slow	0.5–2.0	1.389 ×10⁻⁴ 5.556 ×10⁻⁴			X	X		
Moderate	2.0–6.5	5.556 ×10⁻⁴ 1.806 ×10⁻³				X		
Moderately high	6.5–12.5	1.806 × 10⁻³ 3.472 ×10⁻³						
High	12.5–25.0	3.472 ×10⁻³ 6.950 ×10⁻³						
Very high	>25.0	>6.950 ×10⁻³					X***	

* According to ASTM classification, for ML soils.
** For adobe with 5% AC cement, the value is 5.238×10^{-5} cm/s, and for special reinforcement mortar MRD (with a/c ratio $= 0.50$) it is 9.371×10^{-9} cm/s [28].
*** For concrete it has a value of 1.5×10^{-11} cm/s, according to the Bureau of Reclamation [29]. For porous concrete it has a value of 2.342×10^{-1} cm/s with 11% voids [30].

than 4 weeks, then taking the dimensions of the face of the block that will be in contact with the water, the suction surface is determined, the dry weight of each of the samples is recorded using an electronic balance with an accuracy of 0.5 g. To carry out the test, a completely flat transparent tray with a depth of not less than 25 mm is required to contain the water. The tray should contain holes to maintain the required constant water level.

The suction is determined as the variation of the weights between the initial state and the final state of the block considering the water absorbed during 1 min of contact with the water, inversely proportional to the area of the base of the block, considering the normalized suction of a surface of $200 \, \text{cm}^2$. Based on the tests performed, the average results are determined (10 specimens in each case), where it is observed that the percentage of suction is 22.39% and that of the *Ch'ampa* is 45.74%, which implies that the latter absorbs almost twice as much water as the traditional adobe because the *Ch'ampa* block has roots and naturally compacted soil, therefore its absorption is greater, but this does not affect its stability due to the rigidity provided by the roots.

4.2   Absorption

The measurement of masonry block permeability is usually taken as a measure of porosity as it measures the probable seepage through masonry blocks and the indication of disintegration when wet blocks are subjected to freezing and thawing.

Therefore, a porous masonry block will not be as resistant as a block with a higher density in its composition, an aspect that influences the application of loads, or resistant enough to the passage of time or any other weathering phenomenon.

This test is adapted to NTP-399.613, using three whole units dried for at least four weeks, which are immersed in water (See Fig. 3) to report what happens as a function of time, taking records of their weights, including the weight of water absorbed, the water must be clean and at a temperature between 15.5 and 30 °C.

Fig. 3. Immersion of traditional adobe and *Ch'ampa* blocks.

The test results (10 specimens in each case) showed that the traditional adobes disintegrated before the first measurement, making it impossible to perform the corresponding measurements, but in the case of the *Ch'ampa* this value increased until it was completely saturated while maintaining its stability (See Table 3 and Fig. 4) because the root lattice gives it an additional property that makes it resistant to long periods in contact with water.

4.3   Erosion

Using as a reference the Mexican standard NMX-C-508 (2015) and the Spanish AENOR UNE 41410 (2008), which establish the erosion called "SAET: Swinburne accelerated erosion test" developed by the University of Swinburne [31], whereby at least two whole blocks must be tested randomly, cured for 28 days before the test, and the masonry block measures the depth of the hollowness in millimeters, and the values between 0 to 5 are considered high strength, between 5 to 10 is a medium strength, between 10 to 20 is low medium and greater than 20 is considered inadequate, based on the Swinburne accelerated erosion test which drops a continuous stream of water on the block for 10 min through a 5.0 mm in diameter, connected to a constant level water tank, the head of which is 1.5 m above the face of the block. This is kept inclined at 27° for the horizontal and the erosion depth is measured with a 3 mm diameter rod.

The purpose of this test is to analyze the behavior of the masonry blocks to the erosion of their surface [32] caused by the continuous contact of water on one of the faces of the masonry units (See Fig. 5), simulating the consequences of heavy and prolonged rainfall.

In the test results (10 specimens in each case) it could be seen that the results are similar, being classified as low or null since the erosion level has an average between 20 to 23 mm for both the traditional adobe and the *Ch'ampa* (See Table 4), but the latter is much more resistant over time, due to the presence of roots.

Table 3. Average of suction tests.

Block	Dry weight (gr)	Saturated weight (gr)							
		1 hr	%	6 hr	%	12 hr	%	24 hr	%
Ch'ampa	2,889	3,881	34.34	3,932	36.11	4,281	48.27	4,393	52.13
Traditional Adobe	5,743	Disintegrated specimens (impossible to measure)							

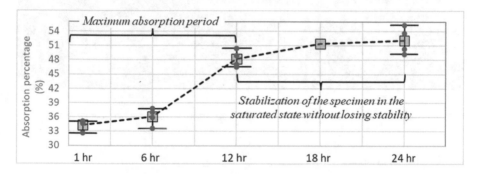

Fig. 4. Absorption of *Ch'ampa* during time.

Fig. 5. Swinburne accelerated erosion (SAET) for traditional adobe and *Ch'ampa* blocks.

Table 4. Average of the accelerated erosion tests.

Block	Flow rate (ml/min)	Time (min)	Hollowness/Erosion (mm)	Resistance level
Ch'ampa	625	10	23.25	LOW TO NONE
Traditional Adobe	625	10	20.50	LOW TO NONE

5   Experiences in Reality

The results confirm the existence of an impermeable property that was antic-
ipated based on empirical knowledge for the construction of *Putuco* and show
why this material has lasted over time and withstood extreme flooding events
that house built with adobe cannot withstand, as we can see in Fig. 6, therefore the traditional empirical knowledge lasts over time, although to date it is
being lost since there are no master builders who can transmit this traditional
knowledge, which is also reinforced by research based on laboratory results that
rather strengthen and cement a new line of research with the primary desire to
revalue our cultural essence of the area of Huancané, Taraco, and Samán.

Fig. 6. Stability of *Putuco* exposed to extreme flooding compared to other housing.

6   Conclusions

Impermeability is a property that is absent in adobe and tapia, but curiously
this does not occur with *Ch'ampa*, with a permeability coefficient (K_{20}) that
fluctuates between 7.77×10^{-7} cm/s and 3.80×10^{-6} cm/s, which makes it practically impermeable, even comparable to concrete and some special reinforcement mortars (see Table 2), allowing rainwater to flow efficiently, corroborated
by the resistance to erosion where the average value is between 20 mm to 23
mm, which, although not efficient, the presence of roots considerably reduces its
disintegration and therefore maintains the stability of this traditional material.

These results demonstrate the resistance of the *Ch'ampa* block to rainfall
and floods that are very frequent in the study area (banks of the Ramis river,
Taraco, Samán, and Huancané, in the Andean highlands of the Puno city in
Peru), unlike adobe or mud walls which do not have this property, and, as can
be seen in Figure 6, the stability of a *Putucos* is significantly better than houses
built with adobe, lasting for long periods of time even up to 80 and more than
100 years of life.

It is preliminarily proven that the characteristics of the earth block masonry
called *Ch'ampa* are adequate for the construction of traditional rural houses
known as *Putucos*, with an adequate capacity of resistance to extreme rainfall
and floods, which occur very frequently in December to February, extended its
useful life, being necessary its revaluation and diffusion of the ancestral traditions
with technical sustenance, which I call traditional constructive ethnoengineering.

References

1. El Fgaier, F., Lafhaj, Z., Chapiseau, C., Antczak, E.: Effect of sorption capacity on thermo-mechanical properties of unfired clay bricks. J. Build. Eng. **6**(1), 86–92 (2016)
2. Houben, H., Guillaud, H.: Earth Construction. Intermediate Technology Publications, London (1994)
3. Delgado, M.C.J., Guerrero, I.C.: The selection of soils for unstabilised earth building: a normative review. Constr. Build. Mater **21**(2), 237–251 (2007)
4. Morel, J.C., Mesbah, A., Oggero, M., Walker, P.: Building houses with local materials: means to drastically reduce the environmental impact of construction. Build. Environ. **36**(10), 1119–1126 (2001)
5. Pacheco-Torgal, F., Jalali, S.: Earth construction: lessons from the past for future eco-efficient construction. Constr. Build. Mater. **29**(1), 512–519 (2012)
6. Shukla, A., Tiwari, G.N., Sodha, M.S.: Embodied energy analysis of adobe house. Renew. Energy **34**(3), 755–761 (2009)
7. Zami, M.S., Lee, A.: Economic benefits of contemporary earth construction in low-cost urban housing - state of the art review. J. Build. Appraisal **5**(1), 259–271 (2010)
8. Lustosa, T.C., Iano, Y., de Oliveira, G.G., Vaz, G.C., Reis, V.S.: Safety management applied to smart cities design. In: Iano, Y., Saotome, O., Kemper, G., Mendes de Seixas, A.C., Gomes de Oliveira, G. (eds.) BTSym 2020. SIST, vol. 233, pp. 498–510. Springer, Cham (2021). https://doi.org/10.1007/978-3-030-75680-2_55
9. de Oliveira, G.G., Iano, Y., Vaz, G.C., Chuma, E.L., Negrete, P.D.M., Negrete, J.C.M.: Structural Analysis of Bridges and Viaducts Using the IoT concept: an approach on dom pedro highway (Campinas-Brazil). In: Brazilian Technology Symposium, pp. 108–119. Springer, Heidelberg (2022). https://doi.org/10.1007/978-3-031-08545-1_10
10. de Souza, C.F.C., Iano, Y., de Oliveira, G.G., Vaz, G.C., Reis, V.S., Neto, J.M.: Institutional Development Index (IDI): calculation for municipalities in the metropolitan region of Campinas (Brazil). In: Brazilian Technology Symposium, pp. 245–255. Springer, Heidelberg (2022). https://doi.org/10.1007/978-3-031-08545-1_23
11. de Oliveira, G.G., Iano, Y., Vaz, G.C., Chuma, E.L., Negrete, P.D.M., Negrete, J.C.M.: Prop walls: a contextualization of the theme in a case study in the city of Campinas (Brazil) BT. In: Proceedings of the 7th Brazilian Technology Symposium (BTSym 2021). Presented at the (2022)
12. Vitulas Quille, Y.T., Reynoso Machaca K.B.: Ancestral construction and mystical conception of the putucos of the peruvian highlands. In: Antioquia Research Institute, Chapter, Colombia, 5th edn., pp. 65–73 (2020)
13. Rivera-Salcedo, H., Valderrama-Andrade, O.M., Daza-Barrera, A.A., Plazas-Jai-Mes, G.S.: Adobe como saber ancestral usado en construcciones autóctonas de Pore y Nunchía. Casanare. Revista de Arquitectura (Bogotá) **23**(1), 74–78 (2021)
14. Al-Sakkafl, Y.K., Abdullah, G.M.S.: Soil properties for earthen building construction in Najran City, Saudi Arabia. Comput. Mater. Continua **672**(1), 127–140 (2021)
15. Villacampa Crespo, L., García-Soriano L., López-Manzanares F., Mileto C.: Constructive techniques of the past for a sustainable future. the case of traditional earthen architecture in aragon (Spain). Int. Jo. Latest Trends Eng. Technol. **11**(3), 30–36 (2018)

16. Duarte Carlos, G., Alcindor, M., Correia, M.: Arquitectura tradicional de tierra en Europa: un patrimonio de entramado y encestado, adobe, tapia y pared de mano. Anales del Instituto de Arte Americano e Investigaciones Estéticas **48**(2), 239–256 (2018)

17. Sturm, T., Ramos, L.F., Lourenço, P.B.: Characterization of dry-stack interlocking compressed earth blocks. Mater. Struct. **48**(1), 3059–3074 (2015)

18. Cid, J., Mazarrón, F.R., Cañas, L.: The earth building normative documents in the world. Informes de la Construcción **63**(523), 159–169 (2011)

19. Gabril, N.: Thermal Comfort and Building Design Strategies for Low Energy Houses in Libya: Lessons from the vernacular architecture, PhD thesis University of Westminster Faculty of Architecture, Central London (2014)

20. Cuitiño Rosales, M.G., Rotondaro, R., Esteves, A: Análisis comparativo de aspectos térmicos y resistencias mecánicas de los materiales y los elementos de la construcción con tierra. Technol. Environ. Sustainabil. (Revista de Arquitectura Bogotá) **22**(1), 138–151 (2020)

21. Wieser, M., Onnis, S., Meli, G.: Desempeño térmico de cerramientos de tierra alivianada, Posibilidades de aplicación en el territorio peruano. Technol. Environ. Sustainabil. **22**(1), 164–174 (2020)

22. Castillo Valencia, W., Areiza Palma, G., Coral Moncayo, H.: Comportamiento físico mecánico de la tapia por pandeo y conexión de esquina, Caso Teatro Imperial de Pasto. INGE CUC **14**(2), 81–96 (2018)

23. Peralta, F., Guerra, C., Capia, C., Soncco, R., Choquechambi, J.: Huaylla: Construcción de viviendas rurales Tipo Putucos. Citado por Andrea Lissy Gamio Felipa, Peru (2010)

24. Quille, Y.V.: Identification of soil characteristics for the extraction of Ch'ampa as earth block masonry. In: BTSym 2021, Smart Innovation, Systems and Technologies, vol. 207, pp. 512–520. Springer, Heidelberg (2023). https://doi.org/10.1007/978-3-031-04435-9_53

25. Alfaro, D.C.A., Mora, F.A.: Modelo físico para la medición de la permeabilidad en suelos cohesivos (cabeza variable). [Thesis] Prog. de Ingeniería Civil, Fac. de Ingeniería, Universidad Católica de Colombia, Bogotá (2014)

26. Angelone, S., Garibay, M.T., Casaux, M.C.: Permeabilidad de suelos (1.a ed.). Rosario, Santa Fe, Argentina: Universidad Nacional de Rosario, Facultad de Ciencias Exactas, Ingeniería y Agrimensura (2006)

27. Fierro Losada, J.A., Parra Gómez, A.F., Vásquez Olaya, C.A.: Determinación del coeficiente de permeabilidad de las comunas 1, 3 y 5 del municipio de Girardot - Cundinamarca. [Thesis] Universidad Piloto de Colombia, Alto Magdalena (2017)

28. Pérez, G., et al.: Evaluación de las propiedades físicas del adobe reforzado y de sus materiales componentes y su influencia en el comportamiento electroquímico. Revista Mater Construcc **54**(274), 5–16 (2004)

29. Wainzstein, M., Sota, J.D.: Permeabilidad en hormigones. Serie **II**(134), 116–133 (1975)

30. Vélez, L.M.: Permeabilidad y Porosidad en Concreto. Tecno Lógicas **1**(25), 169–187 (2010)

31. Cid Falceto, J.: Durabilidad de los bloques de tierra comprimida. Evaluación y recomendaciones para la normalización de los ensayos de erosión y absorción. [Doctoral Thesis] Universidad Politécnica de Madrid (2012)

32. Cabrera, S., González, A.: Wet erosion resistance in compressed earth blocks, evaluation of different methods for the analysis of results. Revista Tecnología y Ciencia **1**(40), 49–62 (2021)

Contribution of the Synchronous and Asynchronous Mode in Virtual Education in a Peruvian Higher Educational Institution During the COVID-19 Pandemic

Janet Aquino⑩, Carlos Valdivia⑩, Jessie Bravo(✉) ⑩, and Roger Alarcón⑩

School of Computer and Informatics Engineering, Pedro Ruiz Gallo National University, Lambayeque, Peru

{jaquino,cvaldivias,jbravo,ralarcong}@unprg.edu.pe

Abstract. COVID-19 caused universities around the world to adapt their educational models to the new virtual modality. In Peru, higher education institutions integrated teaching-learning activities, integrating synchronous and asynchronous modes, through online classes and virtual learning spaces. The research aimed to identify the level of contribution of synchronous and asynchronous modes in virtual education, demonstrating the influence of five dimensions: psychological, technological, communication, pedagogical, and academic activities. With a quantitative approach, non-experimental design, and a sample of 1519 students at a public university, using an instrument based on a Likert scale. As a result, the synchronous mode had a greater contribution to virtual education, evidenced in the ease of use of technological tools, motivation, response time to queries, and effective communication, however, the asynchronous modality developed better research skills of the students, due to the autonomy and the better control of their time. The analysis by groups of careers and modes did not determine greater significance. The proceeds will serve universities as a contribution towards a new hybrid educational model.

Keywords: Virtual education · Synchronous mode · Asynchronous mode · Higher education · COVID-19

1 Introduction

Since the beginning of the pandemic, institutions in the education sector have adapted their academic and administrative processes, enhancing their technological infrastructure in order to provide an adequate virtual modality. According to Arias Ortiz et al. [1], 26% of teachers in public universities in Latin America felt little or nothing prepared for the use of digital tools in their courses, 38% of universities report that they do not have training programs in digital technologies and 30% of teachers in Peru did not have access to internet service, being the main obstacle to virtual education. In addition, UNESCO [2] said that "prioritizing the recovery of education is fundamental to avoid

Y. Iano et al. (Eds.): BTSym 2022, SIST 353, pp. 409–418, 2023.
https://doi.org/10.1007/978-3-031-31007-2_38

a generational catastrophe". Many authors talk about virtual education, its impact, and the perceptions of both students and teachers, but few focus on a differentiated analysis of the two modes of virtual learning, synchronous and asynchronous, which makes it difficult for higher education to establish ideal strategies for each mode in terms of the use of information technologies, training of its teachers in educational didactics and teaching-learning methodologies for this new educational scenario.

Teaching in public universities had been developing mostly in person, but due to the COVID-19 pandemic, as stated by Biwer et al. [3], the change was violent in such a way that the digital divide had to be shortened in both teachers and students in order to be able to continue education despite the lockdown.

Given this context, in Peru, universities have adapted to this modality of virtual teaching, which integrates modes: synchronous and asynchronous, where the form and time allocated by mode have defined by each university and embodied in its educational model, in many cases without precedents, criteria were identified for this new normality: times allocated to online classes, virtual environments, academic activities, mixed methodologies, communication tools, however, their effectiveness and influence on the teaching-learning process.

Then, under the perception of the student, who constitutes the key element in this modality of virtual teaching, the purpose of this study was determined through the research questions: To what extent have the psychological, technological, communication, pedagogical, and academic activities dimensions influenced the virtual teaching-learning process in both the synchronous and asynchronous modality? Which mode has a greater contribution to the virtual teaching-learning process? Based on these questions, a guide can be determined that supports the feedback of its educational model towards a hybrid educational model and achieve educational quality in the University environment.

2   State of the Art

According to Baber [4], virtual education has been accepted by students despite the inconveniences that had to be overcome, likewise, Tuma et al. [5], in a cross-sectional study in a university medical school, found that 69% of students and teachers perceived better results with virtual education than with traditional methods, despite the fact that 51% had problems in technology and connectivity. As for learning modes, Nguyen et al. [6] state that students felt more motivated in synchronous mode; however, Tuma & Aljazeeri [7] found that asynchronous education holds promise for the future of teaching by being innovative and providing more advantages to users by being able to develop anywhere, anytime. According to Shi et al. [8], there is a close relationship between synchronous teaching work and students' commitment to motivation as a mediator; therefore, they must take into account social, technical, and pedagogical capacities, where the most influential linked to motivation was pedagogical.

As Cardona & Sánchez propose [9], the process of virtual education can be evaluated through five indicators: institution, pedagogy, technology, context, and services, which evaluate e-learning, allowing to know if the student has internalized the contents and if the transfer of knowledge has been carried out appropriately. Other authors have evaluated different aspects of virtual education. In addition, Ramirez et al. [10] state that the perception of satisfaction depends on the connection and the computer equipment with which the student develops his virtual education. In the pedagogical aspect, the teacher had to adapt to a new educational model that should be 100% virtual in their academic processes. According to Norman-Acevedo & Daza-Orozco [11], the transition to virtual teaching has had aspects that favor and disfavor the relationship between digital learning and student motivation, where the psychological aspect can affect motivation and student performance, as stated by Shah et al. [12]. In the same way, Son et al. [13] state that students when going through emotional and motivational stress boxes affected their adaptation to remote learning. Finally, in the aspect of academic activities and communication, Ojeda-Beltran et al. [14] tell us that education is par excellence a way of communication where the teacher without students does not exist and vice versa, it is for this reason that social networks become allies to establish a communicative channel in this change of educational model, taking into account Martínez & Jiménez [15] who say that teacher must design his virtual classroom according to the guidelines of pedagogical practice with activities that lead to compliance of the expected learning outcome.

3 Materials and Methods

The population was made up of 11600 students enrolled in the virtual semesters 2020-I and 2020-II of a Peruvian public university, with a sample of 1519 students.

The research was carried out under the non-experimental, cross-sectional, and descriptive quantitative approach. A questionnaire was used, validated with Cronbach's alpha reliability analysis of 0.898 with a pilot test of 85 respondents, obtaining good internal consistency. Likewise, the instrument was validated with expert judgment, which allowed the identification of internal validity and reliability.

The instrument was composed of five dimensions: technological, pedagogical, psychological, academic activities, and communication, as can be seen in Table 1.

The 28 professional careers were grouped into five groups: engineering, economic sciences, medical sciences, social sciences, and pure sciences, for the inferential analysis developed.

Table 1. Dimensions of the instrument.

Dimension	Objective	N° questions
Technological	Identify the level of access to the technologies and technological tools used in the virtual teaching-learning process	7
Pedagogical	Identify the level of perception about the methodology, contents, and motivation given by teachers	6
Psychological	Recognize the degree to which episodes of stress, anxiety, irritability, and depression have affected the development of virtual classes in students	4
Academic activities	Identify the level of perception about how academic activities were scheduled in terms of time, quantity, development, and feedback	10
Communication	Identify the perception of the communication tools used by teachers and their effectiveness	3

4   Results

4.1   Descriptive Analysis

In the technological dimension, 65% of students have adequate equipment for the development of virtual classes; in addition, 46% of them occasionally have a good connection to the internet, and 19% rarely, this being an indicator of the main obstacles to the correct development of virtual classes. Among the technological tools most used by teachers in synchronous sessions is Google Meet with 99.6%, complemented by the use of Jamboard (24.7%), Google Forms (21.8%), and 3.1% used other tools such as digital whiteboards and applications typical of your professional career.

Finally, in the asynchronous sessions, students manifest that, in terms of the activities programmed in the virtual classroom, tasks were used first, followed by the forums and essays, and lastly, questionnaires and chats. Regarding resources, teachers used more videos and files, followed by URLs and folders. The ease of use of technological tools had a 46% perception in synchronous mode and 43% in asynchronous mode.

In the pedagogical dimension, an important aspect was the domain of the courses by the teachers, the students found 75% of teachers with this domain, however, 45% consider inadequate the methodology applied, this could be due to the rapid change from the face-to-face mode to the virtual mode.

Likewise, 67% found courses with updated content in synchronous mode and 61% in asynchronous mode, considering 38% that such content could be improved. Regarding the opportunity to deliver activities out of time, 45% of students indicate that teachers did provide opportunities in synchronous mode, as did 55% perceived in the asynchronous mode, which could reflect that some teachers did not contemplate support for their students due to lack of empathy, very attached to the regulations or other reasons.

Finally, in the aspect of motivation to students in the development of classes and activities, 55% perceived it in the synchronous mode and 44% in the asynchronous mode, which could indicate a lack of knowledge of traditional motivational methods and techniques adapted to the new normality.

In the psychological dimension, 89% of students presented at least one episode of stress, anxiety, irritability, or depression, due to the new form of virtual education, compared to 11% who rarely or never had it, which shows us that behind the screen we can find an endless number of factors that teachers must take into account in order to reach the student properly. In addition, 67% of students say that these episodes have affected their academic performance, 19% do not know if this was the cause, and 14% that never or almost never had an impact on their academic performance.

Regarding the attention paid to virtual classes, 25% never had difficulty maintaining this attention in synchronous mode and 35% in asynchronous mode.

In the dimension of academic activities, the perception of the order of the contents and activities was 65% in the synchronous mode and 62% in the asynchronous mode, which reflects the effort that teachers have made to adapt the learning contents to the new modality. As for the time allocated by teachers to the development of activities, 52% consider it appropriate in the synchronous mode and 50% in the asynchronous mode, in addition to the number of programmed activities were perceived in excess by 49% in the synchronous mode and 55% in the asynchronous mode, however not all activities were qualified, as stated 79% in the synchronous mode and 74% in the asynchronous mode, despite the qualified ones, 50% in both modes did not have feedback from their teachers.

Likewise, it was found that the activities of greater weight in the synchronous mode were expositions (40%) and oral interventions (23%) and, in asynchronous, tasks (47%), essays (20%), questionnaires (16%), and forums (15%).

In the dimension of Communication between students and teachers, 79% perceived that their queries were answered quickly in synchronous mode and 57% in asynchronous mode. In addition, 69% consider the communication tools used by the teachers in synchronous mode to be effective, and 63% in asynchronous mode.

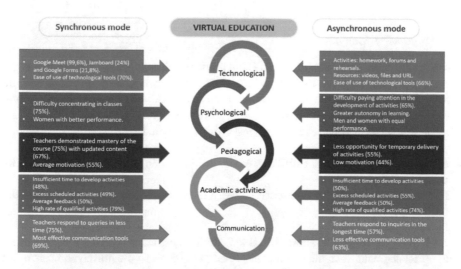

Fig. 1. Study dimensions analyzed in synchronous and asynchronous modes.

The results of the five dimensions with less or greater influence according to their components, both in synchronous and asynchronous mode, are summarized in Fig. 1.

To determine to what extent the dimensions under study have influenced virtual education both in its synchronous and asynchronous modality, the average scores of the questions in each dimension were used, obtaining the results of Fig. 2, where it was evidenced that the technological, communication, pedagogical and academic activities dimensions had a greater influence on the synchronous mode than in asynchronous mode, contributing to the virtual teaching-learning process, however, the psychological dimension influenced more in the synchronous mode affecting the academic performance of the students.

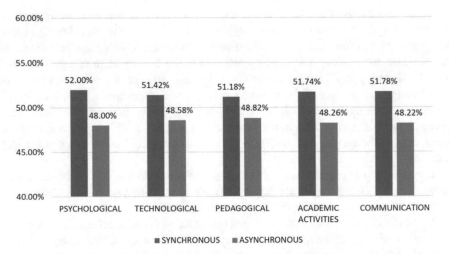

Fig. 2. Study dimensions and their influence on synchronous and asynchronous modes.

4.2 Inferential Analysis

Relationship between career groups and synchronous and asynchronous modes. A comparison was made between the scores categorized by questions of both modes and the career groups, for which the analysis of variance (ANOVA) was used, which allows the comparison of the differences in the means of 3 or more groups.

The following hypotheses were proposed to be evaluated:

- H_0: There is no significant difference between scores in the career groups and the modes.
- H_1: There is a significant difference between the scores in the career groups and the modes.

According to the results shown in Table 2, for the synchronous mode, the probability value (PR) is greater than the significance level ($\alpha = 0.05$), so the null hypothesis is not

Table 2. Analysis of Variance: Career Modes and Groups.

Synchronous	sum_sq	Df	F	PR(>F)
C(Group)	180.61	4.00	1.36	0.25
Residual	50443.28	1514.00	NaN	NaN
Asynchronous	**sum_sq**	**Df**	**F**	**PR(>F)**
C(Group)	119.94	4.00	0.81	0.52
Residual	56187.15	1514.00	NaN	NaN

rejected, that is, no significant difference was found in the synchronous scores in the career groups.

For the asynchronous mode, a probability value (PR) greater than the level of significance ($\alpha = 0.05$) was obtained, so the null hypothesis is not rejected, it is concluded that no significant difference was found in the asynchronous scores in the career groups.

Concluding that both the synchronous and asynchronous modes at the level of professional career groups contributed in similar conditions to virtual education, however complementing with the previous descriptive analysis at the level of dimensions; it was possible to show that the use of technological tools was easier for the engineering and medical sciences career groups, the pedagogical and academic dimensions were better adapted for the social sciences group, and the communication dimension was less effective in the economic and medical sciences groups.

4.3 Contribution Relationship in the Teaching-Learning Process of Synchronous and Asynchronous Modes

Total categorized scores were used for both modes, using the Wilcoxon–Mann–Whitney test, where the following hypotheses were raised.

- H_0: The contribution level of the asynchronous mode is equal to the contribution level of the synchronous mode.
- H_1: The contribution level of the asynchronous mode is lower than the input level of the synchronous mode.

With the results shown in Table 3, we can conclude that there is statistical evidence that the level of contribution of the asynchronous mode is lower than the level of contribution of the synchronous mode (Sig. Statistics < 0.05). Therefore, the synchronous mode is the one that best contributes to the virtual teaching-learning process and therefore to the academic performance of the students.

Table 3. Comparison analysis of the level of perception of synchronous and asynchronous modes.

Test statistics[a]	
	Asynchronous scoring − Synchronous scoring
Z	−21.65[b]
Asymptotic significance (bilateral)	.00
a. Wilcoxon signed rank test	
b. It is based on positive ranges.	

5 Discussion

In the discussion of the results, [3] state that students who went through stress, cognitive, emotional, and motivational aspects of learning, experienced difficulties in adapting to remote learning, however, in our research, it was obtained that women despite having a greater affectation in the psychological aspect their adaptation was better in the synchronous mode [16, 17].

According to [6], it is considered that the synchronous mode has more acceptance in students, while [7] indicates the asynchronous mode as a broad concept of learning, our results show that students perceive both modes as complementary in their virtual teaching process, but considering the synchronous mode as the one with the greatest influence on some key aspects of the teaching-learning process and the asynchronous mode as the one that most contributes to his investigative skills.

Finally, [14] argues that connectivity, access to technologies, and economic resources affect the virtual teaching process. Our results show that 65% of students have adequate equipment, while only 31% have an adequate internet connection, which shows that it also influences the virtual teaching-learning process, although they perceive that are more affected in the synchronous modality than in the asynchronous one.

This study could be complemented by the perception of the university teacher on the development of their activities in the synchronous and asynchronous modes and allow it to be a guide that supports the feedback of the university educational model [18].

6 Conclusions

The dimensions of the present study allowed us to identify in a segmented way, based on dimensions, its influence on the virtual teaching-learning process and the academic performance of the students, thus we found in the technological dimension, there was an ease of use of tools by teachers in the planning and development of their activities, as well as students who achieved good performance in the use of virtual environments; likewise, in the pedagogical dimension, the most remarkable thing is that there was motivation on the part of students and teachers to adapt to this new educational normality, however, the percentages of perception indicate that it can still be improved.

The psychological dimension was present in a transversal way throughout the teaching-learning process influencing manifestations such as stress and anxiety in the attention of students in online classes, however, women adapted better to virtual education despite being the most affected by psychological factors.

In the dimension of academic activities, the perception of the students highlights the excess of activities and scheduled tasks, the non-commensurate times for the delivery of activities, and the feedback that was not effective in many cases.

In the communication dimension, the tools used between teachers and students were considered effective.

Likewise, through the statistical analysis, it was determined that the level of perception of the synchronous mode is greater than the asynchronous, which indicates that the teaching-learning process received a better contribution of the synchronous mode and all the activities that made it up: online activities through Google Meet, collaborative documents, digital whiteboards, presentations of works and the tools of communication. This is not to say that the asynchronous mode did not generate input, however statistical evidence indicates that some of its activities should be improved: excess planned activities, delivery times, qualification of all activities, and the form of communication.

Finally, the study dimensions analyzed through the career groups showed that they did not have a significant influence on the teaching-learning process, on the contrary, they contributed to conditions similar to virtual education.

Therefore, with the study carried out, it has been shown that the synchronous mode contributed more effectively to the academic training of the students in virtual education, where online interaction with teachers was important in the accompaniment of their learning and the asynchronous mode strengthened the investigative skills for this process, since they were able to autonomously manage their time for the review of material in their virtual classrooms, digital libraries and information from the internet.

With the analysis of the dimensions of study, a significant contribution is made to virtual education, based on the perception of the students and how they were participants in the accelerated change from the face-to-face mode to the virtual mode, in order to not affect their academic training; therefore the results found in this research will serve as support for the universities make the necessary adjustments in those training indicators (use of technologies, motivation, planning of activities, communication, etc.) that require it and in those that worked properly, carry out a continuous improvement, which contributes towards the development of a hybrid educational model for the institutions of higher education.

References

1. Arias, E., Escamilla, J., López, A., Peña, L.: COVID-19: Tecnologías Digitales y Educación Superior¿ Qué opinan los docentes? Centro de Información para la mejora de los aprendizajes CIMA. Inter-American Development Bank IDB (2020)
2. UNESCO: Education: From disruption to recovery. https://en.unesco.org/covid19/education response. Accessed 22 Nov 2004
3. Biwer, F., et al.: Changes and adaptations: how university students self-regulate their online learning during the COVID-19 pandemic. Front. Psychol. **12**, 642593 (2021)
4. Baber, H.: Modelling the acceptance of e-learning during the pandemic of COVID-19-A study of South Korea. Int. J. Manag. Educ. **19**, 100503 (2021)

5. Tuma, F., Nassar, A.K., Kamel, M.K., Knowlton, L.M., Jawad, N.K.: Students and faculty perception of distance medical education outcomes in resource-constrained system during COVID-19 pandemic A cross-sectional study. Ann. Med. Surg. **62**, 377–382 (2021)
6. Nguyen, T., et al.: Insights into students' experiences and perceptions of remote learning methods: from the COVID-19 pandemic to best practice for the future. In: Frontiers in Education, p. 91. Frontiers (2021)
7. Tuma, F., Aljazeeri, J.: Asynchronous group learning in learn from the learner approach: a learning object that enhances and facilitates distance self and shared learning. Ann. Med. Surg. **67**, 102535 (2021)
8. Shi, Y., Tong, M., Long, T.: Investigating relationships among blended synchronous learning environments, students' motivation, and cognitive engagement: A mixed methods study. Comput. Educ. **168**, 104193 (2021)
9. Cardona, D.M., Sánchez, J.M.: Indicadores Básicos para Evaluar el Proceso de Aprendizaje en Estudiantes de Educación a Distancia en Ambiente e-learning. Form. Univ. **3**, 15–32 (2010)
10. Ivonne, R., Carla, J., Bernarda, M.R., Ingrid, O.: Percepciones universitarias sobre la educación virtual. Red docentes IB. **3**, 1–6 (2020)
11. Acevedo, E.N., Daza-Orozco, C.E.: Construction of Content for Virtual Education: Lockdown's Circumstantial Challenges. Panorama. 14 (2020)
12. Shah, S.S., Shah, A.A., Memon, F., Kemal, A.A., Soomro, A.: Online learning during the COVID-19 pandemic: Applying the self-determination theory in the 'new normal.' Rev. Psicodidáctica (English Ed.) **26**, 168–177 (2021)
13. Son, C., Hegde, S., Smith, A., Wang, X., Sasangohar, F.: Effects of COVID-19 on college students' mental health in the United States: Interview survey study. J. Med. internet Res. **22**, e21279 (2020)
14. Ortega-Alvarez, D.D., Boom-Carcamo, E.A.: Análisis de la percepción de estudiantes presenciales acerca de clases virtuales como respuesta a la crisis del covid-19. Espacios. 41, 81–92 (2020)
15. Martínez, G.A., Jiménez, N.: Análisis del uso de las aulas virtuales en la Universidad de Cundinamarca. Colombia. Form. Univ. **13**, 81–92 (2020)
16. Negrete, J.C.M., Iano, Y., Negrete, P.D.M., Vaz, G.C., de Oliveira, G.G.: Sentiment analysis in the ecuadorian presidential election. In: Brazilian Technology Symposium, pp. 25–34. Springer (2023) https://doi.org/10.1007/978-3-031-04435-9_3
17. Negrete, J.C.M., Iano, Y., Negrete, P.D.M., Vaz, G.C., de Oliveira, G.G.: Sentiment and emotions analysis of tweets during the second round of 2021 ecuadorian presidential election. In: Brazilian Technology Symposium, pp. 257–268. Springer (2023) https://doi.org/10.1007/978-3-031-04435-9_24
18. Demanboro, A.C., Bianchini, D., Iano, Y., de Oliveira, G.G., Vaz, G.C.: 6G networks: An innovative approach, but with many challenges and paradigms, in the development of platforms and services in the near future. In: Brazilian Technology Symposium, pp. 172–187. Springer (2023) https://doi.org/10.1007/978-3-031-04435-9_17

Using Thermal Wheels for LAFIQ/Fiocruz Air Conditioning System Heat Recovery

Lucas José Paskevicius Rabecchi[1] , Maria Thereza de Moraes Gomes Rosa[2] ,
and Míriam Tvrská de Gouvêa[1](✉)

[1] School of Engineering, Mackenzie Presbyterian University, Campinas, Brazil
miriamtg_br@yahoo.com
[2] Center of Science and Technology, Mackenzie Presbyterian University, Campinas, Brazil

Abstract. Thermal wheels are heat exchangers whose function is to recover process heat that has been recently applied in heat and ventilation air conditioning systems (HVAC) to increase energy efficiency. The objective of the present work was to evaluate the reduction in thermal load of the HVAC of the Physical Chemistry Laboratory of Fiocruz in Rio de Janeiro (LAFIQ) that could be achieved by incorporating thermal wheels in the HVAC. The model of the HVAC presented in this study is based on mass and energy balances and on a model of efficiency to represent the operation of the thermal wheels. Correlations were derived for the evaluation of the effectiveness of the thermal wheel, which is based on experimental data from the literature. The proposed model was used to simulate different operational scenarios in order to investigate the reduction in the thermal load promoted by the usage of enthalpic wheels. Reduction in the thermal load varied in the range of 40% to 60% depending on the simulation scenario, showing that incorporating thermal wheels is desirable for increasing energy efficiency.

Keyword: Air Conditioning · Enthalpic Wheel · Pharmaceutical industry

1 Introduction

The pharmaceutical industry experiences continuous growth, which has been made even larger due to the COVID-19 pandemic. Generally, in the pharmaceutical industries, conditioned air is provided by a central water-air conditioning system and air quality must be assured by rigorous norms of the sector, which contributes to high energy consumption by air conditioning systems of the order of 47.3% of the total energy demand. The interest in applying energy efficiency policies is, however, relatively recent in that sector [1, 2]. Energy is mainly consumed in the compressor of the vapor compression system of the air conditioning system, which is dependent on the thermal loads of the climatized zones, particularly laboratories [3, 4].

Thermal wheels are rotatory heat exchangers positioned within supply and exhaust air streams and are shown to be a powerful tool to reduce energy consumption and are being applied in hot and humid climates in air-conditioning systems [5]. Those heat exchangers are cylindrical in shape and contain packed small air passages parallel to the axial direction of the cylinder [5], as illustrated in Fig. 1.

© The Author(s), under exclusive license to Springer Nature Switzerland AG 2023
Y. Iano et al. (Eds.): BTSym 2022, SIST 353, pp. 419–427, 2023.
https://doi.org/10.1007/978-3-031-31007-2_39

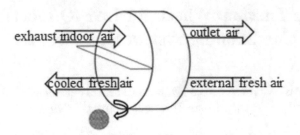

Fig. 1. General scheme of a rotatory thermal wheel.

External air exchanges sensible and latent heat with exhaust air from the climatized zones in the thermal wheels. Though contamination between external air and exhaust air may occur, it can be minimized and controlled by using highly efficient filters (HEPA type H13) [6, 7]. Consequently, it is important to consider the usage of thermal wheels in air conditioning systems in the pharmaceutical industry sector.

In this work, the usage of thermal wheels to reduce energy consumption by the air conditioning system of the physical chemistry laboratory LAFIQ of Fiocruz in Rio de Janeiro, where the Oxford/Astrazeneca vaccines are produced, is investigated. Process simulation of a thermal model of the current and modified air conditioning system of the laboratory is applied to analyze the reduction of thermal load that would be achieved if thermal wheels were used [8]. The effect of the external air flow rate on the thermal load of the air conditioning system is also analyzed.

2   Description of the Air-Conditioning System and the Proposed Mathematical Model

Figure 2 shows the air-conditioning simulation flowsheets of the LAFIQ laboratory considered here. In Fig. 2a, the current configuration of the LAFIQ laboratory is considered. The air in the laboratory is conditioned by a central air-water conditioning system. Both figures focus on the air streams and do not show the chiller that produces refrigerated water for the fan coil that serves LAFIQ and other laboratories of the Fiocruz pharmaceutical industry in Rio de Janeiro, Brazil. According to the scheme shown in Fig. 2b, fresh external air enters the thermal wheels through stream 0 and exchanges sensible and latent heat with exhaust air from the laboratory (stream 10). Stream 1 is mixed with the return laboratory air stream 9 and enters the fan coil that serves LAFIQ, where it is cooled to stream 3, and water is condensed (stream 12). The fan coil uses cold water that is refrigerated in a central vapor compression system not shown in Fig. 2. In the real plant, there are also air filters before the fan coil. The cold air from the fan coil (stream 3) is divided into streams 4 and 5. Stream 5 enters the terminal heater and stream 4 is a bypass stream. The warm stream from the terminal heater is mixed with the bypass stream used to control the air temperature of the LAFIQ laboratory and the mixed stream enters the LAFIQ laboratory. All air streams leaving LAFIQ are mixed in both diagrams of Fig. 2, and the combined stream is represented by stream 8, which is divided into the return and exhaust streams 9 and 10. The latter may enter the thermal wheels for heat recovery (Fig. 2b), while stream 9 is mixed with the external air stream (passing or not through the thermal wheel).

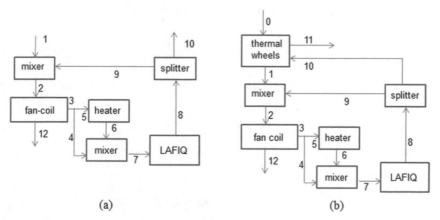

(a)   (b)

Fig. 2. Simulation flowsheet of the LAFIQ air conditioning system: (a) current configuration (b) inclusion of thermal wheels into the HVAC system.

The proposed model of the process diagrams in Fig. 2 is composed of mass and energy balances, which are presented in Eqs. 1 to 14. All pipes are considered adiabatic and flow through fans is considered isothermal. The following nomenclature is adopted in the process model. The dried air mass flow rates and specific enthalpies of each stream j ($j = 1, \ldots, 11$) are represented, respectively, by $\dot{m}_j$ and h_j. UA_j is the humidity ratio of stream j. Q_{heater}, Q_{fc}, and Q_{total} are, respectively, the thermal loads of the terminal heater, fan coil, and LAFIQ laboratory. The condensed water mass flowrate and specific heat are represented by $\dot{m}_{12}$ and $cp_{w,l}$. Since the temperature of stream 6 is controlled by manipulating the bypass flow rate, Eq. 13 is used to evaluate the thermal heat consumption of the terminal heater. Q_{total} encompasses both the sensible and latent heat of the LAFIQ laboratory. In accordance with specifications applied to the pharmacological sector, design values for the temperature of stream 6, return air flow rate, laboratory total, and sensible heats are, respectively 25 °C, 4414 m³/h, 29.86 kW, and 26.48 kW. Because pipes are assumed adiabatic, specific enthalpies of streams 8, 9, and 10 are identical and are equal to the specific enthalpy inside the laboratory. LAFIQ air thermodynamic state is to remain at a dried bulb temperature of 20 °C and relative humidity of 50%. The fan coil of the system is designed to provide exit air stream 3 at 10 °C and 95% relative humidity. Air properties, the specific heat of liquid and vapor water, and dried air and vaporization enthalpy of water at 0 °C are modeled or considered as described by [9].

$$\dot{m}_0 - \dot{m}_1 = 0 \tag{1}$$

$$\dot{m}_{10} - \dot{m}_{11} = 0 \tag{2}$$

$$\dot{m}_1 + \dot{m}_9 - \dot{m}_2 = 0 \tag{3}$$

$$\dot{m}_2 - \dot{m}_3 = 0 \tag{4}$$

$$\dot{m}_2(UA_2 - UA_3) - \dot{m}_{12} = 0 \tag{5}$$

$$\dot{m}_3 + \dot{m}_5 - \dot{m}_4 = 0 \tag{6}$$

$$\dot{m}_5 - \dot{m}_6 = 0 \tag{7}$$

$$\dot{m}_4 + \dot{m}_6 - \dot{m}_7 = 0 \tag{8}$$

$$\dot{m}_7 - \dot{m}_9 - \dot{m}_{10} = 0 \tag{9}$$

$$\dot{m}_0 h_0 + \dot{m}_{10} h_{10} - \dot{m}_1 h_1 - \dot{m}_{11} h_{11} = 0 \tag{10}$$

$$\dot{m}_1 h_1 + \dot{m}_9 h_9 - \dot{m}_2 h_2 = 0 \tag{11}$$

$$\dot{m}_2(h_2 - h_3) - \dot{m}_{12} cp_{w,l} T_3 - Q_{fc} = 0 \tag{12}$$

$$\dot{m}_4 h_3 + \dot{m}_5 h_5 - \dot{m}_7 h_7 + Q_{heater} = 0 \tag{13}$$

$$\dot{m}_7(h_7 - h_9) - Q_{total} = 0 \tag{14}$$

The sensible heat of the laboratory can be evaluated by Eq. 15, where h_I is the specific air enthalpy evaluated at the humidity ratio of stream 7 and the dried bulb temperature of stream 9.

$$\dot{m}_7(h_7 - h_I) - Q_s = 0 \tag{15}$$

The heat exchanged between external and exhaust air in the thermal wheels was predicted by an effectiveness model, for which effectiveness correlations were established based on the experimental data published by [6], which considered 3 types of effectiveness, namely, total, sensible and latent effectiveness.

Figure 3 and Fig. 4, 5 show the experimental data provided by [6] and the adjusted correlations proposed in this work. Total and latent effectivenesses are dependent on the thermal wheels speed, while sensible effectiveness is mainly dependent on the airflow rate and dependency on the external air temperature is not significant accordingly to experimental data presented in [6]. Since the experimental data provided by the authors consider a thermal wheel operating with flowrates from 400 m³/h to 1200 m³/h, in the current work, six thermal wheels operating in parallel are considered in order to process the external air design flowrate of 6003.3 m³/h. The minimum and maximum flow rates of each thermal will are considered as 400 m³/h to 1200 m³/h. In the present work, the correlations in the effectiveness ε_L and ε_T were used to evaluate the humidity ratio and dried bulb temperature of stream 1 assuming each thermal wheel operating at 400 m³/h and the effectiveness of sensible heat correlation was used to adjust the temperature of stream 1 to meet the real air flow rate through the thermal wheel. Because of the absence of additional experimental data, no further adjustments were made to the humidity ratio of stream 1. The nominal thermal wheel speed was considered to be 15 rpm and the nominal latent effectiveness was considered to be 85%.

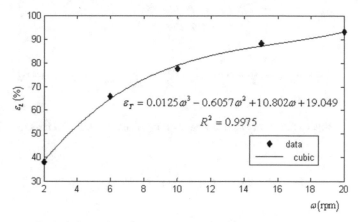

Fig. 3. Effect of thermal wheel's speed on latent effectiveness.

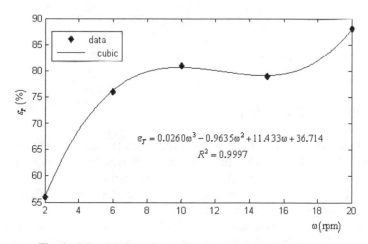

Fig. 4. Effect of thermal wheel's speed on total effectiveness.

Equations 16 to 19 show how the effectiveness evaluated by the proposed correlations was used to estimate the thermodynamic states of stream 1. Enthalpy h_1^* and temperature T_1^* are related by the air-specific enthalpy ASHRAE model [9] presented in Eq. 20, where, λ, cp_{air}, and $cp_{w,v}$ are, respectively, the latent heat of vaporization of water at 0 °C and specific heats of dried air and water vapor.

$$UA_1 = UA_0 + \varepsilon_L(UA_0 - UA_{10}) \tag{16}$$

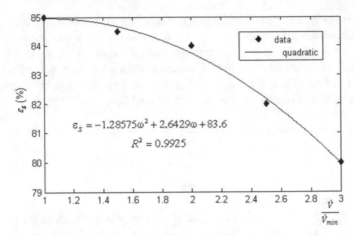

Fig. 5. Effect of external air flow rate on sensible effectiveness.

$$T_1 = T_0 + \varepsilon_s \frac{\varepsilon^*}{85}(T_0 - T_{10}) \tag{17}$$

$$\varepsilon^* = \frac{T_0 - T_1^*}{T_0 - T_{10}} \times 100\% \tag{18}$$

$$h_1^* = h_0 + \varepsilon_T(h_0 - h_{10}) \tag{19}$$

$$h_1^* = cp_{air}T_1^* + UA_1\left(\lambda - cp_{w,v}T_1^*\right) \tag{20}$$

3   Results and Discussion

The model presented in Sect. 2 was solved using Excel™. Table 1 presents simulation results for the following variables: dried air mass flowrate entering the laboratory ($\dot{m}_7$), external air volumetric flowrate ($\dot{V}_o$), return air volumetric flowrate ($\dot{V}_9$), thermal loads of the fan coil (Q_{fc}), and terminal heater (Q_{heater}). Simulation results include an evaluation of the nominal operating point and six different scenarios.

In scenario 1, the external air flow rate is decreased by about 10%, and the return air flow rate is increased to maintain the mass flow rate into the laboratory constant. Thermal wheels are neither considered in scenario 1 nor the nominal point. The thermal load of the terminal heater remained the same as for the nominal point because the air thermodynamic state at the exit of the fan coil is controlled and therefore the bypass ratio is not altered, as well as the thermodynamic state of the laboratory. The reduction in the fan coil thermal load was 7,6%. However, a reduction in external air flow rate may compromise laboratory air quality.

Scenarios 2 to 6 show simulation results with the usage of thermal wheels. Scenario 2 corresponds to maintaining design external and return air flow rates. A drastic reduction in the thermal load of the fan coil of 57% can be seen. This result clearly shows that including thermal wheels in the process largely reduces the energetic demand.

Simulations 3 to 5 explore the effect of not using return air. The idea is to augment external air flowrate to increase air quality control in the laboratories. However, one must have in mind that although no return air flow rate is used, contamination of the inlet laboratory stream may still be possible because of air contamination that may occur in the thermal wheels. Therefore, it is essential to remain using air filters before the fan coil.

In scenarios 3 and 4, the mass inlet flow rate into the laboratory was maintained at the nominal operating point. In case 3 the thermal wheel´s speed was maintained at the nominal assumed operating value and, in case 4, it was increased to 20 rpm. We can still observe a significant decrease in the thermal load of the order of 40% for case 3 and about 51% for case 4. Hence, a significant reduction in energy consumption would be achieved, while augmenting air quality, since the smaller the return air flow rate and the higher the external air flow rate, the better air quality. However, since the external air flow rate was significantly increased, 9 or 10 thermal wheels would be needed, increasing the capital investment. Simulation results of case 4 show that manipulating the thermal wheel´s speed is important to achieve a higher reduction in the fan coil thermal load. Since the increase in external air flow rate facilitates air quality control, it is not necessary to maintain the design value inlet flow rate in the laboratory. When the inlet flow rate to the laboratory is reduced, the bypass ratio must be increased to maintain the temperature of the laboratory at the specified value.

The last two simulations explore operating scenarios with higher external air flowrate in regard to the nominal operating point and with a bypass ratio of 100%. Obviously, when the bypass ratio is 100%, the terminal heater will not be used. The thermal wheels´ speeds are maintained at 15 rpm for simulation cases 5 and 6. Scenario 5 corresponds to the maximum external air flowrate that can be introduced with a bypass ratio of 100% and without using return air, while in scenario 6, the bypass ratio is also maintained at 100%, but return air is used so that external air flowrate corresponds to the maximum value that can be used with only six thermal wheels with a maximum capacity of 1200 m^3/h. Inlet-dried air mass flow rate into the laboratory is evaluated by the simulator as 2.59 kg/s for both scenarios 5 and 6. Reduction in energy consumption is significant. In scenario 5, the reduction in the thermal load of the fan coil is 55% in regard to the nominal point and in scenario 6 it is 59%. The observed values in a reduction in the thermal load in the range of 40 to 60% are in accordance with reported values for other case studies [5, 10–12].

Simulation results showed a clear reduction in thermal load when using thermal wheels. The usage of the latter also enables the increase in external air flow rate, which is an interesting strategy to control air quality. However, there are implementation costs associated with the insertion of thermal wheels in the air conditioning plant. Noteworthy is the fact that reducing energy consumption also contributes to the reduction of CO_2 emissions. So, further research will focus on the economical viability of incorporating thermal wheels in the air conditioning system of LAFIQ. One last comment is worthy.

Table 1. Evaluation of thermal loads

Simulation scenario	$\dot{m}_7$ (kg/s)	$\dot{V}_O$ (m³/h)	$\dot{V}_9$ (m³/h)	Q_{fc} (kW)	Q_{heater} (kW)
Nominal point	3,29	6003	4412	125,84	7,09
1	3,29	5379	4986	116,26	7,09
2	3,29	6003	4412	53,62	7,09
3	3,29	10776	0	75,34	7,09
4	3,29	10776	0	62,26	7,09
5	2,59	8483	0	56,78	0
6	2,59	7200	1191	51,25	0

The electricity consumption of the air conditioning system is dependent on both fan coil and terminal heater loads but is not identical to the sum of those thermal loads, since the thermal load of the fan coil will affect the operation of the chiller of the air conditioning system and variations in the thermal load will mainly impact the energy consumption of the chiller's compressor.

4 Conclusions

This study showed that a significant reduction in the thermal load of the fan coil of the air-water conditioning system of the LAFIQ laboratory could be obtained if thermal wheels were incorporated into the air-conditioning system. If the external air flow rate and the inlet air flow rate into the laboratory were maintained at design values, a reduction in the fan coil thermal load would be 57%. If no return air was used, still a large reduction of the order of 40% would be observed in the thermal load. This promising result motivates further research that will focus on the estimation of the payback period and on an economic viability assessment of implementing thermal wheels.

Acknowledgment. The authors thank engineer Eduardo Rein of Reintech company for supplying the information necessary to perform the evaluations presented in the current work.

References

1. Chaturvedi, U., Sharma, M., Dangayach, G.S., Sarkar, P.: Evolution and adoption of sustainable practices in the pharmaceutical industry: An overview with an Indian perspective. J. Clean. Prod. **168**, 1358–1369 (2017)
2. Capparella, J.: Energy benchmarking in the pharmaceutical industry. Pharm Eng. **33**, 1–6 (2013)
3. Lee, K.-P., Cheng, T.-A.: A simulation–optimization approach for energy efficiency of chilled water system. Energy Build. **54**, 290–296 (2012)

4. Siegle, A.R., Iano, Y., Gomes, G., de Oliveira, G., Vaz, C.: Proposal of mathematical models for a continuous flow electric heater. In: Iano, Y., Saotome, O., Vásquez, G.L.K., Pezzuto, C.C., Arthur, R., Gomes de Oliveira, G. (eds.) Proceedings of the 7th Brazilian Technology Symposium (BTSym'21): Emerging Trends in Human Smart and Sustainable Future of Cities (Volume 1), pp. 213–228. Springer International Publishing, Cham (2023). https://doi.org/ 10.1007/978-3-031-04435-9_20
5. Herath, H., Wickramasinghe, M.D.A., Polgolla, A., Jayasena, A.S., Ranasinghe, R., Wijewardane, M.A.: Applicability of rotary thermal wheels to hot and humid climates. Energy Rep. **6**, 539–544 (2020)
6. Kassai, M., Al-Hyari, L.: Experimental investigation on operation parameters of 3Å molecular sieve desiccant coated total energy recovery wheel for maximum effectiveness. Therm. Sci. **24**, 2113–2124 (2020)
7. O Futuro da Refrigeração – Leonardo Energy Brasil. https://leonardo-energy.org.br/noticias/ o-futuro-da-refrigeracao. Accessed 20 May 2018
8. de Lima, L.B., et al.: Mathematical modeling: a conceptual approach of linear algebra as a tool for technological applications. In: Brazilian Technology Symposium, pp. 239–248. Springer (2023) https://doi.org/10.1007/978-3-031-04435-9_22
9. Ashrae. Handbook of Fundamentals. ASHRAE Inc. (2017)
10. Azevedo, J.D.A.L.: Sistemas dedicados ao tratamento do ar de renovação no condicionamento de ar. Universidade Federal do Rio de Janeiro (2013). https://docplayer.com.br/144 43103-Sistemas-dedicados-ao-tratamento-do-ar-de-renovacao-no-condicionamento-de-ar- joao-d-anuzio-lima-de-azevedo.html. Accessed 20 May 2018
11. O'Connor, D., Calautit, J.K.S., Hughes, B.R.: A review of heat recovery technology for passive ventilation applications. Renew. Sustain. Energy Rev. **54**, 1481–1493 (2016)
12. Niemann, P., Schmitz, G.: Air conditioning system with enthalpy recovery for space heating and air humidification: an experimental and numerical investigation. Energy **213**, 118789 (2020)

A Data-Driven Methodology for Analyzing Field Nonconformities in Semiconductor Production Applied to a Brazilian Manufacturer

Jorge M. de Souza[1] , Giovanni M. de Holanda[1] , Fabrício Cristófani[1(✉)] ,
Luana A. Sartor[2] , and Paulo C. Sardinha[2]

[1] FITec – Technological Innovations, Campinas, Brazil
{jmdsouza,gholanda,fabriciocristofani}@fitec.org.br
[2] Brasil Componentes – Multi, Extrema, Brazil
luana.sartor@grupomulti.com.br, paulo.sardinha@multilaser.com.br

Abstract. The stages of the semiconductor production chain range from design and production to field monitoring and customer service. Failure analysis of products on the market is essential to provide feedback for production and in- crease process quality. This paper presents an analytical methodology based on customer semiconductor failure data, which integrates a specific system to manage these failures (the Sigequalis) and adds efforts to control the manufacturing process, extending analytical capabilities to the final stages of the production chain. It includes an approach for analyzing reliable offenders and a key indicator, whose monitoring reinforces the use of 8D methodology for corrective actions of nonconformities. Such analyses allow for identifying batches of devices with problems, directing actions that may anticipate the occurrence of problems for customers, and providing feedback to the manufacturing process. The methodology and its corresponding tool combine and expand the information collected from customers, enabling a big picture of possible offending elements in order to act correctively and predictively, improving the quality of semiconductor production.

Keywords: Quality analysis · Data intelligence · Semiconductor manufacturing

1 Introduction

The production of semiconductors is responsible for an essential role in the densification of the production chain of the electronic complex, which is responsible for the production of several final goods in the Brazilian market [1]. The production stages of an integrated circuit (IC) range from the semiconductor design, that is, the definition of features and component design, going through the front-end process (foundry), encapsulation/assembly/test (back-end), and chip integration, up to the end customer service.

This expanded production chain reflects the technological and business complexity of the semiconductor industry, with the participation of multiple agents, characterizing what Bampi [2] calls the "productive and technological ecosystem". In this environment,

© The Author(s), under exclusive license to Springer Nature Switzerland AG 2023
Y. Iano et al. (Eds.): BTSym 2022, SIST 353, pp. 428–438, 2023.
https://doi.org/10.1007/978-3-031-31007-2_40

with different levels of collaboration in the production cycle, some companies assume the role of more than one agent, verticalizing part of the process in its own factory structure, cf. [3].

Once the chips are encapsulated, the integration into equipment and the sale of the product can be done both by those who encapsulate the chips and by third parties in the electronics sector, densifying the production chain. In any situation, it is essential to feedback to the production team with information on defective items detected by customers. Such feedback is based on information generated at some inspection points, which feed control loops to reduce losses, improve the quality of items produced, and increase the efficiency of the production process. Indicators aimed at evaluating this manufacturing process usually focus on yield (effective production), quality (suitability to specifications and use), production time, and productivity, among others (e.g., [4]).

Continuous monitoring of manufacturing indicators allows visibility and more effective control of the process, leading to corrective and preventive actions, maintenance planning, time reduction, more efficient use of the production line, and, of course, customer satisfaction. Consequently, the checkpoints that feed control loops, the analytical tools that support decisions, and course-correcting actions must permeate not only the initial stages of production but also the end of the chain, i.e., customer service.

Like other manufacturing sectors, the semiconductor industry has the production goal of minimizing cost and maximizing quality and reliability. Quality can be achieved with stable and controlled processes. In turn, reliability depends on reducing manufacturing faults, which can be detected at production line control points – a lower corrective cost situation – or when failures are reported by customers [5–8].

Analysis methodologies play an important role in ensuring reliability, not just at line quality-check points to reduce process variability [9], but also to enable improved reliability by taking actions in advance of failures. Such actions are based on data collected from the laboratory and production line by monitoring the product during its initial use (cf. [10]).

Brasil Componentes - Multi is one of the agents that participate in the semiconductor production chain and integrate the electronic complex in Brazil. This paper presents an analysis methodology developed for this company, based on semiconductor failure data reported by customers via a customer relationship system. This methodology integrates a specific system to manage these failures (the Sigequalis) and adds efforts to the statistical treatments already developed to control the production process [9], extending analytical capabilities to the final stages of the production chain. It includes two methods of analyzing reliability offenders and a key indicator, whose analytical monitoring makes it possible to identify device batches with problems, directing actions that anticipate the occurrence of problems for customers and that, at the same time, can provide feedback to the manufacturing process.

The paper is structured as follows. Section 2 brings a brief discussion of the literature on statistical treatments of monitoring and control aimed at raising the level of factory production quality. Section 3 summarizes the basic dynamics of nonconformity management performed by the Application Engineering team at Brasil Componentes - Multi. Section 4 presents the approach for critical analysis developed for Sigequalis, in terms of identifying faulty components and providing quality monitoring of devices and production batches. Section 5 brings the essence of the methodology and the analysis of the results achieved to a conclusion, highlighting the current stage of development, the prospects for the evolution of the approach, and its potential for contribution to the quality of semiconductor production.

2   A Brief Discussion of the Literature

For a semiconductor manufacturing company, a product failure detected by the customer has negative implications in several dimensions: economic, environmental, product acceptance, and corporate image. Statistics play an important role in ensuring the reliability of manufacturing processes (see, for example, [11]).

There are many studies and approaches in recent literature applying statistics and data intelligence to detect defects, identify root causes of failures and improve the reliability of semiconductor production [12–18]. Zero defect targets are increasingly seen by semiconductor manufacturers as potentially achievable [13]. Machine learning and big data have proved to be important techniques to bring this scenario closer [13, 19–22].

The combination of statistical methods with reliability growth models has also been of significant value in improving the quality of semiconductor manufacturing [23, 24]. Another important combination for the methodology presented here is the application of the 8D methodology with statistical analysis capabilities to identify non-conformities and analyze root causes in manufacturing processes [25–27]. The 8D methodology establishes a permanent corrective action based on a statistical analysis of the problem and focuses on the origin of the problem by determining its root causes.

Zhou et al. [28] merge the 8D methodology with six sigma programs, based on after-sales customer complaints, to improve product quality and improve the company's image, helping decisions in terms of performance criteria and process capability. The six Sigma concept refers to how many standard deviations there are between a process's average result and its target outcome. The merging of 8D, Six Sigma, and other analytical tools [29] has shown promising results in root cause analysis and in reducing the rate of defects in industrial production.

Therefore, it is observed in the literature, the practice of combining these methodologies and analytical resources to work statistically on the quality indicators of semiconductor products and support decisions to improve the quality of the production process. In the work herein addressed, such application occurs in the formulation of indicators molded to the operational and traceability specificities of the products we need to monitor in the 8D flow, combined with statistical techniques to detect root causes of defects and to enable confidence in inferences and trends from calculated results.

3   Quality Management of Nonconformities

The scope of this methodology comprises the monitoring and treatment of failures in semiconductor components being used by customers, among them, memory modules, UFD-COB, eMMC, eMCP, Micro SD Cards, and SSDs, embedded in various products, such as smartphones, tablets, pen drives, cameras, computers, and car stereo. The relationship with customers has as its central element the RMA (Return Merchandise

Authorization), from which the analyses begin by verifying the quality targets that may indicate the need for a detailed treatment of nonconformities of the reported products.

The quality indices used in contracts with customers are reliability-oriented, such as "Yield Rate", "Defect per Million" (DPM), and Customer Satisfaction or Failure Rate, and are measured by the customer himself during material incoming, mass production, and after-sales. During the first contact with the company support, the customer reports the SKU (Stock Keeping Unit), part number and serial number, the number of samples used in the evaluation, the deviations from the expected values for these indicators, etc. The Application Engineering team carries out an analysis to verify the need to open a corrective action report (the RAC, in the acronym in Portuguese), in case the values reported by the customer are not in accordance with the contracted DPM.

Nonconformity (NC) management applies the 8D methodology [30–32]. An important phase in this methodology is that the problem encountered by the customer is recorded (Phase D2, "Problem description") with all information regarding the component, usage, environment, product type, etc. Such information is recorded by the customer with the support of the Application Engineering team and is part of the records during the opening of the RAC. In the root cause analysis (Phase D3, "Develop Containment Plan"), the Quality & FAE (Field Application Engineering) team carefully analyzes the information recorded in the RAC and the NC history of a component to give a quick solution to the customer, to define and implement interim containment actions to isolate the problem from any current customer as well in future demand.

In addition, RMA provides a complementary index based on the percentage of returns (RMAs) compared with the number of products in the batch sent to the customer. The batches have identification and are monitored when the percentage of returns reaches a specified upper limit. It is an additional screening of the quality process that acting together with the RAC process can be used to flag potential nonconformity outcomes and to go further when some products do not achieve the contractual agreements. Quality actions can be resumed by the following points: i) open a RAC for the products not in accordance with the contractual agreement, ii) identify if there are other RACs related to the product and to which customers it was sold, iii) verify where the raw materials used by the non-compliant product are present, and iv) analyze the batches for which the percentage of batch return (RMA) reaches the defined upper limit.

The ultimate objective of product quality management is to identify critical products and guide action plans to eliminate problems and work on prevention rather than correction. To support this objective a software tool, Sigequalis, is under development to register and organize data related to the RAC and RMA processes and to evaluate the corresponding quality targets.

4 Methods for Analyzing Critical Components

In the context of this methodology, a product is characterized by three ways, where each one reveals different levels of detail: i) The SKU contains the product's main information such as product type, density, form factor, BOM (Bill of Materials) information, ODM (Original Design Manufacturer), and Controller brand; ii) The Part number (PN) contains additional product details, such as product form factor, flash type, capacity, speed information, and BOM; iii) The Serial Number (SN) contains additional product production information, such as work year, work week, flash sourcing, production line, capacity, supplier, and BOM.

As the RAC and RMA processes share those data, the quality targets of each process can be used to flag critical products still in stock or already in the field, based on the quality recorded data of its components, aiming to support a predictive action plan.

4.1 RAC Process - Yield Rate

The RAC template is filled by the customer and includes the data used for the yield rate evaluation as well as the serial number of non-conforming products. Based on the product SN, the BOM can be identified, and therefore all the batches sent to different customers can be detected as well as the component's PN. Figure 1 displays an example, which is related to the batches with the same BOM along with the components' PN (SSD, memory, and controller).

Date	Batch	Product code	PN Memory	PN Controller	BOM ID
10/abr	PGT314	A	YMN08TE1B1HC3B	AS2258-BM	58
13/mai	PGT319	A	YMN08TE1B1HC3B	AS2258-BM	58
24/jun	PGT321	A	YMN08TE1B1HC3B	SM2258XT	63

Fig. 1. Data from the Application Engineering database.

If, for example, the RAC reports the product/BOM A/58 as nonconforming, its components (memory, controller) must also be analyzed if they are present in other BOMs, aiming to anticipate or mitigate similar complaints from another possible customer. This is the case shown in Fig. 1, where BOM 63 and 58 contain the same memory.

The steps of the methodology for reliability analysis based on the RAC data can be summarized as follow: i) identify the BOM ID of nonconforming products, based on the product SN, and systematize the procedure that is currently performed; ii) search for the batches having the same BOM ID and identify the customers with products related to it; iii) record the measured yield rate of the non-conforming products; iv) record the yield rate requirement of identified customers; v) search for BOMs with the same component PN, since this component may be in other BOMs, as illustrated in Fig. 1; and vi) report the results for quality analysis and mitigation actions.

4.2 RMA Process – Percentage of Returns

The percentage of batch returns (RMA/M) expresses the ratio between the number of returns (RMA count) and the total production over a period (months) spanning between the batch that was sent to the customer and the current date. When $RMA/M > 0.2\%$, the batch is considered critical, triggering a quality analysis of the attributes of the corresponding products (BOM and component PNs). A first analysis can be carried out by sorting the critical batches as shown in Fig. 2 for $RMA/M > 0.2\%$ spanning over the years 2020 and 2021 for the SSD products.

Date	Batch	Product code	Memory PN	Controller PN	BOM ID	Total production	% RMA mensal
08/12/2020	PGT296	A	SDTNCIAMA-032GB	AS2258-BM	27	43,000	1.97%
08/12/2020	PGT296	B	SDTNBIAMA-064G	AS2258-BM	26	6,000	1.25%
10/04/2021	PGT314	A	YMN08TE1B1HC3B	AS2258-BM	58	15,000	1.17%
13/05/2021	PGT319	A	YMN08TE1B1HC3B	AS2258-BM	58	34,000	0.96%
22/02/2021	PGT299	B	SDTNBIAMA-064G	AS2258-BM	26	10,500	0.92%
22/02/2021	PGT299	B	SDYNBIAMA-064G	AS2258-BM	49	2,500	0.92%
08/12/2020	PGT296	C	SDTNBIAMA-064G	AS2258-BM	26	2,000	0.9%
17/11/2020	PGT105	B	30-POQA0HP981	22-3111CE1130	44	5,000	0.35%
16/09/2020	PGT097	D	30-POQA0HP986	22-3111CE1130	44	2,000	0.33%
22/02/2021	PGT299	A	SDTNDIAMA-032G	AS2258-BM	53	43,000	0.23%

Fig. 2. Critical batches based on the RMA/M screening and extracted from the database.

As in the RAC process, the BOM attribute identifies the component PNs of the critical batches. The result can be tabulated by eliminating repeated values.

The sorting result does not allow a search for critical components based on the BOM attribute, since the same BOM ID can appear several times in different ranks of the sorting, as shown in Fig. 2. This renders difficult a joint analysis of the results related to RAC and RMA processes. To overcome this issue the proposed solution is to define a weighted index, namely Weighted Return Index (*WRI*), based on the total production attribute. For attribute *A*, *WRI*(*A*) is defined by Eq. (1)

$$WRI(A) = \frac{\sum_{i=1}^{N} TotalProduction_A(i) \cdot \frac{RMA}{M_A(i)}}{\sum_{i=1}^{N} TotalProduction_A(i)} \tag{1}$$

where N is the number attribute A recorded in the analyzed period. As an illustration, the *WRI* for BOM 26 is defined by Eq. (2).

$$WRI(BOM\,26) = \frac{6,000 * 1.25\% + 10,500 * 0.92\% + 2,000 * 0.90\%}{18,500} = 1.025\% \tag{2}$$

Table 1 shows the weighted index for all the batches recorded in the database.

Table 1. WRI for the batches of Fig. 2.

BOM	Total production	WRI%
27	43,000	1.970
26	18,500	1.025
58	49,000	1.024
49	2,500	0.920
44	7,000	0.344
53	43,000	0.230

For products with several components, they can also be independently ranked by WRI using its PN. Figure 3a and 3b show the Pareto graph of the WRI for memory and controller PN.

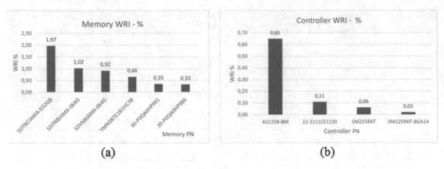

Fig. 3. Memory PN ranked by WRI.

This raises a question about the influence of the components on the BOM behavior as, for example, the controller AS2258-BM runs with different memories (see Fig. 2). The WRI correlation between the components and BOM highlights the memory as the main influencer in the BOM behavior as shown in Table 2.

Table 2. BOM vs. component correlation

	Mem	Contr	BOM
Mem	1.000	0.444	0.964
Contr	0.444	1.000	0.511
BOM	0.964	0.511	1.000

The steps of the RMA rank analysis using WRI are resumed in Fig. 4.

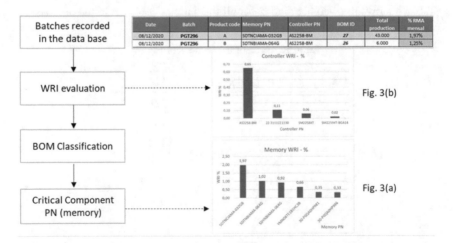

Fig. 4. RMA rank analysis.

4.3 RAC and RMA Processes in Concert

In the RAC and RMA processes, the BOM attribute is the central element. It is indicated in the product SNs attached to the RAC report and is a piece of information recorded in the RMA control. Therefore, it is possible to resume the targets related to the BOM in a consolidated report to give a broad picture of the product quality parameters. Figure 5 depicts a joint report of the BOM 58.

RAC - RMA Report					WRI%	
RAC	Product SN				1	0.66
BOM	58				2	0.65
Contratual YR	0.04%		Components		BOM correlation	
Measured YR	0.11%	1	YMN08TE1B1HC3B		1	96%
RMA Branches	PGT314, PGT319	2	AS2258-BM		2	51%

Fig. 5. BOM 58 RAC – RMA Report.

The joint report makes it possible to relate BOM, contractual information, batches, critical components, WRI, and the correlation of the BOM with the components in the same analytical framework, facilitating the identification of offending components and subsidizing corrective and predictive actions.

5   Conclusion

This paper presented an analysis methodology developed with a basis on semiconductor failure data reported by customers aiming to allow the identification of faulty semiconductor components and provide feedback to the quality engineering and customer service processes. This methodology includes the proposition of a specific indicator (the Weighted Return Index - WRI) for the characteristics of the follow-up process of corrective actions and is part of the quality management system, Sigequalis, which is the object of an ongoing R&D project. It has as a starting point the information reported by customers, which is sequentially detailed in two forms: RAC and RMA, according to contractual quality requirements.

With the application of this approach, it is possible to include new information and gather it in a single analytical framework, allowing i) identify the BOM ID of noncon- forming products; ii) search for the batches having the same BOM ID, and identify the customers with products related to it; iii) search for BOMs with the same component PN, since this component may be in other BOMs; and iv) report the results for quality analysis and mitigation actions. The combined analysis of RAC and RMA – encompassing the WRI – enables a big picture of the possible offending elements in order to act corrective and predictively, improving the quality of semiconductor product & process and strengthening the sector's production chain.

For a sharper and more advanced statistical analysis, a more significant volume of failure data is required, aiming to establish other reliability-oriented indicators, such as failure rate, confidence level, and reliability growth, and thus generate results with greater accuracy and applicability in the unfolding of the 8D methodology. Providing this analytical upgrade and improving data quality is one of the goals foreseen for the future evolution of Sigequalis.

Acknowledgment. The authors thank the Brazilian Ministry of Science, Technology, and Innovations for the financial support to this project through the PADIS (Program of Support for the Technological Development of the Semiconductor and Displays Industry).

References

1. Filippin, F.: Estado e desenvolvimento: a indústria de semicondutores no Brasil (2020)
2. da Silva Bueno, A.K.: Políticas setoriais de fomento à indústria microeletrônica no Brasil: descrição e resultados. GESTÃO DA SUSTENTABILIDADE Organ. 133
3. Aita, B.H.: A cadeia produtiva da indústria de semicondutores: um estudo exploratório. (2013)
4. Zhu, L., Johnsson, C., Varisco, M., Schiraldi, M.M.: Key performance indicators for manufacturing operations management–gap analysis between process industrial needs and ISO 22400 standard. Procedia Manuf. **25**, 82–88 (2018)
5. Demanboro, A.C., Bianchini, D., Iano, Y., de Oliveira, G.G., Vaz, G.C.: 6G networks: an innovative approach, but with many challenges and paradigms, in the development of platforms and services in the near future. In: Brazilian Technology Symposium, pp. 172–187. Springer (2023). https://doi.org/10.1007/978-3-031-04435-9_17
6. Izario, D., Brancalhone, J., Iano, Y., de Oliveira, G.G., Vaz, G.C., Izario, K.: 5G-automation of vertical systems in the industry 4.0. In: Brazilian Technology Symposium, pp. 35–43. Springer (2023). https://doi.org/10.1007/978-3-031-04435-9_4
7. Bonello, D.K., Iano, Y., Neto, U.B., de Oliveira, G.G., Vaz, G.C.: A study about automated optical inspection: inspection algorithms applied in flexible manufacturing printed circuit board cells using the mahalanobis distance method 1. In: Brazilian Technology Symposium, pp. 198–212. Springer (2023). https://doi.org/10.1007/978-3-031-04435-9_19
8. Nishimura, E.H., Iano, Y., de Oliveira, G.G., Vaz, G.C.: Application and requirements of AIoT-enabled industrial control units. In: Brazilian Technology Symposium, pp. 724–733. Springer (2022). https://doi.org/10.1007/978-3-031-08545-1_72
9. de Souza, J.M., de Holanda, G.M., Henriques, H.A., Furukawa, R.H.: Modified control charts monitoring long-term semiconductor manufacturing processes. In: Iano, Y., Saotome, O., Kemper, G., Mendes de Seixas, A.C., Gomes de Oliveira, G. (eds.) BTSym 2020. SIST, vol. 233, pp. 80–87. Springer, Cham (2021). https://doi.org/10.1007/978-3-030-75680-2_11
10. Doganaksoy, N., Meeker, W.Q., Hahn G.J.: Reliability and the role of Statistics. In: Doganaksoy, N., Meeker, W.Q., Hahn, G.J. Achieving Product Reliability: A Key to Business Success (1st edn.). Chapman and Hall/CRC (2021)
11. May, G.S., Spanos, C.J.: Fundamentals of semiconductor manufacturing and process control. Wiley, Hoboken (2006)
12. Farayola, P.O., Chaganti, S.K., Obaidi, A.O., Sheikh, A., Ravi, S., Chen, D.: Detection of site to site variations from volume measurement data in multisite semiconductor testing. IEEE Trans. Instrum. Meas. **70**, 1–12 (2021)
13. Bergès, C., Bird, J., Shroff, M.D., Rongen, R., Smith, C.: Data analytics and machine learning: root-cause problem-solving approach to prevent yield loss and quality issues in semiconductor industry for automotive applications. In: 2021 IEEE International Symposium on the Physical and Failure Analysis of Integrated Circuits (IPFA), pp. 1–10. IEEE

14. Al-Kharaz, M., Ananou, B., Ouladsine, M., Combal, M., Pinaton, J.: Evaluation of alarm system performance and management in semiconductor manufacturing. In: 2019 6th International Conference on Control, Decision and Information Technologies (CoDIT), pp. 1155–1160. IEEE (2019)
15. Tran, T., Gundala, S.R., Soni, K., Baker, A., Fogle, A., Chandrashekhar, S.: No trouble found (NTF) customer return analysis. In: 2020 IEEE International Reliability Physics Symposium (IRPS), pp. 1–6. IEEE (2020)
16. Cho, M., Park, G., Song, M., Lee, J., Lee, B., Kum, E.: Discovery of resource-oriented transition systems for yield enhancement in semiconductor manufacturing. IEEE Trans. Semicond. Manuf. **34**, 17–24 (2020)
17. Azamfar, M., Li, X., Lee, J.: Deep learning-based domain adaptation method for fault diagnosis in semiconductor manufacturing. IEEE Trans. Semicond. Manuf. **33**, 445–453 (2020)
18. Jiang, D., Lin, W., Raghavan, N.: A novel framework for semiconductor manufacturing final test yield classification using machine learning techniques. IEEE Access. **8**, 197885–197895 (2020)
19. Kim, D., Kim, M., Kim, W.: Wafer edge yield prediction using a combined long short-term memory and feed-forward neural network model for semiconductor manufacturing. IEEE Access. **8**, 215125–215132 (2020)
20. Long, H., Ma, M., Guo, W., Li, F., Zhang, X.: Fault diagnosis for IGBTs open-circuit faults in photovoltaic grid-connected inverters based on statistical analysis and machine learning. In: 2020 IEEE 1st China International Youth Conference on Electrical Engineering (CIYCEE), pp. 1–6. IEEE (2020)
21. Fan, S.-K.S., Hsu, C.-Y., Tsai, D.-M., He, F., Cheng, C.-C.: Data-driven approach for fault detection and diagnostic in semiconductor manufacturing. IEEE Trans. Autom. Sci. Eng. **17**, 1925–1936 (2020)
22. Espadinha-Cruz, P., Godina, R., Rodrigues, E.M.G.: A review of data mining applications in semiconductor manufacturing. Processes. **9**, 305 (2021)
23. Zhu, L., Jin, X., Burkhart, C., Roham, S.: Reliability engineering for high-value low-volume complex equipment. In: 2019 Annual Reliability and Maintainability Symposium (RAMS), pp. 1–7. IEEE (2019)
24. Jin, T., Yu, Y., Huang, H.-Z.: A multiphase decision model for system reliability growth with latent failures. IEEE Trans. Syst. Man, Cybern. Syst. **43**, 958–966 (2013)
25. Rathi, R., Reddy, M.C.G., Narayana, A.L., Narayana, U.L., Rahman, M.S.: Investigation and implementation of 8D methodology in a manufacturing system. Mater. Today Proc. **50**, 743–750 (2022)
26. Pacana, A., Czerwińska, K.: Improving the effectiveness of proceedings with disagreements in a production process with applying of report 8D. Qual. Prod. Improv. **2**, 172–179 (2020)
27. Kumar, T.S.M., Adaveesh, B.: Application of "8D methodology" for the root cause analysis and reduction of valve spring rejection in a valve spring manufacturing company: a case study. Indian J. Sci. Technol. **10**, 1–11 (2017)
28. Zhou, F., Wang, X., Mpshe, T., Zhang, Y., Yang, Y.: Quality improvement procedure (QIP) based on 8D and six sigma pilot programs in automotive industry. In: First International Conference Economic and Business Management 2016, pp. 275–281. Atlantis Press (2016)
29. Sharma, M., Sharma, S., Sahni, S.: Structured Problem Solving: combined approach using 8D and Six Sigma case study. Eng. Manag. Prod. Serv. **12**, 57–69 (2020)
30. de Figueiredo, D.L.: Gestão da Manutenção: Metodologias e Ferramentas para Análises de Falhas (2019). https://aprepro.org.br/conbrepro/2019/anais/arquivos/10202019_011052_5da bdc30a9927.pdf. Accessed 02 Nov 2022

31. Dziuba, S.T., Ingaldi, M., Kozina, A., Hernes, M.: 8D report as the product improvement tool. Sist. Gest. **16**(2), 157–165 (2021). (in Portuguese)
32. de Oliveira Chies, S., Buneder, R.: A APLICAÇÃO DA FERRAMENTA 8D PARA A RESOLUÇÃO DE PROBLEMAS DE QUALIDADE NO CLIENTE. Cippus. **7**, 87–103 (2019)

Shelf Life of Humboldt Squid (*Dosidicus gigas*) Flakes Enriched with Brown Rice

Ana María Guzmán Neyra$^{(\boxtimes)}$ ⓘ, Harold Peter Gómez Cornejo Gonzáles ⓘ, José Isaías Laura Huaman ⓘ, Gustavo Eduardo Benavente Velasquez ⓘ, and Rosario Fausta Choque de la Cruz ⓘ

Universidad Nacional de San Agustín de Arequipa, Arequipa, Perú
{aguzmann,hgomes-cornejo,jlaurah,gbenaventev,
rchoqued}@unsa.edu.pe

Abstract. The insertion of healthy foods based on hydrobiological resources faces a great challenge, since, when they are implemented in healthy eating habits, it is necessary to substitute ingredients high in carbohydrates and fats, knowing the appropriate time for their responsible consumption. Snacks are considered junk food because they have little or no nutritional value, and also contain high-fat content due to the frying process. Currently, healthy foods with high protein value and less fat content are required to avoid oxidation or rancidity of the final product and thus guarantee the shelf life of the product, among them we have the flakes of Humboldt squid enriched with rice flour and fried with corn oil at 180 °C. Extruded or fried products are generally susceptible to lipid oxidation due to their low moisture content and high-fat content, so it is necessary to determine the peroxide value. The shelf life of the Humboldt squid flakes with rice flour fried with corn oil at 180 °C as a function of the peroxide value using the accelerated testing method shows that the product will have a shelf life of 75.32 days equivalent to 2.51 months.

Keywords: Shelf life · Snack · Humboldt squid flake · Frying

1 Introduction

Breakfast cereals comprise a wide variety of products with a wide variety of cereals, shapes, formulations, and technological processes. They generally include an extrusion process (at low - intermediate and temperature above 80° - 95 °C) and drying - roasting (at low and temperature above 150 °C). The Maillard chemical browning and caramelization reactions can occur in the elaboration of these products and will intervene in the sensory quality of such products.

Fish flakes (snack) [1–4], is a snack-type food, with a very extended and thin fried dough, this mixture is starch, fish pulp, shrimp, prawn, and squid flavorings, water, and salt, after being steamed and cut into slices, dried, fried by immersion in oil at temperatures of 185 °C to 190 °C, for a few seconds, producing an expansion phenomenon that gives rise to the crunchiness of the product, which is then packaged in plastic bags,

Y. Iano et al. (Eds.): BTSym 2022, SIST 353, pp. 439–446, 2023.
https://doi.org/10.1007/978-3-031-31007-2_41

offering a certain barrier to the transmission of oxygen and humidity, as mentioned by Guzmán Neyra, "Marketing plan for the commercialization of giant squid flakes: city of Arequipa case" [5]. In Peru, fish flakes are considered a new product, and studies were carried out at ITP using frozen hake pulp, which concluded that different proportions of water confer different textural properties to the final product [5].

There are two types: sweet or salted flakes or snacks [3]. Within the sweet flakes or crispy fruit flakes there are pineapple, mango, apple, banana, and papaya flakes, and, within the salted ones [3], there are crispy flakes of tubers, cereals, and mixtures enriched with fish pulp.

On the other hand, the frying process is a complex physicochemical process in which the product to be fried (potatoes, meat, fish, breaded products, etc.) is subjected to a high temperature with the purpose of modifying the surface of the product, waterproofing it in some way, to control the loss of water from its interior. In this way, it is possible to conserve many of the characteristics of the food, improving in most cases, its flavor, texture, appearance, and color. In this way, it is possible to obtain a more "appetizing" product, which undoubtedly contributes to the success of the consumption of fried products.

Frying is a unitary operation performed by immersion in edible oil or fat at a temperature above the boiling point of water, generally 150 °C to 200 °C. It preserves food by thermal destruction of microorganisms and reduction of water activity. With frying, foods acquire certain pleasant characteristics of color, texture, and aroma that are the result of the Maillard reaction, the absorption by the food of volatile compounds present, and the formation of a crunchy, porous and oily crust, and a moist and cooked interior, all mentioned by Antón [6].

Oil immersion frying is one of the most widely used cooking methods worldwide, where oil plays a critical role in heat transfer and impregnation medium and is the decisive component of the frying process mentioned by Santos Lara [7]. Frying temperatures and time intervals range from 165 °C to 195 °C and from 50 to 90 s [7].

2 Shelf Life

The shelf life of a product depends on environmental factors, humidity, exposure temperature, the thermal process to which it is subjected, and the quality of raw materials, among others. The effect of these factors is manifested through the changes in the qualities of the food that prevent its sale: changes in flavor, color, texture, or loss of nutrients, as mentioned by García [8], who refers to the end of the shelf life of a product when it no longer maintains the qualities required for the final consumer to use it.

The shelf life of food represents that period of time during which the food is kept fit for consumption from the sanitary point of view, maintaining the sensory, functional, and nutritional characteristics above the quality limits previously established as acceptable; quoted by Sullo Ignacio [9]. The shelf life is determined by stressing the product, provided that the storage conditions are controlled. Shelf-life predictions can be made using mathematical models (useful for evaluation of microbial growth and death), real-time tests (for fresh foods with short shelf-life), and accelerated tests (for foods with high stability) where deterioration is accelerated, and then these values are used to make predictions under less severe conditions [9].

The shelf life represents the period in which the meat will maintain all its organolep-tic characteristics, nutritional quality, and safety for human consumption. According to the Campden & Chorleywood Food Research Association, an understanding of the shelf life of a product is essential to ensure the safety and quality of the product at the time of consumption. It is important to consider aspects such as storage, distribution, and marketing, as well as other factors to ensure food safety and quality. The first is temperature control during production and storage. Keeping food under refrigerated conditions guarantees food safety and quality because it reduces the risk of possible growth of microorganisms due to temperature misuse. Another factor to consider is the initial contamination of fresh meat with bacteria from the skin, equipment, and workers, among other sources; cited by Davalos Cuno [10].

Shelf life can be estimated by several methods: values reported in specialized lit-erature for similar foods and under similar conditions to the product of interest can be taken; consumer complaints can be monitored to guide possible shelf life values; food quality attributes that vary during shelf life can be evaluated or by accelerated testing [8].

3   Materials and Methods

The shelf life of the Humboldt squid flakes was calculated based on their peroxide value, using the accelerated temperature test method, working with temperatures of 30 °C, 40 °C, and 50 °C, measuring the value every half hour. These tests were carried out not exceeding the peroxide index limit of 5 meq/Kg. Three different temperatures of 10 °C (30 °C, 40 °C, and 50 °C) were considered, being these the variables to be evaluated for the calculation of the shelf life of the Humboldt squid (Dosidiscus gigas).

The data were analyzed using Friedman's test for which statistical analysis was used with a significance level of 5%. When significant statistical differences were found, Tukey's test was used.

4   Results and Discussion

4.1   Calculation of Shelf Life

In the present experiment, the objective was to find the shelf life of the elaborated product. In this sense, accelerated shelf-life tests were used to achieve this goal, considering three temperatures differentiated by 10 °C (30 °C, 40 °C, and 50 °C), temperatures that were regulated in the accelerated test chambers.

The index that was considered as a determinant for the shelf life of the flakes is the peroxide index, since it was sought to determine the influence of fat oxidation of the processed product, measuring the index every half hour. These tests were performed considering the limit of the peroxide index for fried foods of 5 milli equivalent per kilogram of peroxides, according to the Peruvian Technical Standard NTP 209.226, 1984 [11].

According to Garcia Baldizón [8], to determine the shelf life of a food or product, the chemical or biological reactions that influence its quality and safety must first be iden-tified, considering the composition of the food and the process to which it is subjected, and then the most critical reactions in quality are established; therefore, the peroxide index was considered to evaluate the shelf life for fish flakes subjected to frying. On the other hand, extruded or fried products are generally susceptible to lipid oxidation due to their low moisture content; therefore, the indicated test is to determine the peroxide value.

The results of the peroxide value behavior during the oil tests are in Table 1.

Table 1. Index of peroxide of Humboldt squid flakes with brown rice, frying the rice at 180 °C

Time (hours)	Peroxides Index (meq/kg)		
	30 °C	40 °C	50 °C
0	0.01	0.01	0.01
0.5	0.28	0.64	1.27
1	0.82	0.94	1.54
1.5	1.04	1.15	1.79
2	1.18	1.29	1.86
2.5	1.34	1.49	2.06
3	1.47	1.76	2.13
3.5	1.94	2.03	2.5
4	2.27	2.34	2.91
4.5	2.31	2.41	2.98
5	2.88	2.92	3.39
5.5	2.95	3.23	3.9
6	3.36	3.74	4.37
6.5	3.89	4.07	4.84
7	4.26	4.34	5.31

It can be observed that the tendency of peroxide formation is directly proportional to time and temperature; it is observed that the odor and flavor of the product changes, which is confirmed by García Baldizón [8], who indicates that the shelf life of a product depends on environmental factors, humidity, exposure temperature, the thermal process to which it is subjected, and the quality of the raw materials, among others. The effect of these factors is manifested as the change in the qualities of the food that prevent its sale: change in flavor, color, texture, or loss of nutrients. It is settled that the end of the shelf life of a product is reached when it no longer maintains the qualities required for the final consumer to use it.

The results of the previous table are used to calculate the natural logarithm of the peroxides index in a given time as a function of the initial peroxides index. The results are presented in Table 2.

With the data in Table 2, Ln is plotted versus storage time, obtaining the ratio of Ln vs. average storage (X) shown below in Table 3.

Table 2. Natural logarithm of the peroxides index

Time (hours)	Ln (IP/IP$_0$)			Ln (IP/IPO)
	30°C	40°C	50°C	
0	0	0	0	
0.5	3.33220451	4.15888308	4.84418709	
1	4.40671925	4.54329478	5.0369526	
1.5	4.6443909	4.74493213	5.18738581	
2	4.77068462	4.8598124	5.22574667	
2.5	4.8978398	5.00394631	5.32787617	
3	4.99043259	5.170484	5.36129217	
3.5	5.26785816	5.31320598	5.52146092	
4	5.42495002	5.45532112	5.67332327	
4.5	5.44241771	5.48479693	5.69709349	
5	5.66296048	5.6767538	5.82600011	
5.5	5.68697536	5.77765232	5.96614674	
6	5.81711116	5.9242558	6.0799332	
6.5	5.96357934	6.00881319	6.18208491	
7	6.05443935	6.07304453	6.27476202	

Table 3. Natural logarithm of the peroxides index

Temperature (°C)	30	40	50
Reaction constant rate (k)	0.5257	0.4882	0.4509

Figure 1 is the plot of the natural logarithm of the reaction constant versus the inverse of the temperature in Kelvin. It is important to mention that the "X" axis is K^{-1} (Kelvin raised to the minus 1), and the "Y" axis is dimensionless, since it results from dividing two values with the same unit: the value of peroxides at a given time divided by the value of peroxides at time 0.

With the data of the slope and the intercept, the activation energy (Ea = 1491.9825 cal/mol) and the pre-exponential factor (K0 = 0.04418 h-1) are calculated [12].

With the values found, we proceed to find the reaction rate for each of the temperatures under study:

$$k_{30} = 0.003707 \, hours^{-1}$$

$$k_{40} = 0.004012 \, hours^{-1}$$

$$k_{50} = 0.004321 \, hours^{-1}$$

Analyzing the pre-exponential factor (30, 40, 50), we proceed to calculate the time of duration of the flakes for each of the temperatures according to the peroxide index,

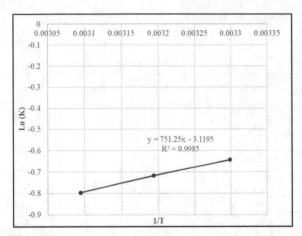

Fig. 1. Natural logarithm (Ln) of the reaction constant vs. the inverse of the temperature in degrees Kelvin (k°).

obtaining: at the time of 30, 40, and 50 (1676.6429; 1549.0749; 1438.2386); consequently with the values obtained we proceed to plot the temperature versus the natural logarithm of the times for each of the temperatures, as shown in Fig. 2.

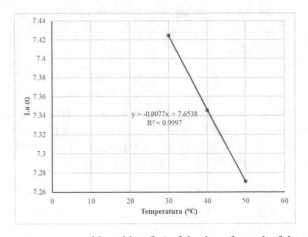

Fig. 2. Temperature vs. natural logarithm (Ln) of the times for each of the temperatures.

From Fig. 2, we extract the slope and the intercept of the equation of the line to calculate the shelf life at different temperatures, expressed in the following formula:

$$\text{Shelf life} = e^{(\text{slope}*T+\text{intercept})} \tag{1}$$

By carrying out Eq. 1, the following values are obtained, expressed in Table 4. It can be noted that the tendency of peroxide formation is directly proportional to time and temperature; these substances change the odor and flavor characteristics of the product, as mentioned by Espínoza [13], who indicates that with increasing temperature the rate of deterioration increases as a function of the oxidation of fats.

Table 4. Shelf life of Humboldt squid flakes with brown rice at different temperatures

Temperature (°C)	Shelf life (hours)	Shelf life (days)	Shelf life (months)
1	2092,47	87,19	2,91
2	2076,42	86,52	2,88
4	2044,69	85,20	2,84
6	2013,44	83,89	2,80
8	1982,67	82,61	2,75
10	1952,37	81,35	2,71
12	1922,54	80,11	2,67
14	1893,15	78,88	2,63
16	1864,22	77,68	2,59
18	1835,73	76,49	2,55
20	1807,68	75,32	2,51

Having all the results, the deterioration rate (k) was determined for the three temperatures in all the time intervals where the measurement was made. Analyzing the preceding values, it can be observed that the product will have a shelf life of 75.32 days, equivalent to 2.51 months.

5   Conclusions

Having all the results, the deterioration rate (k) was determined for the three temperatures in all the time intervals where the measurement was made. It can be observed that the product of Humboldt squid flakes with rice flour fried with corn oil at 180 °C as a function of the peroxide index using the accelerated testing method will have a shelf life of 75.32 days equivalent to 2.51 months.

Develop research on flakes from fishery resources with different moisture percentages because extruded or fried products with low moisture content are susceptible to lipid oxidation [14, 15].

The work carried out is a contribution to the community in the areas of food technology [16–18], for which it is projected in the future to automate the processes in data collection, in order to have better quality products that meet food quality standards. For another part, it is projected to estimate the useful life of other marine resources [19], bringing a contribution to human health.

References

1. Pacco, N.R.Y.: Evaluación de la Operación de fritado en hojuelas de pota (Dosidicus gigas). Universidad Nacional de San Agustin de Arequipa (2006)

2. Llerena, M.S.: Influencia de la cantidad de agua y espesor en las crocantes de las hojuelas de pota (Dosidicus gigas). Universidad Nacional de San Agustin de Arequipa (2006)
3. Villanueva, A.B.P.: Hojuelas dulces de pota (Dosidicus Gigas) usando Edulcorante Stevia enriquecido con Quinua (Chenopodium Quinoa Willdenow) (2013)
4. Alarcon, K.E.E.: Elaboración y determinación de parametros optimos de procesamiento de hojuelas de pescado utilizando sardina (Sardinops sagax). Universidad Nacional de San Agustin de Arequipa (2002)
5. Neyra, A.M.G.: Plan de marketing para la comercialización de hojuelas de calamar gigante: caso cuidad de Arequipa. Universidad Nacional de San Agustin de Arequipa (2013)
6. Lara, M.E.S., Mesa, A.J., T., Martínez, P.C.C., Herrero, M.M.H.: Desarrollo de un método analítico para la cuantificación de acrilamida en tostadas de tortillas de maíz procedentes de Monterrey (México) y estimación de la exposición dietética. Universitat Autònoma de Barcelona, Departament de Ciència Animal i dels Aliments (2017)
7. Baldizón, C.G., Córdoba, M.E.M.: Estimación de la vida útil de una mayonesa mediante pruebas aceleradas. Ingeniería. **18**, 57–64 (2008)
8. Sullo Ignacio, L.Y.: Evaluación de características sensoriales de jamonada de lisa voladora (Cypselurus heterurus) enriquecido con berenjena (Solanum melongena) (2017)
9. Dávalos Cuno, L.M.: Desarrollo de nuggets de bonito (Sarda chiliensis chiliensis) bajos en calorías y con la adición de chía (Salvia hispánica) como antioxidante (2016)
10. Catálogo Normas Técnicas Peruanas | Inacal Perú. https://www.inacal.gob.pe/cid/categoria/catalogo-bibliografico. Accessed 29 Aug 2022
11. Espinoza, K., Acero, D.J.R., Martínez, N.: Elaboración de Snack extruido a partir de Cereales y Concentrado de proteína de pota (Dosidicus gigas) y determinación de su vida útil. In: Anales Científicos. pp. 180–191. Universidad Nacional Agraria La Molina (2021)
12. Santos, P.A., et al.: Analysis of the relationship between maturity indicators using the multivariate linear regression: a case study in the brazilian cities. In: Xu, Z., Alrabaee, S., Loyola-González, O., Zhang, X., Cahyani, N.D.W., Ab Rahman, N.H. (eds.) CSIA 2022. LNDECT, vol. 125, pp. 203–210. Springer, Cham (2022). https://doi.org/10.1007/978-3-030-97874-7_26
13. Antón Bernal, T.L., Saavedra Bravo, P. de J.: Influencia del escaldado en la reducción de acrilamida en camotes (ipomoea batatas) fritos, variedad amarillo (2017)
14. Lin, J., Lin, Z., Liao, G., Yin, H.: A novel product remaining useful life prediction approach considering fault effects. IEEE/CAA J. Autom. Sin. **8**, 1762–1773 (2021)
15. Roohinejad, S., Koubaa, M., Barba, F.J., Saljoughian, S., Amid, M., Greiner, R.: Application of seaweeds to develop new food products with enhanced shelf-life, quality and health-related beneficial properties. Food Res. Int. **99**, 1066–1083 (2017)
16. Correia Peres Costa, J.C., et al.: Study of the microbiological quality, prevalence of foodborne pathogens and product shelf-life of Gilthead sea bream (Sparus aurata) and Sea bass (Dicentrarchus labrax) from aquaculture in estuarine ecosystems of Andalusia (Spain). Food Microbiol **90**, 103498 (2020). https://doi.org/10.1016/j.fm.2020.103498
17. Kato, H.C.A., Peixoto Joele, M.R.S., Sousa, C.L., Ribeiro, S.C.A., Lourenço, L.F.H.: Evaluation of the shelf life of tambaqui fillet processed by the sous vide method. J. Aquat. food Prod. Technol. **26**, 1144–1156 (2017)
18. Villafuerte, U., Obispo, E.O., Maza, S.T., Macavilca, E.A.: Elaboración de snack de maíz amarillo duro (Zea mays L.), enriquecido con calamar gigante (Dosidicus gigas). Cienc. Invest. **18**, 73–77 (2015)
19. Lee, D.S., Robertson, G.L.: Shelf-life estimation of packaged dried foods as affected by choice of moisture sorption isotherm models. J. Food Process. Preserv. **46**, e16335 (2022)

A Portable Device for Obtaining Body Condition Score of Dairy Cattle Based on Image Processing and Convolutional Neural Networks

Edgar Oblitas[ID], Rober Villarreal[ID], Alonso Sanchez[ID], and Guillermo Kemper[(⊠)][ID]

Universidad Peruana de Ciencias Aplicadas, Lima, Peru
{u201316586,u20171a525,pcelasan}@upc.edu.pe,
guillermo.kemper@upc.pe

Abstract. The present work develops an image classifier algorithm to measure the body condition score in Holstein cows. The algorithm aims to reduce the subjectivity that arises when evaluating cattle through visual inspection by specialists. This score measures how thin or overweight are cows in stables, which impacts milk production and the quality of life of the cattle. Although state-of-the-art attempts to solve the subjectivity problem, an efficient and satisfactory method for classification has not yet been found. Moreover, implementations have only considered placing fixed devices in the stables under certain restrictions. Therefore, a portable device with a graphical user interface was designed, and the images were captured and then segmented in a DeepLab3 + convolutional neural network. With this segmented database, the classifier algorithm was trained. For the validation of image segmentation, the Coefficient of Intersection over Union was used, achieving results over 0.9. This finally allowed us to obtain satisfactory results in the calculation of the body condition score.

Keywords: Dairy cattle · Body condition score · Image segmentation · Image processing · CNN · Classification algorithm

1 Introduction

Body condition score (BCS) is a critical measurement used to assess feeding effectiveness on a farm [1]. This system was proposed by E. E. Wildman and describes a 5-level scale to study the relationships between weight, milk production, and carcass measurements of the cow's body [2]. This tool is used to directly estimate the mobilization of energy reserves in the fat and muscle of cattle that meet the requirements of animal welfare and precision farming [3].

In cattle stables, there are many workers who are responsible for the care of the animals. Among these, there are specialists who classify cows according to body condition score and do so by evaluating the specific anatomical zones of the bovine body [4]. However, this score is subjective because different specialists may have different classification criteria, which may produce imprecise results. This subjectivity generates inadequate animal food control criteria due to the number of food rations they receive, resulting in underweight or overweight cows. The inadequate control is further amplified by nonexistent registration systems for livestock feeding. Due to the large number of cows in a barn, it is difficult to monitor the BCS of all the animals, resulting in the impoverishment of bovine health and economic losses in the barn, due to the low productivity of milk and cattle meat.

There are some commercial solutions to the described problem, such as mobile applications to measure BCS, but they do not use any type of artificial intelligence and still depend on the user's criteria. Intellectual property such as patents and utility models also aims to solve this issue. For instance, Bohao Liao and Marilyn Krukowski [5] developed a device using a three-dimensional camera system to capture images of the animal's body and determine the BCS based on the statistically analyzed three-dimensional surface. However, the cameras might be prohibitively expensive.

Moreover, scientific works also propose solutions to the problem. The work [3] develops a linear regression model using ultrasound cow backfat thickness and tests a convolutional neural network-based system that evaluates depth, gray, and phase congruence to automatically extract features. However, the system was more effective in lean cows ($3 < BCS$), while it underperformed for cows with BCS from 3.25 to 3.5.

Authors in [6] developed an automatic system using a Kinect v2 camera. Then, they used the SqueezeNet neural network, achieving a 78% accuracy when considering an estimated BCS within 0.5 units, while resulting in a 94% accuracy when within 0.50 units. However, the device must be fixed 2.8 m above the ground and pointed at an area that would not be exposed to direct sunlight to reduce noise in the images.

The proposal in [7] uses an image collection system using an RFID reader, using the active contour method to segment cows and the Mean Absolute Error (MAE) to evaluate the system performance. However, interference such as noise and corridor barriers have been found in the depth image. The work at [8] uses the Markov clustering method for BCS feature vector classification and applies image processing techniques. To do this, the authors identify 7 anatomical points manually located in the short rib area of the image of the cows and then calculate the seven unknown parameters that the vector will use. However, the solution has not been tested in stables and the user must manually locate the anatomical points on the image. In [9], images and dynamic background models (Gaussian Mixture Model, GMM) were used to separate the cows from the background. The results were acceptable when considering extreme BCS values, increasing the accuracy from 43% to 76%. However, the method has an error of 24%.

With this in consideration, this work proposes an electronic and image processing system. It has a graphical interface to capture the images and enter the necessary data. It also has two stages, one for pre-processing to segment the cow's body, and another for post-processing, to classify it according to its BCS. While most of the previous works must be fixed in a particular place in the barn, the proposed equipment is portable. It works only on Holstein-type cows. Moreover, this equipment also enables users to generate an information history for each evaluated cow and upload it to the cloud [10, 11]. Thus, information will feed a record of each bovine, to see its evolution from time to time.

2 Description of the Proposed Device

Figure 1 shows the block diagram of the proposed method. Each stage, from the acquisition of the image capture to the saving of the database in the cloud, is described in the following sections. For the training and testing of the models, a MacBook Retina 2015 was used, it has an Intel Core i7 processor with 16 GB of RAM.

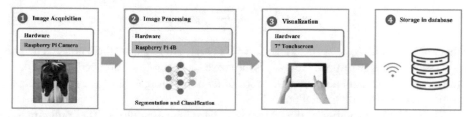

Fig. 1. Block diagram of the proposed system.

2.1 Image Acquisition

The image acquisition subsystem consists of an 8 MP Raspberry Pi v2 camera that uses an IMX219 sensor with a focal length of 3.04 mm [12]. This is located on the lid of the handheld device at a 55° angle, as shown in Fig. 2. The device is placed on the outside of the camera housing and the FFC flat cable passes through a rectangular hole to connect the camera. Camera to the CSI port of the Raspberry Pi 4B 4 GB RAM (5V/3A) single-board computer [13].

Fig. 2. Top view of the printed case and the camera used for image capture.

Images can be captured either by pressing a push button connected to two GPIO pins in the Raspberry Pi or by interacting with the device's graphical interface. To capture the image, the PiCamera and OpenCV libraries are used. The version of OpenCV [14] used is 4.1.0.25. In the image preview visualization, the resolution is 640 × 400 in video mode with a 30 FPS framerate. To aid the user in focusing on the cow, a red rectangle is drawn inside each preview frame. For this, the rectangle function from the OpenCV library is used. The position of the top left corner of the red box is $\left(fprv_x, fprv_y\right)$, defined in Eqs. 1 and 2; the bottom right is $\left(fprv_x + n_{prv}, fprv_y + n_{prv}\right)$ with a width of 3 pixels.

$$fprv_x = \frac{M_{prv}}{2} - \frac{n_{prv}}{2}, fprv_x \in N \tag{1}$$

$$fprv_y = \frac{N_{prv}}{2} - \frac{n_{prv}}{2}, fprv_y \in N \tag{2}$$

where $M_{prv} = 640, N_{prv} = 400$, and $n_{prv} = 200$. M_{prv} And N_{prv} are the width and height of the preview image respectively, n_{prv} is the size of the soon-to-be cropped image. $fprv_x$ And $fprv_y$ are the pixel position of the top corner of the cropped image. Figure 3 shows the preview image with the red box.

The full 8 MP resolution of the camera is used for image capturing. The configuration of the camera resolution is changed to 3264×2024 pixels. The points of the area of interest are calculated again in Eqs. 3 to 7 for the new resolution.

Fig. 3. Preview of the device with the red box that helps with the aiming of the photo.

$$fp_x = \frac{M}{2} - \frac{n}{2}, fp_x \in N \tag{3}$$

$$fp_x = \frac{M}{2} - \frac{n}{2}, fp_x \in N \tag{4}$$

$$Ic_R(x, y) = I_R\left(x + fp_x, y + fp_y\right) \tag{5}$$

$$Ic_G(x, y) = I_G\left(x + fp_x, y + fp_y\right) \tag{6}$$

$$Ic_B(x, y) = I_B\left(x + fp_x, y + fp_y\right) \tag{7}$$

where $x = 0, 1, \ldots, n$, $y = 0, 1, \ldots, n$, $M = 3264$, $N = 2040$, $n = 1019$. I is the original image, Ic is the image cropped, and R, G, and B are the color channels.

2.2 Image Processing

Pre-processing. In this sub-stage, bilinear, nearest neighbor, and area scaling are compared, due to the segmentation neural network having a 512×512 input dimension. To choose one of them, the execution times and the results of the segmentation algorithms are compared. After training three segmentation models with each pre-processing technique, the best one, according to Eq. 8, is the nearest neighbor method. When comparing runtime, the nearest neighbor method takes 1.68 ms on average while the other methods take more than 3 ms.

Segmentation. The DeepLabV3 + [15] segmentation algorithm is used. The model outputs a prediction mask, which is multiplied by the input image, resulting in an image of the segmented cow. The database consists of 648 images with their respective manual segmentation masks. The database was divided into images to train and validate the model. Horizontal flip data augmentation resulted in 1232 training images and 64 testing images. Figure 4 shows the results of the segmentation algorithm.

The intersection-over-union (IoU) metric is used to validate the results of the segmentation algorithm:

$$IoU = \frac{\sum MMM\,\mathbf{AND}MMP}{\sum MMM\,\mathbf{OR}MMP} \tag{8}$$

where *MMM* is the manually created mask and *MMP* is the mask predicted by the algorithm.

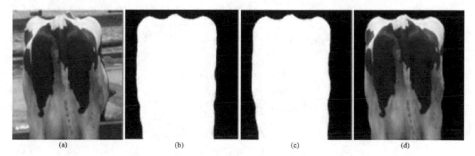

Fig. 4. a) Original input image. b) Mask manually created. c) Mask predicted by the algorithm. d) Segmented image.

This metric is computed over the testing dataset, achieving an average IoU of 0.9775. This may be interpreted as the segmentation algorithm having an accuracy of 97.75%, which is acceptable (see Fig. 5).

Post-processing. A labeling algorithm is used to clean the predicted masks resulting from the segmentation algorithm. This process consists of eliminating 1-valued pixels with no connectivity to the image region corresponding to the cow. A labeling function from OpenCV was used with 4-neighbor connectivity. "connectedComponentsWith-Stats" function returns information from the labeling algorithm, of which the most

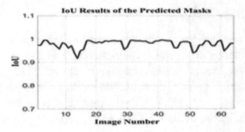

Fig. 5. Plot of the results obtained in the testing of the DeepLabV3 + segmentation model.

important information is the area of each label. The label with the largest area corresponds to the image region of the cow. The pixel value of the label becomes 1 and everything else becomes 0 (clean segmentation's binary mask $M_{lb}(x_e, y_e)$). The labeling algorithm that OpenCV uses is known as Spaghetti Labeling [16].

To change the background of the segmented image to blue, Eq. 9 is used to invert the values of the binary mask. Then, Eq. 10 converts the values 1 to 255, followed by Eq. 11, which describes the concatenation of the binary masks to obtain a (512, 512, 3) RGB array from a (512, 512, 1) array. Using the result of Eq. 11, Eq. 12 is applied to obtain the segmented image, but with a black background. Finally, the result of Eq. 12 is applied in Eq. 13 to obtain the segmented image with the blue background. Figure 6 shows the results of these computations.

$$M_{lb_{inv}}(x_e, y_e) = \begin{cases} 0 \, , \, M_{lb}(x_e, y_e) = 1 \\ 1 \, , \, M_{lb}(x_e, y_e) = 0 \end{cases} \tag{9}$$

$$M_{uint8}(x_e, y_e) = M_{lb_{inv}}(x_e, y_e) \times 255 \tag{10}$$

$$\begin{aligned} Ms_R(x_e, y_e) &= M_{lb}(x_e, y_e) \\ Ms_G(x_e, y_e) &= M_{lb}(x_e, y_e) \\ Ms_B(x_e, y_e) &= M_{lb}(x_e, y_e) \end{aligned} \tag{11}$$

$$\begin{aligned} I_{seg_R}(x_e, y_e) &= I_{e_R}(x_e, y_e) \times Ms_R(x_e, y_e) \\ I_{seg_G}(x_e, y_e) &= I_{e_G}(x_e, y_e) \times Ms_G(x_e, y_e) \\ I_{seg_B}(x_e, y_e) &= I_{e_B}(x_e, y_e) \times Ms_B(x_e, y_e) \end{aligned} \tag{12}$$

$$I_{seg_B}(x_e, y_e) = I_{seg_B}(x_e, y_e) + M_{uint8}(x_e, y_e) \tag{13}$$

where Ms is the segmented RGB image, I_e is the original image of dimensions $512 \times 512 \times 3$, I_{seg} is the segmented image with a blue background, M_{lb} is the labeled image, $M_{lb_{inv}}$ is the inverted labeled image, and M_{uint8}, the labeled image in uint8 format.

Classification Algorithm. An expert zootechnician manually assigned body condition scores to cow images. First, the zootechnician received 361 images and discarded those where the cows are being covered by some external object, such as the wood of the stable corral or the body of another cow, because these artifacts can be detrimental to the classification model. This procedure resulted in 302 valid images.

The specialist classified the body condition score in decimal values, with a difference of 0.25. Figure 7 shows the number of images taken in a cattle barn, classified according to their BCS, in which it is observed that the majority of cattle have a score from 2.75 to 3.75, which indicates that the animal is well, healthier, and more productive. On the other hand, the number of 0 images is because no such type was found.

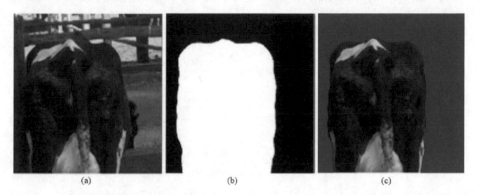

Fig. 6. a) Original image, b) predicted mask, c) final segmented image.

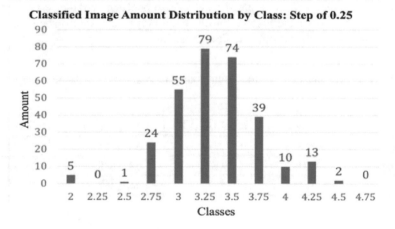

Fig. 7. Distribution graph of the images classified by their class.

Due to the limited number of images classified by the specialist, an approximation of the classified results to integer classes was considered:

$$BCS_1 = \begin{cases} 2, & if\, 2 \leq BCS_{0.25} \leq 2.75 \\ 3, & if\, 3 \leq BCS_{0.25} \leq 3.5 \\ 4, & if\, 3.75 \leq BCS_{0.25} \leq 4.75 \end{cases} \tag{14}$$

where $BCS_{0.25}$ is the classification value delivered by the specialist and BCS_1 is the approximate value with specialist recommendation. The values 2, 3, and 4 represent the largest number of bovines with a body condition score (BCS) found in the barns, since cows with a BCS of 1 or 5 are not common to find.

Then, with the manually classified images, training was carried out in different neural networks. The ResNet50 [17], MobileNetV2 [18], InceptionV3 [19], and VGG16 [20] architectures were trained using the transfer learning technique. The models were trained using 3 different types of input images: binary masks, original images, and segmented images with blue backgrounds. Equations 15 to 17 describe the metrics used to evaluate each model's performance [21].

$$Precision_M = \frac{\sum_{i=1}^{l} \frac{TP_i}{TP_i+FP_i}}{l} \tag{15}$$

$$Recall_M = \frac{\sum_{i=1}^{l} \frac{TP_i}{TP_i+FN_i}}{l} \tag{16}$$

$$Fscore = \frac{(\beta^2 + 1) \cdot Precision_M \cdot Recall_M}{\beta^2 \cdot Precision_M + Recall_M} \tag{17}$$

where TP_i is the true positive, FP_i is the false positive, FN_i is the false negative, and β^2 is the important value of precision over recall. These model accuracy measurement metrics are applied to see which model has the best performance.

As shown in Table 1, 2 and 3, the MobileNetV2 model achieved the best performance when considering recall and F-score for the 3 input types, as well as when considering the 3 metrics for the binary segmentation msask inputs.

Table 1. Table of results of the metrics of the four models trained with the binary segmentation masks.

	ResNet50	MobileNetV2	InceptionV3	VGG16
$Precision_M$	0.430672	0.577778	0.474781	0.231111
$Recall_M$	0.397435	0.594208	0.428686	0.333333
F-score	0.388164	0.585336	0.428447	0.272966

Table 2. Table of results of the metrics of the four models trained with the original images (no segmentation).

	ResNet50	MobileNetV2	InceptionV3	VGG16
$Precision_M$	0.43809	0.63216	0.68724	0.53038
$Recall_M$	0.38301	0.69665	0.55678	0.46715
F-score	0.36846	0.65709	0.59352	0.47874

Table 3. Table of results of the metrics of the four models trained with the segmented images.

	ResNet50	MobileNetV2	InceptionV3	VGG16
Precision$_M$	0.46970	0.58672	0.60548	0.78808
Recall$_M$	0.43920	0.62523	0.48214	0.50515
F-score	0.43683	0.60121	0.48858	0.53484

2.3 Graphical Interface

The graphical interface has 4 main windows. The image capture window, as shown in Fig. 3, allows the user to turn on the camera, and capture and send the image to the next window. Then, the "Image to Process" window shown in Fig. 8 displays the cropped image and asks the user for the cow ID. Once these values have been entered, the image begins to be processed, passing through the segmentation and classification algorithms. After the process is finished, the segmented image and body condition score are displayed in the "Results" window (Fig. 9) and then stored in the device as a record. Figure 10 shows the last "Storage" window where all the records are displayed.

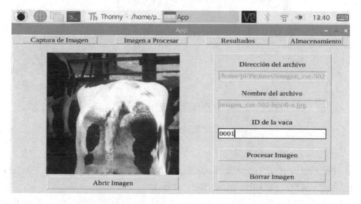

Fig. 8. Image to Process" window.

2.4 Sending Data to the Cloud

The 000webhost server was used, where the records sent from the device are saved, such as the ID of the cow, date and time of classification, body condition score, and the original acquired image. Since the images are a three-dimensional array of values that define the color of each pixel, a base64 encoding was performed, which converts the image file into a text string, to send this information over the network. The JSON format is used to send the information of the records due to its orderly structure. Also, it can contain the encoded image text string and send via a POST send.

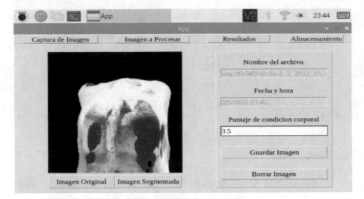

Fig. 9. "Results" window.

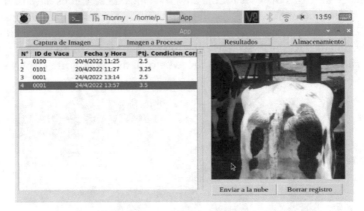

Fig. 10. "Storage" window.

A website of 3 windows for data visualization was developed. The 3 windows represent the main page where all the information in the database is shown, the second page shows a graph of all the scores that has a specific cow ID, and the last page shows which cows have a body condition score outside of a normal range.

3   Results

Testing was carried out in an experimental zootechnical barn at Universidad Nacional Agraria La Molina. To do this, the portable device was used at a prudent distance from the cows in order to center the area of interest over the animal. The execution time of the program took approximately 25 s: 20 s for segmentation and 5 s for classification. A Raspberry Pi 4B with 4GB RAM was used as the hardware platform. The processing times were obtained by comparing the processes in an external computer. The validation population consisted of pictures of the hindquarters of 10 Holstein-type cows. Table 4 shows the IoU of the images taken in the barn, in order to measure the segmentation algorithm performance.

An average IoU of 0.9819 was obtained, which may be interpreted as a highly efficient segmentation algorithm. Moreover, the lower IoU was 0.94. Thus, the worst case consisted of the algorithm having a 94% similarity with respect to the manual segmentation.

Table 4. Results of the calculation of the IoU metric of the captured images.

Cow assigned ID	IoU score
A1	0.9759
A2	0.9732
A3	0.9835
A4	0.9496
A5	0.9892
A6	0.9782
A7	0.9952
A8	0.9912
A9	0.9858
A10	0.9881
A11	0.9742
A12	0.9840
A13	0.9891
A14	0.9895

To measure the performance of the body condition score classifier, the images captured and classified in the barn were compared with the results classified by the zootechnician. To have homogeneity between the results of the specialist and the classifier, a grouping criterion was used; that is, the specialist's results were grouped into 3 groups, using the criteria defined in Eq. 14; this is shown in Table 5.

A success rate (T_A) was applied to the results to obtain the percentage of similarity, comparing the grouped and real results with those obtained by the device.

$$T_A = \frac{Number\ of\ successes}{Number\ of\ evaluations} \cdot 100\% \tag{18}$$

Considering the BCS assigned by the zootechnician (second column in Table 5), a 30% success rate was obtained, which is an indicator that the algorithm needs more training (although the subjectivity of the zootechnician may also play against this result). Additionally, the estimated BCS would need to have 0.25-point variations to improve the success rate. When considering the approximate BCS (third column in Table 5), the success rate obtained was 60%, which shows an improvement with respect to the real result.

Table 5. Results obtained for validation

Cow assigned ID	Specialist result	Approx. Specialist result	Device result
A1	3.75	4	3
A2	3	3	3
A3	3	3	3
A4	4.5	4	4
A5	4	4	3
A6	2.75	2	2
A7	2.75	2	3
A8	4	4	4
A9	3.5	3	3
A10	2.75	2	3

4   Conclusions

A portable device that measures BCS in cows was successfully developed. It includes a graphical interface to visualize the results. A total of 1000 images were taken to train the neural networks, but only 700 images were manually segmented in order to build the training dataset of the segmentation algorithm. This amount turned out to be sufficient, since the IoU showed a segmentation performance of 98% on average, which turned out to be high.

For the classification algorithm, due to the limited availability of zootechnicians, approximately 330 classified images were obtained for network training. For this reason, the classification performance was low, since a 60% F-score of the model was obtained, which coincided with the 60% success rate of the grouped results for validation. The MobileNetV2 architecture showed the best performance among the evaluated architectures, most likely due to having fewer trainable parameters and thus being less prone to overfitting. Due to the small training dataset, models with more trainable parameters might overfit easily.

The F-score of the model with non-segmented inputs was higher than the same metric in the model with segmented input images. This could suggest that segmentation might not be necessary for this classification problem; however, this conclusion should be evaluated with a much larger training dataset. Future work should evaluate this performance difference with segmented and non-segmented inputs because it is likely that the model with segmented inputs should be more accurate. Since the evaluated models in this work were pre-trained in the ImageNet dataset, this might explain the improved performance when using non-segmented inputs. Future work should also consider using at least 100 images for each of the 17 classes obtained by dividing the BCS into 0.25 increments. Moreover, at least 2 zootechnicians should be surveyed to generate the ground truth BCS, due to the high subjectivity in a single technician's score. Finally, adding classifiers for the lateral zone of the cow could increase the accuracy when measuring BCS.

Acknowledgments. The authors would like to thank the Dirección de Investigacion of Universidad Peruana de Ciencias Aplicadas for funding and logistical support with Code UPC-D-2022–2.

References

1. Huang, X., Hu, Z., Wang, X., Yang, X., Zhang, J., Shi, D.: An improved single shot multibox detector method applied in body condition score for dairy cows. Animals **9**, 470 (2019)
2. Wildman, E.E., Jones, G.M., Wagner, P.E., Boman, R.L., Troutt, H.F., Jr., Lesch, T.N.: A dairy cow body condition scoring system and its relationship to selected production characteristics. J. Dairy Sci. **65**, 495–501 (1982)
3. Yukun, S., et al.: Automatic monitoring system for individual dairy cows based on a deep learning framework that provides identification via body parts and estimation of body condition score. J. Dairy Sci. **102**, 10140–10151 (2019)
4. Grigera, J., Bargo, F.: Evaluación del estado corporal en vacas lecheras. Inf. Técnico. www. Prod. com. ar. (2005)
5. Google Patents Homepage. https://patents.google.com/patent/US9684956B2/en, (Accessed 20 Sep 2021)
6. Alvarez, J.R., et al.: Body condition estimation on cows from depth images using Convolutional Neural Networks. Comput. Electron. Agric. **155**, 12–22 (2018)
7. Li, W.-Y., Shen, Y., Wang, D.-J., Yang, Z.-K., Yang, X.-T.: Automatic dairy cow body condition scoring using depth images and 3D surface fitting. In: 2019 IEEE International Conference on Unmanned Systems and Artificial Intelligence (ICUSAI), pp. 155–159. IEEE (2019)
8. Zin, T.T., Tin, P., Kobayashi, I., Horii, Y.: An automatic estimation of dairy cow body condition score using analytic geometric image features. In: 2018 IEEE 7th Global Conference on Consumer Electronics (GCCE), pp. 775–776. IEEE (2018)
9. Liu, D., He, D., Norton, T.: Automatic estimation of dairy cattle body condition score from depth image using ensemble model. Biosys. Eng. **194**, 16–27 (2020)
10. Neto, A.B., et al.: The BFS method in a cloud environment for analyzing distributed energy resource Management systems. In: Brazilian Technology Symposium, pp. 349–362. Springer (2023). https://doi.org/10.1007/978-3-031-04435-9_35
11. Bacega, P.R.d.O., Iano, Y., Carvalho, B.C.S.d., Vaz, G.C., Oliveira, G.G.d., Chuma, E.L.: Study about the applicability of low latency in HAS transmission systems. In: Brazilian Technology Symposium, pp. 73–87. Springer (2023). https://doi.org/10.1007/978-3-031-044 35-9_7
12. Arducan Homepage. https://www.arducam.com/product/arducam-imx219-auto-focus-camera-module-drop-in-replacement-for-raspberry-pi-v2-and-nvidia-jetson-nano-camera/, (Accessed 4 Jul 2022)
13. Omniretro Homepage. https://omniretro.com/tecnologia/raspberry-pi-4-especificaciones-car acteristicas/, (Accessed 04 Jul 2022)
14. OpenCV: Indroduction, https://docs.opencv.org/3.4.16/d1/dfb/intro.html, (Accessed 30 Nov 2021)
15. Chen, L.-C., Zhu, Y., Papandreou, G., Schroff, F., Adam, H.: Encoder-decoder with atrous separable convolution for semantic image segmentation. In: Ferrari, V., Hebert, M., Sminchisescu, C., Weiss, Y. (eds.) ECCV 2018. LNCS, vol. 11211, pp. 833–851. Springer, Cham (2018). https://doi.org/10.1007/978-3-030-01234-2_49

16. Bolelli, F., Allegretti, S., Baraldi, L., Grana, C.: Spaghetti labeling: directed acyclic graphs for block-based connected components labeling. IEEE Trans. Image Process. **29**(1), 1999–2012 (2020)
17. He, K., Zhang, X., Ren, S., Sun, J.: Deep residual learning for image recognition (2015). cite. arXiv Prepr. arxiv1512.03385
18. MobileNet, MobileNetV2, and MobileNetV3.: https://keras.io/api/applications/mobilenet/, (Accessed 13 June 2022)
19. Szegedy, C.,et al.: Going deeper with convolutions. In: Proceedings of the IEEE Conference on Computer Vision and Pattern Recognition, pp. 1–9 (2015)
20. Simonyan, K., Zisserman, A.: Very deep convolutional networks for large-scale image recognition. In: 3rd International Conference on Learning Representations, ICLR 2015 - Conference Track Proceedings, pp. 1–14 (2015)
21. Sokolova, M., Lapalme, G.: A systematic analysis of performance measures for classification tasks. Inf. Process. Manag. **45**, 427–437 (2009)

Aquatic Quantification of Toxic Heavy Metals Due to Physical-Chemical Factors in Meat Production of *Oncorhynchus mykiss* (Rainbow Trout) in Controlled Open Systems Case: Lagunillas-Lampa, Puno

Olger Acosta-Angulo[1,2](✉) ⓘ, Renzo Pepe-Victoriano[1] ⓘ,
Lorena Cornejo-Ponce[3] ⓘ, Jordan I. Huanacuni[4] ⓘ,
and Yorka Yashira Castillo Silva[1] ⓘ

[1] Universidad Arturo Prat, Arica, Chile
oacostaa@unsa.edu.pe, rpepev@unap.cl, yocastillo@estudiantesunap.cl
[2] Universidad Nacional San Agustin de Arequipa, Arequipa, Peru
[3] Tarapaca University of the State of Chile, Arica, Chile
lorenacp@academicos.eta.cl
[4] Universidad Nacional Jorge Basadre Grohmann, Tacna, Peru
jhuanacunip@unjbg.edu.pe

Abstract. Heavy metals in the water can accumulate in the organs of fish, which was reported in various continental fish farms in Peru. The objective of the present study was to know the situational state of the water bodies and their effect on rainbow trout meat, determining the level of contamination by heavy metals. The present investigation was carried out in the Lagunillas lagoon, a high Andean zone of Santa Lucía, Puno. The physicochemical parameters of the water were determined and the quantification of heavy metals in the muscle, kidney, and liver of trout was carried out, by Atomic Absorption Spectrometry in the Testing Laboratory accredited by the Peruvian Accreditation Agency INACAL-DA (CERPER - Certifications of Peru SA). The results in the concentration of Sb (0.002 ml/Kg), As (0.0347 ml/Kg), Cd (0.001 ml/Kg), Cu (0.0024 ml/Kg), Cr (0.003 ml/Kg), Hg (0.0001 ml/Kg), and Pb (0.0004 ml/Kg) are below the maximum permissible limits established by the Ministry of the Environment and SANIPES. It is concluded that the water quality of the Lagunillas lagoon in the district of Santa Lucía, Lampa - Puno, is suitable for the cultivation of rainbow trout meat for human consumption.

Keywords: Inland aquaculture · W · Environmental impact · Water resource

© The Author(s), under exclusive license to Springer Nature Switzerland AG 2023
Y. Iano et al. (Eds.): BTSym 2022, SIST 353, pp. 461–471, 2023.
https://doi.org/10.1007/978-3-031-31007-2_43

1   Introduction

The production of trout meat from aquaculture is an important source of food, healthy and with high protein content; together with that proposed by the Food and Agriculture Organization of the United Nations (FAO) [1].

According to Argota [2], through studies carried out with the species *Gambusia punctata* of the order of *cyprinodontiformes* in the Filé river of Santiago de Cuba, where 282 adult individuals were analyzed, differentiated by sex and measuring between 2.1 and 4 cm of total length to establish reference levels in terms of histology and presence of heavy metals in three organs (brain, liver, and gills), Cu, Cd, Zn, and Pb were quantified by Inductively Coupled Plasma Spectrometry, and histopathological analysis showed that no damage was observed in the tissues of the organs analyzed. The levels of metals were below the threshold value in the brain; low levels of Pb and Cd were also detected in the liver, while in the gills the values were similar to the threshold value, according to the analysis [2].

Londoño and Muñoz [3], investigated heavy metals and the potential risk they can represent to human and animal health, including the trophic chain. The increase of heavy metals such as Cd, Cu, Hg, Cr, etc., was caused by the increase in mining operations, contamination of water, air, soil, and plants, as well as by insecticide fertilizers, climate change, and the greenhouse effect, among others.

Within the national context, in Junín (Peru), a study was carried out on the bioaccumulation of Fe, Zn, Cu, and Pb heavy metals in the liver [4], kidney, and muscle tissues of *O. mykiss* (rainbow trout) obtained from 7 production centers in the province of Yauli, where samples were taken monthly to analyze the presence of heavy metals, and 28 trouts averaging 250 g were used to determine the concentration of metals in the tissues, using atomic absorption spectrometry and the methodology recommended by FAO; atomic absorption spectrometry was used to quantify the presence of heavy metals [5] in the water and tissues of the trouts, finding that the levels of lead, iron, and zinc are higher than the maximum limits allowed by the European Union and the environmental quality standards established by the Peruvian Ministry of the Environment for rivers on the coast and in the highlands for trout farming; on the other hand, copper was the only element that remained below the maximum permitted levels [6].

In 2014 Muñoz [7], identified histopathological lesions present in *O. mykiss*, cultured by exposure to a contaminated environment where 35 specimens were collected at random to obtain samples of gills, liver, and skeletal striated muscle, a liter of water from the lagoon was also sampled. The concentration of heavy metals was determined with atomic absorption spectro-photometry and the levels of heavy metals in water did not exceed the maximum permissible limit (according to Peruvian legislation); however, some values (As, Cd, and Hg) in sediment were above the permissible level; it was mentioned that the regions prone to this high concentration of metals are the areas near the mouths of the effluents of informal mining areas (highlands and jungle), which is why the corresponding studies were carried out, clarifying that the aquatic resources were highly contaminated [8,9].

In contrast, Gamarra and Uceda [10], for the Huancayo region, used the same species of *O. mykiss* to determine the concentration levels of heavy metals in the Chiapuquio de Ingenio river, according to the maximum permissible limit for water. Sixteen specimens and water samples were used to determine the presence of lead and cadmium in gills and liver using the atomic absorption spectrometry method provided with a graphite furnace; physicochemical analyses were performed according to United States Pharmacopeia 39 (USP 39). The results obtained for lead and cadmium in the liver and gills compared to the European Union standard, Codex Alimentarius, and the Peruvian Fish Health Standard, are below the maximum permissible limit. On the other hand, the concentration of lead and cadmium in the water of the Chiapuquio river of Ingenio - Huancayo exceeded the value established by the Ministry of the Environment [11]. The conclusion is that trout organs contain low levels of lead and cadmium allowed by national and international regulations; however, the river water exceeded the established limits.

On the other hand, in the Junín region, Gonzáles [12] demonstrated that the bioaccumulation of cadmium and mercury determined by atomic absorption spectrometry, carried out at the Universidad Nacional Mayor de San Marcos in the laboratory of the Faculty of Chemistry and Engineering, is related to growth in rainbow trout (*O. mykiss*), taking 40 samples of trout from two hatcheries in the Junín region, according to the maximum permissible limits established by the European Union, a quasi-experimental design was used, evaluating the levels of cadmium and mercury bioaccumulation and growth factors of the trout. The results of heavy metal accumulation differed between them. In the Ingenio hatchery, no cadmium or mercury was evidenced, while in the Huayhuay hatchery the European Union limits for cadmium and mercury content were exceeded.

In 2018, the contribution of Zeballos [13], through a study evaluated the significant decrease in the number of rainbow trout in the district of Challhuahuacho- Apurimac.

Within Peru's existing environmental regulations, environmental management instruments are mechanisms designed and implemented to comply with national environmental policy and the country's environmental standards. Peruvian legislation contains various environmental management instruments, including Environmental Quality Standards (ECAs) and maximum permissible limits (MPLs). The former is of general application, that is, for society as a whole, while the latter has been developed to regulate particular activities.

ECAs are indicators of environmental quality. They measure the concentration of elements, substances, or others in the air, water, or soil. Their purpose is to set targets that represent the level at which the environment and human health can be significantly affected. They are not legally required but are used for the establishment of public environmental policies [14].

MPLs measure the concentration of certain elements, substances, and/or physical, chemical, and/or biological aspects found in emissions, effluents, or discharges generated by a particular productive activity, since it is through them that air, water, or soil can be affected [15].

The purpose of setting such limits is to protect the environment and human health from certain elements and/or substances that may represent a risk to them, but unlike ECAs, MPLs establish a limit applicable to emissions, effluents, or discharges into the environment, individualizing the limits by productive activity. Thus, MPLs are enforceable and compliance with them is mandatory for each person or company in each sector [16, 17].

2   Methodology

The present investigation was carried out in the high Andean zone of Santa Lucía, Puno; for the quantification of heavy metals, the technique of Atomic Absorption Spectrometry was used, for which the samples were stored in hermetically sealed bags and kept at 5 °C for analysis in the CERPER - Certificaciones del Perú S.A. laboratory [18], a testing laboratory accredited by INACAL [19]. The content of analyzed heavy metals (antimony, arsenic, cadmium, copper, chromium, phosphorus, mercury, and lead) was quantified, emphasizing the analysis of Cadmium, Mercury, and Lead, which were analyzed in the following trout organs: muscle, kidney, and liver, where the objective results of this research are based.

2.1   Study Area

The Lagunillas lagoon (see Fig. 1) is an aquifer located in the district of Santa Lucía, province of Lampa in the department of Puno - Peru, located at latitude: 15°44'S and longitude: 70°41'W with an altitude of 4,147 m above sea level. This lagoon has a surface area of 66 km^2 and an average depth of 47.6 m. The lagoon's reservoir is supplied by local rainfall, natural runoff from agricultural areas, and other sources. There are currently no baseline studies that indicate the physicochemical characteristics of the lagoon.

Currently, the Lagunillas lagoon is developing rainbow trout farming activities in a floating cage system (see Fig. 2) with more than 150 producers, both formal and informal, generating more than 500 permanent and temporary jobs, with an estimated production of more than 1,000 tons by 2022. With the clarification that due to SANIPES inspection and the consequences of the COVID-19 pandemic, the effect is a decrease in trout meat production.

2.2   Gathering Water Samples

To collect water samples from Lagunillas lagoon, 500 ml glass tanks were used, previously washed with distilled water, of transparent color. Different water samples were taken at each point (A, B, and C) shown in Fig. 2, which contained rainbow trout in floating cages, considering that these samples were obtained for later processing in a specialized and accredited laboratory. After collecting

Fig. 1. Satellite location of the Lagunillas lagoon (Santa Lucía, Puno).

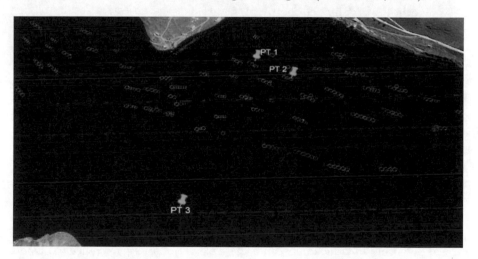

Fig. 2. Satellite location of the sampling points in the Lagunillas lagoon (Santa Lucía, Puno) and location of the sampling zones.

the water samples, the corresponding temperatures were taken and they were hermetically sealed to be placed in a place isolated from the Sun's rays so as not to alter the results. To determine the concentration of heavy metals in the trouts, it was first necessary to anesthetize them in groups of 10 individuals in a container of 20 L capacity with a solution of clove oil, which is an active ingredient, eugenol, at a dose of 12.5 mg of isoeugenol per liter of water [7] and then they were sacrificed by a medullary cut at the level of the joint between the skull and the first vertebra. Then it was verified that all the organs were in perfect condition. Afterward, the liver, kidney, and muscle were removed. The samples were stored in hermetically sealed bags and kept at 5 °C for analysis at the testing laboratory accredited by the Peruvian Accreditation Agency INACAL-DA [19] (CERPER- Certificaciones del Perú S.A.) located in the city of Arequipa.

2.3   Sampling of Study Specimens

We worked with farmed rainbow trout, which had been in the lagoon for 9 months up to the date of sampling, as part of their finishing stage.

During their time in the water, the fish were reared under an intensive system in floating cages, under control conditions in relation to their daily diet. The 150 fish collected at random were obtained from 3 production units of Lagunillas lagoon, with an average of 3000 specimens per cage and taking as a sample 50 specimens from each production unit, corresponding to each sampling point. The specimens obtained reached an average weight of 280 g ± 20 g and an average length of 29 cm ± 3 cm; with these characteristics in weight and length they are considered suitable for the commercialization of this hydrobiological resource.

2.4   Methods of Physicochemical Analysis

The concentration of heavy metals was determined using an atomic absorption spectrometer (AAS), according to Method 245.1 for Hg; and Method 2008 was used to determine As, Cd, Cr, Cu, Pb, and Zn.

Water Temperature. A thermometer with metal grid protection, with graduation from −10 °C to 100 °C, was used to determine the temperature of the surface water, the unit of measurement being °C.

Water Transparency. The Secchi disk, which measures the depth in meters, was used to measure this parameter. The white disk, 30 cm in diameter, when dropped from a boat, becomes invisible.

pH. For its measurement, the electrometric method was used, which is based on the potential difference between a glass electrode and a reference electrode. A Hatch portable digital potentiometer was used.

Dissolved Oxygen. A digital oxygen meter, previously calibrated to standard conditions, was used to measure this parameter.

3   Results

3.1   Physicochemical Characteristics of Water

The analyses that were carried out by the CERPER, in relation to the analyzed water space, are represented in Table 1.

Table 1. Analyses performed by CERPER-Arequipa laboratories [18].

Parameter	Result
Conductivity	11.41 µS/cm
Dissolved Oxygen	7.19 mg/L
Temperature	10.3 °C
pH	8.62
Total Dissolved Solids	761 mg/L
Total Suspended Solids	3.74 mg/L
Sulfides	< 0.001 mg/L
Ammonia	< 0.024 mg NH2/L

3.2 Presence of Heavy Metals at Sampling Points

The first part of the experiment consisted of comparing the number of heavy metals in the three water sampling points of Lagunillas lagoon. This information is important to establish if there is an influence on the bioaccumulation of heavy metals in the trouts cultured in the lagoon. The results of the sampling points are presented in Table 2 below, where the presence of metals can be seen: arsenic, boron, cadmium, copper, chromium, mercury, nickel, lead, selenium, and thallium are below the maximum permissible limits established for water for the cultivation of hydrobiological species in lakes and lagoons Category 2 - C4; making the average analysis versus what is established by the Ministry of the Environment (MINAM) [20].

A comparison was made with that established in MINAM, which gave values below the permissible limits, as can be seen in Figs. 3, 4, and 5, corresponding to the organs muscle, kidney, and liver, respectively. The low levels of heavy metal concentration in the different organs of rainbow trouts allow them not to be histopathologically damaged.

The results were obtained and compared with other researchers from other countries; having as the main contribution that they are below the values established by them, mentioning that for the proposed study the main guideline is

Table 2. Comparison of heavy metals in 3 sampling points; Lagunillas vs. Ministry of Environment (MINAM) [20].

N	Analyzed Metal	WATER: Sampling Points (mg/L)				DS 004-2017-MINAM
		P1 (15°44'41.4" S 70°41'46" W)	P2 (15°44'39.6" S 70°41'49.2" W)	P3 (15°44'53.8" S 70°41'54.8" W)	Average (mg/L)	ECA Quantity (mg/L)
1	Antimony	0.0001	0.0001	0.0003	0.0002	0.6400
2	Arsenic	0.0309	0.0348	0.0386	0.0347	0.1500
3	Cadmium	0.0001	0.0001	0.0000	0.0001	0.0003
4	Copper	0.0049	0.0007	0.0007	0.0021	0.1000
5	Chrome	0.0003	0.0003	0.0003	0.0003	0.0110
6	Phosphorus	———	———	0.0190	0.0190	0.0250
7	Mercury	0.0001	0.0001	0.0001	0.0001	0.0001
8	Plumb	0.0003	0.0002	0.0007	0.0004	0,0025

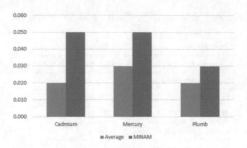

Fig. 3. Comparison of heavy metals concentration in average muscle (mg/Kg); 3 sampling points (average) Lagunillas vs Ministry of the Environment (MINAM) [20].

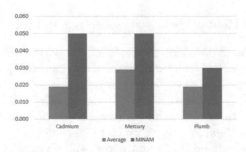

Fig. 4. Comparison of heavy metals concentration in kidneys (mg/Kg); 3 sampling points (average) Lagunillas vs Ministry of Environment (MINAM) [20].

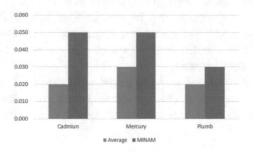

Fig. 5. Comparison of heavy metals concentration in liver (mg/Kg); 3 sampling points (average) Lagunillas vs Ministry of the Environment (MINAM) [19].

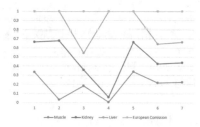

Fig. 6. Comparison of heavy metals concentration found in rainbow trout (Lagunillas) vs European Commission

MINAM [20], and for the rest of the countries the main guideline is the one established by FAO in document N° 764-ROMA [21]; all these data are being represented graphically in Fig. 6.

Within the established international analyses carried out, a comparison is made with those carried out in the European Union (EU) and those carried out in Japan, where it can be inferred that international standards are met, as shown in Table 3 [21].

Table 3. Comparative analyses carried out between SANIPES, the European Union, and Japan. Manual of Health and Safety Indicators for fishery products for the national and export markets. Executive Directorate Resolution No. 057-2016-SANIPES-DE.

	Peru	UE	Japan
Arsenic	———-	1.0	1.0
Cadmium	0.05 mg/kg fresh fish meat	0.05	———
Mercury	0.50 mg/kg fresh fish meat	0.05	0.5
Plumb	0.30 mg/Kg fresh fish meat	0.30	2.0

4   Analysis and Discussion

The analysis of heavy metals in the surface water of Lagunillas lagoon, in the rainbow trout farming area, highlighted the presence of the following metals: arsenic, boron, cadmium, copper, chromium, mercury, nickel, lead, selenium, and thallium. However, they are below the maximum permissible limits established by the Ministry of the Environment (MINAM) [20] for water used for the cultivation of hydrobiological species in lakes and lagoons. In relation to the values obtained in the analysis of trout meat [4], the present work reported similar concentrations of lead (0.0004 ml/Kg) and cadmium (0.0001 ml/Kg); however, our work reported mercury concentrations 5 times higher than those reported by Chui (0.00002 ml/Kg) [4], but within the permissible parameters considered by the Ministry of the Environment (MINAM) [20]. Analyses carried out in areas close to mining establishments reported concentrations of heavy metals that exceed the limits established in the muscle of other aquaculture species [21]. The samples analyzed for cadmium exceeded the limits allowed by the MINAM standard. The samples analyzed for the present investigation, such as muscle, kidney, and liver of rainbow trout [4], gave minimum values to those established by the food safety standard according to FAO.

5   Conclusions and Future Work

The concentrations of heavy metals, such as antimony, arsenic, cadmium, copper, chromium, mercury, and lead in the water and trout organs do not exceed the maximum limits established by the national institutions that regulate aquaculture products; therefore, it is concluded that the meat of the rainbow trout grown in the Lagunillas lagoon in the district of Santa Lucía, Lampa - Puno complies with the standards and is fit for human consumption direct. The use of IoT (Internet of Things) for the collection of data and the creation of an automated database is proposed as future work.

References

1. Fisheries and Aquaculture - Fisheries and Aquaculture - Aquaculture, https:// www.fao.org/fishery/en/aquaculture Accessed 02 Jan 2022
2. Argota, G., Argota, H., Larramendi, D., Mora, Y., Fimia, R., Iannacone, J.: Histología y química umbral de metales pesados en hígado, branquias y cerebro de Gambusia punctata (Poeciliidae) del río Filé de Santiago de Cuba. REDVET. Rev. Electrónica Vet. **13**, 1–11 (2012)
3. Luis, L., Paula, L., Fabián, M.: Los riesgos de los metales pesado en la salud humana y animal. Biotecnol. en el Sect. Agropecu. y agroindustrial. **14**, 145–153 (2016)
4. Chui, H.N., Roque, B., Huaquisto, E., Sardón, D.L., Belizario, G., Calatayud, A.P.: Metales pesados en truchas arcoíris (Oncorhynchus mykiss) de crianza intensiva de la zona noroeste del lago Titicaca. Rev. Investig. Vet. del Perú. 32, (2021)
5. Vargas Licona, S.P., Marrugo Negrete, J.L.: Mercury, methylmercury and other heavy metals in fish in Colombia: risk from Ingestion. Acta Biológica Colomb. **24**, 232–242 (2019)
6. Chanamé Zapata, F.C.: Bioacumulación de metales pesados procedentes de la contaminación minera y metalúrgica en tejidos de oncorthynchus mykiss "trucha arco iris" de los centros de producción de la provincia de yauli-junin (2009)
7. Huancaré Pusari, R.K.: Identificación histopatológica de lesiones inducidas por bioacumulación de metales pesados en branquias, hígado y músculo de trucha arcoíris (Oncorhynchus mykiss) de cultivo en etapa comercial de la laguna de Mamacocha, área de influencia minera, Cajamarca-Perú. (2014)
8. Thiagarajan, Y., Pasupulati, B., de Oliveira, G.G., Iano, Y., Vaz, G.C.: A Simple Approach for Short-Term Hydrothermal Self Scheduling for Generation Companies in Restructured Power System. In: Brazilian Technology Symposium, pp. 396–414. Springer (2022). https://doi.org/10.1007/978-3-031-08545-1_38
9. Chuma, E.L., Iano, Y., Roger, L.L.B., De Oliveira, G.G., Vaz, G.C.: Novelty sensor for detection of wear particles in oil using integrated microwave metamaterial resonators with neodymium magnets. IEEE Sens. J. **22**, 10508–10514 (2022)

10. Gamarra Avila, N.A., Uceda León, R.Y.: Determinación de metales pesados por espectrofotometría de absorción atómica en truchas arcoiris "oncorhynchus mykiss" del río Chiapuquio de Ingenio-Huancayo. (2017)
11. Límite Maximo Permisible (LMP), https://infoaireperu.minam.gob.pe/limite-maximo-permisible-lmp/ Accessed 02 Jan 2022
12. González Alarcón, S.: Determinación espectrofotométrica por absorción atómica de la bioacumulación de cadmio y mercurio y su relación con el crecimiento en truchas arco iris (oncorrhynchus mykiss) de dos criaderos de la Región Junín Perú. (2017)
13. Zevallos De La Torre, S.: Calidad de agua, bioacumulación de metales pesados y niveles de estrés en la trucha arcoíris (Oncorhynchus mykiss) en Challhuahuacho, Apurímac. (2018)
14. Aprueban Estándares de Calidad Ambiental (ECA) para Agua y establecen Disposiciones Complementarias | SINIA | Sistema Nacional de Información Ambiental, https://sinia.minam.gob.pe/normas/aprueban-estandares-calidad-ambiental-eca-agua-establecen-disposiciones, Accessed 02 Jan 2022
15. Reglamento de la Calidad del Agua para Consumo Humano, http://www.digesa.minsa.gob.pe/publicaciones/descargas/Reglamento_Calidad_Agua.pdf Accessed 02 Jan 2022
16. de Souza, C.F.C., Iano, Y., de Oliveira, G.G., Vaz, G.C., Reis, V.S., Neto, J.M.: Institutional Development Index (IDI): Calculation for Municipalities in the Metropolitan Region of Campinas (Brazil). In: Brazilian Technology Symposium. pp. 245–255. Springer (2022). https://doi.org/10.1007/978-3-031-08545-1_23
17. Santos, P.A., et al.: Analysis of the relationship between maturity indicators using the multivariate linear regression: a case study in the brazilian cities. In: Xu, Z., Alrabaee, S., Loyola-González, O., Zhang, X., Cahyani, N.D.W., Ab Rahman, N.H. (eds.) CSIA 2022. LNDECT, vol. 125, pp. 203–210. Springer, Cham (2022). https://doi.org/10.1007/978-3-030-97874-7_26
18. CERPER - Análisis y ensayo, inspección y muestreo, certificación, capacitación, https://cerper.com/, Accessed 30 Oct 2022
19. Instituto Nacional de Calidad - INACAL - Gobierno del Perú, https://www.gob.pe/inacal, Accessed 30 Oct 2022
20. Decreto Supremo N° 004–2017-MINAM.- | Ministerio del Ambiente, https://www.minam.gob.pe/disposiciones/decreto-supremo-n-004-2017-minam/ Accessed 30 Oct 2022
21. Nepal, A.P., Sharma, S., Bhujel, R.C., Bahadur, T.: Condition factor, growth performance, and production of Rainbow trout (Oncorhynchus mykiss) in floating cages in a shallow reservoir in Panauti, Nepal: A preliminary study (2021)

Footprints' Effectiveness as Decision-Making Tools for Promoting Sustainability

Bruna A. Branchi$^{(\boxtimes)}$ (iD), Denise Helena Lombardo Ferreira (iD),
Alan Marcelo Barbosa (iD), and Ana Luiza Ferreira (iD)

Pontifícia Universidade Católica de Campinas (PUC-Campinas), Campinas, Brazil
{bruna.branchi,lombardo}@puc-campinas.edu.br,
alan.mb@puccampinas.edu.br

Abstract. To study the human pressure on the environment, quantitative indicators have been made. Among them, those reunited by the "footprint" label gained a relevant place in promoting consciousness of the unsustainability of our current production and consumption patterns. This paper focuses on a selected group of three indicators: the Ecological Footprint, the Carbon Footprint, and the Water Footprint. The choice has been oriented by their wide application and accurate methodology. With the purpose of discussing their contribution to sustainability by modifying the decision-makers' behavior, their characteristics and methodological similarities and differences are discussed. Footprints are consumer-oriented indicators that share a conceptual simplicity and a straightforward message. These are important qualities for indicators thought to affect the decentralized decision-making process. They play a valuable contribution to increasing public awareness of human pressure on the environment. But they still lack any social and economic discussions. Therefore, their contribution to sustainability is partially downsized.

Keywords: Sustainable development · Water use · Land use

1 Introduction

The current consumption patterns are challenging the planet's boundaries. The effort for reducing the human pressure on the natural environment dates to the 1970 s with the Club of Rome report [1] and the 1972 United Nations Conference on the Environment in Stockholm, and further on with the 1987 Brundtland Commission report [2], when the term "sustainable development" gained impulse as a new vision of development, connecting economic growth with social and environmental dimensions.

Along with this new concept, there is a need to measure human activities' impact on natural resources. The appearance of the Ecological Footprint in the early 1990s [3] gained such widespread recognition that many other types of footprints emerged thereafter [4]. Each of them focuses on a specific environmental issue that can be measured at distinct levels, from micro (product or person) to macro (community, nation, or the entire world). Among them, those with a wide overall use and a well-established methodology are the Ecological Footprint (EF), Carbon Footprint (CF), and Water Footprint (WF) [5].

© The Author(s), under exclusive license to Springer Nature Switzerland AG 2023
Y. Iano et al. (Eds.): BTSym 2022, SIST 353, pp. 472–478, 2023.
https://doi.org/10.1007/978-3-031-31007-2_44

The primary purpose of the paper is to analyze how the above-mentioned Footprints can be correctly used to impact human lifestyle. It starts with a concise description of each one of the three selected Footprints that helps to identify similarities and differences among them. Then, their contribution to effective changes in human behavior to promote sustainability is discussed.

2 Three Relevant Footprints

When first published, the ecological footprint (EF) was meant to measure the land imprint of human consumption decisions. But nowadays footprints gained a wider connotation as "indicators of human pressure on the environment" or Environmental Footprints (EnF) [6].

The EnF are aggregate indicators that share conceptual simplicity and straightforward message that could help to raise the consciousness of our lifestyle [7]. Therefore, they are important instruments for molding and changing human consumption and production patterns [8].

2.1 The Ecological Footprint

First published in 1992 by Rees [3], the Ecological Footprint identified the space (land) necessary to sustain a region's consumption activity. Nowadays, it measures the biologically productive space needed to attend to the current consumption patterns and absorb the associated waste. It includes six distinct types of land: cropland, pastureland, fishing area, forest, space for urban infrastructure, and land to absorb carbon emissions. Therefore, it considers the direct and indirect effects of human activities on natural resources.

Its popularity gained more strength with Earth Overshoot Day, the date on which the annual human demand for natural resources exceeds the Earth's capacity for regeneration. The Global Footprint Network (GFN) institute shows that each year the Earth Overshoot Day is reached faster than in the past. For example, in 2022 it fell on July 28th, much faster than in 1971 when Earth Overshoot Day was reached in December [9]. Such evolution is clearly displayed in Fig. 1.

The EF is nowadays quantified in "global hectares", a theoretical measure of global average production per hectare [10].

Its strength is based on its conceptual simplicity and graphical design that help mass communication. On the other hand, because of its focus on productivity, it does not discriminate among types of land management, or it does not include other impacts such as the reduction of biodiversity and mineral resources depletion [11].

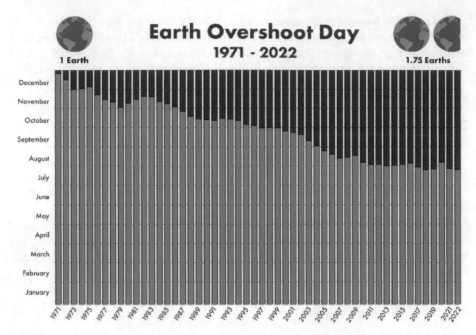

Fig. 1. Earth Overshoot Day Evolution [9].

2.2 The Carbon Footprint

To measure the impact of human activity on global warming different methodologies are resumed under the Carbon Footprint umbrella. In general terms, the CF assesses the climate change impact of Greenhouse Gases (GHGs) defined in the Kyoto Protocol measured in terms of kilograms of CO_2 equivalent. Differences come from the selection of which GHGs are included and the calculation methods, which can be the Life Cycle Assessment or the Input-Output analysis [12]. Therefore, methodological differences can result in different measurements for the same region, potentially generating confusing messages on the footprint of human lifestyle.

On the other hand, it is even easier to be understood by the public in general than the ecological footprint and, consequently, to raise consciousness and change individual behaviors.

2.3 The Water Footprint

Ten years after the Ecological Footprint publication, the Water Footprint appears to measure the virtual water content in goods and services [13]. This is one of the different footprints aimed to assess the impact of human consumption on water, like the water scarcity footprint or the water availability footprint for example [14, 15].

The WF is composed of the green WF to measure the rainwater incorporated by plants or evaporated, the blue WF to assess surface and groundwater, and the gray WF to measure the quantity of freshwater needed to dilute pollution associated with production stages [13].

In synthesis, it measures the water volume consumed, directly and indirectly, and the amount required to assimilate pollution. It is measured in m^3 per unit of time or quantity of product.

3 Their Contributions to Sustainability

The selected Footprints are composite indicators with a well-defined methodology, flexible coverage, and a clear research question [5, 16]. They all aim to measure the environmental consequences of human activity.

Within the DPSIR framework, the Environmental Footprints contribute by measuring and raising consciousness on pressures resulting from human activity on the use of natural resources, such as land, air, or water, and the related pollution and waste (Fig. 2). They can be employed to adjust responses to the impact of human lifestyle on natural resources. But they share a limited contribution to impact assessment since they are environmental instruments and do not include any social considerations, for example [17].

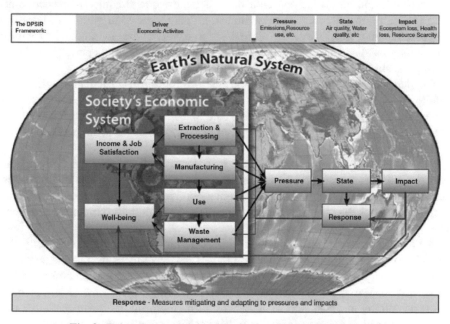

Fig. 2. Driver-Pressure-State-Impact-Response Framework [10].

As composite indicators, they are simplifications of reality, with a focus on specific natural resources suffering from human pressure. The EF highlights the aggregate resource consumption and compares it with the Earth boundary, visualizing the limit of growth. The CF, by measuring the GHGs emissions, evaluates the human impact on rising temperatures. The WF alerts for the amount of water needed to attend to human demand.

The EnF share a consumption-based viewpoint since they all evaluate the impact of consumers' behavior on biocapacity, climate change, or water. But only EF and WF look at the environment as a production input as well as the receiver of waste and pollution from production and consumption processes.

Given their conceptual simplicity, they represent relevant tools to inform decision-makers of the effects of their choices on specific environmental problems.

They can be used by producers, consumers, and society in general. For example, producers can use them in their ESG journey [6, 18, 19]. The final product footprint is therefore the sum of direct and indirect components, that is it includes the impact on the environment from a life cycle perspective. Their main challenges are related to supply chain monitoring and environmental footprints are useful indicators.

Consumers can become more conscious when informed about the environmental impact of their choices. Changing diets, buying locally, and challenging consumerism are relevant strategies to promote sustainability [20, 21].

At the country level, environmental footprints help raise awareness of externalities linked to international trade since the environmental impacts of consumption can happen abroad, impacting water or land in foreign countries.

Footprints can also arise consciousness that more social equity is needed, since some consumption patterns are unsustainable, no matter the contributions of improved and eco-efficient technologies. Therefore, in a finite world, "the environmental footprint of humanity has to reduce toward sustainable levels, and footprints per capita have to converge to similar, more equitable shares" [6].

Challenges related to the use of footprints for monitoring sustainable actions may include the trade-offs between different footprints [16]. Each specific footprint focuses on a specific environmental aspect, water, land, or air. For example, substituting fossil fuels for ethanol reduces the carbon footprint but it increases the ecological footprint if sugarcane crops occupy more land.

Thus, there is a need for an integrated approach that can be built bringing together the three EnF that can create a better instrument to mold decisions, especially because human actions affect simultaneously different natural resources. Examples can be found in studies applying the Life Cycle Accounting or the Multi-Regional Input-Output model [16].

An additional drawback comes along with EnF quality: conceptual simplicity. The idea of measuring consumption impact on the environment by using a single number is not new. Novelty is found in the idea of a footprint. It is a clear "imprint on the planet Earth" that one is making while consuming and producing. At the same time, this image can be potentially misunderstood and misused if the footprints methodology is not well explained. As a global aggregate indicator, it is based on simplification, assumptions, and uncertainty. For correct use and interpretation, their methodologies must be published, publicized, and discussed.

4   Final Considerations

The climate changes we are facing nowadays reinforce the importance of having good indicators to monitor human impacts, drive decision-making, and bring consciousness to global society. The United Nations Environment Program highlights relevant risks and issues for the global environment, which can bring extremely negative impacts on humanity, such as the mismatch in life cycles, noise pollution, and forest fires, as well as water scarcity, food security, and pollution.

When the primary purpose is to inform society in general and to promote involvement with sustainable actions, footprints are appropriate tools. They share conceptual simplicity, methodological accuracy, and straight interpretation. That is, they can be powerful tools for changing human lifestyle in the move toward sustainable development.

But, on the other end, they are environmental footprints and do not take into account the social dimension of sustainable development. Therefore, there is room for improvement by building a Sustainability Footprint that, based on the EnF´s experience, can have an even larger impact on decision-makers.

Acknowledgments. This study was financed in part by the Coordenação de Aperfeiçoamento de Pessoal de Nível Superior – Brasil (CAPES) – Finance Code 001.

References

1. Meadows, D.H., Meadows, D.L., Randers, J., Behrens, W.W.: The limits to growth. In: Green planet blues, pp. 25–29. Routledge (2018)
2. Brundtland, G.H.: World commission on environment and development. Environ. policy law. **14**, 26–30 (1985)
3. Rees, W.E.: Ecological footprints and appropriated carrying capacity: what urban economics leaves out. In: The Earthscan Reader in Rural–Urban Linkages, pp. 285–297. Routledge (2018)
4. Fang, K.: Environmental Footprints: Assessing Anthropogenic Effects. Springer International Publishing, Cham (2021)
5. Laurent, A., Owsianiak, M.: Potentials and limitations of footprints for gauging environmental sustainability. Curr. Opin. Environ. Sustain. **25**, 20–27 (2017)
6. Hoekstra, A.Y., Wiedmann, T.O.: Humanity's unsustainable environmental footprint. Science (80). **344**, 1114–1117 (2014)
7. Ruberti M, Massari, S.: Ecological Footprint. In: Massari S, Sonnemann G, Balkau F (eds.) Life cycle approaches to sustainable regional development, 47–52 (2017)
8. Thiagarajan, Y., Palanivel, G., Soubache, I.D., Gomes, G., de Oliveira, Y., Iano, G.C., Vaz, H.M.: Design and Fabrication of Human-Powered Vehicle - A Measure for Healthy Living. In: Iano, Y., Saotome, O., Vásquez, G.L.K., Pezzuto, C.C., Arthur, R., Gomes, G., de Oliveira, (eds.) Proceedings of the 7th Brazilian Technology Symposium (BTSym'21): Emerging Trends in Human Smart and Sustainable Future of Cities (Volume 1), pp. 1–15. Springer International Publishing, Cham (2023). https://doi.org/10.1007/978-3-031-04435-9_1
9. Global Footprint Network (2022) Earth Overshoot Day, https://www.footprintnetwork.org/our-work/earth-overshoot-day/, Accessed Oct 22 2022
10. Wood, R.: Environmental footprints. In: Raa, T. (ed.) Handbook of Input-Output Analysis, pp. 175–222. Edward Elgar Publishing, Northampton (2017)
11. Matuštík, J., Kočí, V.: What is a footprint? A conceptual analysis of environmental footprint indicators. J. Clean. Prod. **285**, 124833 (2021)
12. Hanscom, L.: Working guidebook to the national footprint accounts (2018)
13. Hoekstra, A.Y., Mekonnen, M.M.: The water footprint of humanity. Proc. Natl. Acad. Sci. **109**, 3232–3237 (2012)

14. Thiagarajan, Y., Pasupulati, B., de Oliveira, G.G., Iano, Y., Vaz, G.C.: A simple approach for short-term hydrothermal self scheduling for generation companies in restructured power system. In: Brazilian Technology Symposium, pp. 396–414. Springer (2022). https://doi.org/10.1007/978-3-031-08545-1_38
15. Gregio, R.P., Iano, Y., Mota, L.T.M., Vaz, G.C., Oliveira, G.G., Castro, D.A.P., Frangeto, C.F.: Energy Use in Urban Areas Using Neodymium Magnets. In: Iano, Y., Saotome, O., Kemper, G., Mendes, A.C., de Seixas, G., de Oliveira, G. (eds.) BTSym 2020. SIST, vol. 233, pp. 988–1005. Springer, Cham (2021). https://doi.org/10.1007/978-3-030-75680-2_107
16. Galli, A., Wiedmann, T., Ercin, E., Knoblauch, D., Ewing, B., Giljum, S.: Integrating ecological, carbon and water footprint into a "footprint family" of indicators: definition and role in tracking human pressure on the planet. Ecol. Indic. **16**, 100–112 (2012)
17. Demanboro, A.C., Bianchini, D., Iano, Y., de Oliveira, G.G., Vaz, G.C.: 6g networks: an innovative approach, but with many challenges and paradigms, in the development of platforms and services in the near future. In: Brazilian Technology Symposium. pp. 172–187. Springer (2023). https://doi.org/10.1007/978-3-031-04435-9_17
18. Čuček, L., Klemeš, J.J., Kravanja, Z.: A review of footprint analysis tools for monitoring impacts on sustainability. J. Clean. Prod. **34**, 9–20 (2012)
19. Matthews, H.S., Hendrickson, C.T., Weber, C.L.: The importance of carbon footprint estimation boundaries. Environ. Sci. Technol. **42**, 5839–5842 (2008)
20. Hoekstra, A.Y.: The water footprint of modern consumer society. Routledge (2013)
21. Jackson, T.: Prosperity without growth: Economics for a finite planet. Routledge (2009)

Analysis of Deforestation at an Annual Rate in the Sub-basins of the Mayo River and its Relationship with Precipitation

Medina Torres Carlos Alonso$^{(\boxtimes)}$, Córdova Flores Marvin Paul ,
Carmona Arteaga Abel , and Vereau Miranda Edmundo

Universidad Privada del Norte, Lima, Peru
{n00107395,n00069828}@upn.pe, {abel.carmona,
edmundo.vereau}@upn.edu.pe

Abstract. Deforestation has long been linked as one of the most important causes of decreased rainfall in tropical forests, which are the most affected. This work has been carried out in the Mayo River drainage basin and aims to analyze in detail the amount of area that has been affected annually by deforestation in 20 selected sub-basins of the Mayo River and also determine which sub-basin has presented greater deforestation; On the other hand, we also want to examine what is its relationship with precipitation. The methodology used for this purpose was the application of the ArcGIS program, using the deforestation codes of the Google Earth Engine program and the grilled climate product ERA5 to obtain precipitation data. Finally, based on the results obtained, it can be affirmed that the amount of deforestation area affected has been very considerable, in such a way that it has caused greater rainfall in the sub-basins investigated, causing an alteration in the climatology.

Keywords: Mayo basin · Deforestation · Precipitation · ArcGIS · Google Earth Engine

1 Introduction

Peru addresses the problem of forest degradation. Deforestation is a problem whose scientific evidence only further alarms the state of forests over time. One of the forest ecosystems of Peru, with particular characteristics, but at the same time little knowledge in the scientific community, is the dry forests of the north. This phenomenon consists of the process of destruction and loss of natural forests due to the indiscriminate felling and burning of trees. So, the climate is mainly affected, because its felling affects the amount of precipitation that falls in the area. There is a great concern because deforestation could lead to a significant decrease in precipitation, since it affects part of the course of the hydrological water cycle, which implies that, the less vegetation, the less rainfall [1, 2].

Butler [3] cited an investigation in which he describes the numerous studies that show the effects of tropical deforestation in different places with different scales. In this, it was determined that the decrease in rainfall is not due to deforestation since it

© The Author(s), under exclusive license to Springer Nature Switzerland AG 2023
Y. Iano et al. (Eds.): BTSym 2022, SIST 353, pp. 479–487, 2023.
https://doi.org/10.1007/978-3-031-31007-2_45

only changes its patterns, this is because when deforestation reaches a certain place, the rain would change its patterns and it would rain a lot more in another place than in that deforested, in the same way, if we had a scenario of extreme deforestation, we would appreciate that the rainfall would decrease in the Midwest, Northwest and South America during the growing season, meanwhile the winter rain would have an increase on the east coast [3].

The Amazon basin has a high rate of deforestation. It has marked an index of 15% of the deforested Amazon rainforest since 1970. This is because the rate of deforestation is variant in the regions or tropical cloud forests being these the most vulnerable area. Of the world, 14% belongs to tropical areas and cloud forests (BTN), and 29% of tropical water is in balance. These have high importance in hydrology and biodiversity. On the other hand, the actions to protect and take care of natural resources in Peru are very scarce, these are only limited in specific areas such as Natural Protected Areas (NPA), for example, the protected forest of Alto Mayo, on the other hand, deforestation continues outside the NPA eliminating approximately 10% of BTN during the period 2000– 2012 [4].

Fernández [4] mentioned in her article that informal agriculture is the main source of deforestation in Peru, as in the entire Amazon, causing the degradation of 90% of the forest area. In addition, natural resources such as extracted wood are not used wisely by the community. Illegal mining and land and road construction are other reasons for deforestation. Consequently, today there is great concern at the global level for the flora and fauna that are directly affected by deforestation [5].

The research seeks to analyze in detail the amount of area that has been affected by deforestation that occurs in the sub-basins of the Mayo River at an annual rate and, in turn, examine what precipitation changes occurred due to it.

2 Study Area

The Mayo River drainage basin is located northwest of the San Martín region and northeast of the Amazonas region, being a bioregional basin. It has an extension of 9,774.37 km^2, where 91% corresponds to the San Martín region (approx. 8,897.94 km^2) and 9% (approx. 867.38 km^2) to the Amazonas region.

The basin lies between the following geographical coordinates WGS84: Latitude 6°2′10.5", longitude: 77° 5′ 53.8". The main channel of the Mayo River has an approximate length of 235.43 km. His regime is irregular and stormy. It also has an altitude of 4000 m above sea level and its average altitude is 1295 m above sea level, whose perimeter is 685.73 km, as shown in Fig. 1.

The Mayo River has its origins in the lower hydrographic unit Alto Mayo by the convergence of the Huasta rivers (formed in turn by the suspension of the Delta and Yanayacu rivers), other rivers and tributary streams at more than 2000 m above sea level; the state of conservation of its headwaters is due to the Natural Area Protected by the state called Alto Mayo Protection Forest, which houses cloud forest ecosystems, important for the genesis of water.

In addition, the following rivers are important tributaries in the upper part of the Mayo River basin: Naranjos, Naranjillo, Cachiyacu, Tioyacu, Soritor, Yurayacu, Avisado, Tónchima, Indoche, Huascayacu; in the middle and lower segments of the rivers: Gera, Cumbaza, and Mamonaquihua, as shown in Fig. 2. Its direction is from SE to NW with a continuously wide channel until the middle segment of its route, in the lower part of the basin its channel constricts to later flow into the Huallaga River.

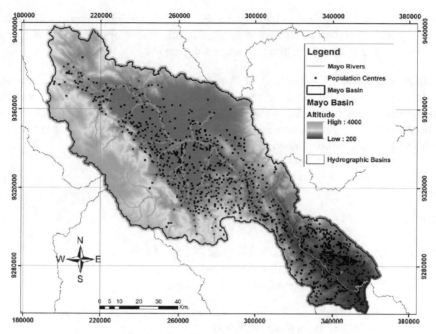

Fig. 1. Mayo River Hydrographic Basin.

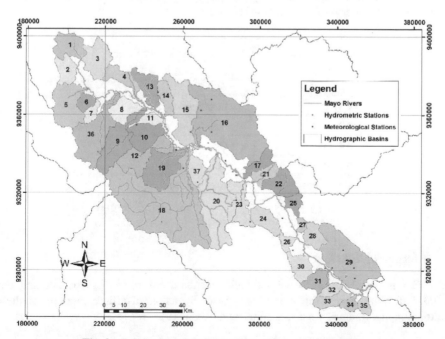

Fig. 2. Sub-basins of the Mayo River Hydrographic Basin.

3   Methodology

3.1   ERA 5 Calibration

The objective of this stage is to identify the values of the model parameters in order to optimally adjust a system as close to the real one that the model represents. The efficiency criterion considered for the calibration stage is detailed below.

Coefficient of Determination (R^2). The coefficient of determination R^2 is a term used in statistics, whose main function is to predict the result of hypotheses. The result can vary between 0 and 1, this means that the closer it is to the one it will be more adjusted to the variable it is trying to test, while the closer it gets to 0 the less reliable it will be because the model will be less adjusted, as shown in Table 1 [2, 6, 7].

$$R^2 = 1 - \frac{Cov(Q0, Qs)}{Sd(Q0).Sd(Qs)} \tag{1}$$

where:

- Cov(Q0, Qs) – Covariance of observed and estimated values.
- Sd(Q0) – Standard deviation of observed values.
- Sd(Qs) – Standard deviation of estimated versions.

3.2   Validation of the Hydrological Model

The objective of this stage is to verify the quality of the calibration settings, using the same efficiency criterion for the analysis of results.

Table 1. Nash – Sutcliffe Criterion reference values [8]

R2	Adjustment
< 0.2	Insufficient
0.2 – 0.4	Satisfying
0.4 – 0.6	Ok
0.6 – 0.8	Very Good
> 0.8	Excellent

3.3   Morphological Data

ArcGIS. It is a complete software that facilitates the use of models, maps, and balloons in 3D. It also has a large set of integrated bases, which are available to all users, these are topography, images, streets, terrains, and oceans [6].

In the present work, the software was used for the zoning of the sub-basins of the Mayo River, as shown in Fig. 2, generating shape files of each sub-basin investigated, in such a way that it was used in the Google Earth Engine code to obtain deforestation data and meteorological precipitation data. Likewise, with this program it was possible to determine the area of the basin called "Mayo River Basin" as shown in Fig. 1, having an area of 9 774.37 km^2, later it was possible to determine the coordinates of the Basin, the length of its main channel, the average slope, its perimeter, its geographical coordinates, as well as, its maximum and average altitude.

3.4 Weather Data

Google Earth Engine (GEE) is a cloud-based geomatics platform that allows users to visualize and analyze multispectral imagery and climate records collected by satellites orbiting our planet [9]. Through this database, the ERA5 precipitation records were obtained at the annual step of each sub-basin, calculated in millimeters (mm/year). Similarly, the deforestation code was used to obtain deforestation records at an annual pace for each sub-basin of the Mayo River, and thus be able to find how much of the accumulated area has been deforested between 2001–2019 and analyze where deforestation is greatest.

As shown in Fig. 3, the growth of deforestation in all the mentioned sub-basins is detailed, in 2006 an oscillation of 0 to 35 is observed while in 2011 it is from 0 to 90, and in 2016 and subsequent years it is from 0 to more than 140 km^2/year.

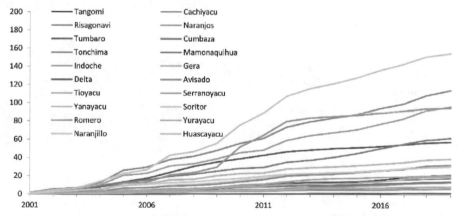

Fig. 3. Record of Accumulated Deforestation at an annual rate in (km^2/year) in the period 2001–2019 of the sub-basins investigated.

As shown in Fig. 4, precipitation ERA5 is observed at an annual rate. The amount of precipitation in 2006 is in a range of 1.1 to 3 mm/year, in 2011 from 1.7 to 3.1 mm/year, and 2016 from 1.5 to 3.5 mm/year.

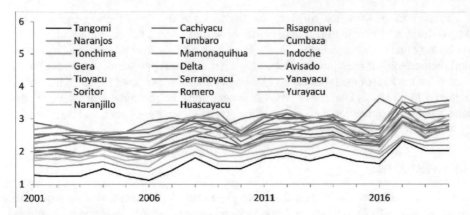

Fig. 4. Record of Precipitation ERA5 at an annual rate in (mm/year) in the period 2001–2019 of the sub-basins investigated.

4   Results

Next, in Fig. 5, the coefficient of determination of the Yurayacu sub-basin will be found between the deforestation data collected in the period 2001–2019, with the meteorological precipitation data obtained from the grilled product ERA5 in the same period.

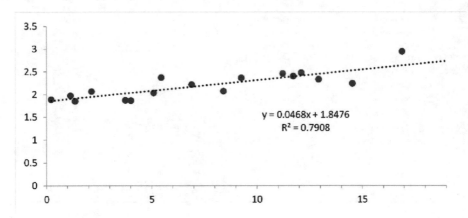

Fig. 5. Correlation R^2 between deforestation annual (km^2) with the annual precipitation (mm) in the period 2001–2019 in the Yurayacu sub-basin.

As shown in Fig. 6, the coefficient of determination of the Romero sub-basin will be found among the deforestation data collected in the period 2001–2019, with the meteorological precipitation data obtained from the grilled product ERA5 in the same period.

Below are the data of the R2 Correlation in Table 2, which contains each value obtained in all the sub-basins investigated in the period 2001–2019.

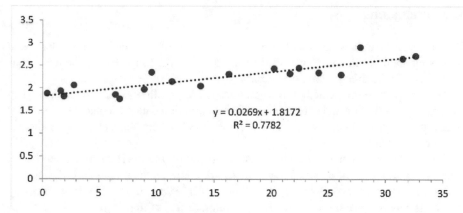

Fig. 6. R2 correlation between annual deforestation (km^2) with annual precipitation (mm) in the period 2001–2019 in the Romero sub-basin.

Table 2. Sub-basins investigated of the Mayo River

N°	Name	m	B	Correlation coefficient R^2
1	Yurayacu	0.047	1.848	0.791
2	Romero	0.027	1.817	0.778
3	Naranjos	0.060	2.405	0.752
4	Avisado	0.006	1.937	0.752
5	Tonchima	0.007	1.887	0.752
6	Naranjillo	0.029	1.762	0.748
7	Tangomi	0.040	1.251	0.732
8	Soritor	0.027	1.710	0.725
9	Indoche	0.007	1.496	0.700
10	Huascayacu	0.004	2.209	0.667
11	Delta	0.442	2.679	0.655
12	Tumbaru	0.013	1.926	0.647
13	Serranoyacu	0.125	2.497	0.621
14	Gera	0.016	1.691	0.587
15	Tioyacu	0.025	2.345	0.539
16	Yanayacu	0.075	2.623	0.532
17	Mamonaquihua	0.044	2.051	0.431
18	Cachiyacu	0.031	2.502	0.415
19	Risagonavi	0.073	2.202	0.375
20	Cumbaza	0.009	2.523	0.273

5 Conclusions

The present research work has allowed an evaluation of how deforestation has been increasing annually in a large part of the sub-basins of the Mayo River, and how it has been affecting the precipitation of the Basin.

With respect to the grilled climate product ERA5, it allows us to collect historical records of precipitation and temperature. The precipitation data presented the coefficient of determination with a maximum value of $R^2 = 0.791$ which, being close to 1, indicates that our results are safe.

The sub-basin that presented the highest deforestation was the Huascayacu sub-basin, with an accumulation of deforested area of 154,638 km^2 in the period 2001–2019.

Deforestation in the sub-basins investigated has been considerable, in such a way that it has caused greater rainfall, causing an alteration in climatology.

The sub-basin that presented the lowest deforestation compared to the other sub-basins investigated, has been the Serranoyacu sub-basin, with an accumulation of deforested area of 6,434 km^2 in the period 2001 - 2019.

Finally, according to our results obtained and our research sources, we can assure that the decrease in precipitation is not a consequence of deforestation, but rather changes in their behavior patterns. If deforestation can reach a high level, land that normally receives rain could be scarce of it, while others would receive more abundant rainfall.

References

1. de Souza, C.F.C., Iano, Y., de Oliveira, G.G., Vaz, G.C., Reis, V.S., Neto, J.M.: Institutional development index (idi): calculation for municipalities in the metropolitan region of campinas (Brazil). In: Brazilian Technology Symposium. pp. 245–255. Springer (2022). https://doi.org/10.1007/978-3-031-08545-1_23
2. Santos, P.A., et al.: Analysis of the Relationship Between Maturity Indicators Using the Multivariate Linear Regression: A Case Study in the Brazilian Cities. In: Xu, Z., Alrabaee, S., Loyola-González, O., Zhang, X., Cahyani, N.D.W., Ab Rahman, N.H. (eds.) CSIA 2022. LNDECT, vol. 125, pp. 203–210. Springer, Cham (2022). https://doi.org/10.1007/978-3-030-97874-7_26
3. Butler, R.A.: La deforestación tropical podría perturbar la lluvia globalmente. https://es.mongabay.com/2015/07/la-deforestacion-tropical-podria-perturbar-la-lluvia-globalmente/, Accessed Sep 15 2022
4. Gonzales Inca, C., Llanos, R.: Evaluación de los efectos de la deforestación en la hidrología y pérdida lateral de carbono orgánico del suelo de la cuenca del Alto Mayo (2015). https://www.conservation.org/docs/default-source/peru/carlos_gonzales_inca.pdf?Status=Master&sfvrsn=ef831abf_5, Accessed Sep 9 2022
5. "La principal causa de deforestación es la agricultura ilegal" I PERU I EL COMERCIO PERÚ, https://elcomercio.pe/peru/principal-causa-deforestacion-agricultura-ilegal-266589-noticia/?ref=ecr, Accessed 18 Sep 2022
6. Arteaga, A.C.: Tendencias, validación y generación de caudales usando la data grillada pisco para las cuencas del río Biabo (2019). https://repositorio.lamolina.edu.pe/handle/20.500.12996/4214, Accessed 23 Sep 2022

7. Sampaio, I.A., Iano, Y., Leite, A.R., de Oliveira, L., da Silva, M., Vieira, R., da Silva Júnior, Gabriel Gomes de Oliveira, Gabriel Caumo Vaz, Polyane Alves Santos, Kelem Christine Pereira Jordão,: The Use of the Elman Preconditioner in the Early Iterations of Interior Point Methods. In: Iano, Y., Saotome, O., Vásquez, G.L.K., Pezzuto, C.C., Arthur, R., Gomes, G., de Oliveira, (eds.) Proceedings of the 7th Brazilian Technology Symposium (BTSym'21): Emerging Trends in Systems Engineering Mathematics and Physical Sciences, Volume 2, pp. 355–363. Springer International Publishing, Cham (2022). https://doi.org/10.1007/978-3-031-08545-1_34

8. Cabrera, J.: Calibración de Modelos Hidrológicos. http://www.imefen.uni.edu.pe/Temas_int eres/modhidro_2.pdf, Accessed Sep 23 2022

9. Perilla, G.A., Mas, J.-F.: Google earth engine - gee: a powerful tool linking the potential of massive data and the efficiency of cloud processing. Investigaciones Geográficas **101**, e59929 (2020)

A Machine Learning Study to Classify the Type of Anemia in Children Under 5 Years of Age

Oscar J. M. Peña-Cáceres[1]([⊠]) [iD], Elmer A. Chunga-Zapata[1] [iD],
Teobaldo Raúl Basurco-Chambilla[2] [iD], Guido Humberto Cayo-Cabrera[2] [iD],
and Andrea D. Villegas-Paz[3] [iD]

[1] Facultad de Ingeniería de Sistemas, Universidad Cesar Vallejo, Piura, Peru
ojpenac@ucvvirtual.edu.pe, echunga@ucv.edu.pe
[2] Facultad de Ingeniería de Mecánica Eléctrica, Electrónica Y Sistemas, Universidad Nacional del Antiplano, Puno, Peru
{trbasurco,ghcc_telematic}@unap.edu.pe
[3] Sociedad Agrícola Rapel, Piura, Peru
avillegas@verfrut.pe

Abstract. In the last years, machine learning has emerged as a support in decision-making for the diagnosis of various diseases, particularly in geographical areas with a high population incidence. The objective of this study was to make use of machine learning algorithms, including Decision Tree, Random Forest, Naive Bayes, Vector Support Machine, and Logistic Regression, to classify the type of anemia in children under 5 years. The data set used corresponds to the year 2019 and represents 45,764 rates of anemia diagnoses in the Piura region, in Peru. Information was obtained through the Open Data platform of the Peruvian Government. The Python programming language and the Google Golab cloud service were used for the coding and execution of each of the models. The results obtained show us that the random forest algorithm represents an accuracy of 100% for the training data set and 93% for the test data. The model was validated by performing 400 tests, the results of which were acceptable. It is still necessary to strengthen this type of study, introducing new variables that enrich it by developing these computational techniques associated with the experience of the human being.

Keywords: Algorithms · Machine Learning · Anemia · Children · Health

1 Introduction

Anemia is one of the most relevant health problems in the world. According to the World Health Organization, the prevalence of anemia in the world is 24.8% and it is estimated that 1,620 million people have anemia [1]. Peru is no stranger to this type of problem, with more than 40% of children suffering from anemia, which affects their brain function and cognitive processes during their development, even into adulthood [2]. Despite Peru's wealth in variables such as maritime diversity, agricultural, and farm exploitation, it is a latent gap that has begun to be reflected in the educational system

Y. Iano et al. (Eds.): BTSym 2022, SIST 353, pp. 488–497, 2023.
https://doi.org/10.1007/978-3-031-31007-2_46

with significant results in terms of school desertions and low academic performance. The socio-demographic and nutritional factors associated with anemia in children aged 1 to 5 years in Peru, independently, have been characterized by low wealth, absence of a degree or primary education level of the mother, age of the mother less than 19 years, not giving birth in a health facility, not consuming antiparasitic drugs and living at an altitude greater than or equal to 4000 m above sea level [3].

Ignorance about this disease, its causes, and preventive measures, has gained ground and, in this scenario, Piura, the second most populated region of Peru, represented by 1 million 856 thousand inhabitants, faces 36.7% of cases of anemia in children under 5 years of age. In most cases, some of the characteristics that influence the results of this disorder are due to lack of access to services such as drinking water, sanitation, living in rural areas, micronutrient deficiencies, low birth weight, and prematurity [1]. In addition, studies show that there are lower hemoglobin values in children living in municipalities with a higher population rate and fewer medical centers, health posts, polyclinics, and hospitals [4].

In relation to the support provided by the Peruvian Government through the Integral Health System, home visits, and evaluation of growth and development control, it is not significantly reflected, so it is necessary to establish public reforms that contribute to not expressing unreasonably high percentages of anemia or results that underestimate it and can lead to making wrong decisions such as giving unnecessary iron supplements or eliminating them to those who need it, particularly in children who live at higher geographical altitudes [5]. In some cases, micronutrient powder supplementation showed an impact on reducing anemia and increasing hemoglobin levels in children who consumed 60 or more micronutrient packets over a six-month period [6].

Research related to this problem shows that it is possible to develop decision support systems using data mining, under the application of computational techniques that are executed in a database whose composition is related to nutritional factors in children [6]. It is essential to consider that this main way should be exploited to provide alternatives and proposals that help to make immediate decisions within the current parameters for the benefit of citizens in general, particularly children.

It is necessary to mention that currently there are no recommendation systems that involve the diagnosis and its classification immediately according to the type of anemia related to the characteristics of a patient. It is necessary to begin to manage current solutions that contribute to the optimization of this type of task, so it is important to indicate that there are six different methods of automatic learning: artificial neural networks, support vector machines, random forest, logistic regression, naive Bayes, and decision tree, which are classification algorithms. In many cases, the decision tree reflects better behavior in this type of scenario compared to the artificial neural networks [7].

Machine learning has become one of the ideal computational principles, widely used to solve various problems of social reality, all of this is possible, whether there are potential sources of data, reliable and secure in the integrity of your data to get acceptable results. On the other hand, most machine learning problems are inherently optimization and, more not precisely, multi-objective optimization problems [8, 9].

The present study aims to use machine learning algorithms based on artificial intelligence criteria to classify the type of anemia in children under 5 years of age in the geographical area of the Piura region and to know the algorithm with the highest accuracy.

2 Related Works

There are significant advances in machine learning, however, not many of them are linked to medical treatment in children under 5 years of age, in this case, we describe findings that motivate the present study.

For example, the authors [10], in their publication entitled 'analysis and investigation of the fuzzy expert system for the prediction of childhood anemia', indicate that the development of fuzzy expert systems could be used to investigate criteria linked to medical diseases and this could be strengthened with machine learning methods and techniques that reduce the risk of making a diagnostic decision. In their work. [11], they show that in the past, statistical methods were used to predict anemia among children and to identify the associated factors; however, machine learning techniques are a good opportunity to explore the knowledge of the social factors associated with childhood anemia.

In [6], the authors reported that previously, systems were developed on the computer using the advice of medical experts, which were later translated into algorithms. However, this method was very time-consuming. Decision tree techniques and association rule mining reflect significant results for solving problems in the health sector.

As can be seen, many of the studies analyzed in the literature focus on several areas, such as decision support systems, which have been the support to continue with the present study.

3 Classification Algorithms

3.1 Decision Tree

A decision tree makes the best decisions from a probabilistic point of view. Its objective function is to interpret results from observations and logical constructs. This technique is widely explored in data mining to obtain as much hidden information as possible. The field of medicine is one of those where many remains to be explored [12].

3.2 Random Forest

It is a classification algorithm that employs starting computational methods to select a data set. It belongs to the collection of decision trees, as they are linked to a set of start-up samples that are generated from the original data set [13]. A scenario that allows adopting exploratory activities in the health area, in the interest of knowing results that could be potential for this study.

3.3 Naive Bayes

It is known as a probabilistic classifier by which it provides an effective classification of a volume of data when they are entered in real-time compared to another algorithm. It also requires a minimum amount of data for training [14].

3.4 Logistic Regression

An analytical technique that functionally relates a dichotomous variable to a set of independent variables. It has been applied especially in research associated with the socio-health sector, without neglecting the fact that it has a long way to go because it directly calculates the estimate of the probability of the event occurring and this could be linked to the health sector [15].

3.5 Vector Support Machine

It allows exploiting a multiclass classification and is considered a new classification technique. Its role is to find the optimal way to classify among several classes [16]. Among other algorithms, its contribution is linked to medicine in conjunction with medical staff, greater accuracy in the diagnosis of diseases, better treatment suggestions, and drug doses.

4 Methodology

This section discusses the treatment of the data set, its characterization, and the tools used to determine the best algorithm to classify the type of anemia in children under 5 years of age.

4.1 Data Set

Table 1 shows the dispersion of anemia cases corresponding to the year 2019 and represents an index of 45,764 diagnoses. Its characterization starts from a normal condition, mild anemia, moderate anemia, and severe anemia in children under 5 years of age in the Piura region. 50.85% of the population corresponds to the male gender.

4.2 Data Characterization

After knowing the global values of the data set, it was necessary to establish a description of the eight variables that are represented in Table 2, to be clear which are the most predominant and should be considered for the model.

Table 1. Cases diagnosed by type of anemia in the eight provinces of the Piura region.

Province	Mild Anemia	Moderate anemia	Severe anemia	Standard
Ayabaca	1159	448		2858
Huancabamba	1043	421	5	2038
Morropon	668	210	2	4061
Paita	173	58		1325
Piura	2376	914	3	15737
Sechura	469	238	2	2635
Sullana	782	264		5510
Talara	411	169		1785

Table 2. Characterization of the data source variables.

Variables	Description
Province	Administrative territorial demarcation of a region
District	Demarcations that subdivide the territory of a province to distribute and order the exercise of civil and political rights
Gender	Composed of Male and Female gender
Age	Set in months
Weigh	Represented in kilograms
Size	Expressed in centimeters
Hemoglobin	Protein of red blood cells in "g/mol"
Anemia Diagnosis	Classified into normal condition, mild anemia, moderate anemia, and severe anemia

4.3 Algorithm Coding and Validation

Currently, there are several programming languages that allow the development of proposals related to the execution of machine learning algorithms; however, we chose to use the Python programming language, as it is one of the most potential technological means [17] that contributes to solving optimization and multivariate complexity problems, considering that it is free and open source [18].

On the other hand, we resorted to using Google Collaboratory, a cloud-based service that allows writing Python code in a web browser [19], in some cases, also known as Colab. This service is inspired by Jupiter Notebook to do machine learning and deep learning operation. Google Colab is useful for developing proposals framed in computer vision, in addition to running algorithmic models because of its robust architecture and easy domain [20].

In this context, artificial intelligence techniques are strengthened by means and services that have been introduced in various areas of the medical field not to replace the staff, but to act as a complement and support in decision-making [21] and above all to achieve results in acceptable times.

Figure 1 describes the eight phases that must be developed for the coding and execution of the automatic learning algorithms, considering that each proposal has its procedures for the fulfillment of the proposed objective.

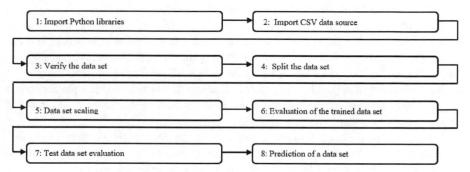

1: Import Python libraries	2: Import CSV data source
3: Verify the data set	4: Split the data set
5: Data set scaling	6: Evaluation of the trained data set
7: Test data set evaluation	8: Prediction of a data set

Fig. 1. Algorithm coding and execution stages.

As is well known, there are libraries that Python offers and are generally used to exploit large data sources, which is why in phase 1, the following libraries were imported: pandas, numpy, matplotlib.pyplot, and seaborn. The libraries were used to prepare the environment for loading the data set. In phases 2 and 3, the data set was imported and corroborated, which consisted of a representation of five input variables and one output variable, as shown in Fig. 2.

```
# vamos a leer ese archivo de datos y asignarlo a una variable
df= pd.read_csv(io.BytesIO(uploaded['data_anemia.csv']))
print(df)

       Sexo EdadMeses  Peso  Talla  Hemoglobina        Dx_Anemia
0         0        51 22.00  106.0         12.3           Normal
1·        0        53 16.00  104.0         13.0           Normal
2         0        48 15.00  101.0         13.0           Normal
3         0        50 17.20   98.0         12.9           Normal
4         1        48 20.00  109.0         13.0           Normal
...     ...       ...   ...    ...          ...              ...
45759     0         6  7.50   68.0         12.3           Normal
45760     0        11  7.40   69.1         10.3      Anemia Leve
45761     0        10  9.10   71.0         11.2           Normal
45762     0        14  9.23   73.5          9.5  Anemia Moderada
45763     1        21 10.00   77.5         11.2           Normal

[45764 rows x 6 columns]
```

Fig. 2. Imported data set

In phase 4, inferences related to data segmentation were performed, so 20% was set aside for testing and 80% for training. The programming style offered by Python allows executing this type of method to exploit desired quantities and in many cases to apply custom functions [22].

Data integrity is fundamental for the development of algorithmic models based on machine learning, considering that this type of attitude allows a better classification of the output variable. In the merit of this, among the actions that were performed in phase 5, there was the scaling of the data under the application of a closed method that is reflected in values confined between the range of 0 and 1.

After having approached the first five phases, the execution of the Decision Tree, Random Forest, Naive Bayes, Logistic Regression, and Vector Support Machine algorithms was carried out to know which is the most optimal algorithm against a monitoring scenario on the health of children under 5 years of age. The evaluation criteria were based on the application of approximation metrics, among them the confusion matrix stands out, where the analysis of the test and training dataset illustrated acceptable results in the predictions made, culminating in phases 6 and 7.

Figure 3 shows the execution procedure of one of the most optimal models, the same one that starts with the entry of five data that correspond to the variables of sex, age in months, weight, height, and hemoglobin. Data that is later scaled with the purpose of standardizing values between a range and that through the 'dtree.predict' instruction it is possible to obtain the prediction. The result was Mild Anemia, a correct response to a real case.

```
dato_nuevo = [[1, 26, 14, 88,10]]
dato_nuevo_scaled= scaler.transform(dato_nuevo)
nueva_prediccion= dtree.predict(dato_nuevo_scaled)
print(nueva_prediccion)

['Anemia Leve']
```

Fig. 3. Test runs on trained models

5　Results and Discussion

Machine learning has shown to have a potential development in the use of classification algorithms oriented to the health sector [8], and in this context, we report the performance of each of the models run according to Table 3.

The random forest algorithm expresses a better accuracy in relation to the other models, without leaving aside that the other models have also represented a significant performance against the training and test data set.

It is important to specify that it is not enough to know the most optimal algorithm for the development of tasks related to health in children under 5 years of age, but rather to corroborate it in real-world events. To make the level of effectiveness visible, a set of data from the year 2020 was chosen that corresponds to 400 cases of anemia on various scales evaluated in the geographical area of the Piura Region.

Table 3. Accuracy of models by training and test data.

Data Set	Decision Tree	Random Forest	Naïve Bayes	Logistic Regression	Vector Support Machine
Training	100%	100%	97%	90%	90
Test	88%	93%	85%	90%	91%
Optimus					

In this context, Fig. 4 illustrates the development of the Random Forest algorithm and the approach it has in predicting the level of anemia in children under 5 years of age.

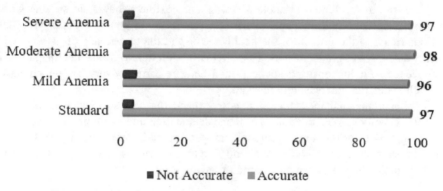

Fig. 4. Results of the 400 tests performed on the random forest model.

The results obtained ratify the importance of relying on the use of these computational means to contribute to strengthening the topics related to the health sector. Machine learning has broken, in part, this paradigm and has allowed many of these problems to be solved without the machines being programmed with algorithms, but in a general way, with experience and a set of data that contributes to their development and allows for acceptable results [23], without forgetting that machine learning is considered a subset of artificial intelligence [24].

Organizations and public institutions of the state must adopt and recognize the importance of data analysis and its benefits. All that, in combination with the benefits available to each of these institutions, can solve problems of permanent need and contribute to reducing the development time of the procedures that are framed in the health sector, particularly when one wants to know the conditions of the child or older adult [25, 26].

6 Conclusions

The diagnosis of anemia in children under 5 years of age is possible using traditional techniques that start with the requirement of a complete blood count, which, when finding a decrease in the value of hemoglobin, hematocrit, or red blood cells, requires a positive case of anemia. Sometimes, it is necessary to study a bone marrow sample to confirm the above. This type of clinical procedure requires experience, costs, and time, which in some cases is limited by the geographical area where the population resides.

This article represents an attempt to reduce the gaps expressed above, however, it is disclosed that the application of machine learning algorithm techniques to classify the type of anemia in children under 5 years of age with easily accessible variables such as sex, age in months, weight, height, and hemoglobin, it is possible thanks to the extensive set of data available from health institutions. The random forest algorithm represents an accuracy of 100% according to the training data set and 93% on the test data, being considered the best model after the decision tree algorithm.

In order to validate the development of the model, the diagnosis was made on a data set corresponding to 400 cases. 96.90% of the results were correct on the classification of the type of anemia in children under 5 years of age. It is important to specify that machine learning techniques denote a strong and flexible behavior in solving world problems, without any limits, and confirm the possibility of generating new proposals that contribute to the growth of the health sector and the experience of patients with correct diagnoses at prudent times. This alternative solution to immediate diagnoses is intended to be a guide for future studies, since there are currently very few, which makes research in this field increasingly relevant.

It is recommended for future studies to expand the data set, which involves the twenty-six regions of Peru, to have a better data source and more global results that can be applied according to the geographical space, in addition to introducing two new variables such as socioeconomic level and skin characteristics that contribute to better accuracy in the diagnosis and processing of the algorithms.

References

1. da Silva, L.L.S., Fawzi, W.W., Cardoso, M.A.: Factors associated with anemia in young children in Brazil. PLoS ONE **13**, e0204504 (2018). https://doi.org/10.1371/journal.pone.0204504
2. Zegarra-Valdivia, J.A., Viza Vásquez, B.M.: Hemoglobin and anemia levels in children: implications for the development of executive functions. Rev. Ecuatoriana Neurol. **29**, 53–61 (2020)
3. Ramírez, J.E.P., et al.: Prevalencia de anemia en la parroquia San Miguel. Cienc. Lat. Rev. Científica Multidiscip. **5**, 8814–8821 (2021)
4. Silva, D.L.F., et al.: Individual and contextual predictors of children's hemoglobin levels from Southern Brazilian municipalities in social vulnerability. Cad. Saude Publica. 36, (2021)
5. Aparco, J.P., Bullón, L., Cusirramos, S.: Impact of micronutrient powder on anemia in children aged 10–35 months in Apurimac, Peru. Rev. Peru. Med. Exp. Salud Publica. **36**, 17–25 (2019)
6. Meena, K., Tayal, D.K., Gupta, V., Fatima, A.: Using classification techniques for statistical analysis of Anemia. Artif. Intell. Med. **94**, 138–152 (2019)
7. Yıldız, T.K., Yurtay, N., Öneç, B.: Classifying anemia types using artificial learning methods. Eng. Sci. Technol. an Int. J. **24**, 50–70 (2021)
8. Rezaei, N., Jabbari, P.: Chapter 5 - Introduction to machine learning. Presented at the (2022)
9. Oliveira, G.G. De, Iano, Y., Vaz, G.C., Chuma, E.L., Arthur, R.: Intelligent Transportation: Application of Deep Learning techniques in the search for a sustainable environment. In: Proceedings of the 2022 5th International Conference on Big Data and Internet of Things, pp. 7–12 (2022)

10. Boadh, R., et al.: Analysis and investigation of fuzzy expert system for predicting the child anaemia. Mater. Today Proc. **56**, 231–236 (2022)
11. Saihood, Q., Sonuç, E.: The Efficiency of Classification Techniques in Predicting Anemia Among Children: A Comparative Study. In: Liatsis, P., Hussain, A., Mostafa, S.A., Al-Jumeily, D. (eds.) TIOTC 2021. CCIS, vol. 1548, pp. 167–181. Springer, Cham (2022). https://doi.org/10.1007/978-3-030-97255-4_12
12. Díaz-Martínez, M.A., Ahumada-Cervantes, M. de los A., Melo-Morín, J.P.: Decision trees as a methodology to determine academic performance in higher education. Rev. Lasallista Investig. **18**, 94–104 (2021)
13. Suthaharan, S.: A cognitive random forest: An intra-and intercognitive computing for big data classification under cune condition. In: Handbook of Statistics, pp. 207–227. Elsevier (2016)
14. Mosquera, R., Castrillón, O.D., Parra, L.: Support vector machines, naïve bayes classifier and genetic algorithms for the prediction of psychosocial risks in teachers of colombian public schools. Inf. tecnológica. **29**, 153–162 (2018)
15. Correa M, J.C., Valencia C, M.: The problem of separation in logistic regression, a solution and an application. Rev. Fac. Nac. Salud Pública. **29**, 281–288 (2011)
16. Russell, R.: Machine Learning: Step-by-Step Guide To Implement Machine Learning Algorithms with Python. (Knxb) (2020)
17. Vidal-Silva, C.L., Sánchez-Ortiz, A., Serrano, J., Rubio, J.M.: Academic experience in rapid development of web information systems with Python and Django. Form. Univ. **14**, 85–94 (2021)
18. Quiroz Burga, L.A.: Espectroscopia de terahercios en el dominio del tiempo para el Análisis de materiales con Python (2022)
19. Kuroki, M.: Using Python and Google Colab to teach undergraduate microeconomic theory. Int. Rev. Econ. Educ. **38**, 100225 (2021)
20. Gujjar, J.P., Kumar, H.R.P., Chiplunkar, N.N.: Image classification and prediction using transfer learning in colab notebook. Glob. Trans. Proc. **2**, 382–385 (2021)
21. Fong-Mata, M.B., Inzunza-González, E., García-Guerrero, E.E., Mejía Medina, D.A., Morales Contreras, O.A., Gómez-Roa, A.: Deep vein thrombosis in lower extremities: review of current diagnostic techniques and their symbiosis with machine learning for timely diagnosis(2020)
22. Hagh, V.F., Sadjadi, M.: rigidPy: Rigidity analysis in Python. Comput. Phys. Commun. **275**, 108306 (2022)
23. Véliz, C.: Machine learning. Introduction to deep learning. The Editorial Fund of the Pontifical Catholic University of Peru, Lima, Peru (2020)
24. Izadkhah, H.: A review of machine learning. En: Deep Learning in Bioinformatics. pp. 9–30. Elsevier (2022). https://doi.org/10.1016/B978-0-12-823822-6.00009-3
25. Demanboro, A.C., Bianchini, D., Iano, Y., de Oliveira, G.G., Vaz, G.C.: 6G Networks: An Innovative Approach, but with Many Challenges and Paradigms, in the Development of Platforms and Services in the Near Future. In: Brazilian Technology Symposium, pp. 172–187. Springer. (2023) https://doi.org/10.1007/978-3-031-04435-9_17
26. Santos, P.A., et al.: Analysis of the Relationship Between Maturity Indicators Using the Multivariate Linear Regression: A Case Study in the Brazilian Cities. In: Xu, Z., Alrabaee, S., Loyola-González, O., Zhang, X., Cahyani, N.D.W., Ab Rahman, N.H. (eds.) CSIA 2022. LNDECT, vol. 125, pp. 203–210. Springer, Cham (2022). https://doi.org/10.1007/978-3-030-97874-7_26

Appreciation of Virtual Teaching Compared to Face-to-Face Teaching During the SARS-Cov-2 Pandemic by Clinical Students in Undergraduate Dentistry

Vilma Mamani-Cori(✉) iD, Yudith Evelin Taco-Hanccoccallo iD,
Tania Carola Padilla-Cáceres iD, Luz Marina Caballero-Apaza iD,
and Sheyla Lenna Cervantes-Alagón iD

Universidad Nacional del Altiplano, Puno, Peru
{vmamani,tpadilla,lmcaballero,slcervantes}@unap.edu.pe,
ytacoh@est.unap.edu.pe

Abstract. The purpose of this research was to evaluate the appreciation of virtual teaching in contrast to face-to-face teaching by undergraduate clinical students of Dentistry. The research was conducted with a quantitative, descriptive, and prospective approach, the population was undergraduate Dentistry clinical students, and the sample was collected according to selection criteria: undergraduate Dentistry clinical students who agreed to participate voluntarily, who have taken and completed at least two clinical subjects virtually during the SARS-Cov-2 pandemic, who have taken and completed at least two clinical subjects face-to-face before the SARS-Cov-2 pandemic. Single variable appreciation of virtual teaching in contrast to face-to-face teaching was measured by a questionnaire validated in 2021. The questionnaire applied had a Cronbach's $\alpha = 0,979$; in addition, it showed that 30,4% of clinical students disagreed/strongly disagreed with virtual teaching in contrast to face-to-face teaching and only 26.1% agreed, although 43.5% were undecided. It is concluded that a considered percentage of Dentistry clinical students disagreed/strongly disagreed with virtual teaching in contrast to face-to-face teaching. However, most clinical students had a confused appreciation.

Keywords: Dentistry · Face-to-face teaching · SARS-Cov-2 · Undergraduate · Virtual teaching

1 Introduction

At the beginning of 2020, the world has been involved in a problem caused by the appearance of the SARS-Cov-2 virus, which was first discovered in the city of Wuhan China in December 2019. Due to its high lethality rate, worldwide mandatory isolation has been decreed as a measure to control the spread of the virus [1]. This measure was also adopted by Peru, a decision that affected the continuity of face-to-face teaching at all educational levels; with a sudden and mandatory migration to virtualization of teaching in basic, technical-productive, and higher education. The SARS-Cov-2 pandemic

Y. Iano et al. (Eds.): BTSym 2022, SIST 353, pp. 498–505, 2023.
https://doi.org/10.1007/978-3-031-31007-2_47

has involved a transformation in university education systems worldwide, revealing the demand for students and professors to have skills and competencies for the development of the teaching-learning process virtually through technological tools [2–6]. However, as virtual education was implemented, certain difficulties became evident, such as restricted access to technologies and limited access due to low Internet coverage [1–5, 7]. Faced with this problem, some universities provide training on virtual academic resources to professors [8, 9] and provide Internet packages (chips with data) to students in order to guarantee the virtual teaching-learning process. All this would not be enough, but it would also require that teachers and students act with discipline and responsibility and develop skills for the proper management of information and communication technology (ICTs) resources [10–15].

The study programs related to the health area have very peculiar pre-professional training, especially the undergraduate clinical subjects in Dentistry. These subjects, due to their practical nature require the development of practical skills and abilities in patients, practices that were affected by virtualization, forcing teachers to redesign the clinical subjects and include technological educational resources and dental simulators for the practices in the teaching sessions [16].

The purpose of university education is to train highly competent individuals for the benefit of society. Therefore, it is important to know how students perceived this teaching modality adopted in clinical subjects during the SARS-Cov-2 pandemic. In this sense, this research was proposed to assess the appreciation of virtual teaching in contrast to face-to-face teaching by clinical students in undergraduate Dentistry.

2 Methodology

This research has a quantitative, descriptive, and prospective approach. The population consisted of undergraduate Dentistry clinical students. The sample was collected according to the selection criteria: undergraduate Dentistry clinical students who agreed to participate voluntarily, who had taken and completed at least two clinical subjects virtually during the SARS-Cov-2 pandemic, and who had taken and completed at least two clinical subjects in a face-to-face manner before the SARS-Cov-2 pandemic.

The single variable studied was the appreciation of virtual teaching in contrast to face-to-face teaching. It was measured using a Likert-type questionnaire that has been validated by [7] with a Cronbach's alpha ($\alpha = 1,00$). This questionnaire has two dimensions; the first dimension contains 19 questions that measure appreciation of planning and teaching, and the second dimension consists of 5 questions that measure appreciation of learning and results. The dimension that measures the perception of planning and teaching is composed of 4 indicators: design of the subject or subject matter (5 questions), characteristics of the classes (5 questions), quality and teaching (6 questions), technological and social skills of the teacher (3 questions). The learning and results dimension is composed of the learning indicator (5 questions). There are a total of 24 questions, with a scale for measuring the answers to each question: $1 =$ Strongly disagree, $2 =$ In disagreement, $3 =$ Undecided, $4 =$ In agreement, and $5 =$ Strongly agree.

The questionnaire was applied virtually by Google Forms form that included: the title and presentation of the research, as well as the informed consent of voluntary acceptance. Also, 2 excluding questions were posed for the fulfillment of the aforementioned selection criteria, and 4 sociodemographic questions were included: age, gender, geographic area where they usually lived in the SARS-Cov-2 pandemic, and usual type of internet connection in the SARS-Cov-2 pandemic. Finally, in order for the student to direct their answers according to reality and without any pressure, the questionnaire was anonymous and the response option was limited to 1. The questionnaire was available for 30 calendar days.

The guidelines of the Declaration of Helsinki were applied throughout the research. The data were coded and subjected to analysis using descriptive statistics in the Excel program.

3 Result

The sample consisted of 46 participants who met the selection criteria (Fig. 1). Of these, 54.3% were male and 82.6% were over 22 years of age. Regarding the area of residence and usual internet connection between 2020–2022, 78.3% indicated having an urban area of residence, while the most frequent internet connection was prepaid mobile data recharge (50%) and home internet (37%) as shown in Table 1.

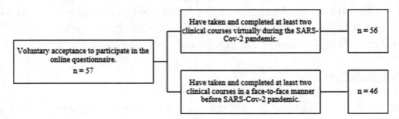

Fig. 1. Selection of the sample.

Table 1. Sociodemographic characteristics of undergraduate Dentistry clinical students.

Characteristics		n	%
Gender	Male	25	54.3
	Female	21	45.7
Age (years)	> 22	38	82.6
	≤ 22	08	17.4
Area of residence 2020 – 2022	Urban area	36	78.3
	Rural area	10	21.7
Connection to Internet 2020 – 2022	Prepaid mobile data recharge	23	50.0
	Home Internet	17	37.0
	Postpaid mobile data	05	10.9
	Mobile data provided by the university	01	2.1
Total		46	100.0

3.1 Questionnaire

The questionnaire used obtained an excellent level of reliability (Cronbach's $\alpha = 0,979$). The appreciation of virtual teaching in contrast to face-to-face teaching by Dentistry clinical students obtained a total average of 3.2 ± 0.9, which indicates that the clinical students showed an undecided appreciation in this regard. However, in reference to whether the students appreciated that in virtual teaching they had a better development of the skills and competencies expected in the clinical subjects in the learning dimension, the students showed a certain disagreement with a mean of 2.9 ± 1.0 (all questions with their respective means and standard deviation are listed below).

- Design of the subject or subject matter

1. Were the organization and sequence of the clinical subjects more adequate and adjusted to the teaching conditions? (3.3 ± 1.1)
2. Was the pace of the clinical subjects more adequate and relevant to the benefit of effective learning? (3.1 ± 1.2)
3. Were the level of academic demands within the clinical subjects more appropriate to the economic and social circumstances, and the teaching model? (3.1 ± 1.1)
4. Were the commitments and tasks assigned within the clinical subjects more in line with the socio-economic needs of the moment? (3.4 ± 1.2)
5. Was the bibliography recommended and sent as part of the clinical assignments more adequate, relevant, and interesting? (3.6 ± 1.0)

- Characteristics of the classes

6. Were the teachers' explanations of the basic contents and other topics during the classes of the clinical subjects more interesting and attractive? (3.3 ± 1.1)
7. Did the lectures of the teachers of the clinical subjects awaken the students' interest in the contents and topics? (3.3 ± 1.2)
8. id the classes of the teachers of the clinical subjects promote more active and dynamic participation of the students? (3.2 ± 1.2)
9. Did the lectures of the teachers of the clinical subjects promote greater motivation in the students? (3.3 ± 1.1)
10. Were the educational resources and media used by the teachers of the clinical subjects during the development of the classes more relevant and attractive? (3.1 ± 1.0)

- Quality and teaching

11. Were the attitude of the teachers of the clinical subjects more adequate and coherent with the needs of the students and did they promote their teaching? (3.3 ± 1.1)
12. Were the teachers of the clinical subjects more empathetic with the students, promoting teaching? (3.5 ± 1.0)

13. Were the contents and information used and selected by the teachers of the clinical subjects more attractive and conducive to teaching? (3.4 ± 1.1)
14. Did the procedures designed by the teachers of the clinical subjects enhance the teaching of the students' skills and competencies? (3.1 ± 1.2)
15. Was the discourse of the teachers of the clinical subjects (expressive language) during their classes clearer, more precise, and more interesting? (3.3 ± 1.1)
16. Was the management of the classes of clinical subjects by the teachers more adequate and satisfactory? (3.2 ± 1.1)

- Technological and social skills of the teacher

17. Did the teachers of the clinical subjects show a greater capacity for the management of the educational resources that mediated the classes? (3.2 ± 1.0)
18. Did the teachers of the clinical subjects show greater skills in the management of communication networks to favor dialogue and formative processes? (3.3 ± 1.1)
19 Did teachers of clinical subjects employ better use of virtual and digital resources to support the training process of students? (3.3 ± 1.1)

- Learning

20. As a result of the teaching of the teachers of the clinical subjects, was student autonomy better promoted? (3.3 ± 1.0)
21. As a result of the teaching of the teachers of the clinical subjects, was the effective learning of the students better promoted? (3.2 ± 1.1)
22. As a result of the teaching of the teachers of the clinical subjects, did the students better develop the skills and competencies expected for the course? (2.9 ± 1.0)
23. As a result of the teaching of the teachers of the clinical subjects, did they better promote the management and control of the students' emotions? (3.1 ± 1.1)
24. As a result of the teaching of the teachers of the clinical subjects, am I more satisfied with the learning achieved? (3.0 ± 1.1)

Overall clinical students evaluated (n = 46), 30,4% disagreed/strongly disagreed with virtual teaching in contrast to face-to-face teaching and only 26.1% agreed, although, 43.5% were undecided. According to the gender of the clinical students, 32.0% (male) and 28.6% (female) disagreed/strongly disagreed. Also, 36.1% of the clinical students who lived in the urban area during the SARS-Cov-2 pandemic, indicated that they disagreed/strongly disagreed (Fig. 2).

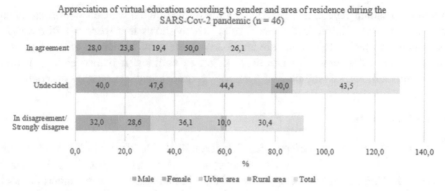

Fig. 2. Appreciation of virtual education according to gender and area of residence during the SARS-Cov-2 pandemic.

4 Discussion

University professors generally show a preference for traditional classroom teaching; however, the SARS-Cov-2 pandemic has forced them to migrate untimely to virtual teaching [17–19]. Some studies such as that of Manchado et al. [20] indicate that most medical teachers did not perceive difficulties in adapting to the use of virtual tools during the SARS-Cov-2 pandemic; however, 92.2% acknowledge the institutional training received for the achievement of such adaptation to active methodologies in the virtual environment. While, a study by Medina et al. [21] indicates that teachers report having had a faster adaptation to the planning and execution of training processes in the virtual environment than their students, in this study the undergraduate students of Dentistry have a hesitant appreciation in terms of satisfaction with the learning constructed (3.0 ± 1.1). Also, as Medina et al. [21] and Ávila et al. [22] indicate that pedagogically teachers and students have shown flexibility in virtual teaching, the results of this study also show that students appreciated empathy on the part of teachers, which favored their teaching (3.5 ± 1.0).

Studies conducted before the pandemic by Castro and Lara [4] on postgraduate students in Dentistry indicate that 97% were satisfied with the inclusion of the virtual approach, they even considered it as a support to the planning of face-to-face activities that saves time. Also, the study conducted by Melgarejo and Rivas [23] on master's degree students in nursing had a moderately favorable perception of the virtual approach (73%). However, the undergraduate dental students in this study, after having experienced virtual teaching during the SARS-Cov-2 pandemic, were mostly undecided about the virtual approach (43.4%), 28.1% agreed, while 20.4% disagreed or strongly disagreed. Similar results were found by Castellano et al. [5] since they indicate that virtual teaching does not favor the fulfillment of collaborative tasks 72%, despite the fact that it is easier to carry out work autonomously. However, Avila et al. [22] indicate that students attribute moderate success to e-learning at the university level during the SARS-Cov-2 pandemic.

Even though the teachers during the virtual teaching by SARS-Cov-2 have had a prompt adaptation of the planning and curricular execution of the clinical courses due to the health emergency, using various technological resources, the appreciation of the students is hesitant. The purely practical nature of the clinical subjects in undergraduate dentistry may have influenced these results, which shows that there is still a need to investigate new technologies that are applicable in the virtual teaching of these subjects that allow the achievement of practical skills and abilities. It is also clear that these permanent challenges in the field of pedagogy require constant updating of teachers.

5 Conclusions

In general, a considerable percentage of undergraduate Dentistry clinical students disagreed/strongly disagreed with virtual teaching in contrast to face-to-face teaching. Regarding planning and teaching, most of the clinical students were uncertain about the questions, and the same happened with respect to learning and results. However, relative to the question about the development of skills and competencies expected in clinical subjects, they showed some disagreement. Also, they recognized the empathy perceived on the part of the teachers, which favored their teaching.

References

1. Maguiña Vargas, C., Gastelo Acosta, R., Tequen Bernilla, A.: El nuevo Coronavirus y la pandemia del Covid-19. Rev. Médica Hered. **31**, 125–131 (2020)
2. Calvo, S.T., Cervi, L., Tusa, F., Parola, A.: Educación en tiempos de pandemia: reflexiones de alumnos y profesores sobre la enseñanza virtual universitaria en España, Italia y Ecuador. Rev. Lat. Comun. Soc. 1–21 (2020)
3. Díaz-Ronceros, E., Marín-Rodriguez, W.J., Meleán-Romero, R.A., Ausejo-Sánchez, J.L.: Enseñanza virtual en tiempos de pandemia: Estudio en universidades públicas del Perú. Rev. Ciencias Soc. **27**, 428–440 (2021)
4. Castro-Rodríguez, Y., Lara-Verástegui, R.: Percepción del blended learning en el proceso enseñanza aprendizaje por estudiantes del posgrado de Odontología. Educ. Médica. **19**, 223–228 (2018)
5. Gil, J.M.C., Lominchar, J.A., Pucha, Á.B.F.: Percepción estudiantil sobre la educación online en tiempos de COVID-19: Universidad de Almería (España). Rev. Sci. **6**, 185–207 (2021)
6. Marrufo, R.M., Espina, W.P.: Estrategias de enseñanza virtual utilizadas con los alumnos de educación superior para un aprendizaje significativo. SUMMA. Rev. Discip. en ciencias económicas y Soc. **3**, 1–28 (2021)
7. Avendaño, W.R., Luna, H.O., Rueda, G.: Educación virtual en tiempos de COVID-19: percepciones de estudiantes universitarios. Form. Univ. **14**, 119–128 (2021)
8. Purizaca-gallo, A.V., Jolay-Benites, J.A.: Retos de la Educación Superior en la educación virtual en tiempos de Covid-19. Pol Con **7**(6), 145–159 (2022)
9. Saporitti, F.O., et al.: La contribución de las TICS a la articulación universidad-escuela ya la articulación interna en la Facultad de Odontología UNLP. In: IV Jornadas Argentinas de Tecnología, Innovación y Creatividad (Universidad CAECE, Mar del Plata, 7 y 8 de noviembre de 2019) (2019)
10. Arab, S., Malekshah, S.N., Mehrizi, E.A., Khanghah, A.E., Naseh, R., Imani, M.M.: Effect of fixed orthodontic treatment on salivary flow, pH and microbial count. J. Dent. (Tehran). 13, 18 (2016)
11. Oyarce-Mariñas, V.A., Chicana, E.M., Solís-Trujillo, B.P., II.: La enseñanza virtual, una necesidad educativa global. Ciencia Latina Revista Científica Multidisciplinar 5, 7200–7218 (2021)

12. Norman-Acevedo, E., Daza-Orozco, C.E.: La construcción de contenidos para la enseñanza virtual: retos coyunturales en el confinamiento. Panorama. **14**, 5–13 (2020)
13. Callasaca-Goyzueta, J., et al.: Percepción sobre educación virtual en estudiantes universitarios de Ciencias de la Salud, en tiempos de COVID-19. Rev. Médica Basadrina. **15**, 3–15 (2021)
14. Negrete, J.C.M., Iano, Y., Negrete, P.D.M., Vaz, G.C., de Oliveira, G.G.: Sentiment analysis in the ecuadorian presidential election. In: Brazilian Technology Symposium. pp. 25–34. Springer (2023). https://doi.org/10.1007/978-3-031-04435-9_3
15. Negrete, J.C.M., Iano, Y., Negrete, P.D.M., Vaz, G.C., de Oliveira, G.G.: Sentiment and Emotions Analysis of Tweets During the Second Round of 2021 Ecuadorian Presidential Election. In: Brazilian Technology Symposium. pp. 257–268. Springer (2023)
16. Demanboro, A.C., Bianchini, D., Iano, Y., de Oliveira, G.G., Vaz, G.C.: 6G Networks: An innovative approach, but with many challenges and paradigms. In: the development of platforms and services in the near future. In: Brazilian Technology Symposium, pp. 172–187. Springer (2023)
17. Arrieta Vergara, K., Díaz Cárdenas, S., Verbel Bohórquez, J., Hawasly Pastrana, N.: Factores asociados a sintomatología clínica de miedo y ansiedad en pacientes atendidos en Odontología. Rev. clínica Med. Fam. **6**, 17–24 (2013)
18. Guo, Y.-R., et al.: The origin, transmission and clinical therapies on coronavirus disease 2019 (COVID-19) outbreak–an update on the status. Mil. Med. Res. **7**, 1–10 (2020)
19. Mera-Mosquera, A.R., Mercado-Bautista, J.D.: Educación a distancia: Un reto para la educación superior en el siglo XXI. Dominio las Ciencias. **5**, 357–376 (2019)
20. Machado de Barros LC, Bitar Portella M, da Silva Brito DM, dos Santos Gorayeb AL, Carvalho de Andrade M.: Percepção dos docentes sobre o ensino remoto em medicina durante a pandemia pela Covid-19. Res. Soc. Dev. **11**(1), e52411125205 (2022)
21. Medina Gual, L., et al.: El impacto de la pandemia en la educación media superior mexicana: un análisis desde lo pedagógico, psicológico y tecnológico. Rev. Iberoam. Educ. 86, 125–169 (2021)
22. Avila, E.C., Abin, G.J., Bien, G.A., Acasamoso, D.M., Arenque, D.D.: Students' perception on online and distance learning and their motivation and learning strategies in using educational technologies during COVID-19 pandemic. In: Journal of Physics: Conference Series, p. 12130. IOP Publishing (2021)
23. Melgarejo Solis, G., Rivas Díaz, L.H.: Percepción de la Calidad del Proceso enseñanza-aprendizaje según las dimensiones planificación, ejecución y evaluación en estudiantes de maestría de enfermería. Rev. Cubana Enferm. **37**, (2021)

Influence of Adaptive Traffic Lights for Delay and Conflict Reduction Applying the SSAM Model at an Urban Intersection

Andy Breña⬥, Junior Vasquez⬥, Manuel Silvera⁽⊠⁾ ⬥, and Fernando Campos⬥

Universidad Peruana de Ciencias Aplicadas, Lima, Peru
{u201621298,u201522788,manuel.silvera,pccifcam}@upc.edu.pe

Abstract. Undoubtedly, conflicts on intersection roads leading to accidents are very often observed. This is due to the ineffectiveness of fixed-cycle traffic lights that do not adapt to changing urban traffic situations. Based on this, the present research evaluated as a case study an intersection located at Habich Avenue with Tupac Amaru Avenue in Lima, Peru. The article also looks for alternative solutions based on the microscopic representation of the intersection using microsimulation programs such as VISSIM and SSAM. In addition, a codification of traffic light cycles was implemented to allow a continuous flow to the Bus Rapid Transit (BRT) system, indirectly reducing the number of conflict points in urban transport. Moreover, the relationship between the reduction of delays and conflicts was identified. The results indicate that a direct relationship between the evaluation parameters was found from the improvement in the traffic light phases. Delays on the east access decreased by 42% and on the west access by 31%. What is more, 12679 rear-end conflicts and 1727 lane change conflicts were reduced.

Keywords: Conflicts · Delay by control · Adaptive traffic lights

1 Introduction

Intersections in the city of Lima operate with fixed-cycle traffic lights. The problem arises because the signals are not aligned with the existing traffic conditions. In this context, when the number of vehicles increases, more congestion is generated, as the traffic lights are programmed for a standard traffic flow [1]. This results in distinct types of accidents generated by queues, collisions, speeding, sudden lane changes, and others [2]. In this situation, it is necessary to use software with the capacity of generating a traffic accident frequency model at intersections, to identify areas of high accident risk [3]. There is a surrogate safety evaluation model considered by the Federal Highway Administration (FHWA) [4]. This becomes important because it can be applied to a microscopic model, making it possible to connect risk factors with consequences [5]. In addition to the existing problems, there is a lack of road safety culture among drivers and pedestrians who despite being educated, do not understand the importance of road safety [6]. It should be noticed that if an intersection shows a decrease in the number of collisions, both accidents and delays should be reduced, increasing access capacity and

© The Author(s), under exclusive license to Springer Nature Switzerland AG 2023
Y. Iano et al. (Eds.): BTSym 2022, SIST 353, pp. 506–516, 2023.
https://doi.org/10.1007/978-3-031-31007-2_48

quality of service [7]. Referring to the mentioned before, the objective of the present research is based on finding a relationship of influence on adaptive traffic lights for the reduction of delays and vehicular conflict points at an urban intersection [8, 9].

2 State of Art

A microsimulation-based study indicates that signal control strategies give priority to buses at signalized intersections [10]. The purpose of this is to reduce vehicle delays at traffic lights and, indirectly, to reduce accidents resulting from conflicts between urban and private transport units. Thus, the authors opt to consider microsimulation as an evaluation method for optimizing urban roads [11]. Also, Lin shows that queue reductions of an average value of 5 min can be obtained after implementing a directed signal control model with control and suppression strategies in a Bus Rapid Transit (BRT) system [12].

Other studies show a relationship between reduced conflicts and delays. Along these lines, Zhang implemented an algorithm that allowed vehicles to be synchronized with traffic light cycles, decreasing conflicts and delays by up to 36 s [13]. In another article, Ren was able to reduce bus travel time by 32.9% of the travel time by allowing buses to pass through continuously by optimizing BRT schedules [14].

3 Methodology

The research methodology was developed as shown in Fig. 1, which describes the processes used to arrive at the results, as well as the development of the current and proposed microsimulation model.

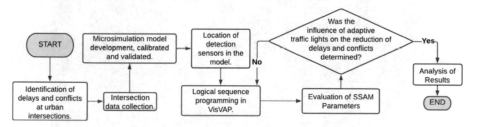

Fig. 1. Flowchart of the research methodology

The methodology was evaluated at the intersection of Habich and Tupac Amaru Avenues, located in the city of Lima, Peru. This is composed of exclusive BRT lanes located on the east and west access, as well as lanes for public and private transportation (see Fig. 2). In this place, we sought to determine the relationship between the reduction of BRT delays and the reduction of conflicts at the intersection.

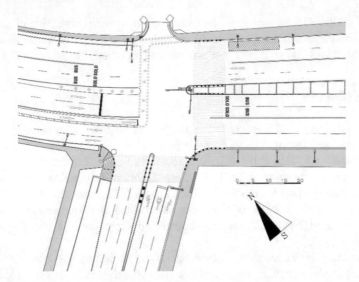

Fig. 2. Drawing of the intersection of Av Habich with Av. Tupac Amaru

3.1   Identifying Delays and Conflicts at the Intersection

It was identified not only the presence of BRT delays due to the red phase at the intersection but also the existence of vehicular conflicts near the crossing area. Figure 3 shows how one vehicle obstructs the movement of another, preventing it from turning in the southern direction, which generates an increase in traffic congestion.

Fig. 3. Vehicle impedes turn and causes congestion

3.2 Data Collection

Field data collection of the intersection was conducted using drone recording. These not only served for the collection of vehicular capacity, but also for the collection of samples that allowed the calibration and validation of the microsimulation model. Figure 4 shows the flowchart of the intersection during rush hour, whose assigned values are visible in Table 1, Table 2, and Table 3.

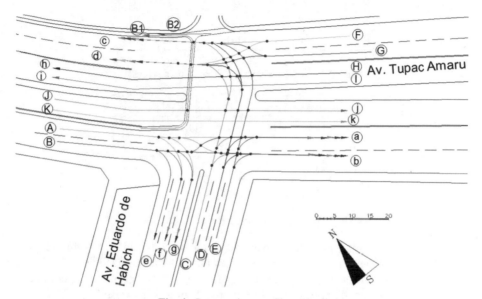

Fig. 4. Intersection conflict points

Field visits were also made to record phases and measure traffic light cycles. The intersection has two phases, and the duration of the traffic light cycle for vehicles and pedestrians is 140 s. For vehicles, the first phase activates the movement of BRT vehicles in the west-east direction and vice versa. For other vehicles, the permitted movement is the same, with the addition of the turn-on from the west to the south access. The second phase provides turning movements for vehicles on the south access to the west and east direction.

Table 1. Vehicle Capacity Table to West Access

Straight ahead		Turn Right		BRT		Bicycle	
A-a	1189	A-e	0	J-j	196	B1	28
A-b	114	A-f	24	K-k	84		
B-a	260	A-g	8				
B-b	642	B-e	15				
		B-f	107				
		B-f	20				

Table 2. Vehicle Capacity Table to South Access

Turn Left		Turn Right	
C-c	50	C-a	150
C-d	29	C-b	12
D-c	6	D-a	110
D-d	19	D-b	170
E-c	3	E-a	20
E-d	0	E-b	49

Table 3. Vehicle Capacity Table to East Access

Straight ahead		BRT		Bicycle	
F-c	583	H-h	98	B2	32
F-d	83	I-i	238		
G-c	216				
G-d	720				

3.3   Development of the Microsimulation Model

The microsimulation model of the current situation was developed. For this purpose, the VISSIM 9.0 program was used, where, based on the tools provided by the software, the lanes, conflict areas, stops, vehicular capacity, and collected phases were added. Also, speed frequency diagrams were incorporated for a better description of vehicle trajectory. Figure 5 shows the model of the current situation.

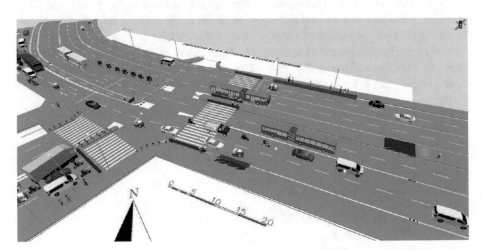

Fig. 5. Microsimulation model of the intersection

3.4 Model Calibration and Validation

Statistical analyses were developed to calibrate and validate the model by collecting the results from thirty samples. The objective is to determine statistically the similarity between one model and the other to give a better representation of the vehicle flow. Initially, the parameters corresponding to the Wiedemann, and Reiter tracking algorithm model shown in Eq. 1 must be determined. From this, the product of the addition between the additive (bx_{add}) and multiplicative (bx_{mult}) part of the safe distance is added to the desired average distance between stopped vehicles (ax).

$$d = ax + (bx_{add} + bx_{mult} * Z)\sqrt{v} \qquad (1)$$

Subsequently, the thirty runs are performed by iterating values for each of the parameters. These results are compared with those obtained in the field through the parametric statistical test (T-Student test), where the t-statistic value should be less than the critical values of one and two tails; also the probability of one tail should be greater than 0.05 (95% confidence) and the non-parametric test (Randomisation test for different means), where it is verified that the mean obtained is within the central zone of the graph (see Fig. 6). From the results, it was determined that the parameters correspond to the value of 0.5 for each one (Eq. 2).

$$d = 0.5 + (0.5 + 0.5 * Z)\sqrt{v} \qquad (2)$$

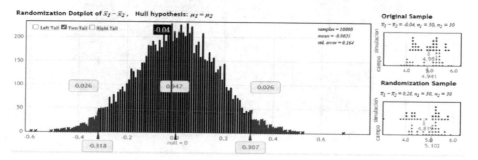

Fig. 6. Non-parametric test for E-W BRT crossing times

3.5 VisVAP Programming

After the placement of detection sensors, new durations for the red and green phases will be obtained, giving a longer time to the latter (86 s for phase 1, and 46 s for phase 2). In addition, the VisVAP code will determine the activation of the phases by sensors located 60 m from the area where the phase change is expected. This code will use the conditionalities set in its programming (see Fig. 7), which determine a minimum green time when the BRT priority phase is activated for the second time.

512　　A. Breña et al.

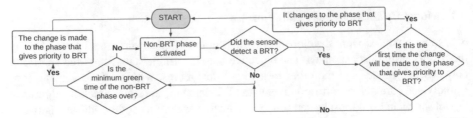

Fig. 7. VisVAP programming flowchart

4　Results

4.1　Assessment of SSAM Parameters

Prior to conducting the thirty runs within the VISSIM software for both the current and proposed situations, the SSAM option was activated within the evaluation tab, which allowed a *.trj extension file to be generated for each iteration, which stores the conflict points developed in the simulation model. Subsequently, in the SSAM software, each of these extensions was imported, which together generated a map of conflict points for the current situation (see Fig. 8) and for the improved situation (see Fig. 9).

Fig. 8. Conflict points mapping of the current situation at the intersection

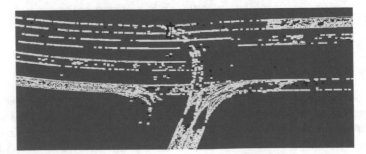

Fig. 9. Conflict points mapping of the proposed situation at the intersection

Three types of conflicts represented by three colors could be observed on the maps The red dots represent a direct collision between vehicles. On the other hand, the blue dots indicate rear-end collisions, in which nearby vehicles hit the peripheral part of the other vehicle. Finally, there are the yellow dots, which correspond to lane change collisions. As can be seen in Figs. 8 and 9, these are the most frequent points within the intersection. Table 4 shows the number of cases corresponding to each type of conflict for both the current and proposed situation. It shows an increase in the number of collisions by ninety-seven cases. However, this number becomes insignificant when compared to the reduction in rear-end and lane change collisions (12679 and 1727 cases respectively). Additionally, the results can be observed in line graphs for each of the runs in the current vs. proposed condition. Figure 10 compares the direct collision conflicts for both scenarios. A reduction in cases is observed in some of the models runs. On the other hand, Fig. 11 shows the rear-end collisions, where a significant improvement of the proposed with respect to the curre

Table 4. Results by type of conflict for Current Situation vs Proposed Situation

Type	Crossing	Rear end	Lane change
Current Situation	169	79051	11269
Proposed Situation	266	66372	9542
Proportion	97	−12679	−1727
Proportion %	57%	−16%	−15%

nt situation can be seen. This case is repeated for the lane change collision type (see Fig. 12).

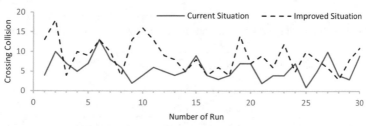

Fig. 10. Comparative graph of conflict type: crossing collision, for the current situation vs. the proposed.

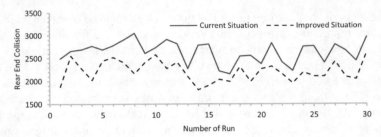

Fig. 11. Comparative graph of conflict type: rear-end collision, for the current situation vs. the proposed.

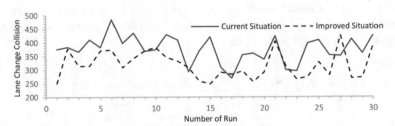

Fig. 12. Comparative graph of conflict type: lane change collision, for the current situation vs. the proposed.

4.2 Delays at the Intersection

Table 5 shows the time taken for delays between traffic lights for both the current and proposed situations. For this, the bus delay time from the traffic light to the intersection crossing was initially measured. Subsequently, the free-flow delay was measured (see Fig. 13). With the difference in these data, the delay generated by the traffic light is calculated. After the application of the adaptive signals, a reduction of 41.7% was achieved for the east access and 30.8% for the west access.

Table 5. Table of delays for each access for the current vs. proposed situation

Direction	Traffic Light Delay Proposed Situation (s)	Traffic Light Delay Current Situation (s)	Difference (%)
E-W	12.61	21.64	41.73
W-E	13.3	19.22	30.80

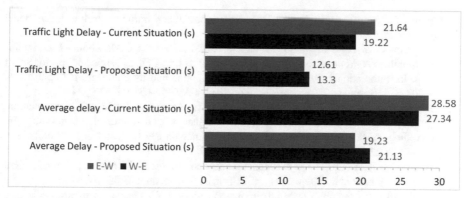

Fig. 13. Delay graph for each access for the current vs. proposed situation

5 Conclusions

A relationship was established between delay reduction and conflicts generated at the intersection, based on the application of adaptive traffic signalization. The VISSIM 9.0 and SSAM programs were used for the evaluation. Based on microsimulation, the vehicle behavior of the intersection was studied, and a logical sequence was generated to give priority to the BRT vehicles that circulate in that area. This resulted in a total reduction of 14309 conflict points. Likewise, a 41.7% reduction in traffic signal control delay was obtained for BRT moving in the E-W direction and 30.8% for BRT moving in the opposite direction. Therefore, it is concluded that there is a relationship between reduced delays and reduced conflict points because of traffic light coding complemented by conflict mapping. In future research, we seek to expand the range of applications of the proposed model to any type of intersection with the same or distinct characteristics as the case study. In view of this, a modification in the traffic light programming will have to be generated to allow greater adaptation to any context.

References

1. Miao, L., Leitner, D.: Adaptive traffic light control with quality-of-service provisioning for connected and automated vehicles at isolated intersections. IEEE Access. **9**, 39897–39909 (2021)
2. Rodríguez Licea, M.A., Vazquez Rodríguez, E.A., Perez Pinal, F.J., Prado Olivares, J.: The rollover risk in delta tricycles: A new rollover index and its robust mitigation by rear differential braking. Math. Probl. Eng. **2018**(1), 1–14 (2018)
3. Abdulhafedh, A.: Crash frequency analysis. J. Transp. Technol. **6**, 169–180 (2016)
4. MUTCD - 2003 Edition (PDF) - FHWA MUTCD, https://mutcd.fhwa.dot.gov/pdfs/2003/pdf-index.htm, Accessed Jan 1 2022
5. Astarita, V., Giofré, V.P.: From traffic conflict simulation to traffic crash simulation: introducing traffic safety indicators based on the explicit simulation of potential driver errors. Simul. Model. Pract. Theory. **94**, 215–236 (2019)
6. Pacheco Cortés, C.M.: Traffic Security and Lifelong Learning in the Digital Era. Diálogos sobre Educ. Temas actuales en Investig. Educ. **8**(15), (2017)

7. Grether, D., Neumann, A., Nagel, K.: Simulation of urban traffic control: a queue model approach. Procedia Comput. Sci. **10**, 808–814 (2012)
8. de Oliveira, G.G., Iano, Y., Vaz, G.C., Negrete, P.D.M., Negrete, J.C.M., Chuma, E.L.: Intelligent Mobility: A Proposal for Modeling Traffic Lights Using Fuzzy Logic and IoT for Smart Cities. In: International Conference on Soft Computing and its Engineering Applications. pp. 302–311. Springer (2022). https://doi.org/10.1007/978-3-031-05767-0_24
9. Oliveira, G.G. De, Iano, Y., Vaz, G.C., Chuma, E.L., Arthur, R.: Intelligent Transportation: Application of Deep Learning techniques in the search for a sustainable environment. In: Proceedings of the 2022 5th International Conference on Big Data and Internet of Things, pp. 7–12 (2022)
10. Zhou, L., Wang, Y., Liu, Y.: Active signal priority control method for bus rapid transit based on vehicle infrastructure integration. Int. J. Transp. Sci. Technol. **6**, 99–109 (2017)
11. Kotagi, P.B., Asaithambi, G.: Microsimulation approach for evaluation of reversible lane operation on urban undivided roads in mixed traffic. Transp. A Transp. Sci. **15**, 1613–1636 (2019)
12. Lin, Y., Yang, X.T., Wang, Q.: New transit signal priority scheme for intersections with nearby bus rapid transit median stations. IET Intell. Transp. Syst. **14**, 1606–1614 (2020)
13. Zhang, P., Gao, S., Wang, P., Li, W.: Cooperative Optimization Model of BRT Speed and Timing Based on Dual Station at an Intersection. Symmetry (Basel). **12**, 1814 (2020)
14. Ren, Y., Zhao, J., Zhou, X.: Optimal design of scheduling for bus rapid transit by combining with passive signal priority control. Int. J. Sustain. Transp. **15**, 407–418 (2021)

Influence of the Earthquake-Generating Mechanism of Peru, Chile, the United States, and Italy on Their Respective Seismic Isolation Standards

Manuel Barra Cier[ID], Brian Cordova Lluen[ID], and Javier Moreno Sánchez[(✉)][ID]

Universidad Peruana de Ciencias Aplicadas, Lima, Peru
{u201414196,u201619416,pccijmor}@upc.edu.pe

Abstract. The use of base isolation is being implemented worldwide in seismically active countries. However, not all of these countries have an isolation
standard and use a foreign one for the design of the isolation device. Using a
foreign code does not reflect the seismic behavior of the country that needs to opt
for that system, since a seismic standard is developed in response to the seismic
generating mechanism of each country. Therefore, the objective of this research
is to show the differences that exist in the seismic generating mechanism of Peru,
Chile, the United States, and Italy and how these are related in their respective
seismic isolation standards. The comparative analysis was carried out based on the
historical seismicity of each country mentioned, the focal mechanism, and their
frequency contents. It was determined that the seismic generating mechanism of
Peru and Chile are similar, since they are countries that have the same seismogenic
source. In addition, it is shown that the seismicity of the United States and Italy
differs from the Peruvian and Chilean seismicity with respect to seismic duration
and frequency content. It is also shown that the displacements of the United States
earthquakes are larger than those of the other analyzed countries.

Keywords: Regulations · Seismic isolation · Frequency content · Seismicity ·
Focal mechanism · Displacements

1 Introduction

Seismic-resistant codes establish that structures in the event of severe earthquakes should
present structural failures without collapsing; however, buildings such as hospitals should
not present any failure, since this would interrupt their operation [1]. In view of this,
there are anti-seismic techniques that guarantee that a structure does not present structural
damage or damage to its contents after a severe earthquake. One of these techniques is
seismic isolation, which "isolates" the base of a structure from the ground where it will
be located.

This technique is applied in the most seismically active countries; however, not all of
them have a seismic isolation standard, which means that if one of these countries requires

© The Author(s), under exclusive license to Springer Nature Switzerland AG 2023
Y. Iano et al. (Eds.): BTSym 2022, SIST 353, pp. 517–529, 2023.
https://doi.org/10.1007/978-3-031-31007-2_49

the implementation of base isolation, a foreign standard must be used for the design of the system [2]. This may result in the structure not being adequately subjected to seismic forces, since the use of a foreign standard does not consider the earthquake-generating mechanism of the country [3].

One of the isolated structures that were designed with foreign standards is the UPC library at the Villa Campus, in which the design of the isolation level was carried out with the U.S. standard ASCE 7–16 and the Chilean code NCH 2745 [4]. Likewise, Piscal and López [2] determine that the ASCE 7–16 standard, which is used in the design of seismic isolation in Colombia, does not reflect the seismicity of that country.

Using a foreign standard or adapting it is a common practice, however using regulations from other countries does not optimally contemplate the level of seismic demand, since a foreign standard does not reflect the seismic behavior of the country that requires the use of this standard. This is an important factor, since the seismic behavior in one country may vary from another.

The purpose of this scientific article is to carry out a comparative analysis of the mechanism that generates earthquakes in countries with seismic isolation standards such as Peru, Chile, the United States, and Italy, in order to show the differences that exist in the seismicity of these countries and how these are reflected in their respective standards.

2   Method

In order to determine the seismic differences between Peru, Chile, the United States, and Italy, it is shown how to determine their seismic generating mechanism, the zone of greatest seismic activity, its type of fault, and its frequency content.

2.1   Seismicity of Peru

The earthquake-generating mechanism in Peru is produced by the convergence between the South American and Nazca plates through a process called subduction [5]. Figure 1

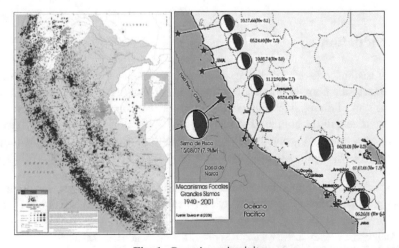

Fig. 1. Peruvian seismicity

shows the historical seismicity, where the highest magnitude earthquakes are located on the Pacific coast, with shallow depth and reverse fault type.

2.2 Seismicity of Chile

The greatest seismic activity in Chile is due to the interaction between the Nazca plate and the continental plate located on the Pacific coast due to the subduction process [6]. In Fig. 2, it is shown that its earthquakes occur at a shallow depth of less than 60 km and that its fault type is of inverse shape.

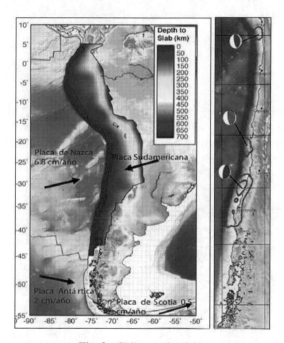

Fig. 2. Chilean seismicity

2.3 Seismicity of the United States

The seismic genesis in the United States is mainly due to the interaction between the North American plate and the Pacific plate (San Andreas fault), which is located in the western part of the country [7]. This is visualized in Fig. 3, where it is shown that the West Coast has high seismic activity. The U.S. focal mechanism presents different types of faults, the most common ones being the rupture faults and the normal faults.

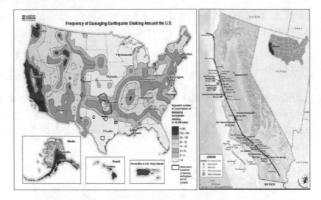

Fig. 3. U.S. seismicity

2.4 Seismicity of Italy

In Italy, earthquakes are caused by the interaction between the African and Eurasian plates [8]. Figure 4 shows its seismic hazard map. Zone 1, which is located in the south-central part, is the one with the highest seismic risk. In addition, it is shown that the historical seismicity of Italy presents normal-type faults according to their focal mechanism.

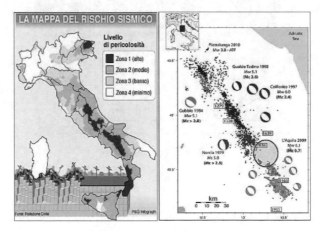

Fig. 4. Italian seismicity

2.5 Seismicity Summary

Table 1 shows a summary of the seismicity of the selected countries, where Peru and Chile present similar genesis of their earthquakes. A common point is the hypocenter, which is superficial (h < 60 km).

Table 1. Seismicity summary

	Peru	**Chile**	**United States**	**Italy**
Proc. Seismic	Subduction	Subduction	Frictional	Subduction
Hypocenter	Superficial	Superficial	Superficial	Superficial
Epicenter	Coast	Coast	Continent	Continent
Fault	Reverse	Reverse	Transforming	Normal

2.6 Seismic Records

Table 2 shows the seismic records used, where the choice was based on Table 1 and a rigid soil (Vs > 500 m/s). From these records, we show the differences in the form of frequency content and the duration of the seismic recordings.

Table 2. Selected seismic records

Peru	**Chile**	**United States**	**Italy**
Lima 74	Tocopilla	Imperial Valley	Friuli
Lima 66	Maule	Loma Prieta	Norcia
Ático 01	Tarapacá	San Fernando	Irpinia
Pisco 07	Iquique	Northbridge	Umbria

Figure 5 shows the record of the 1974 Lima earthquake with a duration of 100 s and a PGA of 0.196 g.

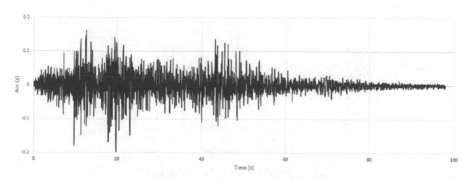

Fig. 5. Seismic record of Lima, Peru 1974

Figure 6 shows the 2010 Concepción, Chile earthquake, which had an approximate duration of 100 s with a PGA of 0.477 g.

The 1994 Northbridge, USA seismic record, which had a duration of 25 s and a PGA of 0.426 g, is shown in Fig. 7.

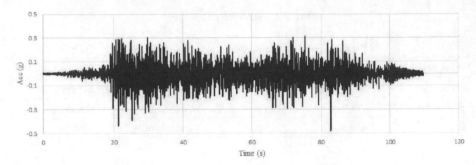

Fig. 6. Seismic record of Concepcion, Chile 2010

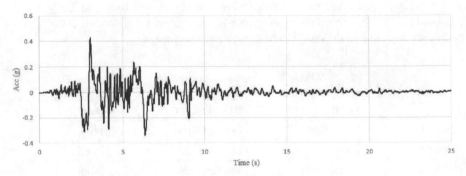

Fig. 7. Seismic record of Northbridge, United States 1994

Figure 8 shows the 1976 seismic record from Friuli, Italy, with a duration of 35 s and a PGA of 0.375 g.

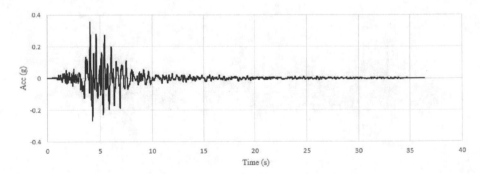

Fig. 8. Seismic record of Friuli, Italy 1976

3   Validation and Results

The comparative analysis was carried out based on earthquake records (Table 2) from Peru, Chile, the United States, and Italy. Based on this, a frequency analysis was carried

out and the displacement and pseudo-acceleration spectra were determined in order to
determine the seismic differences between the four selected countries.

3.1 Frequency Content Analysis

Figure 9 shows that the 1974 Lima earthquake has high frequencies (3.308 Hz) and
its predominant ground period is 0.302 s, which means that this earthquake must have
affected three-level structures due to the resonance effect.

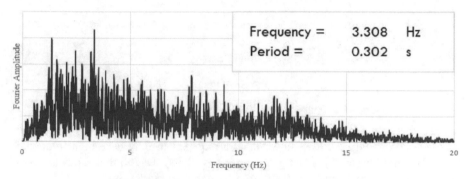

Fig. 9. Frequency analysis of the Lima earthquake

Figure 10 shows that earthquakes in Chile have high frequencies (2.832 Hz) and
a predominant ground period of 0.353 s, which affects more 4-level structures due to
resonance.

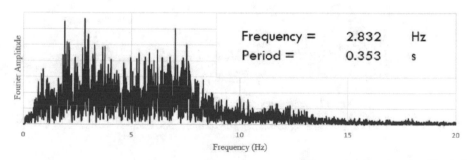

Fig. 10. Frequency analysis of Concepcion earthquake

According to Fig. 11, it is evident that the Northbridge earthquake has low frequencies (0.83 Hz) and high ground periods, whose value is 1.205 s. This is why this type of earthquake affects more 12-level structures due to the resonance effect.

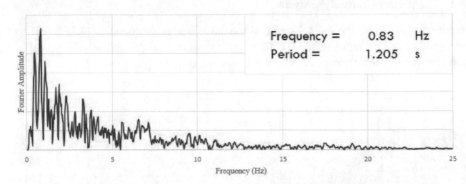

Fig. 11. Frequency analysis of the Northbridge earthquake

According to Fig. 12, it is shown that earthquakes in Italy have high frequencies (2.002 Hz) and low predominant ground periods (0.5 s). Due to the resonance effect, this earthquake affects small structures to a greater extent (5 levels).

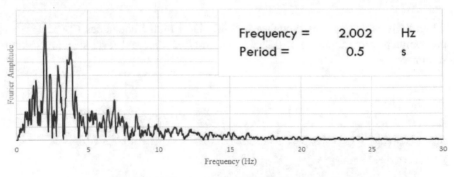

Fig. 12. Frequency analysis of Friuli earthquake

3.2 Displacement Spectrum

The displacement spectra were made with the records of the earthquakes in Table 2 and compared with the spectra of their respective seismic standards.

According to Fig. 13, the earthquakes produced in Peru present a zone of constant displacements, which is determined by the "TL" factor of the E.030-E.031 standard. This is a relevant factor, since it indicates that Peruvian seismicity generates low displacements of about 30 cm.

The displacement spectrum of Chilean standard NCH 2745 establishes that the period indicating the zone of constant displacements for rigid soil is 2.51 s according to the

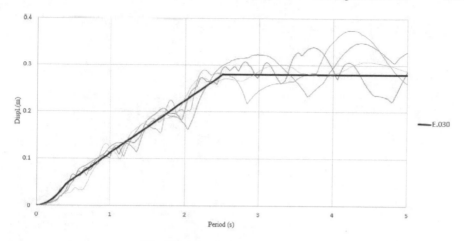

Fig. 13. Peru displacement spectrum

factor "Td". It is also shown in Fig. 14 that the earthquakes of the Chilean country present low displacements with an approximate value of 25 cm.

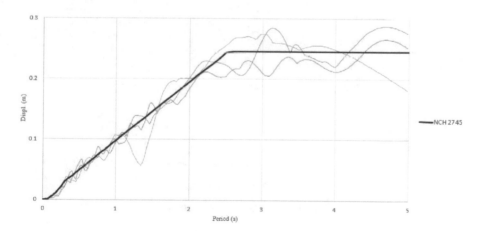

Fig. 14. Chile displacement spectrum

According to Fig. 15, earthquakes in the United States present displacements with values of up to 60 cm, which is why the ASCE 7–16 standard establishes that the "TL" factor presents high values of up to 16 s according to the seismic map of said standard.

The displacements produced by earthquakes in Italy are low with values of 20 cm for rigid soil according to Fig. 16, in which we can see how the spectra envelop the spectrum of its norm.

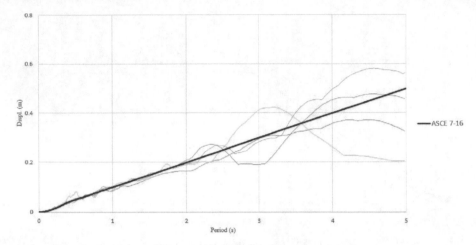

Fig. 15. US displacement spectrum

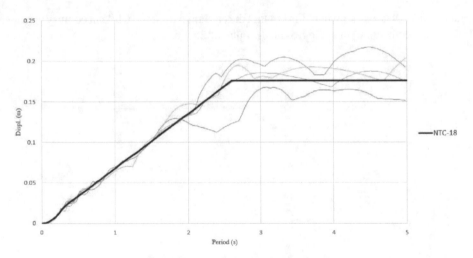

Fig. 16. Italy displacement spectrum

3.3 Pseudo-accelerations Spectrum

The response spectrum was performed according to the earthquakes in Table 2 and compared with the spectrum given by the respective seismic standard. The results obtained are presented below.

Figure 17 shows that the spectrum of the Peruvian standard optimally encompasses the spectra of its historical earthquakes, in which the maximum acceleration occurs in short periods.

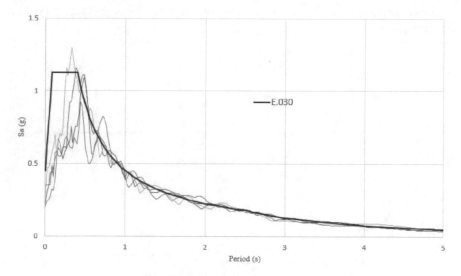

Fig. 17. Response spectrum of Peru

According to Fig. 18, it is determined that the seismic records of Chile have the same shape as the response spectrum of its standard. In addition, it reaches peak acceleration values up to 1.5 g.

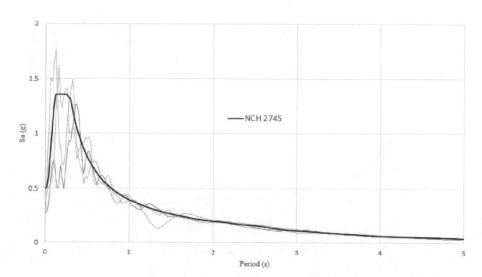

Fig. 18. Response spectrum of Chile

According to the data of the seismic records of the United States, it is evident in Fig. 19 that two of the earthquakes present maximum accelerations of 2.0 g. However, the spectrum of its standard indicates that the maximum acceleration is 1.0 g due to the fact that the most common earthquakes present similar values. The spectrum of the North American standard does not include accelerations of 2.0 g, since these are considered rare earthquakes.

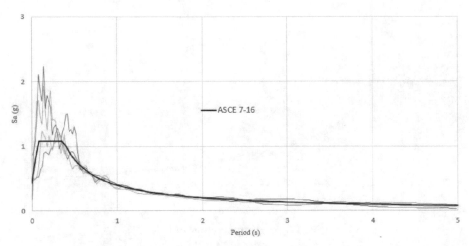

Fig. 19. Response spectrum of USA

Figure 20 shows the maximum accelerations of the historical earthquakes in Italy and their norm spectra, which have values of about 0.85 g.

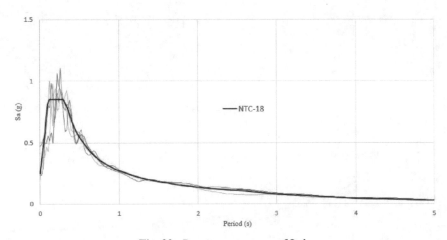

Fig. 20. Response spectrum of Italy

4 Conclusions

According to the seismic records presented, there are differences in their shapes, duration, and peak acceleration value (PGA). These differences are due to the seismic process and its focal mechanism. According to Figs. 5 and 6, it can be deduced that the typical earthquakes occurring in Peru and Chile are similar, since they have the same seismic process (subduction), the same type of reverse fault, and the plates (Nazca and South American) that originate their earthquakes are the same.

The frequency analysis shows that the earthquakes in Peru and Chile have high frequencies with low predominant periods of 0.35 s on average, which means that these earthquakes affect structures of 3–4 levels. On the other hand, in the United States, they present low frequencies with predominant ground periods of 1.2 s, which affects structures of 12 levels.

According to the displacement spectrum, the earthquakes in Peru and Chile have values of 30 cm at most, since these countries have the same earthquake-generating mechanism. However, the United States presents high displacements with values of up to 60 cm. Therefore, if a country with similar seismicity to Peru and Chile uses the U.S. standard for the seismic analysis of a structure, it will be designed to support large displacements, causing the structure to be over-dimensioned.

According to the analysis carried out, it is concluded that there are differences in the seismic generating mechanism of Peru and Chile with those of the United States and Italy. Therefore, if a country needs to use the U.S. standard in the application of seismic isolation, it should be careful with chapter 11 of this standard, since it is in this chapter where the U.S. seismicity is reflected and therefore where the greatest differences in seismic parameters with respect to the other standards are presented.

References

1. COINESED Homepage, http://www.coinesed.com.pe/munoz.pdf, Accessed 15 July 2022
2. Piscal, C., Lopez, F.: Consequences of the possible application to Colombia of the most current standards on seismic isolation of buildings. Int. J. Struct. Eng. **21**(4), 415–436 (2016)
3. de Oliveira, G.G., Iano, Y., Vaz, G.C., Chuma, E.L., Negrete, P.D.M., Negrete, J.C.M.: Prop Walls: A Contextualization of the Theme in a Case Study in the City of Campinas (Brazil). In: Brazilian Technology Symposium. pp. 128–139. Springer (2022). https://doi.org/10.1007/978-3-031-08545-1_12
4. Peru Construye Magazine Homepage, https://issuu.com/cvillenat/docs/pc20/70, Accessed 27 July 2022
5. GOB Homepage, https://www.gob.pe/institucion/igp/noticias/127394-cinturon-de-fuego-del-pacifico-activacion-en-cadena, Accessed 13 Aug 2022
6. Radkia, S., Rahnavard, R., Tuwair, H., Gandomkar, F., Napolitano, R.: Investigating the effects of seismic isolators on steel asymmetric structures considering soil-structure interaction. Structures **27**, 1029–1040 (2020)
7. Gino, D., Anerdi, C., Castaldo, P., Ferrara, M., Bertagnoli, G., Giordano, L.: Seismic upgrading of existing reinforced concrete buildings using friction pendulum devices: A probabilistic Evaluation. Appl. Sci. **10**, 1–17 (2020)
8. Sunagar, P., Bhashyam, A., Shashikant, M., Sreekeshava, K., Chaurasiya, A.: Effect of different base isolation techniques in multistoried rc regular and irregular building. Lect. Notes Civil Eng. **99**, 391–403 (2021)

Antibacterial Effect of the Ethanolic Extract of *Curcuma longa L.* and *Erythroxylum coca var. Coca* at Different Concentrations Against *Streptococcus mutans*: Comparative Study in Vitro

Sheyla Lenna Cervantes-Alagón⬤, Tania Carola Padilla-Cáceres⬤,
Luz Marina Caballero-Apaza$^{(\boxtimes)}$ ⬤, Ruth Flores-Atencio⬤,
and Ruvaly Mamani-Zambrano⬤

Universidad Nacional del Altiplano, Puno, Peru
{slcervantes,tpadilla,lmcaballero}@unap.edu.pe, {rufloresa,
rmamaniz}@est.unap.edu.pe

Abstract. The purpose of this research was to compare the in vitro antibacterial effect of ethanolic extract of *Curcuma Longa L.* and *Erythroxylum coca var. Coca* in concentrations of 100%, 75%, 50%, 25%, and 12.5% against *Streptococcus mutans*. Materials and Methods: Experimental, comparative, and longitudinal study. The ethanolic extract was obtained by the maceration method with an alcoholic solution, the McFarland method was used for the dilution of the bacterial load to 0.5% turbidity, and the Kirby Bauer method to see the sensitivity of the inhibition halo. Data analysis was performed with a statistical t-test, ANOVA analysis of variance test was used to determine significance, and Tukey's comparison tests were made for comparison. Results: The best antibacterial effect is recorded by the extract of *Curcuma longa L.* at 100% at 48 h with 16.05 mm of inhibition halo with an effectiveness of 93.04%, the lowest average is by the extract of *Erythroxylum coca var. Coca* (coca) at a concentration of 12.5% in 24 h with 10.73 mm of inhibition halo with an effectiveness of 62.20%. Conclusions: Both extracts have an inhibitory effect against *Streptococcus mutans*. Curcuma extract (*Curcuma longa L.*) has a greater antibacterial effect than coca leaf extract *(Erythroxylum coca var. Coca) against Streptococcus mutans* at 24 and 48 h. In addition, the antibacterial effect of the active ingredients of both extracts increases after 48 h.

Keywords: Antibacterial effect · *Cúrcuma Longa L.* · *Erythroxylum coca var. Coca* · *Streptococcus mutans* · Ethanolic extract

1 Introduction

Dental caries is an ecological imbalance of the biofilm, caused by the excessive consumption of sugar, it is irreversible, and the process is dynamic, chronic, infectious

Y. Iano et al. (Eds.): BTSym 2022, SIST 353, pp. 530–539, 2023.
https://doi.org/10.1007/978-3-031-31007-2_50

post-eruptive, transmissible, and multifactorial, characterized by a gradual dissolution and destruction of mineralized tissues of the teeth. Most prevalent in humans and is one of the main public health problems in the world [1]. *Streptococcus mutans* [2] has been considered the main cause of dental caries because it participates in the process of biofilm formation [3].

Currently, the study of the active principles of natural origin produced in our country by inhabitants of the region and frequently consumed by the Andean population is of great interest. These frequently used medicinal plants such as Turmeric (palillo) and Coca Leaf. The first is an herbaceous plant of the *Zingiberaceae* family native from Southeast Asia, commonly known in traditional Indian medicine, with beneficial properties for health: antibacterial, antioxidant, anti-inflammatory and strengthens the immune system [4]. Likewise, coca belongs to the *Erythroxylaceae* family, native to the Amazonian Andes, typical of South America, with proven medicinal properties [5].

One of the most prevalent diseases of the oral cavity is dental caries, one of the biggest public health problems in Peru. There are currently various protocols for the prevention and treatment of caries; furthermore, the use of antibacterial agents such as chlorhexidine [6]. In this way, the challenge of finding new alternatives of easily accessible plant-based antibacterial agents arises from ability and low cost. Thus, traditional or complementary medicine works to find other alternative solutions for oral diseases, especially the most prevalent ones. Since ancient times, these medicinal plants have been considered the origin of therapy for the prevention or maintenance of health. Since then, this initial empirical knowledge has developed to the present day and plants have become important sources of industrialized biologically active natural products [7].

In Peru, specifically in Puno, several recent studies have been carried out on different medicinal plants, looking at the properties of their components such as antibacterial, antihemorrhagic, analgesic, anti-inflammatory, and other properties [8]. Among them is turmeric (*Curcuma Longa L.*) [9]. The medicinal plant is used as a colorant in food preparation and has had high nutritional value since ancient times, with antibacterial, anti-inflammatory, antioxidant, parasitical, and hypoglycemic properties [10]. The coca leaf (*Erythroxylum coca var. Coca*) is a plant native to Peru and the Andes of Bolivia, it has been cultivated since ancient times known for its medicinal effects, with antibacterial, anesthetic, analgesic, antidiarrheal properties and natural coagulant [11].

The clinical importance of this research relies on using complementary medicine to treat infections of bacterial origin with plant products [12] frequently consumed in our high Andean population and that help fight against microorganisms during an established infection such as *Streptococcus mutans* bacteria [13] that constitutes the first cause of dental caries [14].

2 Methodology

It is an experimental, comparative, prospective, and longitudinal study. The type sampling is non-probabilistic, for convenience, according to inclusion and exclusion criteria. The ethanolic extract was obtained by the maceration method [15] with an alcoholic solution, the McFarland method [16] was used for the dilution of the bacterial load to 0.5% turbidity, and the Kirby Bauer method [17] to see the sensitivity of the inhibition halo.

The observation was carried out in 60 Petri dishes for each extract, with 12 repetitions for the concentrations 100%, 75%, 50%, 25%, and 12.5%, thus having 5 experienced units plus a positive control group (chlorhexidine at 0.12%) all these worked against the strain of *Streptococcus mutans*, isolated in the Laboratory of Microbiology and Parasitology of the Faculty of Human Medicine of the UNA-Puno.

The technique used is direct observation, and measurement of the inhibitory halo (mm) of the concentration at 100%, 75%, 50%, 25%, and 12.5% of *Curcuma longa L.* and *Erythroxylum coca var. Coca* and as a control group chlorhexidine 0.12% against *Streptococcus mutans* at 24 and 48 h; the data obtained were recorded in a data collection form.

Data analysis was performed with the statistical t-test, the ANOVA analysis of variance test was used to determine the significance, and Tukey's comparison tests were made for the comparison of extracts.

2.1 Procedure

Acquisition of *Curcuma Longa L.* and *Erythroxylum coca var. Coca*, the rhizomes of turmeric were obtained from the District of San Juan del Oro, Province of Sandia, Department of Puno, quantity 2 kg. It was transferred in kraft paper bags for selection and sampling. The most preserved coca leaves were selected and the deteriorated leaves were removed, which were washed with running water and then with distilled water in the Laboratory of Microbiology and Parasitology of the Faculty of Human Medicine of the "Universidad Nacional del Altiplano".

Preparation and elaboration of the ethanolic extracts of *Curcuma longa L.* and *Erythroxylum coca var. Coca* at concentrations of 100%, 75%, 50%, 25%, and, by means of the conventional method of maceration with alcoholic solution, which consists in putting the solid matrix in contact with the solvent in a certain time [15].

Preparation of the culture medium for the isolation of the *Streptococcus mutans* strains in the laboratory, the sample was collected and the microorganisms were distributed in the blood agar so that they could develop and multiply, the process was repeated in 5 Petri dishes. Once the seeding was done, it was incubated at 37 °C for 24 h in anaerobiosis and 24 h in aerobiosis, after this time the results were observed and the plates that presented the greatest development of colonies were selected, using the McFarland method, to determine the turbidity in the preparation of suspensions of microorganisms with a standard 0.5 is applied in the preparation of bacterial inocula in sensitivity tests [16].

Preparation of the nutritive broth for the replication with Trypticase soy for the development and storage of the strains, and then putting them in the incubator at 37 °C for 24 h so that the collected microorganisms develop in greater quantity and can multiply.

Observation and collection of the strain in order for the appropriate bacteria to develop and reach the required purity. After sowing in the selective culture medium, it was again observed microscopically and a 99% pure *Streptococcus mutans* strain was determined.

Preparation of the selective blood agar culture medium, a distribution was made in 5 cold sterilized Petri dishes, when the culture medium solidified, the sample that was in the culture broth was seeded in the Petri dishes. After sowing, the Petri dishes were stored in an anaerobic box and the strain was incubated for 24 h at 37 °C in anaerobiosis and 24 h in aerobiosis.

Preparation of Mueller Hinton blood agar at 5%, once the culture medium was autoclaved, it was allowed to cool and distributed in 40 Petri dishes. It was allowed to gel at room temperature. After the gelation process, the strains were seeded by the exhaustion method, making lines in the form of striations in three different directions to achieve a uniform distribution. Ten minutes after sowing, the disc diffusion method was applied and wells were made in agar with a punch and sterile filter paper discs No. 4 were distributed in each of the wells, making a total of 6 discs for each Petri dish, distributed with a minimum distance of 20 mm between each well (the diameter of the discs according to INS standards was 6 mm), the Petri dishes were grouped in groups of 5 (12.5%, 25%, 50%, 75%, and 100%). Filter paper discs were distributed in each of the dishes and the extract of both plants was inoculated in the center of them with 0.12% chlorhexidine as a positive control.

After the process of inoculation of the extracts, the control dishes were placed in an anaerobic box and stored in the incubator at a temperature of 37 °C for 24 h, proceeding later to data collection. After 24 h and after collecting the data, it was left to incubate for a further 24 h to carry out the 48-h control.

After the process of inoculation of the extracts, the control dishes were placed in an anaerobic box and stored in the incubator at a temperature of 37 °C for 24 h, proceeding later to data collection. After 24 h and after collecting the data, it was left to incubate for a further 24 h to carry out the 48-h control. Then the Kirby Bauer method is applied to observe the sensitivity of the inhibition halo, it serves to verify the susceptibility to antibiotics between bacterial species based on different cell structures and their resistance [17].

2.2 Ethical Considerations and Legal Aspects

The procedures performed were executed according to the guidelines of the General Health Law of Peru (Law No. 26842) and Biosafety Law No. 27104 of the Peruvian health regulations.

2.3 Statistical Analysis

Data analysis was performed with the t-statistical test, the ANOVA analysis of variance test was used to determine the significance, and Tukey's comparison tests were made to differentiate the inhibition halos.

3 Result

The averages of the treatments that have an inhibitory effect are observed, where it can be seen that the highest average is registered in the treatment with *Curcuma longa L.* extract. (turmeric) at a concentration of 100% at 24 h with 15.66 mm of inhibition halo with an effectiveness of 90.78%, the lowest average is the treatment with *Erythroxylum coca var. Coca.* (coca) at a concentration of 12.5% at 24 h with 10.73 mm of inhibition

Table 1. Comparison of the in vitro antibacterial effect of the ethanolic extract of *Curcuma longa L.* (turmeric) and *Erythroxylum coca var. Coca* (coca leaf) against the bacterium Streptococcus mutans

Time	Application	Concentration	Average	Effectiveness	Difference of growth
24 h	Turmeric	100%	15.66 mm	90.78%	0.22%
		75%	14.98 mm	86.84%	3.16%
		50%	13.95 mm	80.86%	19.14%
		25%	13.02 mm	75.47%	14.53%
		12.5%	12 mm	69.56%	30.44%
		Control+	17.15 mm	99.42%	0.58%
	Coca	100%	14.7 mm	85.21%	4.79%
		75%	13.46 mm	77.97%	22.03%
		50%	12.65 mm	73.33%	26.67%
		25%	11.65 mm	67.53%	32.43%
		12.5%	10.73 mm	62.20%	37.82%
		Control+	17.15 mm	99.42%	0.58%

halo with an effectiveness of 62.20%. There is a difference between the largest and smallest of 4.93 mm (Table 1).

The averages of the treatments that have an inhibitory effect, where it can be seen that the highest average is recorded in the treatment with *Curcuma longa L.* extract (turmeric) at a concentration of 100% at 48 h with 16.05 mm of inhibition halo with effectiveness of 93.04%, the lowest average is the treatment with extract *Erythroxylum coca var. Coca* (coca) at a concentration of 12.5% at 48 h with 11.15 mm of inhibition halo with an effectiveness of 64.74%. There is a difference between the largest and smallest of 4.90 mm (Table 2).

The results of the data analysis with the statistical test of analysis of variance (ANOVA), with a Coefficient of variability of 1.17, being the $F_{calculated}$ greater than the $F_{tabular}$, which indicates that there is a significant difference between the concentrations of the extracts of *Curcuma longa L.* and *Erythroxylum coca var. Coca* (coca) against the *Streptococcus mutans* bacteria at 48 h, for which the data was submitted to the Tukey comparison test and an alpha probability of 0.05, where it is observed in the bar diagram, LSD = 0.14673, df = 230, and experimental error of 0.0257, resulting in the greatest inhibition halo occurring at the 100% concentration of the *Curcuma longa L.* (turmeric) extract. (Fig. 1.)

Averages of the treatments that have an inhibitory effect at 24 and 48 h, where it can be seen that the highest average is registered in the treatment with ethanolic extract of *Curcuma longa L.* (turmeric) at a concentration of 100% with 15.66 mm of inhibition halo with an effectiveness of 90.78%, the lowest average is the treatment with *Erythroxylum*

Table 2. Comparison of the inhibition zone at 48 h in the treatment with ethanolic extract of *Curcuma longa L.* (turmeric) and *Erythroxylum coca var. Coca* against *Streptococcus mutans.*

Time	Application	Concentration	Average	Effectiveness	Difference of growth
48 h	Turmeric	100%	16.05 mm	93.04%	6.96%
		75%	15.33 mm	88.86%	11.14%
		50%	14.35 mm	83.18%	16.82%
		25%	13.39 mm	77.62%	12.38%
		12.5%	12.41 mm	71.94%	18.06%
		Control+	17.25 mm	100%	0.0%
	Coca	100%	15.21 mm	88.17%	11.83%
		75%	13.95 mm	80.82%	19.18%
		50%	13.16 mm	76.34%	23.66%
		25%	12.14 mm	70.51%	29.49%
		12.5%	11.15 mm	64.74%	35.26%
		Control+	17.25 mm	100%	0.0%

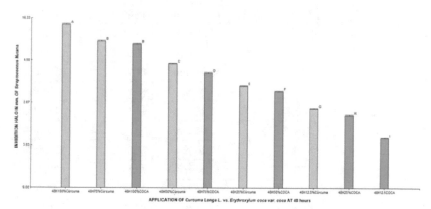

Fig. 1. Contrast of means with Tukey's statistical test of the in vitro inhibitory effect of the ethanolic extract of *Curcuma longa L.* (turmeric) and *Erythroxylum coca var. Coca* (coca) in its concentrations of 100%, 75%, 50%, 25% and 12.5% against the bacteria *Streptococcus mutans* at 48 h.

coca var. Coca (coca) at a concentration of 12.5% at 24 h with 10.73 mm of inhibition halo with an effectiveness of 62.20% (Table 3.)

Submitted the data of the application of the extract of *Curcuma longa L.* (turmeric), *Erythroxylum coca var. Coca* (coca), and the positive control (chlorhexidine 0.12%) to the statistical test of analysis of variance (ANOVA), gives a result that the coefficient of

Table 3. Sensitivity of the *Streptococcus mutans* bacteria to the extract of *Curcuma longa L.* (turmeric) and *Erythroxylum coca var. Coca* (coca) and the positive control at 24 and 48 h.

Time	Application	Concentration	Average	Effectiveness	Difference of growth
24 h	Turmeric	100%	15.66 mm	90.78%	0.22%
		75%	14.98 mm	86.84%	3.16%
		50%	13.95 mm	80.86%	19.14%
		25%	13.02 mm	75.47%	14.53%
		12.5%	12 mm	69.56%	30.44%
		Control +	17.15 mm	99.42%	0.58%
	Coca	100%	14.7 mm	85.21%	4.79%
		75%	13.46 mm	77.97%	22.03%
		50%	12.65 mm	73.33%	26.67%
		25%	11.65 mm	67.53%	32.43%
		12.5%	10.73 mm	62.20%	37.82%
		Control +	17.15 mm	99.42%	0.58%
48 h	Turmeric	100%	16.05 mm	93.04%	6.96%
		75%	15.33 mm	88.86%	11.14%
		50%	14.35 mm	83.18%	16.82%
		25%	13.39 mm	77.62%	12.38%
		12.5%	12.41 mm	71.94%	18.06%
		Control +	17.25 mm	100%	0.0%
	Coca	100%	15.21 mm	88.17%	11.83%
		75%	13.95 mm	80.82%	19.18%
		50%	13.16 mm	76.34%	23.66%
		25%	12.14 mm	70.51%	29.49%
		12.5%	11.15 mm	64.74%	35.26%
		Control+	17.25 mm	100%	0.0%

variability (CV) is 1.88, and the calculated F is greater than the $F_{tabular}$, which shows that there is a significant difference between the applications in different concentrations (Fig. 2.)

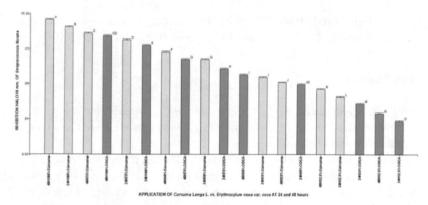

APPLICATION OF *Curcuma Longa L. vs. Erythroxylum coca var. coca* AT 24 and 48 hours

Fig. 2. Contrast of means with Tukey's statistical test of the in vitro inhibitory effect of the ethanolic extract of *Curcuma longa L.* (turmeric) and *Erythroxylum coca var. Coca* (coca) in its concentrations of 100%, 75%, 50%, 25% and 12.5% against the bacteria *Streptococcus mutans* at 24 and 48 h.

4 Discussion

The present experimental investigation compared the in vitro antibacterial effect of the ethanolic extracts of *Curcuma longa L.* and *Erythroxylum coca var. Coca* against strains of *Streptococcus mutans*, using concentrations of 100%, 75%, 50%, 25%, and 12.5% compared to the positive control (0.12% Chlorhexidine), were measured and evaluated in 24 and 48 h. Based on the findings found, we accept the research hypothesis that establishes that the *Curcuma Longa L.* extract has a greater antibacterial effect than *Erythroxylum coca var. Coca* against strains of *Streptococcus mutans*.

Jalaluddin M. et al. [18] evaluated the antimicrobial activity of *Curcuma longa L.* (CLE) extract on periodontal pathogens where 70 patients were sampled and grouped into three groups: Group I: patients treated alone with scaling and root planing (SRP), Group II: patients treated with SRP followed by subgingival irrigation with 1% CLE solution and Group III: patients treated with SRP followed by subgingival irrigation with 0% chlorhexidine (CHX) solution, 2%, it was concluded that *Curcuma longa L.* has great antimicrobial efficacy against bacteria. Our study agrees that the greatest antibacterial activity is that of turmeric, also using chlorhexidine for the positive control, but at 0.12%. Likewise, Tazeena H. Islam et al. [19] investigated the antimicrobial activity of medicinal plants on *Streptococcus mutans*, they showed that *Curcuma longa L.* at 100% has a greater inhibitory effect and less than 3.125%, compared to our research the greatest antibacterial effect was found in the concentration 100% and the lowest 12.5%, which show that the higher the concentration, the greater the antibacterial effect.

Loyola et al. [5] studied the ethanolic extract of *Erythroxylum coca Lam*, another type of species similar to ours, which is *coca var.* Showed that a concentration of 75% for its ethanolic extract also achieved greater antimicrobial activity against *S. mutans* but it is not as effective as chlorhexidine, in our study we showed that the ethanolic extract of coca has lower antibacterial properties than turmeric in the same concentrations. However, we must mention that coca will continue to be widely used, such as the hydroalcoholic extract of the coca leaf, presenting favorable antibacterial activity against other microorganisms such as black-pigmented bacilli at concentrations of 100% and 12.5% [20].

5   Conclusions

Treatment with ethanolic extract of *Curcuma longa L.* (turmeric) has a greater antibacterial effect compared to the coca leaf extract *Erythroxylum coca var. Coca* (coca) in all its concentrations and observation times.

Traditional Andean medicine through the use of plant products is used to treat bacterial infections. In addition, these active ingredients will be used as inputs in the industrialization of toothpaste, mouthwashes, and other dental products for the benefit of people's oral health.

References

1. Calle-Sánchez, M.J., et al.: Teorías de caries dental y su evolución a través del tiempo: revisión de literatura. Rev. Científica Odontológica. **6**, 98–105 (2018)
2. Gol, S., Pena, R.N., Rothschild, M.F., Tor, M., Estany, J.: A polymorphism in the fatty acid desaturase-2 gene is associated with the arachidonic acid metabolism in pigs. Sci. Rep. **8**, 1–9 (2018)
3. Santos, V.R.d., et al.: Effect of S. mutans combinations with bifidobacteria/lactobacilli on biofilm and enamel demineralization. Braz. Oral Res. **35** (2021)
4. Ariza, L.L.G., Quim, J.H.O.M., Acevedo, J.I.S., Sanabria, L.P.: Biological activity of three curcuminoids from Curcuma longa L. (turmeric) grown in Quindío, Colombia. Rev. Cuba. Plantas Med. **22**, 1–14 (2017)
5. Loyola, D., et al: Ethanol extract of Schinus molle L.(molle) and Erythroxylum coca Lam (coca): Antibacterial properties at different concentrations against Streptococcus mutans: An in vitro study. J. Int. Soc. Prev. Community Dent. **10**, 579 (2020)
6. Cui, T., Luo, W., Xu, L., Yang, B., Zhao, W., Cang, H.: Progress of antimicrobial discovery against the major cariogenic pathogen Streptococcus mutans. Curr. Issues Mol. Biol. **32**, 601–644 (2019)
7. Nawirska-Olszańska, A., Zaczyńska, E., Czarny, A., Kolniak-Ostek, J.: chemical characteristics of ethanol and water extracts of black alder (Alnus glutinosa L.) Acorns and their antibacterial, anti-fungal and antitumor properties. Molecules **27**, 2804 (2022)
8. Hirakawa, K., Mori, M.: Phenothiazine dyes induce NADH photooxidation through electron transfer: kinetics and the effect of copper ions. ACS Omega **6**, 8630–8636 (2021)
9. Di Salle, A., et al.: Antimicrobial and antibiofilm activity of curcumin-loaded electrospun nanofibers for the prevention of the biofilm-associated infections. Molecules **26**, 4866 (2021)
10. Figueira, L.W., de Oliveira, J.R., Camargo, S.E.A., de Oliveira, L.D.: Curcuma longa L.(turmeric), Rosmarinus officinalis L.(rosemary), and Thymus vulgaris L.(thyme) extracts aid murine macrophages (RAW 264.7) to fight Streptococcus mutans during in vitro infection. Arch. Microbiol. **202**, 2269–2277 (2020)
11. Espeza, L.P.L., Figueroa, N.L., Siancas, E.E.A.: Efecto de la masticación de la hoja de coca sobre las estructuras de la cavidad oral. Odontol. sanmarquina. **22**, 283–286 (2019)
12. Reis, A.C.M., Regis, W.F.M., Rodrigues, L.K.A.: Scientific evidence in antimicrobial photodynamic therapy: An alternative approach for reducing cariogenic bacteria. Photodiagnosis Photodyn. Ther. **26**, 179–189 (2019)

13. Ferrillo, M., et al.: Periodontal disease and vitamin D deficiency in pregnant women: Which correlation with preterm and low-weight birth? J. Clin. Med. **10**, 4578 (2021)
14. Zhang, Y., et al.: Effects of Rhein-8-O-β-D-glucopyranoside on the Biofilm Formation of Streptococcus mutans. Curr. Microbiol. **78**, 323–328 (2021)
15. Duarte-Trujillo, A.S., Jiménez-Forero, J.A., Pineda-Insuasti, J., González-Trujillo, C.A., Garcia-Juarez, M.: Extraction of bioactive substances from Pleurotus ostreatus (Pleurotaceae) by dynamic maceration. Acta Biol. Colomb. **25**, 61–74 (2020)
16. Cona, T.: Condiciones para un buen estudio de susceptibilidad mediante test de difusión en agar. Rev. Chil. infectología. **19**, 77–81 (2002)
17. Schiller, H., Young, C., Schulze, S., Tripepi, M., Pohlschroder, M.: A twist to the kirby-bauer disk diffusion susceptibility test: an accessible laboratory experiment comparing haloferax volcanii and escherichia coli antibiotic susceptibility to highlight the unique cell biology of archaea. J. Microbiol. Biol. Educ. **23**, e00234-e321 (2022)
18. Izui, S., et al.: Antibacterial activity of curcumin against periodontopathic bacteria. J. Periodontol. **87**, 83–90 (2016)
19. Islam, T.H., Bin Azad, A.H., Akter, S., Datta, S.: Antimicrobial activity of medicinal plants on Streptococcus mutans, a causing agent of dental caries. IJERT **1**, 1–6 (2012)
20. Deza, C.P.E.: Estudio in vitro de la actividad antibacteriana del extracto de Erythroxylum coca sobre bacilos negro pigmentantes (2016)

Management of Family Businesses in the Face of the New Scenario of Global Digital Transformation

André Luiz Caulit Silva[1] (ID), Wandercleiton Cardoso[2]([envelope]) (ID),
Thiago Augusto Pires Machado[3] (ID), Danyelle Santos Ribeiro[4] (ID), Marcelo Margon[5] (ID),
and Ernandes Scopel[3] (ID)

[1] Fucape Business School, Vitoria, Brazil
[2] Università degli Studi di Genova, Genoa, Italy
wandercleiton.cardoso@dicca.unige.it
[3] Instituto Federal do Espirito Santo, Vitoria, Brazil
[4] Università degli Studi Niccolò Cusano, Rome, Italy
[5] Pontifícia Universidade Católica, Belo Horizonte, Brazil

Abstract. The main objective of this article is to evaluate the reputation of family businesses in the new scenario of digital transformation and how digital transformation can benefit family businesses. Family businesses have a stigma of being unprofessional and allowing intra-family relationships and conflicts to enter the business environment. They are also often seen as centralized, with power concentrated in the hands of the founder or his successors and with inadequate control mechanisms. The fact is that this stereotype of the family business greatly obscures the strengths of these organizations. As privately held companies with agile decision-making processes and a long-term vision guided by consolidated family values, such organizations have demonstrated better performance than many publicly traded companies. In this sense, family businesses are fundamental to economic and social life. On the one hand, they behave strategically differently from other companies and sometimes make decisions that go beyond the interests of profitability or the expediency of the business. On the other hand, they stand out for their strong commitment to their workers and employees, both in human and social terms, and for the high socioeconomic value they create. Both by virtue of their weight and economic representation, and by virtue of their commitment and contributions to the area and communities in which they operate, as well as their pursuit of stability and consistency over time, they are an essential factor in the socioeconomic development of any region around the world.

Keywords: Family businesses · Digital Transformation · Management

1 Introduction

The greatest challenge that these companies have had to face in recent years has been the great change that corporatization has brought, that is, giving up the place that belongs to each individual and reconciling the complex dynamics that occur in the triple situation

Y. Iano et al. (Eds.): BTSym 2022, SIST 353, pp. 540–547, 2023.
https://doi.org/10.1007/978-3-031-31007-2_51

of the family, shareholders, and workers. All this with the aim of surviving the third generation, when most family businesses are in crisis or even disappear [1].

The experience of many of these companies in recent years shows that on the way from a family business it is necessary to identify and have the best human resources to make the company sustainable [1, 2].

Despite its particular challenges, the family business does not escape the major changes that society faces, from the opening to foreign capital to the need to internationalize and respond to new social trends [2, 3].

We are living in a new reality, a moment of upheaval in many economic and social sectors caused by digital transformation. While it is normal for a family business to ask itself to what extent technology is affecting the development of the business, it is generally not so common for them to analyze how this digital disruption can have a great impact on the reputation of the family from the perspective of the communication of the business and the good name of the owners [2–4].

The digital transformation has turned the forms of relationships 180°; hyper-connectivity has given way to an excess of transparency, and those who are not able to adapt to a transparent context risk losing their own reputation [3–6].

Reputational risks related to the level of legal security in many countries, corruption scandals, or the simple fact of being cited in an investigation, even as a witness, can create a stigma that goes beyond personal reputation and can affect the entire family business [7].

On the other hand, from a business perspective, reputation management will or should become a primary axis of work to ensure the sustainability of the business in the face of any unexpected situation. Reputation management can lead stakeholders to grant a second chance in case of a reputation problem. For this, it is important to do things well and inform them clearly so that these stakeholders are willing to continue to grant this second chance [6, 8].

In a third area, it is obvious that society has more opportunities to influence every day. Thanks to social networks and all the platforms available on the Internet, citizens can increasingly voice their concerns and fears. If we are not attentive, if we do not listen to them and decode them by actively listening to conversations, issues, and domains, we will not be able to adapt to their needs [7, 9].

Listening is a tool for collaboration and a generator of participation, and it will always help promote transparency. Therefore, when we talk about how we should adapt to the needs of citizens, we are not just referring to a product or service, but to the very existence of the company, as even the social license to act may be affected [8, 10].

2 Materials and Methods

A bibliographic review of national and international authors dealing with family businesses was conducted. In order to solve the problem and in accordance with the authors' guidelines, we propose a mixed qualitative and quantitative research approach as well as an evaluation of the aspects and characteristics of family businesses in the face of the digital transformation scenario.

3   Characteristics of Family Businesses

In general, we refer to family businesses as those in which the ownership or actual control of the businesses is in the hands of the same family. Organizations of this type have a great weight in the global market. Most family businesses transfer their specific values to their organizations, thus shaping the corporate culture [10].

For this reason, the reputation of the company is a key element that distinguishes this type of company from others in the sector. This so characteristic social and unique value between family and company, as well as the way the business is managed, is a factor that in many cases hinders professionalization and affects the competitiveness and survival of some of these businesses [7].

Family businesses have peculiarities and greater complexity compared to other businesses. In a world where the brand is one of the most important assets of the company, we know that family businesses are closely linked to the image and reputation of the company. Therefore, managing communication is important to maintain and protect the reputation of family businesses. Many family businesses do not have a professional or protocol communication strategy, so we know that communication remains one of the gaps in many family businesses [6].

In today's world, where markets and society increasingly demand transparency, building trust and reputation in the collective imagination and the business world has become one of the strategic assets of companies [2].

Communication professionals are aware that products and companies are evaluated not so much by what they were or are, but by what they mean to customers, consumers, and the environment in which they operate [1].

One of the keys to the success of family businesses lies precisely in how they are perceived as companies that integrate a community, convey a human and close image, and contribute to the economic and social development of the territory [6].

Today's brands want to be perceived as positive experiences that offer not only functional but also emotional benefits. To this end, they use intelligent communication and strategies to align expectations with shared beliefs and significantly improve reputation [6].

Family businesses have traditionally been recognized for their credibility, integrity, and contributions, but they need to better manage their image and, most importantly, their transparency. Reputation is an intangible asset, a recognition granted by stakeholders or communities. Therefore, it is necessary to implement a bold and intelligent strategy to protect it [2].

4   Communication Methods in Family Businesses

A good communication strategy is essential for any business, but it is especially important for family businesses. The management of ownership, administration, and family becomes a strategic challenge for the good development of the company and a central element of the family's commitment to the company. For this, it is essential to pass on the fundamental values and contribute to their continuity with a correct succession and transfer of ownership to the next generations [9].

The first and most specific reason is the importance of correct communication management within the family or between the different branches of the family. This is particularly important to unify the different perceptions between the generations living in a company [8].

In many companies, there are currently founding members who manage companies that belong to a generation that has little or nothing in terms of form or content to do with the new generations that will be the natural successors of these companies in the coming years [3].

In a decade, countless family businesses will face the challenge of creating leadership positions for a new generation that sees the world from a different perspective than their predecessors, which is a major obstacle to business transformation [4].

Therefore, it is not only important to plan for the future legacy of the family, but also to build a culture of family communication that accompanies the process of building values and shared corporate culture in a coherent and comprehensive way [8].

Apart from who is in charge, family members must have a sense of belonging to the company so that not only the future but also the present is attractive to the next generation [4].

Another fundamental aspect of maintaining the reputation of family businesses, and especially the reputation of the owning families, is to be skillful in the communication between the family and the business. In other words, they must properly communicate the purpose of the business and the values that the family instills in its employees and staff in order to create the culture of the business [8].

As the management of the company passes to successive generations, it becomes an increasingly complex task to balance the legacy of the previous generations, that of the founders, with the purpose of the company and the goals of the new generations. All this is challenging when there are different interpretations or conflict zones between owners or managers belonging to the family [3, 4].

In some family businesses, there is often a difference or lack of cohesion that is transmitted and projected within the business, especially to employees and collaborators, which raises doubts about the direction and efficiency of management and, above all, undermines the credibility of all family members [8, 9].

Therefore, it is necessary to have an internal communication strategy that communicates the values and goals of the company in a clear and understandable way, even if there are different opinions about them within the families. To this end, it is necessary to professionalize communication in order to avoid transferring informality from family relationships to the internal processes of the companies [8].

One of the main challenges is to develop an employee engagement policy aimed at increasing employees' pride of belonging and commitment to the company and the family project, which, in short, is the best guarantee for increasing productivity, efficiency, and continuity of companies [9].

Employee engagement is the emotional attachment of employees to the company they work for and the goals it defines. An engaged employee is someone who shares the vision of the company to which they belong, who sees meaning in their work, and who is willing to voluntarily do more than is required of them [3].

Actions aimed at strengthening this positive internal feeling have an impact not only on the inside of companies by improving the work environment, but also on numerous external variables such as consumer satisfaction, turnover, and, above all, the company's ability to attract new employees. Talent that guarantees the competitiveness of family businesses [2].

When we talk about engagement, we are not just talking about employee satisfaction. We are talking about engagement, about the connection they have with the purpose and values of the company and ultimately with the values of the owner families and their contribution to the reputation of the family and the company. Currently, no one disputes the key role of employees as a credible source when it comes to reporting what is happening in the company, especially when it comes to conflicts or differences between the owner's families [1].

Therefore, a smart internal communication strategy that focuses on employee engagement is essential for any business, and even more so for family businesses. In other words, active listening and the creation of an open and participative work environment are basic requirements for communication and reputation policies in companies of this type [9].

Many family businesses are traditionally reserved in their communication policies. The characteristics of these companies with closed and unlisted structures meant that they did not have strategies or policies for corporate communication or did not believe in their necessity. Traditionally, their communication was based on a modest presence on the Internet, starting from a website with basic corporate information and contact with the media that focused heavily on the products and services they offered and tried to manage their presence in the media to guarantee and control what was published about them [8].

In the age of the attention economy, communication has become a crucial resource, both for business performance and competitiveness and for building a solid reputation [4].

Communication is an indispensable tool to adapt to new times and operate in markets increasingly characterized by conversation. This is characterized by the communicative empowerment of different stakeholders or interest groups, the speed of transmissions in an online and live world, and the increasing access to data [1].

Therefore, the main challenge for family businesses is to communicate the updated and modernized founding purpose, transform it and convey it to the territories and communities in which the business operates, and create a narrative that engages the various stakeholders. This is because today's communication skills require the ability to be transparent, which can only be learned and developed with a proactive mindset. Some family businesses are increasingly putting the citizen, the consumer, and the customer at the center of their decisions [3].

However, they are still unable to understand that new information and communication technologies give consumers and the public control over the conversation about us, twenty-four hours a day, through different channels and formats. Social media is the place where brands and businesses can be created or destroyed. Therefore, you must not only listen, but also participate in the conversation by creating the appropriate narrative based on a clear and shared goal with the company [2].

It is advisable to leave outdated thoughts behind, such as the claim "if we are not on social media, no one will talk about us." In a hyper-connected world, there will always be someone who will comment positively or negatively. This forces us to be ready to communicate, listen, and interact to protect the reputation of the company and the good name of the family [1].

There are some examples of good practices where family businesses have invested in creative and intelligent communication strategies to create a solid and strong image that benefits both the reputation of the business and the family [4].

In any case, business communication should be the axis and the integrating element of the family business report. The change in the business paradigm and communication environment poses new and complex challenges for companies to meet the traditional and new exceptions in the business model and the value proposition of companies to their stakeholders [6–9].

Therefore, the main challenge is to identify these new trends and expectations at an early stage in order to respond to them immediately. Reputation and digital transformation will be the variables that will move the world in the coming years, and the family business must be able to manage this efficiently [1].

The growing interconnectedness of citizens and increasing democratization have led to an era that cannot be understood without the value of transparency, certainly not in companies that seek to defend their family values on a daily basis by projecting them into the future [4].

Economic and social change is occurring at a rapid pace. New trends replace, change or condition other models. Consumers see less and less differentiation in products and services, but increasingly value differentiation in the reputation and good name of companies [6].

5 Final Considerations

10 years ago, the world's population could not imagine using a portable, rectangular object that fits in a pocket, is lightweight, and at the same time has more functions than a computer, i.e., a smartphone, and no one could imagine that we would have access to information through means other than television or the newspaper.

These are just some of the big changes that the digital age has brought to the world. Within 5 to 10 years, all companies had to adapt to a new reality, and even more, they had to understand their audience and the market with a new view [9].

According to the literature, 9 out of 10 companies (87%) have struggled with digital transformation. On the one hand, digital transformation caused anxiety in some companies, but on the other hand, it offered the opportunity to gain more flexibility, make companies more dynamic and achieve faster results with a good digital strategy. Moreover, the companies that could anticipate consumers' needs were clearly ahead [1–4].

Focusing on small and medium-sized family businesses, we notice a key advantage in this whole innovation process: less bureaucracy and more agility in the face of change. Thanks to the digital age, small and medium-sized companies now have the same access to information as large companies that used to be ahead of the market. It is much easier for them to implement, learn about, miss, and try again new ideas and processes. You should know how to leverage your strengths and take new actions to improve the digital presence of the corporate brand [3–5].

Look for reputable software and social networks to increase family business productivity. For constant growth in the digital environment, it is important for the family business to be present in as many social networks as it can manage [2, 3].

When a customer perceives that someone is always ready to help them, and even more so in a channel they are comfortable and familiar with, such as Facebook or Instagram, the chances of providing 5-star service increase. Bigger and greater. However, it is necessary to invest in sponsored posts, videos, and content that always speak to the family business and customers [3–6].

As we have seen, adapting and responding to the demands of a market with increasingly frequent changes is not an easy task. However, it is also not overly complicated [2].

Whether large or small companies, the marketing budget must provide for a minimum investment in social media. Social media has already established itself as a highly effective means of maximizing profits, improving relationships with the public, and enhancing brand image [1, 2, 4–6].

One study showed that companies that invested in social media grew by 18% in one year, while those that invested less in the networks experienced an average 6% decline in revenue over the same period [2].

Social media has become an excellent relationship channel between a company and its customers and is a way to generate brand awareness and engagement. And the greater the number of active and engaged users, the greater the reach and effectiveness of strategies targeted at this channel [4].

The benefits of social media are not only monetary, but also include brand image and relationship with the public, which are essential for the success of any business.

In addition, it is possible to use machine learning techniques in social networks, such as famous robots. This type of technique is present in all commercial and industrial sectors. For example, there are several publications explaining how to manufacture steel using artificial intelligence [11–13]. In this context, it is crucial for family businesses to experience this new digital transformation.

Social media allows brands to show a more human side and explore other ways of approaching users. Whether with a striking image or a video that tells a story, this format allows for reaching the right audience with the right type of media at the right time, improving conversion rates and content efficiency [5].

The open and participatory nature of social media allows the public to interact in a simple and immediate way. Moreover, it is possible to measure the success and commercial appeal of campaigns and brands based on user engagement and constant interaction. In this way, companies can gain valuable information that can be used to improve products, services, and the company as a whole [4].

There are many ways to improve your brand image through social media. One of the most common is to present a more human side, ready to help and listen to the public wherever needed. In this way, users' trust and respect grow, which has a positive effect on sales [3–5].

Another way is to provide useful and relevant content to users, thus increasing the authority and awareness of the brand. The possibilities are many.

References

1. Randerson, K.: Conceptualizing family business social responsibility. Technol. Forecast. Soc. Change. **174**, 121225 (2022)
2. Calabrò, A., Frank, H., Minichilli, A., Suess-Reyes, J.: Business families in times of crises: The backbone of family firm resilience and continuity. J. Fam. Bus. Strateg. **12**, 100442 (2021)
3. Gregori, P., Holzmann, P.: Digital sustainable entrepreneurship: A business model perspective on embedding digital technologies for social and environmental value creation. J. Clean. Prod. **272**, 122817 (2020)
4. Strange, R., Chen, L., Fleury, M.T.L.: Digital transformation and international strategies. J. Int. Manag. 100968 (2022)
5. Samper, M.G., et al.: Digital transformation of business models: influence of operation and trade variables. Procedia Comput. Sci. **203**, 565–569 (2022)
6. Wu, H., Xu, Z., Skare, M.: How do family businesses adapt to the rapid pace of globalization? a bibliometric analysis. J. Bus. Res. **153**, 59–74 (2022)
7. Kayid, W.A.L., Jin, Z., Priporas, C.-V., Ramakrishnan, S.: Defining family business efficacy: An exploratory study. J. Bus. Res. **141**, 713–725 (2022)
8. Bresciani, S., Ferraris, A., Huarng, K.H., Malhotra, A.: Digital transformation as a springboard for product, process and business model innovation. J. Bus. Res. **128**, 204–210 (2021)
9. Porfírio, J.A., Carrilho, T., Felício, J.A., Jardim, J.: Leadership characteristics and digital transformation. J. Bus. Res. **124**, 610–619 (2021)
10. Deferne, M., Bertschi-Michel, A., de Groote, J.: The role of trust in family business stakeholder relationships: A systematic literature review. J. Fam. Bus. Strateg., 100501 (2022)
11. Cardoso, W., Di Felice, R.: A novel committee machine to predict the quantity of impurities in hot metal produced in blast furnace. Comput. Chem. Eng. **163**, 107814 (2022)
12. Cardoso, W., di Felice, R., Baptista, R.C.: Artificial neural network for predicting silicon content in the hot metal produced in a blast furnace fueled by metallurgical coke. Mater. Res. 25 (2022)
13. Izario, D., Brancalhone, J., Iano, Y., de Oliveira, G.G., Vaz, G.C., Izario, K.: 5G-Automation of Vertical Systems in the Industry 4.0. In: Brazilian Technology Symposium, pp. 35–43. Springer (2023)

Assessing the Early-Age Drying Shrinkage Cracking in Polyamide and Alkali Resistant Glass Microfibers Reinforced Concrete

Nicolas Jorge Vianna[1]([✉]) [iD], Nádia Cazarim da Silva Forti[1] [iD],
Sarah Valente Tavares[1] [iD], Ana Elisabete Paganelli Guimarães de Avila Jacintho[1] [iD],
Lia Lorena Pimentel[1] [iD], and João Batista Lamari Palma e Silva[2] [iD]

[1] Pontifical Catholic University of Campinas, Campinas, Brazil
{nicolas.jv1,sarah.vt}@puccampinas.edu.br, {nadia.cazarim,
anajacintho,lia.lp}@puc-campinas.edu.br
[2] State University of Campinas, Campinas, Brazil
j095353@dac.unicamp.br

Abstract. Cracking in concrete structures is an unsettling pathological manifestation that might compromise its esthetic or indicate a lack of durability. The development of cracks occurs when the internal stresses exceed the material's tensile strength. Different factors are involved in the cracking phenomenon. At early ages, volume changes are associated with thermal effects and shrinkage. Concrete exhibits a low tensile strength at early ages, thus the risk of cracking shall be seriously considered. Hence, an experimental study was conducted to investigate the influence of polyamide and alkali-resistant glass microfibers on the cracking susceptibility of conventional concrete at early ages due to drying shrinkage. The ring test methodology] was adopted in order to attain the objective stated. In total, three dosages have been studied – plain concrete (PC), glass fiber reinforced concrete (GFRC), and polyamide fiber reinforced concrete (PAFRC). A dosage of 0.9 kg/m^3 of micro-fibers was adopted. The PAFRC developed the first crack on the 5th day, which occurred before the conventional concrete (on the 7th day). The glass microfibers delayed the crack formation in eight days, proving to be more effective in controlling cracking when compared to the other samples. A significant reduction in crack width was observed in the microfiber reinforced concretes.

Keywords: Microfiber · Ring test · Drying shrinkage

1 Introduction

In order to provide satisfactory integrity for concrete structural elements, it is crucial assessing the risk of cracking and its intervening factors [1]. For this reason, it is vital to determine in advance the potential of cracking on cementitious materials as a preventive measure to avoid any adverse future repair [2].

Nowadays, there are different aspects of concrete related to early-ages properties that have been an interest of research [3]. At early ages, cracking develops mainly with regard the restraints (either external or internal), rough environmental conditions, and the phenomenon of shrinkage. Mehta and Monteiro [4] describe drying shrinkage as a consequence of the loss of water from the concrete in an attempt to achieve a water potential equivalent to its external environment. This study focuses exclusively on drying shrinkage cracking.

In view of the aforementioned factors, the inclusion of fibers has been pointed out as an alternative to overcome the limitations regarding plain concrete structures [5–7]. The addition of discontinuous discrete fibers collaborates towards reducing crack propagation and width because of the bridging effect [8]. Particularly, microfibers should not replace reinforcements. In principle, they tend to reduce cracking at early- ages and improve serviceability [9].

The early-age cracking in cementitious materials due to drying shrinkage might be evaluated through the ring test, whose methodology consists of casting samples of concrete on a ring mold form. The inner steel ring provides restraint to the concrete ring. Consequently, tensile stresses are developed and cracking occurs when the strength of the material is exceeded [10–12].

Therefore, an experimental study was carried out to determine the cracking potential on alkali-resistant glass and polyamide microfibers reinforced concrete at early ages through the methodology standardized by ASTM C1581/C1581M [13].

2 Methodology

2.1 Concrete Mix Design

A total of four natural aggregates were employed in this study. The granulometric composition, density, and water absorption are described in Table 1.

Table 2 summarizes the physical properties of both microfibers. The alkali-resistant glass monofilament microfiber was designed to provide plastic shrinkage crack control [14], while the polyamide microfiber is a polymer-based monofilament that provides effective crack control against short-term plastic shrinkage and long-term drying shrinkage [15]. The technical data sheets provided by the companies recommend a minimum dosage of 0.6 kg/m^3.

The concrete mixture was designed for floors on-ground application. Three different variations were studied: plain concrete (PC); alkali-resistant glass microfiber-reinforced concrete (GFRC); and polyamide microfiber-reinforced concrete (PAFRC). The mix proportions are presented in Table 3 for all mixtures.

The loss of workability due to the incorporation of fibers has been well-established in the literature [9]. Hence, intending to keep similar workability between the mixtures without affecting the water/cement ratio, a higher consumption of plasticizer was required for the microfiber reinforced concretes. The slump cone test, according to NBR NM 67 [16], was performed to assess workability.

The concrete was prepared using a tilting drum mixer. The constituents were loaded in the following order: (*i*) coarse aggregates and 1/3 of the water; (*ii*) cement and 1/3 of the water; (*iii*) fine aggregates, followed by the remaining water with the plasticizer. Also, exclusively for GFRC and PAFRC batches, the microfibers were gradually and

Table 1. Size distribution and properties analyses of aggregates

Mesh sieve size [mm]	Coarse aggregate		Fine aggregate	
	#1	#2	#1	#2
25.00	0%	0%	0%	0%
19.00	0%	0%	0%	0%
12.50	18%	0%	0%	0%
9.50	72%	5%	0%	0%
6.30	98%	46%	0%	0%
4.75	99%	73%	1%	0%
2.36	99%	97%	8%	0%
1.18	99%	99%	17%	2%
0.60	99%	99%	33%	7%
0.30	99%	100%	69%	43%
0.15	99%	100%	92%	87%
0.075	99%	100%	99%	100%
Bottom (<0.075)	100%	100%	100%	100%
Fineness modulus	7.65	5.73	2.19	1.39
Maximum size [mm]	12.5	9.50	4.75	1.18
Specific gravity [g/cm^3]	2.93	2.77	2.60	2.51
Water absorption [%]	0.80	0.95	0.39	0.30

Table 2. Physical properties of employed microfibers.

Parameters/Microfiber	Polyamide 6.6 [15]	Alkali-resistant Glass [14]
Specific gravity [g/cm^3]	1.14	2.68
Diameter [μm]	27	14
Tensile strength [MPa]	900	>1,000
Young's Modulus [GPa]	–	72
Length [mm]	12	12
Dispersion [filaments/kg]	111,000,000	200,000,000

randomly dispersed during the last step. To ensure homogenization, a mixing cycle of 120 s was adopted between each loading period.

The compressive strength, tension strength in flexure, and elasticity modulus (Young's Modulus) were performed in accordance with NBR 5739 [17], NBR 12142 [18], and NBR 8522–1 [19], respectively. It should be noted that a low dosage of fibers does not change significantly either the elastic properties or compressive/tensile strength.

Table 3. Concrete mixture design.

Materials	Mixture abbreviations		
	PC	GFRC	PAFRC
Cement [kg/m^3]	370.00	370.00	370.00
Water [kg/m^3]	185.00	185.00	185.00
Coarse aggregate #1 [kg/m^3]	830.00	830.00	830.00
Coarse aggregate #2 [kg/m^3]	275.00	275.00	275.00
Fine aggregate #1 [kg/m^3]	535.00	535.00	535.00
Fine aggregate #2 [kg/m^3]	285.00	285.00	285.00
Plasticizer [kg/m^3]	2.22	2.96	2.96
Fibers [kg/m^3]	–	0.900	0.900

Hence, it is expected that the fiber-reinforced concrete cracks at a similar magnitude of stress and strain to the plain concrete [9].

The statistical significance for outlying observations (outliers) was tested according to Grubbs [20] criteria, adopting a significance level of 0.05. Table 4 summarizes the results at 28 days of age.

Table 4. Mechanical properties for 28 days of age.

Group	N	Average	Standard Deviation	Coefficient of Variation
Compressive strength [MPa]				
PC	5	56.356	8.253	0.146
GFRC	5	58.695	3.247	0.055
PAFRC	5	57.608	8.551	0.148
Tension strength in flexure [MPa]				
PC	2	6.742	0.305	0.045
GFRC	3	7.222	0.636	0.088
PAFRC	3	8.951	0.089	0.010
Elasticity modulus [GPa]				
PC	3	46.777	7.807	0.167
GFRC	5	42.086	3.257	0.077
PAFRC[1]	–	–	–	–

---

[1] Based on the argument given by Grubbs [20], "When the skilled experimenter is clearly aware that a gross deviation from prescribed experimental procedure has taken place, the resultant observations should be discarded […]", those data were discarded due to experimental incoherence.

A one-way ANOVA (Analyses of Variance) was applied to determine if there is a statistically significant difference between the groups of concrete. Similar compressive strength and Young's modulus for the specimens were verified. However, the tensile strength in flexure differed up to 2 MPa and also indicates that there is a significant difference between them (p-value of 0.00422 <0.05).

2.2 Ring Test

The restrained drying shrinkage test was performed accordingly to the methodology prescribed by ASTM C1581/C1581 [13]. There was cast one test specimen for each material. They were made by filling the mold in two approximately equal layers and compacted by applying 75 strikes with a 10 mm rod and then consolidated for 90 s on a vibrating table.

Immediately after casting, the test specimens were stored in the testing environment, which consisted of boxes made of 1.5 cm thick plywood panels coated externally with aluminum foil and internally with 2.5 cm expanded polystyrene (EPS) sheets. The external temperature was monitored with a lambda probe. In turn, the environment inside the boxes was determined with a wireless sensor – HTP.xw Sensor. It has an accuracy of ± 1.5%RH and ± 0.1 °C for relative humidity and temperature, respectively.

The strain development was measured using two strain gages (PA-06-125BA-120L) diametrically opposite to each other bonded at midheight on the circumferential direction on the interior surface of the inner steel ring. It should be mentioned that those strain gages were waterproofed using an epoxy coating. The strain gages communication cables were connected to the data acquisition system (HBM QuantumX MX840B), starting to monitor and record both the strain and time at intervals of one minute.

All the specimens were moist-cured using wet burlap for about 24 h. At the end of curing, the outer steel ring was loosened and the top surface of the concrete rings was sealed with a thin layer of paraffin wax. In those conditions, the drying process happens through the outer circumference of the concrete ring.

3 Results and Discussions

Figure 1 plots the steel ring strain against the specimen age. The dashed line represents the time recorded after sealing the test specimen, also known as the 'Initial age of drying' (approximately one day). During the first 24 h, it can be noted an expansive strain tendency, which might be caused by the heat of hydration [6].

The strain development resembles a sawtooth wave – an upward trend followed by a sharp drop. It is therefore believed the reason for this behavior is the positioning of the resistances near the data acquisition system. Hence, the resistances were exposed to the external environment instead of that within the boxes and a wider temperature range was recorded outside the boxes.

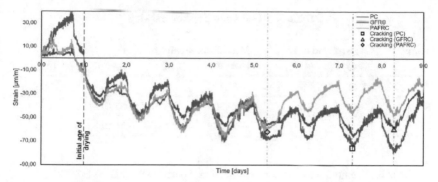

Fig. 1. Plots of Steel ring strain versus time for all specimens.

Figure 2 shows both the internal and external testing environment conditions recorded over the experiment. On the first day, the relative humidity has risen due to the curing method applied to the concrete rings. The sudden drop indicates the time at which the boxes were opened for operations and maintenance of the rings.

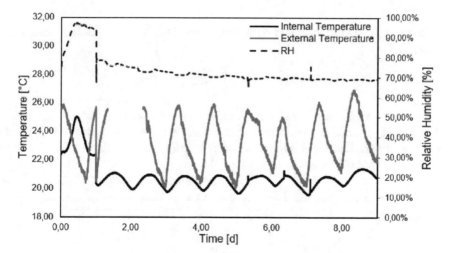

Fig. 2. Testing environment (internal and external).

Data markers and dash-dotted lines indicate the cracking age for each test specimen in Fig. 1. Also, the compressive and tension in flexure strengths were also tested at the age of cracking. Table 5 summarizes the main data for each material. A classification for cracking potential is given by ASTM C1581/C1581 [13] based on the net time-to-cracking (t_{cr}) and the stress rate at cracking (q), as provided in Table 6.

Table 5. Results at the age of cracking.

Mixture	Age at cracking [days]	Maximum strain [μm/m]	f_{ckj} [MPa]	$f_{ct,f}$ [MPa]
PC	7.31	−75.728	50.51	8.03
GFRC	8.29	−59.501	55.01	8.77
PAFRC	5.31	−61.989	46.01	8.50

Table 6. Potential for cracking classification. Source: ASTM C1581/C1581 [13].

t_{cr} [d]	q [MPa/d]	Potential for cracking
$0 < t_{cr} \leq 7$	$q > 0.34$	High
$7 < t_{cr} \leq 14$	$0.17 \leq q < 0.34$	Moderate-High
$14 < t_{cr} \leq 28$	$0.10 \leq q < 0.17$	Moderate-Low
$t_{cr} > 28$	$q < 0.10$	Low

The stress rate in the specimen at the time of cracking was calculated in accordance with Eq. 1.

$$q = \frac{G|\alpha|}{2\sqrt{t_r}} \tag{1}$$

where G is a constant equal to 72.2 GPa, t_r refers to the elapsed time (difference between each recorded time and the age drying was initiated), and α (Strain Rate Factor) is the slope of a straight line fitted through linear regression analysis of the plot Net strain versus Square root of elapsed time (see Fig. 3).

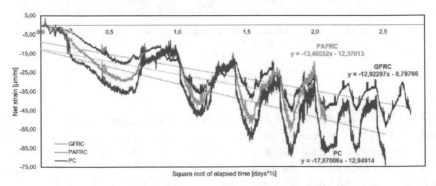

Fig. 3. Linear regression of Net strain versus Square root of elapsed time.

Results are shown in Table 7 for each composite. It should be mentioned that the least favorable classification has been adopted.

Table 7. Potential of cracking for the different mixtures

Mixture	t_r [d]	α [(μm/m)/d$^{1/2}$]	q [MPa/d]	Potential for cracking
PC	6.32	−17.87006	0.257	High
GFRC	7.29	−12.92297	0.173	Moderate-high
PAFRC	4.31	−13.46052	0.234	High

The cracking pattern on the specimen is depicted in Fig. 4. A digital microscope was used to measure the crack width along its extension. Prior to any measurement, a clear card with specified width marks closest to the surface was used to calibrate the microscope. Then, the cracking widths at the top, middle, and bottom have been registered. Also, it has been determined its propagation on the cross-section (see Fig. 5). The results are listed in Table 8. It can be noted that the addition of both fibers promoted better control of crack opening.

Fig. 4. Cracking pattern.

Table 8. Average crack width analysis.

Mixture	Top [mm]	Middle [mm]	Bottom [mm]	Cross-section [mm]
PC	0.15	0.14	0.14	30.29
GFRC	0.12	0.05	0.02	2.56
PAFRC	0.13	0.10	0.08	5.38

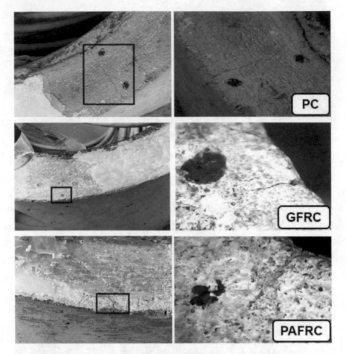

Fig. 5. Cracking throughout the cross-section.

4 Conclusions

An experimental study was conducted to evaluate the cracking potential on plain and microfiber reinforced concretes due to drying shrinkage. Based on the restrained ring test results, the following conclusions were gathered:

Although the polyamide fiber reinforced concrete (PAFRC) cracked prior to the plain concrete (PC), the polyamide microfiber promoted a narrower cracking width. In general, both microfibers were able to delay the cracking development due to the bridging effect.

A similar crack width was verified at the top of the specimen for all the mixtures analyzed. The PC presented a wider crack along its extension, while the microfiber reinforced concretes had an average crack width lower than 0.10 mm at the middle and bottom of the crack. In addition, a deeper crack on the cross-section was verified on the PC.

The alkali-resistant glass microfiber significantly affected the potential for cracking. The glass fiber reinforced concrete (GFRC) was classified as having a Moderate-high potential for cracking, while the other mixtures were classified as a high potential because their net time to cracking was lower than 7 days.

Acknowledgment. This study was financed in part by the Coordenação de Aperfeiçoamento de Pessoal de Nível Superior – Brasil (CAPES) – Finance Code 001.

References

1. do Santos S.B.: Fenômeno térmico do concreto: Fundamentos e aplicações práticas. 1 edn. Editora Interciência. Rio de Janeiro (2019). ISBN 978–85–7193–419–1. [in portuguese]
2. Dobson, G.: Concrete floor slabs: recognizing problems before they happen. Concr. Int. **17**, 45–47 (1995)
3. Safiuddin, M.D., Kaish, A.B.M.A., Woon, C.-O., Raman, S.N.: Early-age cracking in concrete: Causes, consequences, remedial measures, and recommendations. Appl. Sci. **8**, 1730 (2018)
4. Mehta, P.K., Monteiro, P.J.M.: Concrete: microstructure, properties, and materials. McGraw-Hill Education (2014)
5. Shah, H.R., Weiss, J.: Quantifying shrinkage cracking in fiber reinforced concrete using the ring test. Mater. Struct. **39**, 887–899 (2006)
6. Ehrenbring, H.Z., de Medeiros Quinino, U.C., Oliveira, L.F.S., Tutikian, B.F.: Experimental method for investigating the impact of the addition of polymer fibers on drying shrinkage and cracking of concretes. Struct. Concr. **20**, 1064–1075 (2019)
7. dos Santos Motta, M., Souza, L.M.S., de Andrade Silva, F.: Early-age shrinkage of cement pastes with polypropylene and curaua fibres. Adv. Cem. Res. 33, 156–167 (2021)
8. Lawler, J.S., Wilhelm, T., Zampini, D., Shah, S.P.: Fracture processes of hybrid fiber-reinforced mortar. Mater. Struct. **36**, 197–208 (2003)
9. IBRACON/ABECE: Prática recomendada IBRACON/ABECE: Projeto de estruturas de concreto reforçado com fibras. 1 edn. IBRACON/ABECE. São Paulo. (2016). ISBN 978-85–98576–26–8. [in portuguese]
10. ACI Committee 231: Report on early-age cracking: Causes. measurement. and mitigation (ACI 231R-10). American Concrete Institute. Farmiton Hills. Michigan. January. 2010 (2010)
11. de Oliveira, G.G., Iano, Y., Vaz, G.C., Chuma, E.L., Negrete, P.D.M., Negrete, J.C.M.: Structural Analysis of bridges and viaducts using the IoT concept. an approach on odm Pedro highway (Campinas-Brazil). In: Brazilian Technology Symposium, pp. 108–119. Springer (2022)
12. de Oliveira, G.G., Iano, Y., Vaz, G.C., Chuma, E.L., Negrete, P.D.M., Negrete, J.C.M.: Prop walls: a contextualization of the theme in a case study in the city of campinas (Brazil) BT - In: Proceedings of the 7th Brazilian Technology Symposium (BTSym'21). Presented at the (2022)
13. American Society for Testing and Materials: Standard Test Method for Determining Age at Cracking and Induced Tensile Stress Characteristic of Mortar and Concrete under Restrained Shrinkage (ASTM C1581/C1581M – 18a). ASTM International. West Conshohoken. PA. (2018). https://doi.org/10.1520/C1581_C1581M-18A
14. Anti-CRAK HD Dry-Use Chopped Strand | Owens Corning Composites, https://www.owenscorning.com/en-us/composites/product/anti-crak-chopped-strands-hd, last accessed 2022/05/18
15. MICRO FIBERS – Kratos, https://kratosreinforcement.com/en/micro-fibers, (Accessed 31 Aug 2022)
16. Associação Brasileira de Normas Técnicas (ABNT): NBR NM 67: Concreto – Determinação da consistência pelo abatimento do tronco de cone. Rio de Janeiro (1998)
17. Associação Brasileira de Normas Técnicas (ABNT): NBR 12142: Concreto – Determinação da resistência à tração na flexão de corpos de prova prismáticos. Rio de Janeiro (2010)
18. Associação Brasileira de Normas Técnicas (ABNT): NBR 5739: Concreto – Ensaio de compressão de corpos de prova cilíndricos. Rio de Janeiro (2018)

19. Associação Brasileira de Normas Técnicas (ABNT): NBR 8522–1: Concreto endurecido – Determinação dos módulos de elasticidade e de deformação. Parte 1: Módulos estáticos à compressão. Rio de Janeiro (2021)
20. Grubbs, F.E.: Procedures for detecting outlying observations in samples. Technometrics **11**, 1–21 (1969)

Author Index

Printed in the United States
by Baker & Taylor Publisher Services